STUDENT HOUSING AND RESIDENTIAL LIFE

Roger B. Winston, Jr.
Scott Anchors
and Associates

STUDENT
HOUSING AND
RESIDENTIAL
LIFE

A Handbook for Professionals
Committed to Student
Development Goals

Foreword by Harold C. Riker

Jossey-Bass Publishers · San Francisco

Substantial discounts on bulk quantities of Jossey-Bass books
are available to corporations, professional associations, and other
organizations. For details and discount information, contact the
special sales department at Jossey-Bass Inc., Publishers.
(415) 433-1740; Fax (415) 433-0499.

For sales outside the United States, contact Maxwell Macmillan
International Publishing Group, 866 Third Avenue, New York,
New York 10022.

Manufactured in the United States of America

The ink in this book is either soy- or vegetable-based and during the
printing process emits fewer than half the volatile organic compounds
(VOCs) emitted by petroleum-based ink.

Library of Congress Cataloging-in-Publication Data

Student housing and residential life : a handbook for professionals
    committed to student development goals / Roger B. Winston, Jr.,
    Scott Anchors and Associates ; foreword by Harold C. Riker.
        p.   cm. — (The Jossey-Bass higher and adult education series)
    Includes bibliographical references and index.
    ISBN 1-55542-507-0
        1. College students—Housing—United States—Handbooks, manuals,
    etc.   2. College student orientation—United States—Handbooks,
    manuals, etc.   3. Residence and education—Handbooks, manuals, etc.
    I. Winston, Roger B.   II. Anchors, Scott.   III. Series.
    LB3227.5.S78   1993
    378.1'98'710973—dc20   92-37735
                                                              CIP

FIRST EDITION
HB Printing   10 9 8 7 6 5 4 3 2 1   *Code 9311*

The Jossey-Bass

Higher and Adult Education Series

Consulting Editor
Student Services

Ursula Delworth
University of Iowa

Contents

═══════════

Foreword

===========

Student Housing and Residential Life is a theory-based, practice-focused hand-book for housing professionals who believe that residential living can be a quintessential part of students' educational experience. In Chapter Two, Winston and Anchors maintain that "effective residence halls are not educa-tionally neutral" but rather should promote student residents' development academically, socially, physically, and spiritually, in addition to providing them with safe and comfortable living accommodations. This is similar to views I stated thirty years ago: "Two primary functions of college housing—as distinguished from other kinds—are, first, to provide a satisfactory place for *students* to live, and second, to help students to learn and to grow, since this housing is part of an educational institution" (Riker, 1965, p. v).

There has been considerable progress in that direction in recent decades, but this point of view has also been met with passive, if not negative, attitudes on the part of many administrators and faculty members, including governing board members. The negative attitudes have been influenced by past attempts to use college residences primarily as a means of controlling student conduct, under the supervision of "mature persons," who sometimes had limited educational backgrounds and no notion of being "educators."

The educational potential of residence halls was either unenvisioned or neglected. Few in higher education today, however, would disagree that students learn *where* they live, with or without assistance. That learning may be negative or positive, and for many years, learning in the control-oriented environment was negative for a substantial number of students. Residence hall facilities and programs have improved markedly but have yet to realize their full potential for contributing to students' education.

Over the past thirty years, there have been substantial changes in the housing field. These changes were caused principally by the introduction into residence life programs of professionally educated staff members who were charged with giving leadership to educational activities. The most notable result has been the creation of offices that focus on "student development." Another significant change has been the increased intensity and sophistication of the training provided for student staff members in understanding individual residents' growth and development and creating open communication and helpful interactions.

The professionalization of housing programs over the past thirty years becomes most evident through an examination of the literature on housing. Before 1960, few books or journal articles related to student housing were published. In addition, there was virtually no sound research into the effects of residential living on students' academic and personal development or the effects of different social and physical environments on residents' satisfaction, adjustment to college, and development. While the field has come a long way, significant problems still exist with regard to research on housing. To begin with, there have been few well-designed and controlled longitudinal studies about the differential impact of residence life programs on learning and behavior change. Also, little is known about the environmental variables that produce change in individuals. Moreover, few studies have successfully isolated the effects of residential living on students' intellectual, moral, and psychosocial development. But the number of studies and research projects has continued to grow, and the conscientious efforts being made to discover which housing practices and programs contribute most to students' development are to be applauded and encouraged. In my opinion, one of the many merits of this handbook is the effort the writers and editors have made to bring together and synthesize relevant research.

Milestones in Student Housing

Tremendous progress has been made in student housing. Particularly noteworthy milestones during the past thirty years include the following:

- Development of programs that encourage students to personalize rooms and public spaces
- Introduction of suites and apartment-like units that allow for greater privacy and autonomy

- Access to campus computers through terminals and modems in the residence halls
- Creation of standards and guidelines for minimum professional practice in housing programs
- Development of statements of ethical standards for resident staff
- Recognition that student residents are human beings with rights, needs, and feelings (brought about to a large degree by court decisions declaring that students possess the same constitutional rights as other citizens)
- Inclusion of residents in administrative decision making
- Recognition that housing is a professional field that requires extensive preparatory education of practitioners
- Expanded professional preparation programs with greater substance and higher standards

Housing and the Future

In the years ahead, housing programs should help contribute to the solution of certain educational and social problems. For example, the United States is currently experiencing a crisis in its health care system. A partial solution to the problem is for individuals to assume greater responsibility for their own health. This objective can be furthered during the college years through expansion in residence halls of wellness programs that emphasize regular physical exercise, good nutrition, and avoidance of self-destructive behaviors such as overeating, smoking, abuse of alcohol, unprotected sex, and use of addictive drugs.

Another area of both present and future importance is ethical standards and moral leadership, concern for which will lead to a greater emphasis in the country on justice and trust. Housing staff members have a significant opportunity to help create residential communities in which students discuss moral and ethical issues and apply an ethical code both as individuals and as group members. When combined with classroom discussions, such experiences should have a lasting effect on students' postcollege lives.

As housing professionals look to the future, one challenge they face is determining, in generalizable terms, the characteristics and needs of coming generations of students. Surveys of today's high school and community college students could be helpful. For example, recent studies of those students indicate that they are often already sexually active and using alcohol or prohibited drugs. Many do not have intact families. In the search for expressions of love and respect, this generation of students responds positively to staff members who show care and concern for their welfare. Institutional leaders should be educated about this. For example, reliance on regulations against the use of alcoholic beverages to control or change the behavior of students who have been drinking for years before enrolling in college is destined to fail. Other means, such as education about the dangers and negative health effects of alcohol consumption, are more likely to produce an effect.

Another challenge that housing professionals face is convincing top-level administrators that residence halls are valuable resources for enhancing student learning. They can serve to improve academic achievement, promote responsible citizenship, and heighten students' concern for the well-being of others. Much remains to be accomplished, however, if residential facilities are to fulfill that function. (1) Housing programs need to assess themselves in the light of the student development goals proposed by Winston and Anchors in Chapter Two and the standards developed by the Council for the Advancement of Standards in Student Services/Development Programs (CAS) and the Association of College and University Housing Officers-International (ACUHO-I) (see Resources A and C), and to institute activities in areas in which they fall short. (2) Housing professionals must communicate more frequently with institutional leaders and faculty members about students — individually and collectively — and their needs and problems in learning and in adapting to campus life. (3) Increased communication should lead to greater involvement of the housing staff in the campus community. This strategy should include inviting faculty members to participate in research projects with the housing staff. (4) Faculty members should be invited to use residential facilities in connection with academic activities such as teaching or advising. (5) Housing staff members should seek opportunities to become better acquainted with faculty members and academic administrators on a more informal basis, such as at cultural, social, and athletic events and through involvement in local community civic activities.

In recent years, the construction of new housing facilities has been limited. Consequently, many buildings need to be renovated or razed. The new living arrangements created in the next decade should provide opportunities to affect students' education more effectively. Planners should be strong in their resolve to prevent replication of past mistakes. The mistakes have included construction of high-population-density (high-rise) buildings, even when they were not required in order to save space; long, double-loaded corridors without adequate community space for recreation and study; built-in furniture; ineffective sound-deadening construction; and inadequate living accommodations and office space for professional staff. Planners should also anticipate new developments in computers, consumer electronics, and telecommunications and make sure that new residential facilities can accommodate current and forecast future electronic and computer technology. It will generally be desirable to plan space that allows for holding class in the halls.

A goal for the future should be to make the residence hall experience a part of the curriculum. This experience could be partly utilized in classes dealing with group behavior, leadership and individual responsibility, ethical issues, health promotion, and environmental concerns. Such classes might be organized into a specific educational program that could be titled

"Living in Tomorrow's World." Such a program should be interdisciplinary, including faculty from areas such as liberal arts, architecture, ecology, and education, as well as the residential life staff. The cost of the courses might become part of the charges for room and board.

What are the prospects that student residences on campus will be included as an important part of higher education in the future? The prospects are good for several economic and educational reasons. From trustees and administrators' point of view, student residences represent a substantial capital investment, which must be protected. Using facilities to improve retention of students will also represent a significant financial advantage. And faculty will be more likely to favor residence hall programs that increase student persistence and foster new academic activities. If such programs improve student readiness for learning in other classes, faculty will tend to be supportive.

If as much progress is made in student residences in the next thirty years as has been made in the past thirty (and I think that is a safe assumption), the results will be both startling from today's perspective and rewarding to all concerned — students, faculty, administrators, student development educators, and parents. This book may well become a stimulus to new achievements in the field.

Reference

Riker, H. C. *College Housing as Learning Centers*. Washington, D.C.: American College Personnel Association, 1965.

January 1993   Harold C. Riker
                                                  Professor of Education Emeritus
                                                  University of Florida

Preface

======

Student Housing and Residential Life was designed to be a comprehensive handbook summarizing and synthesizing current thinking about and research on student residential facilities, programs, administrative practices, and personnel on college campuses. The book is based on four important premises: (1) College residence halls exist to provide relatively low-cost, safe, sanitary, and comfortable living quarters; to promote the intellectual, social, personality, physical, career, educational, and moral development of those who live there; and to supplement and enrich students' academic experiences. (2) Efficacious residential life programs are not educationally neutral or value neutral; they intentionally structure or influence environments and design proactive interventions to enhance the academic experience and to enrich the personal lives of residents. (3) Residential life programs committed to the goals of student development are purposely intrusive. (4) Residential life programs have a responsibility to provide civic education, to promote active citizenship, and to sensitize students to their responsibilities to society.

Collegiate housing facilities and programs are strategically placed within the academic environment to influence the quality of students' educational experiences and personal development. Because residential students sleep and spend more of their waking hours in residence halls than in any other part of the institution, many more opportunities arise there than in the formal classroom to teach students valuable lessons that can affect the course of their future lives. Unlike in some classes, where students may fail to see the relevance of what is taught, in residence halls, learning can be immediate and relevant.

Residence halls as "laboratories for living," however, have frequently failed to realize their potential on many campuses. There are numerous reasons for this; chief among them are (1) lack of commitment to goals of student development, (2) lack of adequately educated personnel who understand how to structure environments and create programs that promote significant learning, (3) lack of courage in confronting certain social issues and political constituencies, (4) hostility on the part of some elitist faculty toward addressing noncognitive development, (5) lack of a tradition of excellence in the institution, (6) refusal or inability to invest adequate resources, (7) reluctance to state moral positions and values and to act on them, (8) aging physical facilities that, for lack of funds, have not been adequately maintained, (9) poorly designed facilities that were built to contain the largest number of beds but that militate against optimal interaction and learning among students, and (10) difficulty in attracting and retaining well-educated, gifted staff members, because of low pay, the unattractiveness of "living in," given the lack of privacy and around-the-clock responsibilities, and difficulty of career advancement past the mid-management bottleneck.

This is not intended to be an operating manual. It is called a handbook because we have eschewed simple answers to complex questions and formulaic, checklist-like advice. We have also sought to make the book comprehensive in its coverage, to ground it in theory, and to provide guidance for conceptualizing, planning, and evaluating residential life programs that make a real difference in students' lives. As much as possible, the chapter authors have supplemented arguments and assertions with research findings, examples, and references to existing programs. The book addresses the full range of concerns faced by colleges and universities with residential facilities—from identifying goals and purposes, to understanding the theoretical foundations for effective interventions, to organizing and managing programs and facilities in an uncertain economic world made more complex by competing educational priorities, legal mandates, and political ideologies. Varied theoretical perspectives that can inform professional practice are summarized, principles to guide practice are enumerated, and examples of applications are described. The book covers administrative concerns related to building maintenance, repairs, and renovations; room assignments; budgeting; legal considerations; organizational patterns and strategies; compensation of personnel; selection, training, and evaluation of professional, support, allied professional, and paraprofessional staff; and fiscal management.

We undertook the project because we felt that housing professionals had no up-to-date, comprehensive resource to consult as they went about their work. Even though a great deal has been written about residential life in the last thirty years, the last book-length, general work on housing was published more than a decade ago (DeCoster and Mable, 1980). Much has changed in higher education and student affairs since that time.

Terminology

As in other areas of student affairs, there is no universally accepted terminology in housing programs. Consequently, we developed a set of operational definitions, which authors of the separate chapters were requested to use for the sake of consistency. We do not claim that these are the best or only acceptable definitions.

College is used as a general name for all kinds of postsecondary educational institutions. *University*, on the other hand, denotes an institution that comprises multiple undergraduate colleges, has an extensive research emphasis, and awards the doctorate.

Student development refers to a group of theories that purport to describe or explain how students change as they mature and as they respond to the collegiate environment. The term *student development* may also refer to a somewhat heterogeneous collection of interventions (ranging from policy formulation and implementation to environmental design to educational programming to individual counseling) whose purpose is to facilitate students' realization of their potential, to enhance or enrich students' educational experiences, or to overcome obstacles that inhibit the realization of their full potential as educated persons and citizens. *Student development* is not used in organizational unit names or in position titles.

The term *student development goals* refers to a broad set of educational outcomes that are not directly or exclusively related to the acquisition of the knowledge and skills taught through the formal curriculum (see Chapter Two). Howard Bowen (1977) asserts that higher education embraces both the formal curriculum and the extracurricular life of the academic community, and he groups the outcomes of higher education into three categories: *cognitive learning* (expanding knowledge and intellectual powers), *affective development* (enhancing moral, religious, and emotional interests and sensibilities), and *practical competence* (improving performance in citizenship, work, family life, consumer choice, health, and other practical matters). "Insofar as these three goals are achieved, they are the ingredients for the flowering of the total personality. In varying combinations—reflecting individual differences and uniqueness of persons—they define the ideal personalities to which many educators aspire for their students" (Bowen, 1977, p. 39). Student development goals are those that fall outside the formal curriculum (principally the last two categories of Bowen's goals) or are areas of knowledge, skill, or competence that are needed to supplement the formal curriculum.

Housing program, housing department, or *housing division* (the terms are used interchangeably) refers to the total residential operation (including programming, facility operations and maintenance, and professional and support services) and all the personnel employed in the accomplishment of its mission. Consequently, a housing staff member could be anyone from the department director to a hall director, a resident assistant, an accountant, or a custodian.

Residential life or *residence life* (the terms are again used interchangeably) refers to the programs and attendant personnel dedicated to creating environments and organizational structures and other interventions that promote the personal development and education of residents; maintain sufficient order to allow for adequate study, sleep, and socializing; and support the academic mission of the institution. A residential life staff member is a person whose primary position responsibilities entail staff selection, training, and supervision; program development, implementation, and evaluation; and environmental assessment, design, and management to further student development goals. She or he may be a member of the professional, allied professional, support, or paraprofessional staff.

For the purpose of this book, we have elected to use the definitions of personnel categories proposed by Winston and Miller (1991) for classifying staff positions.

Professional staff members are persons who hold at least a master's degree in a relevant academic discipline (usually student personnel, counseling, or higher education), who hold membership in and ascribe to the ethical and professional standards of one or more student affairs professional associations, and who have responsibility for the education of students outside the classroom.

Allied professional staff members are persons who are responsible for, or indirectly support, educational functions outside the classroom but who have been extensively educated in specialized professions other than student affairs. Housing personnel in this category, for example, include accountants, clergy, engineers, counselors, interior designers, and attorneys.

Support staff members are persons who perform the myriad activities that enable professionals and allied professionals to provide essential services and educational interventions. Housing personnel in this category include receptionists, secretaries, maintenance workers, custodians, and security officers.

Paraprofessionals are students who are selected, trained, and supervised in the performance of specific functions that generally would be accomplished by professionals. They are given compensation in money or in kind. Examples of paraprofessionals in housing are students who function as resident assistants or resident advisors, peer counselors, minority assistants, peer sexuality educators, or tutors. Students who are employed to fill such

essential support roles as desk assistant, file clerk, salesperson, or maintenance assistant would not be classified as paraprofessionals.

Specialized programs that seek to expand the educational impact of
residence halls on students tend to fall into four broad categories: living-
learning centers, service-learning units, cultural-emphasis units, and
common-interest units.

Living-learning centers are living units (such as a floor or wing of a
residence or a collection of buildings) in which academics in general or in-
depth study in a particular subject area is emphasized. This emphasis may
take the form of designating areas that have extended study hours and
recognizing residents who achieve high GPAs; making available resource
materials, computers, and tutors to building residents; grouping together
students who share one or more classes; encouraging residents to participate
in extensive extracurricular activities such as writing or artistic performance;
or some combination of these approaches.

Service-learning units are living units in which residents contribute to
worthy causes or programs. Activities may involve regular and systematic
philanthropic pursuits such as fundraising for a charitable organization (for
instance, the Salvation Army or a women's shelter); providing volunteer
services to a local organization (such as Habitat for Humanity, a crisis hotline,
or a homeless shelter); or instituting a service program (such as a Big Brother/
Big Sister program for children in a public housing project, or a tutorial
program for a class in a neighborhood school).

Cultural-emphasis units generally include those in which residents concentrate on the study of a particular foreign language and the culture of
countries in which that language is spoken (residents may, for instance, be
required to speak only that language when in the unit) and units in which the
culture of a particular ethnic-cultural group, such as African Americans or
Americans from Puerto Rico, is emphasized. These units usually provide
frequent in-house cultural programs and invite speakers to address their
unique interests.

Residents of *common-interest units* elect to live in the unit because of
shared interests and usually commit to a certain level of participation in the
unit's activities as a condition of their assignment to the unit. The common
interest may be academic or cultural (as in living-learning centers or cultural-
emphasis units), or avocational—for instance, outdoor activities (such as
camping, sailing, or hiking), athletic activities (skiing, golf, fitness, or weight
training, for instance), travel, or hobbies (such as photography, needlework,
or collecting).

Audience

This book will be of interest primarily to housing professionals—the single
largest component of student affairs staff. It should be of interest to entry-
level professionals as well as mid-level and senior administrators who wish to

update their knowledge. It has considerable potential for use in graduate preparation programs and in training and educating graduate student staff members in housing programs. As a basic reference, it should also be of interest to chief student affairs administrators and college presidents on residential campuses.

Contents

Student Housing and Residential Life is organized into three basic parts, which are preceded by a chapter that identifies many of the challenges housing programs face today. In Chapter One, Gregory S. Blimling identifies eight groups of challenges that housing programs face on most contemporary campuses and that require immediate attention: (1) multiculturalism, (2) student mental and physical health concerns, (3) campus violence, (4) institutional finances, (5) deteriorating physical facilities, (6) changing student attitudes, (7) demands for greater accountability, and (8) staffing issues.

The next five chapters—which make up Part One of the book—review the theoretical and historical foundations for contemporary professional housing practice. In Chapter Two, Roger B. Winston, Jr., and Scott Anchors explore what it means to speak of a residential life program committed to goals of student development. They review the research on the effects of housing programs on students and suggest guidelines for creating programs that are most likely to have significant influence on students' personal and educational development. David B. White and William D. Porterfield (Chapter Three) summarize the major theories of student psychosocial development, analyze the reported research, and offer recommendations for using the theories to improve understanding of students and to design effective interventions. In Chapter Four, Marcia B. Baxter Magolda considers the major theories of intellectual, ethical, and moral development and proposes ways to use these theoretical perspectives to create programs and environments that will benefit students. She also offers important insights into the role that gender plays as students make meaning of experiences. C. Carney Strange (Chapter Five) presents an overview of the major theories of person-environment interaction and provides guidance for housing professionals in their use of these perspectives and research findings to create more successful residential environments. In Chapter Six, Charles F. Frederiksen presents a brief history of collegiate housing; he offers important insights into the evolution of housing as a professional field of practice in student affairs.

Part Two, which is composed of ten chapters, discusses issues related to organizing and administering housing programs. In Chapter Seven, M. Lee Upcraft addresses such important concerns as creating viable administrative structures, examining differences that derive from institutional size and type of control (public versus private), and determining appropriate staffing patterns. Daniel A. Hallenbeck (Chapter Eight) writes about budgeting, organizing the operational components of housing, and managing the physical facilities. In Chapter Nine, Paul Fairbrook explains how food service programs can contribute significantly to the overall quality of housing programs and to residents' health and general satisfaction. He supplies guidelines for estimating the quality of food service operations and provides a good overview for neophytes in this aspect of residential life. In Chapter Ten, James C. Grimm outlines many of the alternative accommodations in student housing today. He examines features and implications of various living arrangements (such as double-loaded corridors, suites, and apartments) and programmatic emphases (for example, coed versus single-sex halls, theme units, and cooperative living units). Finally, he looks at family housing programs and suggests strategies for improving the quality of the educational experiences of students in those programs.

The next three chapters are devoted to staffing. Patricia A. Kearney (Chapter Eleven) describes the principal roles professional staff members should play, provides guidance for the staff selection process, and discusses professional staff development, training, supervision, and evaluation. In Chapter Twelve, Sue A. Saunders explains the essential roles that allied professional staff (such as accountants and psychologists) and support staff (such as secretaries and custodial personnel) play in creating high-quality residential life programs. She discusses the unique aspects of staff selection, training, supervision, and evaluation for those personnel categories. Roger B. Winston, Jr., and R. Thomas Fitch (Chapter Thirteen) discuss the utilization of students in paraprofessional roles. The authors identify a variety of roles appropriate for student personnel and propose guidelines for their selection, training, supervision, and evaluation.

The final three chapters in Part Two discuss legal considerations, the application of professional standards, and strategies for assessing student needs and determining program effects. In Chapter Fourteen, Donald D. Gehring outlines the constitutional issues housing professionals confront daily, summarizes the federal regulations that directly affect housing programs, and considers liability issues regarding personal safety, alcohol consumption, and security. Guidelines for limiting or managing risks are offered. Theodore K. Miller and Michael E. Eyster (Chapter Fifteen) describe standards of professional practice and illustrate how housing professionals can use them to improve their programs. Miller and Eyster also deal with statements of ethical standards and discuss their distinctive application in residential life programs. Finally, in Chapter Sixteen, Robert D. Brown and Diane L. Podolske provide a primer on conducting useful needs assessments, valid program evaluations, and well-conceptualized research studies.

Part Three examines many of the pressing issues that residential life programs currently face and describes a wide variety of successful responses to concerns and problems. In Chapter Seventeen, John H. Schuh and Vicky L. Triponey deal with the nuts and bolts of program design and execution. They present a model process for developing programs for personal enrichment, education, and social and recreational activities that include student development goals. Fred Leafgren (Chapter Eighteen) provides an overview of wellness as a unifying theme for residential life programs. He describes how the concept has been used to integrate programming efforts and to communicate the importance of holistic development to residents. In Chapter Nineteen, Scott Anchors, Katie Branch Douglas, and Mary Kay Kasper consider the practical aspects of community development (for example, theme units, ethnic-cultural centers, group development activities, living-learning centers, and service-learning units) and milieu management programs (such as room and hall personalization and creation of specialized-use areas—for example, weight rooms and TV lounges). Charles J. Werring, Diana L. Robertson, and Carolyn V. Coon (Chapter Twenty) take up some of the most difficult contemporary social problems, including interpersonal conflicts about sexual violence, racism, homophobia, roommate problems, and other causes of social tension. The authors analyze the issues, offer guidelines for addressing them, and describe successful interventions used in housing programs across the country. In Chapter Twenty-One, Steven M. Janosik addresses the increase in criminal behavior (rape and other forms of assault, theft, vandalism, and drug abuse) in residence halls and suggests responses.

In the conclusion (Chapter Twenty-Two), Charles C. Schroeder identifies problems facing higher education in the coming decade and proposes steps that student affairs divisions and their housing programs can take to resolve them.

Acknowledgments

We wish to express our appreciation to the chapter authors. They have been resourceful, energetic, creative, and very cooperative throughout this process. We sought contributors who we were convinced possessed the background and experience needed to address adequately the important issues facing today's housing programs. Even though the authors are basically in agreement with the overarching ideas that motivated us to undertake the project, differences of opinion and approach are also evident from chapter to chapter. We have not tried to homogenize the differences or to impose our views but instead have honored individual opinions and convictions as much as possible.

We also wish to thank Gale Erlandson, editor for the Higher and Adult Education Series at Jossey-Bass, for her support and encouragement from the time we proposed the original idea through the final editing process. She has made the often tedious aspects of producing an edited work of this length less onerous.

January 1993   Roger B. Winston, Jr.
                                                                 Athens, Georgia

                                                                 Scott Anchors
                                                                 Orono, Maine

References

Bowen, H. R. *Investment in Learning: The Individual and Social Value of American Higher Education*. San Francisco: Jossey-Bass, 1977.

DeCoster, D. A., and Mable, P. (eds.). *Personal Education and Community Development in College Residence Halls*. Washington, D.C.: American College Personnel Association, 1980.

Winston, R. B., Jr., and Miller, T. K. "Human Resource Management: Professional Preparation and Staff Selection." In T. K. Miller, R. B. Winston, Jr., and Associates, *Administration and Leadership in Student Affairs: Actualizing Student Development in Higher Education*. (2nd ed.) Muncie, Ind.: Accelerated Development, 1991.

The Authors

===

Roger B. Winston, Jr., is professor in the student personnel in higher education program and graduate coordinator in the Department of Counseling and Human Development Services, College of Education, University of Georgia. He received his A.B. degree (1965) in history and philosophy from Auburn University and his M.A. degree (1970) in philosophy and Ph.D. degree (1973) in counseling and student personnel services from the University of Georgia. Before assuming a teaching position at the University of Georgia, he was dean of men at Georgia Southwestern College, where he was responsible for the men's residential life program.

He is author or editor of seven other books: *Developmental Approaches to Academic Advising* (1982, with S. C. Ender and T. K. Miller), *Developmental Academic Advising: Addressing Students' Educational, Career, and Personal Needs* (1984, with T. K. Miller, S. C. Ender, and T. J. Grites), *Students as Paraprofessional Staff* (1984, with S. C. Ender), *Fraternities and Sororities on the Contemporary College Campus* (1987, with W. R. Nettles and J. H. Opper), *Promoting Student Development Through Intentionally Structured Groups: Principles, Techniques, and Applications* (1988, with W. C. Bonney, T. K. Miller, and J. C. Dagley), *Administration and Leadership in Student Affairs: Actualizing Student*

Development in Higher Education (2nd ed., 1991, with T. K. Miller), and *Using Professional Standards in Student Affairs* (1991, with W. A. Bryan and T. K. Miller).

He is also coauthor of published assessment instruments: *Student Developmental Task Inventory* (1973, 1979, with T. K. Miller and J. S. Prince), *Student Developmental Task and Lifestyle Inventory* (1987, with T. K. Miller and J. S. Prince), and *Academic Advising Inventory* (1984, with J. A. Sandor).

Honors and recognitions he has received include Outstanding Contribution to Research on Academic Advising (by the National Academic Advising Association, 1984); senior professional, Annuit Coeptis Dinner (by the American College Personnel Association [ACPA], 1987); Melvene D. Hardee Award for outstanding contribution to the student affairs field (by the Southern Association for College Student Affairs, 1989); Senior Scholar (by the American College Personnel Association, 1989); and Outstanding Contribution to Knowledge (by the American College Personnel Association, 1990).

Scott Anchors is director of campus living and cooperative professor of education at the University of Maine, Orono. He received his B.A. degree (1972) in interdisciplinary social science from the University of South Florida and his M.A. (1974) and Ph.D. (1987) degrees in higher education from Iowa State University.

Throughout his professional career, Anchors has worked in a variety of capacities in residence halls at both large public and small private institutions, in addition to having responsibility for family housing. While at Iowa State University (1972–1974 and 1984–85), he worked as program adviser in an all-men's residence and as program coordinator for family housing, respectively. At Auburn University (1976–77), he served as program coordinator for several campus living-learning programs; he then served as director of residence life and assistant dean of students at Mercer University (1977–1980). He has spent most of his career in posts at the University of Maine, where he has worked in various aspects of residential life administration, including as area coordinator, assistant director for staff development, and acting director of dining services. He currently is director of campus living, the unit of student affairs responsible for all campus residence and dining halls, campus video services, and related auxiliary enterprises.

His major publications include *Making Yourself at Home: A Practical Guide to Personalizing Residence Halls* (1978, with C. C. Schroeder and S. G. Jackson) and *Applications of the Myers-Briggs Type Indicator in Higher Education* (1987, with J. Provost). He was the recipient of the Association of College and University Housing Officers-International's "Outstanding Manuscript of the Year" award in 1986.

Gregory S. Blimling is vice-chancellor for student development at Appalachian State University in North Carolina, where he is also professor of human development and psychological counseling. He earned his B.A. degree (1972) in sociology and speech and his M.S. degree (1974) in college student personnel administration from Indiana University and his Ph.D. degree (1988) in educational policy and leadership in higher education and college student personnel work from Ohio State University. He is the author of *The Resident Assistant: Working with College Students in Residence Halls* (1980, 1984, 1990, with L. Miltenberger) and *The Experienced Resident Assistant* (1990, with L. Miltenberger).

Robert D. Brown is Carl A. Happold Distinguished Professor of Educational Psychology at the University of Nebraska, Lincoln. He is former president of the American College Personnel Association and former editor of the *Journal of College Student Development*. He has published numerous books and research articles on program evaluation and on college student development.

Carolyn V. Coon is a doctoral student in higher education administration and an administrative assistant for the Department of Housing and Dining Services at Kansas State University. She earned her B.S. degree (1982) at Bethel College in business administration and economics and her M.S. degree (1988) at Wichita State University in health sciences administration. Coon was formerly director of residence life at McPherson College.

Katie Branch Douglas is a Ph.D. student in the higher education and student affairs program at Indiana University, Bloomington. Her emphasis is on person-environment interaction, especially multicultural education. She earned her B.A. degree in student affairs in higher education and her M.A. degree in journalism from Ohio State University. She worked as community development coordinator at the University of Maine and residence hall director at Ohio State. In 1991, she was the recipient of the National Association of Student Personnel Administrators Region I Outstanding New Professional Award for the state of Maine.

Michael E. Eyster is director of housing at the University of Oregon and has actively participated in the Association of College and University Housing Officers-International, having been the chair of its Professional Standards Committee and its representative on the Council for the Advancement of Standards. He holds a B.S. degree (1970) in education and an M.A. degree (1972) in educational psychology from the University of Nebraska, Lincoln. Eyster was director of housing and residential life at Indiana University of Pennsylvania and has worked in housing positions at the University of Delaware, the University of Chicago, and Cornell University.

Paul Fairbrook is a nationally known consultant and lecturer specializing in college and university food services. He is the author of *Food on Campus*,

The College and University Food Service Manual, and *Public Relations and Merchandising in College Food Service*. He was director of food services for over twenty-five years at the University of the Pacific in California.

R. Thomas Fitch is assistant professor in the student personnel in higher education program, Department of Counseling and Human Development Services, University of Georgia. He received his B.S. degree (1979) in history and economics and his M.Ed. degree (1981) in counselor education from the University of Virginia and his Ph.D. degree (1987) in counseling and student personnel services from the University of Georgia. He has been head resident at the University of Tennessee, coordinator of residence education at Mercer University, and dean of students at the Atlanta College of Art.

Charles F. Frederiksen is director of university housing and food service and assistant professor in the Hotel, Restaurant, and Institutional Management Department at Iowa State University. He received his B.S. degree (1953) and his M.S. degree (1954) from Iowa State University. He has served as secretary, newsletter editor, and president of the Association of College and University Housing Officers-International and was one of two recipients of its first Leadership and Service Award.

Donald D. Gehring is professor and chair of the higher education doctoral program at Bowling Green State University. He received his B.S. degree (1960) in industrial management from the Georgia Institute of Technology, his M.Ed. degree (1966) in mathematics education from Emory University, and his Ed.D. degree (1971) in higher education from the University of Georgia. His books include *The College Student and the Courts* (1977, with D. P. Young), and *Administrating College and University Housing: A Legal Perspective* (1983, with others).

James C. Grimm is director of housing at the University of Florida. He holds B.S. and M.S. degrees from Bowling Green State University. He has worked in the housing field since 1954 at Bowling Green State University, the University of Miami, and the University of Florida, where he has been since 1977. Grimm is a past president of the Association of College and University Housing Officers-International and is currently chair of its Research and Educational Foundation.

Daniel A. Hallenbeck is associate vice president for student affairs at the University of Georgia, where he was previously director of housing. He received his B.A. degree (1964) in junior high school social studies from the University of Northern Iowa, his M.A. degree (1965) in college student personnel administration from Michigan State University, and his Ph.D. degree (1974) in higher education administration from Iowa State University. He is former president of the Association of College and University Housing

Officers-International and has held housing positions at the University of Northern Iowa and Iowa State University.

Steven M. Janosik is the associate dean of students and director of judicial programs at Virginia Polytechnic Institute and State University. He earned his B.S. degree (1973) in business administration from Virginia Polytechnic Institute and State University, his M.Ed. degree (1975) in student personnel in higher education from the University of Georgia, and his Ed.D. degree (1987) in higher education administration from Virginia Tech. He has published widely on campus crime, higher education law, judicial affairs, liability and risk management, residence life, and student development. He is former editor of the *Journal of College and University Student Housing* and a member of the ACPA Media Board.

Mary Kay Kasper is currently an Ed.D. candidate in the Department of Counseling Education at the University of Maine, Orono, and an area director at the University of Southern Maine. Her areas of research include supervision, community development, and multiculturalism. She received her M.Ed. degree (1989) in student personnel in higher education from the University of Maine. In 1989, she received the ACPA Outstanding Graduate Student Residence Staff Member Award.

Patricia A. Kearney is assistant vice-chancellor for student affairs and director of housing at the University of California, Davis. She is former president of the American College Personnel Association and has twice served as a faculty member at the National Housing Training Institute. She received her B.A. degree (1965) in psychology from Michigan State University and her M.S. degree (1966) in higher education from Indiana University, and she is a Ph.D. candidate in college student services administration at Oregon State University.

Fred Leafgren is currently serving on the board of directors of the National Wellness Institute and is a human relations consultant. He received his B.S. degree (1954) in chemistry from the University of Illinois, and his M.A. degree (1959) in counseling and guidance and his Ph.D. degree (1968) in counseling psychology and student personnel administration from Michigan State University. He is the cofounder of the National Wellness Institute and coauthor of the *Life Style Assessment Questionnaire*.

Marcia B. Baxter Magolda is associate professor of educational leadership at Miami University. She received her B.A. degree (1974) in psychology from Capital University and her M.A. (1976) and Ph.D. (1983) degrees in college student personnel services from Ohio State University. She developed and validated a measure of college students' intellectual development and conducted a longitudinal study on intellectual development of both women and men. She is the author of *Knowing and Reasoning in College: Gender-Related Patterns in Students' Intellectual Development* (1992) and *Assessing Intellectual Development: The Link Between Theory and Practice* (1988, with W. D. Porterfield). Before joining the faculty at Miami University, Baxter Magolda was a student affairs practitioner at Ohio State University.

Theodore K. Miller is professor of counseling and human development services at the University of Georgia, where he is also coordinator of the student development in higher education preparation program. He earned his B.S. degree (1954) in business and English and his M.A. degree (1957) in counseling and guidance at Ball State University and his Ed.D. degree (1962) in counseling and student personnel services from the University of Florida. Miller has coauthored or edited eight professional books, including *Using Professional Standards in Student Affairs* (1991, with W. A. Bryan and R. B. Winston) and *Administration and Leadership in Student Affairs: Actualizing Student Development in Higher Education* (2nd ed., 1991, with R. B. Winston). In addition, he is former president of both the Council for the Advancement of Standards and the American College Personnel Association. He has received the American College Personnel Association's Outstanding Professional Service Award and the National Association of Student Personnel Administrators' Robert H. Shaffer Award for Academic Excellence as a Graduate Faculty Member.

Diane L. Podolske is a doctoral student in college student development at the University of Nebraska, Lincoln (UNL). She is a graduate assistant in the leadership development area of the UNL Campus Activities and Programs Office. Her research interests include leadership development training, evaluation processes, and ethical issues in student affairs.

William D. Porterfield is a partner in Diversity Associates, a management and educational services consulting firm with headquarters in St. Petersburg, Florida. He works with businesses and health care and educational organizations on affirmative action and assessment programs. He received his B.A. degree (1980) in political science and communications from the University of North Carolina at Chapel Hill, and his M.A. (1982) and Ph.D. (1984) degrees in educational administration from Ohio State University.

Diana L. Robertson is area coordinator for the Department of Housing and Dining Services at Kansas State University. She earned her B.A. degree (1986) in management science and English from Buena Vista College and her M.S. degree (1990) in college student personnel from Western Illinois University. Robertson was the recipient of the Gerald Saddlemire Award (1991) for master's-level research on homophobia. In 1992, she was one of the emerging professionals honored by ACPA at the Annuit Coeptis dinner.

Sue A. Saunders is the dean of students at Longwood College. She received her B.S. degree (1972) in journalism and her M.Ed. degree (1973) in counseling from Ohio University and her Ph.D. degree (1979) in counseling and student personnel services from the University of Georgia. Her publications include *Students Helping Students* (1979, with S. C. Ender and T. K. Miller) and numerous journal articles and book chapters. She has held housing positions at Bethany College and the University of Georgia. She is currently chairperson of American College Personnel Association Commission I.

John H. Schuh is associate vice president for student affairs and professor of counseling and school psychology at Wichita State University. He earned his Ph.D. degree at Arizona State University and has held administrative and faculty positions at Arizona State and at Indiana University. Schuh has served as a member of the executive board of the Association of College and University Housing Officers-International, the executive council of the American College Personnel Association, and the board of directors of the National Association of Student Personnel Administrators. He is a member of the editorial boards of the *Journal of College Student Development* and the *Journal of College and University Student Housing*. The author, coauthor, or editor of over one hundred publications, he has received awards from the American College Personnel Association and the National Association of Student Personnel Administrators for contributions to the student affairs literature.

Charles C. Schroeder earned his B.A. degree (1967) in psychology and history and his M.A. degree (1968) in student personnel and counseling psychology at Austin College; he earned his Ed.D. degree (1972) in college student personnel administration at Oregon State University. He has been vice president for student development at Saint Louis University, dean of students and assistant professor of psychology at Mercer University, director of men's housing at Auburn University, director of counseling services at Western New England College, and counselor at Austin College. He is former president and president-elect of the American College Personnel Association and has published widely on residential life.

C. Carney Strange is professor and chair of the Department of Higher Education and Student Affairs at Bowling Green State University. He received his B.A. degree (1969) in French literature from Saint Meinrad College of Liberal Arts and his M.A. degree (1976) in college student personnel and Ph.D. degree (1978) in college student personnel and higher education from the University of Iowa.

Vicky L. Triponey is associate dean of student life and services at Wichita State University. She has held student affairs and student activities positions at the University of Virginia, the University of Georgia, and the University of Pittsburgh, Johnstown. She received her B.S. degree in psychology from the

University of Pittsburgh, Johnstown, her M.A. degree in student personnel from Indiana University of Pennsylvania, and her Ph.D. degree in higher education administration from the University of Virginia.

M. Lee Upcraft is assistant vice president for counseling services and program assessment, affiliate professor of education, and affiliate, Center for the Study of Higher Education, Pennsylvania State University. He is the author of more than fifty publications and serves as associate editor of the New Directions for Student Services sourcebooks. He received his B.A. degree (1960) in social studies and his M.A. degree (1961) in guidance and counseling from the State University of New York (SUNY), Albany, and his Ph.D. degree (1967) in student personnel administration from Michigan State University.

Charles J. Werring is director of housing and dining services at Kansas State University. He earned both his B.S. degree (1974) in biology and his M.Ed. degree (1975) in educational administration at Kansas State University; he earned his Ed.D. degree (1984) in adult education at the University of Georgia. Werring is former chairperson of American College Personnel Association Commission III and has written extensively in the areas of adult education and residential life.

David B. White is staff member in the development office at Asheville-Buncombe Technical Community College in Asheville, North Carolina, with primary responsibilities related to outcomes assessment and institutional research. He received his B.A. degree (1977) in psychology from SUNY, Geneseo, his M.A. degree (1980) in counseling psychology from Trinity Evangelical Divinity School, and his Ph.D. degree (1986) in student development in postsecondary education from the University of Iowa.

Chapter One

New Challenges and Goals for Residential Life Programs

Gregory S. Blimling

At the core of any established student affairs organization at a residential college is a strong residence hall program. Life outside the classroom is amplified here. It provides more opportunities to influence student growth and development in the first year or two of college than almost any other program in student affairs. Although educational opportunities are offered through a variety of student affairs programs and departments, none are as pervasive in scope or have the potential to influence as many students as residence halls do.

Residence halls have always been about teaching. Their origin can be traced backed to the residential colleges of Oxford and Cambridge established for the purpose of educating young men to be "gentleman scholars." It was recognized at an early date that education for a responsible and enlightened citizenship must involve the development of the intellect, the character, and the personality of the student (Rudolph, 1962). Although there have been times in American higher education when some educators have lost sight of the value of the out-of-class experience for students' education, the importance of this experience to the overall education of students is as valuable today as it was when students lived and studied together in residence

1

halls under the watchful tutelage of the faculty at Oxford and Cambridge in the thirteenth century.

Like all of higher education, housing programs are in a period of transition. They are confronted by a changing student population, increased scrutiny by state legislatures, an aging physical plant, and a declining pool of trained personnel to work with students in residence halls. In this chapter, challenges and issues facing housing programs are identified. No attempt is made to posit solutions. The chapters that follow fulfill this task. The chapter is organized into eight major challenges. Under each heading, issues facing housing programs are identified and briefly discussed. The chapter concludes with observations about the direction residence life staff may explore in the future.

Challenge 1: Multiculturalism

The number of Asian Americans, African Americans, and Hispanic Americans in the college-age population in the United States is increasing and will continue to do so (Levine, 1989). In actual numbers, there were more African-American, Asian-American, and Hispanic-American students enrolled in four-year colleges in 1988 than there were in 1976. However, although the total number of people of color enrolled increased, their participation rates in four-year colleges has declined as a percentage of students graduating from high school. Between 1976 and 1988, the proportion of African Americans who enrolled in college declined from 33 to 28 percent; the proportion of Hispanic Americans declined from 36 to 31 percent (American Council on Education, 1990). Asian-American students increased approximately 128 percent. But an increasing percentage of people of color are attending two-year colleges.

On balance, if one looks at all of higher education — two-year institutions through research universities — there are significant changes in the composition of the student population. In 1980, 81 percent of the more than twelve million students enrolled in higher education were white Americans. In 1990, 78 percent of the almost fourteen million students were white Americans. The remaining students in both years were comprised of many other racial groups ("College Enrollment by Racial and Ethnic Group," 1992, p. A35).

These demographic shifts are not uniformly evident across the nation. Certain geographical regions of the United States, urban institutions, and state-supported open admissions institutions have seen noticeable changes in the number of people of color enrolling; other institutions have not seen significant changes. Changes in federally funded financial aid policies, new high school curricula, some public policy decisions, and possibly an increase in the number of students transferring from two-year colleges to four-year colleges may influence future college participation rates for these groups.

Institutions experiencing these changes in the composition of their student body face what Kuh (1990, p. 85) describes as "unprecedented challenges to institutions of higher education in general and to student affairs professionals in particular." There is no place in a college in which these challenges are more keenly felt than in residence halls. There are always conflicts when two eighteen- or nineteen-year-old students are asked to share a twelve-foot by twelve-foot room together—to sleep, socialize, relax, and study in that same space. When students come from different racial, ethnic, cultural, religious, or socioeconomic backgrounds, these adjustments are often more difficult. Most residence staff can recite examples of roommate conflicts stemming from parents discovering that their son or daughter was assigned a room with a student of a different race, ethnic background, or culture. What is surprising is how many of these initial roommate conflicts are resolved after parents leave and the students take time to know one another.

An increase in the number of people of color in residence halls at predominantly white colleges is likely to create more of these conflicts. Most of these conflicts will probably resolve themselves; some will not. One could envision several scenarios that may materialize in housing programs on various campuses. The worst of these would be an increase in hate groups, as some colleges in Pennsylvania, Florida, Minnesota, and Louisiana have experienced with the creation of White Student Unions (Levinson, 1990; Dodge, 1992), and a corresponding increase in hate speech. The best of these scenarios would be an acceptance and an appreciation of multiculturalism. The limited research done in residence halls concerning racial integration issues would suggest that the latter scenario is the more likely outcome (Markley, 1968; Daniels, 1977; Marion and Stafford, 1980).

Given that the highest percentage of students living in college residence halls are first-year students—eighteen and nineteen years old—and that students usually spend part of the first year trying to gain self-confidence and control of their own environment, those who must contend with cultural norms in peer relationships different from their background environment are likely to face adjustment problems. In these circumstances, white middle-class students at what have been predominantly white colleges may experience adjustment difficulties similar to those that students who are members of racial, ethnic, or cultural minority groups have experienced on these campuses for many years.

Residence life staff will bear the brunt of the interpersonal conflicts, and they will need to familiarize themselves with the culture of various groups on their own campuses. Policies appropriate to the circumstances of the institution need to be in place to allow residence life staff to mediate or in other ways intervene in these situations. Training will be an important component for both professional residence life staff and paraprofessionals, who must learn to help students work through these conflicts.

There is a tendency to view the changing demographic features of the student population in terms of race, culture, ethnic background, and similar features and to ignore other important changes emerging among the student population. One of these changes concerns the increased openness and acceptance of students' sexual orientation. Although it is unlikely that there are any more or less homosexual or bisexual students on college campuses today than there were twenty years ago, there is a greater awareness of this issue and a greater number of students who are open about their sexual orientation (Dey, Astin, and Korn, 1991).

Many colleges have adopted policies stating that the institution does not discriminate on the basis of sexual orientation. These policies have sometimes been used to remove ROTC programs from college campuses because of the military's policy of excluding homosexual and bisexual persons from military service. The implementation of institutional policies prohibiting discrimination on the basis of sexual orientation has already influenced residence hall policies on some campuses. Several large research universities currently allow students to indicate a preference for a homosexual roommate. The thinking behind this decision is that two homosexual students living together are more likely to be supportive of one another than two students with differing sexual orientations.

When two openly homosexual students live together in a residence hall, other students in the living unit may feel threatened. In these situations, young male students in the transition to adulthood, grappling with their own sexual identities, can present particularly difficult situations for homosexual students and for the residence life staff. One graphic example of this occurred at a large Midwestern university (Lindsmith, 1991), when two openly homosexual male students living in a male residence hall were harassed and physically threatened by students in their living unit. Repeated attempts to resolve the situation and heroic efforts to ensure the rights of all students in the living unit were unsuccessful. Ultimately, with the assistance of the campus police, the residence life staff had to disband the entire living unit and involuntarily reassign all of the students to other living units on the campus. The decision was unpopular with the students in the living unit and with their parents, and it was the subject of much discussion on campus.

Other colleges and universities have confronted and will continue to confront the same issues. Many factors have the potential to make the implementation of college policies prohibiting discrimination on the basis of sexual orientation controversial when applied to undergraduates living in residence halls. These factors include institutional policies, the constraints of the particular campus housing situation in terms of the number of available rooms, the institution's code of student conduct, the intervention of parents, and the external policies involved with decisions surrounding the situations.

One other demographic change deserves mention. Dey, Astin, and Korn (1991) report that between 1969 and 1990, the proportion of female students enrolling as first-year students increased from 43 to 54 percent. The change in the proportion of male and female students enrolling as undergraduates is not a problem, but it does present some logistical issues for colleges retaining only single-sex residence halls. This is not a new topic. Every fall, housing administrators balance the population in residence halls by remodeling bathrooms and reassigning residence hall space. Demographics for the student population suggest that these minor adjustments will continue in the future.

Challenge 2: Student Mental and Physical Health

Not only are the demographics of students changing, but so are their attitudes and needs for certain services. Within the past ten years, college campuses have experienced a noticeable increase in students presenting psychological problems. College counseling centers report (Stone and Archer, 1990) that both the number and severity of psychological problems students are bringing with them to college are increasing. In a survey of college counseling centers, Gallagher (1988) finds that 56 percent of the college counseling center directors were seeing students with more severe psychological disorders. Only 2 percent of the counseling center directors saw a decrease, and 39 percent were seeing about the same numbers. Other data support the observation of counseling center directors that overall severity of psychological problems of students is increasing. Studies by Koplik and DeVito (1986), Rimmer, Halikas, and Schuckit (1982), and Johnson, Ellison, and Heikkinen (1989) using standardized psychological testing instruments with various populations of college students show that students are coming to college with more distress and psychiatric problems than the normal adult population or than students who enrolled in college in the 1970s. The most common presenting problems for students that are increasing are the following: eating disorders, substance abuse, sexual abuse and violence, dysfunctional family problems, and acquired immune deficiency syndrome (AIDS) (Stone and Archer, 1990).

Physicians in student health services frequently work with psychologists and psychiatrists to administer and monitor the use of psychotropic drug therapy with students. The legal issues surrounding the behavior of students who have psychological problems, and the recourses colleges have in addressing these issues, have been the subject of several publications (Pavela, 1983, 1985; Weeks, 1983). Students with serious psychological problems manifest these problems in many places on campus. Because most students spend a large portion of their out-of-class time in residence halls, residence life staff are likely to be involved in significant ways with the psychologically troubled student and his or her behavior. The resident assistants (RAs) and residents of the living unit are often befuddled by the inability or reluctance of college officials to address the behavior of these students. Administrators, fearing lawsuits and federal agency intervention, are frequently frustrated in their attempts to intervene. Finding an appropriate balance between protecting the rights and opportunities for recovery of disturbed students and the rights of other residents for comfortable and psychologically "safe" living arrangements will continue to be a challenge for residential life programs.

There is no indication that the number of students with serious mental health problems who enroll in college and live in residence halls will decrease in the future. Residence life staff members (professional and paraprofessional alike) will need more training in dealing with psychologically distressed students and will require greater support from the college mental health professionals.

On the positive side, fewer students are using drugs. In a national study conducted with graduating high school seniors in 1989, Johnston, O'Malley, and Bachman (1990) found a 15 percent decrease in the use of illegal drugs since 1981. They also found that 78 percent of graduating high school seniors view the regular use of marijuana as harmful, and 90 percent view the regular use of cocaine as harmful. These findings are consistent with national survey data on first-year students. Dey, Astin, and Korn (1991) found that in 1977, 53 percent of college freshmen supported the legalization of marijuana. In 1990, only 19 percent supported this proposal.

There is evidence (Charlier, 1990) that the consumption of alcohol by eighteen- to twenty-four-year-olds is also declining. Quoting a study by the Simmons Market Research Bureau, Charlier (1990) reports that between 1984 and 1988, the consumption of vodka fell from 32 to 22 percent in the college-age group. The percentage of college-age students drinking beer fell from 56 percent in 1984 to 47 percent in 1989. This movement toward increased sobriety is supported by Johnson, O'Malley, and Bachman's (1990) research that found 70 percent of high school seniors view taking four or five drinks everyday as harmful, and 25 percent believe that moderate drinking (one or two drinks nearly every day) poses a great physical or mental risk. Increased attention to personal health and wellness, an interest in weight control, and increased social pressure toward moderation are often credited with these trends toward more responsible drinking habits among college students.

Although there are definite indications of a decline in alcohol consumption, 94 percent of all college students reported having used alcohol, 76 percent reported using it within the previous month, and 42 percent reported having five or more drinks consecutively within two weeks prior to completing the survey by Johnson, O'Malley, and Bachman (1990). Most studies are showing that between 21 and 27 percent of college students are heavy drinkers (Rivinus, 1988).

Alcohol also plays a role in many behavioral problems. O'Shaughnessey and Palmer (1990) found that when sexual assaults occurred, approximately 71 percent of the women and 81 percent of the men were drinking. More than 20 percent of students admitted to engaging in unprotected sexual intercourse while under the influence of alcohol (Rivinus, 1988), and alcohol is often involved in property damage, vandalism, and similar acts of destruction in the residence halls.

Two problems with alcohol remain. The first is the continuing problem of alcohol education. This becomes increasingly difficult from year to year because many of the alcohol education programs seem to be routine or redundant. Most students have been exposed to information about alcohol misuse since grade school. Maintaining the enthusiasm in residence halls to do alcohol education programs is a challenge. The second of these problems is the continuing problem of enforcement of college alcohol policies. Because most of the student's leisure time is spent in residence halls, residence life staff and RAs usually make up the vanguard of enforcement for college alcohol policies. It is a strain for residence life staff and RAs to function as both counselors and policy enforcers (see Chapter Thirteen). This is by no means a new role. Many residence life staff who were in college when the states still had eighteen-year-old drinking laws sometimes find it difficult to be convincing in explaining to twenty-year-old students the reasons why they should not be permitted to consume alcohol. The argument that "a law is a law" begins to ring hollow and less sincere the more residence life staff resort to it.

One of the most serious health-related problems that residence life staff will be asked to handle concerns AIDS and the issues surrounding the transmission of the human immunodeficiency virus (HIV). Current studies by the Centers for Disease Control and the American College Health Association indicate that approximately 1 in 500 college students is infected with HIV ("ACHA/CDC Release HIV Sero-Prevalence Data," 1989). Although surveys show that most college students know how to prevent the transmission of HIV, they also show that students often do not take precautions to prevent the transmission of HIV or other sexually transmitted diseases (Carroll, 1991). AIDS education is the responsibility of many college departments and programs. What makes the issue more sensitive in residence halls is the likelihood that a noninfected student may be asked to live with an HIV-infected student. Although there are no documented cases of HIV being transmitted by casual contact, many people remain unconvinced. Students, parents, and college administrators often fear that bloodborne pathogens from HIV-infected students will expose a noninfected student to the virus. The result of this fear has been that some students ostracize those they believe to have HIV or refuse to occupy rooms in the same living unit as an HIV-infected resident.

Recent federal regulations codified as 29 CFR 1910.1030 (1992) under the Occupational Safety and Health Administration (OSHA) require universities, among other agencies, to institute special safety precautions to ensure that personnel who come into contact with blood and other bodily fluids are protected from accidental exposure. These regulations include precautions and training for housekeeping personnel and others, such as housing administrators and residence life staff, who may occasionally come into contact with blood and other bodily fluids subsequent to a student injury.

Accompanying these concerns are a host of ethical issues when residence life staff know that a student is HIV positive and has a roommate assumed to be HIV negative. In most cases, they do not have this information. The issue becomes more complex when the student has AIDS and the disease is in its active state. These students are usually too ill to attend classes, or they fear that exposure to the general population places them at unreasonable risk of acquiring infections. However, some students may continue to remain enrolled and continue to live in residence halls. As this disease spreads throughout the population, residence life staff will have increased occasions to address these and related issues.

Challenge 3: Campus Violence

Violence on college campuses is a serious concern. In high school, many students learned to carry weapons as a means of self-protection or peer status. This dangerous practice has made its way to colleges. At many large universities and colleges in urban communities, college officials have resorted to the use of metal detectors to screen guests at social functions. In residence halls, too many opportunities exist for students with low impulse control to resort to the use of weapons when they feel threatened, and there are numerous opportunities for students to be careless with a weapon when it is in a residence hall. How residence life staff will control this dangerous practice is a serious concern.

Violence against female students in particular is a major issue. Koss (1988) found in a national study that over 20 percent of college women reported that they were forced against their will to have sexual intercourse at some time in their dating history. In another study (Aizenman and Kelley, 1988), 22 percent of college students reported being involved in some form of violence related to a dating situation. A survey by O'Shaughnessey and Palmer (1990) of female students at a large Midwestern university found that 45 percent indicated that they were the victim of some form of date violence, ranging from intimidation to rape. Students in this survey also were asked the locations of these incidents. Most (30 percent) occurred in residence halls. Women's residence halls accounted for 22 percent, and men's residence halls accounted for 8 percent. Fraternity houses were the next most likely location, with 25 percent of the respondents reporting this as the location for the act of dating violence.

At the forefront of responding to these situations are the residence life staff and RAs. These acts of dating violence are destructive to the victims and are threatening and disruptive to the network of friends who support the victim. Confronting the person responsible for the violence through the criminal court system or through the college's disciplinary system presents additional stress that often students choose not to subject themselves to. Residence life staff and RAs frequently find themselves in the middle of these events. Because of the sensitive nature of these situations and the severity of the charges, residence life staff are often used instead of the police to pursue an investigation prior to any decision about whether criminal or disciplinary action may be supportable by facts. These encounters challenge the crisis management and counseling skills of residence life staff and require them to negotiate a circuitous path among legal issues, confidentiality, and the emotional health of students.

Challenge 4: Changing Student Attitudes

Student attitudes and beliefs appear to follow cycles (Levine, 1980), ranging from very liberal views such as were expressed in the 1960s to very conservative views such as were expressed by students in the 1980s. There is some evidence suggesting that a general liberalizing of students' views at enrollment is now emerging. The 1990 annual survey of first-year students (Dey, Astin, and Korn, 1991) documents that 39 percent participated in organized demonstrations in high school the year prior to attending college. This is the highest percentage observed since the survey was begun in 1966. In the late 1960s and early 1970s, only 16 to 18 percent participated in an organized protest during the year preceding college. There is a similar increase in the percentage of freshmen indicating that the chances are "very good" that they will participate in student protests or demonstrations while in college. In 1990, 7 percent of the first-year students who were surveyed indicated that this was likely. This percentage marks an all-time high. During the late 1960s at the height of student protests in college, between 4 and 5 percent of freshmen were indicating a "very good" chance of participation.

What this means for residence life is unclear. If student activism is going to increase, as trends in the annual survey of freshman attitudes research suggest and that some in student affairs are forecasting (Miser, 1988), residence life staff are likely to be thrust into roles as mediators, negotiators, consultants, and policy enforcers. These are not new roles for residence life staff or for other student affairs administrators, but they are roles in the context of student protests that many student affairs administrators have not had to use in many years and that younger staff may never have experienced.

It is difficult to know the issues that might ignite a student protest. Concerns expressed by African-American students, sexual violence and harassment, global political issues, and ecological issues are all likely candidates. Ecological issues are an area of increasing concern for students (Dey, Astin, and Korn, 1991). In housing programs, these issues include concerns about recycling in the residence halls and environmental questions related to the construction of new residence halls in wooded or "green space" areas of a campus. Recycling is something that colleges should be teaching students through the experience of living in residence halls. However, unless it is approached correctly, it can present health and fire safety risks. Given student concern about the environment and local ordinances regarding recycling, housing programs that have not yet addressed the issues of recycling in residence halls may find it appropriate to do so.

Challenge 5: Accountability

At least sixteen states require colleges to document what students are learning through some form of institutional assessment program (*Chronicle of Higher Education*, 1991). Regional educational accrediting agencies in all regions of the United States ask that colleges assess what students are learning and how the institution is using this information in policy and curriculum decisions.

In student affairs, the 1988 Council for the Advancement of Standards for Student Services/Development Programs (CAS) (1988) established standards for student affairs divisions and programs. In housing and residence life, these standards call for "systematic and regular research on and evaluating of the overall institutional student services/development program and the residence life program to determine whether the educational goals and needs of students are met" (p. 28).

The value of living in a residence hall to the education of students needs to be documented on each campus. Residence life staff cannot assume that counting the number of residence hall programs and the number of students who wander through the hall lounge during the program is sufficient to indicate the educational value of residence halls. Numbers of programs and participants do not equal degree of education received by students (see Chapter Sixteen).

There are many ways to assess student growth and development outside the classroom (Erwin, 1991). To share in full membership with the academic community, residence life must be willing and prepared to take a serious look at the educational value of the residence hall experience. As noted in Chapter Two, the research literature on residence halls does not support the contention that simply living in a residence hall has a significant influence on students' attitudes, values, academic performance, or intellectual or psychosocial development (Blimling, 1989; Pascarella and Terenzini, 1991). The literature tends to be highly specific and supports fairly narrow statements about the ways in which residence halls help to educate students. The type of institution, the kind of residence hall situation, and the class standing of students all influence the results. For example, published research on the influence of residence halls on African-American students is almost nonexistent, and there are very few published studies involving small colleges. Most of the research literature is from large research universities in the Midwestern and Southeastern parts of the United States (Blimling, 1989; Blimling and others, 1987).

There is no substitute for research conducted on one's own campus under familiar circumstances. Staff in housing programs that have not yet begun a serious assessment effort face the enjoyable challenge of discovering what they help students learn and what they need to help students learn better. If residential life programs are truly committed to the goals of student development, these programs must become more intrusive and intentional.

Implementation of theme housing units that require major staff involvement and institutional support, such as living-learning centers, service-learning units, and cultural emphasis programs, are program opportunities worth exploring.

Challenge 6: Residence Hall Facilities

There are people in the college community who think of residence halls first as buildings to house students for the purpose of shelter. Student affairs administrators seldom agree. They see residence halls as opportunities to educate students. Residence halls are one tool student affairs administrators have at their disposal to influence the psychosocial development and practical competence of students. These differing views of the purpose of residence halls manifest themselves in disputes over education versus efficiency, teaching versus consumerism, and housing comforts versus programming needs. The only reason to mention these old management issues is that they may rekindle disputes in attempts to address some of the challenges facing housing programs.

One of these challenges concerns what to do with a number of large high-rise buildings constructed in the early 1960s under the Higher Education Facilities Act of 1963 and similar legislation. Bess (1973, pp. 37–38) describes these residence halls as "huge complexes of dormitory residences... with little thought to the ways in which residence life might be integrated into academic life... beset by unwieldy state and federal restrictions on costs per square foot... without [thought to] the educational life of students, let alone their personal living space." These high-rise residence halls are the bane of many housing administrators' lives. Many of the buildings remain under bond obligation, or the revenue is pledged to support other bonds. Frequently, they are a maintenance nightmare. More than one housing administrator has contemplated with glee the solution that the University of Cincinnati implemented on June 23, 1991—when it had the twenty-six-story, 1,300-bed Sander Residence Hall dynamited (Keegan, 1991). Other high-rise residence halls have come to kinder fates when they were converted to administrative offices or the space was redesigned for special life-style programs (Rodgers, 1990). The research on the negative influence of high-rise residence halls on the students is clear (Mandel, Baron, and Fisher, 1980; Wilcox and Holahan, 1976; Ashley, 1982; Bickman and others, 1973). With few exceptions, these buildings are an architectural mistake that needs to be addressed.

As a related problem, many residence hall facilities are in need of repair. After thirty or more years of service, even with good maintenance, most buildings should be renovated. Maintenance costs for elevators, damage from vandalism and normal abuse, the need to comply with new federal regulations to ensure accessibility by disabled students, and the need to comply with more pervasive safety and fire code regulations all are costly routine or special maintenance problems facing housing programs. Addressing these problems requires renovation, and renovation is expensive. To find the funds, room rental charges have to be increased, fund reserves depleted, or money appropriated from educational programming funds. None of these are appealing options. The most common response has been to increase room rental fees. This alternative is becoming less viable as institutions consider the overall cost of education at their institution to first-year students, and as proposed increases in housing fees compete with proposed increases in tuition and other fees. These financial demands on colleges hold the promise of rekindling the debates between facility needs versus educational program needs.

For many students, the traditional residence hall situation — with two students assigned to a room, a common bathroom on the floor with gang showers, and a double-loaded straight corridor — is not a satisfactory housing situation. As the size of families has grown smaller and the number of bedrooms in the average home has grown larger, more students in high school have their own rooms. These rooms are frequently equipped with stereos, televisions, and personal computers. To verify this, watch the next time students and their parents arrive on campus when the residence halls open for occupancy. Minirefrigerators, microwave ovens, and a plethora of electronic gadgetry caravan their way into residence halls. The practical problems associated with this are minor — they consist of occasional power problems in older buildings, an increasing electric bill, and the constant challenge for the residence life staff of maintaining a moderate decibel volume as students listen to their 200-watt-per-channel quadriphonic sound systems. The important issue here is the desire for privacy. Students are accustomed to it. They like it. And they find ways of escaping into their stereos or televisions to find it.

In response to this demand for privacy, institutions have converted double-room space to single-room space. They are building suite-type living arrangements and constructing apartment-style housing. The latter is partially in response to requests for twelve-month housing contracts from international students, older students, and students who either do not have parents or who do not want to spend time with their parents when residence halls are closed for vacation periods.

These changes in student life-style have the potential to fundamentally change the way residence life staff interact with students and the magnitude of the influence that residence halls can have on students. When students move into apartments instead of into traditional halls, the social organization and peer environment change. The kind and degree of mutually shared experiences students have are different and are often confined to a more closed social network. The dynamics of group interaction, the diversity of students with whom students share common experiences, and the power and influence of primary peer associations are redefined by the architecture of the living unit. The interaction of RAs and the kind of programming they create can also change.

The architectural environment influences behavior in important ways. Kurt Lewin (1936) posed this concept as a basic principle of human behavior: behavior is a function of the person in the environment. When students are moved from high-rise to low-rise buildings or from traditional two-person residence halls to apartment-style living, one of the tools that student affairs administrators use to influence student growth and development changes. Residence life educators must learn how to use these new tools to maximize the psychosocial development and practical competence of students.

Challenge 7: Institutional Finances

The financial strain experienced by many colleges frequently places additional burdens on residence halls. Because housing programs are usually treated as a financial auxiliary at state-supported institutions, their funds are separate from other institutional funds. Frequently, housing programs keep sizable financial reserves to address unanticipated major maintenance problems and as insurance against declines in occupancy that could lead to default on bond obligations on residence halls. Tight financial times require "creative" solutions to financial problems. One of these financial solutions for colleges has been to charge housing programs for a variety of on-campus services, including general administrative overhead. Housing programs are being billed for a host of previously unforeseen expenses, including fire-fighting equipment, physical plant equipment, landscaping services, and special administrative costs associated with the billing of electricity, water use, sewage, and steam heat. If higher education continues to experience financial problems, residence halls are likely to continue to be viewed as a "deep pocket" for colleges in their attempt to cope with other institutional costs.

Colleges also are turning to private business to supply services that were previously provided by college personnel. Food services and custodial services are two areas where this is used most in housing programs. Hiring a private company to provide residence life staff, RAs, and general counseling services is the next logical step in the process of institutional privatization. The question of privatization has not gone unnoticed by housing administrators. The Association of College and University Housing Officers-International is studying the issue, its magnitude, and its influence on housing programs (Garry Johnson, president-elect, ACUHO-I, letter to the author, March 1992).

Because of devastating financial problems experienced during periods of economic recession in certain regions of the United States, some colleges have considered selling their residence halls to private businesses as a way to recover capital investment for other financial purposes. Privately operated residence halls are not a new concept. At large universities in some geographical areas, they have been moderately successful; however, there appear to be more examples of their failure. What is new is the idea of treating residence halls as property. Although there were times in the history of higher education when this argument was made (Cowley, 1934), it has been many years since colleges were willing to trade the educational value of residence halls for financial expedience. The implications of such a move are dramatic. It would send a strong message that residence halls are only shelters and that anyone can operate them. It would also say, in a subtle way, that residence halls are not a part of the educational system designed to foster the personal development and education of students.

Research by Astin (1992) shows that students are becoming more informed consumers in higher education. Increasingly, the cost of college and the availability of financial assistance or part-time jobs are major considerations in where a student chooses to enroll. In the 1991 annual survey of American freshmen (Astin, 1992) 28 percent of students indicated that low tuition and availability of financial aid were their primary considerations in selecting a college. This compares with 23 and 20 percent respectively for the freshmen completing the survey in 1990. The cost of room and board as part of the overall cost of education also influences the volume of students applying for admission. Residence halls may soon see a time when they can no longer simply pass along the cost of operations to students in the form of increased room-and-board charges. When this happens, housing administrators will be forced to make difficult choices between facilities issues and student development goals.

Challenge 8: Staffing Issues

A joint task force report of the American College Personnel Association and the National Association of Student Personnel Administrators (1990) on professional preparation shows that there has been an 18 percent decline in the number of graduates from master's, specialist, and doctoral programs since 1970. This report also shows an increase in the number of women entering the field and a decrease in the number of men. Two of the conclusions drawn from this report are that there are many positions in student affairs that are being filled by persons who have not been trained for student affairs work, and that there is a general feminizing of the field. These findings have several implications for housing programs. First is the difficulty of finding qualified personnel to serve in educational roles in residence halls. Because housing programs tend to hire a large number of people in entry-level positions and these new professionals tend to move from these positions within two or three years, there is frequent turnover in staff. In any one year, a housing program may be filling vacancies for as many as half of the entry-level positions as hall directors or area coordinators.

Competition for the best graduates is strong. One common response to the decline in the number of qualified applicants has been for housing programs to reorganize by moving graduate students into hall director roles and residence life staff with graduate degrees in student affairs work into area coordinator roles supervising several residence halls. An outgrowth of this reorganization has been the creation of a recruiting conference in Oshkosh, Wisconsin, for graduate students interested in assistantships as hall directors while they work on graduate degrees. This development has not, however, been accompanied by an increase in the number of full-time faculty members in student affairs preparatory programs or in the creation of new programs.

A second problem for some housing programs has been to find enough males to serve as hall directors in male residence halls. This is more of an issue at institutions that have yet to adopt coed housing or that offer only limited coed housing. Some housing programs have assigned female hall directors to male residence halls; however, this practice tends to be the exception to the traditional way of matching the gender of residence life staff to that of students in residence halls.

One challenge that awaits student affairs is finding more ways to interest students in pursuing careers in this field. RAs often become interested in pursuing careers in student affairs work after serving for a year or two in the RA role. Housing programs are in an excellent position to help funnel interested students into the field generally and residence life specifically.

The social norms governing relationships between unmarried couples are different than they were thirty years ago. Unmarried couples frequently live together, and there is little if any social stigma attached to the relationship. The reason for raising this issue concerns expectations colleges have for unmarried residence life staff who have live-in responsibilities as hall directors or area coordinators. For many years, colleges expected live-in residence life staff to conduct their personal lives as models for student behavior; many institutions still have this expectation. These colleges did not want live-in residence life staff to engage in any behavior that might be embarrassing to the institution or that might be inconsistent with the expectations that parents have for a college employee with responsibility for the life of their son or daughter outside of the classroom.

Within the context of a particular college setting, this expectation may or may not be realistic. Some institutions have reexamined their policies governing the social life of their live-in residence life staff and have determined that this issue does not concern work performance and is not something the institution should attempt to control. Other institutions have reached different decisions. The issue often becomes more complex for institutions when the subject of the sexual orientation of live-in residence life staff and their companions is considered. Although it is one thing for an institution to advance a philosophy of nondiscrimination on the basis of sexual orientation, it is often more difficult to live that philosophy under the scrutiny of the public. Housing administrators are sometimes placed in the awkward position of defending the rights of students to be free from discrimination on the basis of sexual orientation while refusing to extend the same rights to their live-in residence life staff. The debate concerning an institution's role in regulating the social life of its live-in residence life staff will continue to provide a challenge for many housing programs.

With the litany of problems reviewed above, one must ask if the expectations for residence life staff and RAs are unrealistic. How can entry-level residence life staff, graduate assistants, and undergraduate RAs be expected to deal with suicidal students, criminal violence, drug abuse, rape situations, students with dangerous weapons, racial problems, AIDS, and students who are experiencing mental health problems ranging from depression to schizophrenia? The answer is that colleges have always had unrealistic expectations for residence life staff and for RAs, and they will continue to. They have survived these challenges in the past by relying on a network of staff support, by keeping themselves informed on issues, and by training themselves to address these issues. The challenges awaiting residence life staff will require the same dedication.

Comments

There is probably no better training in student affairs work than to spend two or three years living in a residence hall as a hall director or area coordinator. One learns more about student life and gains more practical experience this way than through a host of seminars and workshops. But this experience is valuable only if it can be applied constructively to the education of students. Doing this requires that residence life staff take their role as teachers seriously.

These are not the same educational roles that residence life staff have had in earlier years. The circumstances that students are bringing with them to college require a far more informed and sophisticated approach. Residence life staff cannot become effective teachers with students today without a clear understanding of what they are trying to achieve, how to go about achieving it, and how to know when or if it has been achieved. There is no substitute for understanding and for being able to put into practice knowledge of the psychosocial and cognitive development of students, how people are influenced by their environments, and the dynamics of peer social group formation and support. This background must be coupled with knowledge and experience in counseling, crisis intervention, educational programming, research methods, and good teaching. These are the tools of the trade in residence hall work.

Students deserve not only the nurturing and support offered by residence life staff, but also the skills of dedicated practitioners with knowledge of student development theory and the capability of assisting students in realizing their full human potential. It is no less than is expected of the faculty, who should be able to teach, do research in their field of study, and motivate, advise, and support students. In an ideal world, the line between teaching in the classroom done by the faculty and teaching outside the classroom done by student affairs administrators would disappear. To move in this direction requires progress by both student affairs educators and faculty members. This book brings student affairs educators one step closer toward achieving this goal.

The chapters that follow offer an informed and insightful look at how residence life staff can meet the challenges facing housing programs and residence life and fulfill the goals of educating students in residence halls.

References

"ACHA/CDC Release HIV Sero-Prevalence Data." *Action*, July-Aug. 1989, pp. 9–10.

American College Personnel Association and National Association of Student Personnel Administrators. *Joint Task Force Report: The Recruitment, Preparation, and Nurturing of the Student Affairs Professional*. Washington, D.C.: National Association of Student Personnel Administrators, 1990.

Aizenman, M., and Kelley, G. "The Incidence of Violence and Acquaintance Rape in Dating Relationships Among College Men and Women." *Journal of College Student Development*, 1988, *29*, 305–311.

American Council on Education. "Racial and Ethnic Trends in College Participation: 1976 to 1988." *Research Briefs*, 1990, *1*(3), 1–3.

Ashley, G. M. "The Relationships Between Dormitory Climates, Personality Factors, and Selected Interactions and Freshmen's Ratings of Satisfaction with College." *Dissertation Abstracts International*, 1982, *44*(5), 1379A.

Astin, A. W. *The American Freshman: National Norms for Fall 1991*. Los Angeles: Higher Education Research Institute, UCLA, 1992.

Bess, J. L. "More Than Room and Board: Linking Residence and Classroom." In J. Katz (ed.), *Services for Students*. New Directions for Higher Education, no. 3. San Francisco: Jossey-Bass, 1973.

Bickman, L., and others. "Dormitory Density and Helping Behavior." *Environment and Behavior*, 1973, *5*(4), 465–490.

Blimling, G. S. "The Influence of College Residence Halls on Students: A Meta-Analysis of the Empirical Research, 1966–1985." Unpublished doctoral dissertation, Educational Policy and Leadership Department, Ohio State University, 1988.

Blimling, G. S. "A Meta-Analysis of the Influence of College Residence Halls on Academic Performance." *Journal of College Student Development*, 1989, *30*, 298–308.

Blimling, G. S., and others. *An ACHUO-I Bibliography on Residence Halls*. Columbus, Ohio: Association of College and University Housing Officers-International, 1987.

Carroll, L. "Gender, Knowledge About AIDS, Reported Behavioral Change, and Sexual Behavior of College Students." *Journal of American College Health*, 1991, *40*(2), 5–12.

Charlier, M. "Youthful Sobriety Tests Liquor Firms." *Wall Street Journal*, June 14, 1990, pp. B1, B7.

Chronicle of Higher Education staff. *The Almanac of Higher Education, 1991.* Chicago: University of Chicago Press, 1991.

"College Enrollment by Racial and Ethnic Group." *Chronicle of Higher Education*, Mar. 18, 1992, p. A35.

Council for the Advancement of Standards for Student Services/Development Programs. *CAS Standards and Guidelines for Student Services/Development Programs.* Washington, D.C.: Council for the Advancement of Standards for Student Services/Development Programs, 1986.

Cowley, W. H. "The History of Student Residential Housing." *School and Society*, 1934, *40*(1040), 705–712; *40*(1042), 758–764.

Daniels, O. C. "An Assessment of College Students' Interracial Apperception and Ideology." *Journal of College Student Personnel*, 1977, *18*(1), 45–49.

Dey, E. L., Astin, A. W., and Korn, W. S. *The American Freshman: Twenty-Five Year Trends.* Los Angeles: Higher Education Research Institute, UCLA, 1991.

Dodge, S. "U. of Minnesota Will Not Recognize or Support Student Group That Promotes 'White Culture.'" *Chronicle of Higher Education*, Mar. 18, 1992, p. A34.

Erwin, D. T. *Assessing Student Learning and Development.* San Francisco: Jossey-Bass, 1991.

Gallagher, R. P. *Counseling Center Survey and Directory.* Pittsburgh: University of Pittsburgh Counseling Center, 1988.

Johnson, R. W., Ellison, R. A., and Heikkinen, C. A. "Psychological Symptoms of Counseling Center Clients." *Journal of Counseling Psychology*, 1989, *36*, 110–114.

Johnston, L. D., O'Malley, P. M., and Bachman, J. G. *Monitoring the Future: A Continuing Study of the Lifestyles and Values of Youth.* Institute for Social Research, University of Michigan, Ann Arbor, and National Institute of Drug Abuse, Rockville, Md., 1990.

Keegan, P. "Blowing the Zoo to Kingdom Come." *Lingua Franca: The Review of Academic Life*, Dec. 1991, pp. 15–21.

Koplik, E. K., and DeVito, A. J. "Problems of Freshmen: Comparison of Classes of 1976 and 1986." *Journal of College Student Development*, 1986, 27, 124–130.

Koss, M. P. "Hidden Rape: Incidence, Prevalence, and Descriptive Characteristics of Sexual Aggression and Victimization in a National Sample of College Students." In A. W. Burgess (ed.), *Sexual Assault.* Vol. 2. New York: Garland, 1988.

Kuh, G. D. "The Demographic Juggernaut." In M. J. Barr, M. L. Upcraft, and Associates, *New Futures for Student Affairs: Building a Vision for Professional Leadership and Practice.* San Francisco: Jossey-Bass, 1990.

Levine, A. *When Dreams and Heroes Died: A Portrait of Today's College Student*. San Francisco: Jossey-Bass, 1980.

Levine, A., and Associates. *Shaping Higher Education's Future: Demographic Realities and Opportunities, 1990–2000*. San Francisco: Jossey-Bass, 1989.

Levinson, A. "White Student Unions Stake Claim to Collegiate Mainstream." *South Bend Tribune*, Aug. 16, 1990, p. A9.

Lewin, K. *Principles of Topological Psychology*. New York: McGraw-Hill, 1936.

Lindsmith, B. "An Indelicate Balance." *Ohio State Quest*, Spring 1991, pp. 8, 9, 16.

Mandel, D. R., Baron, R. M., and Fisher, J. D. "Room Utilization and Dimensions of Density: Effects of Height and View." *Environment and Behavior*, 1980, *12*, 308–319.

Marion, P. B., Jr., and Stafford, T. H., Jr. "Residence Hall Proximity to Foreign Students as an Influence on Selected Attitudes and Behaviors of American College Students." *Journal of College and University Student Housing*, 1980, *10*(1), 16–19.

Markley, O. W. "Having a Negro Roommate as an Experience in Intercultural Education." Unpublished doctoral dissertation, Northwestern University, 1968.

Miser, K. M. (ed.) *Student Affairs and Campus Dissent: Reflections of the Past and Challenge for the Future*. Monograph Series, no. 8. Washington, D.C.: National Association of Student Personnel Administrators, 1988.

O'Shaughnessey, M. E., and Palmer, C. J. "Sexually Stressful Events Survey: Summary Report." Unpublished manuscript, Office of the Dean of Students, University of Illinois at Urbana-Champaign, 1990.

Pascarella, E. T., and Terenzini, P. T. *How College Affects Students: Findings and Insights from Twenty Years of Research*. San Francisco: Jossey-Bass, 1991.

Pavela, G. "Therapeutic Paternalism and the Misuse of Mandatory Psychiatric Withdrawals on Campus." *Journal of College and University Law*, 1983, *9*(2), 101–147.

Pavela, G. *The Dismissal of Students with Mental Disorders*. Asheville, N.C.: College Administration Publications, 1985.

Rimmer, J., Halikas, J. A., and Schuckit, M. A. "Prevalence and Incidence of Psychiatric Illness in College Students: A Four Year Perspective Study." *Journal of American College Health*, 1982, *30*, 207–211.

Rivinus, T. "Alcoholism/Chemical Dependency and the College Student." *Journal of College Student Psychotherapy*, 1988, *2*, 13–28.

Rodgers, R. F., "An Integration of Campus Ecology and Student Development: The Olentangy Project." In D. G. Creamer and Associates, *College Student Development: Theory and Practice for the 1990s*. Alexandria, Va.: American College Personnel Association, 1990.

Rudolph, F. *The American College and University: A History*. New York: Vintage Books, 1962.

Stone, G. L., and Archer, J. "College and University Counseling in the 1990s: Challenge and Limits." *Counseling Psychologist*, 1990, *18*(4), 539–607.

Weeks, K. M. "Emotionally and Psychologically Disturbed Students and With-drawal Policies." *Lex Collegii*, 1983, *6*(4), 26–31.

Wilcox, B. L., and Holahan, C. J. "Social Ecology of the Megadorm in University Student Housing." *Journal of Educational Psychology*, 1976, *68*(4), 453–458.

PART ONE

=====

Theoretical and Historical Foundations of Current Housing Practice

We conceptualized this book to be a comprehensive resource and handbook for housing practitioners who are committed to goals of student development for their programs. Because this is a handbook and not an operating manual, we hold that a firm grounding in theories of student development and environmental management, as well as a grasp of research findings and a historical perspective, are essential to *professional* practice. In this section (Chapters Two through Six), readers are provided with a discussion of what the editors mean by *student development*, a synopsis of recent research on the effects of living in residence halls, overviews of important developmental theories, and a brief historical treatment of the evolution of student housing in the United States. Interwoven into each theory chapter is an inquiry into how variables such as gender, cultural/racial background, and age affect applications in the residence environment.

Promoting student development should be a primary goal of today's housing and residential life programs, Winston and Anchors assert. Chapter Two provides a concise, although comprehensive, summary of research findings about the effects of residence hall programs and services on the development of students, as well as a discussion of the conditions that need to exist in a housing program that is serious about pursuing goals of student development. The authors maintain that certain learning environments seem to have greater impact on students than others, and that residence life practitioners must be intentional and intrusive if they are to make a difference in promoting student development.

White and Porterfield explain how psychosocial development theories can be utilized to move from a services model to a model that emphasizes student development. In Chapter Three, they summarize relevant theories of the psychosocial development of college students, describe instruments that measure important constructs, review research findings related to the theories, and discuss how these theories can be used by housing professionals. Guidelines are presented for applying these theories in residence hall programming and management.

Residence hall living provides many unique opportunities to stimulate the intellectual and moral development of students. Chapter Four uses everyday examples in describing relevant theories of intellectual and moral development and explains how students make meaning of their experience and why they sometimes respond to institutional initiatives and programs in unintended ways. Using a case-study approach, Baxter Magolda discusses how housing professionals can use cognitive development theories to promote student development goals and how different segments of the resident population, such as women and ethnic minorities, go about making meaning in ways different from men and European Americans.

A major contemporary challenge for educators in postsecondary education is understanding and structuring the environment for intentional impact on the human development process. Strange, in Chapter Five, presents a comprehensive review of theories about collegiate environments and how students interact with them. He describes how approaches to structuring both the social and physical environment can affect residents' development, summarizes and discusses research findings based on these theories, and suggests strategies housing professionals can use to create healthy, growth-promoting residential environments.

College and university housing activities have not always been the primary responsibility of housing professionals. In earlier years, they were extensions of the faculty role and the overall "paternal" supervision of students exercised by the college. In Chapter Six, Frederiksen traces the evolution of student residences from boardinghouses to dormitories to residence halls and describes how housing has become an area of distinct specialization within student affairs.

Part One lays the groundwork for modern housing practice. As Riker noted in the foreword, in the past thirty years the housing profession has made significant strides in meeting the educational and developmental needs of contemporary college students. Much of this progress can be attributed to the introduction of student development and environmental interaction theories, which have given housing professionals a more sophisticated understanding of students' behavior and helped mold a broader and more educationally relevant mission for housing programs. These are the foundations on which the future of the housing profession must be built.

Chapter Two

Student Development in the Residential Environment

Roger B. Winston, Jr.
Scott Anchors

Over a decade ago, Patricia Cross (1980, p. 1) observed: "Student development is a little like the weather. Everyone talks about it and is interested in it, but no one does much about it. Just as we are pleased when a nice day comes along, so we are happy when a student graduates from college with social and intellectual maturity and a sense of personal direction." She further commented that student affairs professionals, like weather forecasters, have enjoyed some success in predicting what will happen when certain elements are present in the environment, but educators have not consistently demonstrated that they know how to initiate action that will increase the probability of achieving desired ends. She asserted, however, that if we in higher education value "characteristics such as tolerance, autonomy, interpersonal sensitivity, and personal integrity," we can take deliberate actions that will encourage, facilitate, guide, or challenge students to development in certain directions purposefully (p. 2).

If student affairs practitioners subscribe to the belief that they have a responsibility to encourage the kinds of development described by Cross, then residence halls would appear to be the ideal setting for implementing those goals. Only in residence halls is that depth and extent of contact between student affairs professionals and students feasible. In fact, the frequency and intensity of student contacts with housing professionals is likely to be much greater than with faculty members during the first year of college. Because staff members are found "where students live," they can address a wide range of developmental issues and have almost limitless opportunities to influence students' lives and contribute to the enrichment of their educational experience.

In recognition of these responsibilities and opportunities, the *CAS Standards* (Council for the Advancement of Standards for Student Services/ Development Programs, 1986, p. 51) specifies that the mission of housing and residential life programs should include the following. (See Resource A.)

> The residence life program is an integral part of the educational program and academic support services of the institution. The mission must include provision for educational programs and services, residential facilities, management services, and, where appropriate, food services.
>
> To accomplish this mission, the goals of the program must provide:
>
> • a living-learning environment that enhances individual growth and development;
> • facilities that ensure well-maintained, safe, and sanitary housing conditions for students, and otherwise accommodate residential life programs;
> • management services that ensure the orderly and effective administration of all aspects of the program; and
> • food, dining facilities, and related services that effectively meet institutional and residential life program goals in programs that include food services.

These goals of focusing attention on the personal development of residents and creating programs and environments to promote desired outcomes came into prominence during the late 1960s. Mable (1987, p. 1), however, maintains that the focus on student development in residence halls has the "momentum of a vague vision," which seems to have lost much of its direction, creativity, and energy during the last decade. Many in residence life programs continue to talk about "student development," but there is little creditable research evidence published in the past decade that substantiates either that residential life programs view "student development" as an important mission or that interventions actually affect the level, course, or direction of students' development.

In this chapter we reexamine what is meant by *student development*, offer propositions about the necessary and sufficient conditions needed to implement goals of student development through residence life programs, and summarize research findings about some of the known effects of living in residence halls.

What Is Student Development?

The term *student development* has been used in student affairs for decades. In the early years of the profession, however, it had no specific meaning beyond "helping students grow up." *Student development* was principally a description of what ideally happened to students as they progressed through the institution, but it had no identifiable theoretical grounding and did not describe any particular set of principles or practices that student affairs staff members tried to apply or use in systematic ways.

In the late 1960s and early 1970s, this term began to take on additional meaning and became something of a movement. In 1968, Tripp and Grant wrote articles in the *Journal of the National Association of Women Deans, Administrators, and Counselors* (NAWDAC) that used *student development* in a somewhat new way. At about the same time, the leadership of the American College Personnel Association began serious discussions about the future of student affairs as a professional field. These discussions led to the initiation of the Tomorrow's Higher Education (THE) project under the presidential leadership of William Butler. Phase I of the THE project culminated in the publication of a commissioned monograph by Robert D. Brown (1972). Phase II, devoted to model building, led to a working conference at the University of Georgia in 1974, which resulted in publication of the THE model (American College Personnel Association, 1975). This model was further defined and illustrated in *The Future of Student Affairs* (Miller and Prince, 1976).

As Miller (1990) pointed out, the student development movement grew out of years of social turmoil, ferment, and sometimes violence, associated with the civil rights movement and opposition to the Vietnam conflict. It was the student affairs staff on most campuses who were called on to serve in the front lines to keep the peace and ensure that the institution could get on with its missions of teaching, research, and public service without major disruptions. These high-stress times came in the midst of significant increases in the numbers and types of colleges and universities and explosive increases in enrollments in the United States. Due to federal court orders and Great Society programs, many African-American students enrolled for the first time on formerly all-white campuses in the South and elsewhere. In addition, there were many more students (especially first-generation college students) on campuses than was true in the previous decade. Major changes in social attitudes and behavior of young adults, especially in regard to the use of mind-altering drugs and sexual freedom, also accompanied the larger social-political movements. There was an increased willingness to question authority and challenge conventional social propriety on most campuses. To paraphrase a Bob Dylan song of that time that challenged the over-thirty generations (which included most college administrators): if you can't lend a hand, get out of the way because the times are changing.

Many student affairs programs had operated either consciously or unconsciously in loco parentis. With the 1961 decision in *Dixon v. Alabama*, however, this time-honored way of conceptualizing work with college students as acting in the place of their parents was ruled inappropriate at public colleges. (The changes in attitude about the nature of the relationship with students mandated by the federal courts were reflected in varying degrees at private colleges as well.) Many of the questions, therefore, about the future of the student affairs profession voiced in the late 1960s were in response to the need to reconceptualize the philosophical underpinnings of the field and modus operandi for daily activities.

In the THE project, *student development* was defined as "the application of human development concepts in postsecondary settings so that everyone involved can master increasingly complex developmental tasks, achieve self-direction, and become interdependent" (Miller and Prince, 1976, p. 3). Philosophically and historically, the roots of the concept of student development have always been present in the profession's literature — for example, in the *Student Personnel Point of View* (American Council on Education, 1937, 1949) and in the writings of E. G. Williamson, ([1967] 1986), Esther Lloyd-Jones and Margaret Ruth Smith (1954), Kate Mueller (1966, 1968), and Nevitt Sanford (1967).

Uses of the Term "Student Development"

At different times (and often simultaneously) in the past twenty years, the term *student development* has been used to describe a movement, a theoretical perspective, a role description, position titles, and a loosely associated set of goals (Brown and Barr, 1990). During the early years of the THE project, many within the profession were polarized as either movement converts, who "preached" the new ideas with the zeal of true believers, or conventionalists, who argued that the term was simply new jargon signifying nothing unique in terms of either ideas or practices.

Currently, the term *student development* has lost many of its inflammatory connotations. (In fact, this term is used so frequently and indiscriminately by student affairs practitioners that it has lost clear definition.) Many of the early zealots have come to realize that the ideas of student development are not a panacea for all of higher education's and student affairs' ills. Likewise, many of the early detractors have accepted student development theories as useful and constructive ways of looking at college students and as sound foundations for designing effective interventions with students.

As a theoretical perspective, student development emphasizes data-based theories that describe and explain the development of young adults in five primary domains: intellectual development (Perry, 1970), moral development (Kohlberg, 1969, 1984), psychosocial development (Heath, 1968; Chickering, 1969), ego development (Loevinger, 1976), and career development

(Super, 1957). Unfortunately, many of these theories were potentially biased against minority-group members and women (although in generally unknown ways) due to their exclusion from or underrepresentation in the samples studied or due to a failure to adequately take into account the effects of ethnicity and gender in shaping experience. More recently, the field has also become aware of the need to understand how age and sexual orientation of students can significantly shape the direction, content, and pace of developmental processes. Works by Gilligan (1982), Belenky, Clinchy, Goldberger, and Tarule (1986), Kitchener and King (1981), Baxter Magolda (1989), Cass (1979), Chickering and Associates (1981), Schlossberg, Lynch, and Chickering (1989), and Cross (1978), for example, have begun to broaden and further refine the earlier developmental theories.

As a theoretical foundation for student affairs practice, student development theories describe developmental processes and allow practitioners to anticipate some of the issues and concerns that many students will encounter during their academic careers. Because of enhanced understandings of these theories, practitioners are currently in better positions than previously to design programs, services, and policies that will facilitate students' personal development and enhance their formal education. When theories of development are coupled with theories of environments and the interactions of persons with environments, student affairs professionals have tools available to them that can strategically affect the entire collegiate experience of many students. The works of Lewin (1936), Pervin (1967), Barker (1968), Stern (1970), Holland (1973), and Moos (1979) in particular have enriched the understanding of social and physical environments and provided guidance in designing effective interventions.

As a role definition or professional identity, student development has emphasized the adult status of college students, who have a right to be involved in determining the direction of their lives and contents of their education. The THE model (American College Personnel Association, 1975; Miller and Prince, 1976) accentuated the importance of treating students as equal partners in designing programs and services and did much to help student affairs administrators through the transition from in loco parentis, authoritarian attitudes and policies to educator-role perspectives. This perspective stressed that one of the student affairs practitioners' principal roles was that of educator — of equal importance with the traditional faculty, it was asserted. This role of educator called for collaboration with faculty members and involvement in the institution's academic affairs and suggested that the traditional curriculum should become more experiential and should be infused with a new sense of relevance for students.

Acceptance of the educator role for student affairs professionals entailed three basic beliefs or assumptions: (1) a presupposition that a knowledge of developmental principles, processes, and content should undergird student affairs practice — whether in designing programmatic interventions or formulating and administering institutional policy; (2) an assumption that practitioners must possess an expert knowledge of human development, environmental assessment, and management theories (as well as other theoretical areas) and skills in translating theoretical constructs into practical applications with individuals, groups, and organizations — student affairs was no longer a field for amateurs; (3) a belief that student affairs practitioners should design interventions that are intended to influence the direction and quality of all students' intellectual, moral, career, and psychosocial development.

As many cynics during the height of the THE "controversy" forecasted, in general, student affairs' bid for a piece of the educational action was treated with hostility in a few instances, but mostly with indifference by faculty and academic administrators. There were, and continue to be, many instances of successful collaboration between student affairs professionals and individual faculty members (seldom, however, due to an acknowledged "new" role for student affairs). Probably the most successful ventures in this regard have been the advent of "University 101" or continuing orientation courses for freshmen, which involve both student affairs practitioners and faculty members as equal partners. There have also been other instances of successful collaboration, such as the residence hall–based academic advising programs for undecided majors at Miami University and the University of Maine. The creation of living-learning centers and common-interest housing (such as those that focus on using a foreign language and understanding another culture) have been popular with students and effective in increasing the educational impact of residential life programs.

It must also be admitted, unfortunately, that at some public institutions the legal mandate (deriving from *Dixon v. Alabama* and subsequent court rulings) to afford students their Constitutional rights has been used as an excuse to repudiate responsibility for offering guidance to students and has led to a general disengagement from students' lives in all but the most rudimentary formalized, legalistic relationships. For example, on many campuses student disciplinary processes were created that mimic the criminal justice system with rigid and time-consuming legalisms. The focus has become the strict application of a conduct code, rather than helping students examine the implications of their behavior for themselves and the academic community (while also protecting their legitimate due process rights). Boyer (1987, pp. 179–180) comments: "Today, we found on many campuses an uneasy truce. Students still have almost unlimited freedom in personal and social matters. Conduct is generally unguided. And yet, administrators are troubled by the limits of their authority, and there is a growing feeling among students that more structure is required." On some campuses, residence halls have become little more than "cheap" hotels with good locations, with the primary emphasis on providing services that students find attractive or convenient.

Especially in the late 1970s and early 1980s, there was a rush to change position titles to include the term *student development*. On many campuses, these changes were principally cosmetic and did not affect in any significant ways either the kinds of services and programs offered or the ways they were organized, designed, and implemented. Some have argued that this use of the term is inappropriate and has generally led to confusion for students and other constituencies within institutions and for student affairs practitioners themselves as they attempt to make sense of what they do (Crookston, 1976; Miller and Winston, 1991).

Student development has also become identified with a set of goals for higher education outcomes that are not directly (or exclusively) related to the acquisition of the knowledge and skills taught through the formal curriculum. For example, based on three national surveys of undergraduate students carried out by the Carnegie Foundation for the Advancement of Teaching, Boyer (1987) identifies two student development goals—learning to get along with people and formulating values and goals for life—in addition to three other goals more directly associated with the formal curriculum (grasp of a special field of endeavor, training and skills for an occupation or career, and a well-rounded general education).

Bowen (1977) and Astin (1985) assert that higher education should be concerned with the "development of the full potentialities of human beings and of society" (Bowen, 1977, p. 54). Bowen identifies two broad sets of goals: those for individual students and those for society. The individual student goals are summarized in Table 2.1, along with our suggestions for potential residential life interventions that can support accomplishment of some goals and should take leadership in providing the primary institutional intervention for others. As can be noted about a number of the interventions—for example, career decision making or personal crisis intervention—student affairs departments other than housing (in these cases, the career center and counseling center) traditionally have principal responsibilities. On many campuses, however, these activities are addressed by housing staff members and/or through residence hall programs as well. For instance, when a resident is faced with an emotional crisis, residence hall staff members often are the first line of intervention, at least as a means of effecting referrals to the appropriate campus or community mental health agencies.

Kuh, Shedd, and Whitt (1987) suggest that the major dimensions of student development parallel the objectives of a liberal education. As can be seen in Table 2.2, "proponents of liberal education and champions of student affairs work seem to agree that higher education should address the development of students' personal identity, interpersonal skills, and esthetic sensibilities in addition to intellectual and academic skills" (p. 255).

Inspection of these goals for higher education would suggest that a number of legitimate outcomes expected of students will go unaddressed unless student affairs divisions take the initiative to repeatedly and assertively focus the institution's leadership attention on those important outcomes. Within student affairs divisions, residence life programs are often the best positioned to reach and directly affect students' lives.

Table 2.1. Goals of Higher Education for Individual Students.

Categories of goals	Examples of skills/ competencies/knowledge	Feasible residence life interventions
	Cognitive learning	
Verbal skills	Comprehend through reading and listening; speak and write clearly, correctly, and gracefully; organize and present ideas effectively in writing and discussion; acquaintance with a second language	Create an in-house student-run publication; special housing units devoted to the language and culture of a particular country
Quantitative skills	Understand elementary concepts of mathematics, statistical data, and statistical reasoning; rudiments of accounting and use of computers	Cultural programs, speakers, art exhibits, housing units that concentrate on study of a particular subject (for example, folk music, computer technology), living-learning centers
Substantive knowledge	Acquaintance with cultural heritage of the West and knowledge of other traditions; awareness of contemporary philosophy, natural science, art, literature, social change, and social issues; command of vocabulary, facts, and principles in one or more selected fields of knowledge	
Rationality	Ability to think logically on the basis of useful assumptions; disposition to weigh evidence, evaluate facts and ideas critically, and think independently; ability to analyze and synthesize	Service-learning units, student judiciary, residence hall government
Intellectual tolerance	Openness to new ideas; willingness to question orthodoxy; intellectual curiosity; ability to deal with complexity and ambiguity effectively; appreciation of intellectual and cultural diversity; historical perspective and cosmopolitan outlook; understand the limitations of knowledge and thought	Issues forum, faculty speakers, service-learning projects, international living units
Esthetic sensibility	Knowledge of, interest in, and responsiveness to literature, the fine arts, and natural beauty	Speaker programs, exhibits of artworks

Table 2.1. **Goals of Higher Education for Individual Students, Cont'd.**

Categories of goals	Examples of skills/ competencies/knowledge	Feasible residence life interventions
Creativeness	Imagination and originality in formulating new hypotheses and ideas and in producing new works of art	Workshop and darkroom facilities in hall; classes and workshops on creative activities
Intellectual integrity	Understanding of the idea of "truth" and of its contingent nature; disposition to seek and speak the truth; conscientiousness of inquiry and accuracy in reporting results	Staff role modeling
Lifelong learning	Love of learning; sustained intellectual interests; learning how to learn	Service-learning units; living-learning centers
Wisdom	Balanced perspective, judgment, and prudence	

Emotional and moral development

Personal self-discovery	Knowledge of own talents, interests, values, aspirations, and weaknesses; discovery of unique personal identity	Provide opportunities to take developmental assessment instruments followed by interpretation of results and goal setting
Psychological well-being	Sensitivity to deeper feelings and emotions combined with emotional stability; ability to express emotions con-structively; appropriate self-assertiveness, sense of security, self-confidence, self-reliance, decisiveness, and spontaneity; acceptance of self and others	Intentionally structured groups on appropriate topics; creation of caring communities; interaction with and feedback from professional staff members; service-learning projects/units
Religious interest	Serious and thoughtful exploration of purpose, value, and meaning	Religious programming; support of programs offered by campus religious centers
Refinement of taste, conduct, and manners	Understanding of generally accepted standards of etiquette; comfort in social interaction	Etiquette courses, formal social events
Human understanding	Humane outlook; capacity for empathy, thoughtfulness, compassion, respect, tolerance, and cooperation toward others (including persons of different back-grounds); democratic and nonauthoritarian disposition; skill in communication with others	Service-learning activities

Table 2.1. Goals of Higher Education for Individual Students, Cont'd.

Categories of goals	Examples of skills/competencies/knowledge	Feasible residence life interventions
Values and morals	Possess a valid and internalized but not dogmatic set of values and moral principles; moral sensitivity and courage; sense of social consciousness and social responsibility	Intentionally structured groups addressing ethical issues; service-learning projects

Practical competence

Categories of goals	Examples of skills/competencies/knowledge	Feasible residence life interventions
Traits of value in practical affairs	In addition to all the previous goals, which have bearing on practical affairs, (1) need for achievement (motivation toward accomplishment; initiative, persistence, self-discipline); (2) future orientation (ability to plan ahead and to take prudent risks; realistic outlook toward future); (3) adaptability (tolerance of new ideas and practices; willingness to accept change; versatility and resourcefulness in coping with problems and crises)	Service-learning projects, hall government, co-op housing
Citizenship	Understanding of and commitment to democracy; knowledge of governmental institutions and procedures; awareness of major social issues; ability to evaluate propaganda and political argumentation; disposition and ability to participate actively in civic, political, economic, professional, educational, and other voluntary organizations; orientation toward international understanding and world community; ability to deal with bureaucracies; disposition toward law observance	Civic education, service-learning projects, theme housing units, hall government, "intentional democratic community"
Consumer efficiency	Sound choice of values relating to style of life; ability to cope with taxes, credit, insurance, investments, legal issues, and so on	Buyers' club, personal budgeting seminar

Table 2.1. Goals of Higher Education for Individual Students, Cont'd.

Categories of goals	Examples of skills/ competencies/knowledge	Feasible residence life interventions
Economic productivity	Knowledge and skills needed for first job and for growth in productivity through experience and on-the-job training; sound career decisions	Career exploration workshops and other programs
Sound family life	Personal qualities making for stable families; knowledge and skills relating to child development	
Fruitful leisure	Wisdom in allocating time among work, leisure, and other pursuits; interests and tastes in literature, the arts, nature, sports, hobbies, and community participation; lifelong education as productive use of leisure; resourcefulness in overcoming boredom, finding renewal, and discovering satisfying and rewarding uses of leisure time	Craft and hobby instruction; space and equipment for working on crafts, recreational sports program, wellness program
Health	Understanding the basic principles for cultivating physical and mental health; knowledge of how and when to use the professional health care system	Wellness program; facilities for exercise; programs provided by health educators
Direction satisfactions and enjoyments of college experiences	Appreciation for broad and diverse educational experience; make realistic self-appraisals; learn appreciation of "here and now" experiences	Wellness programs, men's/women's awareness groups, programs to increase level of involvement
Avoidance of negative outcomes for individual students	Strengthen academic skills and correct deficiencies; develop skills in time management, efficient study techniques, and decision making; enhance social skills and sense of self-worth; crisis intervention	Tutorial programs, study skills workshops, living-learning centers

Source: Bowen, 1977, pp. 55–58. Feasible residence life interventions are the suggestions of the authors.

Table 2.2. **Comparison of Student Affairs and Liberal Education Objectives.**

Dimensions of student development	Goals and presumed effects of liberal education
Intellectual and academic skills	Intellectual and academic skills
Increased complexity of thinking related to problem solving	Independent thinking
Enhanced capability to distill, analyze, and synthesize information	Critical, analytical thinking
Encouragement of lifelong learning	Learning how to learn
Personal identity formation	Personal identity formation
Sense of purpose, confidence, unified self-view	Personal integration
Examined value system	Self-control for the sake of broader loyalties
Clarity of vocational purpose	Egalitarian, liberal, proscience, antiauthoritarian values and beliefs
Interpersonal skills	Interpersonal skills
Communication skills	
Empathy and trust	
Group interaction skills	
Esthetic development	Esthetic development
Enhanced sensitivity to and awareness of arts	Participation in and enjoyment of cultural experience
Sense of personal skill in appreciation and creation	
Moral reasoning	Moral reasoning
Integration of valid internal criteria	Mature social and emotional judgment, personal integration
Physical well-being	Physical well-being
Physical recreation skills	
Personal responsibility for health	
Social perspective	Social perspective
Movement from ethnocentricity [narrow, parochial perspective] toward an anthrocentric [broader, more humanitarian] perspective	Empathizing, seeing all sides of an issue

Source: Kuh, Shedd, and Whitt, 1987, p. 260. Reproduced by permission of the *Journal of College Student Personnel*, vol. 28, p. 260. *Authors' note:* The "Dimensions of Student Development" were synthesized from Morrill and Hurst (1980) and Delworth, Hanson, and Associates (1980). The "Goals and Presumed Effects of Liberal Education" were synthesized from Winter, McClelland, and Stewart (1982).

Critics of Student Development

The ideas of student development continue to have their critics. Critics can be grouped according to the nature of their objections: (1) using student development theory is manipulative, (2) student development theories are inadequate for use with some populations (for example, women, ethnic minorities, and homosexuals), (3) goals of student development are not in the mainstream of higher education, (4) student development theories are too complex for student affairs practitioners to use effectively, and (5) student development theories are too simplistic and are based on inappropriate assumptions about the nature of reality.

Bloland (1986a, 1986b) charges student development advocates with an excess of "true belief," which leads to "human engineering" and unethical manipulation of students. That is, student development theory is used as a script to "program" student affairs practitioners' interactions with students in a hidden agenda (1986a, p. 1). Rodgers (1991) responds to these charges by pointing out that all human action implies the use of informal theories or theories-in-use. The principal difference between the advocates of student development and the advocates of common sense, or unsystematically guided practice, involves their assumptions and beliefs about the nature of human beings, the purposes of higher education, and the appropriate roles for student affairs within higher education. Advocates of the use of student development theories to guide practice maintain that higher education should be directed toward promoting humane, caring, intellectually in-quisitive, and tough-minded citizens. Through an understanding of how students acquire these characteristics and skills, student affairs practitioners increase the probability of successful interventions. Commonsense practi-tioners apparently advocate a laissez-faire attitude toward students' lives, reacting to problematic situations post hoc by offering assistance to repair or ameliorate difficulties once encountered. Otherwise, student affairs' role is to provide services that sustain the smooth operation of the institution and ensure a minimum of disruptions of the status quo.

The argument that many of the frequently utilized student develop-ment theories have not adequately taken into account important student characteristics, such as gender, ethnicity, and sexual orientation, is freely acknowledged. These shortcomings, however, have been recognized and are being addressed (see Moore, 1990). It is interesting to note that the major developmental theories have withstood these challenges to their applicability rather well, requiring only minor modifications to accommodate the ex-panding understanding of subgroup differences. But continued work is needed to refine developmental concepts and to test how generalizable concepts formulated as a result of studying one segment of the student population can be to others. Staff who wish to base their practice on an understanding of students' development must pay careful attention to the characteristics of the student population with which they work and the exact environmental conditions of their institution. They should repeatedly ask, "How well does this theory fit these students attending this college?"

Plato (1978) and Bloland (1986a) argue that student affairs has at-tempted to sell a "bill of goods" to the higher education establishment but has found few "buyers." They argue that neither students nor faculty see college as a place for developing areas of life other than the intellect and possibly vocational skills. Numerous studies (Britell, Beck, Park, and Peterson, 1973; Markwood, 1985; Gruber, 1987) utilizing the Institutional Goals Inventory (Peterson, 1973) have documented that parents, governing boards, the general public, students, and faculty all subscribe to goals related to personal development and learning beyond the traditional academic disciplines. The summary of goals (Kuh, Shedd, and Whitt, 1987) presented in Table 2.2 and of student outcomes (Bowen, 1977) presented in Table 2.1 would seem to identify areas that student affairs can or should have primary responsibility for addressing within an institution. Rodgers (1991) argues that the hostility to the goals of student development is based in a rigid rationalistic bias held by many in higher education. "Student affairs," he comments, "may be a care-oriented ship negotiating a turbulent, rationalistic, or positivistic sea. Consequently, student affairs' values and methodologies often may be in conflict with assumptions and methodological biases of its host environment" (p. 209). For example, Lyons (1990) argues—in basic agreement with a recent National Association of Student Affairs Administrators statement (1987)— that student affairs' principal justification for existence is in support (or enrichment) of students' academic learning. "Because how students feel cannot be separated from how they think," he writes, "those in student affairs are charged to organize the physical, social, and ethical aspects of the student's collegiate experience" (p. 28). No autonomous educational role seems envisioned for student affairs; it should only complement the development of the intellect. These kinds of arguments implicitly accept the rationalistic bias and reduce student development goals to an ancillary status.

We must also admit that at many institutions, the student affairs division has not made winning arguments that student affairs should be given the authority to pursue personal development goals vigorously and has not been given the resources necessary to accomplish such goals on a systematic, institutionwide basis. Fairness dictates that we acknowledge that many—if not most—student affairs divisions have not consistently influenced the direction or content of students' personal development. In fact, most institutions have little or no idea about what happens to students academically or personally as a result of enrolling. This fact has promoted the recent emphasis on outcomes assessment (Winston and Moore, 1991). Student affairs has not demonstrated in convincing ways that its staff and programs are capable of producing the desired outcomes. On most campuses, there is no systematic, purposive contact between the majority of students and developmentally focused programs and practitioners. And few student affairs divisions in the nation have in place evaluation programs that can document effects, even when student development goals are espoused and acted on. In some instances, ambitious projects with explicit student development goals have failed, often due to a lack of understanding of how to bring about constructive change in complex organizations such as higher education institutions (D. G. Creamer and E. G. Creamer, 1986, 1990; E. G. Creamer and D. G. Creamer, 1986, 1988, 1989).

Other critics of the use of student development theories in student affairs practice—for example, Rhatigan (1975)—argue that because of their complexity, these theories have little practical utility. In response, Rodgers (1991, p. 211) asserts that *"Student development is a complex task requiring complex methods using multiple specific theories.* Reductionistic integration or the desire to find a simple unified student development model to replace complex theories is misplaced energy and an ill-advised goal." Rodgers (p. 210) advocates the use of models for planning and implementing interventions because "a model can inform a practitioner on the steps one needs to take in order to use theory in practice; it can broadly conceptualize the domains of development or the dimensions of relating theory to practice; but it cannot provide substantive content or program guidance."

On the other hand, advocates of the "emergent paradigm" (for instance, Kuh, Whitt, and Shedd, 1987; Caple, 1987a, 1987b) argue that contemporary theories of student development are too simple and do not accurately reflect the reality of individual differences. They argue that some of the basic tenets about the nature of human development—for example, that development is patterned, cumulative, orderly, continuous, and predictable—are not theoretically defensible. They likewise challenge the conviction that student affairs professionals should be proactive (that is, act in anticipation of students' behavior to help them accomplish developmental tasks or to avert barriers to development) and that it is impossible to design interventions that will produce predictable results.

Basic assumptions and tenets of any theory are not empirically testable. Consequently, the assumptions of both the conventional scientific paradigm and the emergent paradigm should be evaluated on the basis of how well they support the theory in which they are enmeshed. The theories in turn must be judged by how well they explain the phenomena that they purport to describe based on the collection of data from appropriate populations. Any serious student of developmental theories will readily acknowledge that all current theories have shortcomings—especially in regard to application to certain student populations and to explaining change processes precisely. There is, however, extensive research that supports many aspects of the major theories (Pascarella and Terenzini, 1991). The new paradigm proponents have presented few data-based studies that would support their alternative view of how students develop or change; they have presented arguments primarily by analogy and anecdote. The emphasis on qualitative research methods has made a contribution that promises—although this promise is so far largely unrealized—to enrich the understanding of developmental processes while keeping in mind the importance of individual differences. (Qualitative studies have been much more fruitful in producing studies of college environments. Examples include the "involving colleges" studies by Kuh, Schuh, Whitt, and Associates, 1991.) As Drum and Lawler (1988, p. 26) note, "though imperfect, conflicting, and incomplete, [human development theories] remain the best guidelines we have in our journey toward fuller understanding of the marvelously complex maturation process of the . . . self."

Student Development and Residential Life

We advocate the use of the term *student development* in three different ways. First, this term should be used to describe the body of theories that purport to describe how students in cohorts change as they move through the college experience. (See Chapters Three and Four, which summarize the major theories and offer suggestions about applications in residential life.) Second, *student development* should be used in connection with specific interventions that are designed to (1) prevent or forestall the onset of problems through anticipation of the consequences of nonaction, or (2) facilitate constructive change by assisting students in developing new skills, acquiring needed information, or resolving critical issues, or (3) repair or reconstruct damage done to the self through unsuccessful or traumatic past experiences (Drum and Lawler, 1988). Third, *student development* should be used to refer to specific outcome goals resulting from attending college and living in college residential facilities. Students are most likely to realize those goals if the residential life staff assist them in developing their talents and realizing their potential as fully functioning human beings. It is through an understanding of developmental processes and the utilization of that knowledge in program development, institutional policy formulization, and administration of programs and services that the goals of talent development and holistic personality growth can most likely be realized.

Residence life programs committed to student development goals should address the following objectives:

1. *Assisting students in the pursuit of becoming literate, liberally educated persons.* This objective may be addressed through helping students overcome academic skill deficits, or find relevance for classroom learning in everyday life, and broaden their experiences with the arts, humanities, and sciences.

2. *Promoting students' development in becoming responsible, contributing members of a society of multiple communities.* Residence life programs should have an explicit, proactive agenda for assisting students in acquiring the knowledge and skills needed to be productive citizen-leaders. Edward J. Blaustein (the late president of Rutgers University) declared: "Making service to others a requirement [for graduation can help students serve usefully as citizens of a democracy, but also may help combat] racism, sexism, homophobia, religious intolerance, and fear and animosity towards foreigners [as well as] providing an alternative to the naked pursuit of individual interest and material gain" (cited in Morse, 1989, pp. 40–41). Residence halls provide an ideal venue for organizing and coordinating civic education. Civic education should become a principal goal of residential life programs.

3. *Advocating commitment to ideals of altruism and social justice.* The organization and administration of residence halls should clearly demonstrate

commitment to these values. Residents should be reminded about these values often, with explicit references that show the connection between staff activity and programming efforts and these values. Behavior of staff or residents that is counter to these values should be challenged by the leaders of the residence life program.

4. *Endorsing the cultivation of a healthy life-style, both physically and psychologically.* All residence hall programs should include components that provide students opportunities to learn how to assess their habits and behavior within a comprehensive model, such as wellness, and to develop healthy behavior patterns and attitudes. (See Chapter Eighteen for examples of diverse approaches.) These programs should provide this information to residents in ways that will encourage them to evaluate their lives carefully, to establish goals, and to take responsibility for their health and personal development.

5. *Encouraging students to examine their religious/faith/spiritual life.* Residence hall programs should actively encourage students to explore the spiritual dimension of life through in-house programs and/or cooperation with off-campus religious centers and academic programs, such as philosophy and religion departments.

6. *Challenging students to confront moral and ethical issues.* An important focus for programming should be consideration of current social problems and the associated moral and ethical issues. Residence halls should be campus centers for dialogue about these issues.

Necessary Conditions for Realizing Student Development Goals

We offer the following propositions as necessary conditions for implementing residence life programs with student development goals.

1. *Outcome goals of the housing program are clearly conceptualized and articulated.* Residence life professionals should clearly communicate to potential residents the goals of the residence life program, including expectations about shared responsibility, contributions to development of a learning community, subscription to certain values (for example, equality, justice, equity, and tolerance), and openness to experimentation. Residence life programs cannot "be all things to all people." It may be necessary to offer a range of residential options that vary from providing basic services (operating basically as a hotel with limited student development goals) to educational programs (designed to facilitate students making connections between classroom learning and applications to their daily lives) and civic education. In the spirit of developmental approaches, students should be provided a range of residential options, given opportunities to make meaningful choices, and held responsible for their decisions.

Clear goals with measurable outcome criteria can serve as the foundation for planning residential programs designed to have an impact on students' personal and academic development. To operate without such goals and objectives is similar to operating a sailboat without sails or rudder. It is unrealistic and wasteful of valuable staff resources to create a completely new set of goals each time new staff members are added. Several professional associations have proposed statements of standards that can help shape the overall direction of programs, but goals need to be congruent with institutional values and the organizational culture and specific enough that they can guide the planning of day-to-day activities. (See Resources A and C.)

An excellent example of clear and consistent goals exists at the University of Florida, where the residence life staff has spent considerable time and effort in developing a ten-year goals-and-objectives manual. The manual is supplied to all residence life staff members, goal attainment is monitored annually, and specific objectives are clearly articulated and evaluated. Goals may be as specific as creating a new professional staff position, or as general as maintaining a commitment to diversity and multiculturalism in programming efforts.

2. *Values are publicly owned and acted on.* Housing programs with student development goals are not value free. Students have a right to know the basic values that the housing program seeks to promote. By implication, then, students who do not appreciate or accept the espoused values can seek an environment more in harmony with their beliefs. The collegiate environment is filled with options, and once again the student, as an adult, is free to choose and is accountable for decisions. It is essential that staff members at all levels own and act on these values. Discrepancies in espoused values and behavior will undermine the most carefully conceptualized and meticulously implemented program.

Values saturate virtually every activity associated with a residential life program. Every intervention planned, every student counseled or confronted, and every policy developed is a direct or indirect statement of values. It is crucial that residential life staff members understand and carefully consider the messages that are communicated through these actions to the academic community.

For example, at the University of Maine at Orono, the residence life program has publicly adopted the principle of affirming and nurturing diversity within its student population. Based on a belief that diversity is integral to developing healthy living-learning communities, a "Statement on Diversity" and another titled "Harassment, Intimidation, Discrimination, and Inequity Protocol" are provided to all students living on campus. These statements serve as a foundation for programming activities as well as for confronting violations and initiating a dialogue with the affected students. These documents are statements of values, an enumeration of behavioral expectations, and a standard against which students' conduct will be measured.

3. *Staff's expectations of students are high.* As Stamatakos (1984, p. 11) notes, "by overtly or tacitly providing students with opportunities to create sanctum sanctorums [in their rooms], . . . we have inadvertently encouraged many of

them to permit their attitudes and values to remain unchallenged and to avoid making new commitment to and with their college." As a general rule, students will live up to high expectations, provided that we catch their imaginations and offer consistent support and encouragement.

It is important that expectations about acceptable and unacceptable behavior be given greater visibility than is often the case—for example, by issuing codes of conduct and including clauses in the housing contract. These documents are essential to maintaining order in residence halls in a litigious society, but they are seldom consulted until violations occur. Residence life programs should foster environments that are self-policing—that is, where residents apply informal sanctions to peers who act in ways that are detrimental to others' welfare or the good of the community. High expectations about positive aspects of student life, such as involvement, service to the community, intellectual integrity, and participation in the arts, are important and can assist students in formulating a vision of what residence hall living *can be.*

Involvement and service to the community are central themes at the University of North Dakota, which has a program titled "International Honorary for Leaders in University Apartment Communities." This program focuses on promoting service through community programs and agencies. The residential staff has built within an apartment community—though such communities are often characterized as isolationist and low in student involvement—high expectations for involvement in the local community. Residents have met the challenge; those who participate are publicly recognized for their work. A program in traditional residence halls with similar goals has proven successful at Northern Illinois University as well.

4. *Professional staff members interact regularly with residents.* Without frequent positive interaction between residents and the professional staff, it is difficult, if not impossible, to design environments that can facilitate accomplishment of student development goals. Paraprofessional and support staff can make invaluable contributions to program and service quality, but if the residence life program is committed to the goals of student development, the expertise of well-educated professionals is needed at the individual resident level. Paraprofessionals, although frequently effective and cost efficient, usually cannot provide the maturity, insight, and life experience that well-educated, highly motivated professional staff members can provide. A knowledge of developmental theories, refined intervention skills, and concern for the welfare of residents combined with teachable moments can create numerous opportunities for making significant, long-lasting impacts on students' lives and educations. Without frequent contact between residents and the professional staff, however, this is unlikely to happen in systematic or predictable ways.

A major way that this interaction can be promoted is through clearly stated expectations in position descriptions. At the University of Southern Maine, residential life position descriptions mandate frequent contacts with residents. Accountability is maintained through performance appraisals that attend to factors such as visibility in the living units, knowing residents by name, and use of theory in interactions.

A simple but effective device for learning about students' lives and getting to know residents in depth is the systematic interview. Residential life staff can select five or six students each week at random and invite them to their offices for informal interviews. The focus should be on *listening* as students are encouraged to talk about their experiences in the institution and what is happening in their personal lives. Having someone truly listen and show concern is rare on most college campuses and can be a powerful developmental intervention in students' lives. Interviews can also help staff members better understand what is happening in the living units and allow them an opportunity to "test" the current theories of student development against the experiences of their own students.

5. *Residence life programs promote active citizenship.* Residence halls should provide multiple opportunities for residents to practice citizenship skills through traditional student organizations, such as hall governments, but also through active involvement in the larger community. As John Dewey (1954, pp. 213, 216) observes, "Democracy must begin at home, and its home is the neighboring community. . . . Whatever the future may have in store, one thing is certain. Unless local communal life can be restored, the public cannot adequately resolve its most urgent program: to find and identify itself." An explicit condition of residence hall living should be a willingness to contribute to the governance of the community and/or to provide service to other worthy causes.

Hannah Arendt (1968, p. 196) argues that "the task of education is to prepare students for the task of renewing a common world." Residential life programs seem strategically placed to challenge students to think about their social and citizenship responsibilities and to provide opportunities for *action* on their convictions. We are convinced that an important contribution that residential life programs can make to helping students create relevance from classroom learning and to addressing some of the many social problems that encircle our campuses is to institute and promote service-learning projects.

Morse (1989, pp. 95–96) offers a number of propositions about how people learn about citizenship that seem to provide further confirmation that service-learning activities should become an integral part of residential life programs.

- Civic preparation occurs when one moves beyond familiar circumstances, outside the curriculum, outside personal values to explore new perspectives, attitudes, and beliefs.
- Civic education is aided by being able to make connections, seeing causal situations and outcomes, and understanding the relationship between the individual and the larger community.

- A sense of our political selves is developed when we see something wrong and join with others to find remedies. . . .
- Civic education includes being able to recognize the interrelationship of issues and look for the implications of the larger system. . . .
- Civic participation is difficult to learn from nonpractitioners [Morse, 1989, pp. 95–96].

At Connecticut College, many aspects of campus living and governance involve students as colleagues in decisions making. Students are challenged to use what they have learned in the classroom in solving day-to-day problems of citizenship on campus. For instances, discipline cases are heard by student-run judicial boards, changes in academic policy require student input, and local community service is an expectation of everyone.

In the student apartment complex at Iowa State University, residents' involvement in governing their community is mandated by an elected council that addresses issues ranging from parking and recreation facilities to child care. A mayor and council members are elected and govern many aspects of the community. A goal of the residential life staff is to replicate community living conditions outside the university that students are likely to encounter after they leave the university.

6. *Facilities are efficiently managed and well maintained.* Before one can speak of designing programs that address student development goals, adequate personnel and resources must be available and utilized to ensure that the physical facilities are safe, comfortable, clean, reasonably esthetically agreeable, and adequately maintained. Until these basic needs are satisfied, neither staff nor students can be expected to address "higher-order" concerns seriously.

As can be seen in Figure 2.1, Riker and DeCoster (1971) have suggested a model based on Maslow's hierarchy of human needs that shows how the facilities management and developmental orientation of a housing program are interrelated.

Riker and DeCoster (1971) suggest that these levels form a continuum, with each level representing a somewhat different set of student needs. Success at one level depends to a large extent on how well lower levels have been addressed. For instance, there is unlikely to be much interest in educational programming (level 4) if students are preoccupied with excessive noise (level 3) or showers that do not work (level 1). Objectives at levels 1 and 2 are met most directly through the operations and facilities personnel; the residence life staff has primary responsibility for objectives at levels 4 and 5; responsibilities are shared at level 3. Only through coordination and cooperation between the residence life staff and the facilities management staff can a program ever hope to be successful in the pursuit of student development goals.

Figure 2.1. General Objectives for College Student Housing.

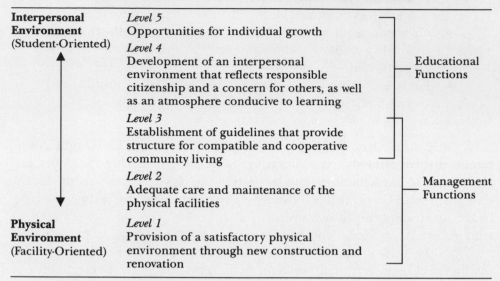

Source: Riker and DeCoster, 1971, p. 2. Reproduced by permission of the *Journal of College and University Student Housing*.

Effects of Residential Life Programs and Facilities

Attempts to determine how residence life programs and facilities affect residents as compared to students who commute or live in quarters in the local community is difficult for a number of reasons. As Pascarella and Terenzini (1991) point out, it is possible to speak of effects in three different senses: direct, net, and indirect. To use a typical residence hall example, there is substantial evidence that residents are more likely to be involved in student organizations than are nonresidents (Astin, 1973; Chickering, 1974; Pascarella, 1984). We might conclude that place of residence has a *direct effect* on organizational membership, probably attributable in large part to physical proximity. On the other hand, a number of factors besides place of residence, such as personality characteristics, financial resources, gender, and ethnicity, also may influence organizational membership. If we were to control (hold constant) these variables, we might find that place of residence drops significantly in importance as a factor affecting membership. If this were the case, the *net effect* of living in a residence hall on membership could be said to be minimal or nonexistent. Living in a residence hall and involvement in student organizations seem to have little effect on academic achievement (Blimling, 1989). These variables, however, have been found to contribute significantly to the social integration of students into the life of the institution (Tinto, 1975, 1987; Pascarella, 1980), which in turn significantly influences student retention and academic achievement. Residence hall living can be said to have an *indirect effect* on achievement, operating through the moderator variable of social integration.

In this section, we briefly summarize research findings about how residence life programs and housing facilities affect students. This summary focuses primarily on research reported in the last twenty years and is based in large part on the exceptionally thorough, well-executed analyses by Benjamin (1988), Blimling (1988), and Pascarella and Terenzini (1991). Five broad categories of effects are reviewed: (1) academic achievement, (2) persistence, (3) satisfaction with the institution, (4) personal development, and (5) living arrangements and architecture.

Academic Achievement

Blimling (1989) identifies twenty-one studies that investigated the effects of residence hall living (where there were no programmed interventions or special groupings, such as floors with special quiet hours or living-learning centers) on grade-point averages. Only ten of those studies, however, controlled for initial differences in academic aptitude or past academic performance when making the comparisons. Those ten studies provide little consistent evidence to support the contention that residential students perform better in classes than similarly gifted students who live off campus. May (1974) and Moos and Lee (1979) found positive effects on grade-point average, but Pike (1989) and Clodfelter, Furr, and Wachowiak (1984) found negative relationships. Pascarella and Terenzini (1982) found a negative relationship for women and a positive relationship for men. The preponderance of the evidence (Grosz and Brandt, 1969; Simono, Wachowiak, and Furr, 1984; Pascarella, 1984; Blimling, 1989)—although not conclusive—suggests that residential students who are not participants in some kind of special program perform similarly to those living elsewhere.

Blimling (1988), however, found that students residing in living-learning centers performed better academically than similar students who resided in conventional residential arrangements. Living-learning center programs usually include some or all of the following characteristics: (1) residents take at least one course together, (2) would-be residents must apply and be selected to live in the center, and (3) some type of enriched cultural or academic experience is associated with the center. Blimling also found that most centers had some form of coed living arrangement—varying from companion single-sex buildings to coed on the same floor. All six studies of living-learning centers found that center residents performed better academically than residents not associated with some kind of special programming effort (Pemberton, 1969; Vanderwall, 1972; Barnes, 1977; Pascarella and Terenzini, 1980, 1981; Felver, 1983).

Findings related to room assignment policies are mixed concerning their effects on academic performance. A variety of schemes have been employed to create homogeneous floor units. Alternatives include using personality variables (Myers-Briggs Type Indicator pairings), academic major, self-reported desire to concentrate on studies (special "quiet floors"), academic classification (typically all freshmen), and academically gifted or honors program participants to create living units of persons sharing one or more characteristics in common. None, however, have produced consistent findings supporting their use as a means of significantly improving academic achievement (Benjamin, 1988; Blimling, 1988; Pascarella and Terenzini, 1991).

Academic Persistence

Even though there is scant evidence that living in residence halls improves or enhances academic achievements or grades, compelling research does support the assertion that residential living positively influences academic persistence. Chickering (1974), in a landmark study, found that on-campus living had a statistically significant positive effect on persistence and completion of the bachelor's degree, even when controlling for initial differences such as socioeconomic status, academic ability, and past academic performance. Other studies have supported these findings (Anderson, 1981; Astin, 1973, 1975, 1977, 1982; Herndon, 1984; Pascarella and Chapman 1983; Velez, 1985).

The principal causal factor underlying this positive influence of residence hall living on persistence is extracurricular and other kinds of campus involvement (an indirect effect of residence hall living). As Astin (1985) found, the more involved students are in the collegiate experience, the more likely they are to be satisfied with the college experience and the more likely they are to persist to graduation. "Living on or near campus while attending college," according to Pascarella and Terenzini (1991, pp. 399–400), "is consistently one of the most important determinants of a student's level of integration or involvement in the social system of an institution. . . . Resident students have significantly more social interaction with peers and faculty and are significantly more likely to be involved in extracurricular activities and to use campus facilities" than are commuters.

Satisfaction with the Institution

Most of the studies that have investigated differences in satisfaction with the institution have found that residential students, in comparison with commuters, were more satisfied with the institution and their educational experiences (Welty, 1974; Lundgren and Schwab, 1979; Goetz, 1983; Pascarella, 1985). Nosow (1975) compared resident seniors with their nonresident counterparts and found that residents were generally more satisfied and had a greater tendency to identify with the institution and peers (which was especially true for women), to find their college education rewarding, and to see the institution as responsive to student needs. Benjamin (1988, p. 23) observes that "residence halls appear to shape the character of interaction and involvement with peers and faculty, leaving academic performance unaffected. These effects appear especially potent during the first two years."

Personal Development

In his meta-analysis of eight studies that investigated differences between residents and students living off campus on personal growth and development dimensions, Blimling (1988) found a significant but relatively low magnitude of differences favoring residents. These findings are consistent with the conclusions drawn by Pascarella and Terenzini (1991).

Wilson, Anderson, and Fleming (1987) and Lundgren and Schwab (1979) report that residents are more trusting, better adjusted, show more initiative, and are less likely to be overly dependent on parents. Miller (1982) found that sophomores who lived on campus a second year compared with those who moved to off-campus apartments after the first year showed greater tolerance for human differences.

There have been inconsistent findings concerning whether residents develop more positive academic self-concepts than commuters. Chickering (1974) found that commuting students showed less positive self-ratings at the end of the freshman year (when initial differences were controlled) on academic self-confidence, public speaking ability, and leadership skills than students living in residence halls. On the other hand, Astin (1977) failed to find significant differences in academic self-concept when data were analyzed for on- and off-campus students.

A number of studies report that residence hall students show larger declines in authoritarianism than their off-campus counterparts (Chickering, McDowell, and Campagna, 1969; Chickering and Kuper, 1971; Matteson, 1974; Rich and Jolicoeur, 1978). These results, however, go counter to the findings of Katz and Associates (1968) and Levin (1967).

In terms of intellectual orientation as measured by the Omnibus Personality Inventory (Heist and Yonge, 1968), several studies have found that residential students show greater gain than off-campus students (Newcomb and others, 1971; Welty, 1976; Lacy, 1978; Tomlinson-Keasey, Williams, and Eisert, 1978; Bennett and Hunter, 1985). Changes in intellectual orientation appear most dramatic for residents of living-learning centers. Pascarella and Terenzini (1991) conclude, however, that the degree of change in intellectual orientation appears principally related to the socialization influences that involve interaction with people—both peers and faculty members. When those kinds of relationships are factored in, the effects of residence hall living approach insignificance. As noted previously, residence hall living appears to have more of an indirect than a direct effect on students' development.

In terms of interpersonal relationships or competence, living in residence halls appears to produce little or no effect (Chickering and Kuper, 1971; Rich and Jolicoeur, 1978; Riahinejad and Hood, 1984). Likewise, there is little evidence that residence hall living differentially affects personal adjustment or psychological well-being (Pascarella and Terenzini, 1991).

The greatest effects on personal development (for example, on personal independence and intellectual disposition) seem produced by living-learning centers in comparison to conventional living arrangements (Pascarella and Terenzini, 1980, 1981). Pascarella and Terenzini (1981) conclude, however, that increases in generalized personal development are more a function of students' interpersonal relations than of where they live. Residential programs that promote development of these relationships both in the living units and across campus seem to provide a means (although not the only means) of effectively promoting these kinds of student change.

Living Arrangements and Architecture

A number of studies have investigated the effects of living on traditional "long halls," which may be operationally defined as a living unit with a single corridor with double-loaded rooms housing from thirty to eighty students, and "suites," which may be defined as a living unit housing four to eight students who share a bath, study/living room, and sleeping rooms designed to accommodate two students each. The consensus of studies is that students living in suites perceive less crowding than long-hall residents (Valins and Baum, 1973; Baum, Harpin, and Valins, 1975; Baum and David, 1980; Huang, 1982). Suite occupants are less inhibited in their interactions with others and develop more social interaction skills in making friends (Baum, Harpin, and Valins, 1975; Harris and Klein, 1980; Miller, Rossbach, and Munson, 1981; Baum, Calesnick, David, and Gatchel, 1982) and are more satisfied with residence hall living, although this variable explains relatively little of the variance (Null, 1980; Miller, Rossbach, and Munson, 1981; Baum and Gatchel, 1981; Stoner and Moss, 1982).

The general consensus in regard to building size is that smaller is better in terms of student development concerns, although high rises may have certain economic advantages over smaller buildings. Studies have found that residents of low-rise halls—operationally defined as buildings of five floors or fewer by Blimling (1988)—compared with residents of high-rise halls (six floors or more) perceive a more positive social climate and report less stress associated with perceived crowding (Sinnett, Sachson, and Furr, 1972; Gerst and Sweetwood, 1973; Holohan and Wilcox, 1979). Sinnett, Sachson, and Furr (1972) report that low-rise residents found the social climate to be friendlier and more intellectual than high-rise residents. Bickman and others (1973) found low-rise residents were more willing to help others living nearby than their high-rise counterparts were. High-rise residents perceived their buildings as being more convenient—though noisier—than low-rise residents, but low-rise residents reported having more social contact in the hall, spending more time in the hall, having more conversations with hallmates, and being more likely to participate in peer groups

(Sinnett, Sachson, and Furr, 1972). A study by Perl (1986) found some contrary results: high-rise residents perceived more support, innovation, and intellectuality than their low-rise counterparts.

In contrast to traditional double-loaded corridors, apartment-style living offers residents opportunities for experiencing a sense of community in the most intimate surroundings of three to five other students. Staff presence is often minimal to nonexistent; thus students are allowed to have virtually complete autonomy and freedom. A frequent negative outcome reported by staff and students, however, is the lack of a sense of community and connections with other residents outside the apartment. Whalen and Morris (1989) found that apartment residents express greater social distance from other residents, are less satisfied with the community environment than residents of traditional halls, and have fewer interactions with students outside their apartment.

Prior to the late 1960s, the norm for most colleges and universities was single-sex residence halls, with strict controls exercised over women's residences in particular, such as sign-in and sign-out rosters, curfews, and bed checks. The sexist attitudes on many campuses supported careful and close supervision of women's conduct, principally as a means of indirectly influencing men's behavior. One effect of the 1960s' sexual revolution, coupled with the entry of the federal courts in requiring that students' Constitutional rights be respected through the provisions of Title IX in the 1970s, was a demand by students for less restrictive parietal rules. Coed or mixed-sex residence halls came into being. *Coed* could mean anything from buildings sharing common lobbies, to those with some floors or wings housing men and others women, to those with suites where men and women shared adjoining sleeping quarters with shared common space (for example, lounges and study rooms).

The principal fear was that such arrangements would lead to increased sexual promiscuity. Greenleaf (1962) early on helped discredit the conventional wisdom of the time. She found few differences in behavior between coed and single-sex halls, except that in coed halls there appeared to be more cross-sex friendships and less stereotypical attitudes toward the opposite sex. Other benefits of coed housing have been found to include increased interpersonal competence and sensitivity toward others, more mature and less destructive behavior (especially by men), less noise, more interest in community and cultural activities, and fewer one-to-one dates and more informal group activities. Coed living arrangements appear not to affect academic performance or level of sexual activity in comparison with single-sex-hall residents (DeCoster and Mable, 1980)—although Lance (1976) found residents of coed halls had more permissive attitudes toward premarital sex than single-sex-hall residents, no research evidence has been presented about actual behavior. The early findings by Greenleaf (1962) have generally been confirmed (Corbett and Sommer, 1972; Brown, Winkworth, and Braskamp,

1973; Schroeder and LeMay, 1973; Duncan, 1974; Reid, 1974; Moos and Otto, 1975).

Summary of Effects

Pascarella and Terenzini (1991) conclude that living on campus may be the most consistent determinant of collegiate impact. They state that "residential living creates a social-psychological context for students that is markedly different from that experienced by those who live at home or elsewhere off campus and commute to college. Simply put, living on campus maximizes opportunities for social, cultural, and extracurricular involvement; and it is this involvement that largely accounts for residential living's impact on student change" (p. 611). A summary of Pascarella and Terenzini's (1991, p. 612) analyses of the effects of residence halls on students is presented in Table 2.3.

The literature about residence halls is extensive. But there remains a scarcity of well-controlled, carefully executed, precisely measured studies that investigate the net effects of residence hall living in comparison to the situation for students living in off-campus apartments or commuting from their parent's homes. It seems safe to also conclude that if residential life programs are serious about attempting to influence the personal development of students directly, well-conceptualized programs such as living-learning centers or service-learning units are required. Most of the positive effects of traditional residence hall living appear attributable to the physical proximity of large numbers of peers and the relationships they develop. Without intentionally designed, effective interventions, the potential power of residence hall living for positively affecting the lives of students will remain marginal.

Recommendations

If housing programs are serious about addressing student development goals, significant changes of priorities on many campuses need to occur. We recommend the following:

1. Purposefully structure residence halls in ways that clearly communicate to residents and potential residents that living in residence halls is intended to be an extension or enhancement of classroom learning. One of the most effective ways to address these goals is to create living units that have a sense of community and whose residents share a transcending common interest. Interests can center on academics (such as interest in a foreign language or culture or activities related to a particular discipline such as archaeology or geology), promotion of general academic achievement (such as living-learning centers), development of talents (such as writing, musical performance, or art), participation in recreational interests (such as camping, rock climbing, skiing, or boating), or social-political causes (such as environmental concerns or women's issues).

Table 2.3. Summary of Estimated Within-College Effects of Living in Residence Halls.

Outcome	Strength of evidence	Direction of evidence	Major rival explanations controlled	Magnitude of net effect
Esthetic, cultural, and intellectual values	Moderate	Positive in direction of on-campus residence	Gender, race, SES, ability, initial values	Unclear[a]
Sociopolitical attitudes and values	Moderate	Positive in direction of on-campus residence	Gender, race, SES, ability	Unclear
Secularism	Moderate	Positive in direction of on-campus residence	Gender, race, SES, ability, initial values	Unclear
Self-concepts	Weak to moderate	Positive in direction of on-campus residence	Gender, race, SES, ability, initial concepts	Unclear, but probably small and indirect via interpersonal relationships
Autonomy, independence, internal locus of control	Weak	Positive in direction of on-campus residence	Gender, ability	Unclear
Intellectual orientation	Moderate	Positive in direction of on-campus residence	Gender, ability, initial level	Unclear
Persistence and degree attainment	Strong	Positive in direction of on-campus residence, especially in living-learning centers	Gender, ability, SES, educational aspirations, high school achievement	Unclear
Moral development	Weak	Positive in direction of on-campus residence	Initial level of moral development	Unclear

Note: SES = socioeconomic status.

[a]"Unclear," as used in this table, means we are acknowledging that the studies do not allow such estimates or that the evidence, though generally consistent, is still sufficiently complex to make an estimate of effect size hazardous.

Source: Pascarella and Terenzini, 1991, p. 612.

Kuh, Schuh, Whitt, and Associates (1991, p. 351) conclude from their study of "involving colleges" that "institutions that provide small, human-scale environments and multiple subcommunities encourage involvement." Common-interest living units would appear to be one way to meet this goal. Once common-interest living units are formed, they should receive continuing support from the professional housing staff and from others on campus, such as interested faculty and staff members. We suggest that before a student is assigned to a particular unit, she or he should sign a contract that clearly details the minimum level of involvement expected of members of the community and the kind and level of support the institution will provide.

It is important, however, not to "overstructure" these communities. There is usually a need for extensive professional staff involvement in assisting these collections of students to come together and to develop a sense of community. Staff members should consciously withdraw as students develop their own ideas about what they want to accomplish and methods of organization. But residential life programs must assume the initial responsibility for making human, technological, and financial resources available and encourage their utilization. To make time for these new initiatives, emphasis should be shifted away from presenting one-shot programs and nonessential services toward encouraging students to take responsibility for expanding and making the most of learning opportunities. Training and supervising paraprofessionals in supporting the "new" communities should also be stressed.

2. Carefully focus attention on the needs of students from underrepresented populations, such as people of color and first-generation college students. The housing staff should clearly articulate a commitment to creating communities that are hospitable to students from varied backgrounds. It is important to know what the experience is like for students from underrepresented populations and to take the initiative in confronting instances of racism, sexism, homophobia, and other conditions that have a chilling effect on learning. Do not wait for an ugly incident to occur or for there to be major complaints.

3. Develop means of providing recognition to individuals and groups who show commitment to and achievements in out-of-class learning. Initially, as housing programs move from viewing residence halls solely or primarily as places to sleep, study, and store belongings to seeing them as learning platforms for experiences that are integral to the total educational experience, there is likely to be resistance from students, "traditional" housing staff members, and perhaps from others on campus who feel threatened by the initiative.

4. As Kuh, Schuh, Whitt, and Associates (1991, p. 348) note, "know your students, how they learn, and the conditions that affect their development." This can be done only when the professional staff has frequent informal contacts with residents and develops schemes for systematically collecting meaningful information from and about students. Once the data are collected, they are of little value, however, if they are not used to shape the way things are done.

5. A clearly stated expectation of students who choose to live in college residence halls should be *active citizenship*. This citizen involvement can be expressed in numerous ways, such as participation in hall or campus government and program development or involvement in community service activities. Ideally, each living unit should be paired with a community service agency that solicits residents' involvement in addressing the needs of the less

fortunate in the local community. Civic education should be a high priority for all residential life programs.

We argued earlier in this chapter that residential living can be an ideal setting for students' personal development to be nurtured and supported. A community context creates important opportunities for students to be contributing members of society, as well as offering a safe climate where they can learn and experiment with developing habits of mind and body that contribute to a healthy life-style. If student development is a goal for residential life, residence hall staff are obligated to be intrusive and intentional in all aspects of their interactions with students. The research summarized in this chapter clearly indicates that simply *living* in residence halls has little direct effect on students' academic or personal development. More intrusive and systematic interventions in the residential environment are called for if this environment is to make a meaningful difference in students' lives.

References

American College Personnel Association. "A Student Development Model for Student Affairs in Tomorrow's Higher Education." *Journal of College Student Personnel*, 1975, *16*, 334–341.

American Council on Education. *The Student Personnel Point of View*. Washington, D.C.: American Council on Education, 1937.

American Council on Education. *The Student Personnel Point of View* (rev. ed.). Washington, D.C.: American Council on Education, 1949.

Anderson, K. "Post-High School Experiences and College Attrition." *Sociology of Education*, 1981, *54*, 1–15.

Arendt, H. *Between Past and Future: Eight Exercises in Political Thought*. New York: Penguin Books, 1968.

Astin, A. W. "The Impact of Dormitory Living on Students." *Educational Record*, 1973, *54*, 204–210.

Astin, A. W. *Preventing Students from Dropping Out*. San Francisco: Jossey-Bass, 1975.

Astin, A. W. *Four Critical Years: Effects of College on Beliefs, Attitudes, and Knowledge*. San Francisco: Jossey-Bass, 1977.

Astin, A. W. *Minorities in American Higher Education: Recent Trends, Current Prospects, and Recommendations*. San Francisco: Jossey-Bass, 1982.

Astin, A. W. *Achieving Educational Excellence: A Critical Assessment of Priorities and Practices in Higher Education*. San Francisco: Jossey-Bass, 1985.

Barker, R. G. *Ecological Psychology: Concepts and Methods for Studying the Environment of Human Behavior*. Stanford, Calif.: Stanford University Press, 1968.

Barnes, S. F. "An Evaluation of the 1971–1972 Live and Learn Program and Its Effect on Residence Hall Social Ecology, Academic Achievement, Interpersonal Growth, and Study and Communication Skills Development of University of Oregon Freshmen." Unpublished doctoral dissertation, University of Oregon, 1977.

Baum, A., Calesnick, L. E., David, G. E., and Gatchel, R. L. "Individual Differences in Coping with Crowding: Stimulus Screening and Social Overload." *Journal of Personality and Social Psychology*, 1982, *43*, 821–830.

Baum, A., and David, G. E. "Reducing the Stress of High-Density Living: An Architectural Intervention." *Journal of Personality*, 1980, *38*, 471–481.

Baum, A., and Gatchel, R. J. "Cognitive Determinants of Reaction to Uncontrollable Events: Development of Reactance and Learned Helplessness." *Journal of Personality and Social Psychology*, 1981, *40*, 1078–1089.

Baum, A., Harpin, R. E., and Valins, S. "The Role of Group Phenomena in the Experience of Crowding." *Environment and Behavior*, 1975, *7*, 185–198.

Baxter Magolda, M. B. "Gender Differences in Cognitive Development: An Analysis of Cognitive Complexity and Learning Styles." *Journal of College Student Development*, 1989, *30*, 213–220.

Belenky, M. F., Clinchy, B. M., Goldberger, N. R., and Tarule, J. M. *Women's Way of Knowing: The Development of Self, Voice, and Mind.* New York: Basic Books, 1986.

Benjamin, M. *Residence Life Systems and Student Development: A Critical Review and Reformulation.* Guelph, Ontario: University of Guelph Student–Environment Study Group, 1988.

Bennett, S., and Hunter, J. "A Measure of Success: The WILL Program Four Years Later." *Journal of the National Association of Women Deans, Administrators, and Counselors*, 1985, *48*, 3–11.

Bickman, L., and others. "Dormitory Density and Helping Behavior." *Environment and Behavior*, 1973, *5*(4), 465–490.

Blimling, G. S. "The Influence of College Residence Halls on Students: A Meta-Analysis of the Empirical Research, 1966–1985." Unpublished doctoral dissertation, Ohio State University, 1988.

Blimling, G. S. "A Meta-Analysis of the Influence of College Residence Halls on Academic Performance." *Journal of College Student Development*, 1989, *30*, 298–308.

Bloland, P. A. "Student Development: The New Orthodoxy? (Part 1)." *American College Personnel Association Developments*, 1986a, *13*(3), 1, 13.

Bloland, P. A. "Student Development: The New Orthodoxy? (Part 2)." *American College Personnel Association Developments*, 1986b, *13*(4), 1, 22.

Bowen, H. R. *Investment in Learning: The Individual and Social Value of American Higher Education.* San Francisco: Jossey-Bass, 1977.

Boyer, E. L. *College: The Undergraduate Experience in America.* New York: Harper-Collins, 1987.

Britell, J. K., Beck, N., Park, E., and Peterson, R. E. *Goals for California Higher Education: Summary of a Report.* Princeton, N.J.: Educational Testing Service, 1973.

Brown, R. D. *Student Development in Tomorrow's Higher Education: A Return to the Academy.* Washington, D.C.: American College Personnel Association, 1972.

Brown, R. D., and Barr, M. J. "Student Development: Yesterday, Today, and

Tomorrow." In L. V. Moore (ed.), *Evolving Theoretical Perspectives on Students*. New Directions for Student Services, no. 51. San Francisco: Jossey-Bass, 1990.

Brown, R. D., Winkworth, J., and Braskamp, L. "Student Development in a Coed Residence Hall: Promiscuity, Prophylactic, or Panacea?" *Journal of College Student Personnel*, 1973, *14*, 98–104.

Caple, R. B. "The Change Process in Developmental Theory: A Self-Organization Paradigm, Part 1." *Journal of College Student Personnel*, 1987a, *28*, 4–11.

Caple, R. B. "The Change Process in Developmental Theory: A Self-Organization Paradigm, Part 2." *Journal of College Student Personnel*, 1987b, *28*, 100–104.

Cass, V. C. "Homosexual Identity Formation: Testing a Theoretical Model." *Journal of Homosexuality*, 1979, *4*, 219–235.

Chickering, A. W. *Education and Identity*. San Francisco: Jossey-Bass, 1969.

Chickering, A. W. *Commuting Versus Resident Students: Overcoming Educational Inequities of Living Off Campus*. San Francisco: Jossey-Bass, 1974.

Chickering, A. W., and Kuper, E. "Educational Outcomes for Commuters and Residents." *Educational Record*, 1971, *52*, 255–261.

Chickering, A. W., McDowell, J., and Campagna, D. "Institutional Differences and Student Development." *Journal of Educational Psychology*, 1969, *60*, 315–326.

Chickering, A. W., and Associates. *The Modern American College: Responding to the New Realities of Diverse Students and a Changing Society*. San Francisco: Jossey-Bass, 1981.

Clodfelter, I., Furr, S., and Wachowiak, D. "Student Living Environments and Their Perceived Impact on Academic Performance." *Journal of College and University Student Housing*, 1984, *14*, 18–21.

Corbett, J., and Sommer, R. "Anatomy of a Coed Residence Hall." *Journal of College Student Personnel*, 1972, *13*, 215–217.

Council for the Advancement of Standards for Student Services/Development Programs. *CAS Standards and Guidelines for Student Services/Development Programs*. Washington, D.C.: Council for the Advancement of Standards for Student Services/Development Programs, 1986.

Creamer, D. G., and Creamer, E. G. "Applying a Model of Planned Change to Program Innovations in Student Affairs." *Journal of College Student Personnel*, 1986, *27*, 19–26.

Creamer, D. G., and Creamer, E. G. "Use of a Planned Change Model to Modify Student Affairs Programs." In D. G. Creamer and Associates, *College Student Development: Theory and Practice for the 1990s*. Alexandria, Va.: American College Personnel Association, 1990.

Creamer, E. G., and Creamer, D. G. "The Role of Leaders and Champions in Planned Change in Student Affairs." *Journal of College Student Personnel*, 1986, *27*, 431–437.

Creamer, E. G., and Creamer, D. G. "Predicting Successful Organization Change: Case Studies." *Journal of College Student Development*, 1988, *29*, 4–11.

Creamer, E. G., and Creamer, D. G. "Testing a Model of Planned Change Across Student Affairs and Curricular Reform Projects." *Journal of College Student Development*, 1989, *30*, 27–34.

Crookston, B. B. "Student Personnel: All Hail and Farewell!" *Personnel and Guidance Journal*, 1976, *55*, 26–29.

Cross, K. P. "Education for Personal Development." In D. A. DeCoster and P. Mable (eds.), *Personal Education and Community Development in College Residence Halls*. Washington, D.C.: American College Personnel Association, 1980.

Cross, W. E., Jr. "The Thomas and Cross Models of Psychological Negrescence: A Review." *Journal of Black Psychology*, 1978, *5*, 13–31.

DeCoster, D. A., and Mable, P. "Coeducational Living and Male-Female Relationships." In D. A. DeCoster and P. Mable (eds.), *Personal Education and Community Development in College Residence Halls*. Washington, D.C.: American College Personnel Association, 1980.

Delworth, U., Hanson, G. R., and Associates. *Student Services: A Handbook for the Profession*. San Francisco: Jossey-Bass, 1980.

Dewey, J. *The Public and Its Problems*. Athens, Ohio: Swallow Press, 1954.

Drum, D. J., and Lawler, A. C. *Developmental Interventions: Theories, Principles, and Practices*. Columbus, Ohio: Merrill, 1988.

Duncan, J. P. "Emphasis on Education in Coeducational Living." In D. A. DeCoster and P. Mable (eds.), *Student Development and Education in College Residence Halls*. Washington, D.C.: American College Personnel Association, 1974.

Felver, J. R., Jr. "A Longitudinal Study of the Effects of Living/Learning Programs." Unpublished doctoral dissertation, Northern Illinois University, 1983.

Gerst, M., and Sweetwood, H. "Correlates of Dormitory Social Climate." *Environment and Behavior*, 1973, *5*, 440–464.

Gilligan, C. *In a Different Voice: Psychological Theory and Women's Development*. Cambridge, Mass.: Harvard University Press, 1982.

Goetz, S. C. "Authoritarianism and Ego Development in Four-Year and Two-Year College Students: A One-Year Impact Study." Unpublished doctoral dissertation, University of Washington, 1983.

Greenleaf, E. A. "Coeducational Residence Halls: An Evaluation." *Journal of the National Association of Women Deans, Administrators, and Counselors*, 1962, *25*, 106–111.

Grosz, R. D., and Brandt, K. "Student Residence and Academic Performance." *College and University*, 1969, *44*(3), 240–243.

Gruber, S. K. "Goal Congruence and Assessment at a Small, Private, Denominational Junior College." Unpublished manuscript, University of Georgia, 1987.

Harris, B., and Klein, K. "The Effect of Dormitory Design on Assertive Behavior." Unpublished manuscript, 1980. (ED 192 184)

Heath, D. H. *Growing Up in College.* San Francisco: Jossey-Bass, 1968.

Heist, P., and Yonge, G. *Omnibus Personality Inventory.* New York: Psychological Corporation, 1968.

Herndon, S. "Recent Findings Concerning the Relative Importance of Housing to Student Retention." *Journal of College and University Student Housing,* 1984, *14*, 27–31.

Holland, J. L. *Making Vocational Choices: A Theory of Careers.* Englewood Cliffs, N.J.: Prentice Hall, 1973.

Holohan, C. J., and Wilcox, B. L. "Environmental Satisfaction in High and Low Rise Resident Settings: A Lewinian Perspective." In J. Aiello and A. Baum (eds.), *Residential Crowding and Design.* New York: Plenum, 1979.

Huang, E.T.Y. "Impacts of Environmental Design on Residential Crowding." *Dissertation Abstracts International,* 1982, *43*(3), 948A. (University Microfilms no. 82-18 991)

Katz, J., and Associates. *No Time for Youth: Growth and Constraint in College Students.* San Francisco: Jossey-Bass, 1968.

Kitchener, K. S., and King, P. M. "The Reflective Judgment: Concepts of Justification and Their Relationship to Age and Education." *Journal of Applied Developmental Psychology,* 1981, *2*, 89–116.

Kohlberg, L. "Stages and Sequences: The Cognitive-Developmental Approach to Socialization." In D. P. Goslin (ed.), *Handbook of Socialization Theory and Research.* Chicago: Rand McNally, 1969.

Kohlberg, L. *Essays on Moral Development, Vol. 2: The Psychology of Moral Development: The Nature and Validity of Moral Stages.* New York: HarperCollins, 1984.

Kuh, G. D., Schuh, J. H., Whitt, E. J., and Associates. *Involving Colleges: Successful Approaches to Fostering Student Learning and Development Outside the Classroom.* San Francisco: Jossey-Bass, 1991.

Kuh, G. D., Shedd, J. D., and Whitt, E. J. "Student Affairs and Liberal Education: Unrecognized (and Unappreciated) Common Law Partners." *Journal of College Student Personnel,* 1987, *28*, 252–260.

Kuh, G. D., Whitt, E. J., and Shedd, J. D. *Student Affairs Work, 2001: A Paradigmatic Odyssey.* Alexandria, Va.: American College Personnel Association, 1987.

Lacy, W. "Interpersonal Relationships as Mediators of Structural Effects: College Student Socialization in a Traditional and an Experimental University Environment." *Sociology of Education,* 1978, *51*, 201–211.

Lance, L. M. "Sex-Integrated and Sex-Segregated University Dormitory Living." *Human Relations,* 1976, *29*, 115–123.

Levin, M. "Congruence and Developmental Changes in Authoritarianism in College Students." In J. Katz (ed.), *Growth and Constraint in College Students.* Stanford, Calif.: Institute for the Study of Human Problems, Stanford University, 1967.

Lewin, K. *Principles of Topological Psychology.* New York: McGraw-Hill, 1936.

Lloyd-Jones, E., and Smith, M. R. *Student Personnel Work as Deeper Teaching.* New York: HarperCollins, 1954.

Loevinger, J. *Ego Development: Conceptions and Theories.* San Francisco: Jossey-Bass, 1976.

Lundgren, D. C., and Schwab, M. R. "The Impact of College on Students: Residential Context, Relations with Parents and Peers." *Youth and Society,* 1979, *10,* 227–236.

Lyons, J. W. "Examining the Validity of Basic Assumptions and Beliefs." In M. J. Barr, M. L. Upcraft, and Associates, *New Futures for Student Affairs: Building a Vision for Professional Leadership and Practice.* San Francisco: Jossey-Bass, 1990.

Mable, P. "Residence Halls: Momentum of a Vague Vision." *ACPA Developments,* Aug. 1987, pp. 1, 18.

Markwood, S. E. "Church-Related Colleges: Significant Differences in Institutional Goals." *Journal of College Student Development,* 1985, *26,* 261–262.

Matteson, D. "Changes in Attitudes Toward Authority Figures with the Move to College: Three Experiments." *Developmental Psychology,* 1974, *10,* 340–347.

May, E. "Type of Housing and Achievement of Disadvantaged University Students." *College Student Journal,* 1974, *8,* 48–51.

Miller, S. "Developmental Impact of Residence Hall Living on College Sophomores." *Journal of College and University Student Housing,* 1982, *12,* 10–14.

Miller, S., Rossbach, J., and Munson, R. "Social Density and Affiliative Tendency as Determinants of Dormitory Residential Outcomes." *Journal of Applied Social Psychology,* 1981, *11,* 356–365.

Miller, T. K. "A Short History of the Tomorrow's Higher Education Project: THE Revisited." Paper presented in the Senior Scholars Program, American College Personnel Association Convention, St. Louis, Mo., Apr. 1990.

Miller, T. K., and Prince, J. S. *The Future of Student Affairs: A Guide to Student Development for Tomorrow's Higher Education.* San Francisco: Jossey-Bass, 1976.

Miller, T. K., and Winston, R. B., Jr. "Human Development and Higher Education." In T. K. Miller, R. B. Winston, Jr., and Associates, *Administration and Leadership in Student Affairs: Actualizing Student Development in Higher Education.* (2nd ed.) Muncie, Ind.: Accelerated Development, 1991.

Moore, L. V. (ed.) *Evolving Theoretical Perspectives on Students.* New Directions for Student Services, no. 51. San Francisco: Jossey-Bass, 1990.

Moos, R. H. *Evaluating Educational Environments: Procedures, Measures, Findings, and Policy Implications.* San Francisco: Jossey-Bass, 1979.

Moos, R. H., and Lee, E. "Comparing Residence Hall and Independent Living Settings." *Research in Higher Education,* 1979, *11,* 207–221.

Moos, R. H., and Otto, J. "The Impact of Coed Living on Males and Females." *Journal of College Student Personnel,* 1975, *16,* 459–467.

Student Development in the Residential Environment

Morrill, W. H., and Hurst, J. C. (eds.), *Dimensions of Intervention for Student Development*. New York: Wiley, 1980.

Morse, S. W. *Renewing Civic Capacity*. ASHE-ERIC Higher Education Reports, no. 8. Washington, D.C.: George Washington University, 1989.

Mueller, K. H. "Three Dilemmas of the Student Personnel Profession and Their Resolution." *Journal of the National Association of Women Deans, Administrators, and Counselors*, 1966, *29*(2), 81–91.

Mueller, K. H. "The Future of the Campus Personnel Worker." *Journal of the National Association of Women Deans, Administrators, and Counselors*, 1968, *31*, 132–137.

National Association of Student Affairs Administrators. *A Perspective on Student Affairs*. Washington, D.C.: National Association of Student Affairs Administrators, 1987.

Newcomb, T., and others. "The University of Michigan's Residential College." In P. Dressel (ed.), *The New Colleges: Toward an Appraisal*. Iowa City, Iowa: American College Testing Program and American Association for Higher Education, 1971.

Nosow, S. "An Attitudinal Comparison of Residential College Seniors with Other Seniors." *Journal of College Student Personnel*, 1975, *16*, 17–23.

Null, R. "A Comparison of Student Perceptions of the Social and Academic Climate of Double Room and Suite Living Arrangements in University Residence Halls." In R. Stough and A. Wandersman (eds.), *Optimizing Environments: Research, Practice, and Policy*. New York: Environmental Design Research Associates, 1980.

Pascarella, E. T. "Student-Faculty Informal Contact and College Outcomes." *Review of Educational Research*, 1980, *50*, 545–595.

Pascarella, E. T. "Reassessing the Effects of Living On-Campus Versus Commuting to College: A Causal Modeling Approach." *Review of Higher Education*, 1984, *7*, 247–260.

Pascarella, E. T. "The Influence of On-Campus Living Versus Commuting to College on Intellectual and Interpersonal Self-Concept." *Journal of College Student Personnel*, 1985, *26*(4), 292–299.

Pascarella, E. T., and Chapman, D. "A Multi-Institutional, Path Analytic Validation of Tinto's Model of College Withdrawal." *Research in Higher Education*, 1983, *19*, 25–48.

Pascarella, E. T., and Terenzini, P. T. "Student-Faculty and Student-Peer Relationships as Mediators of the Structural Effects of Undergraduate Residence Arrangement." *Journal of Educational Research*, 1980, *73*, 344–353.

Pascarella, E. T., and Terenzini, P. T. "Residence Arrangement, Student/Faculty Relationships, and Freshman-Year Educational Outcomes." *Journal of College Student Personnel*, 1981, *22*, 147–156.

Pascarella, E. T., and Terenzini, P. T. "Contextual Analysis as a Method for Assessing Residence Group Effects." *Journal of College Student Personnel*, 1982, *23*, 108–114.

Pascarella, E. T., and Terenzini, P. T. *How College Affects Students: Findings and Insights from Twenty Years of Research*. San Francisco: Jossey-Bass, 1991.

Pemberton, C. "An Evaluation of a Living-Learning Residence Hall Program. Unpublished manuscript, 1969. (ED 077 399)

Perl, H. I. "Prediction and Perception of the Psychosocial Environment by Entering College Students." *Journal of College and University Student Housing*, 1986, *16*, 24–31.

Perry, W. G., Jr. *Forms of Intellectual and Ethical Development in the College Years: A Scheme*. Troy, Mo.: Holt, Rinehart & Winston, 1970.

Pervin, L. P. "Satisfaction and Perceived Self-Environment Similarity: A Semantic Differential Study of Student-College Interaction." *Journal of Personality*, 1967, *35*, 623–634.

Peterson, R. E. *Institutional Goals Inventory*. Princeton, N.J.: Educational Testing Service, 1973.

Pike, G. "Background, College Experiences, and the ACT-COMP Exam: Using Construct Validity to Evaluate Assessment Instruments." *Review of Higher Education*, 1989, *13*, 91–117.

Plato, K. "The Shift to Student Development: An Analysis of the Patterns of Change." *NASPA Journal*, 1978, *15*(4), 32–36.

Reid, E. A. "Effects of Coresidential Living on the Attitudes, Self-Image, and Role Expectations of College Women." *American Journal of Psychiatry*, 1974, *46*, 551–554.

Rhatigan, J. J. "Student Services vs. Student Development: Is There a Difference?" *Journal of the National Association of Women Deans, Administrators, and Counselors*, 1975, *38*(2), 51–59.

Riahinejad, A., and Hood, A. B. "The Development of Interpersonal Relationships in College." *Journal of College Student Personnel*, 1984, *25*, 498–502.

Rich, H., and Jolicoeur, P. *Student Attitudes and Academic Environments: A Study of California Higher Education*. New York: Praeger, 1978.

Riker, H. C., and DeCoster, D. A. "The Educational Role in College Student Housing." *Journal of College and University Student Housing*, 1971, *1*(1), 1–4.

Rodgers, R. F. "Using Theory in Practice in Student Affairs." In T. K. Miller, R. B. Winston, Jr., and Associates, *Administration and Leadership in Student Affairs: Actualizing Student Development in Higher Education*. (2nd ed.) Muncie, Ind.: Accelerated Development, 1991.

Sanford, N. "Developmental Status of the Entering Freshman." In N. Sanford (ed.), *The American College: A Psychological and Social Interpretation of the Higher Learning*. New York: Wiley, 1967.

Schlossberg, N. K., Lynch, A. Q., and Chickering, A. W. *Improving Higher Education Environments for Adults: Responsive Programs and Services from Entry to Departure*. San Francisco: Jossey-Bass, 1989.

Schroeder, C. C., and LeMay, L. W. "The Impact of Coed Residence Halls on Self-Actualization." *Journal of College Student Personnel*, 1973, *14*, 105–110.

Simono, R., Wachowiak, D., and Furr, S. "Student Living Environments and

Their Perceived Impact on Academic Performance: A Brief Follow-Up." *Journal of College and University Housing*, 1984, *14*, 22–24.

Sinnett, E. R., Sachson, A. D., and Furr, S. R. "The Influence of Living Units on the Behavior of College Students." *Journal of College Student Personnel*, 1972, *13*, 209–214.

Stamatakos, L. C. "College Residence Halls: In Search of Educational Leadership." *Journal of College and University Student Housing*, 1984, *14*(1), 10–17.

Stern, G. G. *People in Context*. New York: Wiley, 1970.

Stoner, K. L., and Moss, P. E. "Resident Student Satisfaction and Quality of Life Survey." *Southern College Personnel Association Journal*, 1982, *4*(2), 24–29.

Super, D. E. *The Psychology of Careers*. New York: HarperCollins, 1957.

Tinto, V. "Dropout from Higher Education: A Theoretical Synthesis of Recent Research." *Review of Educational Research*, 1975, *45*, 89–125.

Tinto, V. *Leaving College: Rethinking the Causes and Cures of Student Attrition*. Chicago: University of Chicago Press, 1987.

Tomlinson-Keasey, C., Williams, V., and Eisert, D. "Evaluation Report of the First Year of the ADAPT Program." In R. Fuller (ed.), *Multidisciplinary Piagetian-Based Programs for College Freshmen: ADAPT*. Lincoln: University of Nebraska, 1978.

Valins, S., and Baum, A. "Residential Group Size, Social Interaction, and Crowding." *Environment and Behavior*, 1973, *5*, 421–439.

Vanderwall, W. J. "A Comparison of College Environmental Perceptions, Academic Achievement, and Attrition of Student Participants and Nonparticipants in a Special University Living-Learning Resident Hall Program." Unpublished doctoral dissertation, North Carolina State University, 1972.

Velez, W. "Finishing College: The Effects of College Type." *Sociology of Education*, 1985, *58*, 191–200.

Welty, J. D. "The Impact of the Residence Hall, Off-Campus, and Commuter Living Situations on College Freshmen." Unpublished doctoral dissertation, Indiana University, 1974.

Welty, J. D. "Resident and Commuter Students: Is It Only the Living Situation?" *Journal of College Student Personnel*, 1976, *17*, 465–468.

Whalen, D., and Morris, E. "The Impact of Social Distance on Community in University Apartments." *Journal of College and University Student Housing*, 1989, *19*, 17–22.

Williamson, E. G. "Some Unresolved Problems in Student Personnel Work." In G. L. Saddlemire and A. L. Rentz (eds.), *Student Affairs: A Profession's Heritage*. Alexandria, Va.: American College Personnel Association, 1986. (Originally published 1967.)

Wilson, R. J., Anderson, S. A., and Fleming, W. M. "Commuter and Residential Students' Personal and Family Adjustment." *Journal of College Student Personnel*, 1987, *28*, 229–233.

Winston, R. B., Jr., and Moore, W. S. "Standards and Outcomes Assessment: Strategies and Tools." In W. A. Bryan, R. B. Winston, Jr., and T. K. Miller (eds.), *Using Professional Standards in Student Affairs*. New Directions for Student Services, no. 53. San Francisco: Jossey-Bass, 1991.

Winter, D. G., McClelland, D. C., and Stewart, A. J. *A New Case for the Liberal Arts: Assessing Institutional Goals and Student Development*. San Francisco: Jossey-Bass, 1982.

Chapter Three

Psychosocial Development in College

David B. White
William D. Porterfield

Student development theory has had a significant impact on the housing profession and housing professionals over the past three decades. The service model of housing, which dominated housing practice up to the 1960s, viewed housing professionals as caretakers of facilities and administrators with in loco parentis responsibilities. A developmental model of housing, which has emerged over the past thirty years, views housing professionals as managers of facilities, administrators, and educational specialists with developmental responsibilities associated with the overall mission of the institution. The house mothers and house masters of previous decades have been replaced by the resident directors of the 1990s. Resident directors are now assumed to have a working knowledge not only of housing facilities, but also of the developmental tasks and patterns of the occupants of these facilities.

As this shift from housing service models to developmental models has taken place, a similar shift has taken place regarding the professional tools required to fulfill the changing roles. Previously, when service models predominated, the housing administrator was responsible for facilities and for controlling the behavior of students. In the service model, student development was *incidental* — based on the random occurrences and the relationships between and among residents and residential staff. Student development models of housing view student development as *intentional*, and the role of the housing professional in providing programs, relational opportunities, policies, training, and counseling is key to fulfilling the new mission.

If student development is to be intentional and an integral part of residential living, student development theories should play a vital role. These theories can provide guideposts and road maps for intentional development; they can offer insight about the changes and challenges that are likely to unfold for students during the college years.

Psychosocial development theories have a particular relevance for housing professionals in that these theories describe the developmental changes and challenges students as a group face as they interact with the collegiate environment. Student housing can be a particularly rich and potent force that influences the course of student's developmental lives.

This chapter presents an overview of psychosocial development theory. We begin by taking a broad look at the origins and assumptions of psychosocial theory. The discussion then focuses on the work of a number of theorists who have formulated psychosocial theories of college student development, each from slightly different perspectives. Due to space limitations, we have chosen to limit our discussion of psychosocial theory to a small group of theorists. However, the discussion of assessment techniques, research needs, and application strategies of psychosocial theory to the housing setting goes beyond any particular theory.

Psychosocial Theory

Psychosocial theories, which build on the work of Erikson (1963), suggest that individuals develop through a sequence of stages that define the life cycle. Developmental stages, which involve the formation of new attitudes, skills, and roles, become critical because of the convergence of social expectations and physiological maturation. Unlike other families of theory that focus on single dimensions of development, psychosocial theories combine thinking, feeling, and behavior into a rich and complex picture of the life span.

The basic concepts used in psychosocial theory are stage (or phase), developmental crisis, developmental or optimal dissonance, and developmental task.

Psychosocial theorists suggest that development occurs in stages. Each stage is considered to have unique psychological/biological characteristics and basic conflicts that initiate the need to resolve particular issues and that provide the impetus for development. A *stage* is defined as an interval of time during which an internal change, stimulated through the environment, creates an internal crisis for an individual. Psychosocial stages tend to follow sequential, preset patterns. However, these sequences are not invariant as in cognitive developmental theory. The existence and order of adult psycho-social stages are heavily influenced by sociocultural variables. Psychosocial stages are also cumulative. Each stage contains elements of previous stages. Resolution of the issues and tasks related to early stages of development affects individuals' ability to effectively complete future stages. In successive stages of development, the individual confronts new developmental issues or tasks that require new or more complex modes of adaptation. While each psychosocial stage has a particular time of ascendancy, relearning, regres-sion, and recycling of issues and tasks often occur. The recycling of stages underlies psychosocial theorists' emphasis on lifelong development. Finally, psychosocial stages are concerned with the content of development (tasks), whereas cognitive developmental stages stress the process of development.

Developmental crises occur as a result of the convergence of biological and psychological maturation and social demands. Erikson (1968, p. 96) states that the term *crisis* is used in a developmental sense to connote not a threat of catastrophe, but a turning point, a crucial period of increased vulnerability and heightened potential. Erikson conceptualized develop-mental crises in terms of polar opposites. During late adolescence and early adulthood, for example, biological, psychological, and social forces combine to produce the developmental crisis of identity versus role diffusion. Suc-cessful resolution of the tasks and issues related to this stage of development increases individuals' sense of identity, while failure adds to a sense of role confusion.

Psychosocial theorists suggest that change involves a period of devel-opmental dissonance. *Developmental* or *optimal dissonance* refers to a period of disequilibrium or anxiety, which psychosocial theorists believe provides the catalyst for development. Central to this concept is Sanford's (1966) theme of challenge and support. Sanford proposed that change is facilitated when individuals are challenged to explore new modes of thinking and behavior. The amount of challenge that is developmental, or optimal, is a function of the support that is available. When challenges outweigh the support that is available in the environment, individuals tend to regress to earlier, less adaptive modes of behavior, become rigid in present modes of behavior, attempt to escape the challenging stimuli, or ignore the stimuli if escape is not possible. Psychosocial theorists suggest that when support outweighs the amount of challenge in the environment, people's progression through psy-chosocial stages may be thwarted. The balance of challenge and support involves moving individuals outside the parameters of their comfort zone in order to promote development.

Developmental tasks are the crucial, problematic issues that must be resolved during individual stages of development. The convergence of phys-iological and psychological growth with social demands creates specific developmental tasks that must be confronted and resolved. For example, during Erikson's stage of identity versus role diffusion, young adults must resolve issues related to vocation and personal commitments. Resolution of these issues enables people to develop the experiential base necessary to resolve later developmental tasks. Failure to resolve these and related issues can result in social disapproval and an inability to successfully resolve subsequent developmental tasks.

Psychosocial Theorists

Several representative psychosocial theories of human development are discussed below. The work of Erik Erikson serves as the foundation of psychosocial theory. Marcia (1966), Keniston (1971), and Chickering (1969) have refined and extended Erikson's theoretical concepts in their work with college students.

Erikson

Erikson's work provides the foundation for psychosocial theory. While drawing heavily from Freudian thought, Erikson extends the Freudian model in two respects. Refusing to believe that personality is set during childhood, Erikson argues that development continues throughout the life span. He also emphasizes that development cannot be understood apart from the sociocultural context in which it occurs.

Erikson conceives development, both physiological and psychological, as unfolding according to an epigenetic principle. The epigenetic principle states that "anything that grows has a ground plan, and out of this ground plan the parts arise, each part having its time of special ascendancy, until all parts have risen to form a functioning whole" (Erikson, 1968, p. 92). Hence, Erikson assumes that development follows a prewired master plan. Unlike cognitive developmental changes that occur as the result of cognitive conflict, these prewired changes occur at the time of their ascendancy. At certain times in life, particular issues become ascendant and reach a point where action is required. The ascendancy of a particular issue comes about as a result of the convergence of biological growth, cognitive maturation, and sociocultural demands. Because biological and psychological maturation occur within a particular social and socializing context, the life cycle can be viewed as a series of biological-social (or psychosocial) phases. In childhood and adolescence, biological factors are the dominant forces that provide the impetus for development. However, during early and middle adulthood, psychological pressures for change (the necessity of making decisions related to career, life-style, and values, for example) become predominant.

Erikson describes eight stages of psychosocial development. Each stage can be presented as a particular set of issues or tasks that require resolution. The central tasks associated with late adolescence and young adulthood involve the resolution of identity and the formation of intimate relationships. In American society, the identity crisis of young adulthood centers on a number of personal and societal demands, which include decisions regarding career, life-style, values, sexual identity, and commitment. Erikson's emphasis on the resolution of issues related to identity and intimacy during the young adult years makes his model particularly useful in the study of traditional-age college students.

Psychosocial theorists who focus on the development of college students include Marcia (1966), Keniston (1971), and Chickering (1969). Based on their work with college students, each elaborates on Erikson's stages of identity and intimacy from slightly different perspectives.

Marcia

Marcia (1966) is one of the chief researchers and interpreters of Eriksonian theory. His work is essentially an elaboration and refinement of the process of identity resolution described by Erikson. According to Marcia, the identity resolution process involves the experiencing of a crisis, a period of uncertainty and active searching, and the making of commitments, most importantly in the areas of vocation and ideology. Marcia has developed a matrix of identity concepts, or ego statuses, which represent styles of coping with the task of identity resolution:

- *Achieved identity*. The individual has both experienced a crisis and has made a commitment in areas of vocation and values.
- *Moratorium*. The individual is experiencing a crisis and is actively seeking to clarify his or her identity and purpose.
- *Diffused identity*. The individual has not experienced a crisis and actively avoids commitments.
- *Foreclosed identity*. The individual has not experienced a crisis yet expresses firm commitments.

Based on his work with college students, Marcia has developed an instrument and a structured interview technique for measuring the stage of identity. Research by Marcia and his associates has indicated that achieved identity and moratorium students demonstrate a capacity for intimacy, a respect for individual rights, and an awareness of the complexity of moral judgments. In contrast, diffused identity and foreclosed identity students exhibit superficial interpersonal relationships and are more likely to be conforming and legalistic in their approach to moral issues. Marcia's work suggests that students with different ego-identity statuses are likely to need different experiences to resolve issues related to identity formation.

Keniston

Like Erikson, Keniston asserts that development results from a complex interaction between biological givens and social conditions. Specific stages

of development tend to emerge at particular times because of the convergence of biological patterns of growth and social demands. Keniston
(1971) argues that Erikson's stage of adolescence inadequately describes the
developmental status of present-day college students. He suggests that the
tendency to prolong the education process in American society has created
an extended period of psychological development that he has labeled *youth*.

Keniston suggests that collegiate life is a distinct and unique social
experience that poses unique psychosocial tasks and issues for the young
adult. He states that the central theme of this stage of development is a
tension between the individual and society. The collegiate experience, in
essence, provides a testing ground that allows individuals to struggle with
and reconcile individual needs and societal demands. Keniston's major
contribution to psychosocial theory rests in his treatment of the social
environment of young adults. A complete understanding of the developmental status of college students cannot be achieved if one fails to take into
account the shifting nature of modern society.

Heath

Drawing on literature from anthropology, biology, psychology, and education, Heath (1968, 1978) has created a model of development that attempts to
delineate the many dimensions involved in the process of maturation.
Heath's maturity model outlines development in terms of five growth dimensions along each of four principal sectors of the self. Maturity involves
development in each of these growth dimensions: (1) being able to symbolize
and express (either verbally, through the written world, or via art or music)
one's experiences, (2) becoming allocentric or other centered, (3) becoming
integrated or able to connect various aspects of one's experience, (4) becoming stable (being able to resist disruption and function consistently), and (5)
becoming autonomous. Maturation along each of these dimensions occurs
in four areas of the self: the intellect, values, self-concept, and interpersonal
relations. Based on a series of cross-cultural longitudinal studies, which
employed multiple methods of assessment, Heath has produced a large
amount of data related to changes that students experience in college. He
draws several general conclusions from his studies. First, seniors were more
mature than freshmen on nearly all dimensions of the model, and both
groups were more mature than they were when they entered college. Heath
notes that many major changes in growth and development occurred during
the first half of the freshman year. Second, a consistent pattern of development was observed for most students. The process of maturation is initiated
by instability (internal or external conflict). Over time, individuals respond
to this instability with increased awareness and become increasingly capable
of other-centered thoughts and behaviors. Eventually, an adaptive solution to
the conflict is forged that stabilizes over time, so that the individual begins to
function more autonomously. Heath views this sequence as an unending

process that occurs at different rates in different areas of the personality. Thus individuals cycle and recycle through this process throughout their lives as they are confronted with challenging stimuli. Finally, an over-emphasis or a lag in development along one dimension or in one area of the personality inhibits development in other dimensions or other areas of the personality.

Heath's conceptualization of development or maturity can guide professional practice in several ways. First, the model provides practitioners with a comprehensive set of developmental goals. By beginning at the end point or goal of development—maturity—he has delineated a number of specific developmental goals that can be used to guide the development, implementation, and evaluation of student development programs. Second, his model suggests that a sequential pattern of development may be experienced by college-age individuals in a college context. This sequence involves first the development of the intellect, next the development of interpersonal relationships, and finally intrapersonal development in the areas of values and self-concept. Finally, Heath outlines factors that encourage student development in a college context: close interpersonal relationships, coursework that focuses on values, faculty members who serve as role models of maturity, and a unified and coherent institutional purpose.

Chickering

Perhaps the most widely recognized and popular psychosocial theory of student development is that proposed by Chickering (1969). Chickering's theory, essentially an elaboration of Erikson's stages of intimacy and identity, was derived from a longitudinal study of undergraduate students in thirteen small colleges. Chickering synthesized this research, and the writings of Sanford (1962) and White (1958), to formulate a theory that added greater specificity and concreteness to Erikson's stages of development. Like Keniston, Chickering sees traditional-age college students as individuals in a distinct psychosocial stage. He suggests that the central task of college students is the establishment of identity.

Seven Vectors. Chickering postulates seven vectors or dimensions that comprise the development of identity in young adulthood. Chickering (1969) prefers to use the term *vector* as opposed to *phase* or *stage* because each seems to have direction and magnitude—"even though the direction may be expressed more appropriately by a spiral or by steps than by a straight line" (p. 8). The seven vectors along which development is hypothesized to occur in young adulthood are the following:

1. *Developing competence.* Chickering views competence as being made up of three distinct spheres: intellectual competence, physical and manual competence, and social and interpersonal competence. Likening competence to a three-tined pitchfork, Chickering (1969, p. 20) states that "intellectual competence, physical and manual skills, and interpersonal competence

area the tines, and a sense of competence the handle." Intellectual competence involves several elements, including an individual's general intelligence or ability level, fund of acquired knowledge, and ability to symbolize abstractly the objects and events of experience. Physical and manual competence enables an individual to master previously unattainable skills and to achieve in competition with others. The development of physical and manual skills also provides an individual with the ability to symbolically tie objects and events through direct action. Interpersonal competence involves the development of basic interpersonal skills. The ability to understand the concerns and motives of others, to work effectively in groups, and to manage a variety of social situations provides the foundation for interpersonal competence. Increased skills in each of these areas leads to an increased sense of competence — that is, growing confidence that one can cope with what comes and achieve desired goals (Chickering, 1969).

2. *Managing emotions.* Development along this vector involves an increased awareness of and integration of emotions, which results in flexibility of control and expression. During young adulthood, biological maturation releases a flood of strong impulses. Sex and aggression are the two major impulses that must be managed. An awareness and acceptance of such feelings as legitimate human emotions occurs when habitual response patterns, modeled after parents and associational groups, are identified. An increased sensitivity to and understanding of emotional impulses sets the stage for the complementary task of developing flexible controls. "The integration of emotions refers to the development of flexible controls which are congruent with the self one is and is becoming" (Chickering, 1969, p. 41). An increased awareness and integration of emotions develops as students seek out new modes of emotional expression and assess their consequences.

3. *Developing autonomy.* Becoming autonomous involves establishing emotional autonomy, attaining instrumental autonomy, and recognizing one's interdependence. Chickering (1969, p. 12) defines emotional autonomy as "being free of continual and pressing needs for reassurance, affection, or approval." Emotional autonomy begins to develop with disengagement from parents. Reliance is later transferred to peers and to occupational and institutional reference groups. Gradually, there is less need for such supports as one's own thoughts, perceptions, and values become the primary motivational force in life. Instrumental autonomy is the second task in this vector; it involves "the ability to carry on activities and to cope with problems without seeking help, and the ability to be mobile in relation to one's needs or desires" (Chickering, 1969, p. 12). Chickering states that recognition and acceptance of interdependence is the capstone of autonomy. Having achieved a sense of responsibility for one's own life, one can acknowledge a sense of connectedness with others.

4. *Establishing identity.* Chickering describes the primary element of this vector as a solid sense of self, which takes shape as the developmental tasks of competency, managing emotions, and autonomy are resolved with success.

Drawing from Erikson (1959) and White (1958), Chickering states that "identity is the inner capital accrued from experience, and that fuller, richer establishment, compounded of bodily sensations, feelings, images of one's body, the sound of one's name, the continuity of one's memories, and an increasing number of social judgments delivered through words and behaviors of others" (1969, p. 13). The establishment of identity depends in large part on progress on the three vectors discussed above. The principal components of this solid sense of self are clarification of conceptions concerning physical needs, characteristics, and personal appearance, and clarification of sexual identity and gender-appropriate roles and behavior. The establishment of identity provides a framework for the development of healthy interpersonal relationships, a sense of purpose, and an integrated system of values.

5. *Freeing interpersonal relationships.* During young adulthood, individuals develop an increased capacity for close interpersonal relationships. The freeing of interpersonal relations involves increased tolerance and respect between individuals and a shift in the quality of intimate relationships. Chickering (1969, p. 94) refers to the development of tolerance as "an increasing openness and acceptance of diversity, which allows our own sensitivities to expand and which increases the range of alternatives for satisfying exchanges and for close and lasting friendships." Once a greater sense of autonomy and identity is achieved, relationships become less anxious and defensive, and a shift toward greater trust, openness, independence, and commitment takes place.

6. *Developing purpose.* Chickering (1969, p. 108) states that development of purpose requires "formulating plans for action and a set of priorities that integrate three major elements: (1) avocational and recreational interests, (2) pursuit of vocation, and (3) life-style issues including concerns for marriage and family." Avocational and recreational interests become increasingly stable and tend to be enjoyed as an end in and of themselves. Vocational plans and aspirations begin to take shape. For men, the development of purpose revolves primarily around the clarification of vocational plans and aspirations. Chickering suggests that the importance of vocational plans for women is complicated by issues related to marriage and childbirth. Finally, the development of purpose includes considerations of life-style that revolve around issues related to long-range goals, personal priorities, and commitments to marriage and family. The integration of avocational and recreational interests, career goals, and life-style considerations provides life with direction and meaning.

7. *Developing integrity.* The development of integrity involves three related tasks: the humanizing of values, the personalization of values, and the development of congruence between beliefs and behavior. Chickering borrows White's (1958) term *humanizing of values* to describe the shift from a literal, absolutist view of rules to a more relativistic position where the social purposes of rules are recognized. The personalization of values occurs as

individuals begin to develop a code of values that reflects personal assessments and serves as a flexible guide for behavior. With the development of a
flexible and personal code of values comes an increased awareness of the
relationship between personal values and behavior.

Conditions for Impact. Chickering suggests that development along each of his
seven vectors can be influenced (either positively or negatively) by six major
institutional factors. These factors include: (1) clarity and consistency of
institutional objectives, (2) institutional size, (3) curriculum, teaching and
evaluation, (4) residence hall arrangements, (5) faculty and administration,
and (6) student culture.

In the mid 1980s, Chickering reaffirmed his original conceptualization of college student development (Thomas and Chickering, 1984). He
stated that although the basic structure and sequence of the seven developmental vectors would remain unchanged, minor changes could be made
within the confines of each vector to account for cultural changes and the
demands of an increasingly complex society. The vector of developing competence would incorporate more attention to the areas of intellectual and
interpersonal competence. More attention would also be given to the area of
sense of competence, particularly among women and minority populations.
Managing emotions would have to take into account a greater variability and
ambiguity in cultural norms and the broader range of alternative behaviors
that have become acceptable forms of self-expression. Cultural changes since
the 1960s have made coming to terms with emotions such as lust and hate
more complex. A shift in emphasis to interdependence would characterize
the vector of developing autonomy (which would now be labeled *interdependence*). Although the original formulation of this vector emphasized interdependence as the capstone, Chickering feels that this vector has often been
interpreted as stressing a rugged individualism. The vector of establishing
identity would recognize the increased impact of pluralism and an increased
emphasis on self-fulfillment and self-actualization today. There would also be
a recognition that these identity issues are not unique to college-age populations but that they characterize individuals at other stages of the life cycle as
well. Freeing interpersonal relationships would emphasize the critical importance of the development of tolerance in an increasingly diverse society. The
vector of developing purpose would remain essentially unchanged. There
would, however, be a recognition that the integration of work, leisure, and life-
style orientations has become more difficult given current economic constraints. Finally, the vector of developing integrity would incorporate the
work of Kohlberg, Perry, and Gilligan in the area of cognitive development.
Overall, the orientation of each vector would shift from a focus on the
development of eighteen- to twenty-year-olds to development throughout the
life span.

Each of Chickering's vectors can be viewed as a series of developmental
tasks that define the central concerns of traditional-age college students.

Similar to Erikson's stages, Chickering hypothesizes that resolution of each vector can be positive or negative. Additionally, vectors may recycle throughout an individual's life span. Chickering describes developmental change in terms of differentiation/integration and challenge/response. On each vector, students progress from simple distinctions and relationships toward more complex differentiations and integrations. As they develop, they are able to cope with increasingly complex stimuli. As these more differentiated perceptions and behaviors are integrated and organized, an increasingly coherent self-system emerges. Growth along each vector entails more than a simple maturational unfolding. Borrowing from Sanford (1966), Chickering suggests that change is facilitated through challenge and support. Environmental factors play a major role in providing challenges that stimulate growth and development. However, challenge only proves to be developmental when accompanied by a corresponding amount of support (Sanford, 1966).

Chickering suggests that the seven vectors follow a specific developmental sequence. He postulates that the first three vectors (developing competence, managing emotions, and developing autonomy) ascend simultaneously and prior to the remaining four vectors. A favorable resolution of the initial three vectors is necessary before the fourth vector, establishing identity, can be resolved. The successful resolution of the first four vectors provides the framework for the remaining three vectors (freeing interpersonal relationships, developing purpose, and developing integrity), which ascend simultaneously. Chickering reports that it is most common for freshmen and sophomores to be preoccupied with tasks related to the first three vectors, while tasks related to the remaining four vectors are emphasized during the final two years of college. However, he also points out that individual students often vary substantially in terms of the vectors that are most important at college entrance.

The cumulative data and basic conclusions derived from the wealth of studies that have been conducted to monitor change in student attitudes, characteristics, goals, and behavior generally substantiate the patterns of development hypothesized by Chickering (Bowen, 1977; Feldman and Newcomb, 1969; Widick, Parker, and Knefelkamp, 1978). Work by Loevinger (1976) indicates that ego development encompasses the development of the capacity for interpersonal relationships and the differentiation and integration of emotional responses. These findings closely parallel elements of Chickering's vectors of managing emotions and freeing interpersonal relationships. Kohlberg's (1971) research on moral development substantiates Chickering's hypotheses regarding the humanization and personalization of values. Perry's (1970) research on intellectual and ethical development during college supports Chickering's assumptions regarding the developmental shift from absolutist thinking to relativistic thinking and the development of intellectual competence. Although these studies offer some support for aspects of Chickering's theory, Widick, Parker, and Knefelkamp (1978, p. 30) point out that "one does not find extensive support suggesting that Chickering's model is the best conceptualization of the pattern of developmental changes in young adulthood, nor is there extensive support for the presumed sequence in which students address the vectors." Winston, Miller, and Prince (1979) have also indicated that development may not follow the precise sequence described by Chickering in 1969.

But Chickering's model of student development has remained popular for a number of reasons. Chickering was one of the first theorists to provide student affairs professionals with a comprehensive theory of student development that could be used to guide professional practice. The theory is practical—through the identification of seven vectors of development, Chickering suggests specific tasks that students must resolve in order for their development to continue. The general scheme of development inherent in his vectors can be used to guide the development of programs and policies. In addition, his writings are relatively free of jargon and are easily grasped. And the notion of a vector of development has a certain appeal. It implies a dynamic quality—a quality that student affairs professionals strive for in their day-to-day interaction with college students.

In *Education and Identity* (1969), Chickering attempted to build a conceptual model of college student development that synthesized previous research findings and that would serve as a guide for educational practice. Recently, he has stated that "the book was not written to advance theory per se but rather to improve practice. For this reason the book was organized at a level of abstraction, some would say simplicity, that I hoped would make the ideas generally accessible to practitioners at a level that would be useful to them" (Thomas and Chickering, 1984, p. 394).

Education and Identity is written in a persuasive style that contains a mix of quotations, a synthesis of theory, evidence from empirical research, and a rich supply of illustrations, metaphors, analogies, and direct quotations from students. However, because Chickering's conceptualizations are presented in a global manner, they often lack specificity and precision. Widick, Parker, and Knefelkamp (1978) point out that a major problem with Chickering's theory is the lack of enumeration of specific behaviors and attitudes that would define development along any given vector. Rodgers (1990) points out that the scope and specificity of the phenomena discussed for each vector vary considerably. The inability to precisely define any of Chickering's developmental vectors in terms of specific behaviors and attitudes has hampered the application of the theory to professional practice and has limited the use of Chickering's theory in college student research.

Psychosocial Development of Subpopulations

In recent years, many individuals have suggested that current developmental theories fail to take into account the experiences of a number of subpopulations of students in higher education (Cheatham, 1991; Moore, 1990;

Rodgers, 1990; Evans and Wall, 1991). Although numerous theories have been proposed to account for the changes that individuals experience in college, in many cases, theoretical concepts were derived from and subsequently validated via studies that focused primarily (if not exclusively) on the experiences of white, middle-class, heterosexual men. Indeed, an implicit assumption of much of the research on college student change and development seems to be that the processes underlying development for men and women as well as for white and nonwhite populations are the same. Today, there is a growing body of research that suggests that it is not appropriate to attempt to explain or evaluate the development of subpopulations of students on college campuses using traditional notions of psychosocial development.

Recent literature suggests that the current body of psychosocial theory does not accurately describe the development of women, nonheterosexuals, or members of ethnic groups. Straub (1987) and Straub and Rodgers (1986) report evidence that supports a sequence of development for women that differs from Chickering's theory. They found that women tend to accomplish tasks related to the management of emotions earlier than men, whereas men tend to achieve autonomy before their female counterparts. Their findings also indicate that women develop mature interpersonal relations prior to developing autonomy (the reverse of the pattern of development hypothesized by Chickering). A similar pattern of development for women was observed by Greeley and Tinsley (1988). Taub and McEwen (1991) found differences between white and African-American women related to the development of intimacy and suggest that the application of Chickering's theory and the use of Chickering-based instruments may not be appropriate with female or African-American students. McEwen, Roper, Bryant, and Langa (1990) suggest nine factors that relate to developmental tasks experienced by African-American students that have not been adequately addressed by current psychosocial theory: developing racial and ethnic identity, interacting with the dominant culture, developing cultural esthetics and awareness, developing identity, developing interdependence, fulfilling affiliation needs, surviving intellectually, developing spiritually, and developing social responsibility. Evans and Wall (1991) note that most psychosocial theories describe developmentally appropriate goals in terms of heterosexual roles and thus fail to account for the development of students whose sexual identity is not heterosexual. (For a more in-depth discussion of these issues, see Cheatham, 1991; Moore, 1990; Rodgers, 1990; Evans and Wall, 1991.) Taken together, this literature suggests that (1) it may be inappropriate in many instances to attempt to understand the experiences of significant subpopulations of students within higher education using current psychosocial theory, and (2) a great deal of additional study is needed to sort out the patterns of development experienced by the diverse subpopulations of students on our college campuses.

Assessing Psychosocial Development

The assessment of psychosocial development can be approached in a number of different ways. This section discusses both formal (via standardized assessment instruments) and informal (for example, by observation) methods of assessment. Mines (1982) asserts that the assessment of developmental tasks (for instance, Chickering's vector of developing autonomy) can be considered from three different perspectives: (1) the cognitive complexity needed to resolve the task, (2) the skills needed to complete the task, and (3) task-specific behaviors that are evidence of task resolution. Mines indicates that the best approach to developmental task assessment integrates cognitive stage, skills, and behavioral dimensions. Formal efforts to date, however, have tended to focus on the behavioral dimensions of task development.

The global nature of Chickering's theory presents student development theorists with a complex measurement task. Within each vector, Chickering has postulated specific tasks that must be attained during late adolescence and young adulthood. The attainment of these tasks often requires multidimensional development. Hence, measurement of growth along each of Chickering's vectors necessitates the assessment of multiple dimensions of development. So far, relatively few instruments have been designed to assess Chickering's theoretical concepts. The best-known efforts that have attempted to operationalize Chickering's developmental theory and design instruments that successfully assess relevant aspects of these conceptualizations have been underway at the University of Georgia and the University of Iowa. The following section will review the work of Winston, Miller, and Prince (1979, 1987) at the University of Georgia; it will also survey the studies of Barratt (1978), Erwin (1979), Hood and Jackson (1983a, 1983b, 1983c), and Mines (1977), which have been conducted at the University of Iowa and are therefore collectively known as the *Iowa Instruments*.

Student Developmental Task and Lifestyle Inventory (SDTLI)

Winston, Miller, and Prince (1979) developed the Student Developmental Task Inventory, second edition (SDTI-2), to measure selected developmental constructs proposed by Chickering among traditional-age college students (age seventeen to twenty-four). The SDTI-2 combines basic constructs developed by Chickering with Havighurst's (1953) conceptualization of developmental tasks to formulate a practical assessment instrument. The SDTI-2 is composed of 140 items divided into three tasks: developing autonomy, developing purpose, and freeing of interpersonal relations. Each task represents a sample of behaviors that students can be expected to demonstrate when they have successfully accomplished a given developmental task. During the last decade, the SDTI-2 became the most widely used instrument designed to assess Chickering's developmental theory. Experience and continued research with the SDTI-2 have led to a total revision of the instrument and the development of the Student Developmental Task and Lifestyle Inventory (SDTLI) (Winston, Miller, and Prince, 1987).

The SDTLI is based on, but does not entirely conform to, the original conceptual framework proposed by Chickering in 1969. Several departures from this framework have been dictated by data accumulated from a number of studies with college students. The SDTLI is composed of three developmental tasks (and subtasks) and three scales. Winston and Miller (1987, p. 2) have defined a developmental task as "an interrelated set of behaviors and attitudes that the culture specifies should be exhibited at approximately the same chronological time in life by a given age cohort in a designated context. Successful accomplishment or achievement of a developmental task allows the individual to acquire the experiential base needed to accomplish the developmental tasks that arise in the future." A subtask is accordingly defined as a more specific component of a broader developmental task. Following are brief descriptions of the developmental tasks and scales of the SDTLI.

Establishing and Clarifying Purpose Task

This task assesses (1) the extent to which students have defined and explored educational goals and plans and the extent to which they are active, self-directed learners; (2) students' ability to synthesize knowledge about themselves and the world of work into appropriate career plans; (3) the extent to which students have established a personal direction in their lives (this takes into account personal, ethical, and religious values, future family plans, and vocational and educational objectives); (4) whether students exhibit a wide range of cultural interests and are active participants in cultural events; and (5) students' ability to structure their lives and manipulate their environment in ways that allow them to satisfy daily needs and meet personal responsibilities.

Developing Mature Interpersonal Relationships Task

This task assesses (1) the extent to which students' relationships with their peers are characterized by independence, honesty, and trust; (2) students' appreciation of individual differences; and (3) the extent to which students are free from the need to seek continual reassurance and approval from others.

Academic Autonomy Task

This task assesses students' ability to deal with ambiguity and to monitor and control their behavior in ways that allow them to attain personal goals and fulfill responsibilities.

Salubrious Lifestyle Scale

This scale measures the extent to which a student's life-style is consistent with or promotes good health and wellness practices.

Intimacy Scale

This scale measures the extent to which students have established an intimate relationship with another individual that is based on mutual respect, honesty, and trust. Winston and Miller (1987) note that this scale should be viewed as an experimental scale at present.

The SDTLI also includes a response bias scale that measures students' tendencies to project an unrealistically favorable self-portrait.

The Iowa Instruments

A number of instruments that assess specific aspects of Chickering's theory of student development have been developed at the University of Iowa and are collectively known as the Iowa Instruments. These instruments are the result of the work of several authors who have attempted to assess selected aspects of Chickering's developmental theory. While Winston, Miller, and Prince (1979, 1987) have focused on the assessment of behavioral dimensions of Chickering's vectors, the instruments outlined below were designed to assess attitudinal dimensions of the theory. The studies of Barratt (1978), Erwin (1979), Hood and Jackson (1983a, 1983b, 1983c), and Mines (1977) are summarized below.

Developing Competency Inventory

Hood and Jackson's (1983a) formulation of developing competence includes constructs related to the development of intellectual competence and the development of interpersonal competence. The Developing Competency Inventory consists of seventy items that form three subscales, Competency in Math, Competency in Writing, and Self-Confidence.

Managing Emotions Inventory

The Managing Emotions Inventory (Hood and Jackson, 1983b) consists of sixty items that comprise a single subscale dealing with depression, anger, frustration, happiness, and attraction. Attraction refers to the emotions evoked by personal or physical attraction to another individual. Development in the area of managing emotions entails increased awareness of emotions and the increased ability to manage them effectively.

Developing Autonomy Inventory

Hood and Jackson (1983c) designed the Developing Autonomy Inventory to assess Chickering's vector of developing autonomy. The inventory consists of ninety items that comprise six subscales: Mobility, Time Management, Money Management, Interdependence, Emotional Independence–Peers, and Emotional Independence–Parents.

Erwin Identity Scale

Erwin (1979) developed the Erwin Identity Scale (EIS) to measure Chickering's concept of establishing identity. It is conceptually based on Erikson's original formulations of identity development and Chickering's refinement. The EIS is composed of fifty-eight items that comprise three major subtasks: confidence, sexual identity, and conceptions about body and appearance.

Mines-Jensen Interpersonal Relationships Inventory

Mines (1977) designed the Mines-Jensen Interpersonal Relationships Inventory (MIRI) to assess Chickering's vector of freeing interpersonal relationships. The MIRI consists of forty-two items that represent four content areas—peers, adults, friends, and significant others—on two subscales, tolerance and quality of relationships.

The Developing Purposes Inventory

Barratt (1978) designed the Developing Purposes Inventory (DPI) to assess students' development on Chickering's vector of developing purpose. The DPI consists of forty-five items that are equally divided among the three subtasks: the development of avocational-recreational purpose, the development of vocational interests, and the development of a style of life.

Although the Iowa Instruments are still in the early stages of development, they have yielded promising results. A relatively small but growing body of literature currently exists that attests to the validity and reliability of each of the instruments. Information on how to obtain and use each instrument, a summary of studies that have employed one or more of the instruments, and information pertaining to each instrument's reliability and validity can be found in Hood (1986).

Informal Assessment Methods

In addition to the formal assessment methods described above, psychosocial development can also be assessed utilizing informal methods. These informal assessment methods can be categorized as follows: dialogue analysis, interactional analysis, behavioral trend analysis, and standard report analysis. Even though none of these informal assessment methods could be used as a basis for research studies, each of the methods provides a systematic way for housing professionals to begin to extract developmental clues from the environment. These clues can become useful pieces of information when developmentally mapping a residential environment.

Dialogue analysis is an examination of the types of conversations that dominate a particular environment. The housing professional has any number of ways of doing dialogue analysis, and the primary skills necessary include a good listening ability and an awareness of the components of various psychosocial theories. Dialogue analysis can involve listening to conversations between residents for trends or psychosocial clues. The informal dialogue between a group of seniors, for example, is likely to be very different from the informal dialogue between a group of freshmen. Both dialogues will be rich in developmental clues that suggest the dominant challenges for each group. Dialogue analysis can also be done between various living units, in the residence hall lobby, on different evenings of the week, and at different times during the academic year. The housing professional who is able to do dialogue analysis on an ongoing basis is likely to develop a keen sense of the developmental issues for the students in a particular living unit, without extensive or expensive formalized assessment.

Interactional analysis is an observation of the interactions that occur within a given context. These interactions offer insight into the type of groups and the group norms that exist within the environment (that is, what types of interactions are most frequent, what social activities dominate the environment, what the main *content* of the interactions is). Such interactional analysis can assist the housing professional in understanding the dominant social norms as well as the dominant group norms within the community. We can readily observe the differences in interactional analysis when observing social norming in single-sex living units. For any number of reasons, we readily observe different interactions in female and male environments. Still other interactional differences exist within groups and between different housing units on the campus. Again, the housing professional only needs the skill to observe, listen, and compare observations to developmental constructs in order to develop a sense of the interactional challenges within a particular environment.

Behavioral trend analysis is the examination of the emergent clusters of behaviors within a living unit. Almost all housing programs have some formalized system for recording disciplinary incidents on the hall. A review of these documents, and a coding of these documents according to developmental constructs, can offer an ongoing source of developmental data for the housing professional. As behaviors are grouped together, informal trends may emerge that suggest that a particular group is either acting out a developmental construct or needs support in accomplishing the challenges of the construct. A developmental housing professional will be able to group behavioral data in such a way that incidents no longer appear random, and certain patterns of behavior may actually become more predictable based on past groupings and insights from developmental theories.

Standard report analysis can also be utilized as an informal assessment technique for psychosocial theories. Most housing units have a series of standard reports that may include maintenance requests, incident reports, program reports, student government minutes, and any number of other pieces of data that are collected on a regular basis. Each of these reporting mechanisms can be a potential source of developmental data. Student government minutes may often contain decisions as well as *process* information that provides insight into the psychosocial challenges for that particular group. Program reports allow housing professionals to understand the developmental needs of residents relative to their response to particular topics, as well as providing an understanding of the resident assistants' abilities to present programs on developmental topics. Incident reports offer insights into the stresses and power structures within the community and can be used to design developmental interventions. Reports are often seen as a necessary administrative task. However, these same reports, when grouped together and examined for trends, can also yield important developmental data about the unique challenges and opportunities within a particular community.

In summary, there are any number of methods for informal assessment within the residence hall environment. Informal assessment requires a number of basic skills for the housing professional: (1) the housing professional must be familiar with the constructs of one or more developmental theories to be used as a general map for the environment, (2) the housing professional must be able to unobtrusively observe and listen within the environment, and (3) the housing professional must begin to value reporting mechanisms beyond their administrative value in order to group data from the reports for developmental insight.

Psychosocial Development in College Residence Halls

Since the early 1970s, a number of studies have been conducted that, taken as a whole, tend to show that living in a residence hall has a positive effect on the psychosocial development (for example, in the areas of self-esteem and interpersonal relationships) of college students. In this section, we will briefly review a number of representative studies that have investigated the impact of residence hall life on students' psychosocial development.

A number of studies have investigated the influence of residence halls by looking at differences between students living in the halls versus students living off campus or commuting to college. Chickering (1974) found that the personal development of students who lived in residence halls exceeded that of commuter students. He summarized his findings as follows:

> Residents in response to immersion in a college environment
> change most during the first two years. They decelerate and may

even slightly regress after that, as they move back toward the
home culture as graduation approaches. They change most
quickly in the nonintellectual areas where the differences between high school and college are greatest. . . . In contrast,
commuter change is slower. They are constrained by internal
conflicts and pressures from parents, peers, and prior community. These constraints operate with least force for intellectual
development, where the college experiences of commuters and
residents are most similar. Thus the commuters more quickly
approximate the scores of residents in the intellectual area. But
because substantial differences exist, and persist, in the range of
noncourse experiences and interpersonal relationships, nonintellectual changes occur more slowly [p. 44].

Astin (1973, 1977) also compared students who lived in residence halls
with students who did not. He found that students who lived in residence
halls reported higher levels of participation in social activities (dating, attending parties) and concluded that living in a residence hall had, among
other things, a positive effect on students' self-esteem, as evidenced by reports
of enhanced self-confidence and public speaking ability and similar measures of self-reliance. Astin's work tells us that residence halls have a positive
effect on students' personal growth and development, perception the
campus social climate, participation in extracurricular activities, and persistence in college.

Scott (1975) used the Personal Orientation Inventory (POI)—a standardized instrument designed to measure personal development—to compare students who lived in residence halls to students who lived off campus.
Individuals achieving high scores on the POI are likely to be more fully
functioning, have a more mature outlook on life, and lead less inhibited life-
styles. Scott found that students who lived in residence halls achieved higher
scores on the POI than students who lived off campus or who commuted to
college. He also found that students in leadership roles in the residence halls
scored higher on the POI than other residence students.

A group of residence hall and commuting freshmen were studied by
Welty (1976). Students completed selected scales of the Omnibus Personality
Inventory, the College Student Questionnaire, and the College Experience
Questionnaire prior to matriculation and after the first two quarters. Welty
found that the two groups initially differed on measures of intellectual
disposition, thinking, introversion, estheticism, complexity, autonomy, and
altruism. Residence hall students scored higher on posttest measures of
intellectual and personal growth and developed more rapidly than commuter freshmen. Welty's findings suggest that these differences were attributable, at least in part, to higher levels of participation in extracurricular
activities and greater numbers of friendships formed among residence
students.

Miller (1982) used the SDTI-2 to compare the personal development of sophomores who lived on campus with a group of sophomores who had moved off campus following their freshman year. He found that students who had moved off campus had achieved higher levels of development during their first year in school than students who had remained in the residence halls.

Pascarella (1984, 1985) and Pascarella and Terenzini (1980) have taken a somewhat different approach to studying the influence of residential living. They have devised and tested an explanatory model of college impact. In their model, living on campus is viewed as one of many influences that exist on a college campus. Their research seeks to determine how a variety of campus influences either directly or indirectly impact college students. They have found that living on campus has a significant *indirect* impact on students. Their findings suggest that living in a residence hall is positively associated with student development by promoting higher levels of interaction with peers and faculty.

The relationship between environmental factors and students' psychosocial development has been examined by Janosik, Creamer, and Cross (1988) and by Erwin and Love (1989). Janosik, Creamer, and Cross studied the relationship between student-environment fit in residence halls and students' sense of competence. Using an instrument designed to assess Chickering's vector of competence, they found that higher levels of competence were associated with perceptions that residence life should provide greater emotional support, greater involvement of students in hall governance, and less competition. Erwin and Love (1989) investigated the relationship between environmental factors (housing, financial aid policies, social environment, work, and educational goals) and student development. Using the SDTI-2 to assess the developmental status of students, Erwin and Love found that students living in Greek housing scored higher on the task of autonomy than students living in various types of off-campus housing. Both Janosik, Creamer, and Cross and Erwin and Love indicate that further study is needed to determine the nature of the relationship between students' personal development and environmental influences.

Taken as a whole, most studies tend to show that living in college residence halls has a positive impact on students' personal and social development. See Chapter Two for a more detailed summary of the effects of living in residence halls.

At this point, knowledge of how specific aspects of residence life influence students' psychosocial development is sketchy. The research literature has been largely unable to expose specific hows and whys of development. Well-designed longitudinal studies that include short-term follow-ups are needed to more fully understand specific dimensions of development as well as accompanying environmental factors that either facilitate or hinder development. Future studies must also consider student diversity, since most of the currently reported research has been conducted at large research universities using predominantly white middle-class student populations. For example, we know little about the effect that living in a residence hall has on minority students—particularly minority students who attend predominantly white institutions. Finally, we must be willing to make better use of qualitative research methodologies such as case studies, participant observation, and phenomenological investigations in our assessments of the residence hall environment. Such alternatives have the potential of providing keener insights into the effects of student development intervention programs and are likely better suited to the study of the influence of the hall environment than many of the single-variable empirical studies that have dominated the research literature to date.

Applying Psychosocial Theory

Psychosocial theory can be applied to the residential setting on two levels: the macro level (institutional characteristics, student body characteristics, outcomes assessment) and the micro level (staff training, supervision, policies, programming, discipline). In this section, we discuss both the macro and micro applications of psychosocial theory for housing professionals. Additionally, we identify some of the key components for developmental models of residential housing programs.

Any time that we consider the application of psychosocial theory in any setting, a number of important variables in addition to institutional size emerge. The first variable is the definition of the *environmental unit*. The environmental unit consists of the community examined. The definition of the environmental unit places some parameters on observations and interventions and gives environmental focus to developmental applications. (Environmental units might be classrooms, residence hall areas, buildings, floors, the campus environment, or the institution as a whole.) The second variable that must be considered is the degree of mattering or marginality within the environmental units (Schlossberg, 1989). *Mattering* is the degree to which a student or group of students feel connected and committed to a particular environmental unit. For psychosocial theory, the higher the degree of mattering within the environmental unit, the higher the potential impact of interventions within the unit. *Marginality* is the degree to which a student or group of students feel disconnected from the environmental unit. If there is a low connection to the community (high degrees of marginality), it is unlikely that interventions in the community will influence students' development. The third variable to consider in the application of psychosocial theory is the degree of perceived *challenge* and *support* among the student population under consideration. An appropriate balance of these two variables promotes student development. However, too much challenge or support tends to cause individuals to cling to the familiar and not risk new behaviors. Each of these three variables (environmental unit, mattering or marginality, challenge and support) should be considered when planning educational strategies based on psychosocial theory.

Psychosocial theory and clues about development can be summarized for an educational unit of any size. However, institutional size, or unit size, plays a major role in the use of psychosocial theory on the macro level. Psychosocial theories are concerned with the individual's development as it relates to the environment. Therefore, the environment may best be understood in relation to a particular individual. Even though administrators may feel that the institution, as a unit, represents a particular type of community, it is the individual student's perception of his or her dominant community that is likely to have the most relevance in terms of psychosocial development. Certainly, smaller institutions with residential campuses have increased opportunities for application of psychosocial theory on the macro level because the campus community is likely to be developmentally relevant to the students. However, on larger campuses it is useful to identify various smaller-sized communities within the campus (unions, fraternities, residence halls, floors, classrooms) for application of psychosocial theory.

In applying psychosocial theory on the macro level, it is important to assess broad institutional trends from developmental clues and then to target particular communities for student development challenges. In other words, larger institutions should define any number of *environmental units* within the campus setting for application of theory. While the theory selected might be the same theory for all units, the degree of mattering or marginality for different students and the degrees of challenge and support across different units may suggest multiple application strategies in the larger institutions. An example of the macro issues can also be seen in a multiple-building residential housing program. For example, in a high-rise building of 750 students, there may be any number of environmental units (floors) in which various psychosocial challenges exist. Therefore, when applying theory in this macro setting, the housing staff member must consider several communities, all of which may have different goals. In another building of fifty students, the housing staff member may be able to apply psychosocial theory using the entire building as the environmental unit.

Student characteristics also play a major role in the application of psychosocial theory in the institutional and residential settings. It is important to acknowledge a general limitation of psychosocial theory with respect to gender as well as racial and ethnic populations at this time. For the past decade, student development theorists and practitioners have raised questions about the applicability of various theories to women as well as to racial and ethnic groups (Straub and Rodgers, 1986; McEwen, Roper, Bryant, and Langa, 1990). Serious applicability questions also arise when considering the psychosocial development of gay, lesbian, and bisexual students. This is a critical concern for psychosocial theories since gender, race and ethnicity, and sexual orientation have significant impacts on the definition of residential environments. We know, for example, that some traits of residence hall communities seem to differ along gender patterns. Any residence hall practitioner will be able to note the differences in all-male, all-female, and coeducational residential units. While we cannot, at this point, say emphatically that these differences are attributable to gender differences, we do know that the communities are *different*. Thus, to make generalizations from a theory that may not fully address the issues of gender may be educationally and ethically unsound. Parallel reasoning applies to racial and ethnic groups. It is important for student development researchers to appreciate the impact of gender, race and ethnicity, and sexual orientation when selecting a theory, applying a theory, or assessing outcomes of any intervention.

Student development theory and assessment methods must be sensitive to the gender, race and ethnicity, and sexual orientation of students in order to be generalizable on the macro level and usable on any micro level of application. Theories need to be updated and potentially revised in light of these issues. Assessment techniques must include ways to tap data from these communities. Outcomes assessment methods must also demonstrate a sensitivity to current limitations in these areas. For example, the perceived degrees of mattering and marginality within a particular community may affect the outcomes assessment (Schlossberg, 1989).

With these limitations in mind, there are still any number of micro applications of psychosocial theory that can be useful to today's housing professional. Theory serves a number of functions on the micro level. Theory serves as a framework for understanding student behavior. Theory serves, in some cases, as a predictor of student developmental patterns. Theory can serve as a rationale for policy development and the implementation of student housing procedures. Theory can define and enhance programming efforts. Theory can assist in structuring student discipline processes.

Understanding Patterns

Perhaps the most useful daily application of psychosocial theory is in assisting the practitioner in understanding patterns of student behavior. Through examining what psychosocial theories have to say about the college years, the housing practitioner can readily see that many student behaviors are predictable and patterned along the lines described by theorists. With this information, the housing professional can begin to be proactive in residence hall management, allocating staff energy and resources toward certain patterns of behavior that are likely to to emerge versus reacting to a constant array of seemingly random events. This realization must occur at the residence hall level and the central administrative level simultaneously. However, we are not suggesting that all residence hall behavior is predictable and acceptable. Psychosocial theory provides the housing professional with valuable insight into the likely patterns of student behavior based on community characteristics, student characteristics, and student development research studies.

Training and Supervision

Staff training and supervision are two areas for application of psychosocial theory. Residence hall staff are often motivated to be in helping positions relative to their peers, and training resident assistants in student development theory can assist them in understanding their communities and the ways in which they can assist them. Many residential programs utilize student development theory in training resident assistants about the general characteristics of their respective populations. Another key area for theoretical application of psychosocial development is in the supervisory process. A number of articles underscore how important it is for supervisors to understand the developmental challenges faced by their supervisees in working with students (Ricci, Porterfield, and Piper, 1987; Porterfield and Pressprich, 1988). Essentially, psychosocial theories offer supervisors new perspectives on the ways in which their supervisees may be processing their residential experiences. The supervisory process becomes a micro environmental unit in which the supervisor uses theory to balance the challenge and support ratio and promote the personal development of the staff member.

Policy Formulation

Policies and procedures can also be written in such a way as to enhance student development. Traditionally, student discipline policies have been based on a punitive system of response to student behavior. More recently, student discipline policies have been reviewed to include educational assignments that request certain behavior of the students and then provide a mechanism for processing the assignment in the context of the community itself (Dannells, 1990). These policies and procedures are consistent with a psychosocial model in that the educational assignment can be adjusted to meet the developmental needs of the student, and processing mechanisms provide some means for continuing to tie the behavioral consequences to the affected community. Thus, the person-environment interaction loop is completed within the judicial process. Such a loop can also be adapted to other processes and procedures in the residential setting.

Program Development

Programming is another area that can readily utilize psychosocial theory. Many developmental housing models provide in-house programs as a regular part of the residential education experience. Indeed, programming is one of the criteria that differentiate a service model housing program from developmental models. Developmental theories can be used in programming in two distinct ways. First, an assessment of the developmental needs of a particular community can be used to target particular *program topics* (career exploration or interpersonal conflict resolution, for instance) that both challenge and support community members' needs. Second, developmental theory can offer insights into the most appropriate ways to *deliver programs*. Based on an assessment of potential program participants, the program delivery system can be designed to meet the developmental level of participants. Delivery systems such as lecture, discussion, role play, and group work can be adapted to fit developmental needs of participants.

The transition from service models of housing to student development models of housing raises the question of criteria for a model developmental housing program. The Council for the Advancement of Standards for Student Services/Developmental Programs (1986) provides some useful criteria for assessing developmental housing programs. In addition to noting the service goals of model programs, the *CAS Standards* (p. 51) incorporate the goal of providing a living-learning environment that enhances individual growth and development. This goal can be integrated into the total housing program in a number of ways, which might include (1) a housing administration that grounds overall housing mission statements in developmental theory, (2) a housing training program that is based on some theory of student development and that provides this information to all housing staff, (3) a rationale for providing residence hall programs that acknowledges the developmental needs of the population in the design and delivery of these programs, (4) a system for formally or informally assessing the developmental needs of residential students on an ongoing basis and making this information available to students and staff, and (5) a policy review and update process that balances the needs of the larger institution with the developmental needs of residential students. These broad criteria for a model developmental housing program may assist housing professionals in moving toward a developmental model. It should be noted that movement toward a developmental model is not at the *exclusion* of services. Rather, developmental models of housing acknowledge the dual role of housing professionals to *administer and educate*.

Summary

Psychosocial theory has played a key role in the movement of the housing profession from a service model to a model that emphasizes student development. During the last two decades, the theories outlined in this chapter have provided the housing professional with a rich backdrop for understanding the complex process of human development. Developmental constructs proposed by psychosocial theorists can serve as a road map or guideposts for the intentional structuring of a variety of housing programs and activities, staff training, and the development of hall policies and procedures. While instrumentation to assess psychosocial development must be viewed as being in its early stages of development, a number of practical methods (both formal and informal) of evaluating students' status along a variety of psychosocial constructs currently exist. Our present knowledge about students' psychosocial development and the influence of the residence hall environment on this development can be likened to a jigsaw puzzle. We have been able to piece together enough of the puzzle to be able to recognize the major themes of the picture that has been slowly taking shape before our eyes. However, it is still unclear how many of the pieces that we currently have fit together—and many parts of the puzzle (the specific hows and whys of development) have yet to be found. We are, therefore, in need of well-designed longitudinal studies that will enable us to more fully understand specific dimensions of development as well as accompanying environmental factors that either facilitate or hinder development. Finally, we must continue to work toward a better understanding of the psychosocial development of underrepresented populations if residence halls are to play a significant role in the development of all students.

References

Astin, A. W. "The Impact of Dormitory Living on Students." *Educational Record*, 1973, *54*, 204–210.

Astin, A. W. *Four Critical Years: Effects of College on Beliefs, Attitudes, and Knowledge*. San Francisco: Jossey-Bass, 1977.

Barratt, W. R. *Construction and Validation of the Developing Purposes Inventory*. Technical report. Iowa City: Iowa Student Development Project, University of Iowa, 1978.

Bowen, H. R. *Investment in Learning: The Individual and Social Value of American Higher Education*. San Francisco: Jossey-Bass, 1977.

Cheatham, H. E. (ed.). *Cultural Pluralism on Campus*. Alexandria, Va.: American College Personnel Association, 1991.

Chickering, A. W. *Education and Identity*. San Francisco: Jossey-Bass, 1969.

Chickering, A. W. *Commuting Versus Resident Students: Overcoming Educational Inequities of Living Off Campus*. San Francisco: Jossey-Bass, 1974.

Council for the Advancement of Standards for Student Services/Development Programs. *CAS Standards and Guidelines for Student Services/Development Programs*. Iowa City, Iowa: Council for the Advancement of Standards for Student Services/Development Programs, 1986.

Dannells, M. "Changes in Disciplinary Policies and Practices Over 10 Years." *Journal of College Student Development*, 1990, *32*, 408–414.

Erikson, E. "Identity and the Life Cycle: Selected Papers." *Psychological Issues*, 1959, *1*, 1–171.

Erikson, E. *Childhood and Society*. (2nd ed.) New York: Norton, 1963.

Erikson, E. *Identity: Youth and Crisis*. New York: Norton, 1968.

Erwin, T. D. "The Validation of the Erwin Identity Scale." Unpublished doctoral dissertation, Department of Counselor Education, University of Iowa, 1979. *Dissertation Abstracts International*, 1979, *34*, 4818A–4819A.

Erwin, T. D., and Love, W. B. "Selected Environmental Factors in Student Development." *NASPA Journal*, 1989, *26*(4), 256–264.

Evans, N. J., and Wall, V. A. (eds.). *Beyond Tolerance: Gays, Lesbians, and Bisexuals on Campus*. Alexandria, Va.: American College Personnel Association, 1991.

Feldman, K. A., and Newcomb, T. M. *The Impact of College on Students*. San Francisco: Jossey-Bass, 1969.

Greeley, A. T., and Tinsley, H.E.A. "Autonomy and Intimacy Development in College Students: Sex Differences and Predictors." *Journal of College Student Development*, 1988, *29*, 512–520.

Havighurst, R. J. *Human Development and Education*. White Plains, N.Y.: Longman, 1953.

Heath, D. *Growing Up in College*. San Francisco: Jossey-Bass, 1968.

Heath, D. "A Model of Becoming a Liberally Educated and Mature Student." In C. A. Parker (ed.), *Encouraging Development in College Students*. Minneapolis: University of Minnesota Press, 1978.

Hood, A. B. *The Iowa Student Development Inventories*. Iowa City, Iowa: Hitech Press, 1986.

Hood, A. B., and Jackson, L. M. *Assessing the Development of Competence*. Technical report. Iowa City: College of Education, University of Iowa, 1983a.

Hood, A. B., and Jackson, L. M. *The Iowa Developing Autonomy Inventory*. Technical report. Iowa City: College of Education, University of Iowa, 1983b.

Hood, A. B., and Jackson, L. M. *The Iowa Managing Emotions Inventory*. Technical report. Iowa City: College of Education, University of Iowa, 1983c.

Janosik, S., Creamer, D. G., and Cross, L. H. "The Relationship of Residence Halls Environmental Fit and Sense of Competence." *Journal of College Student Personnel*, 1988, *29*, 320–326.

Keniston, K. *Youth and Dissent*. Orlando, Fla.: Harcourt Brace Jovanovich, 1971.

Kohlberg, L. "Stages of Moral Development." In C. M. Beck, B. S. Crittenden, and E. V. Sullivan (eds.), *Moral Education*. Toronto: University of Toronto Press, 1971.

Loevinger, J. *Ego Development: Conceptions and Theories*. San Francisco: Jossey-Bass, 1976.

McEwen, M. K., Roper, D. R., Bryant, D. R., and Langa, M. J. "Incorporating the Development of African-American Students into Psychosocial Theories of Student Development." *Journal of College Student Development*, 1990, *31*, 429–436.

Marcia, J. "Development and Validation of Ego Identity Status." *Journal of Personality and Social Psychology*, 1966, *3*, 551–558.

Miller, S. "Developmental Impact of Residence Hall Living on College Sophomores." *Journal of College and University Student Housing*, 1982, *12*, 10–14.

Mines, R. A. *Development and Validation of the Mines-Jensen Interpersonal Relationships Inventory*. Technical report. Iowa City: Student Development Project, University of Iowa, 1977.

Mines, R. A. "Student Development Assessment Techniques." In G. R. Hanson (ed.), *Measuring Student Development*. New Directions for Student Services, no. 20. San Francisco: Jossey-Bass, 1982.

Moore, L. V. (ed.). *Evolving Theoretical Perspectives on Students*. New Directions for Student Services, no. 51. San Francisco: Jossey-Bass, 1990.

Pascarella, E. T. "Reassessing the Effects of Living On-Campus Versus Commuting to College: A Causal Modeling Approach." *Review of Higher Education*, 1984, *7*, 247–260.

Pascarella, E. T. "The Influence of On-Campus Living Versus Commuting to College on Intellectual and Interpersonal Self-Concept." *Journal of College Student Personnel*, 1985, *26*(4), 292–299.

Pascarella, E. T., and Terenzini, P. T. "Student-Faculty and Student-Peer Relationships as Mediators of the Structural Effects of Undergraduate Residence Arrangement." *Journal of Educational Research*, 1980, *73*, 344–353.

Perry, W. G., Jr. *Forms of Intellectual and Ethical Development in the College Years: A Scheme*. Troy, Mo.: Holt, Rinehart & Winston, 1970.

Porterfield, W. D., and Pressprich, S. T. "Carol Gilligan's Perspectives and Staff Supervision: Implications for the Practitioner." *NASPA Journal*, 1988, *25*(4), 244–248.

Ricci, J. R., Porterfield, W. D., and Piper, T. D. "Using Developmental Theory in Supervising Residential Staff Members." *NASPA Journal*, 1987, *24*, 32–41.

Rodgers, R. F. "Recent Theories and Research Underlying Student Development." In D. G. Creamer and Associates, *College Student Development: Theory and Practice for the 1990s*. Alexandria, Va.: American College Personnel Association, 1990.

Sanford, N. *The American College*. New York: Wiley, 1962.

Sanford, N. *Self and Society*. New York: Atherton Press, 1966.

Schlossberg, N. K. "Marginality and Mattering: Key Concepts in Community Building." In D. C. Roberts (ed.), *Designing Campus Activities to Foster a Sense of Community*. New Directions for Student Services, no. 48. San Francisco: Jossey-Bass, 1989.

Scott, S. "Impact of Residence Hall Living on College Student Development." *Journal of College Student Personnel*, 1975, *16*, 214–219.

Straub, C. A. "Women's Development of Autonomy and Chickering's Theory." *Journal of College Student Personnel*, 1987, *28*, 198–204.

Straub, C. A., and Rodgers, R. F. "An Exploration of Chickering's Theory and Women's Development." *Journal of College Student Personnel*, 1986, *27*, 216–223.

Taub, D. J., and McEwen, M. K. "Patterns of Development of Autonomy and Mature Interpersonal Relationships in Black and White Undergraduate Women." *Journal of College Student Development*, 1991, *32*, 502–508.

Thomas, R., and Chickering, A. W. "*Education and Identity* Revisited." *Journal of College Student Personnel*, 1984, *25*, 392–399.

Welty, J. D. "Resident and Commuter Students: Is It Only the Living Situation?" *Journal of College Student Personnel*, 1976, *17*, 465–468.

White, E. *Lives in Progress*. Troy, Mo.: Holt, Rinehart & Winston, 1958.

Widick, C., Parker, C. A., and Knefelkamp, L. "Arthur Chickering's Vectors of Development." In L. Knefelkamp, C. Widick, and C. A. Parker (eds.), *Applying New Developmental Findings*. New Directions for Student Services, no. 4. San Francisco: Jossey-Bass, 1978.

Winston, R. B., Jr., and Miller, T. K. *Student Developmental Task and Lifestyle Inventory Manual*. Athens, Ga.: Student Development Associates, 1987.

Winston, R. B., Jr., Miller, T. K., and Prince, J. S. *Student Developmental Task Inventory*. (2nd ed.) Athens, Ga.: Student Development Associates, 1979.

Winston, R. B., Jr., Miller, T. K., and Prince, J. S. *Student Developmental Task and Lifestyle Inventory*. Athens, Ga.: Student Development Associates, 1987.

Chapter Four

——————

Intellectual, Ethical, and Moral Development

Marcia B. Baxter Magolda

Shirley Lang was feeling great about the start of her second year as hall director of Bradbury Hall. Staff training was a huge success, hall opening went smoothly, and community building efforts were working well. That is, until the hall-government-sponsored T-shirt arrived. The shirts, all 350 of them, displayed a scene that was offensive to minority students. Even though the shirts had not been distributed yet, hall government leaders and residents were already involved in heated exchanges. To make matters worse, student government leaders said that the assistant hall director had approved the design before it was printed. The assistant insisted that the conceptual design did not look anything like the final product.

Residence life work is never easy. Situations like the one plaguing Shirley Lang happen without forewarning. They are often perceived as problems that must be solved before staff can return to broader goals, such as fostering community formation and student development. Some staff members would focus on obtaining the facts of the situation and making a decision about the fate of the shirts, an approach certain to alienate some group in the situation. Fortunately, Shirley's professional training in student development theory and application prompts her to see the situation as an opportunity to educate the hall government leaders and the community on issues of diversity. She will use her student development theory training to generate possibilities for how this sequence of events occurred, how various students react, and how to facilitate student interactions to resolve the shirt dilemma and promote growth of residents and the community at the same time.

This chapter describes major theories of intellectual, ethical, and moral development for traditional-age college students and addresses ways of promoting opportunities for students' intellectual and moral development through everyday situations, such as the shirt incident. Residence life offers an ideal setting for development because peer interaction is paramount in student development. Residence life staff have opportunities to shape peer interaction around areas of interest to students such as substance abuse, sexual practices, life-style issues, and everyday incidents. These settings can encourage students to explore individual interests in the context of community interests. Boyer's (1987) vision of community calls for a balance of individual and community interests. Most residence life incidents are about this very issue, since individual interests and rights are constantly crashing into community interests and rights in a group living setting. Thus, this is the ideal setting for students to learn about collaboration and concern for others while meeting their own needs.

Using Theories in Residence Life

Intellectual and moral development theories provide a knowledge base from which to interpret student behavior, analyze the environment, make judgments about the fit between the two, and turn a problem into a learning opportunity. Professional practice hinges on these abilities as well as on the ability to use theory judiciously. Theories represent descriptions of particular persons' development in particular contexts. Generalizing these to other persons and contexts and using them "as is" rather than keeping other possibilities open is tempting. This is dangerous because it leads to overlooking differences among students and the complexity of student development. Theory can be viewed as a framework in which experiences of some groups are shared to provide a context for other groups to discuss their experience, thus generating possibilities for making sense of the latter groups' development rather than fitting it into the previous picture (Frye, 1990). Following this line of thinking, this chapter describes existing intellectual and moral development theory as a foundation for generating possibilities for understanding the development of women and men college students, including those from different cultural backgrounds and age groups. Examples of students' thinking about the shirt incident are viewed from various theoretical standpoints to illustrate possible interpretations of the incident depending on the development of the students involved.

Intellectual or Epistemological Development Theories

Intellectual development as it is discussed here refers to students' assumptions about the nature and certainty of knowledge and limits of one's ability to know. Some theorists refer to the evolution of these assumptions as epistemological development because the evolution is in ways of knowing. The major theories are summarized here along with research on gender, culture, and age differences.

Single-Gender Models

William Perry (1970) offered the first description of college students' assumptions about the limits, certainty, and nature of knowing. Perry's nine-position scheme was not limited to men, but the predominantly male sample resulted in a description of a male version of development. Perry's first five positions reflect qualitatively different sets of assumptions about knowing or five different cognitive structures. The last four positions reflect the development of commitment based on the fifth structure, and they have subsequently been viewed by researchers to represent ethical and identity development more than intellectual development (King, 1978).

The first two positions in Perry's scheme share the assumption that knowledge is certain and is acquired from authorities. Students in these positions see knowledge in absolute, right-wrong terms. Position 2 students believe that teachers sometimes introduce uncertainty to help students learn how to find answers on their own, but this uncertainty is temporary and exists only on the part of the student. Uncertainty of knowledge becomes legitimate in some areas for the first time in position 3, replacing the right-wrong dichotomy with a known-unknown dichotomy. Knowledge in the known category can still be acquired from authorities, whereas the unknown areas require learning a process for finding the right answers. As uncertainty spreads to additional areas of knowledge, students alter their assumptions to believe that most, if not all, knowledge is uncertain. This position 4 structure results in less reliance on authorities because right answers no longer exist. Independent thinking emerges as all views are perceived to be *equally valid*. The ability to judge the merits of various views emerges in position 5, in which knowledge is viewed as contextual. Knowledge claims are validated by supporting evidence relevant to the context surrounding the claims.

Attempts to interpret women's intellectual development with the Perry scheme have raised questions about its applicability to women (Benack, 1982; Clinchy and Zimmerman, 1982). Belenky, Clinchy, Goldberger, and Tarule (1986) identify five epistemological categories, labeled *perspectives*, from their interviews with women. Because only a small portion of the interviews were longitudinal, the authors caution that the perspectives were not necessarily a hierarchical sequence. The first perspective, *silence*, was not common in the college sample but more prevalent in the thinking of women using family agencies to seek assistance with parenting. Women in this perspective do not perceive their ability to learn from their own voices or the voices of others.

The ability to learn from the voices of others is reflected in the second perspective, called *received knowing*, in which the prevalent mode of learning is listening to authorities. The recognition of uncertainty of knowledge and the emergence of the woman's own voice (having one's own beliefs separate from those of authority) are evident in the third perspective, called *subjective knowing*. Subjective knowers rely more on intuition and personal experience than on authorities, even though they often refrain from expressing these sources as justification for their beliefs. *Procedural knowing*, the fourth perspective, is characterized by thinking about knowledge either through a logical, impersonal process called *separate knowing* or through a subjective, empathic process called *connected knowing*. Separate knowers separate their feelings from the analysis of knowledge claims, whereas connected knowers incorporate them in accessing others' experiences to explore knowledge claims. The awareness that truth is a matter of the context in which it is embedded prompts the fifth perspective, called *constructed knowing*. It is at this point that women understand and develop knowledge by examining the circumstances surrounding knowledge claims.

Comparing these two theoretical descriptions yields many similarities. The assumption of certainty of knowledge is evident in early categories in both descriptions, as is the assumption of uncertainty in later categories. The shift from certainty to uncertainty and the accompanying decrease in reliance on authority seems slightly different in these descriptions. The descriptions also allude to a difference in the legitimizing of the student's own voice. These differences can only be clarified by exploring gender-inclusive theoretical models.

Gender-Inclusive Models

The first gender-inclusive model of intellectual development was called Reflective Judgment (RJ) (Kitchener and King, 1981, 1990). The RJ model was constructed using both women and men but did not separate women's and men's contributions to the model, presumably because gender differences were not in the forefront of developmental theory at that time. The seven-stage model, summarized in Table 4.1, provides a more detailed account of the evolution from certainty to uncertainty of knowledge than does either of the single-gender models. The model describes assumptions about knowledge, how it is obtained, and how beliefs are justified for each of the seven stages. Table 4.1 also contains examples related to the shirt incident for the stages typically found in college populations.

In stage 1, all knowledge is certain and can be directly observed. Justification of beliefs is not necessary because knowledge, or reality in this case, can be observed. In stage 2, knowledge remains certain but is not always

Table 4.1. Gender-Inclusive Models of Intellectual Development and Corresponding Examples for the Shirt Incident.

Reflective Judgment (Kitchener and King)	Epistemological Reflection (Baxter Magolda)	Examples
1 All knowledge is certain, accept authorities' beliefs		
2 All knowledge is certain but not always observable, obtain from authorities	*Absolute knowing* All knowledge is certain, some master it, some receive it	(1) Shirt should not be sold because it is wrong to offend others, or (2) shirt should be sold because staff would not have approved an offensive shirt design.
3 Temporary uncertainty emerges, use own biases until absolute knowledge is possible	*Transitional knowing* Some knowledge is certain, some uncertain; some rely on logic, some rely on intuition and experience	Whether shirt is offensive is uncertain; some decide by how many are offended, some decide by whether students find it offensive.
4 Some knowledge is permanently uncertain, idiosyncratic evaluation of data	*Independent knowing* Knowledge is uncertain, student has own voice; some challenge each others' ideas, some open to ideas	Can never tell who will or will not be offended by shirt; all have own opinion on it; challenging each others' opinions or hearing each others' opinions may result in a solution.
5 Knowledge is uncertain, subjective interpretation based on rules of inquiry in particular context		
6 Knowledge is constructed, beliefs based on generalized rules of inquiry	*Contextual knowing* Knowledge is contextual; self-author knowledge based on judging evidence in context	Some opinions about whether to sell the shirt are better than other opinions. Students will use their experience, others' experience, and available evidence to make the best decision in the context.
7 Objective knowledge is obtainable, beliefs better or worse approximations of reality based on evidence		

directly observable. Students still rely on direct observation when it is possible, and when it is not, authorities' beliefs are accepted as justification. Temporary uncertainty in some areas of knowledge emerges in stage 3. Earlier modes of obtaining and justifying knowledge are retained in the certain areas. In the uncertain areas, students return to their own biases for what to believe. This approach becomes increasingly prevalent in stage 4, where some knowledge becomes permanently uncertain. The use of one's own biases as well as those of others, logic, and available data result in idiosyncratic evaluations of knowledge claims. Rules of inquiry replace this idiosyncratic evaluation in stage 5. Although most knowledge remains uncertain, certainty is possible through personal perspectives in specific contexts. Justification of beliefs becomes a matter of subjective interpretation based on rules of inquiry for that context. These rules are generalized in stage 6 to achieve certainty through evaluation of evidence and experts' views. Stage 7 reflects the recognition that some knowledge claims are better than others. Beliefs are viewed as better or worse approximations of reality based on critical evaluation of evidence to support them.

The Reflective Judgment model clearly articulates the evolution of the student voice in the knowing process. It first emerges in stage 3 in the form of biases and expands in stage 4 as biases permeate the idiosyncratic justification of beliefs. This unregulated voice then begins to be regulated by rules of inquiry in stage 5. Believing whatever one wants is replaced by believing what is justifiable based on rules of understanding in that context. The student voice is modulated further in stage 6 by the incorporation of evidence in justification of beliefs. Use of the rules of inquiry evolves into a student voice that makes use of critical judgment and contextual evidence in endorsing knowledge claims. This description of assumptions about knowing suggests that both logic and personal biases play an integral role in evolution to more complex stages.

The role of gender, however, is unclear. Research on gender differences in the RJ model revealed differences in some cases but not in others (Kitchener and King, 1985). When differences did exist, men had higher RJ scores than did women except in one study involving nontraditional-age students (Schmidt, 1985). Welfel and Davison (1986) also found that male RJ scores were slightly higher at the end of a four-year longitudinal study, although the differences were not statistically significant. Statistically significant gender differences did appear with samples of seniors and graduate students (King, Wood, and Mines, 1990), despite some of the differences being within the same RJ stage. These data demonstrate the need for research that includes both genders but that intentionally separates their development to determine the nature of gender differences in epistemological development.

It was with this consideration in mind that I began a longitudinal study of women's and men's epistemological development from college entrance to graduation. The model of epistemological development that emerged suggests that gender differences do not exist in students' sets of assumptions about knowing, but rather in gender-related patterns inherent within these sets of assumptions (Baxter Magolda, 1990a). This model dispels notions that women's development is less complex than men's and illustrates that equally valid, albeit different, pathways lead to the same sequence of epistemological assumptions. The data also reveal that these pathways are gender related rather than gender exclusive. In other words, each pattern was used predominantly, but not exclusively, by one gender.

This model is labeled the Epistemological Reflection (ER) model because it was constructed from students' own reflections on their ways of knowing. Table 4.1 summarizes the four distinct epistemological levels evident in the data. Analysis of individual student change over the five years as well as the percentage of students in each level each year supports viewing the levels as evolving in hierarchical and sequential order (Baxter Magolda, 1992). *Absolute knowing* was most prevalent in the first two years of college. Absolute knowers view knowledge as certain, so that learning is a straightforward process of obtaining information from the instructor. Instructors are responsible for communicating knowledge appropriately and ensuring that students understand it. Peers are expected to share notes and explain to each other what they have learned, but they are not purveyors of knowledge beyond repeating what they have heard. Tests are viewed as means of showing teachers what students have learned. Discrepancies in knowledge claims are interpreted as differences in the way people view a particular situation, not in the truth of the matter per se.

Despite sharing these assumptions, absolute knowers exhibited two distinct patterns. (1) The receiving patterns, used more often by women than by men, involved collecting knowledge. Students using this pattern described listening and recording as their primary role in class, did not expect interaction with the instructor, viewed peers as a support network to help listen and occasionally ask questions, valued evaluation that offered the best opportunity to demonstrate their knowledge, and relied on their own interpretations of discrepancies in knowledge claims rather than consulting authority. (2) The mastery pattern, used more often by men than by women, involved an active attempt to acquire knowledge. Students using this pattern advocated taking an active role in class to demonstrate their interest to the instructor, expected an interchange with the instructor, viewed peers as partners in argument and quizzing each other to master the material, valued evaluation that helped them improve their mastery, and appealed to authority to resolve discrepancies in knowledge claims.

Transitional knowing was present in the first year of college, became increasingly prevalent the second and third years, and decreased slightly the fourth year. The nature of knowledge shifts to partially certain and partially uncertain in this level. Students accordingly shift their focus from acquiring knowledge to understanding it. Instructors are expected to use methods aimed at understanding, many of which include applying knowledge. Peers take on more active roles because understanding requires more exploration than acquisition of knowledge. Evaluation is expected to focus on understanding of the material rather than memorization.

Within transitional knowing, some students—usually women—used an interpersonal approach, whereas other students—usually men—used an impersonal approach. Interpersonal-pattern students were involved in learning through collection of others' ideas, expected interaction with peers to hear their views and provide exposure to new ideas, wanted a rapport with the instructor to enhance self-expression, valued evaluation that takes individual differences into account, and resolved uncertainty by personal judgment. Impersonal-pattern students wanted to be forced to think, preferred to exchange their views with instructors and peers via debate, expected to be challenged by instructors, valued evaluation that is fair and practical, and resolved uncertainty by logic and research. They also demonstrated a dual focus on certainty and uncertainty and wanted to resolve uncertainty when it existed. Interpersonal-pattern knowers, however, tended to focus on those areas that were uncertain and viewed this as an opportunity to express their own views for the first time.

The discovery of the student voice hinted at in interpersonal-pattern transitional knowers' expression of their views is at the center of the third level, *independent knowing*. Independent knowing emerged for a few students in the junior and senior years and was prevalent in the first year after graduation. The nature of knowledge in this level shifts to uncertain, warranting everyone having their own beliefs. This allows learners the freedom to think for themselves and share viewpoints with others. Teaching and evaluation methods that encourage independent thinking and exchange of opinions were valued. Within these shared assumptions, women were more likely than men to use an interindividual pattern and men were more likely than women to use an individual pattern. Interindividual-pattern knowers focused simultaneously on thinking for themselves and engaging others' views. They preferred instructors who promoted this sharing of views and viewed evaluation as a mutual process between student and instructor. Individual-pattern knowers focused primarily on their own independent thinking, with sharing views with peers being secondary. They focused on ways to think independently, expected peers to think independently, wanted instructors to allow students to define their own learning goals, and preferred evaluation based on independent thinking.

A few junior, senior, and fifth-year participants expressed epistemological assumptions beyond those characterizing independent thinking. The small number of students expressing these assumptions warrants caution in describing this level, called *contextual knowing*. Contextual knowers believe that knowledge is uncertain and one decides what to believe by evaluating the evidence in the context in question. Learning for contextual knowers means thinking through problems, integrating knowledge, and applying knowledge in a context. Contextual knowers preferred instructors who focus on application in a context, emphasize evaluative discussion of perspectives, and allow student and instructor to critique each other's ideas. They also wanted this mutual exchange in evaluation, which they defined as working together toward a goal and measuring their progress. The number of contextual knowers was too small to identify gender-related patterns in this level.

Applicability to Diverse Populations

As is apparent in the review of theoretical models of epistemological development, extending these models to women is a recent phenomenon. Even less is known about the epistemological development of nondominant-student cultures. Although literature is available on some aspects of the African-American student experience (Fleming, 1984; Holland and Eisenhart, 1990), it does not address epistemological development. The small number of African-American students in the models reviewed here prohibits construction of their developmental picture. This construction is beginning with a study of African-American students using the RJ model (King, Taylor, and Ottinger, 1989). Because the RJ model involves intensive interviews from which students' epistemological assumptions are extracted, it allows for variations of development to emerge. King, Taylor, and Ottinger found that students' responses were consistent with the RJ categories described earlier and that RJ scores were consistent with scores of other college samples. The RJ scores increased with educational level, as is typical of other RJ studies. They were not attributable to other variables King, Taylor, and Ottinger (1989) measured, including academic and social integration and noncognitive variables (Tracey and Sedlacek, 1984). No gender differences were found in the African-American student sample.

Studies using the Reflective Judgment model also provide insight into the relationship of age to epistemological development. Kitchener and King (1990) conclude from longitudinal studies using the RJ model that education is more consistently related to reflective judgment than is age. Students, therefore, are not necessarily more complex in their assumptions by virtue of age alone. Belenky, Clinchy, Goldberger, and Tarule (1986) also note that the move toward greater autonomy in epistemology is not tied to any specific age. They do, however, suggest that students from advantaged backgrounds are more likely to encounter the experiences that lead to discovering that authorities do not have all the answers than are disadvantaged persons. A study of mothers from socially isolated and impoverished areas notes that these women exhibited the epistemological positions of silence, and received and subjective knowing (Belenky and others, 1990). The women in Belenky and others' (1990) study who were involved in seeking parenting assistance from family agencies in some cases described growth due to experiences with the agency's services.

Collectively, these data suggest that experience, including education, is the key to epistemological development. To the extent that social class, racial or ethnic background, and age influence the type of experiences encountered, they may also influence development in different ways. Although further research is needed to construct developmental pictures for diverse student groups, the current theoretical models offer possibilities for understanding college students from diverse populations. As is the case with all theoretical perspectives, residence life professionals must judge the applicability of a particular theoretical picture to the students with whom they work before using that picture to design residence hall environments intended to promote students' development.

Moral Development Theories

Provoked by greater sensitivity to gender issues, research over the past decade has led to differing perspectives on understanding moral development in both genders. Kohlberg's perspective, labeled the *justice* orientation, was constructed primarily from men's experiences. The *care* orientation, first postulated by Gilligan as an additional possibility for understanding moral development, was constructed largely from women's experiences.

Justice: Kohlberg's Contribution to Moral Development Theory

Kohlberg (1969, 1976, 1984) offered the first comprehensive description of moral judgment. His six-stage description was developed originally from the study of men, resulting in current inquiry regarding potential gender bias in the theory to be discussed later in the chapter. Kohlberg's description contains three levels of moral judgment, each characterized by different points of view from which a person formulates moral judgments. (1) The preconventional level rests on an individualistic point of view, resulting in moral judgments based on what is good for the person making the judgment. (2) The conventional level rests on viewing self in relation to others, resulting in moral judgments based on what is good for those relationships. (3) The postconventional level rests on a view of rights and values prior to social attachments, resulting in moral judgments based on principles. Kohlberg described two stages in each of these levels. Although the entire theory will be overviewed here, particular attention is paid to the conventional level because it describes most adolescents and adults (Colby and Kohlberg, 1987).

Table 4.2 summarizes the six stages. The preconventional level is most typical of children under nine and some adolescents (Colby and Kohlberg, 1987). In stage 1, children obey rules to avoid punishment. They do not recognize that other people have different interests than they do, and they act in accordance with their own interests. In stage 2, children recognize that others do have their own interests, so that what is right is what is in one's best interests, while recognizing that others operate similarly. This sometimes requires equal exchanges, or deals (for example, I will not tell that you cheated on a test if you will not tell that I was called to the principal's office),

Table 4.2. Moral Development Theories and Corresponding Examples for the Shirt Incident in College Populations.

Justice (Kohlberg)	Care (Gilligan, Lyons)	Examples
1 Egocentric, obey rules to avoid punishment	1 Do what ensures individual survival	
2 Aware of others' interests, balance through equal exchange	*First transition* Aware of others' interests, view concern for self as selfish	
3 Interpersonal conformity, do what those close to you expect	2 Good is defined by caring for others	Justice: For or against selling shirt depending on peer approval Care: For or against selling shirt depending on who is hurt
4 Doing one's duty for the benefit of the group		Justice: For or against selling shirt depending on what action fulfills duty (to hall government or students at large)
4½ Relative social standards, choice personal and subjective, except when impinges on others' rights	*Second transition* Question whether self-sacrifice is logical in ethic of care	Justice: Aware that different groups view shirt differently, all views valid, have to consider rights of each group Care: Attempt to consider own as well as others' views in deciding on shirt issue
Postconventional Ethical principles	3 Ethic of nonviolence	

to accommodate conflicts in interests. The conventional level stands in contrast to these two stages due to the shift from an individual to a relationship perspective.

In stage 3, mutual relationships with others take precedence over individual interests. Moral judgments are based on living up to others' expectations, doing what is expected of a particular role such as daughter, brother, or husband, and showing concern for others. Peer pressure in college can be understood in this context as students behave in ways that gain approval of their peers. Students in this stage also work to maintain trust and loyalty within relationships. Stage 4 represents an expansion of the relationship perspective to societal relationships rather than interpersonal ones. The basis for what is right in this stage is fulfilling obligations as a member of society rather than as a partner in an interpersonal relationship. Meeting social duties is necessary to maintain the social system. For example, laws must be upheld, because if everyone violated them, chaos would result. Interpersonal relationships still exist and are important but are placed in the context of the larger social system when moral judgments are made. Kohlberg also described a transitional stage between stage 4 and postconventional thinking, after college students in his studies exhibited thinking that could not be captured in the six-stage system. It reflects an awareness of the relativity of different social standards, making choices of social standards personal and subjective unless the choice impinges on the rights of others.

The postconventional level, reached by only a minority of the adult population after age twenty to twenty-five (Colby and Kohlberg, 1987), is characterized by moral judgments based on the social contract (stage 5) or self-chosen ethical principles (stage 6). Stage 5 individuals view the social system as a contract into which people enter freely to preserve the rights and promote the welfare of all members. Societal laws are developed to protect everyone's rights and thus should be upheld. Stage 6 persons also view laws or social agreements as valid as long as they are based on ethical principles. In the case that the two conflict, moral judgment is based on ethical principles. The scarcity of these two stages in studies of the adult population has led researchers to question their validity. Gibbs and Widaman (1982) argue that there are really two instead of three levels of moral development, eliminating the postconventional. They do offer a theory-defining level beyond stage 4 in which persons develop intellectual or philosophical positions regarding issues of individual and societal rights. They suggest that thinking of this type enriches stage 4 moral judgment but is not necessarily a different stage of moral development.

Care: Gilligan's Contribution to Moral Development Theory

Gilligan (1977, 1982) asserted that Kohlberg's theory was biased toward male development, arguing that Kohlberg's focus on justice and rights did not reflect women's concern with care and responsibility. She proposed a description of women's moral development, centered around an ethic of care, with three levels and two transitions between levels (see Table 4.2). She described the first level as one of individual survival in which women feel alone. Because the woman's primary concern is her own survival, moral judgments are made to ensure survival. Only a conflict in her own needs prompts a moral dilemma. At the first transition, defining oneself in relation to others results in viewing concern for the self as selfish. This in turn prompts a move toward responsibility to others.

Accepting this responsibility as her appropriate role, the woman endorses the level 2 concept of goodness as self-sacrifice. Women in this level make moral judgments based on the needs and feelings of others. Sacrificing one's own needs to care for others is seen as good and a way to gain approval. A dilemma arises in this level, however, since the passivity of dependence on others conflicts with the activity of care. Defining morality as care makes not caring for oneself illogical. The second transition is a time of struggle with this issue. The woman in transition considers the logic of self-sacrifice, debates whether it is responsible or selfish to include herself in the ethic of care, and if she claims equality for herself, shifts from moral judgment based on others' needs to moral judgment based on the intent and consequence of her actions.

The claiming of equality for herself propels the woman into the third level, where the principle of nonviolence resolves the tension between selfishness and responsibility. Moral judgment hinges on considering the needs of others and self equally in an attempt to find a nonviolent solution to moral dilemmas. The woman takes responsibility for her choices as well as recognizing that nonviolent solutions (ones in which no one is hurt) are not always possible.

Justice, Care, and Their Relationship to Gender

Lyons (1983) elaborated on the justice and care considerations in moral judgment and also found them to be related to the way individuals define themselves. Two versions of self-definition emerged from her interview data. One is the separate/objective self, a definition based on impartiality and distancing the self from others, and the other is the connected self, a definition based on interdependence and concern for others. Lyons's data illustrate how these definitions affect moral judgment. Separate/objective individuals tend to rely on justice and fairness in moral judgment because they view relationships with others as reciprocal. Moral problems are thus viewed as conflicting claims between self and others that can be resolved by the use of objective rules and standards. Connected people tend to rely on care because they view relationships as responding to others in others' terms. Thus, moral problems are understood as issues of how to respond to others that can be resolved by action that maintains the relationship and promotes the well-being of others. (See Table 4.2 for examples.)

In an attempt to test Gilligan's hypothesis that these versions of moral considerations were gender related, Lyons (1983) explored the considerations used by women and men in real-life dilemmas. She found that care was the predominant response for 75 percent of the women and 14 percent of the men. Justice was the predominant response for 25 percent of the women and 79 percent of the men. An equal use of the two versions was evident for 7 percent of the men and none of the women. Lyons also reported that 36 percent of the men used no care considerations, whereas all of the male responses included some justice considerations. Similarly, 37 percent of the women used no justice considerations, whereas all of the female responses included some care considerations. Lyons's data also revealed that women were more likely to define themselves as connected (63 percent) and men were more likely to define themselves as separate/objective (79 percent). Finally, in comparing self-definition to modes of moral choice, Lyons found that most of those using care defined themselves as connected and most using justice defined themselves as separate/objective. She concluded that two versions of self-definition and of moral orientation exist and are gender related but not gender exclusive.

Gilligan and Attenucci (1988) reported additional study of the two orientations. They found that one-third of their sample used justice and care equally, with the remaining two-thirds using responses dominated by one or the other. Women's responses were equally distributed, with one-third using care predominantly, one-third using care and justice equally, and slightly less than one-third using justice predominantly. Men's responses revealed one-third used care and justice equally and two-thirds used justice predominantly. Gilligan (Kerber and others, 1986) cited Johnston's (1985) study as another example in which adolescents understood and used both orientations but still illustrated gender differences in orientation use.

Gilligan's assertion of a second version of moral development and studies comparing justice and care to gender sparked considerable debate about gender differences in moral development. The debate is confounded by a number of methodological issues in moral development research. Brabeck (1983) noted that Gilligan's assertions are limited by the small numbers of participants typical of intensive interview studies, that gender differences are often not included in the designs of studies but explored as an afterthought, and that studies designed to explore gender differences vary in instruments to measure moral development. With these cautions in mind, she reviewed research on moral reasoning and caring behaviors (altruism and empathy) and reported that research finds more similarities than differences.

Walker (1984) undertook an extensive review of studies designed to explore gender differences that used Kohlberg's interview measure. He intentionally excluded studies using other measures, studies confounding age and sex, and single-sex studies. This yielded seventy-nine studies divided into three categories: childhood and early adolescence, late adolescence and youth, and adulthood. He concluded that gender differences were rare in the first category. The second, including thirty-five studies of almost 4,000 high school and university students, also revealed infrequent differences, with only ten of forty-six samples yielding significant differences. In adulthood, thirteen studies involving over 1,200 persons resulted in four cases of difference out of twenty-one samples. Walker concluded that the moral development of women and men is more similar than different. He maintained this conclusion after addressing methodological criticisms of his review (Baumrind, 1986; Walker, 1986). Kohlberg (1984) relied heavily on Walker's review to refute Gilligan's assertion of sex bias in his theory. He argued that both orientations emerged from the same structure. Gilligan (1986) responded by citing Langdale's (1983) work, in which persons with care as a predominant moral orientation had lower Kohlberg stage scores than persons with justice as a predominant moral orientation. Bakken and Ellsworth's (1990) data, while not focused on moral orientation, indicated that women had lower Kohlberg stage scores as measured by the Moral Judgment Interview than did men across three adult age groups and three educational levels.

Both Walker and Kohlberg (Colby and Kohlberg, 1987) suggested the possibility of gender differences in orientation or reasoning used within moral stages. This possibility was confirmed by Gibbs, Arnold, and Burkhart (1984). Using the Sociomoral Reflection Measure (SRM) (Gibbs and Widaman, 1982) with 177 men and women, they tested differences in moral stage and within moral stage. The SRM is a written counterpart to Kohlberg's Moral Judgment Interview (MJI) and has high concurrent validity with Kohlberg's interview (Gibbs, Widaman, and Colby, 1982). The scoring manual for the SRM also contains aspects within each stage that persons use to justify their moral reasoning. Because this manual was constructed using both genders, it is reasonable to assume that the aspects are gender inclusive. Results of this study revealed no gender differences in moral stage but significant gender differences in stage aspects. Women used the empathic role-taking and intrapersonal approval or disapproval aspects more than men did in stage 3. Women also used the society-based rights and values aspect more than men did in stage 4. The first two findings are consistent with the assertion that women use care more than men, whereas the last finding shows women in this case using justice more than men.

Although Gibbs, Widaman, and Colby's study does not close the debate on whether the two orientations stem from the same underlying structure or reflect a consistent gender difference, it does suggest that a scoring system built on both genders helps refine our understanding of gender-related differences. Because differences occurred in orientation rather than stage, Gibbs, Widaman, and Colby (1982, p. 1043) concluded that "ascriptions of greater adequacy or maturity to the moral thought of one or the other sex are inappropriate." Hopefully these data will help turn the moral development debate toward building gender-inclusive models. Collectively, the data on moral development suggest that residence life professionals can expect to see both the justice and care versions of development and might find opportunities in peer interactions to help students integrate the two.

Applicability to Diverse Populations

More cross-cultural research exists in moral development than in any other area of cognitive development theory, perhaps because Kohlberg's (1969) claim of universality sparked research to refute it. The volume of cross-cultural research is beyond the scope of this chapter, but an overview of the research is useful in determining the extent to which current theory is appropriate in understanding college students' moral development. Edwards (1985) synthesized much of the cross-cultural research to address whether Kohlberg's interview and scoring system were valid and whether his theory was useful in understanding moral development in other cultures. She found that the interview method was valid when researchers were familiar enough with the culture studied to translate the interview into that language. She also reported that the scoring system readily accounted for cross-cultural data, although subtle distinctions in the higher stages were needed. The studies on which Edwards based these conclusions included cultures from the Americas (outside of mainstream U.S. culture), Asia, Africa, Western Europe, Australia, and Oceania. It is important to note that only foraging societies and Eastern European societies are missing from this list.

These studies, although cross-sectional in many cases, have found moral stage to increase with age during childhood and adolescence and have found no missing stages. They also show that socioeconomic status, residential factors, educational level, school experiences, parental discipline or warmth, and identification with parents are positively related to moral development. These data, along with Kohlberg's (1976) claim that role-taking opportunities are necessary for moral development, suggest that development is influenced by cultural factors despite the occurrence of stages across cultures.

Longitudinal research also supports the applicability of Kohlberg's theory to other cultures. The sequential advance of stages up to stage 4 and similarity of responses to Kohlberg's stages were found in a study of Turkish men from both village and city populations (Nisan and Kohlberg, 1982). Evidence of the developmental sequence, increase in moral development with age, and no sex differences were also reported in a study of kibbutz-born and Middle East adolescents (Snarey, Reimer, and Kohlberg, 1984).

Cross-cultural data offer more in understanding international college students than in understanding diverse U.S. populations. The variable of social class has been studied with adolescents from three low-income neighborhoods. This study (Bardige and others, 1988) involved interviewing white,

African-American, and Hispanic adolescents. A subset of the interviews were used to construct a coding scheme relevant to the group, and then the remaining interviews were coded with that scheme. The results, reported in the form of quotes, suggested that the adolescents (1) used both justice and care orientations, (2) used moral language similar to other populations, with the exception of sometimes describing situations in which it is necessary to do something one has been told not to do, (3) experienced types of moral conflicts similar to other adolescent populations, and (4) exhibited the same gender-related differences found in Gilligan's earlier work. Although this study implies a number of similarities with other populations, the differences are difficult to judge due to the lack of information on the outcome of coding their responses.

Research with African-American return migrants led Stack (Kerber and others, 1986) to suggest that the women and men in her study were more similar than different. She proposed an African-American model of moral development characterized by a collective social conscience manifest in "concern for reciprocity, commitment to kin and community, and belief in the morality of responsibility" (Kerber and others, 1986, p. 324). Stack's model stemmed from studying return migration of African-American women, men, and children from the urban Northeast to the rural South. She noted, however, that the data were collected for another purpose and using other methods than those used by moral development theorists.

Numerous studies also address the relationship of age and education to moral development. Although some studies report a relationship of age to moral development (Bakken and Ellsworth, 1990), White's (1988) data from participants age nineteen to eighty-two showed no age effect. White did find that education had a significant effect on moral development, a finding consistent with Colby and Kohlberg's (1987) data. Bakken and Ellsworth also noted that education was a predictor of moral reasoning level. Rest (1988) argued that experience outweighs age in affecting moral development due to studies finding higher correlations between moral development and education than between moral development and age, studies showing greater moral development in persons going to college than those not attending, and studies showing academic orientation to have some impact on moral development. As was the case with intellectual development, it is possible that educational experiences offer opportunities for moral development.

Because most research has focused on moral stage, differences within stage found in the gender research reported earlier have not been studied with other cultures. Cross-cultural similarity in stage development combined with cultural influences on development make it possible that cultural differences, albeit as yet undescribed, exist within stages. The collective data suggest that educators can rely on the overall moral development picture (including both orientations) for possibilities in understanding college students' moral development, but will need to identify the possible variations by listening carefully to students.

Integrating Intellectual and Moral Development

Separating various strands of development is necessary to gain an in-depth understanding of each, but an integrated view of the whole student is necessary to foster development in practice. Kohlberg claimed that intellectual development was a necessary but insufficient condition for moral development. In other words, certain levels of intellectual development served as prerequisites for certain levels of moral development, although they did not ensure that the corresponding levels of moral development would occur. Research on children offers mixed results on this view (Krebs and Gillmore, 1982; Walker, 1980) but King, Kitchener, and Wood's (1984) longitudinal study with high school and college students supported Kohlberg's view. They found that moral development over a six-year period was partially attributable to development in reflective judgment.

On the basis of two longitudinal studies with college and older women, Clinchy (in press) speculated that women's moral and intellectual development are intertwined because ways of knowing both allow and constrain the development of moral sensitivity. She argues that received knowers are initially constrained by denying that different views exist. However, through their connections with friends who hold different views, they come to acknowledge the existence of different views even though they do not accept them. This acknowledgment of other views opens the door for a subjective stance. Subjective knowers' moral sensitivity is constrained by the view that values are a result of experience and thus everyone has their own experiences and values. The subjective knower allows other views to exist but refuses to make moral judgments because everyone's values result from their own circumstances.

When women move to a procedural stance, they move away from themselves to look at issues from others' perspectives. This approach allows them to see issues as others see them, resulting in moral breadth that truly acknowledges other possibilities. However, the procedural approach continues to constrain judgment, because the knower cannot transcend others' perceptions of moral issues to make a judgment. Constructed knowers are able to step outside their understanding of others' views to judge those views. They not only understand the others' possibilities, but engage in dialogue about these possibilities and their own views that results in constructing their own moral judgments. Clinchy refers to this as attaining moral depth. Thus, ways of knowing for these women mediated their moral meaning making.

Both intellectual and moral development seem to be related to self-definition. Lyons's work (reviewed earlier) illustrated how separate and connected definitions of *self* prompted different conceptions of moral judgment. The gender-related patterns evident in the Epistemological Reflection model support the hypothesis that students' views of themselves play a role in the epistemological pattern they exhibit. Kegan's (1982) theory of self-evolution is a possible foundation for both intellectual and moral development. Of

Kegan's six stages, two are relevant for the college context. He describes self-definition as a balance between dependence and independence, or a truce between yearning for inclusion versus autonomy. The truce most often reflected in late adolescence is interpersonal; persons in this truce define themselves through their relationships with others. The influence of peer pressure can be understood in light of students' inability to define themselves outside of their relationships with friends, lovers, or social groups. Reliance on authorities by absolute knowers may be attributed to their relationship with authorities. This truce seems consistent with interpersonal-pattern transitional knowers' reliance on peers to know and making moral choices based on others' needs (Kohlberg stage 3 and Gilligan level 2). It is possible that men are more likely to orient to relationships with authority, whereas women are more likely to orient to relationships with peers. Clinchy's notion of subjective knowers being open to other views may translate into their being consumed by other views in the interpersonal truce.

The next truce, labeled institutional, occurs when persons begin to define themselves separately from relationships and focus on maintaining their self-identity. This truce is manifest in students who make choices about career, identity, and social issues regardless of others' opinions. This is compatible with independent knowing and with moral choice that genuinely acknowledges diverse possibilities and struggles to take the self into account (Gilligan's second transition, Kohlberg's stage 4½, Clinchy's moral breadth). Kegan's last truce, interindividual, reflects a self-definition that allows balancing autonomy and connectedness. It is most compatible with contextual knowing, Gilligan's level 3, Kohlberg's postconventional level, and Clinchy's notion of moral depth, and as such is probably uncommon in undergraduate populations. Thus, development in college must be viewed as an intertwining of self-definition and intellectual and moral development. Table 4.3 summarizes the hypothesized connections among these three strands of development. The task of fostering the development of the self was addressed in Chapter Three. The remainder of this chapter addresses how to provide opportunities for intellectual and moral development in the context of the integrated view of development.

Translating Theory into Practice in Residence Life Programs

Students regularly report that their cocurricular environment is of equal if not greater importance in their development than their academic environment (Chickering, 1969; Baxter Magolda, 1990b). Students report that exposure to divergent perspectives, moral conflicts, and assuming new responsibilities aid their moral development (Pascarella and Terenzini, 1991). Residence life offers an ideal context for fostering development because intensive interactions with peers can lead to questioning one's way of looking at issues, moral values, and even identity. Despite these conditions, there are few formal, published examples of theory-based residence life programs.

Table 4.3. Integration of Self, Intellectual, and Moral Development in College Populations.

Self-development	Intellectual development		Moral development	
Kegan	ER	RJ	Care	Justice
Interpersonal	Absolute knowing	Stage 2	Level 2	Stage 3
	Transitional knowing	Stage 3		Stage 4
Institutional	Independent knowing			
		Stage 4	Second transition	Stage 4 ½
		Stage 5		
Interindividual	Contextual knowing	Stage 6	Level 3	Postconventional level
		Stage 7		

Among the principal reasons for this are the intensity of residence life work, a shortage of actual examples to guide translation of theory into practice, lack of understanding of the changes required by traditional student affairs organizations, and lack of support for this function from the university community.

Interwoven with these issues is the perception of theory and its application as abstract and detached from the everyday lives of students and residence life staff. Theory is often written in the abstract, without student quotes to illustrate its meaning. Application of theory is often viewed as manipulating students without their input. In these forms, theory and application do not automatically appeal to residence life staff, who are generally interpersonal in nature. Increased interest in pursuing theory and application from a naturalistic or interpretive perspective may heighten the chances that theory will be used to guide practice. This approach recognizes that development is a complex and dynamic process, that a variety of factors interact to influence development, and that theory can guide but not dictate practice (Kuh, Whitt, and Shedd, 1987). Approaching application from this perspective is consistent with viewing theory as a means of generating possibilities and is more interpersonal in its focus on listening to students. Although published applications of theory are not necessarily written from this perspective, they do offer rich insights and new possibilities for using theory to guide practice. Those efforts are summarized next, followed by a framework for translating theory into practice and examples using the framework as well as insights from published applications to illustrate its use in residence life.

The Literature on Theory to Practice in Residence Life

The largest literature base on intentional environmental design to foster intellectual and moral development focuses on instructional contexts rather than student life contexts. (For a report on Alverno College's comprehensive effort in instructional application, see Mentkowski and Doherty, 1984; also see Penn, 1990, for a longitudinal study of a direct approach to fostering moral development through instruction.) Student life literature can be summarized in four categories: (1) implications of theory for practice, (2) conceptualizations of theoretically based designs, (3) applications to foster development in general, and (4) specific theory-based applications.

The first category consists of translating the meaning of theory for practice and suggests that theoretical ideas ought to be considered in shaping practice. Contributions in the second category play out these implications in conceptual examples of what practice should look like based on development. Thomas (1987) provided examples of fitting the handling of student behavior issues to an integrated picture of student development. He argued that student life has come to view handling of student behavior as a discipline system, which should be replaced by a system of values education to promote development. Hurt and Pratt (1984) proposed an intervention model that specified the target, purpose, and method of intervention to translate theory into practice and discussed examples of these various strategies in academic advising. Evans (1987) advocated a comprehensive framework for moral development interventions defined by target (individuals or institutions), type (planned or responsive), and approach (explicit or implicit). She provided examples of various combinations of interventions. Hotelling and Forrest (1985) outlined counseling strategies for men and women based on Gilligan's theory. Finally, a comprehensive conceptualization of staff supervision based on student development theory has been developed by Ricci, Porterfield, and Piper (1987). This conceptualization specifies characteristics of staff according to intellectual development levels, implications for staff of these characteristics, and strategies for supervisors. For example, staff members who see the world in absolute terms believe only one point of view can be correct. They need considerable support as they encounter the complexity of working with students. Supervisor strategies include providing moderate diversity and helping the staff member analyze conflicting issues. For staff who acknowledge that some uncertainty exists, less support to face uncertainty is needed, but more help in making choices is important. Supervisor strategies include providing increasing diversity and encouragement of self-responsibility. Finally, staff who view the world contextually will need less structure, since they have criteria on which to make decisions. Providing extensive diversity and encouraging commitment become the most appropriate supervisor strategies. Ricci, Porterfield, and Piper (1987) articulated this difference in strategies for views on authority, the learning process, peer acceptance, and staff evaluation.

The third category of literature contains actual applications based on general student development, such as providing the balance of challenge and support that fosters development. Discussing creating conditions for student development, Schroeder and Jackson (1987) highlighted various aspects of the physical living environment that could be adjusted to be supportive of

students and also reported policy strategies implemented in living environments. For example, matching roommates according to their personality
types to create supportive atmospheres resulted in a 65 percent decrease in
room change requests. Locke and Zimmerman's (1987) peer mentor training
program, based on the notion that role-taking opportunities foster moral
development, resulted in slightly higher moral development scores after the
peer mentor experience.

The fourth category, intentional theory-based designs that have been
implemented and evaluated, is small. The three best examples are the Sierra
project (Whitely and Associates, 1982), the Evans Hall Democratic Community (Ignelzi, 1990), and the Olentangy project (Rodgers, 1990). The Sierra
project was intended to foster character development, defined in part by
Kohlberg's theory of moral development. The project was set in the context of
a residence hall, and students agreeing to live in the hall did so with the
condition that they would concurrently enroll in an undergraduate class on
moral development. The authors emphasize the importance of the residence
hall context in this project, saying: "Community as it develops is enhanced by
the twenty-four-hour day living arrangements; the hours per week devoted to
the formal class are few by comparison" (Whitely and Associates, 1982,
p. 102). However, no specific strategies within the hall are reported except
using professional hall staff as instructors of the course and hiring undergraduate staff from previous Sierra project participants.

The specific intervention was a curriculum composed of eleven units.
The survival skills unit taught learning skills for academic success. The
empathy/social perspective-taking unit sought to enhance students' ability to
understand others' points of view and communicate that understanding.
Community building was aimed at creating an open, trusting, and supportive atmosphere characterized by democratic decision making to resolve
conflicts. Sex-role choices dealt with societal expectations and their implications for relationships. The units of assertion training and community service aided students in asserting their own rights and applying their collective
skills in a social-action setting, respectively. A unit on conflict resolution in
society addressed conflict resolution skills as well as principles of fairness
and justice. Race-role choices challenged students to understand stereotyp-
ing, its impact on relationships, and its role in prejudice. Three other units—
conceptions of life-style, career decision making, and life-style planning—
were also included but were not part of the character development focus of
the project.

The moral development of Sierra project participants, all of whom
were first-year students, was assessed prior to and after their first year in the
project. Their development was also contrasted with two control groups. The
moral development of the Sierra participants increased slightly during their
freshman year, and as a group, they showed more growth in moral development than did those in the control groups. These data suggest that the units

encountered by Sierra students may be useful in promoting moral development. In cases where it is inappropriate to offer these units in the form of a
course, they could be integrated into residence life programming.

Unlike the Sierra project, the Evans Hall Democratic Community
(Ignelzi, 1990) intervention focused on the residence hall environment per se
to foster moral development. This project implemented Kohlberg's Just
Community approach in a women's residence hall to promote ethical development, ethical reasoning, and translation of reasoning into ethical action.
Because the Just Community approach advocates voluntary participation,
students applied to join the community and those selected based on interest
and political commitment to the community were assigned to Evans Hall the
following year. At the outset of that year, the community members were asked
to set up a vehicle for discussing and deciding on issues facing the community, since the Just Community approach involves the entire membership of
the community. The seventy-five community members of the Evans Hall
Democratic Community decided to meet for ninety minutes each week to
discuss community matters. They chose to make decisions by consensus
whenever possible and to use public vote only if necessary. Different members facilitated each meeting to maintain equal participation.

Consistent with the Just Community approach, the students were given
authority and responsibility for community policies, including room assignments, visitation, alcohol use, and study/quiet hours. Advisors to the community played educator and facilitator roles. Even though the advisors commented on the weekly discussions and considerations of justice and
responsibility not addressed by students, they stated that they "tried to avoid
using our positions as adult authorities, and to avoid indoctrination; instead,
we appealed to ethical reasoning and community spirit in articulating the
shared ideals of the group" (Ignelzi, 1990, p. 195). A fairness committee
consisting of a small group of community members whose membership
rotated every two months handled violations of community norms and
policies. This group discussed violations and developed resolutions, which
were then reviewed by the entire community. This committee represented the
Just Community component of community members sharing responsibility
for holding each other accountable to established community norms.

Ignelzi (1990) reported that the community handled these responsibilities effectively. One incident recounted in detail by Ignelzi illustrated how
the community handled a theft of a ring from one of the members. After the
first community discussion, the community was considering individually
contributing to replace the ring in order to restore trust in the community.
Despite the ring's anonymous return before this decision was final, the
community response was one of shared responsibility. No thefts occurred in
the remaining seven months of that year, leading Ignelzi to believe that such a
community does lead toward more just and responsible environments.

The Olentangy project, also focused on residential living, was initiated to balance the challenge-support characteristics of a high-rise residence complex (Kalsbeek and others, 1982). Of the multiple dimensions of the project, the portion directed toward intellectual development is of primary interest here. Assessment of students' intellectual development revealed that they used positions 2 and 3 of the Perry scheme to make meaning of their experiences. Widick, Knefelkamp, and Parker's (1975) criteria for facilitating intellectual development were used to assess the nature of the environment. It was determined to be relativistic because it was characterized by extensive diversity (students lived in sixteen-person suites) and low structure (the staff-to-student ratio of 1 to 91 limited staff involvement).

The residence hall environment was redesigned to facilitate intellectual development by matching the environment more closely to the students' ways of making meaning. Widick, Knefelkamp, and Parker's (1975) criteria guided the redesign, which was characterized by high structure, encountering moderate (rather than extensive) diversity, concrete and experiential experience of diversity, help from authority to structure and process experience, and a trusting and collaborative atmosphere. Rodgers (1990) summarized two interventions based on these principles. The first was implementation of a new process for negotiating standards for living together in the suites. The process was structured in that staff introduced the process in a two- to three-hour suite meeting, facilitated a structured dialogue between suitemates, shared samples of previous standards, facilitated the negotiation of actual standards, and conducted a minimum of three follow-up meetings throughout the year. Moderate diversity was introduced by providing only two samples of previous standards. Staff facilitators, viewed as authorities, helped students work through the process and intentionally tried to create an open, sharing atmosphere.

The second intervention involved assigning students to suites based on their Myers-Briggs Type personality profiles. In some suites, all students had identical types, in others only dominant functions were the same (such as sensing or thinking), in some suites only the external (judging or perceiving) function was the same, and some suites were assigned randomly for comparison purposes. Rodgers (1990) reported that 65 percent of the students in the Myers-Briggs Type–matched suites showed increased intellectual development at the end of the year, whereas only 28 percent of those in random suites (including suites that used both the new and old negotiation of standards process) did so. Results were not reported separately for those using the new and old negotiation process. Rodgers concluded that the combination of matching types and the new negotiation process fostered intellectual development. Kalsbeek and others (1982) reported increases in students' perceptions of support in the Myers-Briggs Type suites, particularly those in suites of identical types. Logically, this dimension of support would match students' reported ways of making meaning.

These three applications, along with the conceptualizations of translating theory into practice, offer rich insights into using theory to guide residence life practice. Integrating these insights into a framework for translating theory into practice both in long-term planning and everyday practice is the task to which we now turn.

A Framework for Translating Theory into Practice: Informed Dialogue

Strange and King (1990) proposed Lewin's (1936) $B = f(P \times E)$, or behavior is a function of person-environment interaction, as a theoretical framework for the practice of student affairs. Effective translation of intellectual and moral development theory to practice requires integrating it with person-environment theory (Rodgers, 1990). This entails understanding students' development, the impact the environment has on development, and the particular interaction between a given student and environment. Rodgers (1990) revised Lewin's equation to read $Bp = f(Pd \times Es)$, in which Bp reflects the probability of facilitating a particular kind of development, Pd reflects the development of the person, Es reflects the external stimuli of the environment as described by the developmental criteria for fostering development, and $\times$ reflects the interaction defined by the compatibility between person and environment based on the criteria for fostering development.

Viewed from the context of development as a dynamic, complex, and multifaceted phenomenon, Rodgers's formula takes into account the particulars of the person's development, the context of the environment, and the mutually shaping interaction between the two. Generating possible opportunities for students' development then requires understanding in the following areas:

1. Students' intellectual and moral development, including gender patterns, and how change takes place in this type of development
2. How to assess students' developmental levels and patterns at a given point in time in a given context
3. Possible connections between environmental characteristics and intellectual and moral development
4. Possible interactions between these characteristics and students' various developmental levels
5. How to assess the environmental characteristics in relation to the students in the environment
6. How to redesign environments (practice) to offer opportunities for intellectual and moral development

Much of the understanding needed in each of these areas can be obtained through informed dialogue with students. The term *informed dialogue* suggests two important notions. First, student affairs professionals cannot redesign practice without engaging in a continuing dialogue with students to understand the possibilities for development, the potential impact of various environments, and the constantly changing nature of students' interaction with various environments. Second, student affairs professionals must engage in the dialogue from an informed perspective: informed by the current theoretical foundations, their limits, and their utility in creating new possibilities. The first portion of this chapter provided a starting point by summarizing the current theoretical foundation for intellectual and moral development. Entering the dialogue from this base, it is possible to explore where students are developmentally, building minitheories (Kuh, Whitt, and Shedd, 1987) for the particular context in question. Assessing students' development involves using the theoretical base as one possible way to interpret student behavior, adding to this base with the particulars of the context and students. In the context of everyday practice, this assessment can be accomplished through staff-student interaction. For example, if Shirley Lang interpreted her hall government's wish to sell the offensive shirt as stemming from Kohlberg's interpersonal conformity stage, she would ask questions like "What would be the disadvantages of not selling the shirt for hall government?" or "How will hall government leaders suffer from not selling the shirt?" These questions can help determine whether peer approval is the basis for hall government's stance. In the context of long-range planning, written assessment instruments are available for establishing a starting point for students' development.

The Measure of Epistemological Reflection (MER) is a valid and reliable written essay questionnaire to measure epistemological development, and it measures both gender patterns due to its inclusion of both genders in construction of the questionnaire and scoring system (Baxter Magolda and Porterfield, 1988). The Sociomoral Reflection Measure (SRM) is a valid and reliable written essay questionnaire to measure moral judgment and appears to be sensitive to gender patterns due to gender-inclusive construction (Gibbs and Widaman, 1982; Gibbs, Arnold, and Burkhart, 1984). Both of these instruments require that the student produce a response to open-ended questions and thus require training to score. Both offer workbook format training for scoring these instruments. The Sociomoral Reflection Objective Measure (SROM) offers a recognition format, in which the student circles preferred responses, that is self-scoring. Validity and reliability of this instrument are also promising (Gibbs, Arnold, and Burkhart, 1984). A similar version of the MER is currently being evaluated for validity and reliability and is being compared to interviews to explore whether recognition formats reflect the same level of complexity of development that emerges in talking with students. (For a thorough discussion of cognitive development assessment, see King, 1990. Similarly, environmental assessment is summarized by Huebner and Lawson, 1990.)

Informed dialogue with students also aids understanding of possible connections between environmental characteristics and students' intellectual and moral development and how these characteristics interact with students' developmental levels. In this instance, research on how developmental change occurs informs the dialogue. Increased cognitive developmental complexity is prompted by cognitive dissonance (Piaget, 1926; Perry, 1970), or an experience that is inconsistent with the student's current ways of thinking. For example, the white absolute knower who holds stereotypes about students of nondominant races is surprised when his or her African-American roommate does not demonstrate these stereotypes. The white student's positive experience with the roommate is inconsistent with the stereotype, prompting the student to figure out how the two fit together. Initial experiences such as this may not change the student's thinking, because they are easily resolved by becoming exceptions to the rule. Continued experiences of this sort eventually result in changing the rule to accommodate the new information and simultaneously changing the student's thinking.

The degree to which the student judges inconsistencies as exceptions versus changing the rules depends on the student's readiness to change and whether support exists to aid in facing these challenges. Kegan (1982) suggested that growth is enhanced when the environment offers confirmation, contradiction, and continuity. He described confirmation as supporting the student in his or her current way of making meaning, contradiction as challenging that way of making meaning, and continuity as staying with the student while he or she makes the transition to a new way of making meaning. The theoretical descriptions of students' thinking provide a starting point for identifying what constitutes confirmation and contradiction. For example, Widick and Simpson (1978) suggested that students initially are supported by high structure, but as they become more complex, support comes from less structure. Likewise, challenge is initially moderate diversity but later on requires extensive diversity to adjust to the students' new perspectives. The gender patterns outlined earlier suggest that collaborative discussion would confirm interpersonal knowers, whereas debates would contradict their reasoning patterns. These informed assumptions about how the environment affects students can be checked through the continuing dialogue with students, which simultaneously generates new information about how students and their environment interact. Dialogue with students is essential to assess what to offer by way of confirmation and contradiction, which to offer, and how to balance the two given the particulars of the situation.

Dialogue needs to occur on another level was well—between and among students. Cognitive dissonance, confirmation, contradiction, and continuity can all emerge when students interact with each other. Kohlberg (1976) suggested that moral development depended in part on role taking, or the ability to be aware of others' thoughts and feelings and put oneself in their place. Tappan and Brown (1991) proposed that telling their own moral stories leads students to reflect on their experience from their own moral perspective, increasing their sense of authority and responsibility for action. Opportunities for role taking in moral arenas and sharing one's own moral stories abound in residence life, as students encounter various perspectives on alcohol and drug issues, responsibilities in relationships, sexual practices, academic honesty, diverse life-styles, and community norms. Experiencing various dilemmas in college, either directly or through experiences of close friends, provides the opportunity for students to struggle with moral conflict and reorganize their moral thinking to accommodate these experiences. Staff can create opportunities for dialogue of this nature to occur and can also facilitate such dialogue by creating confirming or contradicting conditions.

Informed dialogue serves as the basis for designing various aspects of residence life practice to offer opportunities for development. These include policy, organizational structure, staff training and supervision, programming, behavioral norms and their management, group advising, and counseling. Examples in each of these areas are explored next to illustrate how this dialogue might vary with students with different developmental levels in different contexts.

Policy

Policy is established in students' best interests, but they are rarely involved in its development. Because involvement heightens investment in an idea, student support of policy could be enhanced by their participation in its development, and such participation could also foster intellectual and moral development.

Policies aimed at safety are a good illustration. Most residence halls lock external doors except the main entrance to restrict the flow of visitors to residents and their guests. This is intended to increase safety, but students often view it as an inconvenience, resolvable by blocking the doors open. A developmental approach with absolute or transitional knowers would involve gathering students to discuss two or three possible plans for creating a safe environment in their hall. We will use men in this example, because they may have less initial interest in safety issues than women.

The dialogue might begin with students hearing from another student who has been assaulted by a stranger in his hall or hearing a campus security officer present data for men's halls on the campus on loss of student property as a result of strangers in the halls. Introducing two or three safety plans would offer contradiction. A structured debate on convenient access versus security of the hall would allow the men to argue their viewpoints and interact with staff authority figures—both forms of confirmation. These absolute and transitional knowers would also reflect Kohlberg stage 3 in our integration and would be interested in choosing a plan that their peers endorse. Staff setting parameters for possible plans yet simultaneously encouraging student responsibility for choosing plans within the parameters would both increase investment in the final safety plan and help students encounter the diversity necessary for intellectual and moral growth. Both enhance the sense of community in the hall. This same strategy could be translated to policies regarding room personalization, use of public space, room changes, and visitation.

Staff Training and Supervision

Training and supervising paraprofessional staff who are independent knowers can be frustrating, because they have their own ideas about how things should be handled. But this can be advantageous once they are able to make wise judgments about diverse situations. For example, both training and supervision geared toward independent knowing and Gilligan's second transition (using a female staff) would involve discussion of multiple courses of action (extensive diversity) for handling roommate conflicts. Having staff sharing their experiences in these situations, exploring their ideas for resolving them, and openly collaborating to arrive at evaluating various approaches for various circumstances would provide both confirmation and contradiction. The focus on evaluation is a necessary challenge to learn how to make judgments, but the group can be supported by freedom to determine their own process for working through judgments about the situations. The supervisor can offer confirmation by acknowledging the legitimacy of staff ideas, validating their ability to come to judgments, and helping them struggle with the conflicts of caring for all concerned that are inherent in roommate dilemmas. Roommate conflicts with moral dimensions (substance abuse or life-style issues) would give staff opportunities to take the role of students in these situations as well as hear peer staff members' views.

Student Group Advising

Despite the enthusiasm of student groups such as hall government at the beginning of the year, most advisors and group leaders soon complain that a few students do all the work. Because absolute and transitional knowers often want to be told what to do, advisors often relent to this preference. A combination of lack of investment and lack of knowing what to do yields student apathy. Advising a group of absolute or transitional knowers, who are also probably in Kohlberg's stage 3 or Gilligan's second level assuming a coed group, requires offering only two or three options about how the group should function. A balance of role playing and watching role plays demonstrating effective group functioning would offer confirmation and contradiction for both gender patterns. High structure would be essential for the group to discuss how to run meetings, delegate responsibilities, and make decisions. With a coed group, focusing this structure toward the interpersonal pattern of building trust and collaboration while moderating the mastery-pattern knowers' tendency toward debate is probably more likely to keep both groups invested in the discussion. A debate focus will result in withdrawal of receiving- or interpersonal-pattern students. Rewarding both active and reflective participation and striving for a balance in these two styles would balance confirmation and contradiction. Facilitating active student exchanges within the context of a relaxed atmosphere would similarly confirm both gender patterns.

Programming

One of the most needed and most difficult areas in programming is celebration of diversity. The students who staff think need this experience the most are the same students most hesitant to attend. This dilemma can also be approached from a developmental perspective. Students are often hesitant to attend programs on diversity because they are too challenging to their absolute view of diversity. Men who do not necessarily relish the chance to talk about feelings may be particularly hesitant. The peer influence characteristic of Kohlberg's stage 3, however, can be used to overcome these hesitancies if the environmental characteristics are connected to students' development. Contradiction in this case might translate to starting with less emotional topics like differences between urban and rural students or Myers-Briggs Type personality differences rather than racism, sexism, or homophobia. Although the latter topics are very important, students are sometimes not ready for them until they have experienced interacting with people different from themselves and have come to a developmental level that allows considering others' differences without challenging self-identity.

Moderate diversity would be encountered through interactions between students representing the difference in question or role plays reflecting these differences or stereotypes about them. This active interchange would be highly structured to allow the men to share their views and challenge each other's thinking. The authority figure would also endorse appreciation of differences to model this value. Staff would offer confirmation by encouraging students to speak openly and master understanding of differences. Discussions of this sort lead up to the more challenging topics and lay the foundation for exploring the moral implications of racist, sexist, and homophobic viewpoints.

Behavioral Norms and Their Management

Behavioral norms are intended to protect individuals' rights. They can simultaneously be a context for community development and retention of more complex students in residence halls, albeit at the increased discomfort of staff and administrators. Staff and administrators are most comfortable specifying behavioral norms when students arrive. This has the same potential for affecting student apathy as described in the "Policy" and "Student Group Advising" examples. Student endorsement of behavioral norms would save many staff headaches related to enforcement of these norms. Independent knowers are most frustrated with explicit behavioral norms and might

tend to move out of the residence due to this mismatch with their development. These same students' moral development in our integrated model
(Kohlberg stage 4 or Gilligan second transition) ought to enhance their
interest in the good of their community.

To approach behavioral norms from a developmental standpoint in a
coed hall of this nature, staff would need to establish minimum parameters
for student behavior. These might include criteria such as respecting others'
rights, respecting student and college property, having equal opportunity to
use hall facilities, and adhering to state law. Students would then be encouraged to discuss multiple plans to meet these criteria and investigate various
plans used elsewhere. They would be challenged to make decisions on
behavioral norms, through both debating implications of options and collaborating on coming to conclusions. In this case, the gender patterns may
be complementary, because debate may clarify the issues for both, whereas
collaboration may move the group toward a choice.

Support for this negotiation of behavioral norms would allow students
the freedom to develop skills in negotiation and to choose an outcome as
long as it remained consistent with the minimum criteria. Again, both
genders' involvement could provide a balance of fairness and care in developing community norms. Staff skill would be needed to balance validating
initiative and encouraging sharing of ideas. Moral story telling and role
taking are inevitable as this discussion turns to norms governing visitation or
sexual conduct. Despite the uncertainty of this process, students at this
developmental level are capable of arriving at community norms, which they
then enforce through peer pressure. The potential result of decreased discipline and increased community and development is worth the discomfort of
giving students freedom to influence their environment. This approach is
not limited to independent knowers. Changing the environmental characteristics to address absolute and transitional knowing also makes this approach relevant to those students.

Counseling

Students approach staff for individual assistance on a wide range of topics.
Often their concern stems from some encounter with information or experience that is inconsistent with their way of seeing the world. This is
particularly true of absolute knowers when uncertainty is first encountered.
Transitional knowers might also seek assistance in handling uncertainty or
the implications of becoming knowers for the first time. For example, consider a receiving-pattern absolute knower who approaches her hall director
about the deterioration of her relationship with her boyfriend. Although she
does not feel she can be herself in the relationship, she tries hard to please
her boyfriend (Gilligan level 2) in order to maintain the "right" relationship.
The hall director might ask the student to describe her interactions with her

boyfriend to learn more about the situation. The director could then introduce moderate contradiction by generating with the student what her options are at this point for handling the situation. The student could be encouraged to explore these options by talking to others who have had similar experiences and resolved them in the relationship or by talking to students who have ended relationships to maintain their own identity. The woman's reliance on her peers at this point makes this approach particularly useful.

Confirmation would take the form of showing concern for the student and building trust to enhance the counseling interaction. A high level of structure would also be needed in talking through options and how to implement each one. For example, if the student chose to work through issues in the relationship, the director could offer guidelines on how to approach this. Sharing the director's own struggle with self versus other needs, perhaps in a global context to avoid too much self-disclosure, would also support the student in knowing she is not alone.

Organizational Structure

The input of student groups (undergraduate staff, hall government, student organizations) in hall management is often minimal. Yet this area offers an opportunity to foster development and increase the sense of community in the hall. The illustrations under "Policy," "Student Group Advising," and "Behavioral Norms and Their Management" reflect how students can be guided in influencing their community effectively. These approaches require an organizational structure within the hall that allows student participation in the framework of environmental characteristics appropriate to their development. This in turn requires freedom to use this organizational structure from the larger residence life system.

As is evident from the preceding pages, environmental redesign can take a number of forms. The Olentangy and Sierra projects illustrate redesign in the context of long-term planning and research. The examples of interaction of student development levels and environmental characteristics in various residence life areas illustrate redesign in the context of everyday (or night, as is the case in residence halls) practice. (See Chapter Five for more detailed discussions of environmental design.) The long-term planning context is useful because it prompts proactive planning for policy, practice, and staffing to provide opportunities for student development. It does require time, expertise, and systemwide support to implement but has the potential to make residence life communities significantly more developmental for students.

The long-term planning context requires residence life and student affairs personnel to take the initiative in promoting residence life as an environment for community, intellectual, and moral development. This presupposes more than understanding the theory and translation framework presented here. It requires understanding organizational behavior and change and how to approach the collegiate community about planned change aimed at student development. Creamer and Creamer's (1990) discussion of a planned change model is essential for staff who wish to implement the ideas proposed in this chapter. The everyday practice context is equally useful for practitioners who need to balance proactive planning with reaction to everyday unexpected events. These interactions with students prompt student development even if the overall system is not developmental in its intention and design. Everyday practice that is developmental, however, can be used to garner support for long-range plans, and when long-range plans are in place, there is greater support for everyday practice that is developmental.

The Challenge for Student Development Professionals

The urgent need for further research to describe the development of diverse populations and clarify gender issues cannot be ignored. Because student development professionals work directly with diverse students, their contributions in this area are essential. However, the use of the developmental theory base that currently exists cannot be ignored either. We know that many college students make meaning of their experience from absolute or transitional perspectives. Within those, the gender-related patterns of receiving or mastery and interpersonal or impersonal exist. We know that most college students conceptualize moral issues in terms of the reactions of others. The justice focus entails doing what is expected to gain approval from peers, whereas the care focus entails caring for others to be perceived as good. Most of these students simultaneously define self through relationships with friends or social groups. This developmental profile gives us valuable information with which to direct our practice.

Useful models to translate theory into practice have existed for years. Student development professionals are highly skilled at interacting with and understanding students. Although formal assessment tools may be somewhat complicated to use, they are available. Both informal interaction and formal assessment allow interpretation of student behavior via theory as well as expanding theory via sustained interaction with students. Yet few examples are available in the literature of using developmental theory in practice, and few residence life practitioners trained in developmental theory actually use it in practice (Piper, 1990). Changing this predicament requires changing individual practice and taking initiative to change divisional and institutional practice.

Student development professionals who understand theory can use it to guide their everyday practice of staff supervision, advising groups and individuals, program planning, policy decisions, and counseling with few additional resources. Those who are unfamiliar with theory have an obligation to become familiar with it to enhance their practice. Practitioners must not only use theory in practice but must demonstrate its value to the campus community. This requires taking initiative to teach colleagues how theory helps solve recurring problems in residence living, enhances student and staff life, and promotes student development. It requires planning everyday practice, recording its effectiveness, and articulating orally and in writing the plan and its outcome. It requires the confidence to propose thoughtful, theory-based alternatives to less effective practice.

As campus constituents search for community to solve pressing concerns about students' ability to function in intellectually and morally complex ways, no one is in a better position than the residential life staff to offer leadership. Current concerns about the quality of campus life offer the opportunity, and the obligation, to share with campus constituents what is known about student development, campus environments, and the interaction between the two.

References

Bakken, L., and Ellsworth, R. "Moral Development in Adulthood: Its Relationship to Age, Sex, and Education." *Educational Research Quarterly*, 1990, *14*, 2–9.

Bardige, B., and others. "Moral Concerns and Considerations of Urban Youth." In C. Gilligan, A. V. Ward, J. M. Taylor, and B. Bardige (eds.), *Mapping the Moral Domain: A Contribution of Women's Thinking to Psychological Theory and Education*. Cambridge, Mass.: Graduate School of Education, Harvard University, 1988.

Baumrind, D. "Sex Differences in Moral Reasoning: Response to Walker's (1984) Conclusion That There Are None." *Child Development*, 1986, *57*, 511–521.

Baxter Magolda, M. B. "Gender Difference in Epistemological Development." *Journal of College Student Development*, 1990a, *31*(6), 555–561.

Baxter Magolda, M. B. "The Impact of the Freshman Year on Epistemological Development: Gender Differences." *Review of Higher Education*, 1990b, *13*(3), 259–284.

Baxter Magolda, M. B. *Knowing and Reasoning in College: Gender-Related Patterns in Students' Intellectual Development*. San Francisco: Jossey-Bass, 1992.

Baxter Magolda, M. B., and Porterfield, W. D. *Assessing Intellectual Development: The Link Between Theory and Practice*. Alexandria, Va.: American College Personnel Association, 1988.

Belenky, M. F., Clinchy, B. M., Goldberger, N. R., and Tarule, J. M. *Women's Ways of Knowing*. New York: Basic Books, 1986.

Belenky, M. F., and others. "Mothers' Ways of Knowing and Their Conceptions of Parenting." Paper presented at the annual meeting of the American Educational Research Association, Boston, Apr. 1990.

Benack, S. "The Coding Dimensions of Epistemological Thought in Young Men and Women." *Moral Education Forum*, 1982, 7(2), 297–309.

Boyer, E. L. *College: The Undergraduate Experience in America*. New York: Harper-Collins, 1987.

Brabeck, M. "Moral Judgment: Theory and Research on Differences Between Males and Females." *Development Review*, 1983, *3*, 274–291.

Chickering, A. W. *Education and Identity*. San Francisco: Jossey-Bass, 1969.

Clinchy, B. "Ways of Knowing and Ways of Being: Epistemological and Moral Development in Undergraduate Women." In A. Garrod (ed.), *Emerging Theories in Moral Development*. New York: Teachers College, in press.

Clinchy, B., and Zimmerman, C. "Epistemology and Agency in the Development of Undergraduate Women." In P. Perun (ed.), *The Undergraduate Woman: Issues in Educational Equity*. Lexington, Mass.: Heath, 1982.

Colby, A. and Kohlberg, L. *The Measurement of Moral Judgment*. Vol. 1. Cambridge, Mass.: Cambridge University Press, 1987.

Creamer, D. G., and Creamer, E. G. "Use of a Planned Change Model to Modify Student Affairs Programs." In D. G. Creamer and Associates, *College Student Development: Theory and Practice for the 1990s*. Alexandria, Va.: American College Personnel Association, 1990.

Edwards, C. P. "Cross-Cultural Research on Kohlberg's Stages: The Basis for Consensus." In S. Modgil and C. Modgil (eds.), *Lawrence Kohlberg: Consensus and Controversy*. Philadelphia: Falmer Press, 1985.

Evans, N. J. "A Framework for Assisting Student Affairs Staff in Fostering Moral Development." *Journal of Counseling and Development*, 1987, *66*, 191–194.

Fleming, J. *Blacks in College: A Comparative Study of Students' Success in Black and in White Institutions*. San Francisco: Jossey-Bass, 1984.

Frye, M. "The Possibility of Feminist Theory." In D. Rhode (ed.), *Theoretical Perspectives on Sexual Difference*: New Haven, Conn.: Yale University Press, 1990.

Gibbs, J. C., Arnold, K. D., and Burkhart, J. E. "Sex Differences in the Expression of Moral Judgment." *Child Development*, 1984, *55*, 1040–1043.

Gibbs, J. C., and Widaman, K. *Social Intelligence: Measuring the Development of Sociomoral Reflection*. Englewood Cliffs, N.J.: Prentice Hall, 1982.

Gibbs, J. C., Widaman, K., and Colby, A. "Construction and Validation of a Simplified Group Administerable Equivalent to the Moral Judgment Interview." *Child Development*, 1982, *53*, 895–910.

Gilligan, C. "In a Different Voice: Women's Conceptions of Self and of Morality." *Harvard Educational Review*, 1977, *47*, 481–517.

Gilligan, C. *In a Different Voice*. Cambridge, Mass.: Harvard University Press, 1982.

Gilligan, C. "Remapping Development: The Power of Divergent Data." In L. Cirillo and S. Wapner (eds.), *Value Presuppositions in Theories of Human Development*. Hillsdale, N.J.: Erlbaum, 1986.

Gilligan, C., and Attenucci, J. "Two Moral Orientations: Gender Differences and Similarities." *Merrill-Palmer Quarterly*, 1988, *34*(3), 223–237.

Holland, D. C., and Eisenhart, M. A. *Educated in Romance: Women, Achievement, and the College Culture*. Chicago: University of Chicago, 1990.

Hotelling, K., and Forrest, L. "Gilligan's Theory of Sex-Role Development: A Perspective for Counseling." *Journal of Counseling and Development*, 1985, *64*, 183–186.

Huebner, L. A., and Lawson, J. M. "Understanding and Assessing College Environments." In D. G. Creamer and Associates, *College Student Development: Theory and Practice for the 1990s*. Alexandria, Va.: American College Personnel Association, 1990.

Hurt, J. C., and Pratt, G. A. "Enhancing Students' Intellectual and Personal Development." In R. B. Winston, Jr., T. K. Miller, S. C. Ender, T. J. Grites, and Associates, *Developmental Academic Advising: Addressing Students' Educational, Career, and Personal Needs*. San Francisco: Jossey-Bass, 1984.

Ignelzi, M. "Ethical Education in a College Environment: The Just Community Approach." *NASPA Journal*, 1990, *27*, 192–198.

Johnston, K. "Two Moral Orientations — Two Problem-Solving Strategies: Adolescents' Solutions to Dilemmas in Fables." Unpublished doctoral dissertation, Graduate School of Education, Harvard University, 1985.

Kalsbeek, D., and others. "Balancing Challenge and Support: A Study of Degrees of Similarity in Suitemate Personality Type and Perceived Differences in Challenge and Support in a Residence Hall Environment." *Journal of College Student Personnel*, 1982, *23*, 434–442.

Kegan, R. *The Evolving Self: Problem and Process in Human Development*. Cambridge, Mass.: Harvard University Press, 1982.

Kerber, L. K., and others. "On *In a Different Voice*: An Interdisciplinary Form." *Signs*, 1986, *11*, 304–333.

King, P. M. "William Perry's Theory of Intellectual and Ethical Development." In L. Knefelkamp, C. Widick, and C. A. Parker (eds.), *Applying New Developmental Findings*. New Directions for Student Services, no. 4. San Francisco: Jossey-Bass, 1978.

King, P. M. "Assessing Development from a Cognitive-Developmental Perspective." In D. G. Creamer (ed.), *College Student Development: Theory and Practice for the 1990s*. Alexandria, Va.: American College Personnel Association, 1990.

King, P. M., Kitchener, K. S., and Wood, P. K. "On the Development of Intellect and Character: A Longitudinal Sequential Study of Intellectual and Moral Development in Young Adults." Paper presented at the annual meeting of the Association for Moral Education, Columbus, Ohio, Nov. 1984.

King, P. M., Taylor, J. A., and Ottinger, D. C. "Intellectual Development of Black College Students on a Predominantly White Campus." Paper presented at the annual meeting of the Association for the Study of Higher Education, Atlanta, Nov. 1989.

King, P. M., Wood, P. K., and Mines, R. A. "Critical Thinking Among College and Graduate Students." *Review of Higher Education*, 1990, *13*(2), 167–186.

Kitchener, K. S., and King, P. M. "Reflective Judgment: Concepts of Justification and Their Relationship to Age and Education." *Journal of Applied Developmental Psychology*, 1981, *2*, 89–116.

Kitchener, K. S., and King, P. M. "Reflective Judgment Theory and Research: Insights into the Process of Knowing in Adulthood." Unpublished manuscript, 1985. (ED 263 821)

Kitchener, K. S., and King, P. M. "The Reflective Judgment Model: Ten Years of Research." In M. L. Commons, T. A. Grotzer, and J. Sinnott (eds.), *Adult Development, Vol. 2: Models and Methods in the Study of Adolescent and Adult Thought*. New York: Praeger, 1990.

Kohlberg, L. "Stage and Sequence: The Cognitive Developmental Approach to Socialization." In D. A. Goslin (ed.), *Handbook of Socialization Theory and Research*. Skokie, Ill.: Rand McNally, 1969.

Kohlberg, L. "Moral Stages and Moralization: The Cognitive-Developmental Approach." In T. Lickona (ed.), *Moral Development and Behavior: Theory, Research, and Social Issues*. Troy, Mo.: Holt, Rinehart & Winston, 1976.

Kohlberg, L. *Essays on Moral Development, Vol. 2: The Psychology of Moral Development*. San Francisco: HarperCollins, 1984.

Krebs, D., and Gillmore, J. "The Relationships Among the First Stages of Cognitive Development, Role-Taking Abilities, and Moral Development." *Child Development*, 1982, *53*, 877–886.

Kuh, G., Whitt, E., and Shedd, J. *Student Affairs 2001: A Paradigmatic Odyssey*. Alexandria, Va.: American College Personnel Association, 1987.

Langdale, S. "Moral Orientations and Moral Development: The Analysis of Care and Justice Reasoning Across Different Dilemmas in Females and Males from Childhood to Adulthood." Unpublished doctoral dissertation, School of Education, Harvard University, 1983.

Lewin, K. *Principles of Topological Psychology*. New York: McGraw-Hill, 1936.

Locke, D. C., and Zimmerman, N. A. "Effects of Peer-Counseling Training on Psychological Maturity of Black Students." *Journal of College Student Personnel*, 1987, *28*, 525–532.

Lyons, N. P. "Two Perspectives: On Self, Relationships, and Morality." *Harvard Educational Review*, 1983, *53*, 125–145.

Mentkowski, M., and Doherty, A. "Abilities That Last a Lifetime: Outcomes of the Alverno Experience." *American Association of Higher Education Bulletin*, 1984, *36*(6), 5–14.

Nisan, M., and Kohlberg, L. "Universality and Cross-Cultural Variation in Moral Development: A Longitudinal and Cross-Sectional Study in Turkey." *Child Development*, 1982, *53*, 865–876.

Pascarella, E. T., and Terenzini, P. T. *How College Affects Students: Findings and Insights from Twenty Years of Research*. San Francisco: Jossey-Bass, 1991.

Penn, W. Y., Jr. "Teaching Ethics—A Direct Approach." *Journal of Moral Education*, 1990, *19*, 124–138.

Perry, W. G. *Forms of Intellectual and Ethical Development in the College Years: A Scheme*. Troy, Mo.: Holt, Rinehart & Winston, 1970.

Piaget, J. *The Language and Thought of the Child* (M. Gabian, trans.). London: Routledge, 1926.

Piper, T. D. "A Study of the Congruence Between Theory Purported to Be Known In-Depth and One's Implicit Theory-in-Use." Unpublished doctoral dissertation, Department of Educational Policy and Leadership, Ohio State University, 1990.

Rest, J. R. "Why Does College Promote Development in Moral Judgment?" *Journal of Moral Education*, 1988, *17*, 183–194.

Ricci, J. P., Porterfield, W. D., and Piper, T. D. "Using Developmental Theory in Supervising Residential Staff Members." *NASPA Journal*, 1987, *24*, 32–41.

Rodgers, R. F. "Recent Theories and Research Underlying Student Development." In D. G. Creamer and Associates, *College Student Development: Theory and Practice for the 1990s*. Alexandria, Va.: American College Personnel Association, 1990.

Schmidt, J. A. "Older and Wiser? A Longitudinal Study of the Impact of College on Intellectual Development." *Journal of College Student Personnel*. 1985, *26*, 388–394.

Schroeder, C. C., and Jackson, S. G. "Creating Conditions for Student Development in Campus Living Environments." *NASPA Journal*, 1987, *25*, 45–53.

Snarey, J., Reimer, J., and Kohlberg, L. "The Sociomoral Development of Kibbutz Adolescents: A Longitudinal, Cross-Cultural Study." *Developmental Psychology*, 1984, *21*, 3–17.

Strange, C. C., and King, P. M. "The Professional Practice of Student Development." In D. G. Creamer (ed.), *College Student Development: Theory and Practice for the 1990s*. Alexandria, Va.: American College Personnel Association, 1990.

Tappan, M. B., and Brown, L. M. "Stories Told and Lessons Learned: Toward a Narrative Approach to Moral Development and Moral Education." In C. Withrell and N. Noddings (eds.), *Stories Lives Tell*. New York: Teachers College Press, 1991.

Thomas, R. L. "Systems for Guiding College Student Behavior: Punishment or Growth?" *NASPA Journal*, 1987, *25*, 54–61.

Tracey, R. J., and Sedlacek, W. E. "Noncognitive Variables in Predicting Academic Success by Race." *Measurement and Evaluation in Counseling*, 1984, *16*, 171–178.

Walker, L. J. "Cognitive and Perspective-Taking Prerequisites for Moral Development." *Child Development*, 1980, *51*, 131–139.

Walker, L. J. "Sex Differences in the Development of Moral Reasoning: A Critical Review." *Child Development*, 1984, *55*, 677–691.

Walker, L. J. "Sex Differences in the Development of Moral Reasoning: A Rejoinder to Baumrind." *Child Development*, 1986, *57*, 522–526.

Welfel, E. R., and Davison, M. L. "The Development of Reflective Judgment

During the College Years: A 4-Year Longitudinal Study." *Journal of College Student Personnel*, 1986, 27(3), 209–216.

White, C. B. "Age, Education, and Sex Effects on Adult Moral Reasoning." *International Journal on Aging and Human Development*, 1988, 27(4), 271–281.

Whitely, J. M., and Associates. *Character Development in College Students*. Schenectady, N.Y.: Character Research Press, 1982.

Widick, C., Knefelkamp, L., and Parker, C. A. "The Counselor as a Developmental Instructor." *Counselor Education and Supervision*, 1975, *14*, 286–296.

Widick, C., and Simpson, D. "Developmental Concepts in College Instruction." In C. Parker (ed.), *Encouraging Development in College Students*. Minneapolis: University of Minnesota Press, 1978.

Chapter Five

===

Developmental Impacts of Campus Living Environments

C. Carney Strange

An idea modeled after the English college system, the residential campus has been a core feature of the first three centuries of American higher education. Variously labeled *dorm, zoo, living-learning center, house,* or a *home away from home,* the college residence hall has played a significant and powerful educational role in the lives of generations of undergraduates. What makes it function as it does? How does the residence life experience contribute to the educational mission of an institution? What are the factors that make for a positive residential experience? This chapter presents a number of theories that have addressed these questions in an attempt to explain the consequences of a group of individuals who live together, share common purposes, and pursue common activities in a campus setting called a *residence hall.* These theories and concepts are important for understanding effective practices of residence life professionals.

Consider the following scene on entering "Williams Hall" at Midwest University for the first time (a fictitious setting for purposes of illustration). The vaulted ceiling, warm colors, comfortable furniture, potted trees and plants, and rich oak woodwork of the entry lobby strike you immediately as an inviting place to be. At once, recognizing you as a novice to the building, a friendly voice behind a bright countertop inquires, "Can I help you find someone?", to which you reply, "I'm just here for the day and am interested in seeing one of the residence halls on campus; this was the first one I walked into." "Let me call Kelly, one of our RAs; she'll give you a quick tour if you'd like." "Great!. . . thanks," you reply. Meanwhile, a group of ten residents walk by, all with distinctive T-shirts proclaiming "Do It Right at Williams Night."

"Let's go this way," suggests Kelly when she arrives, explaining that Williams is one of the older halls on campus (recently renovated though), housing 125 males and 150 females (coed on each corridor) with a special wing dedicated to the student-faculty fellows program. Dorothy Williams, now retired and whose name endorses the hall, apparently was a well-known faculty member on campus who challenged students to seek the most of their learning opportunities, both in and out of the classroom. Her interaction with, dedication to, and impact on students over the years left a legacy of spirit and values that shape the living-learning mission and goals of Williams Hall today. Large bulletin boards announce events of the week at every turn, a distinctive corner of each reserved for business of the "Williams Student Initiative" (a term for their resident student association). Elections for new officers, representatives, and committee coordinators are just around the corner. A real excitement is obvious, since posters everywhere tout the virtues and skills of various residents vying in a spirit of friendly competition and honor for these valued positions.

"Williams is an exciting place to live on campus," Kelly says as she recounts the extensive application and interview process she survived to get in, including production of a personal statement of philosophy and goals for learning. "And there's just something about the place," she continues, describing how important it is for her and how much she has learned from being a contributing member of the many committees, projects, and events that always seem to be going on around the hall. ("Williams Carnival" is one event she has just completed, she further explains.) These experiences are particularly relevant to her career goals, being a human resource management major, and they have challenged her to develop many of the skills and competencies she anticipates will be important for acquiring an entry-level position in the field. This kind of involvement led her to think about applying for, and now getting, one of the resident assistant positions available for the coming year, a highly prized and well-respected leadership role acknowledged at the annual Williams Community Banquet in the spring.

"It's really a home," she says, knocking at one of the residents' doors to ask permission to see one of the rooms. More than I expected, the inside looks quite roomy — actually three distinct rooms — with private space for each of the two residents and a common area as well. All the furniture is movable and, as the residents explain, was selected by them at the beginning of the year from a range of five different options of color, style, and configuration. "We were encouraged to design and create our own space here," they say with pride, pointing to several features that make their "home" unique and different from others on the floor. I ask about the "Williams Code" referred to in a handout in the lobby earlier and framed on all the walls adjacent to entrances or exits to each floor. The students explain the honor system of rights and responsibilities all residents agree to as a social contract of mutual respect and commitment to the Williams way. "It works fairly well," they say, and new members quickly come to value these standards of community living. The standards seem to create a very supportive atmosphere, where trying something different is encouraged, contributing talents is expected, and volunteering to help out is a way of life. Students appear to study hard, work hard, and play hard, with a deep sense that now is a very important time in their lives and there is so much to be gained. I thank them for the quick tour and accept Kelly's invitation to get some lunch with them, where I meet several faculty members who are participants in the student-faculty fellows program. They too acknowledge that Williams Hall is not an ordinary place to live, but rather a place where "ordinary students do extraordinary things"—apparently a well-deserved reputation, from what I've seen.

Is Williams Hall real? Where are all the loud stereos, damaged lounge furniture, inconsiderate visitors, and inebriated roommates in the middle of the night? Where are the complaints about lack of privacy, apathy, and excessive noise? Those conditions are all too real in many places. But so are the features of Williams described above. What makes one residence different from another? How does a residence hall develop the distinctive character of a place like Williams Hall? Are there certain programs and policies that can be implemented to make a difference? Will they work with all students? What attracts certain students to live in certain halls? What encourages them to stay? This brief tour and description of Williams Hall (albeit an idealized description) illustrates that residence halls are complex human educational environments whose features are a function of (1) their physical structure and design, (2) the characteristics of individuals who live in them, (3) the way residents organize themselves, and (4) their collective perceptions of the living environment, which, in turn, influence how they evaluate and respond to those features.

These four aspects correspond to the four sets of concepts or "theories" presented here as explanations for how residence halls function. They are: (1) *physical models*, which address the natural and synthetic features of human environments, noting the limits they set on the behavior that can occur within them; (2) *human aggregate* models, which emphasize that the dominant features of environments are transmitted through people and reflect the collective characteristics of the individuals who inhabit them; (3) *structural organizational models*, which underscore the goals and purposes of environments and the consequent organizational structures that, in turn, enhance or inhibit certain environmental characteristics and outcomes; and (4) *perceptual models*, which acknowledge the importance of individuals' subjective interpretations of the environment as a critical element in understanding how they respond to its key features.

Physical Models of Residence Environments

Models of the physical environment focus on how natural and synthetic physical features of the environment influence behavior. Obvious natural physical features include elements such as location, terrain, and climate. For example, the natural wooded setting providing the environmental backdrop for the University of the Redlands may influence students to behave in very different ways from those at the University of Chicago, ensconced in the middle of a massive urban metropolis. Synthetic physical features include elements such as architectural design, space, amenities, and distance. There is a different "feel" to the design and spatial arrangement of a fifteen-story hall with 1,200 residents than to a much smaller "house" arrangement where fifteen students occupy a single floor structure. Both natural and synthetic features, through varying conditions of light, density, noise, temperature, air quality, and accessibility, combine to create a powerful influence on a student's attraction to, satisfaction with, and stability within a particular setting.

According to Michelson's (1970, p. 25) model of "intersystems congruence," at the very least the physical environment sets broad limits on the phenomena that can occur in any given setting, making some behaviors more or less likely to occur than others. Aspects of the physical environment, natural and synthetic, interact with other features of the setting—social systems, for example—to affect the probability of various phenomena occurring. For example, increased use of indoor campus recreation facilities is an inevitable correlate of inclement weather or a change of seasons, particularly among a young, physically active student population. At times, the physical features may limit certain behaviors, such as the frequency of interaction between residents of two wings of a floor separated by a set of stairs and a closed fire door. On the other hand, they may encourage certain behaviors, as is evident on many campuses where bare worn paths (instead of sidewalks) chart the shortest distance between two points. Although the physical environment may not directly cause specific behaviors or attitudes, its limitations present challenges that must be negotiated by those within.

Campus residence halls offer a classic study of the complex influences of the physical environment. The number of floors, the location of stairwells and elevators, the design of inner spaces (suites versus double-loaded-corridor room arrangements, for example), the use of amenities, and distances to communal facilities all play an important role in the quality of students' campus experiences and can be a positive force for development in students' lives (Strange, 1983). In the interest of creating residence hall environments that enhance the student development mission of the institution, attention has been directed toward application of the concepts of territoriality (Schroeder, 1979b), personal space (Anchors, Schroeder, and

Jackson, 1978), and the development of community (Ender, Kane, Mable, and Strohm, 1980) to encourage students to assume greater responsibility for individualizing their own living space.

Since the dramatic growth of campus housing began over twenty years ago, several reviews of extant research (Blimling, 1988; Heilweil, 1973; Moos, 1986, 1979) have addressed the topic of the effects of various physical features of campus residence halls. In response to the period of student activism in the late 1960s, when student complaints about living-group regulations were second only to issues related to the war in Vietnam, Heilweil (1973) provided a review of the factors related to student dissatisfaction with residential living focusing on four areas of research: (1) privacy and isolation versus enforced social interaction, (2) proximity and social relations, (3) study activities, and (4) individualization. Concerning issues of privacy, Heilweil concluded that the commonly expressed goals of fostering sociability and community in a residence hall may have their costs and that "many of the problems and dissatisfactions that do arise, arise in response to enforced sociability and the absence of opportunity for solitude and privacy" (p. 384). Residence halls undoubtedly offer conditions of "close living," and their design features—for example, common dining facilities, "gang showers," doors opposite rather than staggered on an open corridor, and limited personal space—often challenge students to seek creative solutions to satisfying their need for privacy.

With respect to proximity and the formation of relationships, Heilweil's review concluded that "patterns of friendship tended to be defined by adjacency and traffic flow" (p. 387), noting the importance of the concept of "functional distance" (Festinger, Schachter, and Back, 1950)—that is, "the distance which must actually be traveled rather than the sheer physical distance" (p. 386). Such factors become important when considering the effects of high-rise (usually more than five stories) versus low-rise structures on the interactions of students and their use of facilities. A number of studies reviewed by Heilweil document the importance of residence halls in students' academic activities. Given that students spend up to 80 percent of their study time in their rooms, issues of privacy, freedom from noise and other distractions, and provision of adequate and appropriately designed space are paramount. Finally, Heilweil noted the role of personalization of space, through the arrangement and replacement of furniture and other amenities, as an important tool in support of the institution's goal of developing students' individual potential.

Moos summarized a range of empirically supported, tentative conclusions about the effects of physical environments. Among these conclusions are two that illustrate the impact of physical space on the behavior of students living in residence halls. He noted that "complaints about lack of space and privacy are related to the social composition of the living unit rather than the number of occupants only" (1976, p. 404). He also concluded that there appear to be consistent gender differences in reaction to crowding, with males responding more unfavorably to crowded conditions than do females. Both of these conditions focus on issues of density and crowding. The decision whether to expand campus housing facilities is currently a precarious one for a number of residential campuses, due to highly competitive and fluctuating enrollment trends. Some are faced with the problem of "overbooking" current residence facilities, with the expectation that not all admitted students will show. However, when matriculation rates exceed available spaces, the placement of students in lounge areas and other temporary facilities as a short-term solution may result. Although such overcrowded conditions are never desirable, these two conclusions may yield clues as to how best to handle such a situation. Accordingly, the keys to minimizing complaints about lack of space and privacy lie in the social and gender composition of the affected group. If possible, students with similar characteristics—for example, similar academic majors or hometowns—might be assigned to temporary overflow space, since the potential for congruence and satisfaction is maximized in such a homogeneous grouping (see the discussion of human aggregate models that follows). Likewise, such conditions might prove more successful (questions of equity aside) with female students involved rather than male students. On the other hand, these conclusions also suggest that crowded conditions, particularly those involving males, may warrant special proactive interventions, such as additional staff and workshops on "negotiating differences" or "managing conflict," to prevent potential problems from arising.

Blimling (1988) carried out a meta-analysis of twenty years of research on the effects of various residence hall designs and features. He found that "long corridors"—arrangements with a single, double-loaded corridor where twenty to forty rooms are located across from one another—resulted in student perceptions of greater crowding, greater inhibition in their interaction with others and in the acquisition of social skills, and perceptions of a lesser quality of social climate than was the case with suite-style living arrangements. Results of studies examining the influence of floor location in a high-rise residence hall, defined as a building with at least six floors, indicated that students who occupy the upper one-third to one-half of the building perceive their environment to be less crowded and as having a better quality of social climate and satisfaction than those students occupying the lower floors. Additionally, a number of studies examining the effects of high-rise versus low-rise designs, with five or fewer floors, found that low-rise residence halls reported a better social climate but not necessarily more satisfaction with the overall residence hall experience.

Blimling also examined issues of territorial control of residence hall room space, and the degree of openness or spaciousness of the residence hall room, finding "strong support for the hypothesis that students living in residence hall rooms with greater room flexibility, that is, more freedom to decorate their own room, and a more spacious atmosphere are more satisfied and comfortable than students living in less flexible rooms with a less spacious atmosphere" (1988, p. 294). "Room flexibility" and "atmosphere" incorporated variables such as "desk location in a residence hall room, view from the residence hall room window, room furniture arrangement, amount of sunlight entering the room, movable versus nonmovable room furniture, the number and type of wall decorations in a residence hall room, having bunk beds versus a twin bed arrangement, and the degree of control students can exercise over decorating their rooms" (p. 294).

Noting the effects of proximity of students' rooms both to the formation and maintenance of friendships and to changes in attitudes and beliefs, Blimling found support for the hypothesis that "students who live close to one another are more likely to form and maintain friendships than students who live further apart" (p. 444). In addition, he found support for the idea that "white students living in proximity to black students or in proximity to international students adopt more favorable attitudes toward the respective group" (p. 448). Finally, reviewing studies focusing on the effects of freedom given students to control their own residence living unit environment, such as painting the walls and building unique physical structures like ramps, slides, and lofts, Blimling found that "increasing territorial control students have over a residence living unit produces a more favorable social climate than giving students less control" (p. 450).

A larger number of studies have examined the effects of residence hall room social density—that is, the temporary assignment of three people to rooms designed for occupancy by two—on academic performance, satisfaction with the residence experience, and social climate. Although Blimling (1988) found some support for the hypothesis that overassignment is detrimental to academic performance in the case of small residence hall systems (fewer than 4,000 on-campus students), no such relationship was supported for all institutions regardless of residence hall system size. With respect to the effect of social density on satisfaction with the residence hall experience, he found evidence that "students living in two-person residence hall rooms which were not overassigned are more satisfied with their residence hall experience than students living in three-person rooms which are overassigned" (p. 410). In addition, this "degree of satisfaction appears to differ with the different expectations of male students and female students" (p. 410)—females perceive such conditions as more crowded than males perceive them to be. Finally, Blimling's review of several other studies indicated an inverse relationship between social density and quality of social climate, defined as the organizational, interpersonal, intellectual, and social atmosphere of a living unit, with students living in two-person rooms reporting a better quality of social climate than those in overassigned rooms.

Human Aggregate Models of Residence Environments

Human aggregate models focus on the collective characteristics of the people within an environment. These theories assume that the characteristics of an environment are collectively transmitted through its inhabitants; therefore, the dominant characteristic of the individuals within an environment determines its dominant feature. Measuring and understanding the nature and influence of an environment, then, involves assessing the various characteristics of its inhabitants. Models developed by Astin (1968), Holland (1985), and Myers (1980) exemplify these assumptions.

Astin (1962) assumed that activities of individuals in an environment constitute the only legitimate source of observable stimulus in an environment. For example, the extent to which a residence hall environment creates a press toward intellectual or academic interests (such as might be desirable in developing an honors hall or living-learning center) would be reflected in observable and quantifiable behaviors such as formal and informal discussions about course material, books read, and faculty-student interactions. Differences in strength of environmental press from one setting to the next are reflected in different frequencies of such behaviors. Measurement of these environmental features involves self-reports of participants' activities and behaviors in the setting, and their collective effect constitutes the dominant feature of the environment. For example, in a living-learning center, 90 percent of the students might report frequent informal discussions about course materials and assignments, in contrast to another type of residence, where only 15 percent report such discussions.

Holland (1985) claimed that information about individual personalities in the environment is the key to understanding its dominant feature, because individuals' activities and behaviors are assumed to be a direct reflection of their personality and interests. Assessment of the various interests represented among the environmental occupants, as is done in using the Environmental Assessment Technique (EAT) (Astin and Holland, 1961), provides an adequate measure of that environment. Six different environmental occupational interest patterns are identified in Holland's model: (1) *realistic* environments, such as those dominated by engineers, demand the explicit, ordered, or systematic manipulation of objects, tools, machines, and animals; (2) *investigative* environments encourage scientific and scholarly activities and offer opportunities for observation and symbolic, systematic, creative investigation of physical, biological, or cultural phenomena, as might be found in an anthropology department; (3) *artistic* environments, such as those characterizing a theater department, are recognized by the dominance of demands and opportunities that entail ambiguous, free, and unsystematized activities and competencies to create art forms or products; (4) *social* environments encourage understanding, cooperation, and sociability and present opportunities that entail the manipulation of others to inform, train, develop, cure, or enlighten, such as a department of counseling; (5) *enterprising* environments demand the manipulation of others to attain organizational or self-interest goals, as is true in many business settings, and people tend to see themselves as aggressive and confident; and

(6) *conventional* environments, like an accounting firm, entail the explicit, ordered, systematic manipulation and organization of data according to a prescribed plan, and they encourage people to see themselves as conforming and orderly.

According to Holland, environments are distinguished by their degree of *differentiation* and *consistency*. A highly differentiated (or focused) environment is characterized by the dominance of one type of individual. For example, a highly differentiated social environment would be in evidence in a residence hall suite where five out of six residents were social work or other related helping profession majors. Consistency refers to the similarity of interests and opportunities in an environment. Adjacent types in Holland's hexagonal arrangement, in order—realistic, investigative, artistic, social, enterprising, and conventional—are those most similar and consistent. For instance, social activities and interests are most similar to and consistent with enterprising and artistic opportunities, but very dissimilar to and inconsistent with conventional, realistic, or investigative activities and interests.

Environments that are highly differentiated and consistent seem to have the most powerful effect over time, and they tend to reinforce and accentuate their own characteristics. This "press toward conformity" (Astin and Panos, 1969) influences the extent to which an individual is likely to be attracted to and remain satisfied and stable within an environment. Fraternities and sororities often exhibit this dynamic in the attraction and selection of new members. "Rush parties" or gatherings allow potential pledges to experience, if only briefly, the dominant characteristics of the current members of the organization. Usually candidates most attracted to the particular unit, and invited to pledge, are those who already share the most similarities with the existing aggregate. By joining they will then, in turn, reinforce the existing dominant characteristic(s), and the accentuation effect continues. In many ways, a similar mutual selection process occurs on an informal basis in a residence hall unit, where the characteristics of those who are returning to the same unit the next academic year tend to establish the dominant pattern, which new residents will likely conform to if they constitute a minority of the occupants. This accentuation effect is also evident in the power of small homogeneous institutions, such as single-sex colleges or specialized single-purpose schools, which often attract and retain over time a highly consistent student body.

Holland further contended that person-environment *congruence*—for example, a conventional person in a conventional environment—is the best predictor of individual satisfaction and stability in an environment. He also noted that individuals respond to situations of person-environment incongruence by (1) leaving the environment and seeking a new, more congruent environment; (2) attempting to change the current environment to make it more compatible; or (3) adapting to the current environment. Which option a person selects is usually a function of the degree of differentiation and consistency of the individual's interests and the degree of differentiation and consistency of the environment. For example, a person with a very undifferentiated interest pattern—that is, having many different interests of equal strength—would most likely adapt to the dominant feature of an environment, as may be the case with an undecided student who elects to major in business after rooming with two business majors. On the other hand, a highly differentiated person might attempt to change an undifferentiated environment, as may be illustrated by a highly committed social work major who convinces an undecided roommate of the merits of her field. Or such a person could leave a differentiated but inconsistent environment, as in the case of a theater student who requests a change in room assignment after a semester with two roommates who are highly committed accounting majors.

Myers (1980) employed a similar set of assumptions. Through application of the Myers-Briggs Type Indicator (MBTI) (Myers and McCaulley, 1985), this model describes individual differences in terms of four dichotomous personality dimensions: (1) the *extraversion-introversion* (EI) dimension assesses whether an individual prefers to direct mental activities toward the external world of people and things (extraversion) or toward the inner world of concepts and ideas (introversion); (2) the *sensing-intuition* (SN) dimension assesses whether the person prefers to perceive the world in a factual, realistic way (sensing) or to perceive inherent, imaginative possibilities (intuitive); (3) at one end of the *thinking-feeling* (TF) dimension, an individual prefers to arrive at decisions by logical analysis (thinking), and at the other end, by appreciating personal and interpersonal subjective values (feeling); and (4), the *judging-perception* (JP) dimension assesses an individual's preference for taking either a judgmental attitude (judging) or a perceptive attitude (perceiving) toward his or her environment.

The various combinations of these dimensions yield sixteen different personality types, each with a unique set of preferences, approaches, and styles. Again, consistent with the tenets of human aggregate models, an environment dominated by the presence of a particular personality type would likely convey the characteristics of that type. For example, much like Holland's social type, a residence hall environment dominated by feeling types would place a premium on being aware of other people and their feelings. In contrast, a residence environment dominated by sensing types would likely be distinguished by a set routine and an emphasis on detail and precision. This model, however, differs somewhat from Holland's typology with respect to how each handles the problem of opposite types. Holland concludes that opposite types—for instance, artistic versus conventional—are inherently incongruent and a source of potentially mutual stress and dissatisfaction. The MBTI model, on the other hand, emphasizes the concepts of balance and complementarity of types. Although individuals develop a dominant preference on each of these four dimensions, the opposite traits are necessary to supplement and to provide balance for the dominant trait. The same dynamic is assumed to function with respect to human aggregates. For example, a work environment dominated by intuitive types, with their characteristic enthusiasm for new problems and solutions, may well benefit from the perspective and skills of a sensing type to keep things realistic and on track.

Moos (1986) acknowledged several tentative conclusions from the empirical research on human aggregates that have interesting implications for educational practice in residence halls. The first conclusion is that "students who are congruent with the majority are more satisfied and stable in terms of their vocational plans than are incongruent students. However, . . . congruence effects may be stronger for women than for men. Congruence, homogeneity, and consistency have important effects [and should be taken] into account in selecting environments" (p. 412). The second conclusion notes the potentially negative consequences of incongruence: "People have a tendency to become more like their environments [progressive uniformity]. . . . [However, people who] do not share the dominant racial, religious, or socioeconomic characteristics of the population have high rates of mental illness and associated symptoms" (p. 413). Both of these conclusions from the human aggregate literature speak directly to the importance of person-environment congruence or "fit." Assuming that successful attraction, matriculation, and retention of students are desirable goals for all campuses, those in charge of recruitment and admissions need to pay special attention to degree of institutional fit for any potential student. Careful and accurate presentation of the institution's or various departments' dominant features is crucial in encouraging an informed decision that will result in maximum consistency and congruence. This is particularly true of residence hall environments, where most traditional-age students spend much of their first year or two of the college experience.

A similar dynamic is reflected in the second conclusion and is especially significant in addressing issues of minority recruitment and retention. First, it suggests that stress and associated symptoms due to person-environment incongruence are additional burdens that any students who do not share the dominant characteristics of the institution's population must carry as they matriculate into the college experience. Higher attrition rates and incidences of adjustment problems can be expected under such conditions. Campus administrative models for addressing such issues range from a centralized approach, where a single "umbrella" office provides most services in a culturally focused manner—for example, an Office of Multicultural Affairs—to a decentralized approach, where representative minorities are located throughout existing campus offices. Considering the above conclusions, a highly focused, centralized model, which might also include a multicultural wing or floor in a residence hall, may be most effective in initially acclimating minority students to campus, since such an arrangement provides a visible, homogeneous unit where cultural ethnic consistency and congruence are maximized. For purposes of identity recognition and support, this arrangement is likely to result in the highest level of initial satisfaction and stability. A similar conclusion can be argued in support of the creation and maintenance of other specialized units on campus that are organized to meet the needs of particular populations who depart from the typical student norm — for example, an Adult Learner Support Service or an International Student Center or hall. These, too, can offer a highly differentiated source of congruence at a critical point of transition in these students' lives.

Blimling's (1988) meta-analysis examining various aspects of human aggregate applications in residence halls found that homogeneous roommate assignment by academic major did not lead to better academic performance or a better quality of social climate. On the other hand, assignment of students by Holland type, by academic selectivity (to an "honors program" residence hall, for instance), or by class level (such as to an all-freshman residence hall rather than with upper-class students) enhances academic performance. Blimling's review also determined that coed residence aggregates resulted in perceptions of a better social climate and more social involvement with the opposite sex, but observed no effects on academic performance, personal growth and development, or involvement in extracurricular activities. Apparently students assigned to single-sex units perform just as well on these measures. Finally, matching or selecting roommates with the same birth order, with demographic and personal trait similarities, or with the same or similar MBTI profiles enhances compatibility. Furthermore, evidence supports the conclusion that "the academic performance of a student influences the academic performance of that student's roommate" (Blimling, 1988, p. 434), a factor that might also have some bearing on roommate selection or assignment.

Structural Organizational Models of Residence Environments

A basic premise of these approaches is that environments are purposeful — that is, they have goals, explicit or implicit, that give them direction and that give rise to organized structures that affect inhabitants' behaviors and attitudes. Most students spend a good deal of time, from day to day, in explicitly purposeful environments (Etzioni, 1964), such as residence halls, classrooms, or offices. These environments are designed to achieve certain ends, and their success is often gauged by the extent to which they do so or, in other words, by their effectiveness. The tendency to *get organized to get things done* is a natural one, and in accomplishing such a task, there are a number of decisions that must be made along the way. Who is in charge? How will decisions about spending resources be made? By what rules, if any, will we function? What must be accomplished and how fast? The decisions made with respect to these questions create a variety of organizational structures in an environment that, in turn, affect an individual's attraction to and satisfaction within that setting. On many campuses, developing a response to such questions, especially within a residence hall setting, offers an ideal opportunity for students to assume leadership and responsibility for their immediate environment and to exercise value judgments in the context of peers. It is also a critical time to engage students as involved members of the campus community.

Hage and Aiken (1970) offered a model of complex organizations that is useful in understanding these various structural organizational aspects of the environment. The authors posited that organized environments can generally be characterized along a continuum, one end of which is described as dynamic and the other end as static. Dynamic environments respond to change; static environments resist change. The extent to which an organized environment is likely to exhibit dynamic or static characteristics can be determined with reference to six basic organizational structures: (1) the degree of organizational *complexity*, or the number of occupational subunits and specialties in an organization, as well as the intensity and extensity of their knowledge and expertise—that is, a measure of their degree of professionalization; (2) the degree of *centralization*, the way in which power is distributed in an organization, from highly centralized units where few share power to decentralized units where all share power equally; (3) the degree of *formalization*, the number and specificity of enforced rules; (4) the degree of *stratification*, the differential distribution of rewards in a system; (5) the degree of *production*, the relative emphasis on quantity or quality of products or services; and (6) the degree of *efficiency*, the relative emphasis on cost reduction of the organization's products or services.

The structural arrangement of dynamically organized environments combines a high degree of complexity with low centralization, formalization, stratification, and efficiency, and a relative emphasis on the *quality* of products or services. According to Hage and Aiken (1970), such an environment is highly conducive to change and innovation. On the other hand, static environments, which tend to discourage change and innovation, are characterized by a low degree of complexity, high centralization, formalization, stratification, and efficiency, and a relative emphasis on the *quantity* of products or services. The importance of this distinction lies in the notion that developmental educational environments are those that exhibit characteristics of a dynamic organization, where individual differences are appreciated, participation is expected, interactions are personal rather than functional, and risk taking is encouraged (Strange, 1983).

Perhaps no one in the residence life literature has addressed these issues more directly than Crookston (1974, p. 57), in his proposal for the development of an "intentional democratic community" (IDC) as a model for campus residential living (which is still employed at the University of Connecticut where it was first created). Crookston defined the critical characteristics of such a community (much like Hage and Aiken's dynamic environment) as including shared power and decision making, open communications, flexibility, and organizational and individual symbiosis. Thus,

Crookston argued, "as the individual contributes to the enrichment of the community, so the community is able to enrich the individual" (p. 58). A crucial mediating factor in all of this, of course, is environmental scale or size, with large systems generally exhibiting more characteristics of a structured, static environment (or "bureaucracy") than smaller ones. The key to student learning and involvement in residence halls, regardless of size, is to create dynamic organizational structures that encourage participation and responsibility.

The degree to which an organized environment is static or dynamic can also affect the morale of participants in the setting, depending on individual differences. For example, consider a static classroom environment, where the professor makes all the decisions about the timing and content of what is taught (high centralization), where assignments are governed by highly specific and inflexible rules (high formalization), where few questions or comments are encouraged for fear of wasting time (high emphasis on production and efficiency), and where examinations assess simple recall of information (low complexity). That classroom environment may be comforting to some students at one level of development—for example, at the level of intellectual dualism (Perry, 1970) or dependent/conforming (Harvey, Hunt, and Schroder, 1961). But it may be very boring and unchallenging to other students with a different set of assumptions about what it means to learn—for example, those who fall in the categories of intellectual relativism (Perry, 1970) or independent/self-reliant (Harvey, Hunt, and Schroder, 1961). Various personality styles may respond differently to this same environment as well. Sensing types (Myers, 1980) or conventional types (Holland, 1985) might enjoy the routine and standardization of such a class, but the consequent high structure may frustrate intuitive and artistic types. As another example, student organizations structured around a hierarchical model of constitutionally based roles and powers may be less attractive to female students, who tend to emphasize the ethic of care and "connectedness" (Gilligan, 1982; Forrest, Hotelling, and Kuk, 1986).

The same sort of person-environment dynamic applies to understanding attraction and satisfaction of students in the residence hall setting. The overall degree of organizational structure in the hall, as is reflected in the way goals are set, rules implemented and enforced, policies decided, and resources expended, may or may not be compatible with the characteristics of the students living there. For example, residents who are not familiar with the fundamentals of organizational leadership and participation, or who are simply inexperienced, may not be immediately ready to assume the responsibilities of an intentional democratic community. A more highly structured organizational environment may be appropriate in that case. On the other hand, a more advanced student group, whose talents and styles have been tested in a variety of settings, may become disinterested and "turned off" by a highly structured system that allows for little student input and involvement. It is, therefore, critical for residence life professionals to have an accurate understanding of the developmental characteristics of residents as a source of information for encouraging an appropriate organizational environment.

In a discussion of organizational environment factors related to size, Moos (1986) drew attention to two tentative conclusions (among others) supported in the empirical research: (1) "As . . . group size increase[s], morale and attitudes become less positive, and absenteeism is more frequent" (p. 410), and (2) "Certain behavioral and attitudinal consequences occur when environments are 'undermanned' [see Wicker, 1973]. People perform more activities in undermanned settings and they are required to accept more positions of responsibility. These settings have a greater 'claim' on people, because they require more effort and because relatively more difficult and important tasks are assigned to the occupants. It is less likely that a person will achieve great proficiency at any one task, since each person must fulfill several tasks. Each person has greater functional importance in the setting, more responsibility, and a greater feeling of functional self-identity" (p. 408). Banning (1989, p. 59) concurred in his analysis of the impact of college environments on freshman students: "The point of manning theory is that the ratio of persons per setting is critical to what happens to the people within the setting. In the undermanned setting, people more frequently serve in responsible positions, engage in actions that are challenging, perform activities that are important to the setting, engage in a wide range of activities, see themselves as important and responsible for the setting, and work hard to maintain the function of the setting."

The college campus offers numerous illustrations of the organizational dynamics highlighted in these observations. "Fighting the bureaucracy" becomes a rallying cry for all too many students attempting to negotiate the barriers inevitable in the large organized systems of a modern university. Endless long lines, numbers instead of names, and forms in quadruplicate all take their toll on the human spirit at a time in students' lives when questions of identity and purpose (Chickering, 1969) demand, and are better served by, a high degree of personalism and support (Widick, Knefelkamp, and Parker, 1975). Even the overt goals of the academy—the development of intellect and reason—are jeopardized by the limitations of size. What are the chances of any individual student posing a question, expressing a comment, exchanging a point of view, or writing a position statement in a classroom with 600 students? What are the chances of any individual student assuming a position of responsibility in a residence hall where 900 students compete for only six available governance committee vacancies? The implications of this conclusion on organizational size are clear and consistent: bigger is not better when it comes to education. Perhaps it is no secret why large institutions tend to have higher attrition rates than smaller ones. The challenge to many institutions is to compensate for the problems of oversizing with the intentional development of smaller subenvironments—that is, residence hall units, student organizations, and class discussion sections—that more fully engage students in meaningful ways.

For example, at Iowa State University, a campus of over 26,000 students, a "house system" has been in effect for over forty years, where large residence halls are divided into smaller, more manageable living units ("houses") with sixty to eighty students. Each house has a distinctive name and separate governance structure that encourages and expects wide participation of the residents (Schuh, 1991).

Moos's conclusions illustrate another point about the relative size of an institution or, for that matter, of a residence hall, a class, or a student organization. An "undermanned" environment (Wicker, 1973) exists when there are too few people for the number of tasks to be accomplished. The opposite condition, an "overmanned" environment, exists when there are too many people for too few opportunities for meaningful involvement and achievement. Chickering (1969) identifies this as a condition of "redundancy." Generally speaking, large institutions, and large residence halls, tend to be "overmanned" and "redundant" and smaller institutions tend to be "undermanned." Consistent with Astin's (1984) observations about student involvement, smaller campuses tend to have a greater claim on students, just as small residence halls, small classes, or small organizations do, and the resultant sense of functional importance and functional self-identity is probably a significant factor in the higher retention rates experienced by these institutions. The importance of human-scale organization was also underscored in a recent study as a key feature of institutions that are perceived to be highly successful in encouraging a high quality of student involvement and learning in out-of-class experiences (Kuh, Schuh, Whitt, and Associates, 1991). A general implication for administrative practice here is that strategies must be employed to maintain manageable campus subenvironments where individuals can experience a sense of functional importance and self-identity. This is especially desirable in the residence hall setting, where functional importance is a critical developmental condition for undergraduates as they respond to the inevitable challenges of growth. The merits of this approach, particularly when combined with a special organizational focus such as a living-learning center, are well documented in the literature; it has been associated with better academic performance, a better social climate, a more intellectual atmosphere, and a higher student retention rate (Blimling, 1988). If colleges are to survive as dynamic educational institutions, the organizational structures of their various subunits, especially residence hall settings, must be examined in light of their ability to respond to changing circumstances and to the individual developmental needs of the students they serve (Strange, 1981, 1983).

Perceptual Models of Residence Environments

Perceptual models of the environment recognize that a consensus of individuals characterizing their environment constitutes a measure of environmental climate that, in turn, exerts a directional influence on behavior

(Moos, 1986). Simply stated, environments are defined by the collective perceptions of the individuals within them. Unlike the three previously described models, the perceptual approach focuses on the subjective view of the participant observer. Thus, an environment can be measured objectively as being 70°F, but may seem "warm" to one person and "cool" to another. Likewise, the same human aggregate may seem both "friendly" and "overbearing," depending on perceptual differences, or a high degree of formalization may be reassuring to one participant, yet confining to another. The key point demonstrated by these models is that perceptions of an environment are critical in understanding how individuals are likely to react to that environment.

Murray (1938), Stern (1970), and Pace and Stern (1958) are among those who established the foundational principles of this environmental approach. According to Stern (1970), an environmental "press" can be inferred from consensual self-reports of environmental activities by either participants ("beta press") or observers ("alpha press") of an environment. For example, if 90 out of 100 sampled residents report that students frequently spend time studying in their rooms, a strong "press toward academic achievement" might be inferred. The various identified "presses" in an environment may or may not correspond to individual participant's "needs," or those "organizational tendencies that seem to give unity and direction to a person's behavior" (Stern, 1970). For example, an academic achievement "need" is inferred from an individual's high level of studying and intellectual activities. A close correspondence (or congruence) between individual need and environmental press is said to be *anabolic*, or growth producing. A *catabolic* need-press combination, where significant dissonance exists between need and press, is growth inhibiting and contributes to dissatisfaction and turnover.

Pervin (1968), another perceptual theorist, focused on the importance of personal goals and self-concept in understanding an individual's perception of and response to an environment. According to his "transactional approach," human behavior can best be understood in terms of the interactions (cause-effect relationships) and transactions (reciprocal relationships) between the individual and the environment. Furthermore, high performance and satisfaction are associated with environments that tend to reduce the discrepancies between an individual's perceived actual self and perceived ideal self. Three basic assumptions underlie this model. First, "individuals find painful and unpleasant large discrepancies between their perceived actual selves and their perceived ideal selves." Second, "individuals are positively attracted toward objects in the perceived environment which hold potential for moving them toward their perceived ideal selves; conversely, individuals are negatively disposed toward stimuli that hold potential for moving them away from their ideal selves." Third, "similarity in regard to objects of importance to the individual is desirable where the individual has a low actual self/ideal self discrepancy and undesirable where the individual has a high actual self/ideal self discrepancy" (Walsh, 1973, p. 158).

Consider the example of an "undecided" student as an illustration of the dynamics of Pervin's first two assumptions. First of all, being undecided is difficult in a setting organized around academic and professional departments and where students often introduce themselves in terms of their majors. Not having selected a major may be tantamount to identity diffusion in the eyes of some. In such a case, the discrepancy between the actual self (that is, "undecided") and the ideal self (in this case, "decided") may be large and a source of pain and anxiety to the individual student. The longer the indecision persists, the greater the pressure from others to make a choice and the greater the anxiety experienced. According to Pervin's second assumption, then, an undecided student would be positively disposed toward an environment that would assist him or her in selecting a career major—for example, a Career Life Planning class—because this environment is likely to move the student toward his or her ideal self and therefore remove the source of anxiety associated with such discrepancies.

The third assumption offers an additional refinement of Sanford's (1966) classic prescriptions for challenge and support. According to Sanford's model, because of a natural tendency toward balance and stability (homeostasis), we need to be *challenged*, or placed in situations where we must generate responses not previously used, for growth to occur. Because change always involves an element of risk, such a challenge is more readily accepted under conditions of *support*, that is, personalism and structure. Pervin's third assumption suggests that the timing of challenge and support, or "similarity of objects of importance" to the individual, must be considered with respect to where students are in terms of meeting their personal goals ("ideal self"). When a student has reached an important set of goals, "similarity of objects of importance," or high support, is appropriate. When the discrepancy between actual self and ideal self is large, similarity of objects of importance in the environment—in other words, an overly supportive environment—would not sufficiently challenge that individual toward the goal of ideal self. Implicit in Pervins's assumptions is that individuals need accurate information about themselves (actual self) and a vision of what they want to be (ideal self) before they can judge the appropriateness or relevance of any given environment. Also implicit in Pervin's model is that individuals who have not yet defined an "ideal self" may be at risk in an environment, since they lack an important referent for judging the appropriateness of the setting. The higher incidence of attrition found among students who have not yet declared a major tends to support such a claim.

Moos (1979), a more recent perceptual theorist, offered a model of *social climate* that describes the nature and effect of various "environmental personalities." Social climate, according to Moos, is comprised of three sets of dimensions found in any environment: (1) *relationship dimensions*, which assess "the extent to which people are involved in the environment, the extent to which they support and help each other, and the extent to which there is spontaneity and free and open expression among them" (Moos, 1974, p. 11);

(2) *personal growth and development dimensions*, assessing the "basic directions along which personal growth and self-enhancement tend to occur . . . depending upon their [the environment's] underlying purposes and goals" (Moos, 1974, p. 13); and (3) *system maintenance and system change dimensions*, assessing "the extent to which the environment is orderly, clear in its expectations, maintains control and is responsive to change" (Moos, 1974, p. 14).

These three dimensions manifest themselves in specific ways depending on the environment being examined. For example, Moos (1979) identified ten aspects of residence hall environments important to understanding the environmental impact of specific residence units. Two aspects focus on relationship dimensions within living units:

> *Involvement*, the "degree of commitment to the house and residents [and] amount of interaction and feeling of friendship"
> *Emotional support*, or "manifest concern for others in the house, [the extent of] efforts to aid one another with academic and personal problems, [and] emphasis on open and honest communication" (p. 29)

Personal growth or goal orientation dimensions are reflected in five different aspects:

> *Independence*, the "emphasis on freedom and self-reliance versus socially proper and conformist behavior"
> *Traditional social organization*, the "stress on dating, going to parties, and other traditional heterosexual interactions"
> *Competition*, the "degree to which a wide variety of activities, such as dating and grades, are cast into a competitive framework"
> *Academic achievement*, the "prominence of strictly classroom and academic accomplishments and concerns"
> *Intellectuality*, the "emphasis on cultural, artistic, and other intellectual activities" (p. 29)

Finally, three aspects comprise the system maintenance and change dimensions of living units:

> *Order and organization*, the "amount of formal structure, neatness, and organization (rules, schedules, established procedures)"
> *Student influence*, or the "extent to which student residents formulate and enforce rules and control use of the money, selection of staff, roommates, and the like"
> *Innovation*, the "organizational and individual spontaneity of behaviors and ideas [and] number and variety of new activities" (p. 29)

Moos (1979) identified, by assessment with the University Residence Environment Scale (Moos and Gerst, 1974), six characteristic environments or "personalities" he attributed to various living groups: (1) *relationship oriented*—units characterized by a supportive relationship orientation that strongly values emotional support and involvement, with some stress on dating and cultural pursuits but little emphasis on doing new and different activities; (2) *traditionally socially oriented*—units that "give priority to dating, going to parties, and other traditional heterosexual interactions, as well as to aspects of formal structure and organization, such as rules, schedules, established procedures, and neatness" (p. 55); (3) *supportive achievement oriented*—units that place "their highest emphasis on the relationship dimensions of involvement and emotional support and on the personal growth dimension of academic achievement [in a] noncompetitive context [but with] very little focus on independence" (p. 56); (4) *competition oriented*—where there is "high stress on competition [with] very little involvement or emotional support" (pp. 56–57); (5) *independence oriented*—units that "encourage a wide diversity of student behaviors without specific social sanction and do not value socially proper or conformist behavior" (p. 57); and (6) *intellectually oriented*—relatively rare units consisting "primarily of theme houses and living-learning and cooperative units composed largely of students in the humanities and social sciences" (p. 58) and emphasizing intellectuality and independence. Moos found that male units tended to be more competition oriented, female units more traditionally socially oriented, and coed units independence and intellectually oriented. Supportive achievement– and relationship-oriented units tend to be almost exclusively female or coed (Moos, 1979). Even architectural aspects seem to have an effect, with units comprised of a greater proportion of single rooms more oriented toward competition and less toward supportive achievement, independence, intellectuality, or relationships.

Moos (1986) highlights two empirically supported conclusions related to the social climate of campus environments. First, "students feel more secure, interested, and satisfied in classrooms that emphasize involvement, affiliation, and support" (p. 414). Second, "colleges that emphasize relationship dimensions (faculty-student interaction, peer cohesion) have a positive impact on students" (p. 414). The implications of these two conclusions are obvious: institutional environments (including residence halls) most satisfying, secure, and productive to humans are those that emphasize involvement, affiliation, and other relationship dimensions. This is particularly true of educational institutions, where some degree of transformation of personal identity is almost always an expected outcome for students, whatever their age. Transformations, whether from late adolescence to young adulthood, from full-time homemaker to full-time career, or from a job in one field to a career in another, all contain elements of risk. Changing goals, unexpected barriers, or challenging opportunities are less difficult to negotiate in a more personalized atmosphere of individualized acceptance and support. Consistent with the *Student Personnel Point of View* (American Council on Education, 1937, 1949), colleges that emphasize relationships and involvement, both within and outside the classroom, from admissions and orientation, through residence life and student organizations, to placement and alumni development, are those that most likely attract, satisfy, sustain, and retain students to a greater degree than those institutions that ignore such dimensions.

A final set of perceptual ideas that enhance understanding of human environments comes from the literature on organizational culture. Growing attention has been focused recently on applying concepts of organizational and institutional culture to understanding colleges and universities (Kuh and Whitt, 1988). "Culture," with roots in anthropology, sociology, and social psychology, is inherently a perceptual construct, in that the culture of an environment reflects the assumptions, beliefs, and values inhabitants of that setting use to interpret and understand the meaning of events and actions. Schein (1985, p. 9) refers to culture as "a pattern of basic assumptions—invented, discovered, or developed by a given group as it learns to cope with its problems of external adaptation and internal integration—that has worked well enough to be considered valid and, therefore, to be taught to new members as the correct way to perceive, think, and feel in relation to those problems." Culture, then, is essentially "a social construction" (Chaffee and Tierney, 1988, p. 10) and is reflected in various artifacts, including traditions, stories, ceremonies, history, myths, heroines and heroes, interactions among members, policies and practices, symbols, mission, and philosophy.

In the earlier illustration of Williams Hall, the spirit and values of Dorothy Williams permeate and sustain the traditions and practices of its residents. Culture serves to solve group problems of both external adaptation and internal integration (Schein, 1985)—that is, the question of what a group must do to survive in a changing environment and what it must do to maintain internal relationships and functioning. This calls to mind the play *Fiddler on the Roof*. In response to the question, How do we keep our balance?, the character Tevye says emphatically, "That I can tell you in one word . . . Tradition!" Problems of *external adaptation* include tasks of establishing a core mission, specific goals derived from that mission, a means to attain the goals, criteria for measuring success, and strategies for remediation when goals are not being met. *Internal integration* tasks include establishing and maintaining a common language and set of concepts, determining criteria for membership, deciding how power is used, delimiting relationships, discerning the nature of rewards and punishments, and defining an ideology that helps the group face inexplicable events (Schein, 1985).

From the paradigm of culture, it can be argued that residence halls are themselves cultures that assist occupants—staff as well as students—in making meaning of the college experience. In effect, the residence hall culture is a powerful tool in socializing students to the goals and purposes of higher education, what it means to be a member of a community, and how to go about the business of being a college student. At times, these cultures are at cross-purposes with the educational goals of the institution—for example, in the case of the stereotypical "zoo" or "animal house" culture, where students place a premium on disruptive and hedonistic activities (Moffatt, 1989). At other times, residence halls are expressly supportive of institutional goals, as in the case of an honors hall or living-learning program.

Understanding residence halls from a cultural perspective entails application of the tools of qualitative inquiry—personal interviews, participant observation, and document analysis. The meaning of various events, personalities, regulations, programs, traditions, symbols, stories, and interactions must be discovered, described, and understood, from the perspective of the members of those environments, as reflections of a core set of beliefs and assumptions that is organizational culture. For example, at the University of Michigan, it is important to understand the assumptions of selection, membership, and participation in Martha Cook Hall, where formal sit-down dinners, rather than the more usual cafeteria-style meals, are regular fare for its all-female occupants. As another example, at the University of Virginia, fourth-year students vie for the prestige of living in one of forty-seven nine by eleven-foot single rooms on "the Lawn," forsaking the convenience of a personal bathroom, as recognition for their academic achievements and overall contributions to the university. Finally, at Morehouse College in Atlanta, the room numbers assigned to Martin Luther King, Jr., and other noted "Morehouse men" as undergraduates in Graves Hall are committed to memory by many students. Participant perceptions of situations of this type are an important source of information for designing responsive educational environments, and educators must be particularly sensitive to any discrepancies between their views of the institution and those of students.

Assessing Residence Environments

Assessment of the characteristics of campus residence environments entails the application of a variety of measurement techniques, both quantitative and qualitative, from each of the four perspectives reviewed. Assessment of the physical features of a residence hall must be done in the context of program philosophy, mission, and purpose. Various conditions of density, privacy, spatial arrangement, distance, color, light, noise, ventilation, and flexibility can either enhance or inhibit certain behaviors and outcomes in the living environment, the consequences of which may or may not be desirable. To what extent are relationships and sense of community affected by the building shape and design? What features seem to promote a sense of community? What aspects inhibit community? What about issues of privacy and personal identity? In what ways do the facility's design features promote a sense of ownership and "territory"? Are the amenities sufficiently flexible to allow personalization of space and individual expression? Which aspects of the physical environment can be changed and which must be adjusted to? How do the residents respond to these various features? These are the types of assessment questions that can be posed in the context of the residence hall's mission and purpose. Answers to these questions will obviously differ depending on the context and the extent to which other aspects of the particular residence hall environment, such as human aggregate and organizational features, serve to compensate for or accentuate aspects of the physical design. For example, with a "theme house" like an athletic hall, an international hall, or a sorority or fraternity, where emphasis is placed on attracting a more homogeneous aggregate of residents, developing a sense of community may be easy regardless of the physical design, because of the accentuation and reinforcement of the dominant characteristics of the people in the environment.

The essential task of assessing human aggregates is to accurately describe as many features as possible of the individuals in an environment and then to discern the dominance of any one or several features that may be present. In addition to the typical demographic information that is usually available through institutional records—gender, ethnic identification, birthdate, hometown, major, grade-point average, and so on—a number of quantitative measures of various personality dimensions have been useful for understanding human aggregates. Among these are the Strong Interest Inventory, a 325-item, self-report questionnaire measuring vocational-personal interest with respect to the six Holland vocational interest types described earlier, and the Myers-Briggs Type Inventory (Myers and Mc-Caulley, 1985), a 126-item, self-report questionnaire assessing personality type with reference to four dichotomous dimensions of functioning, also described earlier. Both of these instruments and their applications have aroused considerable interest among researchers and practitioners; they can be used for a variety of purposes, including roommate matching and staff development (Schroeder, 1979a, 1979b; Schroeder, Warner, and Malone, 1980; Kalsbeek and others, 1982). For that matter, any psychometric tool that is amenable to the description and evaluation of individual persons, whatever the dimension(s) being measured, is appropriate for assessing the aggregate characteristics of an environment. Determining if any patterns of dominant characteristics exist is essential to understanding the potential effects of the aggregate on any given individual within the environment.

From an organizational perspective, a number of quantitative assessment tools have been applied to business organizations and reported primarily in the literature on the sociology of complex organizations (Price, 1972; Price and Mueller, 1986). Most of these materials would require some adaptation to the specific setting but would be conceptually appropriate for guiding an assessment of the various organizational structures described earlier. For example, to measure the organizational environment of a student affairs division or specific office, Strange and Heineman (1984) created the

Organizational Dynamics Questionnaire, based on the conceptual foundations outlined in Hage and Aiken's (1970) model of complex organizations and adapted to assess the views of student affairs staff. A qualitative approach to understanding organizations can be found, for example, in Schein (1985), which offers a comprehensive review of the culture and leadership aspects of organized environments, including several chapters on assessment methods and procedures.

The perceptual models have generated several tools and approaches for assessing residential environments. The University Residence Environment Scales (URES) was developed by Moos and Gerst (1974) for purposes of measuring the ten aspects of living-group social climate described earlier. The URES, a 100-item, true-and-false, self-report instrument is designed for use in three different forms. Form R (real) assesses occupants' perceptions of the current social climate dimensions of the living-group setting, which may focus on an individual floor or an entire residence hall. Form I (ideal) of the URES assesses occupants' perceptions of their ideal living-group social climate. Finally, Form E (expected) is appropriate for assessing potential occupants' expectations about what it will be like to live in a particular setting. All of these forms are constructed in the same parallel format, and they can be used separately or in combination to address a variety of perspectives and concerns. For example, examination of scale discrepancies between Form R and Form I can yield clues as to what aspects require attention to increase satisfaction and functioning of current residents. If residents score high on the Form I emotional support subscale but low on that same subscale as measured by Form R, this may imply the need for some staff intervention in terms of creating programs and activities that will contribute to a higher degree of emotional support. Readministration of Form R at a subsequent point in time and examination of what discrepancies have been reduced can provide useful evaluative information as to the effects of the interventions.

Another interesting use is a combination of the Form E and Form R forms. Understanding what students expect to find in a particular living group can be an important source of information for planning and anticipating their arrival. For example, if students have high expectations for student influence and innovation, perhaps various mechanisms and programs can be created to engage their involvement in the design of the residence organizational environment prior to their coming to campus. Again, the subsequent administration of Form R and the examination of any subscale discrepancy between the two forms (E and R) can alert staff as to whether expectations are being met.

Finally, each of these forms can be used alone, with a focus on potential interunit and intraunit subgroup differences. For instance, does one residence hall differ from another? Do the residents of one floor have different expectations of these dimensions of social climate than another floor? Do males describe a different ideal living-group social climate than do females?

Are there any differences, real, ideal, or expected, related to racial or ethnic membership? What differences, if any, are related to academic major? What about those who drop out; did they come with expectations and ideals that differed from those who persisted? All of these various perspectives provide important information for student affairs and residence life professionals to understand how their constituents perceive and interact with the living environments they create.

A host of materials addressing the particulars of qualitative and naturalistic assessment have appeared in the literature and contribute to an understanding of these environmental issues (Goetz and LeCompte, 1984; Lincoln and Guba, 1985; Marshall and Rossman, 1989; Merriam, 1988; Miles and Huberman, 1984; Patton, 1990; Schein, 1985). A case illustration of the type of assessment information that can be assembled from such an approach is found in Moffatt (1989), where an anthropologist applied his craft over a period of time in describing and understanding the dynamics of several living-group units on the campus of Rutgers University. One advantage of these qualitative methods—that is, personal interviews, focus groups, and observations—is that they allow assessment of the complex interactions between participants and the various environmental components. Even more important, they make it possible to uncover meaning ascribed by members of the environment rather than how much or how little of a particular, predetermined dimension is present in the environment. By virtue of their professional training in counseling and interpersonal dynamics, many residence life professionals have a ready-made set of skills that can be, and *are* in the course of their day-to-day work, put to use doing qualitative assessment on an informal basis.

Regardless of methods or specific tools used (see Huebner and Lawson, 1990, for a current review of additional instruments and methods), environmental assessment, both formal and informal, is an important tool residence life professionals can use to be more responsive to the students they serve and to create campus living environments that are educationally alive. With the influx of new students each year, the aggregate characteristics of a residence hall are likely to change, as are the collective perceptions of the inhabitants with respect to the hall's physical features, peer environment, and organizational structures. What may work one year may not work in subsequent years. All the more important is the regular application of environmental assessment, as a form of introduction to the residence environment and as part of the processes of formative and summative evaluation throughout the year.

Student Development and Campus Residence Halls

If a typical college student spends about forty-eight hours a week attending class and studying, as Boyer (1987) observed, a good portion of the remaining time for most traditional-age students, above and beyond the usual fifty hours sleeping, is spent in a residence hall pursuing the lessons of human interaction, communication, individual differences, and communal living. The residence hall is an exceptionally powerful educational environment, perhaps even more so than the classroom, in terms of the residual effects of college attendance. Considering the general education goals espoused by most colleges—for example, "development of a personal value system"—the residence hall is unmatched in terms of the potential it has as a learning environment, particularly during the first year (Zeller, Fidler, and Barefoot, 1991). In these theories and concepts about human environments lie important clues about how to tap that potential in creating meaningful educational environments (Strange and King, 1990).

Moos (1979) identified five key strategies for applying theories about human environments in an educational setting. The first of these applications involves using theories as conceptual frameworks for organizing information about campus environments and for giving feedback to students and soliciting it from them. Each of these environmental perspectives offers a set of ideas that explains some aspect of how individuals interact with and are affected by human environments. For example, communicating to prospective and current students the nature of the physical, aggregate, and organizational features of the residence hall they will occupy, or explaining to them the dynamics of the social climate dimensions they are likely to encounter, may better educate them about the aspects of the environment that will have a significant effect on their satisfaction.

Too often information is collected from students but is rarely fed back to them for purposes of discussion and insight as to potential action and understanding. Using these environmental models to communicate to students their collective perceptions of their respective living environments can prove helpful in their initial adjustment to college. For example, a residence hall director could administer the URES (Form E or Form I) (Moos and Gerst, 1974) to assigned residents prior to their arrival on campus or during the orientation process, for purposes of understanding students' expectations of what on-campus living will be like. This report or profile can be an important source of information for organizing programming that will meet their needs or for correcting those expectations that may be unrealistic. Six to eight weeks into the term, following up that assessment with the URES (Form R), or simply engaging in a guided group discussion of the URES subscale framework and definitions, can help identify sources of discrepancy between what students expected, or ideally sought, and what they found. This simple give-and-take of information and feedback, which can be organized from floor to floor, accomplishes several important learning goals: (1) students learn about the nature and design of their environment in terms of a conceptual framework that will continue to prove helpful to them as they make decisions about living environments in the future; (2) students learn how they individually may differ from and share perspectives with their group of peers on what they perceive to be the desirable aspects of a living environment; (3) residence hall staff members gain an important source of information for purposes of planning and programming in the discrepancies students perceive between what they expected and what they found to be the case; and (4) students learn that staff value their perspective as one source for planning a living-learning experience and that they must become involved in the processes of community change and goal setting.

A second application of these theories of human environments involves promoting and evaluating environmental change (Moos, 1979). This knowledge based on human environments, Moos argued, is helpful in facilitating and assessing the consequences of environmental change on campus, whether that involves changing social climate or changing architectural and organizational characteristics. Campus change is sometimes unexpected and at other times intentional. It can be both revolutionary and evolutionary. The importance of these environmental models lies in their descriptive value for monitoring the nature and direction of those changes. In concert with some of the established environmental process models, such as ecosystem design (Aulepp and Delworth, 1976; Huebner, 1979; Western Interstate Commission for Higher Education, 1973), these environmental models can serve as a powerful tool for facilitating desired changes. For example, some campuses are turning to the living-learning center as a model for the design of residence environments. What is an appropriate model for implementing such a program or design as thoughts are given to staff and resident selection, programming, and organization? A review of Moos's (1979) six living-group social climate profiles might suggest that an emphasis on the dimensions of an intellectually oriented unit—that is, high levels of involvement, emotional support, intellectuality, student influence, and innovation—would likely achieve the living-group goals of a living-learning center. Such a profile can serve as an environmental template to guide the development of a purposeful educational environment.

A third application, Moos (1979) suggested, involves implementing educational consultation. The lives of many students are significantly influenced during the college years by their participation in one or more campus groups, whether it be through a formal student organization or a residence hall floor. In these groups they learn the lessons of interdependence and group life, critical tools for later survival and success in the world of work. It is also in this context that many student affairs educators have the opportunity to do their "teaching." As in the case of the living-learning center example above, the framework provided by these environmental models can be helpful in sorting out issues of group functioning and in responding to the needs of students who participate in them. Also similar to the earlier example, where students' expectations of a residence hall environment were assessed and fed back to them, application of these models accomplishes several important learning goals. Students learn about the nature of effective group environments, they learn how their views compare with others, and they learn that administrators value and expect their involvement in making decisions about their learning environments.

A fourth type of application of this environmental knowledge base involves formulating ecologically relevant case descriptions (Moos, 1979). Students arrive on campus as part of an intact life ecology, bringing with them interacting systems of family, peers, culture, and hometown. To that they join the existing campus ecology, which usually includes a residence hall environment, various classroom environments, a social or task group environment, and often a work environment, all distinct settings addressed by Moos's (1974) social climate model. The various applications of this model offer a framework for resident directors, advisers, and counselors to understand more fully the nature of each student's ecology. For students experiencing transitional adjustment problems, for example, Moos's social climate model could be useful in cataloguing specific concerns and issues relevant to personal functioning in a variety of environments. Is the issue one of inadequate emotional support (a relationship dimension) or limited opportunities for student influence and participation (a system maintenance and change dimension)? Are the personal growth and development goals of the student's residence environment compatible with those encouraged by the classroom or work environment? How do the relationship dimensions differ across the various environments the student interacts with, and how do they affect his or her satisfaction and stability?

The impact of these environmental components on a student's behavior is also an important consideration. Moos (1979) delineated five different though related notions of the way the environment works; these vary on a positive-negative continuum. At one end are powerful positive environments that (1) stimulate and challenge, facilitating personal and social growth, or environments that (2) release individual capacities, supporting and allowing behavior to occur. In the middle are environments that simply (3) select and favor certain organisms. At the other end are powerful negative environments that (4) limit, resist, and inhibit, and environments that are (5) actively stressful. In terms of understanding students, it is helpful to distinguish between concerns that are actively stressful, requiring immediate relief—that is, a powerful negative influence—and those that are a matter of normal anxiety and frustration in response to a developmental challenge, a powerful positive influence. such approaches can help those who work closely with students build a more complete and relevant picture of how they are adapting to and coping with the campus environment.

Finally, Moos (1979) examined the implications of enhancing environmental competence. In this fifth application, Moos talked about teaching students how to create, select, and transcend environments, how to maximize person-environment congruence when support is the goal, or how to seek an appropriate amount of challenge and incongruence when the goal is personal growth. The overall intent is to help students understand more fully the impact of the environment on their lives. Perhaps no other place on campus equals the residence hall setting in terms of the opportunities it presents to learn the lessons of community building, tolerance, interdependence, and cooperation, all important keys to a future society that promises growing diversity and individual differences. Enhancing environmental competence is a goal that encompasses the basic purposes and outcomes of higher education. From a developmental perspective, the typical entering student might be characterized by a simplistic, categorical view of the world, dependent on external authorities for certainty, and lacking both the motivation and skill for self-directed learning. This view might reflect Perry's (1970) "dualist" or Harvey, Hunt, and Schroder's (1961) "dependent/conforming" stage. It can be argued that such a posture is incompatible and ineffective in a world environment where little is certain and change is constant. Through a general education core, students are challenged to examine the world environment in all its contexts, historical, cultural, physical, and interpersonal, and to develop the basic tools of inquiry and communication to be able to pursue further examination of a select part of that environment through completion of an academic major. The college outcome research consistently supports the finding that students who persist in this process emerge with a more complex view of the world, are more appreciative of its subtleties, and are more capable of sorting through the maze of opinions, facts, and interpretations necessary for making adequate judgments about life and the environment surrounding them (Kitchener, King, Wood, and Davison, 1989; Pascarella and Terenzini, 1991).

Understanding Environments:
Essential for Competent Residence Life Practice

In summary, the literature on human environments indicates that a more complete understanding of the dynamics and consequences of any environment lies in an examination and assessment of four key aspects: (1) the physical features of the setting, (2) the collective characteristics of the people within, (3) the organized structures associated with the goals of the setting, and (4) the subjective perceptions and interpretations of the participants. Collectively, these four interactive elements can serve as a framework for assessing and describing an environment, as well as a basis for implementing environmental change. The challenge to higher education professionals today is the development of institutional learning environments that encourage developmental processes in students. At the very least, those aspects of the college environment that are actively stressful or limiting and resisting ought to be changed or eliminated. However, the ultimate goal is to be a powerful positive influence in students' lives, where the campus and its various subenvironments stimulate and challenge them individually to personal and social growth. Student affairs educators, and in particular those whose "classroom" incorporates the mission and design of a campus residence hall, with their focus on the whole student, their professional commitment to human development, and their knowledge of these developmental processes in educational environments, can play a critical role in bringing this perspective to the campus community.

References

American Council on Education. *The Student Personnel Point of View.* American Council on Education Studies, series 1, vol. 1, no. 3. Washington, D.C.: American Council on Education, 1937.

American Council on Education. *The Student Personnel Point of View.* (Rev. ed.) American Council on Education Studies, series 6, no. 13. Washington, D.C.: American Council on Education, 1949.

Anchors, S., Schroeder, C., and Jackson, S. *Making Yourself at Home: A Practical Guide to Restructuring and Personalizing Your Residence Hall Environment.* Washington, D.C.: ACPA Media, 1978.

Astin, A. W. "An Empirical Characterization of Higher Educational Institutions. *Journal of Educational Psychology,* 1962, *53,* 224–235.

Astin, A. W. *The College Environment.* Washington, D.C.: American Council on Education, 1968.

Astin, A. W. "Student Involvement: A Developmental Theory for Higher Education." *Journal of College Student Personnel,* 1984, *25,* 297–308.

Astin, A. W., and Holland, J. L. "The Environmental Assessment Technique: A Way to Measure College Environments." *Journal of Educational Psychology,* 1961, *52,* 308–316.

Astin, A. W., and Panos, R. *The Educational and Vocational Development of College Students.* Washington, D.C.: American Council on Education, 1969.

Aulepp, L., and Delworth, U. *Training Manual for an Ecosystem Model: Assessing and Designing Campus Environments.* Boulder, Colo.: Western Interstate Commission for Higher Education, 1976.

Banning, J. H. "Impact of College Environments on Freshman Students." In M. L. Upcraft, J. N. Gardner, and Associates, *The Freshman Year Experience: Helping Students Survive and Succeed in College.* San Francisco: Jossey-Bass, 1989.

Blimling, G. S. "The Influence of College Residence Halls on Students: A Meta-Analysis of the Empirical Research, 1966–1985." Unpublished doctoral dissertation, Ohio State University, 1988.

Boyer, E. L. *College: The Undergraduate Experience in America.* New York: Harper-Collins, 1987.

Chaffee, E. E., and Tierney, W. G. *Collegiate Culture and Leadership Strategies.* New York: American Council on Education/Macmillan, 1988.

Chickering, A. W. *Education and Identity.* San Francisco: Jossey-Bass, 1969.

Crookston, B. B. "A Design for an Intentional Democratic Community." In D. A. DeCoster and P. Mable (eds.), *Student Development and Education in College*

Residence Halls. Washington, D.C.: American College Personnel Association, 1974.

Ender, K. L., Kane, N., Mable, P., and Strohm, M. *Creating Community in Residence Halls*. Washington, D.C.: ACPA Media, 1980.

Etzioni, A. *Modern Organizations* Englewood Cliffs, N.J.: Prentice Hall, 1964.

Festinger, L., Schachter, S., and Back, K. *Social Pressures in Informal Groups*. New York: HarperCollins, 1950.

Forrest, L., Hotelling, K., and Kuk, L. "The Elimination of Sexism in the University Environment." Paper delivered at the 2nd annual symposium on Student Development Through Campus Ecology, Pingree Park, Colo., July 1986. (ED 267 348)

Gilligan, C. *In a Different Voice: Psychological Theory and Women's Development*. Cambridge, Mass.: Harvard University Press, 1982.

Goetz, J. P., and LeCompte, M. D. *Ethnography and Qualitative Design in Educational Research*. Orlando, Fla.: Academic Press, 1984.

Hage, J., and Aiken, M. *Social Change in Complex Organizations*. New York: Random House, 1970.

Harvey, O. J., Hunt, D. E., and Schroder, H. M. *Conceptual Systems and Personality Organization*. New York: Wiley, 1961.

Heilweil, M. "The Influence of Dormitory Architecture on Residence Behavior." *Environment and Behavior*, 1973, *5*, 377–412.

Holland, J. L. *Making Vocational Choices: A Theory of Personally and Work Environments*. (2nd ed.) Englewood Cliffs, N.J.: Prentice Hall, 1985.

Huebner, L. A. (ed.). *Redesigning Campus Environments*. New Directions for Student Services, no. 8. San Francisco: Jossey-Bass, 1979.

Huebner, L. A. and Lawson, J. M. "Understanding and Assessing College Environments." In D. G. Creamer and Associates, *College Student Development: Theory and Practice for the 1990s*. Alexandria, Va.: American College Personnel Association, 1990.

Kalsbeek, D., and others. "Balancing Challenge and Support: A Study of Degrees of Similarity in Suitemate Personality Type and Perceived Differences in Challenge and Support in a Residence Hall Environment." *Journal of College Student Personnel*, 1982, *23*, 434–442.

Kitchener, K. S., King, P. M., Wood, P. K., and Davison, M. L. "Sequentiality and Consistency in the Development of Reflective Judgment: A Six-Year Longitudinal Study." *Journal of Applied Developmental Psychology*, 1989, *10*, 73–95.

Kuh, G. D., Schuh, J. H., Whitt, E. J., and Associates. *Involving Colleges: Successful Approaches to Fostering Student Learning and Development Outside the Classroom*. San Francisco: Jossey-Bass, 1991.

Kuh, G. D., and Whitt, E. J. *The Invisible Tapestry: Cultures in American Colleges and Universities*. ASHE-ERIC Higher Education Report Series, no. 1. Washington, D.C.: Association for the Study of Higher Education, 1988.

Lincoln, Y. S., and Guba, E. G. *Naturalistic Inquiry*. Newbury Park, Calif.: Sage, 1985.

Marshall, C., and Rossman, G. B. (1989). *Designing Qualitative Research*. Newbury Park, Calif.: Sage, 1989.

Merriam, S. B. *Case Study Research in Education: A Qualitative Approach*. San Francisco: Jossey-Bass, 1988.

Michelson, W. *Man and His Urban Environment: A Sociological Approach*. Reading, Mass.: Addison-Wesley, 1970.

Miles, M. B., and Huberman, A. M. *Qualitative Data Analysis: A Sourcebook of New Methods*. Newbury Park, Calif.: Sage, 1984.

Moffatt, M. *Coming of Age in New Jersey: College and American Culture*. New Brunswick, N.J.: Rutgers University Press, 1989.

Moos, R. H. *The Social Climate Scales: An Overview*. Palo Alto, Calif.: Consulting Psychologists Press, 1974.

Moos, R. H. *Evaluating Educational Environments: Procedures, Measures, Findings, and Policy Implications*. San Francisco: Jossey-Bass, 1979.

Moos, R. H. *The Human Context: Environmental Determinants of Behavior*. Malabar, Fla: Krieger, 1986.

Moos, R. H., and Gerst, M. *The University Residence Environment Scale Manual*. Palo Alto, Calif.: Consulting Psychologists Press, 1974.

Murray, H. *Exploration in Personality*. New York: Oxford University Press, 1938.

Myers, I. B. *Gifts Differing*. Palo Alto, Calif.: Consulting Psychologists Press, 1980.

Myers, I. B., and McCaulley, M. H. *Manual: A Guide to the Development and Use of the Myers-Briggs Type Indicator*. Palo Alto, Calif.: Consulting Psychologists Press, 1985.

Pace, C. R., and Stern, G. G. "An Approach to the Measurement of Psychological Characteristics of College Environments." *Journal of Educational Psychology*, 1958, *49*, 269–277.

Pascarella, E. T., and Terenzini, P. T. *How College Affects Students: Findings and Insights from Twenty Years of Research*. San Francisco: Jossey-Bass, 1991.

Patton, M. Q. *Qualitative Evaluation and Research Methods*. (2nd ed.) Newbury Park, Calif.: Sage, 1990.

Perry, W. G. *Forms of Intellectual and Ethical Development in the College Years: A Scheme*. Troy, Mo.: Holt, Rinehart & Winston, 1970.

Pervin, L. "Performance and Satisfaction as a Function of Individual-Environment Fit." *Psychological Bulletin*, 1968, *69*, 56–68.

Price, J. L. *Handbook of Organizational Measurement*. Lexington, Mass.: Heath, 1972.

Price, J. L., and Mueller, C. W. *Handbook of Organizational Measurement*. Marshfield, Mass.: Pitman, 1986.

Sanford, N. *Self and Society: Social Change and Individual Development*. New York: Atherton Press, 1966.

Schein, E. H. *Organizational Culture and Leadership: A Dynamic View*. San Francisco: Jossey-Bass, 1985.

Schroeder, C. C. "Designing Ideal Staff Environments Through Milieu Management." *Journal of College Student Personnel*, 1979a, *20*, 129–135.

Schroeder, C. C. "Territoriality: Conceptual and Methodological Issues for Residence Educators." *Journal of College and University Housing*, 1979b, *8*, 9–15.

Schroeder, C. C., Warner, R., and Malone, D. R. "Effects of Assignment of Living Units by Personality Types on Environmental Perceptions and Student Development." *Journal of College Student Personnel*, 1980, *21*, 443–449.

Schuh, J. H. "Making a Large University Feel Small: The Iowa State University Story." In G. D. Kuh and J. H. Schuh (eds.), *The Role and Contribution of Student Affairs in Involving Colleges*. Washington, D.C.: National Association of Student Personnel Administrators, 1991.

Stern, G. G. *People in Context: Measuring Person-Environment Congruence in Education and Industry*. New York: Wiley, 1970.

Strange, C. C. "Organizational Barriers to Student Development." *NASPA Journal*, 1981, *19*, 12–20.

Strange, C. C. "Human Development Theory and Administrative Practice in Student Affairs: Ships Passing in the Daylight?" *NASPA Journal*, 1983, *21*, 2–8.

Strange, C. C., and Heineman, D. "An Empirical Analysis of Organizational Dynamics, Staff Morale, and Press Toward Innovation in Student Affairs Units." Unpublished manuscript, Department of Higher Education and Student Affairs, Bowling Green State University, 1984.

Strange, C. C., and King, P. "The Professional Practice of Student Development." In D. G. Creamer and Associates, *College Student Development: Theory and Practice for the 1990s*. Alexandria, Va.: American College Personnel Association, 1990.

Walsh, W. B. *Theories of Person-Environment Interaction: Implications for the College Student*. Iowa City, Iowa: American College Testing Program, 1973.

Western Interstate Commission for Higher Education. *The Ecosystem Model: Designing Campus Environments*. Boulder, Colo.: Western Interstate Commission for Higher Education, 1973.

Wicker, A. W. "Undermanning Theory and Research: Implications for the Study of Psychological and Behavioral Effects of Excess Populations." *Representative Research in Social Psychology*, 1973, *4*, 185–206.

Widick, C., Knefelkamp, L., and Parker, C. "The Counselor as Developmental Instructor." *Counselor Education and Supervision*, 1975, *14*, 286–296.

Zeller, W. J., Fidler, D. S., and Barefoot, B. O. *Residential Life Programs and the First-Year Experience*. Monograph Series, no. 5. Columbia, S.C.: National Resource Center for the Freshman Year Experience, 1991.

Chapter Six

======

A Brief History of Collegiate Housing

Charles F. Frederiksen

Almost from the beginning of American higher education, some form of student housing has existed. Housing and residential life programs have grown with higher education and have become professionalized just as other areas of student affairs have. This chapter traces the development of higher education in America and describes how housing programs fit into the educational picture (or how, during some periods, they faced attempts at eradication). The evolution of student housing as a profession is chronicled, and the professional and student organizations that have promoted that development are acknowledged.

Evolution of Student Housing in the United States

The roots of residential education are found in the universities of Europe, which date back to the twelfth century. During these earlier centuries, two basic educational systems emerged that have had a major impact on American higher education — the English and German systems.

The English educational system is represented by the universities of

Oxford and Cambridge. This system is based on residential colleges committed to the education and development of the total student. Faculty and
students share time and lodgings during out-of-class hours as well as coming
together during formal instruction.

The German educational system is based on instruction and research.
In earlier periods, facilities for housing and food service were not provided
on campus. Students were expected to make their own private living arrangements in rooming and boarding houses in the city, while the university
concentrated its efforts on creating the finest centers for scholarship in
Europe.

Influence of the English Educational System

In the United States, the history of collegiate housing began with the history
of higher education in general. Early American higher education was patterned after the colleges of Oxford and Cambridge, beginning with the
founding of Harvard College in 1636. Because many of the leading citizens of
early New England were alumni of Oxford and Cambridge, it was a predictable decision to pattern Harvard after these colleges. The English pattern of
the residence unit being the center of both informal and formal education
became the organizational standard of the American college. Other factors
were also important in the support of the residential college system. According to Cowley (1934) and Shay (1964), students of higher education during
the colonial period were very young, they typically had to travel long distances to reach the few existing colleges, and their parents were supportive of
having them under the disciplinary supervision of college officials. In addition, the supply of rooming houses in the small communities in which the
colleges were located was inadequate to meet the needs of the college
population. The residence unit provided the atmosphere in which a social
organization could be built around the students and faculty. Thus, the
residence hall was essential to the pre–Civil War American college for both
philosophical and practical reasons. This organizational structure gave rise
on American campuses to the in loco parentis approach, which involves
regulation or supervision by administrative officers and faculty of a college
acting in the place of a parent.

The English residential concept continued to shape American colleges
until about the time of the Civil War. This period was the first of three phases
in the development of student housing in the United States.

Influence of the German Educational System

The second phase was relatively short, lasting from the Civil War until the
early 1900s. During this period, the German influence flourished in the
United States.

Cowley (1934) suggests that by the nineteenth century, the residence unit had not fulfilled its purpose of being an extension of the classroom, but rather was only a shelter for students. There were also many student-faculty conflicts and student rebellions during the first half of the nineteenth century, resulting in a temporary decline in residence hall popularity and effectiveness as an educational tool.

A number of educators returned from German universities in the mid-nineteenth century and popularized the German belief that housing students was not the responsibility of the institution. During the latter half of the nineteenth century, several major American colleges were led by very strong presidents who denounced residence halls as inappropriate and a waste of money. These leading educators included Wayland of Brown in 1842, Barnard of Columbia in 1855, Tappan of Michigan in 1852, and Eliot of Harvard in 1869. In his first annual report to the Michigan board of regents, President Tappan (1853, pp. 11–12) commented as follows: "The dormitory system is objectionable in itself. By withdrawing young men from the influence of domestic circles and forming them into a separate community, they are often led to contract evil habits, and are prone to fall into disorderly conduct. The difficulties of maintaining a proper discipline are thus greatly increased. It is a mere remnant of the monkish cloisters of the middle ages, still retained in England indeed, but banished from the Universities of Germany." Presidents Barnard and Eliot also believed residence halls were not vital to a university. These presidents led their institutions away from the collegiate heritage toward their view of the university of the future.

In the process, residential education declined. These educational leaders believed student life should be left to develop in its own way without interference from the institution. This contradicted the traditional view that college students need to be supervised. Tappan and Eliot believed in treating students as adults. Adults were expected to make their own housing arrangements; therefore, students should too. The practice of in loco parentis declined in these institutions during this time.

The primary purposes of these leading universities were teaching and research—as in the German system. According to Cowley (1934), Brubacher and Rudy (1958), and Rudolph (1962), so widespread was this feeling that many state universities in the West that opened their doors during the nineteenth century did not include residence halls in their construction plans. The timing of this influence was even more significant, because the number of state universities being created in the West was stimulated by the passage of the Morrill Act and the founding of state land-grant colleges and universities. Any available money at these new educational institutions was needed for instruction. Residence halls were expensive to build, and state university administrators, anxious for their institutions to become the equals of those in the East, put all of their funds into salaries, classrooms, and laboratories.

The move to abolish residence halls from the campuses of major colleges and universities, however, led to major difficulties by the end of the nineteenth century. The supply of rooming houses and boardinghouses was inadequate to handle all student needs in many college towns. Students were crowding into private homes, where they often experienced few comforts or amenities. The cost of quality accommodations also increased as quality deteriorated.

Appearance of Fraternities and Sororities

This period resulted in a great growth in the popularity of fraternities. Many beautiful chapter houses were built, which resulted in a great disparity in the quality of housing for students attending these institutions. These organizations housed a large number of students, because educational institutions for the most part could not or would not provide housing facilities.

The fraternity movement of the nineteenth century and the introduction of sororities in the latter half of the century also inspired competitive collegiate activities. During this time, intercollegiate and intracollegiate activities began to prosper, as students became as interested in the extracurricular activities as in the academic aspects of collegiate life (Cowley, 1934).

Land-Grant Movement

Other important changes were taking place in American higher education at this time. Women were beginning to seek enrollment in institutions of higher learning. The advent of the land-grant movement and the opening of women's colleges such as Wesleyan (Georgia), Wellesley, Vassar, Smith, and others all gave women the opportunity to attend institutions of higher education (Cowley, 1934). These institutions were founded on a residential basis. The new residential-based colleges, the overcrowding and inadequacy of rooming houses, the dissatisfaction of students and their parents with the quality of off-campus housing, and the increased interest on the part of students in extracurricular activities all resulted in a shift toward a policy of providing housing facilities and programs similar to the traditional residential university.

This resurgence in the popularity of the residential college brought to a close the second phase in the development of student housing in the United States and a decline in the influence of the German system.

Resurgence of Residence Hall Construction

The presence of strong university presidents again played a significant role as they gave leadership to campus residence hall construction at both urban and rural universities. Harper at the University of Chicago, Schurman at Cornell University, and Woodrow Wilson at Princeton University are examples of presidents who strongly supported the construction of residence halls on their campuses. By the turn of the century—or more precisely,

1986–1915—institutions such as Cornell University, the University of Pennsylvania, the University of Minnesota, Columbia University, Iowa State University, and the University of Illinois all subscribed to the residence hall movement and built residential campuses for their students. According to Cowley (1934), by 1915 residence halls were being built at a faster rate than at any other time in the history of American higher education.

Stretching limited funds was always a challenge for the presidents of the early universities. A. H. Diamond (1957) found that the majority of residence halls built before the Depression of the 1930s were built through the aid of private gifts. States were much less interested in supplying funds for residence halls than for academic purposes. Thus, the cost of constructing residence halls during the third phase of the development of student housing in the United States was a major obstacle that had to be overcome.

Several states—such as Wisconsin in 1925 and 1928, Minnesota in 1926, Oregon in 1928, and North Dakota in 1928—tried to pass laws permitting them either to use state monies or to sell bonds to finance the construction of residence halls. However, all attempts failed (Chambers, 1931).

With the Great Depression and the New Deal programs of the 1930s, a new force in the construction of dormitories or residence halls—the federal government—appeared on the scene.

Involvement of the Federal Government

An unusual shortage of housing facilities existed on the fifty-two land-grant college campuses, according to a study published in *School and Society* ("Student Housing Facilities at Land-Grant Colleges," 1931). State funds were simply inadequate to meet all the needs of the depressed areas of the economy. Several institutions were able to get general state laws enacted that gave them the right to construct residence halls and additions through the issuance of bonds or financing by corporations set up for that purpose. Institutions affected by such laws included Iowa State University, the University of Kentucky, the University of Minnesota, Oregon Agricultural College, Pennsylvania State College, and Washington State College. The governments of several other states passed legislation specifically designed for particular residence hall construction projects to help alleviate the shortage of housing units for members of the collegiate community. Residence and dining halls were built under such legislation at the University of Idaho, Michigan State College, Mississippi A&M College, Oklahoma A&M College, and Virginia Polytechnic Institute, according to the 1931 study.

Changing state laws on the financing of residence halls, however, was not enough. In 1933, President Franklin D. Roosevelt signed an executive order establishing the Federal Emergency Administration of Public Works. This act attempted to reduce unemployment through construction and other public works. The housing division of the Public Works Administration (PWA) promoted a program of low-cost housing and slum clearance projects.

Many public colleges and universities qualified for loans and grants under this program and were able to increase their housing facilities in this way. For the first time since the beginnings of American higher education, the federal government played a major role in residence hall construction. Its influence was positive during this time, and the success of the PWA grant programs set the stage for increased intervention of the government in the affairs of local colleges and universities throughout the nation.

Impact of World War II

During world War II, college enrollments declined significantly, which resulted in a temporary halt in residence hall construction. Then came the dramatic change following World War II. Public Law 346 of the 78th Congress had the greatest single impact on the number of veterans entering or returning to colleges and universities. The Serviceman's Readjustment Act, commonly called the "GI Bill of Rights," became law. It resulted in rapidly increasing enrollments and pressing problems concerning the housing and feeding of students. The significant increase in the number of married students attending college further complicated the situation.

The housing crisis was present on both small and large campuses and on public as well as private ones. It was clearly a national problem, with the federal government emerging from the war years as the most influential contributor to student housing at American colleges and universities. To ease the nearly impossible situation, the government made former war facilities available to veteran students. Thousands of temporary structures were turned over to colleges throughout the United States.

College enrollments were predicted to continue to increase in the 1950s and 1960s. A more permanent solution to the collegiate housing shortage was needed. In response to this need and faced with pleas from many college administrators, Congress passed Title IV of the Housing Act of 1950, known as "Housing for Educational Institutions." This housing program offered financial assistance to educational institutions in providing loans for housing repairs and additions as well as for the construction of new facilities for students and faculty. The low interest rates and long periods of amortization were attractive to both public and private institutions. A massive program of student housing construction followed during the 1950s and 1960s.

The major shortage of collegiate housing, the desire for a fast solution to this shortage, and conditions on the use of the federal loan money resulted in the construction of many dormitories rather than residence halls. The dormitories were built to house and feed students and to maximize the number of beds constructed for the dollars available, with little or no regard for the quality of students' educational experiences and personal development. Dormitories were designed for low-cost maintenance, not livability. For example, the decision was often made to affix furniture to the building to make the project eligible for federal loan money. As a result, wardrobes, dressers, desks, and even beds were constructed as part of the building, leaving no flexibility for student residents to create living environments that would contribute to their personal development and respond to their life-style needs.

Educational Value of Collegiate Housing

As housing capacities began to catch up with increasing enrollments in the 1970s, the concern for maximizing the educational experience of students living in university housing received more attention from housing and student affairs professionals. There was a realization that dormitories and other housing facilities were not fulfilling their potential as living-learning centers.

Residence halls, rather than dormitories, are needed on college campuses. Residence halls, as described throughout this book, are designed to provide students with low-cost, safe, sanitary, and comfortable living accommodations and to promote students' intellectual, social, moral, and physical development. Collegiate housing facilities and programs can and do influence the quality of students' educational experiences and personal development (Riker and DeCoster, 1971; Chickering, 1969, 1974; Astin, 1984; Kuh, Schuh, Whitt, and Associates, 1991). Astin (1984) reports the positive effects of living in the residence halls during the freshman and sophomore years as increasing the probability that students would complete their college programs, increasing students' feelings of self-confidence, and increasing overall student satisfaction with the college experience. Chickering's (1974) studies on resident versus commuter students consistently show that resident students tend to take more credit hours, have higher grade-point averages, persist and graduate with greater frequency, use campus resources with greater frequency, are more involved in campus clubs and activities, and in general show more satisfaction with their undergraduate education than do commuter students. The positive benefits students receive by actively participating in the campus community, including residence halls, are widely acknowledged by leaders throughout higher education (Kuh, Schuh, Whitt, and Associates, 1991). There is now renewed emphasis on the integration of residential living as an integral part of the educational experience of students. This emphasis has grown out of the movement that created a philosophy of student development.

Needs of Student Residents in the 1990s

Housing professionals in the 1990s must respond to students in many new ways. Most students are legal adults and deserve to be treated as such. Students are customers who expect to receive a level of services consistent with the cost of those services. Student residents expect housing professionals to be accountable for their room-and-board dollars. The litigious nature of American society in the past ten years has increased the need for fair and consistent administration of housing and food service policies, judicial procedures, contract and lease terms, and student-university relationship matters in general.

Many of today's students and their parents are again expecting a more structured living environment, with behavioral policies and enforcement similar to the in loco parentis framework of earlier years. The freedom from control and supervision espoused by many students in the late 1960s and 1970s has changed today to a more moderate and structured living environment, with a heightened concern for safety and security. The freedoms demanded during the 1960s included abolishing curfews or hours for women; eliminating dress codes in dining rooms, in formal lounges, and at social events; the offering of coeducational housing for men and women; permitting the consumption of alcoholic beverages in the residence halls by persons of legal drinking age; eliminating the requirement for chaperons at registered social functions; and permitting the visitation in student rooms of persons of the opposite sex. The current concern for safety and security relates directly to housing policies and their consistent enforcement in areas of alcohol and other drug use and abuse and to visitation policies where men and women may be present in one another's residence hall rooms. This concern is also expressed in terms of the presence of security staff and policies relating to the locking of residence hall exterior doors. The administration of student residential facilities and residence life policies in today's environment presents a real challenge to the housing professionals in colleges and universities throughout the United States.

The closing decade of the twentieth century offers collegiate housing professionals the opportunity to intentionally create residential learning environments that will enhance the academic experience and enrich the personal lives of the student residents. Individual student development is now the central theme of residential living in American colleges and universities.

Professional Specialization in Housing

The evolution of student housing in the United States has a parallel evolution in the career field of student housing in higher education.

Faculty Members as Housing Professionals

In the first phase of development, early American college housing professionals were faculty members. These faculty members lived with, ate with, supervised, and taught students in their residential colleges. But within a few years, student-faculty conflicts and student rebellions caused many faculty members to become disinterested in the residential housing experience. This growing disinterest coincided with an emphasis on specialization and the development of the "research university." This new emphasis placed additional pressure on faculty members. They began to question the appropriateness of their roles as housing staff, disciplinarians, and "substitute parents" for resident students. They believed they were spending too much time away from their teaching and research responsibilities, and they wanted to be relieved of their live-in residential responsibilities.

Role of Housemothers in Student Housing

The second phase occurred during the period of the decline in residential housing as a central factor in higher education. The influence of the German educational system prevailed, and students were made responsible for their own room-and-board arrangements in private rooming houses and boardinghouses. The need for student housing staff declined, and what was to become a housing career field was at a low point in its development. During this period, when faculty members were leaving their residential housing positions, a number of nonfaculty persons were appointed to positions in residence units. They included coaches and housemothers. Housemothers were most often older women and were present in fraternities, sororities, and residence halls. They provided a control factor, a parental factor, and a social graces factor. They were key staff members in the institution's implementation of in loco parentis.

Emergence of the Housing Career Field

It has been during the third phase of the development of student housing in the United States that the housing career field has emerged as an area of professional specialization, typically within the student affairs area of colleges and universities.

The massive construction program of building dormitories in the 1950s and 1960s resulted in leadership predominantly by the business area of colleges and universities. As a result, many housing administrators reported to the business area during these years. These housing professionals had primary responsibilities in the areas of administration and facilities maintenance—not usually in the area of residence life.

The renewed emphasis on residential education during the past twenty years has resulted in housing professionals becoming living-learning specialists in addition to being housing and food service administrators. Overall, concern for student development and student services within a division of student affairs has emerged as a preferred organizational arrangement and staffing pattern at most colleges and universities in the United States. Student housing is now a basic student development service and is a full-fledged partner with other student affairs departments.

The massive growth of student housing facilities since 1950 was accompanied by administrative staff growth typically separated into two divisions, one for men and one for women. Housing staff and dean of students staff were frequently organized into these two separate organizational clusters. In addition, rules, policies, supervision, and even facilities were different for men and women on the same campus. This divided administrative pattern was prevalent until about 1970. Since 1970, the emphasis on student development and out-of-class educational experiences has resulted in the merger of the men's and women's housing staffs as well as deans of men and women into single administrative units for all students. A major influence that speeded the changes that were already taking place on many campuses was Title IX of the Higher Education Act of 1965, which was passed by Congress in 1973. This act mandated that women and men should receive equal treatment in higher education (for example, parietal rules had to be the same for men and women and residential facilities had to be comparable in quality) at all institutions that received federal financial support (including individual student financial aid).

Many housing organizations at large universities developed and expanded into major autonomous housing divisions with responsibility for housing administration, residence life, food service, and facilities maintenance. These large and diverse housing organizations encompass a staff, programs, and services representing a variety of specialty career fields.

In addition, the housing and residence life career field has become a primary provider of basic student affairs professional work experiences and in so doing offers an excellent experience foundation for other career fields within student affairs.

Thus, the housing career field of the 1990s has expanded and matured into four basic specialty areas: residence life, administration, maintenance, and food service. Other subgroup special areas include conference services, apartment housing, and marketing services.

Student housing is a respected career field with its own unique body of knowledge, statement of standards, ethical codes, and professional organizations. (See Resources.)

Student Housing Professional Organizations

The rapidly rising tide of enrollment in colleges and universities after World War II brought with it immediate and pressing problems concerning the housing and feeding of students. The overcrowding of facilities and the need to take care of large numbers of married students resulted in focusing the attention of college and university administrators on housing problems never before faced. The problems of student housing had become national in scope, and the need to discuss housing problems on a national level became quite evident.

National Housing Organization Formed

S. Earl Thompson, the director of housing at the University of Illinois at Champaign-Urbana, originally proposed an association of housing officers of colleges and universities that would meet on a national level to discuss their problems and concerns. He and his staff prepared a program and invited delegates to attend a national housing conference at the University of Illinois during the summer of 1949.

Sixty-two official delegates representing thirty-three colleges and universities attended the first National Housing Conference. During the business meeting of this first conference, and after much discussion, the group present proposed to have a similar meeting the next year and to delay consideration of a permanent organization until that time. Eighty-six delegates from sixty colleges and universities attended the second meeting in the summer of 1950. The question of a permanent organization was again discussed, resulting in the appointment of a committee on organization chaired by J. C. Schilletter, director of residence at Iowa State University. The committee made the following recommendations at the third meeting, held in 1951: (1) that a non-dues-paying organization be established; (2) that officers consisting of a president, a vice president, and a secretary be elected at this meeting; and (3) that the elected officers be charged with the responsibility of appointing necessary committees, drawing up a constitution, and recommending an official name for the organization. The recommendations of the committee were adopted unanimously. The first officers were elected at this meeting, with S. Earl Thompson being elected to serve as the first president.

In 1952, delegates adopted the official name of National Association of College and University Housing Officers and voted to establish annual dues. The first constitution was adopted in 1953, and the name was changed to Association of College and University Housing Officers (ACUHO).

During the seventh annual conference, in 1955, four committees or service areas were identified as a result of requests for services from member institutions. They were a research committee, a displays committee, a placement service, and an expanded newsletter. Two additional committees were added in 1956—a membership committee and the Federal Housing and Home Finance Administration advisory committee. The important role of the federal government in supporting the financing of college housing programs necessitated the appointment of this advisory committee. This committee developed a relationship with the federal government and the college housing program officials that continues to this day.

The services and activities of ACUHO were recognized by other related professional associations, resulting in many collaborative efforts and benefits to the members of both associations. These joint efforts occurred as early as 1957, when ACUHO, the American College Health Association, and the Campus Safety Association collaborated on the development of a set of health, safety, and sanitation standards for off-campus student housing. Also during 1957, the Federal Office of Education asked ACUHO to assist in the development of a basic curriculum in quantity food preparation.

By 1958, three regional associations scheduled their own meetings and considered ACUHO as the parent organization. They were the Northeast, Rocky Mountain, and Western associations. Membership had grown to over 200 institutions by 1959, with the growth including foreign universities from Lebanon, Canada, and Australia. By 1960, all states except Alaska and Hawaii were represented in the association, and the first National Training Institute was sponsored by ACUHO.

Additional professional collaborations occurred in 1962, with the ACUHO research committee working with the Education Facilities Laboratories to conduct research on various phases of college housing. Half of a $60,000 grant was committed to ACUHO research projects. In 1964, arrangements were made with the American College Personnel Association for ACUHO to copublish a monograph on college housing centers.

The first ACUHO library was established in 1963 at Emory University in Atlanta, Georgia, to provide a repository for all ACUHO publications and other publications related to residence hall operations. The ACUHO Award, the highest honor that ACUHO can bestow on a former member, was established in 1964. The first recipient was S. Earl Thompson, the original proposer of a national organization for housing officers.

The first lobbying or political influence action occurred in 1966, with the members of ACUHO who attended the annual conference voting to send a resolution to President Lyndon B. Johnson, the chairpersons of appropriate congressional committees, the secretary of Housing and Urban Development, and others having an interest in college housing. The resolution recommended that $600 million be appropriated by Congress to fund the College Housing Program. Such actions and collaborations with other professional organizations increased the visibility and credibility of the new housing professional organization.

Changes in the National Housing Association

In 1969, twenty years after the first meeting of ACUHO, an ad hoc committee (later called the evaluation committee) was appointed to study the past, present, and future of ACUHO. Their report recommended a redefinition of the purposes and goals of ACUHO and ways of broadening member opportunities for participation in its affairs.

The first issue of the *Journal of College and University Housing* was published in 1971 as a project of the research committee. This was another milestone in the development of a recognized professional organization for persons in the student housing career field.

Significant changes were made to the ACUHO constitution in 1972 to emphasize the association's commitment to fairness based on sex, race, color, creed, and national origin and to extend membership opportunities to junior and community colleges that have housing operations.

The first annual conference of ACUHO to be held outside the United States was hosted at the University of British Columbia for the 1973 silver anniversary year meeting. The Canadian members presented ACUHO with a "Talking Stick," a sign of authority carried when a meeting of chiefs is in session. This stick is displayed at each annual conference and serves as the symbol of friendship and leadership as it is passed from president to president each year. The *Talking Stick* also became the new name of the association newsletter in 1983. The displaying of services and products by commercial exhibitors was permitted for the first time at this annual conference, and institutional membership increased to 425 members.

The professional standards committee of ACUHO prepared a statement of professional and ethical standards for housing officers that was accepted and approved as an official code of ethics for the association in 1976. In 1980, this committee also developed a set of guidelines for the development of a professional preparation program for housing officers that was distributed to graduate schools throughout the United States.

Further Changes in the Housing Association

In 1980, the evaluation committee was charged with the responsibility of completing a second self-study of the association that would include purposes and goals, organizational structure, services and programs, regional-international relationships, and finances. After two years of study, seventeen recommendations for change were presented to the membership and were approved at the 1982 annual conference for implementation over the next two years. The official name of the association was changed in 1981 to incorporate the word *International*, with the new acronym *ACUHO-I* now representing the association. The approved recommendations included significant new directions for ACUHO-I, such as the establishment of a central office to provide support services, restructuring the committee organization, dropping the position of second vice president, and adding four district representatives to the executive board in place of the two members-at-large.

The 1982–83 year was a time of major transition because of implementing the recommendations of the self-study. A decision was made in 1983 to locate the central support services office at Ohio State University, and Rhea Dawn Smith was hired as the first manager of the central office, which opened in 1984. A further change occurred with the appointment of an executive director to give leadership to the ACUHO-I central office and to the newly formed ACUHO-I Research and Educational Foundation. (Gary Schwarzmueller was appointed to this new administrative position in 1991.) The ACUHO-I *Statement of Standards* was also adopted in 1984 to be used as a tool for evaluating housing programs during accreditation visits and for self-study or general improvement of housing programs by member institutions.

Housing professionals can take pride in the evolution of ACUHO-I into a respected professional organization representing all aspects of college and university housing—administration, residence life, food service, and maintenance. ACUHO-I has meaningful relationships with other student personnel professional organizations as well as other professional business management organizations. It has built its success on a foundation of broad volunteer membership participation and contributions. Even though current membership is now over 800 institutional members and 90 associate members, it is the involvement, leadership, and contributions of individual members that continue to distinguish ACUHO-I as a professional organization. More detailed information about ACUHO-I can be found in the *Purpose and History of the Association of College and University Housing Officers-International* (Association of College and University Housing Officers-International, 1985).

Other organizations besides ACUHO-I have provided and continue to provide professional association opportunities for housing staff members. The American College Personnel Association established Commission III: Student Residence Programs in 1966 with the intent of pulling together residence life professionals, both theoretical and applied, to focus on the enhancement of the residence hall experience through programs and intentional student development efforts. Harold Riker from the University of Florida served as the first commission chairperson. Current membership totals more than 700 individuals.

The goals of this commission include providing leadership for student development in college residence halls in cooperation with the American College Personnel Association and the profession in general; communicating innovative ideas, suggestions for problem resolution, and research information with a broad base of individuals throughout the country who are involved in resident education; cultivating professional development experiences through sponsoring and implementing convention programs and regional workshops; assisting in developing a set of professional standards for staffs working in residence halls; and maintaining a working relationship with other professional organizations and student associations that have similar or overlapping objectives.

The broad range of professional staff career fields included in the overall housing areas of administration, residence life, food service, and maintenance results in housing professionals belonging to, participating in, and giving leadership to many other professional organizations. They include the National Association of Student Personnel Administrators, the National Association of College and University Food Services, the College and University Machine Records Association, the Association of Physical Plant Administrators, the National Association of College Auxiliary Services, the National Association of Educational Buyers, the National Association of College and University Business Officers, and the Environmental Management Association. Many collaborative efforts are conducted among two or more of these associations in the areas of workshops, surveys, studies, research, training, and publications.

Professional organizations are available to support the continued development of all professional staff in the housing career field.

Student Organizations Related to Housing

The management of collegiate housing facilities and the leadership of residence life educational programming are the responsibilities of housing professionals. However, these responsibilities do not rest solely with housing staff members. Successful housing programs also depend on the participation and leadership of resident students.

The quality and effectiveness of student involvement in self-governance and developmental programming are enhanced by the communication and exchange of information with student leaders from other universities. This need for sharing of programs, services, and student government experiences led to the formation of regional associations of colleges and universities. These associations were geographically based and frequently were made up of institutions in the different intercollegiate athletic conferences or institutions in an individual state. These student associations date from the early and mid-twentieth century.

The National Association of College and University Residence Halls, Inc. (NACURH) is the national voice of residence hall students across the United States. The purpose of NACURH is to design and facilitate programs and informational services to promote the educational goals of residence hall students. NACURH was founded on the precept that students active in the residence halls are in a position to make positive contributions to the total educational process. This reflects the belief that residence hall living can and should supplement the formal experience of a student in the classroom.

The parent organization to NACURH was founded in 1954 at Iowa State University. It began as the Midwest Dormitory Conference, with student representatives from five Midwestern universities in attendance. The first meeting was organized because Iowa State University residence hall student government officers believed that such an organization was needed to encourage the exchange of ideas and information. At the second annual conference, in 1955, the delegates from twelve universities revised the constitution to rename the organization the Association of College and University Residence Halls (ACURH). The association took on a formal stature at this meeting, with a basic constitution passed, officers elected, and a 1956 site selected. Discussions were also held on subjects such as the association purpose, planned programs and activities, and the need for an advisor. This organization continued to grow into a large regional student government association.

In 1961, the Intermountain Residence Hall Association voted to affiliate with ACURH, and ACURH voted to accept the affiliation. The association
changed its name by adding the word *National*, resulting in a two-region
national association made up of the Midwest and Intermountain regions.
Three years later, in 1964, three new regional organizations were created.
They were the Pacific Coast, North Atlantic, and South Atlantic Associations
of College and University Residence Halls. Another organizational change
occurred in 1968, when the very large Midwest Association was divided into
the Great Lakes and a smaller Midwest Association of Residence Halls. This
resulted in NACURH being made up of six regional associations. The final
organizational change occurred in 1981, when the still large Midwest region
was again divided into a smaller Midwest region and a Southwest Association
of College and University Residence Halls. NACURH continues to have these
seven regional associations. One other significant event occurred in 1971,
when the membership voted to incorporate NACURH under Oklahoma
State doctrines. A NACURH board of directors now provides the leadership
for this organization.

Today, NACURH offers many services to its members. It has given
leadership to a National Residence Hall Honorary, a National Information
Center, and negotiated discount relationships with movie distributors, refrigerator distributors, and a property insurance company. However, it is the
annual national and regional conferences that provide the most significant
benefits to the individual student participants.

NACURH and ACUHO-I have established a meaningful collaborative
relationship over the last decade that has led to the sharing of information
and educational programs. The result is continued progress toward the
overall objectives of the education and development of individual residents
in college and university housing.

Summary

This brief history of the development of collegiate housing in the United
States was divided into four focus areas. The first focus area was a review of
the evolution of student housing in the United States. The initial phase
occurred when American colleges were first established and followed the
lead of the English educational system. The second phase occurred from the
Civil War until the early 1900s, when the influence of the German system was
paramount. The third and last phase was the period after 1930, when
residential housing on college campuses again flourished and there was a
renewed emphasis on residential living as an integral part of the educational
experience of students. The second focus area described housing as an area
of professional specialization within student affairs, which has led to a full-
fledged housing career field. The third focus area presented a brief history of
student housing professional organizations, with an emphasis on the Association of College and University Housing Officers-International. The last

focus area provided a brief history of student organizations related to housing.

This review of the 350-year history of collegiate housing in the United States serves as a framework and foundation for the other chapters in this volume.

References

Association of College and University Housing Officers-International. *The Purpose and History of the Association of College and University Housing-International.* Columbus, Ohio: Association of College and University Housing Officers–International, 1985.

Astin, A. W. "Student Involvement: A Developmental Theory for Higher Education." *Journal of College Student Personnel,* 1984, *25,* 297–308.

Brubacher, J. S., and Rudy, W. *Higher Education in Transition: An American History: 1636–1956.* New York: HarperCollins, 1958.

Chambers, M. M. "Law and Administration." *Journal of Higher Education,* 1931, *2,* 195–203.

Chickering, A. W. *Education and Identity.* San Francisco: Jossey-Bass, 1969.

Chickering, A. W. *Commuting Versus Resident Students: Overcoming Educational Inequities of Living Off Campus.* San Francisco: Jossey-Bass, 1974.

Cowley, W. H. "The History of Student Residential Housing." *School and Society,* 1934, *40,* 705–712, 758–764.

Diamond, A. H. "College Housing Program—Its History and Operation." *Educational Record,* 1957, *38,* 204–220.

Kuh, G. D., Schuh, J. H., Whitt, E. J., and Associates. *Involving Colleges: Successful Approaches to Fostering Student Learning and Development Outside the Classroom.* San Francisco: Jossey-Bass, 1991.

Riker, H. C., and DeCoster, D. A. "The Educational Role in College Student Housing." *Journal of College and University Student Housing,* 1971, *1,* 1–4.

Rudolph, F. *The American College and University: A History.* New York: Knopf, 1962.

"Student Housing Facilities at Land-Grant Colleges." *School and Society,* 1931, *33,* 522–523.

Tappan, H. P. *Report to the Board of Regents of the University of Michigan.* Ann Arbor: Board of Regents, University of Michigan, 1853.

PART TWO

===

Organizing and Managing Residential Life Programs

The role of the housing and residential life administrator has become increasingly difficult and complex in the past thirty years. The need for increased responsiveness, combined with new responsibilities and demands, has resulted from increasingly consumer-oriented students, more ethnically and socially diverse student populations, greater fiscal challenges, and new social issues and movements. Today's housing staff must have skills and competencies that include personnel management, entrepreneurial initiatives, personal crisis intervention, and organization development. Staff at all levels of the organization must have increased knowledge and theoretical sophistication to be effective. Part Two includes chapters that cover topics ranging from nuts-and-bolts operational matters, considerations in staffing, and determining resident needs and program effectiveness, to legal parameters and professional standards that define today's housing world.

Paramount to a successful housing and residential life program is a responsive organization and leadership structure that promotes creativity, allows change, and supports diversity. In Chapter Seven, Upcraft deals with the practical aspects of the organization and administration of departments situated in both private and public institutions and addresses how variables such as institutional size, historical development, staff composition, and mission influence administrative structures. He also tackles the sometimes sensitive relationships between housing and business affairs and housing and physical plant operations. Staffing patterns, organizational structures, and the integration of fiscal management, maintenance, and programmatic functions are topics discussed.

Chapter Eight addresses practical aspects of managing physical facilities and fiscal operations. Hallenbeck maintains that residents' basic shelter and security needs must be met through appropriately maintained and staffed buildings, backed up by preventive maintenance programs and sound fiscal management, which allows the housing program to offer living accommodations at reasonable rates. The issues addressed range from student contracts, room assignments, and budgeting, to the practical aspects of building renovations and new construction.

Often college and university dining services are a grossly underestimated and misunderstood aspect of campus living. In Chapter Nine, Fairbrook maintains that intellectually stimulating dialogue, relaxation, and education about eating habits are some of the important products of well-conceptualized food services programs. The role of the food service director, contracting with outside companies versus self-operated programs, maintaining quality, providing education about nutrition, integrating dining services and housing programs, and responding to special food needs of students are topics covered in this chapter.

"Variety is the spice of life" is how Grimm introduces Chapter Ten, on residential alternatives. He asserts that individual student development is often directly related to choices and options in living arrangements. Because residents respond differently to physical facilities and programming emphases, a key to successful housing programs is to provide a diversity of programs and living arrangements, which will maximize the probability of providing an optimal match between individuals and their environment. Theme housing, co-op buildings, house systems, coeducational facilities, living-learning centers, and family housing units are some of the options described, with the accompanying benefits and problems identified.

At the heart of every housing program is its staff. Regardless of the type of residential facilities, campus, or student body, it is the staff that usually makes the ultimate difference in the quality and impact of the housing program. Chapters Eleven through Thirteen deal with the definition of roles, selection, training, supervision, and evaluation of the professional, allied professional, support, and paraprofessional housing staff.

In Chapter Eleven, Kearney maintains that the professional staff is primarily charged with setting the tone and overall direction of the housing program. The selection of professional staff members, she maintains, is probably the most important determinant of success for residential life programs. As a result, she outlines procedures that can increase the probability of making "good" decisions.

In Chapter Twelve, Saunders argues that the allied professional and support staffs generally have the first and most frequent contact with students. Consequently, they often have a great deal of influence on students' satisfaction with the housing program and success in the institution. Careful selection, extensive training, and constructive supervision are required to ensure that staff members in these categories maintain a high level of concern for residents, provide high-quality services, and sustain positive attitudes.

In Chapter Thirteen, the crucial roles student paraprofessionals can play in the success of a housing program are analyzed. Winston and Fitch argue that paraprofessionals can play major roles in facilitating their peers' development, implementing residential life programs, and identifying potentially devastating resident problems early. They maintain, however, that successful paraprofessional programs require careful conceptualization, thorough and extensive training, and ongoing supervision. Failure in any of these functions can spell disaster for a housing program.

Housing programs today are faced with a Gordian knot of individual, family, and community problems that students bring with them at enrollment and that sometimes are complicated by the local community surrounding the campus. A complex set of statutes, case law, and regulations has grown up in American higher education over the past thirty years that prescribes much of contemporary housing practice. In Chapter Fourteen, Gehring outlines the legal parameters of contemporary housing practice, briefly describes the ever-increasing number of government regulations that affect housing programs, and offers suggestions for ways to minimize risks while not abandoning goals of student development.

One of the most significant advances in the professionalization of student affairs has been the adoption of standards that identify minimal criteria for acceptable practice and define the parameters of ethical conduct. In Chapter Fifteen, Miller and Eyster describe multiple ways to use professional practice standards (including self-studies, program planning, and staff development) and explore practical applications of statements of ethical standards.

Finally, in Chapter Sixteen, Brown and Podolske present a primer on needs assessment, program evaluation, and research. They recommend strategies for conducting useful needs assessments that can have immediate utility for program design and implementation and offer advice about constructing valid program evaluations. Both theoretical issues (for example, conceptualizing problems and selecting research or evaluation designs) and practical considerations (such as selection and/or construction of instruments and methods of analysis) are addressed.

Chapter Seven

_____

Organizational
and Administrative
Approaches

M. Lee Upcraft

How should we organize and administer residence halls so that they are efficiently managed, affordable, safe, well maintained, and perhaps most important, contribute to the personal and academic development of residents? To answer this question, we must look at what organizational models are available and at how residence halls should be staffed. This must be done within the context of the issues we face in the 1990s and beyond if we are to offer high-quality residential services and programs that meet the personal and academic needs of students and if we are to provide facilites that meet their "creature comfort" needs as well.

In this chapter, I discuss the mission and goals of residence halls, the contextual issues that must be considered in organizing residence halls, the choices available in making decisions about organizational structure, and the ways residence halls should be organized to meet the challenges of the 1990s and into the twenty-first century.

Note: The author is deeply indebted to and most appreciative of the help provided by Gary North and Thomas Gibson, whose advice was invaluable in writing this chapter. Most of the sample organizational charts were derived from the actual residential organizational structure of Pennsylvania State University.

Mission and Goals

Before discussing how residence halls should be organized and administered, one must first ask the question, "organized and administered for
what?" According to the *Standards and Guildelines for Housing and Residential
Life Programs* developed by the Council for the Advancement of Standards for
Student Services/Development Programs (CAS) (1986, p. 21), "The residential
life program is an integral part of the educational program and academic
support services of the institution. The mission must include provision for
educational programs and services, residential facilities, management services, and, where appropriate, food services."

To accomplish this mission, individual and group educational and
developmental opportunities must exist, and there must be residential facilities that are kept clean, safe, well maintained, reasonably priced, attractive,
and comfortable. Further, management functions must include planning,
personnel, property management, purchasing, contract administration, and
financial control. And finally, food services, where applicable, should provide high-quality, nutritious, and reasonably priced meals (Council for the
Advancement of Standards for Student Services/Development Programs,
1986).

So the challenge becomes how to organize and administer residence
halls so that this mission is accomplished and these goals met. For the
purposes of this chapter, I will assume that this mission is viable for all
institutions. I will also assume that institutions have a responsibility to meet
each of these goals in a fiscally responsible and developmentally supportive
way, given the contextual factors described below.

Contextual Factors in the Organization of Residence Halls

Before discussing the organizational models available, one needs to consider
the contextual factors that influence how residence halls should be organized. First, the size of the institution affects organizational structure. For
example, an institution with 10,000 residential students will organize its
residence halls differently from a small college with two residence halls and
300 students. Large institutions require bureaucracies with specialized support services and programs staffed by specialists; small institutions are often
able to get along with less bureaucracy and are staffed by both generalists and
specialists.

Second, the mission of the institution influences the organizational
structure. If the institution has a strong developmental, out-of-class mission,
its residence halls should be organized in a way that devotes considerable
resources to the creation of a residential climate that promotes individual
growth and healthy community environments. If the institution sees residence halls mostly as a place to eat and sleep, its residence halls probably will

be organized in a way that devotes more resources to facilities management, food services, and management services.

Third, even though all students need certain basic services, programs, and facilities, the characteristics of the students who enroll in an institution are also a defining factor in organizational structure. For example, an institution that has a strong engineering, mathematics, and science emphasis may want to organize its residence halls to meet the unique needs of a primarily vocationally and professionally oriented residential population. On the other hand, an institution with a strong liberal arts emphasis may want to organize in a way that can meet the unique (and generally much broader) needs of liberal arts students.

Fourth, the class mix of students who live in residence halls has an impact on organizational structure. For example, if first-year students make up the critical mass of residents, more time and attention must be given to assisting in college adjustment concerns than if the residential population is more balanced among first-year and upperclass students. In the first instance, much more time, energy, and resources must be spent orienting first-year students to the living-environment expectations. In the second instance, upperclass students "know the ropes" and require much less time and attention, both in creating a positive learning environment and in assuming responsibility for the maintenance of safe, clean, and quiet facilities. That is not to say that first-year students are more important than upperclass students, but rather that first-year students have needs in the residential environment that require more time and attention than upperclass students. Also, students who have a successful first year are more likely to earn higher grades and graduate than those who have an unsuccessful first year (Upcraft, Gardner, and Associates, 1989).

Fifth, organizational structure might be affected by whether or not students are required to live in residence halls. In general, it is much more difficult to develop a positive residential environment if residents resent living there. Students forced to live in residence halls as a result of institutional residence requirements generally require more attention and supervision than students who live in residence halls by choice.

And finally, the racial and ethnic mix of residents influences the ways an institution organizes its residence halls. In general, residential populations with a heterogeneous mix of races and ethnicities require more resources than those that are more homogeneous. For example, in the former instance, race and ethnicity sometimes become a factor in such issues as roommate relationships, intra- and interfloor conflicts, relationships between students and resident assistants (RAs), damage, and violence and therefore require more time, energy, and skill from the professional staff.

All these factors must be taken into consideration in deciding how residence halls should be organized. So what are the choices, and how do they relate to these contextual factors?

Choices in Organizational Structure

The first choice is whether the goals of residence halls described in the above excerpt from the *CAS Standards* are to be implemented through a unitary (integrated) organizational structure or through a bifurcated (split) structure. In the *integrated model*, one organization is responsible for student life programs, facilities, and management services, with food services typically reporting through the business affairs organization but sometimes reporting through the student affairs organization. A second model has those responsible for creating and maintaining the living-learning environment reporting to the student affairs organization, whereas those responsible for facilities operations, management services, and food services report to the business affairs organization. This model is referred to in this chapter as a *split system*.

Integrated Model

The most obvious advantage of the integrated model is that the four CAS goals are implemented within one organization, with a commonality of mission and purpose, leadership, structure, chain of command, and accountability path (Figure 7.1). In short, under this model, there is a greater likelihood that things will get done more efficiently. Also, the leadership can change personnel, processes, policies, and organizational structures more quickly in response to changing conditions.

Figure 7.1. Residence Halls Integrated System: Sample Organizational Chart.

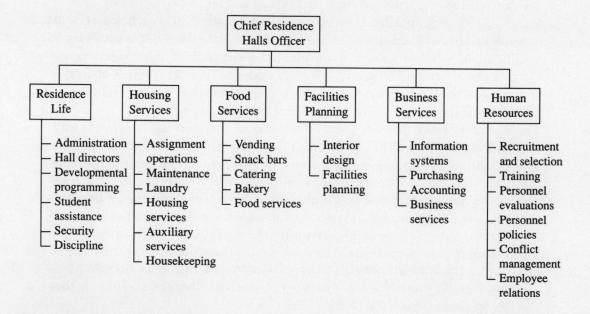

Figure 7.2. Residence Halls Split System: Sample Organizational Chart.

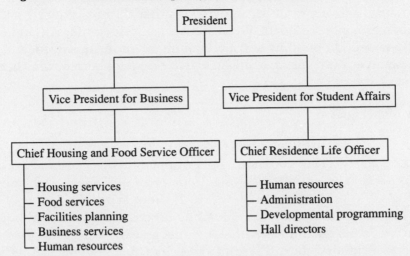

The downside of the integrated system is that too often, the fiscal bottom line may take precedence over the developmental bottom line, particularly if the organization is placed within the business side of the institution. In this instance, facilities, management services, and food services may take precedence over living-learning goals. For example, business-dominated residential organizations, in the name of increased revenue generation, may be inclined to overcrowd facilities by assigning three students to a room, or housing students on a temporary basis in floor lounges. The problem, of course, is that there is some evidence that overcrowding has a detrimental effect on academic achievement, retention, and interpersonal relationships, a fact that may be unimportant to a business-dominated organization.

Split System

This model separates residence life services and programs from the other three functions (facilities, management services, and food services). (See Figure 7.2.) In this model, staff efforts toward programs and services designed to fit student needs are likely to be the major, if not the only, concern. Fiscal matters are the priority of others, resulting in time being available for a strong student advocacy role. In fact, the residence life staff may take an advocacy role with those responsible for residence hall business administration, supporting student concerns and issues. The dynamic tension between the business types and the student affairs types may lead to an appropriate balance of developmental and fiscal concerns, with residents as the primary beneficiaries.

On the less favorable side, this model can fragment the development of a residential program. When business and student affairs types do not agree, students may suffer because of inaction, stalemates, and unresolved conflicts.

In the event of a lack of consensus, too many issues may be brought to upper-level administrators, resulting in decisions that do not properly take into account the reality of student life. In addition, considerable time and energy are often spent on building and maintaining relationships needed to make this system work—time that might better be spent serving the needs of students.

Which Model Is Best?

In part, the answer to this question depends on the contextual considerations described above. There does not, however, appear to be a national consensus on this issue. A recent report by the Association of College and University Housing Officers-International (ACUHO-I) summarizes the results of a survey of organizational structures of housing programs. Of 290 institutions in the survey, 72 percent indicated that the chief housing officer reported to the chief student affairs officer, 6 percent to the chief business officer, 3 percent to both, and nearly 19 percent reported elsewhere. Of those chief housing officers reporting to the chief business affairs officer, 88 percent were in public institutions (Ploskonka, 1990).

In my opinion, the integrated model probably works best in smaller, single-purpose institutions with a homogeneous student population, where the primary goal is to safely house and feed students. The "split" system model probably works best in larger, multipurpose institutions with a more heterogeneous student population and where developmental goals are more primary. But this choice also depends on the values of the leadership of the institution. The integrated model is probably preferred, if the leadership of the institution and residence halls is committed to giving equal support to the developmental and fiscal bottom lines. One way this balanced commitment might be reinforced is for the chief operating officer of residence halls to report to the chief student affairs officer. Or a chief operating officer of residence halls can be appointed whose training and experience is in student affairs but who reports to the chief business officer.

Organizing Residence Life

The second choice is how to organize the living-learning or residence life aspect of residence halls. (See Figure 7.3.) The choices are about the same regardless of whether the organization is integrated or split. Because most residence hall systems rely on students who serve as RAs for the delivery of many direct services to students, discussion will begin at that level and move upward.

Resident Assistants

Regardless of the institution, RAs are typically expected to (1) provide personal help and assistance; (2) manage and facilitate groups; (3) facilitate

Figure 7.3. Residence Life Programs: Sample Organizational Chart.

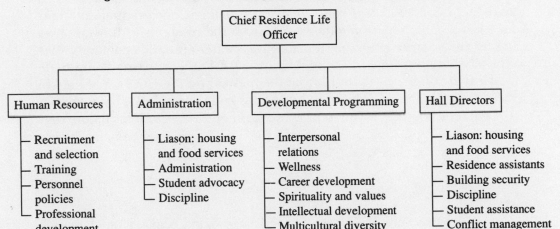

social, recreational, and educational programs; (4) inform students or refer them to appropriate information sources; (5) explain and enforce rules and regulations; and (6) maintain a safe, orderly, and relatively quiet environment (Upcraft and Pilato, 1982). (See Chapter Thirteen for a more complete analysis of the role of the RA.) Usually RAs are assigned to a floor or wing of a residence hall, but how many students an individual RA should be assigned depends on many factors. According to a survey by ACUHO-I, among the factors that affect student-RA ratios are (1) characteristics of the resident population (typically upperclass halls have a higher resident-RA ratio than freshman halls), (2) concern for the amount of individual attention given to residents, (3) increased need for student-staff contact, (4) amount of discipline needed to maintain an orderly environment, and (5) financial/budget concerns (typically the student-RA ratio increases when fiscal resources are strained). Because of the many factors that influence student-RA ratios, there appears to be no national consensus, although a survey by Duerst and Welch (1988) revealed that the mode ranges from 26:1 to 35:1.

Who should be hired as resident assistants? Most institutions hire junior and senior undergraduates to fill these positions, although graduate students are sometimes hired. The rationale behind hiring undergraduates is to make the best use of the peer influence, which can be very powerful for undergraduates. When properly recruited, selected, trained, supervised, and evaluated, they can make a major contribution to the personal and academic development of students, as well as help maintain a safe, orderly, and supportive residential environment (Upcraft and Pilato, 1982). Undergraduate RAs, however, sometimes have difficulty separating themselves from the peers for whom they are responsible, because to be an undergraduate RA means having one foot in studenthood and the other in the administration. This partial separation is necessary if the RA is to be effective.

The rationale behind hiring graduate students is that residents need an older and more mature role model to guide them, and graduate students have less trouble separating themselves from the residents with whom they live. However, since graduate students face greater academic demands, they typically have less time to spend doing the RA job. Furthermore, graduate students are often new to the campus themselves and therefore are limited in their ability to orient students to the campus and the residence halls. Finally, it is often difficult to recruit, select, and train graduate students before they take on the RA position. Based on my own experience, I recommend the use of undergraduates as RAs.

Second-Level Staff

RAs must be recruited, selected, trained, supervised, and evaluated, which leads us to the next level of staffing. These positions are variously titled head resident, resident adviser, or hall director. At this level, other administrative duties may enter in, such as room assignments, damages, recordkeeping, public relations, and so on. Providing direct services and programs to students may also be a part of this level of staffing. Choices include (1) whether to employ professionally educated entry-level staff or to seek persons who have administrative experience and good interpersonal skills, regardless of academic background, (2) whether the position is part time or full time, and (3) if part time, graduate students enrolled in student affairs preparation programs may be used — if the institution has such a program — or upper-class undergraduates may be used.

These decisions tend to be based on contextual and fiscal considerations, but the goal is to hire persons who fit the job. For example, if supervision of RAs is important, someone with good supervisory skills should be hired. If the administration of a hall or block of halls is important, someone with good administrative skills should be hired. If programming and counseling are important, someone with good interpersonal and group skills should be hired. Again, based on my experience, if the job is primarily supervision, programming, and counseling, someone with professional training and experience should be hired. If, however, the job is primarily administrative and clerical in nature, someone with administrative skills and experience — possibly with a bachelor's degree — should be hired. In my opinion, under no circumstances should an undergraduate student be given the sole responsibility at this level of staffing, because even the best and most experienced undergraduate generally lacks the personal maturity, judgment, and professional skills needed to function effectively. I tend to favor full-time persons over part-time persons, because they can devote more of their time and energy to the job. Part-time staff have other responsibilities that may conflict with their job. And perhaps more important, due to the nature of the job, even if it is defined as part time, it often becomes almost a full-time job. I also tend to favor persons trained in student affairs or related fields, because they are better prepared to pursue the living-learning goals of residence halls and to build supportive residential communities. It might also be argued that residence hall programs have a professional obligation to provide practical experience opportunities for graduate students who plan a career in student affairs through paid internships or assistantships.

Another issue for this organizational level is where staff should live. Most staff at this level are required to live in the residence hall or one of the residence halls for which they are responsible. Living in has many advantages, including the opportunity to be with residents and staff in their own environment and to be accessible to help students. The inability to really get away from the job, even in the most ideal circumstances, however, tends to be disruptive to the privacy of staff and can lead to burnout. Burnout in turn creates an inordinately high rate of turnover, thus inhibiting the development of experienced professional staff support needed at this mid-management level. Creating more structured working hours, providing for more time away from the facilities, and creating joint appointments with other student services and programs are some measures that can help reduce or prevent burnout. Some institutions have even allowed staff at this level to live outside of residence halls, and the job can still get done. But all things considered, in my opinion, the advantages of living in outweigh the disadvantages.

Central Office Staff

The next level of staffing is usually the central residence life office. There is no question that staff at this level should be full time, professionally trained, with extensive residence hall experience. How this level is organized depends on contextual considerations, such as the size of the system. In smaller systems, residence hall staff who are responsible for RAs and buildings may report directly to the director of residence life. In larger systems, they may report to another level of staff who report to the director. The number and type of other staff at the central level are also determined by contextual factors. In some large systems, more specialized functions may be necessary, such as administering discipline, coordinating staff development, coordinating developmental programming, handling crises, and administering information systems and data processing.

Organizing the Business Side of Housing

The third choice is how to organize the business side of residence halls. Regardless of size, there are typically three major functions: housing, food services, and support services. Organizationally, at this central level, there is typically a person in charge of housing, a person in charge of food services, and a person in charge of support functions such as business services, personnel, facilities planning, purchasing, information services, accounting, vending, marketing, and communications (Figure 7.4). This last function

Figure 7.4. Housing and Food Services: Sample Organizational Chart.

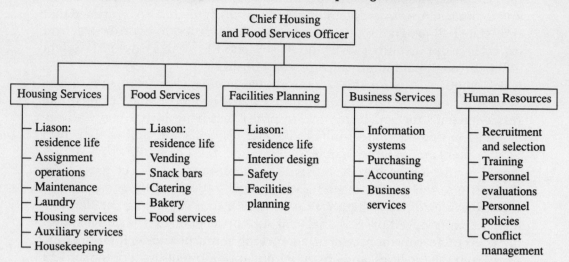

becomes more important as business operations become more customer and consumer oriented. In general, these three functions report directly to a person with business management background, training, and experience.

In the operations or business areas, there are several functions. Facilities need to be planned, constructed, renovated, and maintained. Maintaining safe, clean facilities whose utilities function well and are repaired in a timely fashion is important not only from the standpoint of lengthening the life of buildings but also for the overall morale of residents. Poorly maintained facilities are virtually an open invitation for students to treat these facilities poorly. For example, facilities that go unrepaired for an unreasonable length of time tend to promote malicious damage by students. If the institution does not maintain clean facilities, students are less likely to assume much responsibility for the cleanliness of common areas or their rooms. (See Chapter Eight for further discussions of housing administration.)

Room Assignments

A key aspect of the housing operation is the way students are assigned. At first glance, this appears to be a straightforward clerical function that assigns students to buildings and rooms on the basis of student preference or architectural realities. But there is some evidence that the way students are assigned is associated with their personal and academic development (Ballou, 1991). Important questions include the following: Should upperclassmen and freshmen be assigned together or separately? What about assigning students to buildings, floors, or rooms by academic interests? Is there a way to assign roommates that reduces roommate incompatibility?

Because assignment policies have fiscal as well as developmental implications, assignment policies should be established jointly by the business and residential life staff. In some cases, the assignment operation may report to the student life organization. But in either instance, institutions must realize that the assignment of students has important developmental and academic consequences and should not treat it as a minor administrative task.

Food Services

In the food service area, the first choice is whether the institution should operate its own food services or contract these services to a private vendor. Generally speaking, the smaller the residential operation, the more feasible it is for the institution to hire a private food service vendor. As size increases, it typically becomes more cost effective for institutions to operate their own food services, because large operations allow for the employment of persons with specialized knowledge and expertise that can make the food service program effective and efficient. Smaller programs tend to lack all the necessary expertise to run efficient operations.

If the institution has its own food services, how should they be organized? First, there may be food service operations that are not directly tied to residence halls, such as snack bars at non–residence hall locations, food services in union buildings, food vending operations, and public dining facilities in conference or hotel facilities. Second, in general, there should be one person in charge of one or more food service facilities whose span of control includes menu planning, quality control, equipment maintenance, food preparation, serving, and cleanup. In addition, food service staff must be hired, trained, supervised, and evaluated.

Several critical issues relevant to the integration of food services into the residential and housing program must be considered. First, it is essential that the liaison role between the dining and residential life staff be clear and constructive, aimed at working collaboratively toward meeting student needs. A mechanism for channeling student complaints, input, and feedback must be built into the structure so that student concerns are not fragmented. Second, in each model reviewed previously, fiscal accountability from an institutional perspective was discussed. It is important that the residential life and housing staff work collaboratively in packaging the "room-and-board" rate as a total package, because that is how it is perceived by students and their parents. The organization and presentation of rates deserve careful consideration so that fiscal accountability to students is ensured. (See Chapter Nine for more detailed discussions of food service.)

Selecting a Model

Readers are reminded that an organizational structure is a product, not only of what needs to be done, but also of the institutional and contextual factors in which it is found. Consequently, there is no one preferred organizational structure for student life, housing, and food services. There is, however, one caveat about tailoring organizational structures and personnel to the institution. Whatever model or structure that is adopted should ensure racial/ethnic diversity and gender equity of housing, food service, and residence life staff. As women and racial/ethnic minorities gain more access to higher education, it is important for institutions to promote greater diversity in their housing and food service staffs. It is not only the right thing to do, it is the necessary thing to do if we want to educate and serve students effectively.

Financing of Residence Halls

In discussing many of the above choices, "fiscal constraints" were frequently mentioned as a factor in making choices. As mentioned in Chapter Eight, most residence halls are financed exclusively by room-and-board charges to residents and are typically budgeted as an auxiliary enterprise (at almost all public institutions). That is, all expenses must be covered by income. General funds of institutions are rarely used to finance residence halls—usually only temporarily, in instances where not enough income is generated to sustain programs, services, and facilities.

Auxiliary enterprises are not simply a matter of dividing the cost of services and programs by the number of residents. First, from an expenses perspective, many housing systems borrowed money to build residences, so that debt retirement may be a substantial portion of expenses. Second, there are typically overhead expenses such as heating, plumbing, and electricity. Third, even though most institutions cover fringe benefits for employees from central sources, auxiliary enterprises are often asked to cover these costs from income, and so the expense line for staff is salary *plus* benefits. Fourth, a reserve fund is necessary to cover unexpected expenses, or capital improvements, so that expenses must include this item. And finally, on the expense side of the ledger, there is the actual cost of providing services, programs, and facilities.

On the income side of the ledger, several factors must be taken into account. First, rates must be kept affordable to students. Rates that are too high may force students to choose other, more affordable institutions or to live elsewhere and thus will reduce occupancy and income. It is often difficult to establish a rate that covers the expenses necessary for a high-quality program, while at the same time remaining competitively affordable.

Second, institutions must maintain a fiscally responsible occupancy rate, while resisting the temptation to overcrowd facilities in a way that does not serve the best interests of residents. It may seem logical to start the year with full occupancy and then be underoccupied due to normal attrition. However, it is more fiscally responsible to overcrowd and let normal attrition take occupancy to more acceptable levels, to keep rates affordable. The question is how much overcrowding is acceptable, and how the overcrowding can be done with a minimum of disruption to residents.

And finally, there is almost always a political dimension to the rate structure. For example, if an institution is facing a larger-than-usual tuition increase or a projected reduction in enrollment, residence halls operations may be under pressure to keep rates low, so that the total cost of an education for students remains competitive. In this instance, reserves may be depleted, maintenance may be deferred, programs may be reduced or eliminated, or other cost-cutting measures may be put into effect. By the way, these measures may also be put into effect if occupancy rates, for whatever reason, become too low to provide basic services, programs, and facilities. (See Chapter Eight for a more detailed discussion.)

Organizing and Administering for the Future

What does the future bode for the organization and administration of residence halls? It is difficult to predict, but we can be certain that we must provide affordable student life, housing, and food service programs to students. How we organize to deliver these services may change, due to changing fiscal realities, changing student needs, and changes in society. For example, as student needs change, we may have to reconsider whether the RA model is appropriate. Or if the total cost of education continues to soar, we may need to reconsider how residence halls are financed.

But I sense that there is a renewed surge of "customer demand" that must be met. Gone are the old days when students had no choice but to live in residence halls, eat the food served, and put up with less-than-high-quality services and programs. In the final analysis, housing programs must organize themselves in ways that are more responsive to the demands not only of "resident customers," but to their parents and other family members, who—given rising costs—will demand more accountability for their dollars.

Is there an "ideal" way to organize and administer residence halls? The answer to that question is a resounding no because of contextual choices and organizational choices that are unique to each institution. The bottom line, however, is that institutions that are committed to quality must develop residence halls that are efficiently managed, affordable, safe, and well maintained, and most important, that contribute to the personal and academic development of all residents. Residence halls that do not proactively address students' developmental needs may well be at a major competitive disadvantage in comparison to local apartment complexes. Attention to students' needs and interests from well-qualified, caring professionals can be an excellent "selling point" to students and parents alike.

References

Ballou, R. A. "Assigning First-Year Students to College Residence Halls." In W. J. Zeller, D. S. Fidler, and B. O. Barefoot, *Residence Life Programs and the*

First Year Experience. Columbia, S.C.: Association of College and University Housing Officers-International and the National Resource Center for the Freshman Year Experience, 1991.

Council for the Advancement of Standards for Student Services/Development Programs. *Standards and Guidelines for Housing and Residential Life Programs*. College Park, Md.: Council for the Advancement of Standards for Student Services/Development Programs, 1986.

Duerst, D., and Welch, M. *RA to Student Ratios, RA Attrition, and RA Compensation*. University of Wisconsin–Eau Claire: Association of College and University Housing Officers-International, 1988.

Ploskonka, J. *Organizational Structures of Housing Programs: An Overview*. Columbus, Ohio: Association of College and University Housing Officers-International, 1990.

Upcraft, M. L., with the collaboration of Pilato, G. T. *Residence Hall Assistants in College: A Guide to Selection, Training, and Supervision*. San Francisco: Jossey-Bass, 1982.

Upcraft, M. L., Gardner, J. N., and Associates. *The Freshman Year Experience: Helping Students Survive and Succeed in College*. San Francisco: Jossey-Bass, 1989.

Chapter Eight

=============

Business Operations and Facility Management

Daniel A. Hallenbeck

Conceptually, a comprehensive housing department can be thought of as a tripod with business, facility management, and programming as the three legs. Each leg of the tripod supports the other two. If one leg crumbles, the tripod topples. These functional areas—business, facility management, and programming—must be supportive of one another and must be recognized as equally important. This chapter focuses on two of the three legs of the tripod, business and facility management. (Programming is addressed in detail in Chapter Seventeen.) In the business operations section, the topics of auxiliary enterprises, budget construction and management, assignments, summer conference housing, and marketing strategies are addressed. Topics discussed in the facility management section include deferred maintenance, planning for new construction or major renovation, construction, maintenance, services, and personalization programs.

The practice of involving students in program planning and implementation, in student government, in student staff positions, and as program participants is commonly accepted. Not as common, but equally important, is the involvement of students in the business and facility management

activities of the department. Students, particularly those in leadership positions, desire and deserve active involvement in financial and facility decisions. It is important to have a clearly defined vehicle for involving students
in discussions pertaining to rate increases, use of facilities, renovations,
funding and construction of new facilities, and personalization programs.

Business Operations

Business operations include all the technical and financial aspects of housing operations—that is, everything except programming and educational
and developmental interventions. Especially important in the organization
of business operations in public colleges are *auxiliary enterprises*, which are
used to maintain a separation between state dollars and income generated
from students in the form of fees and charges for services.

Auxiliary Enterprises

At most publicly supported colleges and some private institutions, the service or business units—for example, housing, food service, health service,
bookstore, vending, printing, golf course—are grouped together in a category called auxiliary services or auxiliary enterprises. Auxiliary enterprises
are generally thought of as revenue-generating self-supporting units. At
public institutions, these units are expected to at least break even financially.
Most are required to generate a specified percentage above the costs of
operations to be placed in reserve and/or surplus accounts. The reserve and
surplus money is used for major repairs, renovation, and replacement.
     On the other hand, at private institutions the lines between auxiliary-
type activities and the instructional budget may be less rigid. For instance,
housing may not be expected to be self-sustaining, receiving "subsidies" for
utilities and other indirect costs from the overall college budget. "In turn, the
auxiliaries return excess income to a general [college] reserve to be used as a
budget-supporting mechanism for the entire institution" (Barr, 1988, p. 26).
There is considerable variation among private institutions concerning how
strictly the separation between housing's budget and the general institutional
budget is maintained. (In the remainder of this section, discussion will center
on auxiliary budgeting common at many public institutions.)
     Because they are self-supporting at public colleges, auxiliary enter-
prises must be operated following sound business practices. Financially
successful housing programs effectively integrate program, staff, and facilities to create a community environment through which individual growth is
promoted. Although it may seem costly to develop and deliver educational/
developmental programs, to hire, train, and supervise resident assistants, and
to provide non-revenue-generating spaces, such as recreation rooms, study
lounges, and computer labs, these measures are essential for a successful
program, both financially and programmatically.

By classifying and operating housing as an auxiliary enterprise, the institution is assured that money will not be diverted from the instructional budget to support the housing program. The effective housing program generates revenue to provide funds for the maintenance, repair, and renovation of facilities; educational, developmental, recreational, and social programs; operating supplies; and staff salaries and benefits. Even though the funding source for an auxiliary differs from other parts of the institution, it is required to follow the same personnel policies and other operating procedures as the rest of the institution. As an example, generally an auxiliary such as housing cannot give its employees a higher percentage pay increase than the rest of the institution, even though housing may have had a financially successful year. To do so would create inequities among employees in similar positions across the campus.

Another distinguishing characteristic of an auxiliary is its ability to carry surplus and/or reserve monies forward from one year to the next. In contrast, most nonauxiliary units lose any balance left in their account at the end of the fiscal year. This flexibility provides the housing director with the ability to develop long-range plans for facility improvements and program development without being constrained by a fiscal calendar or the pressure to spend all available funds prior to the end of the year.

Monies carried over at the conclusion of the fiscal year can be placed in surplus and/or reserve accounts, as prescribed by institutional policy or loan covenants. The policies and procedures governing expenditure of these funds are dictated by the governing board and vary from institution to institution and state to state. These monies are used for the repair and renovation of the facilities and the replacement of equipment and furnishings.

One philosophical position argues that because residence hall living plays an integral role in the educational mission of the institution, the programmatic portion of the housing budget should be financed with state monies. This argument continues that since education takes place both in the classroom and in the residence hall, it should be funded from the same source. Even though I agree with and support the premise that residence hall living significantly contributes to the educational and developmental growth of the individual student, the reality of the sitution is that funding for residence hall learning will never be on equal footing with classroom learning. If funding for residence hall programs and classroom instruction are competing for the same dollar, classroom instruction will win more often than not. If faced with budget reductions, which position would be cut first, a residence hall director or a classroom instructor?

Operating as an auxiliary, the housing director has more control over the financial and programmatic destiny of the housing department. By managing a fiscally sound operation, the director has the flexibility to create, delete, or reconfigure positions, facilities, and programs to meet the needs of a changing residential clientele. Consequently, a housing program may be better off not seeking funding for programming positions from the general instructional budget.

Budget Construction and Management

To most new housing professionals, the process of budget construction and budget administration or management is a mysterious process and something to approach with fear and trembling. Most young professionals indicate that the area in which they most need additional training and experience is in "budgets." Although the details of the budget process are institution specific, the general concepts discussed here in an elementary fashion are widely generalizable.

Planning and goal setting are integral to the budgeting process. The budget is a plan or blueprint for reaching the department's goals. The budget should not be viewed as a static document but as a fluid management tool employed to reach desired outcomes. As priorities and requirements change, the budget must necessarily change.

The two basic components of a budget are revenue and expenses. The difference between the two is the net or surplus. In constructing a budget, estimates of the revenue and expenses and a determination of the amount desired in surplus have to be made.

Since it is a self-supporting auxiliary enterprise, the housing department's primary source of revenue comes through the rental of rooms to students. Therefore, revenue projections are necessarily closely tied to the anticipated occupancy. The ideal, from an income standpoint, would be to have every bed filled all the time. However, that is not realistic. Occupancy figures for the last few years should be reviewed to determine a realistic occupancy figure on which to base the projected revenue. In addition to reviewing the historical occupancy data, the housing administrator must also be aware of institutional decisions in the area of enrollment management that may impact occupancy. As a rule of thumb, 95 percent occupancy is used for revenue projections by colleges that anticipate being "full," because there is always some shrinkage and it is safer to underestimate than overestimate revenue. Additional revenue sources might include vending income, interest income, damage reimbursements, and conference income, which should be considered in developing the department's anticipated revenue figures for the coming year.

Operating expense categories are institution specific but generally include the following: (1) personnel—salaries and staff benefits, (2) debt service, (3) utilities, (4) repairs, (5) supplies, (6) overhead charges, and (7) reserve. These categories may be grouped under various headings or titles at different institutions and some institutions will have additional categories, but these basic categories will be found in most housing budgets.

Because housing organizations are labor intensive, one of the department's major expenses will be salaries and staff benefits. It is important to remember that staff benefit costs generally run from 25 to 30 percent of the total staff salaries. Therefore, the 25 to 30 percent needs to be added to total staff costs. These staff benefits include such items as the institution's contribution to health insurance, retirement, and social security.

Principal and interest payments required to retire the debt on the residence halls are categorized as debt service. Many residence halls were built with borrowed funds through the sale of revenue bonds, a federally financed loan program, or private loans. The repayment schedule or amortization schedule lists the annual principal and interest payments over the life of the loan. Many of these loans were amortized over a thirty- to fifty-year period.

Utility costs are another major expenditure in housing budgets. Gas, electricity, water, and sewage may be purchased from the institution's physical plant department or from a community agency. In either case, it costs a substantial amount to heat, cool, light, and supply water to residence halls. Other utility costs, which may or may not be in the budget, are telephone, television cable, and trash collection.

The category of repairs is one over which some control can be exercised. This includes items such as replacing a broken window, mending a jammed door lock, or adjusting a door closer. Generally, these are expenditures that are considered to be caused through normal wear and tear on the facilities. These work orders may be accomplished by an in-house maintenance staff, the campus' physical plant department, or an outside contractor.

The supply category includes both office and custodial supplies. This includes everything from paper clips, letterhead, and brochures to floor wax and cleaning supplies.

Some auxiliaries are responsible for administrative overhead charges, which theoretically cover some of the cost of doing business on the campus. These charges are usually expressed as a percentage of the total operating budget and may run from 2 to 3 percent to as high as 15 to 20 percent. This might cover the use of the mainframe computer, the personnel office, the procurement office, police and fire protection, and campus mail. Many times, a portion of the salary of the vice president to which the auxiliary reports is charged to the operating unit.

Many housing organizations are required—either by the governing board or by their bond covenants—to put a certain percentage of funds in reserve. This is required to ensure the liquidity of the operation should a drop in occupancy occur. In some cases, a full year's operating expenses are required to be held in reserve. In other cases, a certain percentage of the revenue is pledged to reserves each year. For instance, the University System of Georgia requires 5 percent of every dollar earned to be placed in a reserve account. Even if not required, it is a good practice to hold some revenue in reserve for emergencies. Depending on how the budget is constructed, it may be necessary to allocate a certain amount of money to reserves each year.

Institutional or system policies may allow reserves to be used for facility maintenance and equipment purchases.

As mentioned earlier, the net or surplus is the amount of money left over at the end of the year after all the bills have been paid. Assuming there is a positive balance, this money is normally used for major repairs, renovation, and replacement of furnishings and equipment. For instance, when a roof needs to be replaced or when desks for student rooms are needed, the money comes from the surplus account. Different institutions have different regulations guiding the expenditure of these funds, but more often than not, these monies are used in this manner. From a budgetary point of view, it is important to accurately predict the amount needed in surplus to accomplish the desired facility upkeep. A variety of planning tools can be employed to determine the money needed in surplus for facility repair and renovation.

Rental rates are established at a level designed to generate enough money to meet all operating expenses and return the desired amount to surplus. Different rate increase cycles are followed at different institutions based on historical and political considerations. At some institutions, a standard rental rate is charged for all residence hall rooms regardless of amenities offered in a particular hall. At others, the rate is based on the amenities, facilities, and services offered in each particular hall. Differential rates are commonly charged for such things as air-conditioning, lavatories in student rooms, and private or semiprivate bathrooms. Administratively, different rates are more difficult to manage; however, they seem to be more fair and equitable when there is a significant difference in housing facilities.

Monthly operating statements are a management tool designed to assist the housing administrator in evaluating progress toward the departmental goals on which the budget was based. They provide a monthly opportunity to see if revenue and expense projections were accurate. The format of these statements varies from institution to institution but usually includes the revenue and expenses realized for the current month, the cumulative total for the fiscal year, the amount budgeted for the fiscal year, the previous year's actual amount for the year to date, and the previous year's budgeted amount.

Table 8.1 shows a residence hall monthly operating statement. At the top of the table, information on the revenue categories (rent and late fee, laundry, damages, conferences) is provided for both the current and the previous year. Following down the left-hand side of the table, notice the expense categories of personal services, direct expenses, and indirect expenses, as well as transfers and encumbrances. The net amount for the current month, $55,140.40, is obtained by subtracting the sum of the expense categories from the total revenue. Operating statements for an entire housing department would follow the same format.

It is important for the housing administrator to be able to read, understand, and use the monthly operating statement. Due to the complicated nature of some institutional budgeting and accounting systems, this may be difficult to do. If so, be sure to seek assistance from the institution's business or accounting office.

The budget for a housing department should reflect the department's goals. Monies should be expended to meet the department's priorities. Revenue projections are based on anticipated occupancy and the rental rate. Expenses are based on previous experience and inflationary factors. Incremental budgeting, which involves increasing expense categories by a percentage arrived at by examining actual expenses from the previous year and estimating the increase for the coming year, is acceptable. Using this method assumes that the previous year's expenditures were justified and that it is only necessary to justify the anticipated increase. The difference between revenue and expenses is the net that goes into the surplus account.

The challenge for the housing administrator comes when there is a shortfall in revenue, expenses exceed estimates, and unexpected and unanticipated major repairs are required. Any one of these can cause consternation, but all three happening at the same time can be a major source of concern. Planning is essential, but one should expect and anticipate some unexpected and uncontrollable events to supply a management challenge.

Assignments

The orderly assignment of students to specific residence halls and specific rooms is the underlying goal of an application/assignment process. Most institutions have a housing application that the prospective resident completes and submits to the housing office. (At some private institutions where on-campus housing is required of all nonlocal students, there is no housing application. Applicants simply check a box on the admissions application concerning housing plans.) This is usually the first step in reserving a space. Although designed differently and requesting various kinds of information, generally an application will request the following information: name, home address, social security number, date of birth, period of time for which housing is being requested with particular emphasis being given to starting date, any physical limitations or disabilities, and signature. Additional information may be requested that will assist in the assignment process, depending on the specific institution and its philosophy. Examples of these questions might include roommate preference, residence hall preference, academic major, visitation option, personality characteristics, hobbies, personal habits, and desire to participate in housing of one kind or another.

At many institutions, housing applications will only be accepted from individuals who have been admitted to the institution. In other words, a prospective student could not submit a housing application until official acceptance of admission had been received. This procedure is followed to make sure the housing office is not processing and holding applications for assignment from persons who have no intention of attending that particular

Table 8.1. Department of University Housing: Example of Monthly Financial Report.

RESIDENCE HALL: Smith Hall
DATE: January 31, 1992
% Time into Year 58.3

	Current Year				Previous Year		
	Current Month	Year to Date	%	Budget FY 93	Year to Date	%	Budget FY 92
REVENUE:							
Rent and late fee	98,702.77	358,320.82			350,842.88		
Laundry	925.75	6,090.75			6,525.50		
Damages	120.00	265.00			863.61		
Conferences		83,209.86			70,220.00		
TOTAL REVENUE	99,748.52	447,886.43	53.7	833,716	428,451.99	52.2	820,067
EXPENDITURES:							
Personal Services:							
Monthly	6,565.83	37,937.33	33.0	114,924	40,083.10	29.3	136,897
Salaried	1,975.84	14,127.26	37.9	37,228	13,853.47	37.4	37,030
Hourly	2,552.17	22,514.24	70.6	31,870	19,163.82	60.1	31,870
Overtime		186.74	18.7	1,000			
Staff benefits	809.30	7,429.29	46.8	15,881	8,317.24	60.1	13,838
TOTAL PERSONAL SERVICES	11,903.14	82,194.86	40.9	200,904	81,417.63	37.1	219,635
Direct Expenses:							
Supplies	385.09	2,378.28	2.72	8,728	3,054.61	37.1	8,234
Insurance		1,739.00	60.0	2,897	2,897.00	104.5	2,772
Communications	4,415.53	35,069.05	50.6	69,356	30,531.39	56.5	54,019
TOTAL DIRECT EXPENSES	4,800.62	39,186.33	48.4	80,981	36,483.00	56.1	65,025

Indirect Expenses:							
Repairs 22000	2,709.25	22,353.51			25,849.20		
Previous maintenance 23000	154.20	1,903.36			1,943.36		
Specific W/O							
Vehicle							
Indirect purchases (001)		5,102.52			4,563.82		
Total maintenance and repairs	2,863.45	29,359.39	41.0	71,627	32,356.38	47.9	67,573
Total Custodial Labor	7,698.60	57,939.70	52.7	110,002	57,087.00	53.8	106,198
Total Custodial Supplies	210.57	(176.21)	−1.7	10,203	2,454.42	24.1	10,203
Water	1,956.28	10,008.38			7,651.51		
Electricity	2,500.40	26,252.32			35,340.24		
Garbage	390.00	2,730.00			2,310.00		
Steam or gas	833.87	6,460.99			7,188.46		
Sewer tax	1,161.69	7,301.90			7,030.35		
Total utilities	6,842.24	52,753.59	43.9	120,285	59,520.56	49.8	119,565
TOTAL INDIRECT EXPENSES	17,614.86	139,876.47	44.8	312,117	151,418.36	49.9	303,539
TRANSFERS:							
Debt service	4,987.42	22,394.32	53.7	41,686	21,422.60	52.2	41,003
Reserve					576.04		
ENCUMBRANCES	5,302.08	5,302.08					
NET	55,140.40	158,932.37	80.3	198,028	137,134.36	71.8	190,865

institution or who do not meet admissions standards. Because most institutions can only house *students*, it makes sense to only accept applications from those persons who have been admitted. It also allows the assignments staff to concentrate on those individuals who are most likely to be residents.

At institutions where admission to the institution is required before the housing application is accepted, the housing application is usually sent in the same envelope with the letter of acceptance. Once applicants are admitted, they receive the housing application with instructions for completing and returning it.

Another common practice is to require an application fee, housing deposit, or prepayment of some amount with the application. This is an institutional decision. An application fee is normally a nonrefundable fee used to cover the cost of processing the application. The deposit is used by some institutions to ensure that the individual is coming. If the student cancels prior to arriving and prior to receiving a contract, usually a portion of the deposit will be refunded and a portion forfeited. If the individual fulfills the terms and conditions of the contract, the deposit is refunded at the conclusion of the contract period. Sometimes the deposit is used as a reservation/damage deposit, which means that if damages above normal wear and tear are inflicted on the room, a portion or all of the deposit is withheld when the student checks out. A prepayment requirement with the application is an attempt to make sure those individuals who apply for housing really want the space and are coming. The mechanics vary, but the prepayment is applied to the rent at some point during the contract period. It may be during the fall or sometimes not until spring semester. If the student cancels prior to the conclusion of the contract period, some amount of the prepayment is forfeited.

In addition to an application, many successful housing programs have a residence hall contract that covers the entire academic year. As the term implies, the contract commits the student to living in the residence hall for the entire academic year (or as long as she or he remains enrolled) or that portion of the year that remains, should the student begin residence midyear. The contract contains the terms and conditions of occupancy and ensures a fairly constant level of occupancy throughout the year. The contract, once signed by the student and parent or legal guardian, becomes a legally binding document.

If faced with writing a contract, it is highly advisable to confer with the institution's legal counsel to make sure the document's terms and conditions are binding and will hold up in court.

Because most institutions only house students in their residence halls, most contracts indicate that the agreement will be terminated when the student is no longer enrolled. The contract should outline a schedule for rent refunds when a student withdraws from the institution.

The contract should, in most cases, outline the payment schedule. Some institutions send the contract to new students during the summer and require them to sign and return it with the fall term's rent by a specified date. Other institutions require the signed contract to be returned during the summer and require the first term's rent by the first day of classes. Others have a deferred payment plan in which students pay a portion of the rent with the returned contract and the balance in two or three installments throughout the term. From the institution's point of view, it is more profitable to receive the full term's rent prior to the beginning of the term so the money can be invested and earn interest. If the interest income is credited to the housing department, this money can assist in keeping the rental rates down. For students, an installment payment plan is usually more convenient and allows "paying as you go" rather than having to pay a whole term's rent in one payment. (This plan is particularly popular when a large percentage of residents must work to meet their educational costs.) The choice of payment plan is usually not a decision that the housing department can make independently of the institution's business/finance vice president. Payment schedules are normally set by the governing board for the institution to include tuition and all fees.

At times, students face extenuating circumstances that may cause them to request a release from their contract. A procedure for handling these requests is necessary. Three options seem to be the most common. One option is to have some kind of petitioning process. This method allows students to explain their circumstances to an individual or group, either in writing or orally. If the review committee feels a release from the contract is warranted, it makes such a recommendation to the director of housing. In most cases, the deposit is forfeited but the resident suffers no other penalty. Another option is a "buyout," through which the contract is terminated by the resident when a sum less than the full remaining face value is paid. The last option is when no provision is made for release or early termination of the contract. In this instance, the student pays the full face value of the contract regardless of length of occupancy. Of course, a combination of these approaches is possible.

Because the primary source of revenue is the rental of rooms to students, the contract must be written to ensure the highest level of occupancy possible. Because the costs of operating a residence hall are basically the same whether the building is full or three-fourths full, the greatest economy is achieved when the costs are spread over the greatest number of residents. If, in a residence hall housing 200 students, 25 are released from their residence hall contracts, the 175 left will be paying the expense of staff, supplies, and debt service for the 25 who have been released. In fairness to all the students living in housing, those students who leave the halls prior to the conclusion of the contract period should pay some amount to cover part of the continuing fixed costs.

One constant characteristic of the student population is mobility. It is common for students to desire to change living arrangements. This may mean moving from one room to another, or one hall to another. Therefore, it is important to have fair and equitable room and hall change procedures. Room change procedures should be facilitative rather than prohibitive. When a student wants to move, for whatever reason, the process should be as hassle free as possible. Available space should be reassigned on a first-come, first-served basis. If moving from one hall to another effects a change in rental rates, the procedure should be explicit in the computation of the additional charge or the refund.

Some housing professionals argue that students will not learn to deal with people from diverse backgrounds or with uncomfortable situations if allowed to freely change rooms. Operationally, room change procedures are developed that put staff in the position of deciding if the student's reason for wanting a change is valid. If the reason is considered valid, the student is allowed to move. If not, the student is told to work through the situation while remaining in the current living arrangement. Others argue that once a student has elected to move, there is little positive accomplished by denying that request. Furthermore, the request to move does not create a "teachable moment." It seems more effective to facilitate the room change, assist the student in finding a satisfying living arrangement, and, if necessary, develop intervention strategies to promote the student's growth in the new environment.

Because the residence hall population is mobile, an efficient system for tracking residents must be employed. When a move is made, it requires changing records in the registrar's office, housing office, campus directory, and mailroom, just to name a few. Today it is possible to notify all necessary offices with the stroke of a computer key. For campuses not at that point, a good paper trail must be employed.

The system devised for assigning new students to the residence halls must be fair and easily explainable and should give all students an equal chance of obtaining their "ideal" living arrangement. On many campuses, the demand for space in one hall exceeds the supply, and so a fair procedure is needed to determine who gets their choice and who does not. One approach is to use date order, where the order of assignment is based on the date the completed housing application was received in the housing office. Another approach is to match students on various personality characteristics, by interests or hobbies, or by academic major.

Returning residents are customarily given some priority over new incoming students for residence hall space. Some schools encourage residents to return by allowing them to select space before new incoming residents are assigned. In this model, all returners that request housing are accommodated. Other schools employ a lottery system for students who wish to return. A specific number of spaces are reserved for returners. The students are "drawn" through some process or criteria and assigned a space. With the lottery, there are always returning students who want but do not get residence hall space.

Contingent on the method employed for returning students is the policy of requiring new students to live in the halls. Some campuses require all freshmen to live in the residence halls. This reserves a space for each freshman. If space is limited, all returning students may not be able to live in the halls. The freshman residency requirement has caused many campuses to implement a lottery for the space left after all freshmen are assigned. On the other hand, if no one is required to live in the residence halls, it seems particularly important to retain as many satisfied customers as possible. Also, from a programming point of view, it may be important to have upperclass leadership in the halls, so returning students are encouraged to continue their occupancy.

"Community" is much more easily established and maintained with people who are living in residence halls because they want to rather than because it is a requirement. Although a strong philosophical argument can be made for the benefits and value of freshmen participating in a guided group-living experience, it is almost impossible to create a learning environment when the individual loathes being there. The basis for freshman residency requirements in most institutions is financial rather than educational. In other words, the goal is to ensure a high level of occupancy. The other alternative, which may be more acceptable, is to sell the program on its merits by having a program that meets students' needs. A *quality* program keeps the halls full and on sound financial footing.

When new students have been assigned, the assignment information must be communicated to them. Some schools will provide only the name of the hall to which the students have been assigned. In this case, the students are notified of the specific room assignment when they arrive on campus to check in. Other institutions notify them of the hall, room, and roommate's name, telephone number, and address before their arrival on campus. This gives students an opportunity to contact their roommates and become acquainted prior to check-in. It also allows for developing room decorating plans and sharing of room furnishings such as stereo, television, and refrigerator. The roommates may determine, after contacting each other, that they will be incompatible and want a room change. It may be necessary to have a procedure developed to process requests for changes before the residents occupy the hall. There are certainly pros and cons to each approach. It is important to think through each option and develop policies and procedures that are fair and equitable to all concerned.

Generally, not all students who make reservations for the fall actually enroll. These individuals are referred to as "no shows." To maintain the highest level of occupancy throughout the academic year, it is wise to oversubscribe the space. In other words, more contracts than available bed spaces in regular student rooms should be accepted. That way, once the "shake-down period" is over and the no-show spaces recaptured, contracted residents will be available to move into these rooms.

Oversubscription is an option in facilities with community baths by placing beds in lounges, recreation rooms, or study rooms on a temporary basis. This has been referred to as temporary housing. Usually students living in temporary housing will be moved into regular accommodations within two weeks. Another alternative for handling "overflow" assignments is to expand the occupancy of some rooms. An extra bed can be placed in a room that normally houses two persons. This approach is sometimes preferable because it does not take public space — recreational areas, study, and lounge — away from use by the rest of the students in the hall. It also allows the "overflow student" to become involved actively in the floor unit of a particular hall. Oversubscription is a common practice that benefits students by spreading the cost of operation over the greatest number of residents and results in lower rental rates. However, it is important to have a well-developed plan for accommodating those "overflow students." If these students cannot move to regular accommodations within five to six weeks after beginning classes, they should be given a rent rebate or reduction of some kind.

The goal of deposits and prepayments is to keep the no-show rate as low as possible. Because the best time to rent residence hall space is in the fall, a lower no-show rate then will yield higher average occupancy. Typically, enrollments peak during the fall, so that is when the demand is the highest.

Organizationally, it is necessary to determine whether the students' and the department's needs can best be met through having the assignments and room change functions centralized or decentralized. Some schools have found a combination of the two to work most effectively, with all initial assignments made centrally and room changes approved and made at the hall or community level. This arrangement seems to satisfy the student's need for convenience and the department's need for administrative control and recordkeeping. The organizational model employed on a particular campus depends to some degree on departmental history and philosophy.

Summer Conference Housing

With summer comes a reduction in enrollment and reduced occupancy in the residence halls. Many campuses have elected to rent housing space to summer conference groups. This provides an additional revenue source, which assists in meeting continuing expenses while the regular-year students are away from campus. It also can be an effective recruitment tool for the institution. Bringing various youth groups to campus and allowing them to live in the residence halls as part of their program is an effective method of showcasing the institution and its housing facilities.

There are several phases to a successful summer conference housing program: marketing, scheduling, staffing, recordkeeping, and follow-up.

Both adult and youth groups look for low-cost campus housing for summer meetings. It is possible to cater to both groups, but it is probably not wise to house both in the same facility at the same time, since their needs and life-styles are too different. Many of the youth groups are associated with sports, band, or cheerleading and may be directly sponsored by a campus department or organization. Private colleges often serve as the hosts for conferences and organizations associated with the affiliated church or other sponsor. Prior to scheduling youth groups, it is recommended that the institution's legal counsel be consulted to clarify any liability issues involved in housing minors. (See Chapter Fourteen.)

To avoid charges of unfair competition with the local hotel owners, the groups that are recruited should have some connection with the institution. Sponsorship by an institutional agency (such as the athletic department, music school, or honors program) legitimizes the educational nature of the group.

Maintaining a master schedule is particularly important for a well-organized, efficiently run conference operation. Information that should be kept includes the name of the group, the dates of arrival and checkout, the size of the group, and the name and telephone number of the contact person. This master schedule should be set up so that reservations can be accepted several years in advance.

Prior to scheduling groups, some decisions need to be made about how soon after the conclusion of spring term and how close to the beginning of fall term reservations will be accepted. Although the conference business provides some helpful income, the department's primary purpose is to house students who attend the institution. Thus, time must be allowed for students to vacate the premises in the spring and for the housekeeping staff to clean and prepare the facility for conferences. At the close of the summer, it is necessary to allow time to get the facilities in good condition for the opening of fall term.

An additional scheduling concern relates to the type of groups that can be housed together in the same building. In other words, it is not possible to use every bed in every building, because it would be "bad business" to house some groups together. For instance, cheerleading and senior citizen groups usually do not mix well. The keeper of the master schedule must be cognizant of the composition of the groups and any special arrangements or facilities they require.

When the initial reservation is made, a ballpark estimate is given of the number of participants to be housed. As it gets closer to the check-in date, a *firm* number is needed. Some institutions require a guaranteed number from the sponsor so that the college is not left with empty beds. It is important to develop a standardized procedure or timetable for receiving a firm number from the group sponsor, because this will allow for a better utilization of space.

Staffing for summer conferences has some different requirements than during the academic year. For instance, the housekeeping staff is accustomed to students checking into a room and staying for nine months. The normal routine followed by the housekeepers is different than is required when groups are moving in and out after a stay of a few days or weeks. Also, different services may be offered to conferees, such as daily emptying of wastepaper baskets and making beds. It is vitally important that the house-keeping staff receive a thorough orientation regarding expectations of working in a summer conference facility. They must be convinced of the importance of this operation to the housing department and realize the importance of the role they play in making summer conference housing a success.

The staff members who check conferees into the residence hall set the "tone" for the group's stay. Some adult conferees expect hotel/motel service and amenities, so it is important that individuals working in this capacity be trained in customer service philosophy and techniques. In many conference operations, a twenty-four-hour desk is run in the hall. This desk serves as an information/hospitality center and as a security measure. All desk workers need to be helpful, courteous, and attentive to the conferees' needs.

Security for the participants in summer conference groups is another consideration. The twenty-four-hour desk is one security measure, but it is also important to keep the campus security force informed regarding what groups are on campus and which buildings they are staying in. Some groups have specific needs in the security area, such as curfews for participants and times when access to the building is prohibited (especially when housing minors). There may be a need to add extra security workers for some specific groups.

If youth groups or athletic camps are catered to, it is a good idea to hire individuals to live on the floors—much like camp counselors. This provides additional supervision and individuals who can plan some activities and programs for the participants in addition to those offered by the sponsoring group. Minor participants are less likely to become involved in mischievous activities if they are actively involved in planned programs and activities.

Recordkeeping is particularly important in the summer conference business because income is determined by the number of persons who stay for a specified number of nights. Another reason for accurate recordkeeping is that the institution will be required to pay income tax on the revenue generated. This income would be categorized as "unrelated business income," which is taxable. (Institutional counsel should be consulted about the tax implications of conferences.) The necessary recordkeeping is more like that of a hotel or motel operation than a traditional residence hall.

Check-in and checkout procedures usually require forms designed specifically for the summer operation.

Rates ordinarily vary depending on the level of services the group requires. For instance, a room with linens should rent at a higher rate than a room without them. A room that receives daily maid service should cost more than one without it. The length of stay will also often affect the rate. A one- or two-night rental usually carries a higher daily rate than one for a week or two weeks.

Some facility damage is to be expected with the rental of rooms to summer conference participants. It should be considered a normal cost of doing business. However, damage attributable to vandalism or considered beyond normal wear should be charged to the individual or sponsoring organization. It is important to develop a routine procedure for reporting, repairing, and billing for damages. (If at all possible, repairs should be effected while the group is still on campus.) Information regarding damage assessment and billing should be shared with the sponsoring organization when space is reserved. Accurate records need to be maintained in this area.

A comparative measure that has been helpful to many institutions in evaluating their conference business from one year to the next is to record the number of "bed nights." The number of bed nights is determined by multiplying the number of participants in a group by the number of nights they stayed. For instance, if a group of 200 individuals stayed for 5 nights, they would generate 1,000 bed nights. This is a more comparable number than the number of groups or the total number of participants housed over a summer conference season.

It is important to follow up with group sponsors to make sure they were satisfied with their accommodations and reschedule them for the next year. Repeat business is far preferable to having to recruit new groups each year. During the follow-up, problems that surfaced during this year's stay can be addressed and worked out. It gives the institution a chance to evaluate its services and staffing model to ensure the satisfaction of the various groups.

Marketing Strategy

Marketing facilities for the maximum usage and greatest financial return is an important, necessary part of running a successful housing operation. In this section, marketing for the academic year and for the summer session will be explored as separate entities.

Those who reside in the halls for the academic year are the primary focus and reason for the housing operation's existence. In developing a successful marketing strategy, it is important to identify the population that is being targeted and to identify the competition. Once the competition is identified, it is necessary to list the components that make residence hall living unique and different from what the competition offers.

When identifying the target population, consideration should be given to groupings of students, such as new incoming, returning upperclass, graduates, and nontraditional. The amount of campus housing provided by an institution is often determined by a combination of historical, philosophical, and practical considerations. Institutional expectations regarding the percentage of the student body to be housed on campus is an important marketing consideration. Decisions resulting in identification of the group to be targeted and the number of spaces to be marketed are important components in developing a marketing strategy. For instance, if the real emphasis is on housing new incoming students, effort should not be expended in trying to retain the current residents. To develop an effective strategy for marketing residence hall space, it is important to accurately identify the market competition and become familiar with the facilities they rent. The unique features of residence hall living can then be identified and highlighted. Once these items are identified, a marketing strategy can be developed.

As an example, assume that the target group are new incoming students and that off-campus apartments are the competitors. Identify some of the ways in which residence halls are uniquely different from an off-campus apartment. First of all, residence halls provide live-in staff to assist the resident's adjustment to college. Usually resident assistants (RAs) live on each floor in an approximate ratio of one RA for every thirty-five to forty residents. Probably there is also a live-in professional staff member who supervises the RAs, works with the student government organization in the hall, and creates and presents educational/developmental programs. Second, opportunities for involvement in self-government are provided through the residence hall student government. This involvement can be in the capacity of a leader, follower, or participant. Third, numerous educational, social, recreational, and developmental programs are provided in which the residents can become involved. Fourth, the residents have the opportunity to meet and interact with other residents who are going through the same adjustment and frustrations. In other words, the student is offered a guided group-living experience, as opposed to an unguided individual-living experience. Fifth, residence halls are convenient to other campus facilities, programs, and services. Students who live on campus are much more likely to be involved in a broad range of extracurricular activities than are off-campus students (Pascarella and Terenzini, 1991). Market uniqueness!

A significant factor in identifying the competition is an awareness of the perception or reputation of the residence halls throughout the state or area from which most of students are drawn. The informal student network operates in every city and state from which students come. If a particular hall develops a negative reputation among students from a particular area, it will impact the effectiveness of the housing department's marketing efforts. This can be determined through exit interviews with residents who request transfers from that particular hall, from paying attention to the requests for a particular hall by incoming students, and by taking comments from parents into account.

As has already been discussed, the housing of summer conference groups is an excellent source of revenue during periods when the facilities would normally be underutilized. The marketing strategy is determined by the groups being targeted for summer conferences, such as youth groups, professional associations, short course or seminar attendees, or some combination of these. If the focus is youth groups, promotional materials should be prepared for athletic coaches, band directors, cheerleading advisors, yearbook advisors, and church/synagogue groups. If the target is adults who attend professional association meetings, the college deans and department heads should be contacted and encouraged to invite their professional associations and societies to meet on campus and stay in the residence halls.

It is important to note the cry of "unfair competition" that has been raised by hotel/motel associations as a result of colleges housing conference groups during the summer. This might be avoided by developing a liaison relationship with the hotel/motel associations, involving the hotels and motels in housing some conference participants, or by joining the chamber of commerce. Also, in many states conference housing income is classified as unrelated business income, which is taxable. The payment of taxes often deflates the unfair competition argument. If the groups housed are sponsored by an institutional department, this further supports the institution's connection and involvement with the group.

The conference services committee of the Association of College and University Housing Officers-International (ACUHO-I) sponsors a workshop each fall that focuses on issues directly related to hosting and accommodating summer conference groups.

Marketing housing facilities is an important function of a progressive housing department. Because the facilities are used differently during the academic year and during the summer and the competition is different in each "season," separate marketing strategies need to be developed. In creating a specific strategy, it is essential to identify the population being targeted, identify the competition, and build on the uniqueness of the residence hall facilities and offerings.

Facility Management

For many housing professionals who began their careers with a principal emphasis on programming and attention to student development issues, facility management may be viewed as a necessary eveil. Without question, however, if buildings are not properly maintained, little higher-order development is likely to occur. Consequently, facility management is an essential housing function.

Deferred Maintenance

In recent years, significant attention has been focused on the deteriorating physical facilities of American higher educational institutions. The findings of a study commissioned by the Association of Physical Plant Administrators (APPA) and the National Association of College and University Business Officers (NACUBO) are reported by Rush and Johnson (1989). According to this study, it would cost $300 billion to reconstruct the facilities on campuses of higher education today. "Between 1950 and 1975, higher education's physical space tripled in size. More college and university space was constructed during this 25 year period than in the previous 200 years" (p. 6).

Housing facilities are no exception. A majority of residential facilities were built during this period to accommodate the returning World War II veterans and the "baby boomers." During the 1950s and 1960s, the percentage of high school graduates attending college increased dramatically, and campuses were faced with the need to construct classroom and residential space at a rapid rate.

The residence halls built in the 1960s are now twenty-five to thirty years old. Even if they have been well maintained, they were built for students of a different generation who had different needs and expectations than today's students. As Kaiser (1990, p. 9) points out, "Quality of campus life is emerging as a major issue. Facilities acceptable twenty-five or thirty years ago in no way meet today's standards. Conditions such as two students to a room, one bathroom per floor, concrete block walls, and unairconditioned residence halls do not satisfy the current generation. Density of occupancy will have to be reduced, along with requirements for the new life styles."

The life expectancy of building subsystems, such as roofing, elevators, heating, ventilating, and air-conditioning systems, expires over time even if the facilities have received regular care and maintenance. The housing administrator should plan for and allocate resources for replacement of these subsystems. As Dunn (1989b) points out, the subsystems of a building have three characteristics: (1) collectively they constitute the building, (2) each subsystem has a definable useful life, and (3) information on subsystem cost and replacement is available.

The importance of the housing administrator's role as a facility manager is receiving increasing acknowledgment as attention is focused on the institution's facilities. As Boyer (1989) notes, facilities are vitally important in the recruitment of students and faculty. Furthermore, he asserts, the quality of the physical arrangements helps determine how students feel about the place, and good facilities help build a spirit of community on campus. Just as overall campus facilities impact enrollment, housing facilities definitely influence occupancy and the financial health of the housing operation.

As competition for students increases, the condition and appearance of the physical facilities have greater and greater significance. When students and parents make campus visits prior to enrollment, the buildings and the landscaping create an immediate impression of the institution. This first impression is lasting, and as Boyer (1989) points out, 60 percent of high school graduates said campus appearance was crucial in their college choice. From the standpoint of housing administrators, the attention paid to the construction, maintenance, and adaptation of facilities is warranted and required.

In 1986, the Council for the Advancement of Standards for Student Services-Development Programs (CAS) outlined minimal standards and guidelines for student services and student development programs. Regarding residential facilities, these standards recommend a maintenance/renovation program that includes preventive maintenance, a timely and efficient repair program, a procedure for renovating and updating facilities, and a systematic replacement program for equipment and furnishings. Attention to these guidelines is recommended for the housing administrator, because increasingly the *CAS Standards* are employed to evaluate institutional programs and facilities for accreditation self-studies. (See Resource A.)

Planning, construction, and maintenance will be discussed from the practitioner's point of view. For maximum effectiveness, the housing administration must integrate student development principles with practice in creating residential environments that provide facilities and programs to support and encourage the educational and personal development of students.

Planning

The following basic steps are recommended when constructing new or remodeling existing facilities (Hallenbeck, 1991): statement of philosophy, assessment of needs, statement of space usage, creation of blueprints, cost estimates, financing plan, and evaluation.

1. *Statement of philosophy.* This statement should clearly and concisely state the mission of the housing program and the purpose for which this building is intended. Of course, this statement must be in harmony with the institutional mission. Attention should be given to the theoretical foundation on which the department operates, the developmental constructs on which the program is built, and various relationships, such as resident to resident, staff to resident, and facility to program. This statement provides the architect with direction in developing the overall design and in detailing the relationship of one space to another within the facility.

2. *Assessment of needs.* An effective approach to identifying the needs that this building must meet is through a student-and-staff committee. To begin the discussion, it might be helpful to respond to a series of questions such as the following: How many students should this residence hall accommodate? What kinds of students are expected to live in this hall — that is, men, women, coed, specific majors, specific classifications? What programs and services should be offered? What staffing model will be followed in the building? What security requirements must be met? When will the building be needed? What federal and/or state regulations must be met in this project?

Through the dicsussion revolving around the questions and the "what ifs" and "wouldn't it be nice to have" brainstorming, a fairly comprehensive list of needs will be generated. After a thorough review and discussion of the needs in relation to the philosophy statement, a finalized list can be agreed on and summarized in a few paragraphs.

3. *Statement of space usage.* This step specifically addresses the relationship of one space to another within the building in light of the various programs, services, and activities intended for the building. For instance, locating a study room next to an exercise room or television lounge would seem unwise. Attention must be given to this phase of the planning to ensure that the spaces within the facility can be used for the purposes for which they were designed. The relationship of one activity to another needs to be considered when making space designations.

4. *Creation of blueprints.* During this phase of the planning, an architect can translate the information from the statement of philosophy, the assessment of needs, and the statement of space usage into drawings. It is helpful for the architect to spend time with both students and staff to understand thoroughly the programs, services, and activities that are to be accommodated within this facility. Only after a thorough understanding is achieved can the architect design the building to facilitate the intended use. The services of other specialists—such as interior designers, structural, mechanical, and electrical engineers, and environmental safety personnel—are retained by the architect.

5. *Cost estimates.* The most common approach to arriving at the estimated cost of construction is to allow the design to dictate the cost. With this approach, the facility is designed to meet the criteria established in the previous steps and the cost is determined by the square footage costs for this particular type of construction. Another approach is to determine the amount of money available prior to design. The architect is instructed to design a facility that meets the criteria identified in the previous steps within a designated dollar amount.

Regardless of the method used, it is important to remember that these are estimates. The actual cost of the project cannot be known until the bids are received from the contractors. If the bids are above the budget ceiling, it will be necessary to revise the plans to bring the project within the budget or to allocate more money.

6. *Financing plan.* The actual method of financing residential facilities varies from institution to institution and state to state. The following methods of financing housing facility construction or renovation have been employed by institutions that are members of ACUHO-I: (1) surplus and reserve monies, (2) sale of revenue bonds, (3) state appropriations, (4) gifts, and (5) federal grants and loans (Hallenbeck and Ullom, 1980).

7. *Evaluation.* This step allows the housing administrator to review the previous six planning steps to ensure that the planned construction or renovation accommodates the programs, services, and activities intended and that money is available to complete the project. If everything is satisfactory, it is time to move to the construction phase.

Construction

In concert with preparing the blueprints, the architect should prepare a set of specifications that outlines the materials to be used in this project. The specifications and architectural drawings are sent to interested contractors so that they can provide the institution with a sealed bid. This bid is the price for which they would complete the project. After the bids are formally opened, the architect and housing administrator should review all of the bid documents to make sure the bids are based on the specifications outlined. It is also a good idea to evaluate the contractor who submitted the low bid. Consideration should be given to the size of the contractor's work force, reputation of the firm, past performance in meeting construction dealines, and recommendations of the architect. Assuming that this evaluation of the low-bid contractor is positive, the contract can be awarded. If the low bidder is found unsatisfactory, state regulations at state-assisted institutions will dictate procedures to be followed in rejecting the bid and selecting another. Private institutions are not required to select the low bid and may choose construction companies that submit higher bids but that have performed well on past construction projects.

Once construction has begun, the architect is responsible for inspecting the project on a regular basis. When the contractor has a question, it should be answered by the architect. To facilitate the process, weekly contractors' meetings normally are held. It is a good idea for the housing administrator to be present on a regular basis. In addition to the housing personnel and architect, the general contractor and possibly some of the subcontractors may attend the meetings. At these meetings, the progress of the week is reviewed and discussed. Problems that have arisen are considered and decisions reached as quickly as possible so that the contractor will not be held up. These meetings are a way to monitor progress of the project and to be involved in the ongoing decision making that is always part of a large project.

A frequent topic discussed in contractors' meetings is the need for "change orders." Change orders are deviations from the original plans or specifications. Particularly in remodeling projects, contractors find numerous "surprises" as the work progresses. These "surprises" usually require additional work, materials, and money. In new construction, it is not uncommon to discover an oversight that needs to be corrected so the facility can be constructed properly. It's necessary for the housing officer and the architect to review each of the change order requests carefully. Potentially the institution can receive a better product as a result of change orders, but these changes can also cause the cost to exceed the budget significantly.

When the project is near completion, a "final" inspection should be scheduled with the architect, housing administrator, and contractor. During this inspection, items that need to be completed or corrected should be enumerated. This list is known as a *punch list*. Once all the items on the punch list are completed, the building can be accepted by the institution and final payment to the contractor authorized.

Maintenance

As was mentioned earlier, one of the top priorities of the housing administrator is to keep the housing facilities well maintained. A planned routine maintenance program can extend the life expectancy of a facility. The housing department's motto regarding maintenance should be, "Do it now, don't wait!" Deferred maintenance, as outlined in *The Decaying American Campus: A Ticking Time Bomb* (Rush and Johnson, 1989), is costly in terms of time, money, and image. The impression caused by deteriorating facilities is negative and *lasting*. The key to an effective routine maintenance program is trained, attentive maintenance and housekeeping staffs who are sensitized to the importance of repairing items immediately and constantly keeping an eye on the building condition. For instance, if a piece of ceiling tile is broken, it should be replaced immediately. If a light switch is broken, it should be repaired immediately. Regular periodic inspections by the housing administrator with the building supervisor or maintenance chief should be undertaken to evaluate the condition of the building and the level of cleanliness.

Another facet of the maintenance program is preventive maintenance. The intent of a preventive program is to extend the life of equipment and ensure its efficient functioning. Examples of items included in a preventive maintenance program would be checking the oil level in motors, cleaning the filters in air-conditioning units, and checking the belts on motors. Much of the attention in a preventive maintenance program revolves around the mechanical systems of the buildings.

An effective planning tool for major repair, renovation, and replacement of equipment is the five-year plan. This allows the housing administrator to systematically review the projects that need to be completed to keep the facilities in good working order and well maintained. This is where the surplus and reserve funds mentioned earlier would be spent. Basically, this approach lists the repairs, major renovations, and equipment or furniture replacements needed in each residence hall. After all of these items are listed in the year the project is to be completed, it is necessary to develop cost estimates to determine the amount of money needed. Based on the funds available, some projects may have to be moved from one year to the next. The plan should be updated annually.

In developing a five-year plan, several approaches are possible. Items could be listed based on the estimated life cycle or on an observation that they are beginning to wear out, or it is possible to use a combination. As an example, residence hall roofs have a life expectancy of twenty to twenty-five years, mattresses normally last ten years, and corridor carpet wears out after five years. Armed with this knowledge, it is possible to anticipate when various roofs, mattresses, and carpets will need to be replaced. This allows the housing officer to plan what major maintenance costs will confront the department in the next five years.

At the University of Florida, a similar approach was employed to develop a ten-year capital renovation plan. The staff in the division of housing evaluated each residence hall and family housing apartment. They identified needed renovations, derived cost estimates, and developed a prioritized plan. Consideration was given, in establishing individual building priorities, to age, use, efficiency, deterioration, and available capital. The cost estimates were developed by using standard engineering estimating practices, mean square foot cost indexes, and local prevalent labor and materials costs.

A frequently raised issue when discussing maintenance and housekeeping involves the pros and cons of hiring, training, and supervising an in-house staff, as opposed to contracting for the services with an outside firm. The institution must determine the method that yields the best job at the best price. This determination varies geographically and even among institutions of the same type and size within a region. One way is not more "right" than the other. Important considerations in evaluating the options include the following:

- The housing administrator must be in a position to establish priorities for the housekeeping and maintenance program.
- The staff must be able and willing to respond rapidly to changing needs—for example, in going from the academic year operation to summer conference operations or by setting up overflow housing beds in a lounge.
- A system of inspection and evaluation must be established.

Attention needs to be given to the individuals who will be employed to work in the residence halls. Some housing administrators feel more comfortable with employees they have hired rather than those hired by an outside firm and assigned to the residence halls. Because the safety of the residents is a responsibility of the housing administrator, this is definitely a valid concern. Whether to contract with a firm or run a self-operated maintenance and cleaning program is a matter of choice for the housing administrator and is influenced by local labor market demands and overall institutional policy.

Another facet of the housing administrator's job is to provide facilities for students that are safe, clean, comfortable, and well maintained. This means that attention must be directed toward compliance with fire and life safety codes, hazardous materials in the living environment, and issues of sanitation. If the institution has a fire safety officer, that individual should be invited to make regular inspections of all housing facilities to ensure compliance and a safe environment for the residents. Hazardous materials increasingly have become a concern in the last few years. Asbestos, a substance employed to insulate pipes and absorb noise, was commonly used as a building material during the 1950s and 1960s. Asbestos has been classified as a hazardous material; consequently, significant sums of money have been and continue to be spent on its removal. It is important for the housing administrator to be attuned to this and other materials that might be hazardous in the living environment. Of course, sanitation in a group living situation is vitally important to the welfare of the residents. Housekeeping, the cornerstone of sanitation and facility upkeep, is a daily need. The keys to an effective housekeeping program are a definite cleaning schedule, proper training in cleaning methods, high-quality equipment and supplies, systematic supervision, and thorough evaluation.

Another area of government regulation is in the area of facility accessibility to the handicapped. Whenever a major renovation project is undertaken, it is necessary that the newly remodeled facility be accessible to persons with disabling conditions. The housing administrator should explore the existing residential facilities to determine which can be modified to accommodate "differently abled" students.

Services

Kaiser (1989, p. 51) has listed modernizing residence halls as one of the potential projects that can move higher education toward a balance between attractive and adequate space for teaching, study, and student life. He suggests that density needs to be lowered and that more private accommodations, air-conditioning, and social space be provided. In addition, Dunn (1989a, p. 7) states that "significant changes in parent and student attitudes about campus housing have also left many institutions in a quandary about how much money should be reinvested in dormitories, dining halls, and other campus life facilities."

It is clear that expectations about the space and services provided in residence halls have changed and will continue to change. The concept of providing only food and shelter is completely outdated. To compete effectively in the higher education arena, institutions must provide a variety of amenities. Services such as telephones in every room, laundry facilities in convenient locations, vending machines filled with a variety of items from food to stamps, recreational areas including game rooms and exercise equipment, cable television outlets in every room, and close, convenient, secured parking are taken for granted. Attention needs to be given to the residence hall room of the future. Various computer hookups that may require extra telephone lines and work-study stations that accommodate computers and printers are a necessity. As technology advances, the residence hall room must accommodate more technology.

Personalization Programs

Research has shown that personalization programs positively contribute to students' satisfaction with their living accommodations (Hanson and Altman, 1976; Anchors, Schroeder, and Jackson, 1978; Wichman and Healy, 1979; Werring, Winston, and McCaffrey, 1981). Painting one's room, painting the corridor or a common area of the living unit, or building a loft or a room divider allows the student to express some creativity and individuality while exercising some control over the immediate living environment.

Personalization programs have provided a vehicle through which students can deinstitutionalize their living space and eliminate some of the monotony of traditional residence halls. At the same time, these programs raise some questions and concerns regarding the regular building maintenance program. The challenge for the housing administrator is to balance the satisfaction of the residents with quality facility maintenance and upkeep.

Carefully developed procedures and guidelines are the key to a successful personalization program. Involving students and staff in the discussion and development of these procedures and guidelines is an effective approach. Widespread agreement among housing staff members, which can be achieved through participation in establishing guidelines, is important to the success of personalization programs. It is suggested that specific guidelines be developed for each separate personalization activity that is being considered. In other words, separate procedures and guidelines should be developed for painting student rooms, painting corridors or common areas, and in-room construction.

In student room painting programs, the most obvious concern is color and quality of paint. A common approach used by some colleges is to stock a group of acceptable paint colors and give the paint and painting equipment to students. An inspection procedure needs to be implemented to ensure an acceptable job. Guidelines also need to be developed regarding the frequency that a room may be painted. In this vein, it is important to determine how the student paint program will fit in with the department's routine painting cycle.

Painting a living unit corridor with a mural or graphic design is a project that can unify the residents and contribute to a feeling of ownership. Approval of the proposed design as well as supply of the paint and other equipment must be addressed in the procedures and guidelines. Additional considerations include the responsibility for touch-up and repainting when needed, as well as the relationship to the department's routine painting cycle.

Fire and life safety codes need to be evaluated in considering a program that allows students to build lofts, room dividers, or other structures. The codes vary from state to state, and so it is important to review the codes for the particular locale in which the institution exists. Assuming the program can be structured to comply with the applicable codes, issues that need to be addressed include the displacement/storage of room furniture, inspection procedures, and removal at the end of the year.

Because residence hall storage space is usually limited, a common requirement for in-room construction is that the room furniture be incorporated into the design. This also ensures that the furniture is in the room and does not turn up "lost" at the end of the year. It is important to have an inspection procedure to ensure that all structures are freestanding and meet all published requirements for safety. The question of whether returning students will be allowed to leave their lofts or other structures in the room over the summer needs to be addressed.

These questions and issues are not meant to be inclusive but only to give the housing administrator a "flavor" of the concerns that must be addressed to enjoy a successful personalization program. The planning, development, and publication of procedures and guidelines lays the foundation for a successful program.

Recapitulation

Business operations and facility management, two of the three legs on the housing tripod, are central to the responsibilities of the housing administrator in a comprehensive housing program. At many colleges, the housing program is classified as an auxiliary enterprise, since it generates revenue and is self-supporting. Fiscal responsibility is exercised through the process of budget construction and management. Since revenue is tied to occupancy, attention must be paid to the application and contract procedures and the room assignment or room change policies and procedures. Combining an effective assignment program with a summer conference program that maximizes the use of the facilities can result in a financially successful operation. Marketing housing facilities for maximum usage during both the academic year and the summer has become increasingly important. Through highlighting the uniqueness of the facilities and the services that can be offered on a college campus, a successful marketing campaign can be mounted for specific populations.

As the concern about the decaying higher education physical plant has gained public attention, the role of facility manager has increased in importance. Since housing facilities on many campuses represent a substantial institutional investment, the housing administrator's role in facility management is receiving greater recognition. The housing administrator is expected to play an active role in planning new construction and major renovation projects, in developing and implementing effective ongoing facility maintenance and housekeeping programs, and in balancing the needs and desires of the student clientele with principles of effective building management.

References

Anchors, S., Schroeder, C. C., and Jackson, S. *Making Yourself at Home: A Practical Guide to Restructuring and Personalizing Your Residence Hall Environment*. Washington, D.C.: American College Personnel Association, 1978.

Barr, M. J. "Managing Money." In M. L. Upcraft and M. J. Barr (eds.), *Managing Student Affairs Effectively*. New Directions for Student Services, no. 41. San Francisco: Jossey-Bass, 1988.

Boyer, E. L. "Buildings Reflect Our Priorities." *Educational Record*, 1989, *70*, 25–27.

Council for the Advancement of Standards for Student Services/Development Programs. *Standards and Guidelines for Housing and Residential Life*

Programs. College Park, Md.: Council for the Advancement of Standards for Student Services/Development Programs, 1986.

Dunn, J. A., Jr. *Financial Planning Guidelines for Facility Renewal and Adaptation*. Ann Arbor, Mich.: Society for College and University Planning, 1989a.

Dunn, J. A., Jr. "Financial Planning for Plant Assets." In H. H. Kaiser (ed.), *Planning and Managing Higher Education Facilities*. New Directions for Institutional Research, no. 61. San Francisco: Jossey-Bass, 1989b.

Hallenbeck, D. A. "Managing Physical Facilities." In T. K. Miller, R. B. Winston, Jr., and Associates, *Administration and Leadership in Student Affairs: Actualizing Student Development in Higher Education*. (2nd ed.) Muncie, Ind.: Accelerated Development, 1991.

Hallenbeck, D. A., and Ullom, M. "Survey of New Construction, Renovation, and/or Remodeling." *ACUHO News*, 1980, *19*(4), 18–19.

Hanson, W. B., and Altman, S. "Decorating Personal Places: A Descriptive Analysis." *Environment and Behavior*, 1976, *8*, 491–504.

Kaiser, H. H. "Rebuilding the Campus: A Higher Education Priority for the 21st Century." *Educational Record*, 1989, *4*(7), 49–52.

Kaiser, H. H. Chapter Two [no title]. In J. W. Myerson and P. M. Mitchell (eds.), *Financing Capital Maintenance*. Washington, D.C.: National Association of College and University Business Officers, 1990.

Pascarella, E. T., and Terenzini, P. T. *How College Affects Students: Findings and Insights from Twenty Years of Research*. San Francisco: Jossey-Bass, 1991.

Rush, S. C., and Johnson, S. L. *The Decaying American Campus: A Ticking Time Bomb*. Alexandria, Va.: Association of Physical Plant Administrators, 1989.

Werring, C. J., Winston, R. B., Jr., and McCaffrey, R. J. "How Paint Projects Affect Residents' Perception of Their Living Environment." *Journal of College and University Student Housing*, 1981, *11*(2), 3–7.

Wichman, H., and Healy, V. "In Their Own Spaces: Student Built Lofts in Dormitory Rooms." Paper presented at the meeting of the American Psychological Association, August 1979.

Chapter Nine

Food Services
and Programs

Paul Fairbrook

The setting in which students dine, as well as the services they are provided there, can make significant contributions to the out-of-class learning and development of students. Those who are not familiar with campus food services often consider them merely a necessary, but relatively unimportant, service, unrelated to broader institutional goals. The specter of eating "institutional" food and all the horrors that that implies begins to haunt the students from the moment they are accepted into college. Unfortunately, throughout the history of higher education, student culture has held college food and dining services in low esteem. Changing this perception continues to be challenging for food service professionals, despite the overall high quality of service and products offered on many of today's campuses.

Contemporary campus food services offer students a wide variety of food choices—from the hamburgers, hot dogs, and pizzas with which they are familiar to interesting and tasty entrees such as breast of chicken cordon bleu or broiled New England lobster, which many students may not have experienced previously. In addition, students are offered a wide variety of healthful and nutritious alternatives to the standard meat-and-potato fare, including expansive salad bars, vegetarian entrees, and fresh fruit at every meal. There are "deli" counters where the students can have sandwiches made to order, griddles where they can cook their own eggs if they choose to, and, at some schools, waffle irons where they can make their own waffles. Various cold cereals are available at all meals, and freshly baked bread, rolls, and several desserts are the norm rather than the exception. A complete array of beverages awaits the student at every meal, from soft drinks to punch, lemonade, fruit juices, regular and low-fat milk, iced tea, coffee, tea, and hot chocolate.

This impressive list of food and beverages does not tell the whole story. Those who head a quality campus food service (many prefer to call it a *dining service*) see themselves as having a responsibility that is far greater than merely providing nourishment. They view themselves as educators and counselors, as adult friends to an ever-changing group of students of varying ages. Many are growing into maturity under their eyes and through their influence. Modern food service managers consider nutrition education an important part of their job, take a personal interest in the social and educational development of students, and become friends with many of them. In partnership with their colleagues who administer the residence hall program, they are, in almost every sense, educators. If they do their job properly, they will help to further the goals and objectives of the institution of which they are a part.

This chapter provides the residence life and housing professional with an overview of key issues in food services and programs in higher education. A summary of roles of the food service director is followed by a review of critical issues, ranging from how to define quality to whether to contract or not to the need and importance of integration into the total residence program.

Roles of the Food Service Director

Central to the success of a food service organization is the director. This person establishes a tone for the area, defines quality, serves as a liaison to external groups and individuals, and works with staff in implementing and creating quality services, educational programs, and food products.

The roles of the food service director in a college or university, and in particular on a residential campus, generally include the following:

1. To operate a high-quality campus food service in a professional and competent manner
2. To contribute to a good quality of campus life, which can facilitate students' personal development
3. To support and aid faculty members and administrators in carrying out their mission on campus
4. To provide the leadership in creating an atmosphere of trust and friendship so as to inspire trust and loyalty in the food service staff

5. To bridge whatever gap may exist between the administration, the faculty, staff, and students
6. To work toward harmonious town/gown relations and to promote the institution to the outside community (Fairbrook, 1991a)

Self-Operated Versus Contractor-Operated Food Services

In the nineteenth and early twentieth centuries, housing and food services in American colleges were largely copied from the British (Brubacher and Rudy, 1958). There were a variety of "houses," each of which was presided over by a "master" or "housemother" who hired cooks to prepare meals for the students in these houses (the population of which was usually less than 100 students). Dinners were often formal affairs, and even in the late 1950s, women who lived in a residence hall could be observed lining up along the entrance of the dining hall (wearing "Sunday dresses"), waiting for the housemother to make her majestic entrance!

The mass of students who flocked to college after World War II changed student life. Along with the urgent need to provide educational services came the need to expand campus housing and food services. Residence halls became larger, growing from the typical 200- to 300-bed facility to multistory skyscrapers housing as many as 2,000 students. The size of dining halls increased proportionately, and when Brody Hall was built at Michigan State University in 1954, it was one of the largest dining halls ever built on a campus, with a capacity to feed over 2,500 students. Ten years later, Dietrick Hall at Virginia Polytechnic Institute was built to feed 3,500 students.

Until the early 1950s, there existed virtually no "contractor-operated" food service on college campuses. Institutional administrators assumed responsibility for food service, and the term *independent* or *self-operated* referred to a food service operated by the college or university itself rather than by an outside firm that contracted to provide the management (hence the familiar term *management contractor*).

In the late 1940s, two recent college graduates formed a company called Saga Food Services and began to offer their services to a number of small colleges. Their offer was eagerly accepted by many business managers, who regarded food service as an activity that was ancillary to the college's educational mission or who had experienced problems running food services themselves. Management contractors quickly grew in number and also started to provide enhancements previously unknown on most campuses. A steak every Saturday night, unlimited seconds, a choice of two entrees, three vegetables, and four desserts were some of these. By the early 1970s, dozens of food management companies existed that operated food services in over half of the nation's colleges and universities, although most of these schools were small or medium sized. The 1980s saw a period of takeovers and mergers that reduced the number of these companies, so that by 1990, most of the college and university accounts were held by less than a dozen large corporations that managed campus food services, in addition to managing hospital and public school food services and cafeterias in businesses and industrial plants. Because of uncertain economic conditions and changing institutional philosophies, the 1990s began with less than half of the food service operations in the United States being run by contractors. Of the fifty public land-grant institutions, only two are operated by contractors as of the publication of this book.

Deciding Whether or Not to Contract

The decision to contract out services or to administer the program through self-operation must be made by considering each institution's unique needs and characteristics. Among auxiliary enterprise staff in higher education, few issues engender the passion and debate that contracting or privatization of services does. Campus culture, staff skills, and overall institutional philosophy should dictate the decision. Although no one correct approach or method is best, it is essential that the decision be viewed as objectively as possible. This is extremely difficult, since the same points can often be made in arguing for each side.

The "Independent" or "Self-Operated" Campus Food Service

A college that operates its own dining service normally hires a director of food services, who reports to one of three individuals: the chief student affairs administrator, the chief business officer, or a director of auxilary services/enterprises, which is occasionally also the chief housing officer. It is relatively unimportant who the food service director reports to, as long as that person understands and appreciates two important objectives of campus food service: (1) to enhance the students' life on campus and (2) to meet predetermined budget goals. Some argue that there are significant advantages for a college or university to operate its own food service, for the following reasons:

1. Profits are retained on campus. Any surplus after expenses are covered from food service operations remains with the institution and does not go to an outside firm. Such profits (often called "excess of income over expenses") are often substantial, especially on campuses with residential spaces for more than 1,500 students. Because management contractors typically charge from 3 to 5 percent of gross sales to cover their own "general and administrative expenses" and an additional 2 to 4 percent profit, the "independent" institution can save anywhere from 5 to 9 percent of total food service income by operating its own food services. These funds can be returned to the college community through improved services or lower costs.

2. Quality and continuity of management can be assured. Well-run "independent" food services are typically headed by experienced directors who have come up through the ranks and who are familiar with all phases of

college and university dining services. Some argue that having contractors is less personalized ("Contract Management Companies Speak Out," 1991) and that they are not a part of the college in the way a college's employees are. Taken further, the mission is to serve the educational needs of the community, not the profit demands of a company.

It is common for the director of a self-operated food service to have been on his or her campus for many years, gaining valuable insights into the way the college or university works. This lends stability and continuity to the institution, when alumni can return year after year to greet those who have befriended them when they were in college. Most important, perhaps, is that such longevity often brings about a continuous improvement in the services offered—a constant shining of the "jewel" so that ultimately it sparkles! Directors employed by management contractors, on the other hand, generally have an average tenure on a client campus of less than five years, and, when promoted, normally move to another campus.

Many institutions maintain that a self-operated program reflects positively on the concern for maximizing control over the uniqueness and individuality of a college's dining program ("Contract Management Companies Speak Out," 1991). Particularly in large public land-grant institutions, the pride and concern for serving the state and using human and local resources position them well for the self-operated alternative.

The Contractor-Operated Food Service

The same factors that at some institutions argue for self-operation are, at others, a distinct disadvantage. College and university administrators who have opted to contract their food services often do so for the following reasons:

1. There is guaranteed income. Although in very small operations (that is, less than $1 million in sales annually) contractors normally insist on a management fee (a *fixed-fee* contract), most of the contracts for college food services are so-called *profit-and-loss* instruments. The contractor charges a fixed dollar amount per student day or per meal served, or guarantees the college a fixed minimum sum. Any resulting profits above such guarantees are then shared between the institution and the contractor. However, as many housing officers know, enrollments impact this amount, and a set guaranteed institutional payment may be rare. In addition to the impact of enrollments, it is important to note that in many contractor relationships, improvements to services, adjustments to hours, equipment purchases, and other enhancements are the responsibility of the college and often result in an adjustment to the contract.

Such an arrangement shifts the risk from the institution to the contractor. College business officers who may have experienced financial problems with their food services might be relieved to have that burden removed by an outside contractor.

2. Continuity of management is assured. A large management firm often employs dozens or even hundreds of experienced food service managers and directors—many of whom are climbing up a career ladder to larger and more challenging jobs. As they become ready for more responsibility, they are promoted to jobs at larger institutions. Thus, the contractor has a wide array of talent from which to draw. As college and university dining services become more specialized and complicated, the pool of qualified managers is shrinking. The contractor, therefore, can offer a service that could be invaluable to a college, especially to a small one where a qualified replacement to a departing director may not be readily available. Even if management firms cannot always provide directors with the solid experience that might be desired, they do have considerable corporate talent above the level of the food service director to support their programs. First there are the district managers, and then above them the regional vice presidents, as well as staff persons (dietitians, kitchen designers, marketing specialists) who can provide backup and support for the client. Also, many of the management firms institute programs on a corporatewide basis in nutrition education, merchandising, and safety and sanitation. Thus, the individual institution benefits from the corporatewide activities of the management contractor.

3. Labor costs are controlled. An important advantage of some management contractors is their ability to pay lower wages. The freedom to pay prevailing area wages and fringe benefits can keep costs down. Some colleges and universities, especially state institutions with mandated wage scales and fringe benefit packages, do not have that option. By paying only prevailing area wages and thus reducing the food service payroll, such a firm can guarantee significant savings to the institution. However, the resulting problems in employee relations and drop in staff morale is a price the college must be willing to pay if such savings are contemplated. In actuality, the campus may end up having different groups of individuals working at a similar skill level but at lower pay.

In addition to the several nationwide companies, there are also a number of smaller contractors that limit their activities to a narrower geographical region or to a smaller number of accounts. These companies are typically headed by executives who have had previous college or university food service experience, and they can often overcome the disadvantages listed for both the independents and the large contractors—that is, they can provide personal service, continuity, and quality operation as well as assume the financial risk. Many institutions have found the smaller firms to be an acceptable compromise between the two extremes.

Meal Plans

Until the mid 1960s, few if any colleges or universities offered their resident students any meal plan options. If they lived on campus, they were normally required to buy a meal ticket or, as some described it, to "be on the meal plan."

This meal plan varied only to the extent that it may have offered nineteen, twenty, or twenty-one meals per week, depending on whether breakfast and lunch were combined into a "brunch" on Saturdays, Sundays, or both. When students complained that they were missing many meals (especially breakfasts and weekend meals), they were hushed into compliance by being told about "absenteeism." The institution "expected an absenteeism of from 30 to 40 percent," they were told, and without such a "missed meal factor," their board rates would have to be increased significantly. Mandatory full meal plans were also encouraged by the lack of kitchen facilities in most residence halls, as well as by the shortage of cooking appliances that have been replaced by microwaves.

By 1970, however, many colleges had made some concessions. Resident students were offered some additional plan choices, such as fifteen-meal plans and even ten-meal plans. The difference in the cost to the student, however, was minimal, because the food service directors justly claimed that all costs other than food costs remained essentially the same regardless of which plan the students chose. At about the same time, some institutions introduced campuswide use — that is, the ability of students to use their meal ticket freely in any campus dining hall, without having to obtain advance permission to do so. This changed the eating patterns on campus and enabled the food service directors to close some of their dining halls on weekends, thus gaining significant savings in labor and overhead costs.

As "free flow" grew in popularity, some colleges expanded this privilege by allowing students to use their meal ticket in the student union, snack bars, and other "cash operations." To do this, however, they had to set limits on how much the meal ticket holders could buy in such cash operations. Thus the principle of *meal equivalency* was born. While students could normally have unlimited food in the residence halls, they would be limited, in cash operations, to predetermined maximums, and anything purchased above that amount would have to be paid for in cash. In the late 1970s, some food service directors came up with a novel plan. To silence the students' complaints about their missed meals, they would convert that portion of the board money actually spent on food into "points." Each meal carried a number of points (for example, breakfast — 3 points, lunch — 4 points, and dinner — 5 points). Students would be required to pay a fixed sum for the cost of labor and overhead and to buy a minimum number of points for their food; they could supplement this with additional purchases of points (meals) during the academic term. This *point plan* became immediately popular, because it gave the students more flexibility in their eating patterns than ever before.

At about the same time that point plans appeared on American campuses, so did another phenomenon — the computerized meal ticket card, which not only identified the students by having their picture on the card but also kept track of the number of meals eaten. This computerized card made possible yet another refinement of the meal plans offered to the on-campus student: the *declining balance plan*. To eliminate the missed meal factor altogether and allow the students even more freedom, some food service directors assigned point values to the different food and beverage items served (a glass of milk, for example, would cost 12 points and a piece of toast 6 points). A student paying $800 for a semester's meal ticket might start the semester with 35,000 points (the equivalent of $350 worth of food, with labor and overhead being valued at $450), and the computer would help keep track of the declining balance until it was time for the student to purchase more points. This made it possible for a college to offer a wide variety of expensive entrees on a regular basis (including steaks and even lobster), since the students would be charged points according to the cost of the food they chose and how much food they actually purchased.

It is important to note that in most instances the cost of labor and overhead was paid for in advance; thus, the number of points charged for each meal would be based only on the actual *cost of the food*. Some colleges experimented with not charging labor and overhead in advance, but selling the food *at retail prices*. The student who, in the previous example, would get 35,000 points would now get 80,000 points (that is, for $800, the cost of the semester meal ticket). Under this plan, a glass of milk that cost the school 12 cents would now be sold not at 12 points but perhaps at 30 points, and a piece of toast with butter not at 6 points but perhaps at 20 points. Such experiments often ended in failure! Students resented paying such "high prices" for the food and, unless the food service operation was superb or there were no other nearby dining options, deserted the campus food service en masse, thus causing serious financial problems for the college or university. *An institution that plans to switch from standard meal plans to a declining balance plan is well advised, therefore, to approach this step cautiously and to make certain that it will continue to gain the gross income it needs to cover its debt service and other obligations.*

In addition to the point plans just described, there is one other declining balance plan made possible by computerized meal tickets: a *debit card* plan, which enables the students (or their parents) to deposit a certain amount of cash (say $50 or $100) that can be used for in-between or late-evening snacks in the college's cash operations. Such a plan, called by some a *plus* plan (a meal ticket plus snack money), is an attractive option for institutions wishing to retain the standard meal plan but also wishing to benefit from additional cash purchases from the students. The computerized card can be used simultaneously with both types of plans and can even be used for purchases in other campus departments. If this trend continues, more and more colleges may develop *all-campus debit cards*, where students can use their card for meals, copy machines, convenience stores, theater tickets, and admission to athletic events.

Currently, some campuses, such as the University of Georgia, require no meal plan for resident students. This approach may have positive payoffs in terms of encouraging retention and helping give students power to maximize control over costs. This approach, however, requires careful planning and a campus consensus and acceptance that not all dining facilities may be needed. In addition, collaborative work with housing and residential life colleagues is needed to gain acceptance and support as students develop new patterns of dining.

Quality Elements in Campus Food Services

There are a number of factors that distinguish a quality campus food service from an ordinary one. Hot and appetizing food, spotlessly clean kitchens and dining rooms, a friendly and congenial staff, and attractively merchandised food and beverages are some of these ingredients.

Good Food

The food in a *quality* campus operation is every bit as good as that found in a first-class commercial cafeteria or restaurant. The hot food is steaming hot, the cold food is chilled, the salads are crisp, and everything is appetizing and tasty. Recipes are standardized using current computerized technology, and the menus are varied and written so as to meet the needs of diverse student tastes, including those who are vegetarians, who wish to lose or gain weight, who may have modest religious or dietary requirements, or who have specific ethnic preferences.

Clean Kitchens and Dining Areas

Absolute cleanliness is a "must" for any quality food service operation. Colleges and universities, just like hospitals, must not merely meet but actually exceed the minimum standards set by the health department. A clean kitchen has very little junk lying around; there are no empty boxes on the floor, the stainless steel surfaces are mirrorlike, and the floors are spotless. All of the utensils are either being used or are stored away, and the kitchen staff all work in clean, attractive uniforms and wear hats or hairnets. The serving lines are equally clean. The hot food pans are covered when not in use, cleaning rags are stored underneath the counters, and everything is served in an appetizing manner. Dining room tables are shiny and are cleaned with wet and dry cloths throughout the dining period.

Friendly Atmosphere

The development of a sense of campus community is a central theme of this book, and it is important to note that this often takes shape around various dining areas on a campus. Generally, dining facilities are the only out-of-classroom location where community members gather routinely with a common purpose—dining. In these facilities, students, staff, and faculty can have meaningful dialogues around intellectual, social, and other topics. According to Mehrabian (1976), college dining areas should attract students, containing something interesting or compelling to encourage socializing. Quality food is essential; however, a friendly atmosphere is equally important. A joyful and congenial staff can spell the difference between the acceptance or rejection of a food service by its clientele. Ambience is crucial to creating a positive and welcoming atmosphere for dining. This is particularly true on a college campus, since the students have a need to relate in a close and personal way to those who may be perceived as taking the place of their family members. When there is a spirit of joy, of friendly cooperation among the staff, and if the cashiers, servers, and managers all wear name tags and make a special effort to remember students' names, then chances are that students will be pleased with their food service.

Merchandising

Successful business ventures of all types depend on merchandising to "sell" the customers on their products. Food services are no different, and without exception, profitable restaurants and fast food units depend on effective merchandising to maximize their sales. College and university food service directors who want to be modern and successful follow many of the same merchandising practices used in commercial establishments. In the years ahead, many will follow the examples set by modern shopping centers — that is, planning small specialized food counters built around a central eating area or "food court." Each food counter will offer a popular food item, usually cooked fresh before the customers' eyes and garnished with tasty and eye-appealing accompaniments. One counter, for example, will grill a thin Philadelphia cheese steak sandwich with a mound of smothered onions, and another will broil hamburgers on a conveyor broiler while the buns are toasted and buttered simultaneously. Pizzas will be assembled from fresh dough as the customer watches and cooked in seven minutes by a conveyor oven, and all kinds of deli sandwiches will be made to the customers' specifications while an imposing array of various breads and rolls awaits their selection. Salad bars will be as beautiful as a bouquet of flowers, with the green salads, red tomatoes, white cauliflower buds, yellow cling peaches, and pink radishes all displayed in shiny containers set in ice or into refrigerated countertops, all surrounded by kale, watercress, or other decorative greens. Cafeteria lines will serve a variety of entrees and vegetables in small, shallow steam table pans, continuously replenished and refreshed, each steaming hot and decorated with a suitable vegetable or fruit garnish. Pans that are almost empty will be removed to the kitchen, to be replaced with new and appetizing items. Each of the items will be clearly marked — not only on the large menu on the back wall, but also with professionally designed individual menu name cards attached to the sneeze guard or placed in front of each steam table item.

Neglecting the merchandising aspect of food service is inviting disaster—especially since college students are becoming more and more discriminating and expect the same degree of quality and service they can get at local eating establishments. The strong consumer orientation of today's students, combined with the increasing costs of higher education, requires staff responsiveness.

Public Relations

No matter how friendly the service or how tasty the food, *a campus food service has not achieved true excellence unless the students, the faculty, and the staff all perceive this to be a fact* (Fairbrook, 1991b). It is a campus food service director's duty and perhaps his or her greatest challenge to create the perception of excellence in the minds of the customers. "Perception is half the battle!" is a motto that could well guide the college or university food service manager.

Creating such a perception is not done with smoke or mirrors. Instead, it requires a basic understanding of marketing techniques and a willingness to learn about and to use commonly accepted public relations practices. Marketing has been defined as "the process of getting the customer to view the product or service offered in a favorable light." Good public relations and good campus relations, when practiced properly and continuously, will help to accomplish the desired objective.

Here are some of the tools available to the campus food service director in this effort.

- Providing a food service newsletter (often printed on the outside pages of the weekly menu), which highlights special events, tells about staff members, provides nutrition information, answers students' concerns, and is entertaining as well as informative. James Madison University's long-standing dining services newsletter highlights to the entire community menu items, serving hours, and ways to avoid lines, as well as providing dietary advice to consumers.
- Offering monotony breakers, theme dinners, blue plate specials, contests, and other special promotions that cause excitement and fun in the dining halls and in the student center eating places. The University of Maine's optional Friday Lobster Dinners allow students to enjoy a favorite local entree, as well as promoting excitement and a positive image.
- Distributing occasional "samples" of institutional signature items to various campus departments and student groups, which can help in promoting new products as well as the special features of a program.
- Making frequent use of complimentary meal passes to encourage various members of the campus community, as well as parents, to dine on campus. At the University of Maine, students are offered free meal passes if they would like to invite a faculty member to dine with them. Complimentary meal passes can also be used to soothe complaints and deflect criticisms.

- Supporting the overall mission of the institution by cooperating with, and by sometimes even *subsidizing*, various projects that may be important to other campus departments or officials (for example, parents' weekend, pledge and/or finals week snacks, athletic training programs, and campus elections).

- Notifying the campus newspaper, radio station, and public relations department whenever a noteworthy activity is about to occur in dining services, including sending free meal passes to the persons who are to cover the story.

- Actively participating in the parents' orientation program by detailing the special features of the dining services, distributing copies of past menus, and offering other promotional materials.

- Printing, in professional quality, a food service brochure and other fliers that explain various meal plan options, describe the various food service venues, and give costs and other relevant data.

- Operating a high-class, top-quality catering service—that is, one that is as good as or better than any commercial competitor—and making certain, through intense supervision, rigid quality control, and personal involvement of the director, that these high standards are maintained at all times.

- Providing attractive uniforms, aprons, hats or caps, and easy-to-read name tags to the entire food service staff.

- Establishing procedures that enable the students to express their opinions and, when they so choose, to complain about food service matters; also, establishing policies that ensure that when they complain, they receive an honest, straightforward, and individually written reply.

The importance of all the above and other similar activities cannot be overemphasized. Students and their parents often conceive of college and university food services as "institutional." This phrase, to them, describes all the negative aspects that they associate with a large, impersonal dining operation—food that is tasteless or overspiced, monotonous, greasy, full of calories and empty nutrients, lukewarm, and generally unappetizing. The fact that this is probably not true is something they still need to be convinced of.

It is, therefore, essential that every member of the campus community is treated, at all times, like a *valued customer*. This implies much more than merely preparing a variety of popular foods and beverages. Not only must the food look attractive, but every worker must greet the student in a warm and hospitable manner, and a general feeling of warmth and friendliness should prevail. Never should students be made to feel that they are taken for granted, that they are a "captive audience," and that, if they are unhappy with something, they could just "take it or leave it."

Similarly, members of the faculty and staff must be treated not only with courtesy, but with a genuine concern for their welfare. Dining services can, if properly run, become an important part of their lives on campus and thus can enhance the spirit of community that a college seeks to create.

Finally, special attention must be paid to cultivating the support of the institution's president and other top administrators. These individuals are the major policy makers of an institution, having many important problems to solve every day. Dining services should not be one of them.

When all these elements come together—when students, faculty, staff, and administrators are treated as important customers, when dining services are operated as well or better than a commercial establishment, and when excitement and innovation keep everyone's interest alive—the merchandising and public relations program of a college or university dining service can be deemed to be a success.

Special Events and Monotony Breakers

Those who manage residential dining programs have one special factor to consider: students' boredom with the dining program. Dining in a similar environment with the same peers each evening can cause boredom. Food services in student centers and other cash operations normally serve their clients during one meal period, and their customers eat most of their other meals off campus. Variety, while desirable, is not crucial. In a residence hall, however, the students quickly get to know the "menu cycle," and they can tell in advance that on every fifth Monday there will be tomato soup and toasted cheese sandwiches for lunch! This boredom, added to perhaps other problems not connected with food service that cause them frustration, can easily turn into disaffection with dining services. For that reason, campus food service directors must carefully plan special events calendars that introduce excitement and variety into their residence hall dining rooms.

A special dinner should be a novel and exciting experience. The food could be served on a buffet line in the dining room instead of from the cafeteria counter. The tables could be arranged in a different pattern; cloth tablecloths and napkins could grace the tables, and perhaps the places could even be set with silverware, so that nobody would need to use a cafeteria tray at such a special meal (teams of student workers could reset the tables as diners leave). Colored paper streamers and other decorations could grace the walls, the cafeteria workers might be issued special hats for the occasion, and the cashiers could perhaps come in fancy attire, each with a food service–supplied corsage or other special item to mark the occasion. Even more important, live or recorded music could drift through the dining halls. Finally, the food itself must be truly special. Whether it is an international dinner or an old-fashioned American Thanksgiving meal, the food items must be selected with special care and there should be some items in the menu that are unusual. The special meal could also be planned around some outside activity, such as a "Circus Night" or a "Day at the Beach," in which case appropriate props could be borrowed to give the dining rooms a special atmosphere.

In addition to having a special meal on the average of perhaps once a month, the creative food service manager can also plan some "monotony breakers"—that is, simple changes in the menu offerings that do not take much effort but that are appreciated by the students. Such monotony break- ers can be as simple as setting up a specialty food bar in the dining room (for example, a fresh fruit bar, hot potato bar, hot bread bar, Mexican food bar), or having a huge birthday cake (enough for everyone) to celebrate all those whose birthday falls in that particular month. It could be the offering of a late-night pizza and Coke party, serving late-evening snacks during finals weeks, or building a thirty-foot-long sundae in a piece of rain gutter lined with aluminum foil.

The fact that such special efforts cost money should not prevent the dining services from putting them on; instead, these should be considered "essential expenses"—essential in that they are needed to keep the students happy in the residence hall dining program and to make them want to return the following year.

Food Services and Residence Life

If a student's life on campus is to be a happy and constructive one, many diverse elements must come together to bring this about. The physical facilities (rooms, lounges, recreational equipment, furniture) must be clean, pleasant, and attractive; the halls must offer security and a certain amount of privacy; opportunities for study as well as for having fun must be adequate; head residents or resident assistants must be congenial and helpful; and roommates must be compatible. The dining experience should also be satisfying and pleasant. Such ideal conditions do not occur accidentally; they require adequate funding, a lot of planning, and above all a lot of teamwork among those charged with bringing this about. It does not matter whether the housing director or food service director reports to the vice president of student life or the vice president for finance . . . as long as everyone works together collaboratively to achieve a common goal. The residence staff is an important group to work with in providing quality service to students. Their support can range from helping to maintain order in a dining room when students occasionally get rowdy to giving staff feedback on products and services. The food service staff must be assertive in assisting the residence staff. For example, they might provide punch and cookies (often without charge) when head residents need to call meetings of their staffs or to arrange training sessions. *Ideally, the two types of professionals—food service and residence life—consider themselves to be equal partners in a challenging and exciting assignment.* They may occasionally send a representative to attend each other's staff meetings and participate in retreats or similar training experiences. In the ideal situation, the only difference between these two staffs is in what they do, not in what they are trying to accomplish.

Professional Organizations

Most college food service professionals are members of the National Association of College and University Food Services (NACUFS), which has its headquarters in East Lansing, Michigan. In addition to its annual conference, each of its nine regions holds regional and subregional conferences throughout the United States. NACUFS publishes newsletters, journals, and monographs pertaining to college and university food services. Perhaps its most important publication is the *Professional Standards Manual* (2nd ed., 1991), which is a summary of all the essential elements that combine to produce a successful campus food service operation. This book is available not only to its members but also to the public at large and is an essential aid to anyone with responsibility for a college or university food service operation.

Food Services and Institutional Mission

Today's college or university food service directors are not merely cafeteria managers. They can be vital members of the student affairs team, which is dedicated to furthering students' overall development into educated, well-adjusted, and well-informed citizens. Students come to the campus with a variety of concerns. Some are dedicated vegetarians; others have special religious dietary needs; others may suffer from diabetes or anorexia; and while the incoming first-year student may dread the possibility of gaining weight, the football player may insist on it. Some students are accustomed only to eating what is normally known as "junk food," while others are extremely conscious of the principles of good nutrition and insist on eating only "healthy" food. None of these conflicting demands are impossible to meet. On the contrary, a good food service director knows how, within limits, to accommodate these various needs. The crucial requirement is to remember the food service director's main assignment, which is to help fulfill the goals and objectives of the residence hall program and, ultimately, of the institution. Budgets, personnel, menus, and nutrition education are only individual problem areas that require solution; the real goal is to have satisfied students who are happy to live on campus and whose happiness is caused, at least partly, by their continued enjoyment of the on-campus dining experience.

References

Brubacher, J. S., and Rudy, W. *Higher Education in Transition: An American History: 1636–1956*. New York: HarperCollins, 1958.

"Contract Management Companies Speak Out." *On Campus Hospitality*, 1991, *14*(2), 23–25.

Fairbrook, P. *College and University Food Service Manual*. Stockton, Calif.: Colman, 1991a.

Fairbrook, P. *Public Relations and Merchandising: A Handbook for College and University Food Services*. Stockton, Calif.: Colman, 1991b.

Mehrabian, A. *Public Spaces and Private Spaces*. New York: Harper, 1976.

National Association of College and University Food Services. *Professional Standards Manual*. (2nd ed.) East Lansing, Mich.: National Association of College and University Food Services, 1991.

Chapter Ten

Residential Alternatives

James C. Grimm

The phrase "variety is the spice of life" has often been quoted to justify the need for change. This cliché has considerable relevance to living options or residential alternatives in campus residence halls. DeCoster and Mable (1980, p. 50) are emphatic in noting that "living options in college residence halls offer student alternatives, educational and social opportunities for facilitating lifestyle and life preparation. . . . Living options are limited only by the creative and critical thinking of students and resident educators." If students are to have an opportunity to grow in a residential setting, they need some choices in living arrangements. And each person may make different choices. This is why living options can enhance the student service and development programs provided.

There are four premises on which this rationale for residential alternatives is based:

1. The environment in which students live has a direct effect on their development; not all students, however, respond in the same way to a given environment.
2. Variations in housing designs and programs provide opportunities for achieving developmental goals.

3. Monolithic programs and designs for college and university housing no longer meet the needs of today's consumer-minded, high-tech, and television-oriented students.
4. Variety in styles and types of accommodations increases the appeal of residence hall living to a greater number of students.

This chapter examines the effects of living arrangements on students, identifies considerations central to making decisions about which options to provide, and discusses several categories of residential alternatives — namely, thematic housing, coed housing, living-learning centers, co-op housing, house systems, and family housing. Not all alternatives are included, however, due to the limited space for this topic.

Impact of Living Arrangements

The *Student Housing Report*, published by the Educational Facilities Laboratories (1972), emphasizes the individual needs of students. Some students look to their residence halls for social purposes, whereas others are more interested in intellectual activities. These differences are reiterated by Evans (1983). Banning and Kaiser (1974, p. 374) note that "the ecological perspective is based on a trans-sectional view of persons and their environments. It is based on the belief that the environment has an effect on people and their behavior and that people also have an effect on their environment. The perspective also assumes that different people respond differently to different types of environment."

Chickering (1974) and Astin, Green, and Korn (1984) have adequately attested that residential living makes a "real" difference in students' achievement in college. Chickering (1974), Astin (1985), and Pace (1984) have also clearly established that involvement outside the classroom is an essential part of students' education and development. That students learn more out of the classroom than in the classroom has been supported by a number of researchers (Wilson, 1966).

One of the more quoted researchers in the area of the environment and human behavior, Moos (1976, p. 137), notes that "the physical environment we create affects our behavior. By recognizing this relationship and by closely examining both our objectives and the ways in which our designs function, we can create environments that are more congruent with our goals." He also notes that the same environment can elicit opposite reactions from students. Some students find high-density residence halls appealing, whereas others have negative reactions. These reactions are determined in part by the students' background in growing up, individual habits, and experiences. If for no other reason, this justifies the need for variety and options for residential education and development. Moos (1976, p. 403) also supports the premise: "Since different individuals often perceive the same architectural environment quite differently, it is unlikely there exists any simple architectural impact." These researchers have reinforced the idea that a variety of designs and programs is essential to meet the various needs of students and that no one design will be effective for all students.

It is unfortunate that this information was not applied in the 1950s, when over a million bed spaces in halls with double-loaded corridors and a bathroom at each end of the hall were constructed. At that time, the double-loaded corridor seemed to be the best solution to the problem at hand. A balance was needed between the demand for accommodations and the availability of funds to meet the demand. The research in college and university housing facilities prior to 1940 was almost nil. The "dorms" were modeled after the only group-living environment that was familiar—the military. Mehrabian (1976, p. 299) notes that "corridor-type dorms also have another unfortunate environmental spin-off. As a result of their uniform, ordered, regularized, and cost-efficient designs, they tend to encourage a bureaucratic approach to various administrative responsibilities." It was not until pioneers such as Harold Riker, Alice Nelson, Earl Thompson, and others established the importance of residential education and emphasized that a hall was more than a place to sleep that residential research began to flourish.

The facilities of the 1950s were constructed and environments created with the best information at hand. Dynamic programs have been established within the existing facilities primarily because of creative students and staff. Examples have included Schroeder's (1978–79) experiment with territoriality in Magnolia Hall at Auburn and Crookston's (1974) Intentional Democratic Community at the University of Connecticut. Many other valuable programs have been created under not-so-perfect physical conditions as well.

Forrest and Schuh (1976), Becker (1980), and Moore and Ostrander (1980) discuss the impact of living space design on students' college experience. Forrest and Schuh found a difference in attitude toward staff between students whose rooms were located away from the normal student traffic pattern and those whose rooms were located within that traffic pattern. Becker's study showed that students' ability to personalize their environment leads to more positive social interaction as well as the building of community among residents. Both of these factors are directly related to student satisfaction. Moore and Ostrander looked at meeting student needs through the establishment of theme houses. A student satisfaction scale was established based on Maslow's hierarchy of needs and the work of DeCoster and Mable (1980). Social organization and social atmosphere were found to be significantly higher in the theme house than in the nontheme house. Moos (1976) describes physical and functional distance as important factors in determining relationships and use of facilities.

Many students reveal that design, traffic patterns, and decor have an effect on goal accomplishment. A common example of this would be shopping malls. While walking through a shopping mall, it can be seen that the design leads people toward what a store is trying to sell. The layout of aisles in the grocery store is also part of the design to create an environment to assist the shopper and influence choice of purchase.

As previously noted, monolithic programs and designs may no longer fulfill the needs of a high-tech society. A range of options are essential to meet the developmental needs of students, both today and tomorrow. Colleagues might say that students really have not changed. My response would be, "Have you read Alexander Astin's latest documentary on the American freshmen — in particular, his follow-up study relating the freshmen survey results from 1989?" (See Higher Education Research Institute, 1989.) During orientation programs for freshmen during the past four years at the University of Florida, a question posed of all students is, "How many of you have ever shared a bedroom with your brother or sister?" The responses indicate that 96 percent of entering fall freshmen have never shared a bedroom.

Several studies over the years have looked at life-style options within residence halls. Some have been major contributors to the thesis that creating variety in housing programs or structural designs is advantageous to the residence hall function. Wills (1975–76), Armstrong and Martin (1982), and Yunon, Goldenberg, and Neeman (1977) are only a few of the authors who have reviewed the design of residence facilities and found a direct effect on behavior and student interaction. Wills looked at six different residence hall life-style programs and their impact on the stability of student preference. His results confirmed that "resident students do have clearly identified preferences for living arrangements" and that "these preferences remain fairly stable." Armstrong and Martin researched the academic performance of students living in a closed-corridored building as compared to an open-corridored facility. The residents of closed-corridored halls had a 12 percent higher grade-point average than the residents of the motel-type exterior-corridored building. Yunon, Goldenberg, and Neeman (1977, p. 762) note that "friendship formation is influenced by the potential for interaction in the living units." The highest interaction came in halls where facilities were communally shared.

Offering a wide range of living styles (options) can contribute to the growth and development of residents. These ideas are not new to the practitioners who have struggled with the problem of trying to find the right combination of programs to improve the quality of life through participation by residents. Astin (1985) emphasizes that involvement of students in out-of-class activity tends to lead to a more positive college experience. If participation is a major ingredient in a successful education, where is that more likely to happen than in residence halls? In order to create the opportunity for involvement, a variety of programs and designs must be provided to stimulate the interest of students.

The current trend across the country appears to be toward creating small-group housing, but not necessarily in a small building (not a new phenomenon). Apartments, suites, and single rooms seem to be at the top of the construction list for new facilities today. Why is this happening? For one thing, students are being involved in the discussions relating to their environment. Also, students' backgrounds are different now. They bring with them different needs, desires, opinions, political views, and social values than those of students in earlier periods (Astin, 1985). A response to those needs can be made by providing the variety they desire. Students appear to want privacy, more bathroom space, and more amenities (cable television, telephones, message services, refrigerators, and microwaves, for example). As these demands continue to grow, the traditionally designed residence halls will not be able to meet the needs of students. Meeting these needs will require extensive renovations of existing buildings or construction of new facilities.

Housing practitioners should not ignore the research, history, and professional knowledge relating to the effect of community building within the halls. The design must take into account the student's need for privacy and at the same time allow the student to become a viable member of the community (Grant, 1980). Schuh (1988) outlines the opportunities for student involvement in residence halls and discusses ways of maximizing these opportunities. He includes activities such as student government organizations, residence hall leadership organizations (National Association of College and University Residence Halls), peer helper groups (resident assistants and peer advisers), special programs (student management boards, student-operated television channel, student-managed faculty associates program, student-operated businesses or co-ops), and student-initiated programs.

Many housing directors have to make do with the buildings they inherited when they assumed their positions. However, some have been fortunate in being able to build new facilities. (Consult Resource D for references that may be helpful in renovating existing buildings or planning new residential facilities.) Renovation is more restrictive than new construction, but it does not necessarily have to be less creative. Student input for new designs or renovations can be advantageous and pleasantly surprising.

It is easy to be preoccupied by design (bricks and beds) and forget that a program must fit within the structure. On the theory that form follows function, the program should be created before the design is constructed. Program variety is as important as design variety. Putting them together is the ultimate achievement in a residence facility. The following discussion notes a few programs that are "tried and true" and a few that should be considered as possible new ventures on some campuses.

Thematic Housing

Thematic programs are organized around topics like languages or cultures, academic fields, wellness, the environment, and so on. These special housing arrangements can bring together students with a common interest to improve the level and quality of their achievement and participation. Duncan and Stoner (1976–77) compared the grade-point averages of a group of

President's Scholars who were assigned to a specific hall with those of President's Scholars who lived off campus, at home, or in other residence halls. The grade-point averages of the scholars in the specially assigned hall were significantly higher. The students explained the reason as being "an atmosphere conducive to study and the motivation provided by living close to other high achievers" (p. 9).

Themes are limited only by the extent of the imagination. A disadvantage to this type of program is the old conflict of homogeneous group assignments versus heterogeneous assignments. Some faculty have criticized the homogeneous approach for not having enough "honors" or academic interest halls. On the other hand, critics complain about putting all the "smart students" together. If this homogeneous grouping lasted for all four years, these objections might be valid; however, the average on-campus residency of a student is usually two years at most. Moore and Ostrander (1980) looked at the differences between theme and nontheme residence halls by comparing the student satisfaction ratings on an eighteen-point physical and social environment scale. In their summary, they note: "Our research indicates that theme dorms may meet students' social-psychological needs more fully than non-theme dorms because of their emphasis on organized activities. These activities help create a generally positive social climate within the hall" (p. 34). This research appears to support what Chickering (1974) and Astin (1985) and others have been expounding for a number of years: residence hall living brings about a higher level of student involvement and thus a better opportunity for a successful college career.

However, in a study of student interaction within various "programmed environments," Clarke, Miser, and Roberts (1988) found that students housed in halls with formal themes spent more time in formal study groups and were more satisfied with general education courses. On the other hand, they also found that "students' involvement in thematic halls appeared to reduce both interest in career development and satisfaction with friendship, perhaps because thematic halls attracted students with a fairly narrow view of their purpose" (p. 11). It would appear that theme houses can have both a positive and a negative effect on the student. Therefore, it would seem appropriate to be somewhat cautious in the development of thematic programs that involve the student for his or her *total* academic career.

Coeducational Housing

The 1960s saw opposition to the Vietnam War and challenges to many long-held social conventions on college campuses. As a result, many students came to seriously question the time-honored practices of strict separation of men's and women's housing facilities (on many campuses as far apart as possible). There was agitation for a more "natural" living arrangement where the sexes lived together. "Together" could be defined as anything from adjoining buildings to alternate floors or adjoining suites in the same building.

Many campuses began to experiment with coeducational housing. In one of the earlier studies during the most controversial period of coed housing, White and White (1973) noted that residents of coed housing arrangements are likely to develop a greater number of heterosexual platonic relationships than residents of unisexual halls and that the development of such relationships can be an excellent indicator of initial progress in a coed system. Studies like White and White's, along with those of the more prominent authors of that period, such as Greenleaf (1962), Duncan (1974), and Katz (1974), brought a surge of coeducational housing programs to the campuses. Greenleaf (1962) examined coeducational housing in two separate halls with a common lobby. She found no differences in academic achievement between coed and noncoed facilities but did conclude that coed housing was preferable in terms of its impact on the socialization process. Duncan (1974, p. 103) noted that "coeducational living is advocated as a vital component of residential education on the basis of students' developmental needs." He also concluded that coeducational housing is not for everyone. Katz (1974) observed a more mature and positive attitude toward sexuality from students residing in coeducational living situations. Based on this type of research and the changes of attitudes on the American campus in the 1970s, coeducational housing has established itself as a viable living option.

One of the more extensive studies of coeducational living was conducted by Roberts (1990). Through the research and information committee of the Association of College and University Housing Officers-International (ACUHO-I), Roberts reviewed the student affairs literature relating to coeducational housing. Some of the high points of the review are as follows: "Coed halls apparently have little or no effect, either positive or negative, on the academic achievements of residents. Living in coed halls appears to have a positive effect on developing students' maturity level. For the most part, it appears that sexual activity in coed halls is either no different or is less emphasized than sexual activity in single sex halls. The research clearly indicates that residents in coed halls are more satisfied with their living environment than residents in single sex halls" (pp. 19–21).

As Duncan (1974) notes, coeducational housing may not be for everyone. However, considerable evidence seems to show that it has a positive developmental impact. On the other hand, different students have different needs; therefore, the need for single-sex halls exists if alternative housing is a goal of a comprehensive residence hall program.

Living-Learning Centers

There appears to be a revival of faculty acting as in-housing tutors, faculty in residence, teaching in the halls, video classes in lounges, academic advising in halls, and faculty and students sharing common activities. These are all aspects of a living-learning concept. Clarke, Miser, and Roberts (1988) developed a study to look at the effects of programming variables using living-learning structures, faculty involvement, and academic themes. Residents were surveyed in order to identify patterns of interaction within the different types of settings. The results of their study indicated that freshmen in living-learning halls were more likely to "change their career choice, value cultural events, [and] make more progress than other freshmen in developing social skills" (p. 9). Residents in halls that had a program of faculty involvement were found to be more satisfied with college, to spend more time talking with friends, and to be more satisfied with general education courses. Clarke, Miser, and Roberts's results indicated that the students who live in theme units spend more time in study groups, participate more in class discussions, and are less satisfied with relationships. These findings confirm the important benefits realized from bringing faculty members and students together in out-of-classroom experiences. Jackson and Stevens (1990, p. 9) support these findings; they note that "involving faculty and staff with students in the residence halls can have powerful, positive effects."

Michigan State's 1960 venture in living-learning centers was one of the earlier programs of this type. At that university, according to Adams (1974, p. 89), "living-learning residence halls provided students with an opportunity to take full advantage of the residence environment without divorcing themselves from the academic programs and departments of the university." This concept and the living-learning centers like Justin Morrill College were somewhat unique for the time. They were a larger, enhanced version of the "house" system of British universities. Many similar programs across the country continue as living-learning centers to bring faculty and students together under one roof. Riker (1965, p. 5) notes that in future housing programs, "group living will be identified as a part of the curriculum and used in teaching human behavior, development, and relationships." Also, "an on-campus housing assignment will mean in effect registering for an action course based on everyday living experience." An assessment might be in order to determine if there are any housing programs that have realized these lofty goals.

Living-learning programs do not necessarily have to involve faculty teaching as described in the Michigan State program. Previously cited research has supported the idea that lifelong learning experiences, organized and structured within the residence halls, are of major importance to the overall development of the resident. Therefore, programs such as student government, orientation, residence counseling, faculty associates or fellows, student-initiated educational and cultural events, and old-fashioned floor meetings are all avenues that lead to learning. Riker (1965) states that there are three major requirements for an effective living-learning center: (1) programs developed to act and react to student needs, (2) staffing to foster the programs, and (3) facilities designed to meet the group's needs. This formula does not seem to have changed much in the last twenty-five years.

Goldman and Matheson (1989), after reviewing the literature concerning the positive effects of living-learning residence halls, conducted a study to determine if there was any initial difference between the students who selected living-learning residence halls and those who selected conventional housing. The results of their study showed a significant difference in that these living-learning students were younger, had fewer brothers and sisters, consisted of more females, and were mostly from within the state. Living-learning students also had higher verbal SAT scores and received higher grade-point averages in high school. These demographics indicate that in a self-selection residential program, there is a definable population of students that can be attracted to the program. The findings of this study can assist in building a data base for the initial exploration of living-learning residence halls. Determining the clientele first, then determining the program is a sound approach in any feasibility study.

In recent years, there appears to be a reemphasis on faculty programs within the residence halls. The annual ACUHO-I conference at the University of Georgia in 1990 had four different interest program sessions relating to faculty involvement in residence halls. Attempting to bring very busy and overextended faculty into the halls is not easy. Most students desire the more popular faculty, who may be the most difficult to recruit. Faculty involvement programs need to be well planned and carefully developed, with the faculty member and the students benefiting equally. The first objective would be to get the faculty member into the hall and make it a pleasant experience. A positive experience travels well throughout the faculty grapevine. One approach to bringing faculty into the halls might be to encourage faculty members to have office hours in the halls. Many academic departments are pressed for space. Faculty office space could be provided in the halls, and a lounge could be used as a classroom for an hour or two in the morning when they are little used.

Schuh and Kuh (1984) assert that motivation and the student's year in college may be key factors in determining the results of faculty-student programs. Kuh, Schuh, and Thomas (1985, p. 35) looked at methods to encourage student-faculty interaction programs and found that "residence-hall based faculty-student interaction programs do add a richness to the residential experience and can be a positive experience for most participants. However, such programs are not a prescription for dramatically improving a residence hall environment." Planning, training, coordination, an interested student clientele, funding, faculty and staff orientations, and scheduled evaluation meetings are all essential for a successful program of positive interaction. As with other residence hall programs, nothing can replace planning, coordination, follow-up, and old-fashioned hard work. In outlining the pitfalls to avoid in developing such a program, Kuh, Schuh, and Thomas (1985, p. 35) offer some basic strategies in working with faculty. "Most faculty will be unfamiliar with the role of 'Fellow' and like others in new situations, can benefit from some structure and assistance. Indeed, assigning faculty to residence hall floors and telling them to 'interact well with students' grossly underestimates the complexity of human behavior. Faculty can benefit from ideas about programs likely to be favorably received by students." These conclusions should not be unfamiliar to residence hall programmers, because such information is provided to the hall staffs during most preterm staff training programs. The staff does not enter the programming arena without training; neither should the faculty fellow.

An option similar to a faculty fellow program but with more personal involvement is a faculty-in-residence program. Though the interaction between faculty and students is similar, the fact that the faculty members *live* in the hall is significant. Programs at Cornell University, Purdue University, Texas A&M University, the University of Arizona, the University of Pennsylvania, Yale University, and the University of Miami, with some variations, all provide faculty accommodations within the halls. The names of these programs differ; alternatives include *residential colleges* and *residential faculty*. But the basic theme applied in this style of faculty program is interaction through availability. This is not a new approach; the tutors in the British residential system have long been live-in faculty working academically and socially with resident students. Success in this faculty program comes with planning, training, coordination, evaluation, and follow-up with staff, students, and faculty. Because of the live-in nature of the program for all participants, it becomes a partnership. With awareness by all participants of expectations, clearly defined roles, and a common goal, faculty and staff conflicts should be minimal.

Co-Op Housing

In a co-op housing program, students live in an on-campus self-governing community and perform some of the maintenance and custodial work to reduce their expenses. This concept was popular off campus during the 1950s and 1960s. It is an excellent cost saver but can be a difficult situation to supervise. A community developed around a common interest can provide the opportunity for personal growth and leadership. Thus co-ops can have a place on the campus; however, a certain amount of autonomy is needed in order to achieve the level of community necessary for a self-operating system. The program appeals to the low-income student because of the price break. Students looking for freedom and independence may also find the program attractive because there may be fewer staff members in the facility. Another feature of co-op housing is the kitchen. In order for students to prepare their own food and realize the savings, they need proper facilities. Community kitchens are difficult to maintain, however; cleanliness often becomes a problem. Cleanup always seems to be the other person's job. Student leadership will vary. Some years it is strong—some years it is weak. Stability of leadership is a difficult situation over the long run. The University of Florida's experience testifies to this difficulty, having had to close a co-op due to a lack of student participation after nineteen years of operation.

House System

The house system is an example of how to develop a small community within a large building complex. This system can work equally well in situations where there is a small group already in a housing facility that needs to develop community. One of the better-known programs is the Iowa State University house system, established in 1949 and consisting of 149 houses in 19 different residence halls. Simard (1989, p. 6) comments as follows: "A house is a living unit consisting of between 40 and 80 residents. The house is the basic functioning unit of the house government. Areas in the residence halls are not referred to by floors, wings, room numbers, or even halls. They are, instead, referred to by their names . . . Louden . . . Hutton . . . Craner . . . , etc." The house system provides the opportunity to create a small group-living situation where students can interact one on one and establish their identity to and within a small group. It gives them a chance to pursue their interests and utilize their skills, as well as to get involved in the group's activities. As Schuh (1991, p. 34) notes in his review of the Iowa State house system, "students emphasized that the development of community in the house depends not just on events and activities but rather on the process by which many house members are involved in the planning and development of the major events of the house each semester." This environment, along with a trained staff and a well-planned program, gives the student the opportunity to have a positive college experience.

The University of Georgia's approach to personalizing its large campus was to develop small-group neighborhoods and communities. It has the basic ingredients of a house system but a different name. Stanford University approaches the house system in a similar fashion but with an added ingredient—resident fellows. Faculty involvement in residence education has long been considered a desirable program goal. Stanford has thirty-seven resident faculty fellows within its house program whose compensation is usually room and board. If success can be measured by the number of faculty applying for this program, the Stanford program is very successful, because the applications exceed the number of positions available. An important consideration for the faculty member was reported by Gurowitz (1991, p. 68): "Another benefit of the resident fellow program is that participating faculty improve their teaching after seeing at close hand how the course material is processed by students and receiving immediate feedback from them." Gurowitz also notes that this approach reduces the Stanford environment to a more human scale.

Other Innovative Options

Various reports have been published on unique programs in residential halls. Oakland University's Anibal House (a residence hall for eighty-four students) established a wellness residence hall. The program included everything from prohibitions against alcohol and cigarettes to requirements that residents attend seminars on nutrition and stress management. In discussing American freshmen, Astin, Green, and Korn (1984, p. 27) proposed another option: "Should institutions consider the possibility of requiring a 'public service' component in the undergraduate curriculum; one which would promote values of concern for others, generosity, empathy, and community responsibility?" (See Chapter Two for further discussion of this idea.)

What an opportunity for a theme house! Changing the undergraduate curriculum is difficult. However, housing staffs do not have the same constraints as faculty. These values can be developed as keenly in residence facilities as in the classroom, perhaps more so.

Riker (1981) selected several institutions that had established creative programs within their overall housing system. He first reported on the program for freshmen development at the University of Wisconsin, Stevens Point. Through the use of the *Student Developmental Task Inventory* (Winston, Miller, and Prince, 1979) and the *Lifestyle Assessment Questionnaire* (Hettler, Elsenrath, and Leafgren, 1990), freshmen were encouraged to assess their developmental status based on the four elements of wellness: physical, emotional, vocational, and sociological. Seminars were held during the year to assist residents in charting their growth.

In 1972, the University of California, Irvine established the Cooperative Outdoor Program, which emphasized environmental awareness and responsibility. Two undergraduate halls were designated as "outdoor halls." Credit courses on coastal ecology, desert ecology, and mountain ecology were taught in the halls.

A third program, at Empire State College, was developed by a special task force charged with providing greater access to higher education for students who worked, had families, or were in need of retraining. Part of the educational process for the participants included short-term residency, which could consist of a weekend workshop. Bringing these students together, even for a short time, provided some of the advantages of community living, such as increased social interaction, more sharing of ideas, increased knowledge of themselves, and more of a feeling of belonging to the institution.

The fourth program reviewed by Riker (1981) was Syracuse University's Experiment in Intergenerational Living. This program brought together 400 older people and 750 traditional-age undergraduates in a residence hall complex. The reaction from both the older residents and the younger ones was equally mixed, flowing from the extreme of great satisfaction to wanting to be left alone. Riker noted that when this program was planned, the major concern was housing space and not support services.

Even though some of these projects may no longer exist, Riker's point in discussing them was to emphasize the creativity involved and the potential accomplishments when staff and students work together toward a common purpose. Housing programs today need to continue in this great tradition of innovation and experimentation.

Family Housing

For decades, students with families have been a largely overlooked constituency in many housing programs. These students represent a growing population about whom little research exists to assist in developing housing alternatives. Kimble and Levy (1989, p. 1) note that non-traditional-age students are increasing at a dramatic rate: "The U.S. Census Bureau predicts an increase of approximately one million older students (25–46) by the 1990s; at the same time the Bureau predicts a decrease of approximately 800,000 in the enrollment of the traditional age student." Schlossberg, Lynch, and Chickering (1989, p. xiii) point out that "this demographic revolution will create an educational revolution; in many ways and in many institutions, in fact, it already has." The dynamics of this particular population are most challenging and exciting. A logical question for housing officers to ask would be, who are these people and what are some of the specific demographics about them? This section seeks to explain some of the more salient issues related to the housing and education of married students with families.

In describing the demographics of this unique population, Kimble and Levy (1989, p. 3) write that

> they tend to be less than 35 years of age, although the greatest percentage increase is occurring in the over 55 age group. They are more likely to be Caucasian than any member of a minority race. Single adults are more likely to continue their education than married, adults employed full-time are the most likely to continue their education; they usually have family incomes of at least $10,000. The most reliable and best predictor of an adult's likelihood of being a continuing learner is an individual's prior level of education attainment. The more one learns, the more one wants to learn. Adults learn most often for career related reasons.

Given these demographic "facts," if housing is responsible for both service and educational development for single resident students, logic would suggest that a similar rationale would apply to students with families of their own. However, the demographics noted above seem to indicate that approaches to programming for these individuals may need to be different from those for single students.

A review of population growth projections for higher education shows there will be a tremendous increase in nontraditional students in the next decade. This presents a major challenge to housing programs. Research indicates that students with families encounter special problems as they attempt to achieve their goals as adult learners. If housing programs have a responsibility to resident students for their education and development, that obligation must extend to all residents, no matter whether married or single.

Facility Needs

In designing facilities or making renovations, account should be taken of physical structures that can assist students in achieving their academic and personal goals. The design of the individual apartment and the location of specific rooms within that apartment in family housing are important to the success of a program—the environment affects everyone in it. Program assessment is a current operational trend; why not assessment for construction? To sit down with four families and discuss with them the design of a kitchen, bedroom, or living room could be most productive.

Riker and DeCoster (1971) provide a model that includes five general objectives for student housing. Their model was influenced by Maslow's (1959) hierarchy of human needs. Students, like everyone else, try to have their basic needs met. Therefore, the facilities in which they live have a major impact on their overall satisfaction with the quality of life within a housing program.

In the renovation of family housing units, adding extra touches that increase the quality of life without raising the rent should always be a goal. Different color designs in each apartment or a series of color arrangements based on the number of apartments within a building reflect an extra touch. Changing the floor tile design and the carpet color can help make each apartment different. On the other hand, some extras, such as garbage disposals or dishwashers, are less cost effective and debate continues as to their importance. These are high-maintenance items, and the initial installation and upkeep are expensive. Each housing program must weigh how to improve the ambience of its family housing without driving costs out of the range of students' resources.

Quality of life must be balanced against rent levels. This struggle is typified by what happened at the University of Florida when family housing students were allowed to install air-conditioning units at their own expense. With the aid of a federal 50–50 energy grant, the university installed heat pumps with central air in each apartment unit. As a result, it was possible to keep the rent increase minimal and still provide a quality convenience to the residents.

Community space for family housing units is also important. For years, it was often difficult to convince administrators that single students in residence facilities needed such things as recreation space, floor lounges, activity rooms, libraries, and computer labs. It was also frequently assumed that students with families did not need common community space; they lived in an apartment complex, and all the necessary activity space existed in the individual apartments. Current knowledge and resources have taken

Table 10.1. Sample Programs and Services for Family Housing.

Remedial	Preventive	Developmental
Marriage counseling	Employment opportunities fair for teenagers	Family student government
Spouse abuse counseling	Birth control information	Child-care class
Referrals to campus counseling center	Referrals to legal aid society	International student orientation
Child welfare referrals	Tornado warning information	Public school enrollment-readiness program
Food secured for needy families	Dental care	Summer activity information
Clothing secured for needy families	Medical care for spouses and children	Resume workshop
Case conferences with local school district, for emotionally disturbed children	Babysitting exchanges	First aid and safety course
Resolution of sanitary problems in living units	Furniture distribution	Aerobics class
		Dance class for children
		Drama classes
		Sports/athletics/new games
		Music appreciation classes
		Arts and crafts classes for children
		Service activities

Source: Schuh, 1985, p. 29. Reproduced by permission of the *Journal of College and University Student Housing.*

university housing beyond that basic "survival hut" approach. Housing officials are increasingly recognizing that facilities must be designed to meet the special program needs of students with families. Day-care centers, nurseries, English classes, study sessions, and Saturday morning movies for the children are just a few examples. The facilities must be planned to ensure maximum effectiveness. With the right design in the right facility, the program can achieve a higher level of service and education.

Programming Needs in Family Housing

Schuh (1985, p. 29) discusses providing services and developmental programs in family housing in some detail. His review of the literature indicates that many types of programs are possible, as long as staff and financial resources are available (see Table 10.1).

Rei (1988) discusses developing staff and facilities and providing educational programming guidelines through a needs assessment analysis. Both Schuh and Rei stress the importance of a needs assessment before launching into a major program effort. Many housing officers follow this approach in the single-student housing area, and there should be no reason not to follow that same advice in family housing. Beyerlein and others (1982) did an assessment in order to identify promoters and inhibitors in community development in family housing. Questionnaires were sent to sixty family housing operations throughout the country. The findings revealed that the three most important promoters were "1. Responsive, skilled, and friendly staff; 2. Clean, safe, and well-maintained physical environment; 3. Effective process for program development and implementation" (p. 12). The three major inhibitors were run-down physical environments, unresponsive staff, and involvement in the village activities as a low priority. Studies by Brechtel and Cherwak (1978) demonstrated the importance of recreational activities and showed that these activities should be free or at minimal cost. Another study, by Paul, Rei, Ostrow, and Shigetomi (1984) at the University of Utah, used an ecosystem model for an assessment/redesign project. These authors observed that "on the residents' part, from the beginning they were aware that their opinions were valued. More than that, they came to see that the staff members were serious about their commitment to improve the living environment. This methodology resulted in great public relations and a team-building bonus" (p. 14).

The research conducted by Whalen, first with Winter (Whalen and Winter, 1987) and then later with Morris (Morris and Whalen, 1989), looked specifically at the on-campus family housing environment. Whalen and Winter (1987) attempted to identify stress factors among neighbors. They followed a personal interview model and randomly sampled 15 percent of the total on-campus family population. They concluded that "the results suggested that if residents of family housing get to know their neighbors, the frequency with which neighbors are a source of stress may be reduced" (p. 33). The other suggestions the authors presented were not that different from what a staff member might follow in a single-student complex — except for one factor, the socialization of spouses. Many housing officers, and institutions of higher education in general, think only of individuals, not family units, when conceptualizing programs and services. When an institution decides to provide family housing units, it has implicitly assumed responsibility for assisting students' spouses (and children) in adjusting to the college environment. Housing programs do not have the liberty to ignore or fail to address the unique needs of spouses simply because they are not enrolled in the institution. The housing program must deal with the entire family unit.

This finding may have stimulated the further research by Morris and Whalen (1989). In this study, using a similar population of family housing units at the same university, they looked at the impact of social distance on community satisfaction. In discussing their outcomes, the authors noted that the community with the greater social distance was a village where the physical layout was not conducive to neighbor interaction. Also, students and spouses from Asian countries experienced major social distance from all other populations. These outcomes imply that programming approaches in family housing should be similar in some respects to those used in single-student housing. However, different needs still exist; only through a proper assessment can those differences be pinpointed and programs scheduled.

Internationalization of Family Housing

One of America's most valuable exports in recent decades has been graduate education. As more and more students from abroad have chosen to study in the United States, greater pressure has been placed on family housing programs, because graduate students often are married and bring their families with them as they complete their studies. In many instances, these international students have limited incomes and cannot afford the rents charged for adequate housing in the local community.

Both national and on-campus discussions are needed regarding the special problems faced by international students in the family housing population. Some campuses have insufficient accommodations for families, and competition between international and native students for housing space may exist. On many campuses, the international population constitutes the majority of students, and this in itself raises the question of accessibility, especially in state-supported institutions — that is, if all or most family housing units are occupied by foreign students, local students from the state that supports the college with tax dollars are effectively excluded.

International students also present unique programming needs. Programs relating to the health care, childrearing practices, marriage philosophy, and relationships of these students — as well as the ever-present language barriers — should be implemented. A useful source of suggestions on how to create this type of programming is Reiff's book *Living and Learning for International Interchange: A Sourcebook for Housing Professionals* (1986). In their book review, Blansett and Buchan (1987, p. 20) note that "this population offers practical and experiential suggestions for building understanding through improved communication skills and programming." The publication is an excellent staff training manual for most housing operations.

Contemporary Problems in Family Housing

The previously neglected family housing population must be recognized and catered to programmatically, just as the single-student population began to be recognized in the 1960s. The issues today are more complex and far reaching; typical examples include the need for day-care centers and for marital counseling. Few solutions currently exist, due in large part to funding limitations.

One bright light at the end of the tunnel is the special apartments committee appointed by ACUHO-I to redefine the term *family*. As the nature of the family changes, family housing programs must also adjust. For instance, on many campuses there is uncertainty about how to deal with cohabitating but unmarried partners (both heterosexual and homosexual). There may be major political and possibly financial implications for the whole institution, depending on how the family housing program deals with these issues.

Housing Alternatives: Maximizing Fit

This chapter looked at the relationship between the design of the physical environment of a residence hall and the personal development and education of the student. Emphasis should be placed on student differences and their individual responses to the physical environment and the available programs. The key to achieving a successful residence hall program is the ability to meet the students' individual needs with as many residential alternatives as financially and physically possible. Variety may well be the spice of life, but it can also be a model for a successful residential community that provides opportunities for individual student growth — whether the students are single, family, or nontraditional students.

References

Adams, D. V. "Residential Learning Opportunities." In D. A. DeCoster and P. Mable (eds.), *Student Development and Education in College Residence Halls*. Washington, D.C.: American College Personnel Association, 1974.

Armstrong, P., and Martin, D. "The Potential Effect of Residence Hall Design on Student Academic Performance." *Journal of College Student Personnel*, 1982, *23*, 278–279.

Astin, A. W. *Achieving Educational Excellence: A Critical Assessment of Priorities and Practices in Higher Education*. San Francisco: Jossey-Bass, 1985.

Astin, A. W., Green, K. C., and Korn, W. S. *The American Freshmen: Twenty Year Trends, 1966–1985*. Los Angeles: Higher Education Research Institute, University of California, 1984.

Banning, J. H., and Kaiser, L. "An Ecological Perspective and Model for Campus Design." *Personnel and Guidance Journal*, 1974, *52*, 370–375.

Becker, F. D. "The Effects of Different Types of Student Involvement in Dormitory Design Over Time." *Housing and Society*, 1980, 7(1), 4–19.

Beyerlein, M., and others. "Community Development in Family Housing: Identifying Promoters and Inhibitors." *Journal of College and University Student Housing*, 1982, *12*(2), 8–13.

Blansett, S., and Buchan, R. "Living and Learning for International Interchange: A Sourcebook for Housing Personnel" (book review). *Journal of College and University Student Housing*, 1987, *17*(2), 29–30.

Brechtel, J. B., and Cherwak, D. "Recreation Needs in Married Student Housing." *Journal of College and University Student Housing*, 1978, 8(2), 16–17.

Chickering, A. W. *Commuting Versus Resident Students: Overcoming Educational Inequities of Living Off Campus*. San Francisco: Jossey-Bass, 1974.

Clarke, J., Miser, K., and Roberts, A. "Freshmen Residential Programs: Effects of Living-Learning Structure, Faculty Involvement, and Thematic Focus." *Journal of College and University Student Housing*, 1988, *18*(2), 7–13.

Crookston, B. B. "A Design for an Intentional Democratic Community." In D. A. DeCoster and P. Mable (eds.), *Student Development and Education in College Residence Halls*. Washington, D.C.: American College Personnel Association, 1974.

DeCoster, D. A., and Mable, P. "Residence Education: Purpose and Process." In D. A. DeCoster and P. Mable (eds.), *Personal Education and Community Development in College Residence Halls*. Cincinnati, Ohio: American College Personnel Association, 1980.

Duncan, C. M., and Stoner, K. L. "The Academic Achievement of Residents Living in a Scholar Residence Hall." *Journal of College and University Student Housing*, 1976–77, *6*(2), 7–9.

Duncan, J. P. "Emphasis on the Education in Coeducational Living." In D. A. DeCoster and P. Mable (eds.), *Student Development and Education in College Residence Halls*. Washington, D.C.: American College Personnel Association, 1974.

Educational Facilities Laboratories. *Student Housing*. New York: Educational Facilities Laboratories, 1972.

Evans, N. J. "Environmental Assessment: Current Practices and Future Directions." *Journal of College Student Personnel*, 1983, *24*(4), 293–299.

Forrest, S. P., Jr., and Schuh, J. H. "The Effect of Building Design on Student/Resident Perceptions." *Journal of College and University Student Housing*, 1976, *6*(1), 24–29.

Goldman, B. A., and Matheson, M. B. "A Comparison of Students Who Select a Living-Learning Residence Hall with Those Who Select a Conventional Residence Hall." *Journal of College and University Student Housing*, 1989, *19*(2), 16–19.

Grant, W. H. "Humanizing the Residence Hall Environment." In D. A. DeCoster and P. Mable (eds.), *Personal Education and Community Development in College Residence Halls*. Cincinnati, Ohio: American College Personnel Association, 1980.

Greenleaf, E. A. "Coeducational Residence Halls: An Evaluation." *Journal of the National Association of Women Deans and Counselors*, 1962, *25*(3), 106–111.

Gurowitz, W. D. "Commentary: Student Affairs at Stanford University." In G. Kuh and J. Schuh (eds.), *The Role and Contribution of Student Affairs in Involving Colleges*. Washington, D.C.: National Association of Student Personnel Administrators, 1991.

Hettler, W., Elsenrath, D., and Leafgren, F. *Lifestyle Assessment Questionnaire*. Stephens Point, Wis.: National Wellness Institute, 1990.

Higher Education Research Institute. *The American Freshmen and Follow-Up*

Survey, 1989 Freshmen Survey Results. Los Angeles: Higher Education Research Institute, University of California, 1989.

Jackson, S. G., and Stevens, S. "Incorporating Faculty and Staff into Residence Halls." *Journal of College and University Student Housing,* 1990, *20*(1), 7–10.

Katz, J. "Coeducational Living: Effects upon Male-Female Relationships." In D. A. DeCoster and P. Mable (eds.), *Student Development and Education in College Residence Halls.* Washington, D.C.: American College Personnel Association, 1974.

Kimble, G., and Levy, G. "Completing the Formula: Programming for Graduate and Non-Traditional Residents." Paper presented at the 41st annual conference of the Association of College and University Housing Officers-International, Macomb, Ill., July 1989.

Kuh, G. D., Schuh, J. H., and Thomas, R. O. "Suggestions for Encouraging Faculty-Student Interaction in a Residence Hall." *NASPA Journal,* 1985, *22*(3), 29–37.

Maslow, A. H. "A Theory of Human Motivation." In L. Gorlow and W. Kalkowsky (eds.), *Readings in the Psychology of Adjustment.* New York: McGraw-Hill, 1959.

Mehrabian, A. *Public Places and Private Spaces.* New York: Basic Books, 1976.

Moore, L. J., and Ostrander, E. R. "Physical and Social Determinants of Student Satisfaction in University Residence Halls: Theme Dorm Concept." *Housing and Society,* 1980, 7(1), 26–34.

Moos, R. H. *The Human Context: Environmental Determinants of Behavior.* New York: Wiley, 1976.

Morris, E., and Whalen, D. F. "The Impact of Social Distance on Community in University Apartments." *Journal of College and University Student Housing,* 1989, *19*(1), 22–27.

Pace, C. R. *Measuring the Quality of College Student Experience.* Los Angeles: Higher Education Research Institute, University of California, 1984.

Paul, S. C., Rei, J., Ostrow, E., and Shigetomi, C. "A Demonstration of Organizational Change in Family Housing." *Journal of College and University Student Housing,* 1984, *14*(2), 8–14.

Rei, J. "Educational Programming in Family Housing." In J. Schuh (ed.), *Educational Programming in College and University Residence Halls.* Columbus, Ohio: Association of College and University Housing Officers-International, 1988.

Reiff, R. F. *Living and Learning for International Interchange: A Sourcebook for Housing Personnel.* Washington, D.C.: NAFSA Washington, 1986.

Riker, H. *College Housing as Learning Centers.* Washington, D.C.: American College Personnel Association, 1965.

Riker, H. "Residential Learning." In A. W. Chickering and Associates, *The Modern American College: Responding to the New Realities of Diverse Students and a Changing Society.* San Francisco: Jossey-Bass, 1981.

Riker, H., and DeCoster, D. "The Educational Role in College Student Housing." *Journal of College and University Student Housing*, 1971, *1*, 4.

Roberts, G. A. *The Impact of Coeducational Living in College and University Residence Halls*. Columbus, Ohio: Association of College and University Housing Officers-International, 1990.

Schlossberg, N. K., Lynch, A. Q., and Chickering, A. W. *Improving Higher Education Environments for Adults: Responsive Programs and Services from Entry to Departure*. San Francisco: Jossey-Bass, 1989.

Schroeder, C. C. "Territoriality: Conceptual and Methodological Issues of Residence Educators." *Journal of College and University Student Housing*, 1978-79, *8*(2), 9-15.

Schuh, J. H. "Developing Programs in Family Student Housing." *Journal of College and University Student Housing*, 1985, *15*(2), 26-30.

Schuh, J. H. "A Framework for Student Involvement." In J. H. Schuh (ed.), *Educational Programming in College and University Residence Halls*. Columbus, Ohio: Association of College and University Housing Officers-International, 1988.

Schuh, J. H. "Making a Large University Feel Small: The Iowa State University Story." In G. Kuh and J. Schuh (eds.), *The Role and Contribution of Student Affairs in Involving Colleges*. Washington, D.C.: National Association of Student Personnel Administrators, 1991.

Schuh, J. H., and Kuh, G. D. "Faculty Interaction with Students in Residence Halls." *Journal of College Student Personnel*, 1984, *25*(6), 519-528.

Simard, A. C. *Working Within the House System: A Handbook for Hall Advisors*. Ames: Department of Residence Life, Iowa State University, 1989.

Whalen, D. F., and Winter, M. "Neighbor Interaction and Stress in Family Housing." *Journal of College and University Student Housing*, 1987, *17*(1), 28-34.

White, F., and White, J. R. "A Study of Bisexual Relationships Developed by Residents of a Co-Ed Living Arrangement." *Journal of College and University Student Housing*, 1973, *3*(2), 20-23.

Wills, B. S. "Life Style Options: Implications for College Housing." *Journal of College and University Student Housing*, 1975-76, *5*(2), 7-10.

Wilson, E. F. "The Entering Student: Attributes and Agents of Change." In T. Newcomb and E. Wilson (eds.), *College Peer Groups: Problems and Prospects for Research*. Hawthorne, N.Y.: Aldine, 1966.

Winston, R. B., Jr., Miller, T. K., and Prince, J. S. *Student Developmental Task Inventory*. (2nd ed.) Athens, Ga.: Student Development Associates, 1979.

Yunon, Y., Goldenberg, J., and Neeman, R. "The Relationship Between Structure of Residence and Formation of Friendships." *Psychological Reports*, 1977, *40*, 761-762.

Chapter Eleven

Professional Staffing

Patricia A. Kearney

Today, professional staff in the housing department play a central role in addressing the overall mission of higher education. Much of the institution's response to the need for community, the need to appreciate diversity, the need to provide information on specific issues and topics (such as personal safety, acquaintance rape, and health matters), and the need to improve retention (especially through increased faculty-student interaction) is targeted at resident populations. Making decisions about professional staffing in the housing department has never been more important.

What kind of professional staff is needed to carry out the mission of the housing department? Once the decision is made on the kind of staff and the number of staff positions, what can be done to find these important individuals? After the individuals are located, what action can be taken to maximize their effectiveness and keep them at the institution? These are the major questions that will be the focus of this chapter on professional staffing in the housing organization.

No discussion of professional and allied professional staffing can take place without an examination of broader issues. The material in Chapter Seven provides an important context for the issues we examine. The mission and goals of each housing department, the way the institution chooses to organize these positions, the size and type of institution, and the financial resources available all influence professional staffing.

This chapter covers the basic knowledge, skills, and competencies that housing professionals need to perform their jobs successfully. Careful attention is paid to the process of selecting professional staff, supervising them after employment, and evaluating their performance.

Defining Staff Positions

Regardless of the size, type, or financial resources of the institution, certain activities are frequently accomplished within a housing organization. These activities may be arranged in different ways. In larger organizations, individuals specialize in one activity, while in smaller organizations, they may take on a number of activities. In some institutions, many of these activities may be done outside of the housing organization.

Typical Staff Activities

The activities that may be assigned to professional staff in housing are identified in the list below. How many of these activities are the responsibility of the housing program varies considerably from campus to campus.

1. *Leadership.* Set goals, do long-range planning, and determine organizational structure.
2. *Developmental programming.* Integrate theory and practice to provide learning environments that positively affect residents' development.
3. *Multicultural development.* Create multicultural development programming (emphasizing appreciation of differences and elimination of prejudice) and respond to sexist, homophobic, or racist incidents.
4. *Community and individual management.* Handle conflict resolution, provide emergency and crisis management, offer supportive counseling, and do advising.
5. *Group advising.* Provide advising for residence hall governments, student committees, associations, boards, and tenant associations.
6. *Student conduct.* Train and advise student conduct boards, meet with students who are behavior problems, and hold disciplinary hearings.
7. *Student families.* Build, manage, and oversee apartment housing and focused programs.
8. *Child care.* Build and manage child-care centers; coordinate child-care referral services.
9. *Cooperative housing.* Create, manage, and oversee cooperative housing structures and/or programs.
10. *Graduate housing.* Build, manage, and oversee graduate housing structures and focused programs.

11. *Summer conference program.* Use housing facilities during the summer for conference groups and visitors.
12. *Community housing.* Work with off-campus managers and owners, mediation services, model leases, and housing listing services.
13. *Fraternity and sorority housing.* Build, manage, and oversee special living-group structures or programs.
14. *Facilities management.* Oversee custodial and maintenance services.
15. *New building, capital improvements, and major maintenance.* Supervise renovations and new housing construction.
16. *Lease management and contract administration.* Administer lease, property rental, equipment, and consultant contracts.
17. *Financial management.* Be responsible for long-term analysis of cash flow needs, budget development, budget administration, managerial and financial accounting, and handling of accounts payable and accounts receivable.
18. *Contracts and assignments.* Market and manage housing requests and assignments.
19. *Personnel and payroll.* Administer matters related to hiring, payroll, leaves, injuries, disabilities, performance appraisal, and affirmative action.
20. *Faculty and staff housing.* Build, sell, and/or lease homes, condominiums, and apartments for faculty and staff.
21. *Private development housing.* Create, work with developers, and manage and/or administer grounds leases for housing built on university land and owned by private developers.
22. *Food services.* Administer an outside contract or directly provide meals within a board program, cash facilities, catering, and/or a vending program.
23. *Coordination with other campus units.* Work with police, fire, environmental health and safety, campus physical plant department, academic units, and other student affairs offices for the enhancement of residence and campus life.
24. *Coordination with city agencies and government.* Work with police, fire, health care, city planning department, and elected government officials to promote safe, affordable housing and coordinate planning and problem solving.

Staff Structure

An important consideration in staffing is centralization versus decentralization. Who will be responsible for goal setting, long-range planning, decision making, and resource management? The more likely it is that a particular position will be responsible for the items noted above, the more important it is to hire someone with greater skills, knowledge, and ability. A decentralized system, in general, requires higher staffing in a greater number of positions than does a centralized system.

Another consideration is specialist versus generalist. Hiring goals and strategies will be different depending on how specialized the tasks within a given position are. Greater expertise in student development theory and program design is needed if the position requires the holder to spend much of her or his time developing leadership training sessions and developmental interventions than if it requires only small quantities of time in those activities, with assignments in other areas (such as facilities management) taking up significant amounts of time. Frequent errors are made when persons are hired for what we wish the position to be, rather than for what the staff member really must do.

Related to specialization is the issue of role rigidity. Particularly in housing, a quality environment for residents depends on the collaborative efforts of individuals assigned to many different functional roles. If individuals rigidly play their own functional roles and consider them to be the only roles of importance, residential environments suffer. This is also true of divisions between housing and student affairs roles and between faculty and staff roles. The literature over the last twenty years confirms the value of both quantitative and qualitative faculty-student interaction (Pascarella and Terenzini, 1991). A quick way to test for role rigidity is to listen to the problem-solving discussions during a housing staff meeting. Does the person in the residence life/programming position express concern with costs or facilities? Does the facilities/business manager speculate on the impact the decision will have on residents' development? In a "healthy" group of specialists, a stranger may not know what role a person formally occupies when listening to a group discussion (Creamer, 1990; Welfel, 1990).

Developing Position Descriptions: Hiring Proactively

Nearly constant staff turnover is a fact of life in housing programs. As a general rule, entry-level positions change every two to four years, which means that many housing programs have to search for new staff members almost every year. Skill in personnel selection, therefore, is essential to building and maintaining good-quality programs and services.

Position Analysis

The first step in the hiring process is a position analysis. It is important that the position's current and future requirements be identified, not its previous ones. What is the goal of the job? How does it assist in addressing the mission of the department? What tasks must the employee accomplish to achieve this goal? How can these tasks be accomplished? Again, honesty and realism are important. The wish list and professional expectations must be balanced with the constraints of the particular organization. Professionally, one may identify developmental needs and opportunities that should receive major time and attention in the organization (for example, substance abuse programs in all residence halls). However, if this position must spend 50 percent of its time on administrative tasks such as room changes, work orders, key inventories, and the like, the job description should reflect the "real" job and include all components.

Unless a newly created position is being filled, chances are that a job description will likely be on hand for the position. Before beginning the search for the "perfect candidate," one should take a hard look at the job description to make sure that it matches the department's current and future needs and operations. Certain activities and skills not contained in the previous job description may now be crucial to the organization. Important current or future activities may demand skills not presently found in the organization.

There are informal and formal techniques for developing position descriptions (Simms and Foxley, 1980). Formal job analysis is most frequently done through a *job inventory approach*, sometimes referred to as the *task inventory approach*. A job inventory is a "comprehensive list of the tasks that are performed to accomplish a job or set of jobs—a list that is cast in the form of a questionnaire" (Gael, 1983, p. 4). The responses required pertain to the relative importance of each task. "The idea is for the respondent to read the task statement, decide how important the task is compared to all other tasks that the incumbent performs, and select the appropriate number corresponding to the scale" (Gael, 1983, p. 6). Other less formal techniques can be used in analyzing a job, including observing incumbents for a day and interviewing them. As part of these observations and/or interviews, it may be helpful to look at the incumbent's calendar for a month. Another source of information is a review of the chronological correspondence file, if one is kept. The task is to understand the *real* job responsibilities.

With what level of detail should the position description be written? "The well-written job description contains short, factual statements that minimize the need for interpretation" (Moore, 1980, p. 3.50). The job description is intended to be used for hiring and often for evaluation. It is not intended to take the place of on-the-job orientation and training and should not contain procedures, policies, and "how-to-do-it" statements. A desk, position, or department manual should contain such details.

Once the position description is completed, it must be analyzed to determine the knowledge, skills, and ability needed to successfully complete the tasks and activities listed. Upcraft (1988, p. 41) states that "because there are many different routes to the profession through formal training or job experience, formal credentialing is absent as a means of screening and selecting staff. Also, the profession is very diverse, consisting of managers, administrators, counselors, student development specialists, and others." A degree in and of itself or a degree in a particular area does not guarantee that a person will be successful in a position. Some states—for example, California—have policies specifically excluding degrees as a staff screening criterion. One should distinguish between formal education and skills training. Formal education teaches students knowledge and helps them develop an understanding of its meaning. It does not necessarily mean that they can apply this knowledge and understanding in actual situations.

Some examples may help to illustrate the distinctions among knowledge, skills, and ability. A given position might require the following:

- *Knowledge* of concepts and theories of college student development and the impact of a residential living-learning environment on student development
- *Skill* to effectively lead and facilitate group discussions, lead small-group training sessions, engage in public speaking, and design and conduct experiential learning programs
- *Ability* to identify and organize tasks, prioritize duties, and effectively complete the many components of the job
- *Skill* working with multicultural groups and individuals
- *Knowledge* of theories and philosophies of discipline
- *Ability* to work under pressure and uneven time constraints
- *Knowledge* of management techniques of budgeting, managerial accounting, and quantitative decision making

The most successful staff members have a balance of knowledge, skills, and ability. (For a more detailed description of specific housing positions and professional knowledge and skills, see Resources A and C.)

Weiss (1989, p. 13) states that "chemistry does play a role in personnel decisions, not the chemistry between you and the candidate but rather the chemistry between the candidate and certain environmental factors—organization culture, the other people with whom the person will work, or the psychological demands of the job itself." Does the person carry out job tasks by working with others? If so, then a candidate's ability to get along with and communicate with others is a legitimate factor to consider in defining the ideal candidate. Other factors that are frequently not openly stated but that may be crucial to the successful completion of job requirements include the following: preferred method of decision making, method of handling conflict, method of responding to supervision, method of expressing disagreement, willingness to perform repetitive tasks, willingness to adapt to organizational styles (dress, writing, decision making)—to "the way we do things at 'X' University."

Moving Beyond Affirmative Action

The demographics, and therefore the culture, of the United States are changing at a rapid pace. Most large metropolitan areas are racially and ethnically diverse. Some states already have a population composed of a majority of people of color. Some prestigious research universities already have a student body that is over 50 percent non-European-American. Half of the college students in the United States are women. More than half of all students are over age twenty-three. Over 10 percent of college students have other than a heterosexual orientation. Individuals with disabilities are an important part of our campus population. Professional staffing for these new and permanent realities does not call for business as usual.

It is imperative that every staff position be filled with an individual who, in addition to having the knowledge, skills, and ability to do the job, appreciates diversity and is willing to empower diversity. No matter what gender, race, ethnic background, sexual orientation, or level of physical ability an applicant has, one must determine if that candidate has the sensitivity and skill to work with a diverse student and employee population (Pedersen, 1988). This criterion must become fundamental to every hiring process. It goes beyond just hiring methods to the idea of "valuing differences" (Thomas, 1991, p. 24).

It is important that all students have role models. Although it is possible and desirable to mentor and role model across genders, races, cultures, and sexual orientations, this does not take the place of mentors and role models who are like oneself. Particularly for groups new to higher education and those who must overcome negative messages and barriers, like role models are crucial. For educational reasons, a diverse professional staff is desirable. This goal must be all-inclusive. It is important to have male role models and white role models. This is not an affirmative action issue; it is a diversity issue and must be part of an inclusive educational model.

There are many books available on affirmative action and the educational value of diversity. Most colleges have a personnel or employment office that develops and regulates hiring practices. These offices can provide information and assistance. The definitive legal reference on affirmative action is *Employment Discrimination Law* (Schlei and Grossman, 1983). Cheatham and Associates (1991) also provide insight into the educational values of diversity, especially in student affairs.

The way housing programs address the issue of diversity and multiculturalism sends a message regarding how much the institution values differences, as well as promoting the creation of an environment that allows these programs to grow and flourish. Clearly articulated plans to address diversity within residential life are needed to meet diversity goals.

Recruitment and Selection

Throughout the entire recruitment and selection process, the highest ethical behavior is expected of both employers and candidates. Professional associations such as the American College Personnel Association and the National

Association of Student Personnel Administrations publish professional standards. (See Welfel, 1990, and Resources E and F.) At its best, the process is an adult-adult, win-win process. The employer accurately represents the position and seeks diversity in the applicant pool. The employer seeks to find out as much as possible about the candidates to determine if they have the knowledge, skills, and ability to do the job. The candidates accurately represent their knowledge, skills, and ability and seek a diverse work group of professional colleagues. The candidates seek to find out as much as possible about the employer and the goals and tasks associated with the position and institution. The employer should keep all candidates informed about the recruitment process. This can best be done with regular communication throughout the entire recruitment and selection process.

Recruitment Methods

There are a number of ways that candidates can be encouraged to apply for positions. In many cases, multiple strategies can and should be employed. The list below presents common methods and notes potential dangers in overreliance on specific methods.

- *Internal recruitment.* A potential candidate may already be employed at or may be a student in the institution. Internal promotion is important for morale. But exclusive use of this method could result in an "inbred," stagnant organization. If the organization is not currently diverse, it could perpetuate that lack of diversity. Judgment and balance are the key to this decision.
- *Local recruitment.* Depending on the position that is open and the population in a geographical area, a candidate may be close by the campus. A mailing to institutions in the region or an advertisement in a metropolitan newspaper may produce some high-quality candidates.
- *National and regional associations.* A number of national and regional associations offer extensive placement services at their annual conventions. These placement services provide both the employer and the applicant an opportunity to cover more ground in less time than other methods. These services may also provide an opportunity for preliminary interviewing and screening. The major placement services for housing positions are offered by the American College Personnel Association, the Association of College and University Housing Officers-International (ACUHO-I), the National Association of Student Personnel Administrators, and the regional and state divisions of these organizations. In using this method, one should keep in mind that many excellent employers and candidates might not attend any given annual conference. For some institutions and candidates, the cost may preclude participation.
- *Publications.* The *Chronicle of Higher Education* is the major recruitment tool in higher education. It is published weekly and has many pages of

position listings. Some regional and national association newsletters also list employment opportunities. A publication increasingly used to diversify recruitment effort is the journal *Black Issues in Higher Education*. Obviously, only individuals who have access to these publications will see the listing. For some small institutions, the cost of placing advertisements in national publications may be prohibitive.

- *Personal efforts.* Some national organizations will provide mailing lists for all or subsets of their members and subscribers. One can write to known colleagues or all colleges and universities of like size, mission, and so forth. The entire staff of a department can get involved by making positions known through their professional networks. If they are having a good experience at their current institution, they are excellent recruiters. The danger is that many professionals have a tendency to have more relationships with people who are like them than who are unlike them. It is possible to unintentionally perpetuate a lack of diversity by spreading the word through a homogeneous network.

- *Focused recruitment.* If there are positions or units within a department that have persistent unmet affirmative action goals, focused recruitment may be used. This method intentionally attempts to increase the number of underrepresented applicants in a hiring pool. Particular strategies might include using publications for special populations, working with special committees of national and regional organizations (for example, multicultural committee, women's committee, gay, lesbian, bisexual committee), and seeking assistance from campus committees and organizations. Some individuals believe that these focused recruitment techniques should become part of regular recruitment.

- *Dual-career recruitment.* With dual-career couples becoming ever more numerous, trailing spouses and partners offer many opportunities for creative recruitment. Colleges in close proximity may work together to improve recruitment of couples and partners.

As social norms and life-styles have changed, the fishbowl-like living arrangements of live-in staff become an increasing issue. No national consensus exists among institutions of higher education on the permissibility and advisability of live-in staff members having unmarried domestic partners (either same-sex or opposite-sex) in residence. Each housing department must thoughtfully review this issue within the context of state law, social mores of the institution, support of the institution's leadership, and institutional policy. A clear policy about who may live at the work site must be developed. For example, a policy could read: "The professional live-in staff member's apartment is her or his private residence and may be shared by a spouse, partner, or other relative. The staff member is responsible for assuring that the presence of other individuals is congruent with the student interaction and support goals of the institution." Or a policy might read: "Only the professional live-in staff member and his or her legal spouse and children may reside in the residence hall apartment." This policy can be given or mailed to applicants along with job descriptions and other materials. Honest communication in advance of on-campus interviews is essential. In the interest of inclusiveness and diversity, housing professionals are encouraged, unless legal or institutional prohibitions exist, to remove barriers in this area. Excellent staff members can be lost through restrictive policies.

Screening

On most occasions, more applications are received than the number of finalists that can actually be interviewed. At some point, preliminary decisions are needed to concentrate efforts on some subset of the applicant pool. It is important to match screening criteria and timing to the material available and at the right time in the selection process. Throughout the selection and interview process, the goal is to "measure" the difference between applicants, not the differences of reviewers' days, moods, and personal styles. To focus on the difference between applicants, screening and interviewing must be structured. For example, if applicant X, in response to the question "How do you use student development theory in developing your programs?", gives a terrific answer, it cannot be known that the applicant is better in this area than other applicants, if others are not asked the same question.

The criteria for screening should be clearly identified to those involved in the screening process. Written materials provide valuable information but cannot answer all questions. Preliminary screening may take place at regional or national conferences. A single staff member or group of staff members may have short interviews with applicants who are interested in the position. Institutions often use two methods for this type of screening. Most institutions have one-hour interviews where they attempt to interview the candidate and impart information to the candidate about the institution and answer the candidate's questions. Some institutions hold group sessions for about one to one and a half hours. At these sessions, they impart information to approximately eight to twelve candidates about the institution, about its philosophy, and about the department and job. Sometimes audiovisual and written materials are shared. This is followed up by thirty- to forty-five-minute individual interviews that are used exclusively to learn about the applicant. In some cases, a second conference interview with a higher-level staff member is offered to the better-qualified applicants. A few institutions hold a reception for their top applicants to let them meet other staff and reinforce the institution's interest.

Reference checks can take place at this stage in the screening process (prior to identifying final candidates), or they may take place at the end of the interview process prior to making a job offer, or they may happen at both points. One hopes that there are no longer instances of hiring decisions made without reference checks. Two points in time are recommended for reference checks. A reference check prior to the final interview saves time and resources. If travel is involved, the applicant and the institution may be spending considerable money and time to arrange and participate in a campus interview. Ideally, one should believe that every candidate invited to a campus interview is hireable. If the preferred candidate has been identified and a reference is called for the first time immediately before making a job offer, objectivity may be lowered. After all, time and money have been invested in a selection process that produced a person believed to be the best candidate. Will questions to a reference be as aggressive and probing at this point? A second reference check after the interview process can be valuable to clarify any discrepancies between interview experience and past work performance.

Screening the initial applicant pool through the use of written materials, telephone interviews, and/or reference checks can help the decision-making process and ensure fairness. It also saves resources by identifying the best-qualified applicants for the particular position.

References

It is estimated that at least one-third of all application materials are exaggerated, misleading, or false (Norton, 1988). Applicants have been known to falsify degrees, jobs held and dates of employment, and the duties of positions held. It is the responsibility of the hiring authority to check the facts presented by the candidate. A reference check should be planned in advance, and the same information should be asked about each applicant. The reference with the most information should be a person's immediate supervisor. Where multiple references are listed, this supervisor should always be one of the references. The hiring authority has the ability to specify types of references to be provided by candidates. References, however, should not be called without a candidate's permission. If candidates will not or cannot provide required references, they can be disqualified.

Questions should be prepared in advance and must be job related. Many institutions develop a reference check form for each position or type of position. If more than one person is checking references, this information can be standardized and shared. The first series of questions should be the quantitative questions, verifying that the person was employed at that institution, dates of employment, position(s) held, and responsibility and authority that were part of the position held. A second line of questioning is more qualitative. It can give a hiring authority indications of issues or the need for more information but in and of itself should not be used to screen out candidates. The reason for differentiating between the first and second types of reference check questions is that the second may be giving as much information about the reference as about the applicant. If issues arise, these same questions should be asked of the applicant.

Ethics of Reference Checking

Cannon (1989) and Cannon and Brown (1985) offer comprehensive discussions of professional ethics. Employment ethics are a subset of professional ethics. Although many of these matters are thought to be basic, some professionals and employers continue to ignore them. Following are suggested guidelines.

1. If a person is not able to provide a positive reference, the individual requesting the reference should know something about the nature of the reference that will be provided. For example, "Yes, I will be your reference. You do realize that my comments will be in line with feedback that has been given to you previously and my evaluations of you."

2. References may be silent, but they may not mislead. If an employee is mediocre or poor, deal with her or him. Do not dump the employee on a colleague by providing a positive, even glowing reference. Remember, a limitation in one organizational setting could be accommodated in another setting. Speaking about a difficulty that has been previously discussed with the individual will not necessarily bar the person from employment elsewhere.

3. Questions that are illegal or inappropriate in an interview are illegal and inappropriate in a telephone reference check.

References can be a valuable tool in professional staffing. The single best predictor of future job performance is past job performance (Stanton, 1977). Verifying a person's work history and success in previous jobs is an essential part of selecting staff.

Interviewing and Final Decision Making

Most institutions use a campus visit as the final step in the selection process. This is desirable and preferred, since it gives both candidate and employer additional time together and information that is not always available in written materials. But time and/or money may preclude the campus visit. If a campus visit is not feasible, a second telephone interview may be substituted. It would also be important to carry out the preliminary screening and reference checks at a higher level of intensity and detail. Although not preferred, successful hiring decisions have been made without campus visits. With limited time and money, careful attention to all other steps in the process may provide a higher probability of a successful match between candidate and employer.

Campus Interviews

When considering the great variety of information available from the applicant's materials, letters of reference, and preliminary interview(s), it may be questioned whether the hiring authority needs more information to make a decision. There are a number of possible reasons for having an additional campus interview. These include opportunities to:

- Determine personal fit — that is, the compatibility between the candidate and certain environmental factors; observe the candidate's effectiveness in working with individuals and groups
- Provide the candidate with an opportunity to learn about the social/cultural/life-style opportunities in the community and on the campus
- Provide an opportunity for a broader range of staff and students to become involved in the selection process
- More intensely probe and follow up on strengths and weaknesses found in the preliminary interview and reference check
- Begin the socialization process

The interview begins the process of teaching the candidate about the organization and its values. To the extent that some or all of these objectives are the rationale for the campus interview effort, the process should be designed purposefully to enhance these opportunities.

Before applicants are invited to visit the campus, all decisions about resources and financial support related to the applicants' visits should be made. Costs are associated with transportation, lodging, meals, and incidentals. Candidates should know exactly how these costs will be handled before being invited to campus. It is important to follow up with written information in advance of the visit.

Stanton (1977, p. 122) indicates that one of the greatest errors made in interviewing is not taking enough time. The interviewer or interview group should make sure that sufficient time is scheduled to get questions answered. Much of the research concerning the effectiveness of interviewing for predicting future job performance has shown disappointing results. Two factors that seem to improve interview effectiveness are training interviewers (Ghiselli, 1966) and structuring the interview.

Deciding who to involve in the interview process has implications both for selecting the "best" candidate and for how well the person selected adjusts to the institution. It is recommended that these individuals or factors be considered in determining who will interview on-campus candidates: (1) the position supervisor and his or her supervisor, (2) important stakeholders, such as residents, staff at the same level as the position being filled, and support staff who will have frequent contact with the position holder, (3) individuals of political influence who desire to be included or whose goodwill is important, (4) staff inside and outside the housing program with whom the position holder will need to relate regularly, and (5) staff peers across student affairs departments.

In addition, the interview teams should reflect gender and cultural diversity. Remember that a goal is to hire individuals who are committed to the appreciation of differences and multicultural development. The ability to work with and understand students is always an important criterion. Students should be active participants in the interview process. Including faculty in the interview process may establish or cement relationships.

Both group and individual interviews should be scheduled. Many housing professionals do much of their work in groups. Too often the interview process looks only at one-on-one interaction.

In putting groups together, some interview processes keep similar people together. For example, the candidate meets with a group of students, then with a group of people she or he will supervise, then with a group of facilities people, and so forth. A second approach, and possibly a superior one, is to mix groups so that a variety of roles and functions are represented in a group. This method helps interviewers realize the multidimensional aspects of the job (and therefore possibly appreciate why their favorite candidate was not chosen). It also helps the candidate see the richness and complexity of the organization.

An orientation session should be provided for all interviewers. A first step is to distribute and go over materials (minimally—the job description, candidates' applications, and interview schedules). Any special goals (hiring, programmatic, affirmative action, and/or diversity goals) for this particular hiring process should be emphasized. Appropriate interview behavior and questions can be reviewed. A minilecture and/or handout on interview techniques or common interview mistakes can be provided (Stanton, 1977; Uris, 1988). It is important to specifically review appropriate and inappropriate interview questions. The hiring authority has an institutional and ethical obligation to ensure that the interview is legal and fair. Questions such as "Are you planning to have children?" and "What religion are you?" are examples of inappropriate questions. Describe the decision-making process and how each individual or group fits into that process.

The interview should be structured. Remember that the purpose is to determine the knowledge, skills, and ability of the candidates, not the knowledge, skills, and ability of the interviewers. When possible, interviews should be held in the same room or a similar room and should be conducted at the same time of day. It is possible to perceive something different than the candidate's enthusiasm if one candidate meets at 9:00 A.M. and one at 1:00 P.M. The interview groups should remain the same. If different people are interviewing each candidate, unknown variables are introduced into the process. The sequence of the interview should also be kept the same. A candidate at the beginning of the interview process will have less information about the organization than one interviewed at the end.

Individual interviewers should be required to complete a candidate evaluation form prior to the group discussion. If diverse viewpoints are important, all those viewpoints ought to be recorded. The group discussion is valuable and important, but it is different from each individual's standpoint. One person—preferably the supervisor and/or hiring authority—should spend considerable time with the candidate over a variety of settings—

informal, group interview, social activity, and so forth. A single person does not need to be with the candidate at all times, but someone should have an overview of the candidate's behavior in a variety of settings.

The candidate should have structured and free time on the itinerary for exploring the community. Where could I live? What would it cost? How is the public school system? What are the employment possibilities like for my spouse or partner? What is this community like for me (for example, as an African American, a disabled person, a Latino/Chicano American, an Asian American, a gay or lesbian person, a single parent, or a single person)? It is useful to facilitate activities such as tours, obtaining materials, and talking with others who might have information or experience to help a candidate find out if her or his needs can be met at this institution and in this community.

A closing session should be scheduled with the candidate. If possible, the hiring authority should conduct this session. It is appropriate to answer questions, raise issues—if any—from concerns about the candidate generated during interviews, and review the decision-making process and timeline. It is also a potentially valuable opportunity to get feedback on the interview process.

Decision Making

An obvious but sometimes overlooked fact is that ultimately a single individual is responsible for the hiring decision. Whoever is designated as the hiring authority must take all the information from interviews, group evaluations, individual interviews, references, and written materials and combine that with the goals of this hiring process to make a decision. Philosophically, the hiring authority needs to decide in advance about how that decision will be made. Must there be a consensus? Will the candidate with support from the most people be hired? Are there key individuals (frequently at least the immediate supervisor) who must support the decision no matter what level of support comes from others? A composite rather than straight consensus model is preferred. Consensus sometimes brings forward the candidate that everyone can agree on. But perhaps the *safest* choice is not the *best* choice. Looking at all the selection process information, not just information from an interview group, the hiring authority makes a final decision. This decision-making model requires sensitivity and political acumen. Before deciding, the hiring authority should have a discussion with individuals who might have a problem with a candidate. It is important to listen to their concerns, follow up on these concerns, and share other viewpoints.

After deciding on a candidate, the hiring authority should make the job offer. Salary, starting date, and fringe benefits (such as moving costs, health insurance, and retirement plan) should be clearly stated. Some degree of negotiation may be possible. The hiring authority and the candidate must agree on a date when the candidate needs to communicate a decision. This date usually takes into account and balances the candidate's needs and the institution's need to offer the position to another candidate or reopen the search. (The employment offer should be put in writing, and the candidate should be required to accept in writing.) Finally, once a decision is made and the position filled, all who participated in the selection process and others who will be working with the individual should be notified. The orientation process can now be planned.

Supervision, Staff Development, and Evaluation

The majority of individuals holding professional positions in housing organizations supervise others. After a hiring decision has been made, the development and training of individual staff members are as crucial to their success as was the careful hiring process.

Orientation

A planned and purposeful orientation of new staff members at all levels is a must. Introduction to the job and to all significant other staff is a good way of reducing the length of the learning curve and alleviating needless stress for a new employee. Another element of this orientation should be a frank and two-way exchange of expectations. An early part of orientation should include a description of the timing and method of performance appraisals. The objectives of the job and the performance standards that will be used to measure success should be clearly communicated. It is important to emphasize that the job as outlined in the official position description may only be changed by mutual agreement. Orientation is sometimes considered an individual activity—that is, one orients the individual to the job. But orientation should be viewed as an opportunity for team building. The individual must be introduced to the team and its norms and values, and the team must open up to accept the talents and needs of a new staff member. To the extent that this process is explicit and intentional, it becomes team building as well as orientation.

Orientation is a time to emphasize the need for young professionals to network with other staff members. It is also important to encourage new staff members to attend receptions and other campus social activities in order to meet others. A discussion of the difference between the almost automatic connections, supervision, and support of graduate school and the need to work at these activities on a typical college campus is useful.

Coaching: A Foundation for Supervision

Darraugh (1990, p. 1) defines coaching as "the managerial activity that creates, by communication alone, the climate, environment, and context that empowers individuals and teams to generate results." Coaching employees on an ongoing basis about results, rather than personality, is the most helpful supervision method available. Process need not be neglected; however, it must be stated in terms of results. A successful coach might say, for example, "Your interaction with Joan at the meeting seemed to produce defensiveness and resistance. Did you observe that? How do you think you might behave differently in order to get her cooperation in completing your project?" Or "I would like you to try another approach in this kind of situation. I believe you will get better results if you. . . ." An experienced and caring "coach" can be worth many hours of formal management seminars. Coaching, when combined with other techniques, enhances the supervisory process. Other important activities include giving clear direction, providing challenging assignments, giving support and training as needed, communicating a high level of expectation, and giving clear and consistent feedback.

Staff Development

In addition to benefiting from individual coaching, all staff members can profit from planned staff development programs. This can be done in-house, with consultants, or with a combination of the two (Moore and Young, 1987). Small institutions in geographical proximity may want to combine forces to have sufficient resources and numbers to have high-quality staff development programs. Providing funding for staff to attend professional conferences is an important part of the staff development effort. The value of this travel can be enhanced if these staff members are required to share their learning with other staff as part of the next staff meeting. For young professionals, it is important to help them understand that their professional growth is their own responsibliity, not the institution's. "A professional has to take the initiative, not wait for someone to develop them" (Bolger, Crahen, and Herzer, 1987, p. 7).

Evaluation

LeBoeuf (1985, p. 23) states that the greatest management principle in the world is, "The things that get rewarded get done." This can be illustrated in the parable of the woman, the dog, and the duck. This parable is adapted from one presented by LeBoeuf (1985, p. 22). "A woman drifting along in her boat saw a dog with a duck in its mouth. Feeling sorry for the duck, she reached down, gently removed the duck from the dog's mouth, and let the duck go free. But now she felt sorry for the dog. She took out a flask of bourbon and poured a few drops in the dog's mouth. The dog swam back to shore happy, the duck was happy, and the woman was happy for having performed such good deeds. She thought all was well until a few minutes passed and she heard something knock against the side of the boat and looked down. With stunned disbelief, the woman boater saw the dog was back with two ducks."

This fable carries two important lessons: "(1) You get more of the behavior you reward. You don't get what you hope for, ask for, wish for, or beg for. You get what you reward. (2) In trying to do the right things, it's oh so easy to fall into the trap of rewarding the wrong activities and ignoring or punishing the right ones. The result is that we hope for A, unwittingly reward B, and wonder why we get B" (LeBoeuf, 1985, p. 22).

How often does the director of housing set a goal to increase student development programming (A), only to continue to give negative feedback to staff members who spend time on this and do not have all administrative tasks done at exactly the deadline or to reward staff who are not doing student development but are outstanding clerical workers (B)? At the end of the year, the director is shaking her head, wondering why she cannot get staff to address student development. Good leaders strive for congruence in management and performance systems.

Brown (1988) defines performance appraisal as the process of assessing and recording staff performance for the purpose of making judgments about staff that lead to decisions. He defines these decisions as "providing feedback for professional development, assessing individual and group hiring needs, determining who is to be promoted, and making salary decisions" (p. 6). One could add selection and discharge decisions to that list. All of these decisions must be made, and the only real question is whether a planned, formal performance appraisal system should be used to make them. In many institutions, the formal performance appraisal system (frequency, format, criteria, and purpose) is determined by the personnel office and/or legal counsel's office. Fox, an expert on employment and labor law and a partner at Pillsbury, Madison, and Sutro of San Francisco, cautions seminar participants about increasing challenges to performance appraisal systems. These challenges include Title VII, libel and slander, breach of contract, and negligent performance appraisal.

Although the institution may impose a format for the performance appraisal system on all divisions of the institution, this usually does not preclude a department from also using additional techniques. One such technique that has been used by this author for many years is a helping appraisal. It is most useful if it is done "away from" the formal process. It is particularly recommended for early in the tenure of new staff members. It might be introduced as follows: "Here is a list of five questions that should give you an opportunity for meaningful self-appraisal. It is very important that this self-appraisal be thoughtful. It is for your own use. You can choose to keep some of it private; you do not have to share it with me. At our next meeting, we will discuss items that are important to your continued growth and job success."

The five questions are designed to help staff members think broadly about their performance and keep some sense of perspective. The five areas covered in the helping appraisal are listed below.

1. What are your accomplishments? List all of the things you have done on this job that you are proud of. In what ways did you exceed your own expectations or those of others? Did you solve any unusually difficult problems? Did you do anything you feel others would have difficulty doing? By whose standards do you feel you have excelled? Do not be modest; brag but do not exaggerate!

2. What are your current strengths? List the areas in which you feel you possess broad and in-depth knowledge, have outstanding skills, or believe you are highly experienced. Link these to your accomplishments. Consider how you can build on these same strengths in the future.

3. Where are the uncertainties and misunderstandings? Give possible ideas for aspects of your performance that you believe were less than outstanding. Pay particular attention to factors that you believe were outside your control. Did you receive confusing or vague instructions? Did anybody interfere with your performance? Was there a significant change in external factors that created problems for you? Did somebody you were depending on disappoint you? In what ways did things go wrong that you did not anticipate beforehand? Were there any areas where you were uncertain about what was expected of you? Did you misunderstand the expectations of others? Are you uncertain about your own ability to accomplish what is expected of you?

4. What obstacles are in your way? How can I be of help? How can you remove these obstacles? Is there specific information or training that would assist you? Can I or other significant people in your work life behave in a manner that is more supportive of your success?

5. Are there any specific goals or action steps that you would like to formulate as a result of your self-appraisal? When do you want to conclude these activities? How will we know if they have been successfully concluded?

With real effort and a shared value of helping, individuals using this appraisal can develop many ideas and possibilities for improving their professional performance.

Housing as a Career

Hood and Arceneaux (1990) assert that in the past decade there has been increasing specialization and consequently greater separatism in the student affairs field. That same specialization is also taking place within the area of housing. One only has to review the list of activities assigned to professional staff in housing at the beginning of this chapter to see the potential for increased specialization. The concept of student development has tended to provide at least a small unifying force in the face of many other forces that are dividing the field. If this small force is to have greater impact, it is important that it be shared, understood, and embraced by all staff within the housing organization. Ensuring this is primarily the responsibility of the chief housing administrator.

Some institutions have integrated systems that include business and facilities and residence life reporting to a single administrator. Other organizations have separate directors for housing and residence life. The major professional organization in this field, ACUHO-I, has stated a preference for the unified model. If individuals wish to stay in the housing field, they must determine if they want to remain exclusively in residence life, move toward the facilities and business side, or develop the breadth to oversee more complex organizations involving both areas. (See Chapter Seven.)

Most professionals in housing start their career in a live-in position as a head resident or resident director. Young professionals today are not as willing or interested in taking live-in positions with long hours, lack of privacy, and relatively low pay for a person with an advanced degree. There is not a large enough or diverse enough pool of young professionals on a national level to fill all the live-in residence hall positions in the colleges and universities in this country.

Colleges and universities could do more to make the position more attractive. Apartments can be furnished and designed to provide a more attractive and private living space. The institution can help set limits on workload and hours of work. The institution can also review pay scales to make sure they are competitive (always a dilemma for a director of housing who is held accountable for keeping rates low).

The second-level position that many young professionals within housing compete for is area or complex director, or in smaller colleges, assistant director. These positions vary a great deal in terms of the amount of emphasis they place on facilities/business management and residence life programming. This second-level career choice should be congruent with the long-term career aspirations of the professional. It is appropriate to fill in gaps or further develop strengths at this level. Staff development, mentors, classes, professional associations, and internships all offer potential. If one is moving toward the facilities/business side of housing, understanding of financial and managerial accounting, budgets, fundamentals of construction management, contracts, and food service management is important knowledge to acquire.

The third career position may include a similar job at a larger institution or a position as an assistant or associate director of housing. A fourth career position may include moving laterally within or outside of student housing for breadth of experience, moving to another institution with more responsibilities, or for some, returning to school to complete an advanced degree.

A fifth career position may include being director of an entire campus program. Many directors of housing, because they frequently head complex organizations with large budgets and staffs, are very competitive for central student affairs leadership positions as assistant vice presidents or vice presidents for student affairs later in their careers.

Obviously, not everyone goes through a career in the same sequence. Many find deep satisfaction in a certain type of position and choose to stay there. Given the "pyramid" type of organizational structure, with ten to twenty first-year professionals on some campuses and one director-of-housing position, many move into other types of work. Housing staff have successfully made transitions to student activities, wellness programs, fraternity and sorority advising, development offices, budget offices, and institutional business or facility offices. Outside of the higher education, they have moved into human development positions in the private and community sectors. There are as many paths as there are individuals. The American College Personnel Association workbook titled *Residence Education: A Career Beginning or a Career Path?* (Reynolds, Komines, and Mable, 1983) allows for individual assessment of the knowledge bases and motivation, skills, and personal goals needed to continue a career in residence life. In August 1990, all chief housing officers from ACUHO-I member institutions were surveyed regarding competencies needed to become an effective housing professional (Dunkel and Walker, 1990). The ten competencies listed below were chosen as most important from a list of fifty-five.

1. Possess interpersonal communication skills — skills that pertain to the exchange of information between persons
2. Be able to work cooperatively and effectively with a wide range of individuals. Possess the ability to facilitate interactions with a diverse population
3. Be able to supervise staff — that is, to provide them with the appropriate direction to successfully perform their responsibilities
4. Be cognizant of the unique needs of diverse groups — that is, be sensitive to the special needs of racial, ethnic, religious, and cultural minorities, gays, bisexuals, and lesbians, women, and the physically challenged
5. Know how to engage in effective decision making: know who and what are directly and indirectly affected by your decisions, and be able to make timely and wise decisions
6. Know how to train staff — that is, how to give them the knowledge and skills to successfully fulfill their responsibilities
7. Have the ability to maintain qualified staff and adhere to selection policies and procedures
8. Possess crisis management skills — the ability to effectively respond to an unstable person or a crisis situation
9. Have the necessary skill to develop and supervise a budget — that is, understand the basic components of a housing budget and how to effectively provide for each component; know how and where to make allocations for the coming year and administer those funds appropriately

10. Be able to recognize and analyze political processes in higher education: acknowledge different subpopulations who have a vested interest in the institution (faculty, staff, students, administration, parents, trustees, and the community, as examples), know how they interact and affect one another, and be able to apply that knowledge to the housing organization and its operations

Assessment of interests and competencies is important both for choosing a career path and for identifying areas for continuing skill development.

Staffing Makes a Difference

Housing as a work setting offers almost unlimited opportunities to contribute to the education and development of college students. The key to unlocking this potential is the selection and nurturing of a talented and committed group of professional staff. It is a time-consuming process but one that is worth the time and effort. What other single management activity is more important than selecting people to carry out the mission of the department?

References

Bolger, A., Crahen, S., and Herzer, S. "Strategies for Success for the New Professional." Paper presented at the annual convention of the Association of College and University Housing Officers-International, Los Angeles, July 1987.

Brown, R. D. *Performance Appraisal as a Tool for Staff Development*. New Directions for Student Services, no. 43. San Francisco: Jossey-Bass, 1988.

Cannon, H. J. "Guiding Standards and Principles." In U. Delworth, G. R. Hanson, and Associates, *Student Services: A Handbook for the Profession*. (2nd ed.) San Francisco: Jossey-Bass, 1989.

Cannon, H. J., and Brown, R. D. (eds.). *Applied Ethics in Student Services*. New Directions for Student Services, no. 30. San Francisco: Jossey-Bass, 1985.

Cheatham, H. E., and Associates. *Cultural Pluralism on Campus*. Alexandria, Va.: American Association of Counseling and Development, 1991.

Creamer, D. G., and Associates. *College Student Development: Theory and Practice for the 1990's*. Washington, D.C.: American College Personnel Association, 1990.

Darraugh, B. (ed.). "Coaching and Feedback." *Info-Line of American Society for Training and Development*, Alexandria, Va., June 1990, pp. 2-3.

Dunkel, N., and Walker, P. J. "Competencies Necessary to Become an Effective Housing Professional." Unpublished survey supported by the Association of College and University Housing Officers-International, University of Florida, 1990.

Gael, S. *Job Analysis: A Guide to Assessing Work Activities*. San Francisco: Jossey-Bass, 1983.

Ghiselli, E. E. "The Validity of a Personnel Interview." *Personnel Psychology*, 1966, *19*, 389–394.

Hood, A. B., and Arceneaux, C. *Key Resources on Student Services: A Guide to the Field and Its Literature*. San Francisco: Jossey-Bass, 1990.

LeBoeuf, M. *The Greatest Management Principle in the World*. New York: Putnam, 1985.

Moore, L. V., and Young, R. B. (eds.). *Expanding Opportunities for Professional Education*. New Directions for Student Services, no. 37. San Francisco: Jossey-Bass, 1987.

Moore, R. F. *AMA Management Handbook*. New York: American Management Association, 1980.

Norton, T. W. "Righting Resume Fraud." *Security Management*, Sept. 1988, pp. 17–22.

Pascarella, E. T., and Terenzini, P. T. *How College Affects Students: Findings and Insights from Twenty Years of Research*. San Francisco: Jossey-Bass, 1991.

Pedersen, P. "Culturally Biased Assumptions and Their Reasonable Opposites." In P. Pedersen (ed.), *A Handbook for Developing Multicultural Awareness*. Alexandria, Va.: American Association for Counseling and Development, 1988.

Reynolds, E., Jr., Komines, S. B., and Mable, P. *Residence Education: A Career Beginning or a Career Path?* Alexandria, Va.: American College Personnel Association, 1983.

Schlei, B. L., and Grossman, P. *Employment Discrimination Law*. (2nd ed.) Washington, D.C.: American Bar Association, 1983.

Simms, J. M., and Foxley, C. H. In C. H. Foxley (ed.), *Applying Management Techniques*. New Directions for Student Services, no. 9. San Francisco: Jossey-Bass, 1980.

Stanton, E. S. *Successful Personnel Recruiting and Selection*. New York: American Management Association, 1977.

Thomas, R. R., Jr. *Beyond Race and Gender: Unleashing the Power of Your Total Work Force by Managing Diversity*. New York: American Management Association, 1991.

Upcraft, M. L. "Managing Staff." In M. L. Upcraft and M. J. Barr (eds.), *Managing Student Affairs Effectively*. New Directions for Student Services, no. 41. San Francisco: Jossey-Bass, 1988.

Uris, A. *88 Mistakes Interviewers Make and How to Avoid Them*. New York: American Management Association, 1988.

Weiss, D. H. "The Talent Search: Successful Recruitment Interviewing." *Trainer's Workshop*, 1989, *3*(2), 9–64.

Welfel, E. R. "Ethical Practice in College Student Affairs." In D. G. Creamer and Associates, *College and Student Development Theory and Practice for the 1990's*. Washington, D.C.: American College Personnel Association, 1990.

Chapter Twelve

Allied Professional
and Support Staffing

Sue A. Saunders

If we were to ask most chief student affairs administrators to elaborate on the purpose of residence halls, we would likely hear articulate, philosophical discussions of the importance of developing students and efficiently managing a variety of physical environments and organizational systems. Yet the primary transmitters of the organizational philosophy are most often the support staff members, such as secretaries and custodians, and allied professional staff members, such as maintenance engineers, accountants, and clergy. These individuals, even though highly skilled in their areas of expertise, are not likely to have formal educational experiences designed to inculcate a developmental approach to the provision of student services. Furthermore, there is a paucity of written materials available to support the housing professional who wants to encourage these categories of staff members to provide quality services that incorporate both efficient management and systematic attention to student development.

The challenge facing housing administrators is exacerbated by the increased complexity of services required for increasingly sophisticated student populations. Boyer (1990) speaks in complimentary terms about the varied and innovative efforts of student affairs professionals to create campus communities characterized by care, justice, civility, and self-discipline. The demands placed on housing programs have expanded not only because of altruistic desires to more adequately address the needs of individuals and communities, but also because of the increasingly consumer-oriented student population. Over the past two decades, students have become savvy consumers in choosing colleges. The attractiveness, efficiency, and friendliness of an institution's housing operation have become important variables in the college choice process. With a declining cohort of traditional-age students anticipated through the next few years, the pressure to respond to market competition for students will undoubtedly increase. The importance of creating and maintaining an effective support and allied professional staff is becoming more central to the financial health of those institutions that desire to attract traditional-age students.

For many housing operations, exemplary management of support and allied professional staff members is particularly challenging, because these operations rely on a large number of new student affairs professionals functioning in supervisory roles. At entry into their first jobs, few new professionals have had experience working with allied professional and support staff. New student affairs staff members are often younger than the support and allied professional staff they supervise. Furthermore, while the support or allied professional staff members often see themsleves as permanent, consistent elements of the housing operations, new housing professionals are likely to see their first position as a short-term stop on the road to professional advancement, most probably at another college. New housing professionals would be wise to develop skills in supervision and motivation of support and allied professional staff so that relationships characterized by mutual respect can be created. Supervising allied professional and support staff can provide important management experiences for new student affairs professionals and exciting stimulation for support and allied professional staff members.

Effective supervision, evaluation, and team building for support and allied professional staff members are crucial as institutions try to retain talented personnel. Research by Yankelovich and Immerwahr (1984) demonstrated that employees have increased expectations that work will provide them opportunities for personal growth. Therefore, it appears that administrative processes used with staff should creatively address employees' needs for personal fulfillment (Schuh and Carlisle, 1991). The purpose of this chapter is to (1) describe the roles of support staff (such as secretarial, custodial, food preparation, and business operations personnel) and allied professionals (such as faculty members, accountants, and maintenance engineers); (2) present pertinent aspects of the position definition process, staff selection, training, supervision, and evaluation; (3) discuss innovative strategies for maximizing the effectiveness of support staff and allied professionals; and (4) share basic axioms that can be used by administrators in building a cadre of support staff and allied professionals who will be agents of an organizational climate congruent with the mission of student affairs.

This chapter emphasizes general personnel practices appropriate for dealing with support and allied professional staff within many housing operations. Comprehensive discussion of the intricate details of supervising a unionized work force, however, requires specialized skills and expertise that are beyond the scope of this chapter. But some basic principles and fundamental advice for those who work under the auspices of a collective bargaining agreement will be outlined.

Managing Support Staff

Support staff are those individuals who perform the varied tasks necessary for professional student affairs staff and allied professionals to provide services and programs. Position titles found among the support staff classification in housing operations include secretary, receptionist, data entry clerk, custodian, maintenance worker, food service worker, and typist.

Typically, these positions do not require a college degree but are likely to require specialized training through vocational programs or continuing education opportunities (Winston and Miller, 1991). (See the preface for definitions of personnel categories.)

Staffing Patterns

On some campuses, support staff who deal with the billing and accounts receivable functions or upkeep of the residence hall physical plant fall under the auspices of the business affairs or auxiliary enterprises area. Supervision of such frontline residence hall support staff as maintenance or custodial workers by non–student affairs professionals brings several challenges. First, it becomes absolutely necessary for the professional staff in student affairs and business affairs to discuss the educational purposes of college residence halls. Also, it is incumbent on housing administrators to understand and be responsive to the constraints and philosophy of the business affairs operation. Second, housing professionals should be involved in the selection and training of those support staff supervised by business affairs professionals. Third, student affairs professionals should become a conduit between the business affairs operations and students by encouraging attention to areas of student concern and evaluation of student satisfaction with the physical facility's maintenance and upkeep.

Another organizational pattern, particularly on small or medium-sized campuses, is to "contract out" dining, custodial, or maintenance services to a private company that specializes in providing the service. For smaller campuses, hiring an outside vendor to provide these services is often cost effective, because the vendor can buy products in volume and typically has access to highly structured and unified personnel management programs. These patterns, although potentially efficient and effective, create special challenges for the housing administrator. It is helpful if housing professionals, including some entry-level professionals, collaborate with the team that constructs the contract between the vendor and the institution. It is also important that housing administrators keep in close communication with the vendor's district or corporate office as well as with the on-site management. A clear, written statement of the educational philosophy or mission of the residence halls provides potential vendors with helpful information about how to structure their services, and it can reduce confusion in the contract negotiation and reevaluation processes.

Student workers, although not technically support staff, perform many support staff functions, frequently under the supervision of a full-time support staff member. The use of student workers to answer the phones, type materials, file, and perform some maintenance tasks has long been a tradition on many campuses, and this practice will likely expand in the future as a means of keeping costs down and providing indirect student financial aid. Systematic educational programs designed to teach support staff how to supervise student workers effectively should be included in continuing educational programs for support staff.

Determining and Communicating Position Duties

To promote equity and efficiency within a housing operation, the position duties must be clearly defined and communicated. A complete and thorough position analysis should be carried out prior to writing (or rewriting) a position description. The institution's personnel department can often assist in this process, which requires specialized knowledge. Position analysis compares the position duties and responsibilities with the experiences, skills, and knowledge required to perform the tasks (Fortunato and Waddell, 1981).

Complete understanding of the state classification system (at public institutions) or union personnel policies is a prerequisite to creating workable position descriptions. In many institutions, specifics related to support staff position descriptions are controlled, to a greater or lesser degree, by the institution's or state's personnel systems or by the union "master contract."

Support staff positions tend to be more standardized than those of professional or allied professional positions, and therefore the duties described in a classification system or union contract may comprise the position description. In some institutions, it is not possible to elaborate on these descriptions. However, if it is possible to add to the description, the supervisor should develop an addendum to the position description that contains pertinent information for staff working in housing.

Statements of work duties should specify clear behavioral performance standards. For example, a duty statement "typing letters, memos, reports using a word processing system" is not complete because no measurable performance standards are included. In addition to specifying performance standards, position descriptions should contain the following elements (Fortunato and Waddell, 1981; Winston and Miller, 1991): (1) accurate position title that reflects the nature of the work; (2) division in which the position exists and title of supervisor; (3) purpose of the position as related to the housing operation mission or philosophy; (4) working activities, including duties, scope of authority, and materials and equipment used, and a statement that covers additional duties as assigned; (5) position requirements, including education, skills, and prior experience; and (6) conditions of employment, such as salary, benefits, and work hours. It is also helpful for candidates to be aware of the estimated proportion of time spent in various position activities. Including such information in the position description promotes consistency between the description, candidate selection, supervisory monitoring, and performance evaluation.

The articulation of performance standards is the heart of a useful position description. The following example outlines clearly communicated standards:

Duty	*Standards*
1. Type reports, letters, memos	a. Process handwritten drafts with less than five errors per ten pages of text.
	b. Work of less than five pages is completed within one day.
	c. Work is arranged on the page according to standard practice.
2. Complete mailings	a. Using mail merge capabilities, process form letters with fewer than 3 percent errors in addresses.
	b. Maintain up-to-date listings of addresses.
	c. Mailing labels and envelopes are neat and readable.
3. Telephone answering	a. Answer telephone within four rings.
	b. Refer callers to the appropriate offices.
	c. Be courteous and friendly.

If allowable under the classification system or union collective bargaining agreement, current position descriptions should be revised whenever there is a vacancy or, at the very minimum, on a biennial basis. Position descriptions should be rewritten to account for advances in technology that require more advanced or different skills and for any changes in philosophy within the housing unit. Including support staff members in the revision process allows for a more realistic outline of performance standards and encourages support staff to become a more visible part of organizational decision making.

Recruitment and Selection

The day-to-day effectiveness of any housing program depends on the adequacy of the selection process in encouraging the best possible fit between candidate characteristics and organizational needs. The institutional personnel officers and affirmative action officers are likely to have specific institutionwide policies for selection processes. The details of these policies should be carefully studied and communicated in writing to staff involved with the selection process.

A strategy for dealing with issues related to racial and gender equity should be completed prior to beginning the recruitment and selection process. Upcraft (1988) contends that few student affairs organizations have satisfied their commitment to hiring categories of persons legally protected from discrimination. Women and minorities are likely to be overrepresented in the lower levels of the support staff hierarchy and underrepresented in supervisory or management positions. It is advisable, then, to expand "deficient internal candidate pools by regional or national searches and hiring qualified minorities and women when their qualifications exceed or are equal to other candidates" (p. 42).

Although internal promotions are preferable whenever possible (Winston and Miller, 1991), in many cases it is appropriate to seek a larger applicant pool to encourage minority access or to simply inject "new blood" into the system. Most institutional personnel offices have established procedures for advertising support staff positions. Vacancies should be listed with internal institutional publications, with local employment services, and in local or regional newspaper advertisements.

Small search or screening committees should be established for all levels of support staff positions. Even though this is a time-consuming process, committees that include representatives from the professional staff, support staff, and student population include multiple perspectives when interviewing candidates or reviewing credentials. Depending on the supervisor's preference, the task of these committees can be limited to initial review and prioritization of credentials, or this group can actually recommend who should be hired. The function of this committee should be determined and communicated to the members and to other interested parties before the review process begins. It is also important to educate these committee members about the position requirements and housing program's goals.

Members of the search or screening committee and the supervisor should thoroughly discuss the characteristics of the ideal employee for the position. Skills, attitudes, and personality characteristics should be identified. These attributes can then be incorporated as the criteria of a simple rating scale so that committee members can independently rate candidates' qualifications. Based on the independent review, committee members should create a short list of candidates who deserve further consideration.

Contacting those who seem to have the desired characeristics by telephone prior to an on-campus interview is highly recommended. During this telephone conversation, the following should be discussed: (1) specifics about the position and search process that may not have been included in written information, (2) additional questions about candidate qualifications that may have been raised during the review process, (3) permission to contact identified references and the candidate's current supervisor, and (4) whether the candidate is still interested in the position (Winston and Miller, 1991). It is also wise to contact candidate references by telephone prior to determining who should be interviewed. The candidate's current supervisor is a vital resource and should be contacted, if the candidate gives permission.

A specific written plan for the interviews, including possible interview questions as well as rating scales so that interviewers can give detailed feedback, should be created. This plan should be constructed well before candidates arrive so that all interviewers will have an opportunity to discuss their role in the process, determine the questions they want to ask, and decide what answers would be desirable. Many times, interviewers lack training in the interviewing process and need additional information about inappropriate questions (which may not be legally asked) and how to devise meaningful questions designed to elicit subtle information that is likely to be of interest to the supervisor. (Consult Winston and Miller, 1991, for information about "prohibited questions.") Supervisors in housing programs may regard this level of prior planning and training as unnecessary or as simply too time consuming for their schedule. Yet once the initial planning is completed, it can be replicated with minimal revisions for similar position vacancies within the housing division.

A systematic, detailed interview process not only encourages selection of the most qualified candidates, but it also communicates to the candidate and to other support staff members that these positions are valued and worth the expenditure of time and thought. Including support staff members in the interviewing process and on the search committees encourages investment in the housing division and reinforces the message that the opinions of support staff are worthy of consideration.

It is important to work carefully with the search or screening committee to determine who should be hired; then the position can be offered. The search or screening committee should review all interviewer ratings, the candidates' written qualifications, and reference information before constructing a prioritized list for consideration by the supervisor. It is important for the supervisor to reiterate to the committee at this stage that the written documentation about candidates, the content of committee deliberations, and the prioritized list of candidates should remain confidential, because of the potential to harm the credibility of the individual selected and the privacy rights of candidates who were not selected. If the supervisor feels that confidentiality is not possible, the committee's access to certain information should be limited, and they should not be asked to construct a prioritized list but simply to identify strengths and weaknesses of the top two or three candidates.

The conversation in which a position is offered is an event that is remembered by most employees. The supervisor's comments when offering the position set an initial tone for future encounters between employee and supervisor. Therefore, the information presented should be clear and complete, and the particulars of the organizational climate should be articulated. The offer should include specific information about salary, benefits, and starting date; also, the candidate should be given a short time (less than one week) to make a decision. If the first-choice candidate accepts the offer, all other candidates should be informed immediately that they were not selected. If the first-choice candidate does not accept, the supervisor must decide whether to make an offer to the second choice or to reopen the search.

Orientation

Once a candidate accepts an offer, the orientation process should begin. This process sets the tone for the subsequent working relationship and should be planned carefully.

During the period between the acceptance of a position and the starting date, the supervisor should provide the necessary information to help the employee get started. The supervisor should send (or make certain that the institution's personnel office provides) the new employee a small amount of written information about the college or university and information about starting a new position (for example, material on parking permits and on registering for various benefit plans; names, addresses, and phone numbers of co-workers and others who the new employee will encounter during the first few days; and an employee handbook that is typically produced by the institution's personnel office). In addition to supplying information, the supervisor should devise strategies to be certain that the new employee will feel welcomed in the work environment. One method is to ask co-workers to write letters or make phone calls of welcome to the new employee. Another is to make sure that the new employee understands office "traditions" such as coffee clubs, birthday celebrations, group lunches, or staff development activities.

During the first few days of employment, the supervisor should plan a systematic series of orientation activities. An effective orientation plan contains a variety of elements such as the following: (1) becoming acquainted with people in the division, including those individuals from other units who will have regular contact with the new employee; (2) becoming knowledgeable about organizational dynamics, such as supervisor preferences, how work is (or is not) shared among employees, and organizational norms for dress and conduct (assigning an experienced support staff member as a guide can assist in this process); (3) becoming competent in the use of the division's equipment and technology, such as telephones, computers, and maintenance equipment; (4) becoming familiar with division procedures through employee review of the procedures manual and discussion with supervisor (if a detailed procedures manual is not available, it should be a project that has high priority); and (5) becoming knowledgeable about the specific position expectations and performance standards that will be used as criteria for evaluation.

Staff Development

Encouraging new staff to develop attitudes consistent with student development principles and to develop interpersonal skills that are congruent with the organizational climate requires considerable thought and prior planning. Many housing divisions have a program of in-service development that emphasizes student development principles, new issues (such as AIDS, drug-free colleges, and school regulations) faced by housing personnel, results of assessment of student characteristics, or team building. Support staff should be included in some of these experiences as part of an ongoing orientation and education.

One strategy for orienting new support staff about expectations in the area of interpersonal skills is the Connections program (Tschohl, 1988). This structured program has as its premise that support staff attitudes have a direct impact on student satisfaction and retention. The program, which contains a combination of structured exercises, videotapes, and reading material, takes six to eight hours to complete. It is best accomplished in a small group and can be easily facilitated by a student affairs professional staff member. The general objectives of this program can, however, be accomplished by exercises and materials developed internally. Many professional staff members in housing are experienced in creating interpersonal skill development programs for resident assistants and other student workers that are designed to improve resident satisfaction and involvement—for instance, Blimling and Miltenberger (1990) or Upcraft and Pilato (1982). These professionals could develop a similar program to use in support staff orientation.

Although some support staff education should occur in collaboration with professional staff, each unit should allocate resources to design ongoing staff development programs especially for support staff members. Representatives from the support staff groups should be involved with the planning of these events. All too often, housing directors determine support staff educational needs without asking these staff members for their opinions. Upcraft (1988) advocates educating for the organizational needs as first priority and training for individual needs as a lower-level objective. He encourages individualized training plans that ultimately fulfill organizational goals.

It is also important not to neglect individual development, because effective personal development positively affects job performance. Individual staff members should be asked what skills or attributes they would like to learn or improve as a result of participating in the organization. These desires should be incorporated, insofar as possible, into the individual training plan. (Helping support staff improve their skills may allow them to seek well-paying positions. If the training program has been successful and the work environment has been supportive, however, housing's loss may well be some other department in the college's gain.)

One way to build advanced skill development opportunities into an organization is through transferring an existing staff member to a more responsible position within the division (vertical staffing). Frequently, career advancement or even advanced skill development opportunities for support staff within any particular housing unit are limited. Incorporating support staff members into division advisory and decision-making committees is another way to assist these staff in developing a wider variety of decision-making and organizational skills. If the institution allows support staff members to enroll in classes for reduced fees, these initiatives should be supported as a component of the individual's educational development.

Supervision

Although orientation and staff development activities contribute to the effectiveness of support staff, the most critical variable is the individual employee's relationship with the supervisor.

With new staff members, a performance evaluation after the first three months is advisable. This is an opportunity to clarify expectations and to provide timely feedback about whether performance standards are being met, what improvement needs to occur, and how the performance standards and work enviornment could be improved to facilitate effective performance.

The supervisor's leadership style should be clearly articulated. The most critical aspect of supervision involves the leadership style of the supervisor. Upcraft (1988) advises that leaders put their leadership philosophy in writing to reduce misunderstandings. Helping staff members understand the broad perspectives of whether the supervisor functions in terms of emphasizing relationships or tasks is vital, but perhaps it is even more useful to assist staff in predicting the supervisor's response to various situations. For example, staff members should know explicitly how the supervisor will react to missed deadlines, to students who are treated in a less-than-courteous fashion, to incomplete information, to lapses in confidentiality, to intrastaff conflict, and to meritorious performance. There should also be opportunities for support staff to discuss with the supervisor their needs and feelings in response to commonly occurring situations. Small-group retreats (during regular working hours) with participation of all staff members of individual units is a good format for focusing on the team-building process. A model that emphasizes unit planning, as well as the team-building process, has been developed by Harvey, Hezler, and Young (1972). In this retreat format, small groups explore issues and develop detailed plans. However, throughout the experience, facilitators focus on individual behavior and group process.

Structured group experiences, such as those developed by Pfeiffer and Jones (1983), are strategies that can be used at any point throughout the academic year to foster better understanding of supervisor and support staff members' individual behavior and approach to task completion. Understanding one's Myers-Briggs Type (Myers, 1980) is another strategy to help staff understand management and decision-making styles. The Myers-Briggs Type Indicator (Myers, 1962) has been used frequently to improve intrastaff relationships and communications patterns. It should be noted, however, that a highly experienced facilitator must be used in order to derive maximum benefit from this experience.

Soliciting the opinions of support staff when making decisions about housing operations is an important element of building staff morale. Yet housing operations—because of the use of students in key leadership positions that are of short duration (such as resident assistants and hall government officers) and because of the complex organizational patterns needed to provide quality services—require additional strategies to make sure support staff members are an integral part of the division's functioning. Therefore, it is very important that all levels of support staff, from housekeepers to clerical staff members, understand the functions of student leaders and are introduced to those student leaders with whom they are likely to have direct contact. Team morale can also be enhanced by making sure that support staff are well acquainted with the functions and supervisory personnel of offices in student affairs or other departments outside housing with whom they are likely to have contact.

Supervisors should spend a significant amount of energy promoting staff satisfaction with their duties and staff pride in their accomplishments. Perhaps the most straightforward, yet difficult, way to promote high morale is to "care a lot" (Upcraft, 1988). According to Upcraft, this type of care is focused on results and staff satisfaction. Individuals' continuing education needs and personal circumstances should be acknowledged and supported. To be credible, this support must go beyond lip service and include meaningful resource allocation for continuing education for support staff and "adapting work conditions (such as flex-time arrangements), within job expectations, to accommodate personal circumstances" (Upcraft, 1988, p. 47).

Caring for support staff also involves taking risks on their behalf and advocating for their interests with institutional decision makers. Supervisors also need to acknowledge honestly when they do not agree with and will not support the position of the staff.

Evaluation

Performance evaluation is often an experience that supervisors and support staff approach with a distinct sense of foreboding. Making sure that the details of the process are explicitly communicated to all staff is a key to using performance evaluation as a tool to enhance quality services rather than an exercise in judging the character and value of an individual employee.

Establishing performance standards is the first step in effective evaluation. The standards should be created and communicated in part through the position vacancy announcement and in entirety within the position description. These standards should be revised on a regular basis (at least once every two years) to reflect changes in unit goals or operational technology.

Determining an evaluation strategy requires that the supervisor become familiar with a variety of different methods before choosing one. Even if the evaluation strategy is mandated by the classification system or union contract, the supervisor should be aware of the advantages and disadvantages of the method used. Evaluation approaches are varied and can range from unstructured narration to ranking employees in comparison to peers.

Two specific types of evaluation strategies have merit for support staff. The first, more traditional approach is a rating scale in which the employee's performance is given a numerical rating for various position characteristics such as knowledge, initiative, and decision making. The sample evaluation form in Exhibit 12.1 uses an approach similar to a rating scale, but each point on the scale has a particular definition or behavioral anchor.

The behaviorally anchored rating scales (BARS) were developed in response to weaknesses perceived in the more traditional numerical rating scale (Kafry, Jacobs, and Zedeck, 1980). This approach requires supervisors to rate behaviors rather than personality traits. It has the advantage of making feedback to the employee perfectly clear, and because of the specificity of the definitions, it offers the employee additional information about position expectations.

The second approach is tied specifically to performance standards. The supervisor is asked to rate, typically on a scale of one to five, the employee's performance on each of the major position duties using performance standards as criteria. The ratings are then added and a summative rating is given. This approach requires that the supervisor be concrete in constructing standards. The purpose of this type of evaluation is to foster a clear, documentable connection between the standards and evaluation. In

Exhibit 12.1. Performance Evaluation for Secretarial-Clerical Employees.

College or administrative unit _____ Date started at university _____

Title and code number _____ Date started this position _____

Reason for evaluation: ☐ Probationary period _____ step increase movement from _____ step to _____ step

☐ Interim evaluation (first year following C or B step)

☐ Other _____

Appraisal Factors

A. Quality of work — Neatness, accuracy, thoroughness.

☐ Performs poorly. Makes frequent mistakes. Generally unsatisfactory.
☐ Does minimally acceptable work. Accuracy and finish of final product often need revision or correction.
☐ Work meets acceptable standards. Makes only occasional mistakes.
☐ Work is above average. Seldom makes errors.
☐ Work is of exceptionally high quality. Consistently thorough and accurate.

Comments: _____

B. Quantity of work — Volume of work regularly produced; consistency of output and speed.

☐ Produces consistently high volume of work. Extremely productive and fast.
☐ Volume of work frequently above expected level.
☐ Does normal amount of work. Volume is satisfactory. When situation requires, production increases markedly.
☐ Volume is generally below what is expected. Does just enough to get by.
☐ Does not meet minimum requirements. Volume of work generally unsatisfactory.

Comments: _____

C. Job knowledge and learning ability — Degree of understanding of the job and related functions. Rapidity with which the employee has developed.

☐ Complete mastery of all phases of job and related functions. Grasps new methods and procedures immediately. Extremely rapid learner.
☐ Excellent understanding of job and related work. Well informed. Learns quickly.
☐ Adequate knowledge of the job. Can answer most questions. Able to learn new aspects of job.
☐ Lacks knowledge of some phases of work. Experiences difficulty in grasping new ideas.
☐ Poor understanding of job. Fails to grasp new ideas.

Comments: _____

D. Judgment and initiative — Problem-solving capabilities. Ability to analyze facts and circumstances, recognize need for action, and take constructive steps to resolve problems within the limits of established boundaries. Degree of supervision required.

☐ Misinterprets the facts. Fails to take independent action. Makes decisions without regard for consequences. Requires very close supervision.
☐ Recognizes facts only partially. Makes errors in judgment. Seldom acts independently. Requires fairly close supervision.
☐ Good common sense. Generally makes sound decisions. Able to act independently. Moderate degree of supervision required.
☐ Decisions are logical and sound. Frequently takes independent action. Requires only occasional supervision.
☐ Exceptional problem-solving ability. Highly logical. A real self-starter. Minimal supervision required.
Comments: _____

E. Dependability and reliability — Ability to meet deadlines. Punctuality and attendance.

☐ Unreliable. Rarely meets deadlines. Often absent or late.
☐ Sometimes requires prompting. Frequently fails to meet deadlines. Occasionally absent or late.
☐ Takes care of necessary tasks and completes with reasonable promptness. Usually present and punctual.
☐ Exceeds normal work demands. Almost always present and punctual.
☐ Exceptionally dependable. Carries out assignments promptly and efficiently. Always present and punctual.
Comments: _____

F. Attitude and cooperation — Effect upon and willingness to work with and for others. Flexibility, courtesy.

☐ Exceptionally courteous and cooperative. Consistently striving for higher level of achievement.
☐ Above average degree of courtesy. Highly cooperative. Shows high level of interest.
☐ Interested in work. Demonstrates desire to improve. Courteous and cooperative.
☐ Lacks courtesy. Shows limited or sporadic interest in work.
☐ Discourteous and uncooperative. Exhibits disinterest in work.
Comments: _____

G. Supervisory ability — COMPLETE ONLY FOR INDIVIDUALS WITH SUPERVISORY RESPONSIBILITY — Leadership, ability to train and motivate. Ability to communicate.

☐ Exhibits little supervisory capabilities. Inadequately trains and motivates employees. Unable to obtain cooperation or desired results.
☐ Has some difficulty in training and motivating employees. Needs additional development in this area.
☐ Adequately trains and motivates subordinates. Exhibits leadership capabilities.
☐ Generates good work climate. Recognizes and develops individual potential in employees.
☐ Exceptional ability to train, develop and motivate subordinates. Maximizes employee potential.
Comments: _____

Exhibit 12.1. Performance Evaluation for Secretarial-Clerical Employees, Cont'd.

Appraisal Factors

H. Overall evaluation – Composite appraisal of employee's total performance of duties.

☐ Exceptional.
☐ Exceeds requirements.
☐ Meets requirements.
☐ Minimally meets requirements.
☐ Inadequate.

Comments: _____

Summary statement: _____
_____
_____
_____

Employee's comments: _____
_____
_____
_____

Supervisor's signature _____ _____ Date
Reviewed by _____ _____ Date
*Employee's signature _____ _____ Date

*My signature indicates only that the evaluation has been reviewed by me. It does not necessarily signify my concurrence.

Source: Fortunato, R. T., and Waddell, D. G., 1981, pp. 229–232. Used with permission.

using this approach, it can be difficult to compare employees across supervisors, because of the various ways in which the supervisors write performance standards. This approach is currently being used in Virginia among state classified employees. (Further information on this system can be obtained from the Virginia Department of Personnel and Training.)

The process used in communicating evaluation results is frequently more influential in determining the staff member's willingness to improve performance than the results themselves. In the evaluation interview, supervisors should focus on the behavior of the support staff member, not the general character of the person. Weaknesses as well as strengths should be addressed directly, and specific plans for improvement and perhaps for additional training and support should be made. The supervisor should have specific, documentable examples to explain the assessment of strengths and weaknesses. Developing specific examples to use as a rationale for ratings may require that the supervisor carefully observe employee performance and keep records of these observations.

To be fully effective, the performance evaluation interview should provide the support staff member with the opportunity to discuss conditions that may impede performance and to provide feedback about the supervisor's performance. If evaluation is to focus on improving employee performance, the evaluation process must culminate in the creation of specific strategies that the staff member can use to enhance future functioning. Another way to emphasize future professional development is to ask that staff members evaluate their own performance. Self-ratings on the same dimensions used by supervisors or colleagues are highly informative and can serve as a powerful motivational tool (Brown, 1988).

Evaluation should be frequent. Upcraft (1988) recommends evaluating performance every three months. Although it is not feasible for all supervisors to provide formal, highly structured feedback that frequently, general judgments about performance should be discussed three or four times each year. Most institutions require structured evaluation once each year, and many link pay raises with these performance evaluations. Winston and Miller (1991) and Penn (1979) suggest that salary review and performance evaluation should be separate processes, because salary determination involves a variety of considerations, such as division priorities and budgetary allocations. Although breaking the link between these two processes may be counter to institutional policy, frequent performance evaluation mitigates the potential negative effect.

Managing Support Staff Within a Unionized Organization

Unions are a fact of life in many businesses and in some higher education and government agencies. During the past twenty-five years, unions have proliferated at colleges and universities, both public and private. In 1970, the

National Labor Relations Board ruled that labor laws concerning unioniza-
tion applied to private colleges and universities that participate in interstate
commerce and that have budgets of at least $1 million. Also, in many states,
government employees are permitted to unionize. Labor organizers are
currently experiencing considerable success in establishing unions in government agencies (Douglas Fraser, former president of United Auto Workers,
personal communication, Feb. 1992).

Most student affairs professionals have little formal training in personnel management within a unionized environment. Yet dealing effectively
with the special constraints and opportunities presented in academic environments governed by collective bargaining agreements is an important
skill for both the entry-level-professional supervisor and the chief student
affairs officer. "In unionized organizations, supervisors must learn to work
cooperatively with union leaders to make the union's presence an asset"
(Imundo, 1980, p. 102).

Many supervisory responsibilities are the same in both nonunion and
unionized housing operations; however, there are several essential differences in personnel management practices that must be considered. The
following answers to commonly asked questions are not intended to provide
a comprehensive discussion of all labor relations principles, but instead are
meant to assist the housing professional new to unions in becoming more
comfortable in dealing with employees.

What employee activities do union agreements cover? The union contract
typically covers hours of work, various position duties, training requirements,
evaluation procedures, wage structure, promotion opportunities, fringe benefits, seniority determination rules, and grievance procedures. The type of
union representation is also typically included in the agreement. The various
types of union representation can range from a strict "union shop" in which
all employees must join the union to a voluntary membership arrangement
in which employees who voluntarily join the union remain members
throughout the life of the contract (Fortunato and Waddell, 1981).

Can supervisors deviate from the terms of the union agreement? No, the
management tasks must be handled exactly as specified in the agreement. For
example, if an employee is asked to perform tasks not included in the
position description, such as asking a housekeeper to perform minor repairs,
the employee is entitled to file a grievance and request a position upgrade.
Bambrick (1986) cites the example of a supervisor who allowed her staff
additional time off for personal business. When upper-level administrators
stopped this lenient practice, the union representatives protested because
the employees had come to expect this special consideration.

How should supervisors deal with complaints in a unionized environment?
More formal complaints are likely to arise in a unionized organization than
in a nonunionized one (Imundo, 1980). Most employee unions have "shop
stewards"—employees who function as the union's representatives to management. The shop steward will often handle complaints in their early stages,

before formal grievances are filed. It is wise for the supervisor to develop a positive relationship with the shop steward. A good relationship between the supervisor and shop steward will allow disagreements to be resolved early and expeditiously (Preston and Zimmerer, 1983).

Who helps supervisors manage the details of working in a unionized environment? Institutions with unions have personnel managers with expertise in labor relations. These individuals can aid the supervisor in understanding the details of the institution's agreement with the union and may distribute a written manual to assist supervisors in managing unionized employees. It is wise to get to know the personnel manager well and to establish rapport before a problem occurs. In addition, supervisors should obtain a copy of the "master contract" or agreement with the union and memorize important provisions about selection, discipline, and evaluation of employees (Preston and Zimmerer, 1983).

Managing Allied Professionals

Allied professionals in residence hall administration are persons who support the administrative and educational functions and who have specialized education in professions other than student affairs (Delworth and Aulepp, 1976). A variety of professional groups function as allied professionals in student affairs. Some examples of position titles include accountant, maintenance engineer, computer consultant, faculty member, and clergy. In some cases, allied professionals' work with the housing operation constitutes their entire position responsibilities. Often, however, allied professionals work with the housing operation as a part-time responsibility. Clergy and faculty members on some campuses work with the housing program without direct remuneration from the housing budget for their services, even though these services may be part of the individual's position description.

Allied professionals require different recruitment and supervision strategies than do support staff. Typically, these individuals bring extensive formal education, high levels of skill, and expertise in their specialized area. Frequently, however, they do not have formal educational experiences in student development theory and organizational theory as applied to student affairs operations.

Building a commitment to student development goals, an understanding of student affairs administrative processes, and a pattern of incentives that encourages continued performance are all areas that the housing administrator must address in the recruitment, selection, training, and evaluation processes.

The recruitment, supervision, and evluation processes for allied professionals who report directly to the housing division are similar to the processes used for student affairs professionals. The orientation and training of allied professionals should be structured to emphasize the division's philosophy about student development. With some allied professionals, it is a challenge to help them envision their roles as more elaborate than simply providing services. If it is desired that allied professionals participate in the educational mission of residence halls, student affairs professionals need to design "jargon-free" orientation programs that emphasize the practical benefits of a student development approach. With many allied professionals, it is helpful to "ground" philosophical statements and discussions within the context of student satisfaction surveys, retention information, and assessments of student characteristics. Incorporating allied professionals who have successfully made the transition to a student affairs unit as key members of the orientation planning team is an effective way to make the training more relevant for new staff members.

Within some housing divisions, allied professional involvement includes professionals who do not report to the housing unit itself. The use of faculty or clergy as significant, continuing players in the residence hall educational programs has potential for incorporating an active intellectual or spiritual dimension into the daily lives of students. Yet, to be successful, the incorporation of faculty or clergy needs to be very carefully planned in terms of goals, organizational structures, and program evaluation. Also, it is important that the perspectives of student affairs leaders who work with faculty are free from the biases that may distort potentially collaborative relationships (Creeden, 1987).

Setting Program Goals

The goals for faculty or clergy involvement need to be feasible, concrete, and cognizant of the talents these individuals can bring to the residence hall enterprise. Simply asking faculty or clergy to "visit the halls and talk with students" can encourage the development of a program that lacks any potential for long-term success. Faculty or clergy should be part of an ongoing program that utilizes their areas of expertise, such as a speakers' series, academic advising, specialized counseling, or academic course offerings. Constructing program goals should be a collaborative effort involving student leaders and housing personnel as well as faculty or clergy participants. The time spent in reaching consensus about the specific goals and written plans of action will reduce confusion and foster greater ownership within the program. It is also helpful if the program goals are constructed to address particular, identifiable student or organizational needs. If these needs are stated as components or broader institutional goals or strategic plans, the collaborative program has greater potential to encourage continued allied professional involvement.

Defining Organizational Structures

The development of clearly defined organizational structures that support faculty or clergy involvement with students has definite advantages. For example, at Longwood College, the freshman seminar program has a clear link with the residence halls. The one-credit seminar is taught by faculty and student affairs staff. The content of the seminar involves educational planning, academic adjustment, and social transitions. Seminar leaders function not only as teachers, but also as academic advisors to their freshman students.

The assignment of students to seminar sections is based on residence hall placement. Students who live on the same residence hall floor are assigned to the same seminar leaders. Seminar leaders work directly with the resident assistants and other student paraprofessionals on their floor to provide programs in the halls, and student paraprofessionals provide assistance as co-teachers or guest lecturers for the seminar sessions. The seminar leader's relationships with students and student paraprofessionals allow the leader to be involved with the social, as well as the academic, adjustment of the students. This structure also encourages frequent, informal interaction between student and seminar leader that crosses the barriers between academic and social issues. These strong relationships have contributed to a significant increase in freshman retention noted since the start of the seminar program.

Direct support for collaborative programs should be articulated by housing directors and the upper-level supervisors of the faculty or clergy participants. On a smaller campus, support from the president or vice presidents is highly valuable. Housing administrators should also remember to acknowledge the contributions of allied professionals through frequent thank-you letters, recognition events, and public relations vehicles. Verbal or written support, however, is not a sufficient incentive to sustain long-term meaningful involvement. It is highly advisable for allied professionals to receive direct reimbursement for services, credit for promotion and tenure (if applicable), or meaningful reduction of other duties within the institution.

Program Evaluation

Careful evaluation of the program is another important strategy needed to support collaborative programs. The evaluation methods should receive the support of all program planners prior to implementation. A variety of evaluation methods can be used successfully, but it is vitally important that all "stakeholders," including faculty, administrators, and students, have the opportunity to comment on the strengths and weaknesses of the program. Evaluation results should be shared with participants and decision makers on a regular basis (Brown, 1978; see Chapter Sixteen).

In collaborative housing-faculty programs, an effectively constructed program evaluation has the potential to highlight inadequate performance by some participants. Because the housing administrator typically does not

have direct supervisory authority over faculty participants, it is highly problematic to simply eliminate one or more participants. Infrequent communication between the housing administrator and the supervisor of the faculty
or clergy participants prior to the program evaluation clearly exacerbates
this problem. It is important that a strong relationship be established between the housing administrator responsible for the program and counterparts in the academic affairs or religious services areas. Communication
should be frequent and should focus on all aspects of the development of the
program.

Developing Commitment with Support and Allied Professional Staff

The challenges of modern housing programs are increasingly intricate and
complex. The interpersonal sensitivity as well as the technical expertise of
support staff and allied professionals are becoming key variables if residence
halls are to realize their potential as "laboratories for living." Several simple
principles may be useful in building a commitment among these important
staff members.

Emphasize involvement. Many resident life professionals are accomplished facilitators of a sense of community among students. Staff members
should also be encouraged to be part of that community. Involving staff in
decisions about their own training, orientation, and position descriptions
and about broader institutional issues, such as retention, strategic planning,
or budgetary priorities, are ways to reiterate the worth of these vital staff
members.

Promote mastery, not mystery. If support staff and alllied professionals are
to develop a commitment to student development goals, housing professionals must teach what *student development* means. To be effective teachers,
housing professionals should reduce the emphasis on displaying specialized
knowledge in a mysterious way and instead accept the challenge of articulating their craft in a way meaningful to all.

Stick to the knitting. Often the small, simple things—a clean bathroom, a
correct bill, a smile, a name remembered, a friendly voice on the telephone, a
referral to the correct office—make the difference in a student's feeling "at
home" in a residence hall. Yet these "small things" are not articulated as
important expectations. Exceptional support staff, in particular, are masters
with these details that improve students' interactions with the campus. They
should be acknowledged, and others should be encouraged to emulate their
behavior.

Listen carefully. Most perceptive housing administrators have recognized that they have been taught important lessons by their effective support
staff and allied professionals. These individuals have a perspective on feasibility that may often escape the busy housing administrator's attention. Their
troubleshooting ability is worth acknowledging, prior to a failure or a crisis.

Focus on clarity. Communicating one's expectations, leadership style, and responses to commonly occurring situations alleviates confusion. Confusion increases stress, wastes time, and can undermine morale as well as efficiency. Oral communication is critical, but well-crafted, straightforward written documents and procedures are key elements in building a strong housing program.

References

Bambrick, J. "Collective Bargaining and Union Contracts." In J. Famularo (ed.), *Handbook of Human Resources Administration*. New York: McGraw-Hill, 1986.

Blimling, G. S., and Miltenberger, L. *The Resident Assistant: Working with College Students in the Residence Halls*. (3rd ed.) Dubuque, Iowa: Kendall/Hunt, 1990.

Boyer, E. *Campus Life: In Search of Community*. Princeton, N.J.: Carnegie Foundation for the Advancement of Teaching, 1990.

Brown, R. D. "How Evaluation Can Make a Difference." In G. R. Hanson (ed.), *Evaluating Program Effectiveness*. New Directions for Student Services, no. 1. San Francisco: Jossey-Bass, 1978.

Brown, R. D. "Implementing Performance Appraisal Systems." In R. D. Brown (ed.), *Performance Appraisal as a Tool for Staff Development*. New Directions for Student Services, no. 43. San Francisco: Jossey-Bass, 1988.

Creeden, J. E. "Student Affairs Biases as Barriers to Collaboration." *NASPA Journal*, 1987, *26*, 60–63.

Delworth, U., and Aulepp, L. *Training Manual for Paraprofessional and Allied Professional Programs*. Boulder, Colo.: Western Interstate Commission for Higher Education, 1976.

Fortunato, R. T., and Waddell, D. G. *Personnel Administration in Higher Education: Handbook of Faculty and Staff Personnel Practices*. San Francisco: Jossey-Bass, 1981.

Harvey, V. P., Hezler, T. A., and Young, J. W. "The Retreat: Keystone of Staff Development." *NASPA Journal*, 1972, *9*, 274–278.

Imundo, L. V. *The Effective Supervisor's Handbook*. New York: American Management Association, 1980.

Kafry, P., Jacobs, R. R., and Zedeck, S. "Expectations of Behaviorally Anchored Rating Scales." *Personnel Psychology*, 1980, *33*, 595–640.

Myers, I. B. *The Myers-Briggs Type Indicator*. Palo Alto, Calif.: Consulting Psychologists Press, 1962.

Myers, I. B. *Gifts Differing*. Palo Alto, Calif.: Consulting Psychologists Press, 1980.

Penn, J. R. "Staff Evaluation." In G. D. Kuh (ed.), *Evaluation in Student Affairs*. Cincinnati, Ohio: ACPA Media, 1979.

Pfeiffer, J. W., and Jones, J. E. *A Handbook of Structured Experiences for Human Relations Training*. San Diego, Calif.: University Associates, 1983.

Preston, P., and Zimmerer, T. W. *Management for Supervisors*. Englewood Cliffs, N.J.: Prentice Hall, 1983.

Schuh, J. H., and Carlisle, W. "Supervision and Evaluation: Selected Topics for Emerging Professionals." In T. K. Miller and R. B. Winston, Jr. (eds.), *Administration and Leadership in Student Affairs: Actualizing Student Development in Higher Education*. (2nd ed.) Muncie, Ind.: Accelerated Development, 1991.

Tschohl, J. *Practice for Excellence, Path to Success: CONNECTIONS Leader's Guide*. Coralville, Iowa: Noel/Levits National Center for Staff Selection and Development, 1988.

Upcraft, M. L. "Managing Staff." In M. L. Upcraft and M. J. Barr, *Managing Student Affairs Effectively*. New Directions for Student Services, no. 41. San Francisco: Jossey-Bass, 1988.

Upcraft, M. L., with the collaboration of Pilato, G. T. *Residence Hall Assistants in College: A Guide to Selection, Training, and Supervision*. San Francisco: Jossey-Bass, 1982.

Winston, R. B., Jr., and Miller, T. K. "Human Resource Management: Professional Preparation and Staff Selection." In T. K. Miller and R. B. Winston, Jr. (eds.), *Administration and Leadership in Student Affairs: Actualizing Student Development in Higher Education*. (2nd ed.) Muncie, Ind.: Accelerated Development, 1991.

Yankelovich, D., and Immerwahr, J. "The Emergence of Expressivism Will Revolutionize the Contract Between Workers and Employers." In L. Chiara and D. Lacey (eds.), *Work in the 21st Century*. Alexandria, Va.: American Society for Personnel Administration, 1984.

Chapter Thirteen

Paraprofessional Staffing

Roger B. Winston, Jr.
R. Thomas Fitch

Historically, college residential life programs in the United States have made more extensive, ongoing, and frequent use of students as staff members than any other area of student affairs (Ender, 1984). Winston and Ender (1988) indicate, based on a survey of a sampling of four-year colleges, that nearly 95 percent of the housing programs reported using paraprofessionals.

In the early days of American higher education, student staff members could not technically be called "paraprofessionals," because in order to have *paraprofessionals* there must first be *professionals*, which is a relatively modern phenomenon. The use of student staff members in housing has closely mirrored developments in the history of higher education and the student affairs profession. (See Chapter Six.)

In this chapter, we present a short history of the use of paraprofessionals in housing programs, define *paraprofessional* in the context of a housing department that is committed to student development goals, discuss elements of the resident assistant (RA) position, and consider the parameters and dynamics of RA selection, training, supervision, and evaluation.

A Brief History

During the founding of American higher education, especially in New England, the concept of the residential college common to Oxford and

Cambridge took root. Implicit in this model was the assumption that students and faculty would live and learn together. Consequently, residence halls or "dormitories" were seen as essential aspects of the educational experience. By the late nineteenth and early twentieth centuries, however, the concept of educating the whole person—an important precept of early American colleges based on the English residential college model—was almost completely abandoned as many of the "leading" institutions adopted the German university model of focusing on the intellect alone. Dormitories came to be seen as necessary evils in rural areas and often were converted to other uses in urban areas (Blimling and Miltenberger, 1990). These changes in the perceived mission of higher education, and thus of residence halls, also coincided with the spread of coeducational institutions and the creation of the first "student personnel" staff positions. These were held by women who carried titles such as principals, wardens, and matrons and who later came to be known as deans of women (Fenske, 1989, p. 30). Their responsibilities were to supervise women's conduct meticulously and to regulate the social interaction between men and women students vigilantly. A little later, deans of men emerged with responsibilities to supervise the conduct of young men, especially in the fraternity system.

The first use of student staff members in residential life programs cannot be established precisely but probably occurred during the colonial period. Student staffing was a natural outgrowth of the expansion of student housing. It became apparent to those responsible for operating housing facilities that there were not enough "adults" available to monitor what was happening with students. A natural solution to this problem, especially in ensuring that rules and regulations were obeyed, was to use older students residing in the halls. Early titles for student staff members included proctors, monitors, and personnel assistants (Powell, Plyler, Dickson, and McClellan, 1969). They were variously volunteers, quasi-elected officers, or employees paid small stipends or given "free" room and/or board in exchange for performing their assigned duties. The positions, however, were infrequently institutionalized, appearing and disappearing as the supervisory staff changed. Up until the late 1950s and early 1960s, most in-house supervisors lacked any specialized educational preparation or training for performing their duties. The arrival of staff members in larger numbers who possessed graduate educations (usually in guidance and counseling) also heralded the more widespread, institutionalized utilization of student paraprofessionals, who came to be known by such titles as resident assistants, hall counselors, house fellows, or resident advisors.

Resident Hall Paraprofessionals: A Definition

Residents currently are employed to perform a wide range of tasks in housing departments. The most common responsibilities of student staff members include "managing" a living unit, which may entail performing duties such as inventorying furnishings, reporting needed repairs, enforcing rules, promoting a sense of community, encouraging participation in educational and social activities, communicating information from the professional staff, and offering peer counseling. There is not universal agreement, however, about the best title for such staff members; we somewhat arbitrarily have chosen to call them *resident assistants*, one of the more frequently used titles. There are also other paraprofessional positions in some housing programs—for example, minority assistants who attend to the special concerns of a particular population, programming specialists who provide and/or promote participation in programs such as wellness or academic subjects in living-learning centers, peer counselors who are available to assist with personal problems, tutors who assist with academic courses, and peer academic advisors who assist in course selection and other academic matters.

Assuming that the housing program is dedicated to goals of student development (see Chapter Two), what is a paraprofessional in this context? A paraprofessional is defined as a student who is selected, trained, and supervised in assuming responsibilities and performing tasks that are intended to (1) directly promote the individual personal development of his or her peers, (2) foster the creation and maintenance of environments that stimulate and support residents' personal and educational development, and/or (3) perform tasks that ensure the maintenance of secure, clean, healthy, psychologically safe, and esthetically pleasing living accommodations. It is important to note that by this definition, not all student employees in a housing department are paraprofessionals. Essential support functions are provided by students who serve as desk attendants, security personnel, maintenance workers, and office assistants. These functions, however, generally are not intended to promote individual development directly, and consequently, these job holders do not fall into the category of paraprofessionals. A crucial dimension of this definition is the essential roles that selection, training, and supervision play: in the absence of carefully conceptualized, expertly implemented, and systematically pursued training and supervision, potential paraprofessionals simply become at best well-intentioned amateurs whose successes are attributable mainly to forceful personalities and/or fortuitous circumstances.

The remainder of this chapter focuses primarily on the RA position. Many of the considerations and issues discussed also apply to other paraprofessional housing positions and to graduate-level positions as well.

Graduate-Level Positions

Many universities that have extensive graduate education programs utilize graduate students on their housing staff. (We call them hall directors or HDs in this chapter.) Master's-level HDs are often in somewhat ambiguous situations; they are more mature and have greater responsibilities than RAs, but

they lack the status, authority, experience, professional academic preparation, and income of well-qualified housing professionals.

Position responsibilities commonly entail management of a residential
living unit (varying in size from 100 to 500 beds) and supervision of an RA
staff (and in some places supervision of other student staff members, such as
desk clerks). Typically, they are called on to structure the educational and
psychological environment, maintain discipline, ensure smooth administrative functioning, provide counseling for troubled residents, encourage
educational, social, and recreational programming, and provide training
and supervision for RAs (Winston, Ullom, and Werring, 1983). These duties
are typically performed while they are also enrolled in a full load of graduate
courses. Consequently, they frequently are neither fish nor fowl, neither
paraprofessional nor professional, but some amalgam of the two.

Doctoral-level HDs (who have a master's degree in student affairs and
several years of work experience before returning for additional study) may
face other problems, since they may be as educationally qualified (and in
some cases even more experienced) a staff member as the person who
supervises them. For them, the HD position may feel like "professional
regression" in that they are asked to perform duties mastered previously and
"outgrown."

The use of HDs presents a particular challenge to housing professionals. They require as much training and supervision as RAs (although
certainly not the same). Winston, Ullom, and Werring (1983) report that HDs
were most attracted to, and received the most satisfaction from, the position
in terms of the learning experiences available and the personal satisfaction
gained by providing assistance to others and doing a job well. The most
difficult aspects of the position included conflicting time demands among
the job, academics, and personal life; maintaining discipline and enforcing
rules; inconveniences of hall living (for example, noise and lack of privacy);
and routine responsibilities of meetings and paperwork. A significant portion of those surveyed also felt a lack of support from the professional staff.

HDs who were enrolled in student affairs preparation programs valued the position more than HDs who did not plan to pursue a career in
student affairs, because it provided relevant work experiences and opportunities for the integration of academic study with practical experiences.
Overall, HDs who were preparing for student affairs careers were more
satisfied than their counterparts with other career plans enrolled in other
academic programs.

The administrative decision regarding staffing with full-time professionals versus part-time HDs can be one of the most crucial management
decisions a housing director makes. Whereas the former may be more costly,
significant programmatic payoffs may occur as a result of their possessing
sophisticated knowledge and advanced skill levels, higher levels of commitment, and significantly more time devoted to pursuit of departmental goals.
Organizational economic savings may be realized, as well, at other levels of

the organization when only full-time professional staff are utilized. On the other hand, use of HDs allows for lower resident-staff ratios and more programming efforts. And on those campuses that have a student affairs preparation program, employment of graduate students enrolled in that program can be seen as a *professional responsibility*. If housing programs do not provide high-quality training and practical experience for would-be student affairs professionals, where will the "well-prepared" professionals of the future come from? Academic preparation programs cannot do the job of educating student affairs professionals alone. Few would contest that employment in housing can be the best possible preparation for a career working with college students, regardless of the specific setting.

Space does not permit further consideration of the HD position. It should be emphasized, however, that housing programs that utilize HDs must carefully consider many of the same issues inherent in designing both RA training and professional staff development programs.

Designing the Resident Assistant Position

Each housing program must carefully analyze its goals for the total program and then make decisions about which categories of staff can best or most effectively address each function or activity. Frequently, position expectations are uncritically adopted year after year without regard to changing student populations, staff interests and expertise, and institutional or departmental goals.

Table 13.1 presents a listing, although not exhaustive, of possible RA roles and responsibilities. Each housing department should carefully examine the goals for its overall program and how the RA staff fits within that framework. Once goals for the housing program have been established—ideally including methods that encourage participation from all levels of staff—careful consideration is required as to which cadre of staff will have primary, secondary, or ancillary responsibilities in each area. Because of the nature of the RA position—that is, at the interface of individual residents and the housing program and professional staff—RAs often are expected to have involvement in all areas. It is not realistic, however, to expect that RAs can be highly involved everywhere; decisions must be made about what level of involvement is expected in each category of activities.

Involvement can be characterized as a continuum, with four basic levels identified: (1) none, (2) incidental, (3) routine, and (4) intense. After analyzing the goals of the residence life program and staffing patterns, a decision may be made that RAs should not be involved in some kinds of activities. Incidental involvement means that RAs are called on occasionally to perform tasks or provide services, but this is not seen as central to their responsibilities. Routine involvement means that RAs have ongoing responsibilities in this area, but a relatively low level of skills is required or the functions are part of daily activities. Intense involvement means that RAs

Table 13.1. Analysis of Resident Assistant Position Expectations.

Roles/responsibilities	Level of involvement			
	None	Incidental	Routine	Intense
Role model of effective student				
Academic achiever				
Extracurricular organization leader				
Community development				
Socializer				
Organizer				
Environmental manager				
Planner and executer of social activities				
System maintenance and control				
Clerical work				
Rule enforcement				
Disciplinary processes				
Information dissemination				
Custodial tasks				
Leadership and governance				
Hall unit leader				
Campus leader				
Hall council functionary				
Helper/facilitator				
Diagnostician				
Counselor				
Conflict mediator				
Crisis intervener				
Referral agent				
Educational programming				
Promoter				
Sponsor				
Advisor				
Planner and executer				

have primary responsibilities in the area and either need a relatively high level of skills (or careful, ongoing attention) or are expected to make recurring, concentrated efforts for relatively short periods.

Housing programs that utilize student paraprofessionals should create relatively unambiguous statements of position responsibilities and expectations for the sake of the RAs, the professional staff, and the residents. Often one of the major difficulties that RAs encounter is determining whether to act and, if so, the appropriate course of action. Given that most undergraduate RAs fall at the multiplicity positions on the Perry scheme (that is, they often perceive competing opinions or points of view as having equal value), the result can be highly frustrating at best and paralyzing at worst when there is ambiguity about position expectations. (See Chapter Four.) To the extent that the professional staff can lessen ambiguity about expectations for the position, the greater confidence many RAs will evidence as they approach their responsibilities and deal with the unavoidable indeterminism involved in analyzing situations and deciding on the "best" course of action on a daily basis.

Winston and Ender (1988) report that supervisors of RAs ranked the following activities as the most important RA activities: (1) enforce rules, (2) explain policies and procedures, (3) provide information, (4) provide personal counseling, and (5) organize social activities. From a survey of the literature (Davis, Hamer, and Hanson, 1972; Greenleaf, 1974; Mable and DeCoster, 1980; Knouse and Rodgers, 1981; Schuh and others, 1982; Upcraft and Pilato, 1982; Forsyth, 1983; Winston, Ullom, and Werring, 1984; Blimling and Miltenberger, 1990), we have identified six roles or areas of responsibility (listed in no particular order) that may be associated with the RA position on many campuses:

- Being a role model of an effective student
- Fostering community development
- Providing system maintenance and control
- Supplying leadership and governance
- Acting as a helper/facilitator
- Contributing or assisting with educational programming

Being a Role Model of an Effective Student

The engine that powers paraprofessional effectiveness is the force of peer role modeling. Seldom does the RA position carry the authority to compel residents to modify their behavior, attitudes, or opinions. (When RAs must resort to the use of their "authority," their overall effectiveness is generally diminished.) The preeminent power of the RA is directly correlated with his or her ability to persuade or influence residents by the force of example and the quality of personal relationships. It is because the RA is a person that residents view as being effective in most areas of her or his life, as successfully measuring up to the institution's expectations, and as having satisfactorily handled the pressures of young adult life that she or he is worthy of emulation. Because of the positive evaluation of the RA as a person and student, residents assent to the RA exercising influence and providing leadership.

The RA is an institutionally designed role model. That designation alone, however, has little power or magnetism unless the residents independently determine that the person possesses characteristics and has achievements they consider important and worth pursuing. Residents watch RAs' behavior carefully in the performance of official responsibilities, informal social interactions, management of academic obligations, and responses to crises. "How RAs manage their personal lives, perform academically, and approach the college experience teach those with whom they live" (Winston, Ullom, and Werring, 1984, p. 53). It is important, therefore, to select RAs who can comfortably manage the stress associated with a fishbowl existence, which is an essential characteristic of the position (Hornak, 1982).

Because RAs are role models, housing professionals need to consider numerous factors during the selection process. RAs are students first; therefore, requiring a relatively high grade-point average is desirable. Caution needs to be exercised, however, to ensure that students selected to be RAs represent both the demographic characteristics of the residential population and a diversity of personality types. For instance, the most gregarious, outgoing RA candidates may not be most effective in the position, especially in working with shy, introverted residents who may be the ones most likely to benefit from staff attention. The most popular or highly involved students, likewise, may not make the best RAs because of their conflicting commitments outside the residence hall.

Fostering Community Development

For housing professionals committed to the goals of student development, an essential objective of residence life programs is to foster the development of a sense of community among residents. This sense of belonging, fitting in, feeling cared for, and being important is a necessary prerequisite for stimulating the personal development of students in a residential context. (See Chapters Five and Nineteen.) As Sanford (1962) postulates, for optimum development to occur there must be a balance of challenge and support in the student's environment. The creation of caring communities in residence halls can serve as an indispensable support base that gives residents the courage needed to experiment with new behaviors, to examine their attitudes, prejudices, and beliefs critically, and to recuperate when their reach exceeds their grasp or when they make mistakes in judgment. Mable, Terry, and Duvall (1980, pp. 103–104) argue that "as students learn to know and respect each other and to seek mutual goals, they realize both response-ability (the ability to respond positively to one's interpersonal and physical environment) and responsibility (the process of demonstrating accountability and reliability)." Gardner (1989, p. 73) maintains that communities confer "upon . . . [their] members identity, a sense of belonging, and a measure of security. . . . The ideals of justice and compassion are nurtured in communities."

The RA is central to the development of a sense of community within living units. Mable and DeCoster (1980) assert that the fundamental prerequisite for building community is for residents to know each other as persons. It is the RA's responsibility to initiate and encourage this process. The RA as socializer needs to help the living unit through three levels of community building. (1) Getting acquainted (learning names, background information, and personality characteristics) is the first step. Early in the year, it is important to have social and/or recreational activities that encourage residents to establish contact with each other and to accomplish the elementary steps needed to transform the conglomerate of individual residents into a group. (2) Establishing an accepting atmosphere where residents can comfortably articulate personal values, experiences, and aspirations can then follow. "As student staff members through their own skills of self-disclosure assist students to think, feel, act upon self-knowledge, and to discover and cultivate who they are, meaningful interpersonal relationships will emerge" (Mable and DeCoster, 1980, p. 208). (3) Once an atmosphere of acceptance and freedom has been established, the living unit has significant potential to promote the personal development of its members. Gardner (1989, p. 78) maintains that "a good community nurtures its members and fosters an atmosphere of trust. They both protect and give a measure of autonomy to the individual. . . . A healthy community deals forthrightly with dissension and 'we-they' polarities, accepting diversity and dissent but using all the various mediating, coalition-building, and conflict resolution procedures to find common ground." This is essential to accomplishment of many of the student development outcomes espoused by college and universities. (See Chapter Two.)

Providing System Maintenance and Control

Most housing programs require someone to perform a number of somewhat mundane, but essential, clerical and administrative tasks, such as checking residents into their rooms, inventorying furnishings, reporting needed repairs, and requesting supplies. RAs are usually essential links in the communication between housing professionals and residents. They are called on to post notices, deliver messages to residents, announce events and deadlines, and pass along to superiors residents' reactions to proposals or administrative procedures.

Often RAs are also required to act as rule enforcers or disciplinarians to ensure an acceptable level of order. They are expected to help educate residents about house rules and necessary limitations on individual freedom due to the high density of students. Ideally, RAs can help residents understand why rules were made and the consequences of violating them both for the community and for the individual violator. Unfortunately, this role often requires RAs to confront residents who choose not to conform, and these confrontations—frequently exacerbated by the consumption of alcohol— are acrimonious, contumacious, and stress producing. Schuh and Shipton (1983) report that RAs often experience verbal abuse resulting from performing their RA duties, generally in the form of obscenities, threats of violence, and racial slurs. They also found that RAs were subject to physical abuse, most frequently in the form of malicious pranks involving fireworks and damage to personal property.

The disciplinary role presents difficulties because it often conflicts with the helper/facilitator role also expected of RAs. Upcraft and Pilato

(1982) call this built-in conflict the *cop-counselor problem*. They assert: "Regardless of how an RA handles a disciplinary situation, there is bound to be negative fallout. The person who is involved is certainly not going to like what is happening, and other members of the floor may also feel strongly. Certain persons are going to resent the RA for turning in someone, regardless of how well the situation was handled. . . . RAs will never win any popularity contests for enforcing rules, but they may win respect if they handle this role properly" (pp. 143–144).

Upcraft and Pilato (1982) propose eight guidelines to help RAs deal with disciplinary situations.

State expectation in advance. RAs should spell out exactly what the rules are, operationalize them (describe how they will be interpreted), and explain the degree of latitude that RAs have in enforcing certain rules. There also needs to be a discussion of residents' responsibilities in enforcing some rules—for example, quiet hours. The operating procedure may be for the RA to become involved in enforcement of quiet hours only after residents have unsuccessfully attempted to deal with the problem.

Teach residents the rules and how to use the system. RAs need to make sure that residents receive a copy of the conduct code; they should also explain important areas and tell residents how the disciplinary process works before there is a need to use it.

Be consistent. It is important to apply rules consistently across situations, individuals, and time. It is even more important to *appear* to be consistent and unbiased. If residents come to believe that some hallmates are given special treatment because of their relationship with the RA, all actions of the RA become suspect.

Maintain an appropriate attitude. If an RA gives the impression that he or she receives pleasure in disciplining students, residents will resent the attitude and will likely reject everything else he or she tries to do. Residents seldom appreciate shows of authority from RAs. Likewise, it is important not to personalize the situation. The attitude should be: *I am doing my job. I am sorry that you chose to violate the rule and I receive no pleasure from seeing you get in trouble. I am still willing to help you.*

Be honest. It is desirable for RAs to honestly share their opinions of rules, even when they disagree with them, and their feelings of discomfort about acting in the disciplinarian role. Residents also need to understand that the RAs' unfavorable opinion about a rule will not affect their enforcement of it.

Be decisive. RAs must be prepared to act as soon as they discover infractions. Appearances of ambivalence or indecision raise doubt in the residents' minds about the legitimacy of the regulation and/or the RAs' eventual actions, which will usually make the situation more difficult to handle. Training programs using simulations should give RAs opportunities to confront common disciplinary situations, formulate alternative courses of action, and examine probable consequences for each alternative.

Figure 13.1. Adaptation of Tannenbaum-Schmidt Leadership Model.

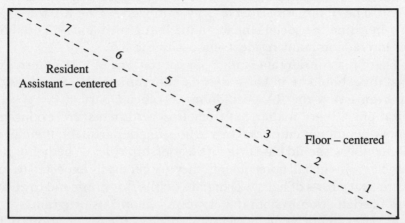

Note: 1 = RA permits floor to function within boundaries defined by institution, group decides; 2 = RA defines boundaries, helps group decide; 3 = RA presents problem, gets suggestions, then decides; 4 = RA presents tentative decision subject to change, then decides; 5 = RA presents decision, invites questions; 6 = RA decides, "sells" decision to floor; 7 = RA decides, announces decision to floor.
Source: Upcraft and Pilato, 1982, p. 127.

Seek help when needed. RAs need to understand that asking for help from fellow RAs or supervisors is not a sign of weakness or incompetence. Supervisors should be careful not to communicate unintentionally that "if you are having problems, you must be doing something wrong."

Abide by the rules. As noted earlier, RAs are officially designated role models. If they violate *any* rule, they forfeit their credibility with residents for enforcing *all* rules. Such instances can also lead to potential extortion. It is essential that RAs not only abide by the rules but also avoid the appearance of violating or ignoring rules. Appearances are as important as the reality.

Blimling and Miltenberger (1990) recommend a five-step procedure when confronted with apparent instances of misconduct: (1) collect the facts, (2) approach the student, (3) listen to the student, (4) take necessary action, and (5) follow up. Follow-up is particularly important if emotions were high at the time of the incident or if the resident was intoxicated. The following day, residents can think more clearly and may well have a different attitude.

Supplying Leadership and Governance

During the selection process, many housing programs look for personal characteristics that will increase the likelihood that the RA can assume leadership roles in the living unit. As a general rule, students who have a highly authoritarian leadership style have considerable difficulty as RAs. On the other hand, students who have difficulty exercising authority and accepting responsibility also have difficulty. Upcraft and Pilato (1982) suggest that an adaptation of the Tannenbaum-Schmidt (1960) model (see Figure 13.1) can be useful in helping RAs understand leadership approaches within a floor unit. The dominant leadership style utilized by the RA will to a large extent determine the social climate of the living unit and will establish the style of interaction many residents have with the RA.

There is a considerable range of expectations of RAs in terms of how involved they should be in hall government organizations. Some residential life programs view the RA position as an official part of the governance organization. Others maintain that hall governments are exclusively for residents who are not employed by the housing department; therefore, RAs, as staff members, should have no active leadership roles. Whether or not RAs have official roles in hall governments, they are generally expected to support programming efforts of hall governments on the floor unit and to encourage resident participation in both the organization and its programs.

Another important consideration involves the expectations of RAs in terms of leadership outside of the residence hall. At small colleges, there is a tendency for a relatively small group of students to dominate leadership positions and to be viewed as outstanding candidates for RA positions. Some programs encourage RAs to be actively involved outside of the halls as a means of giving the residence halls exposure to the larger community and to create a favorable image for the housing program. Residential life programs need to consider the implications of their expectations and should clearly communicate their expectations to students when they apply for RA positions.

Consideration of theories of leadership and the effects of different styles or approaches should be part of the training program for RAs. Simulations and role plays are generally needed to help students translate theory into practice. Exercises designed to help RAs become more flexible in their leadership styles are important. As Hersey and Blanchard (1982) assert, there is no "best" leadership style. Effective leaders are those who can accurately assess the situation, especially the level of maturity of group members in regard to performing a particular task or handling a given issue, and then utilize the leadership style that is most likely to fit the situation. Deluga's (1989, p. 10) findings indicate that "an RA's ability to generate and maintain a favorable group atmosphere, regardless of task-relationship leadership orientation, may prove to be a primary factor affecting RA-student influencing patterns." He also reports that there are significant differences in the ways that men and women residents interact with RAs and attempt to influence their actions. These differences need to be dealt with in training programs, especially for programs that have coeducational arrangements that require RAs to deal with residents of the other sex.

Acting as a Helper/Facilitator

Most residential life programs give at least lip service to the idea that RAs should help students deal with problems of a developmental nature, or what

Table 13.2. Counseling Issues Encountered by Resident Assistants at One University (1980–1986).

Problem/issue/concern	Percentage of units reporting encounter during one semester	
	Women's units[a]	Men's units[a]
Developmental issues		
Dating problems	77	58
Sexual problems of homosexual nature	14	27
Sexual problems of heterosexual nature	24	23
Vocational or career concerns	73	68
Alcohol abuse	22	41
Homesickness	66	45
Family concerns or problems	65	52
Preventive issues		
Pregnancy or birth control	27	8
Abortion needs or concerns	20	8
Health-related problems	73	53
Emotional crisis resulting in referral	63	42
Suicide threat	21	8
Remedial issues		
Roommate conflicts	81	75
Physical confrontation between students	18	40
Rape or other forms of sexual assault	11	1
Alcohol use (disciplinary situations)	74	88
Damage to facilities	49	85
Drug use (disciplinary situations)	23	37
Student in trouble with law enforcement officer	12	53
Student self-reliance or self-responsibility (including quiet hours)	81	66
Student alienated or ostracized by peers	57	59

[a]Means for years 1980, 1983, and 1986 were computed by R. B. Winston, Jr.
Source: Based on data reported by Schuh, Shipton, and Edman, 1988. Classification of problems was made by Schuh, Shipton, and Edman.

Ender (1984, p. 10) calls concerns related to "adjustment, satisfaction, and persistence." How well or how often RAs actually perform in this role is uncertain and generally undocumented (Winkelpleck and Domke, 1977), although Schuh and others (1982) and Kuh and Schuh (1983) report that residents, faculty members, professional staff in housing, parents, and RAs themselves all view acting as a helper or counselor to be an important function of the position. The data presented in Table 13.2 document that RAs are confronted with many problems and issues that they could handle more effectively if they were trained in the use of counseling skills.

Winston (1989) holds that student helpers need to possess the skills and knowledge that will enable them to establish relationships with peers that communicate genuine interest and concern about residents' welfare, promote self-exploration, and facilitate problem solving. Only after the establishment of a warm, caring relationship is effective helping or assistance likely to be possible. Concerns that students bring up in the context of a helping relationship can be conceptualized on a continuum with *developmental* anchoring one end and *remedial* anchoring the other end; in the middle, concerns may be thought of as *unclear* (that is, as not obviously either developmental or remedial or as containing aspects of both).

Cues that concerns are developmental include the following: (1) concerns are predicted by developmental theory for a student at that stage of life or academic career, (2) problems are directly related to the resident's present situation, (3) concerns are centered on interpersonal relationships or a skill or knowledge deficit, (4) student is not incapacitated by the concerns, and (5) student is willing and seems able to initiate action to address the concerns.

Remedial concerns are characterized by one or more of the following: (1) student's behavior is inconsistent with predictions for a person of her or his age and educational level, (2) student is dysfunctional in daily life, (3) problems seem centered in the past, (4) student has chronic psychological or physical complaints or has suffered trauma, (5) concerns seem based on intrapersonal conflicts, or (6) student appears suicidal.

The following cues point to unclear concerns, which are the majority of concerns as they appear when RAs first encounter them: (1) there is a mixture of developmental and remedial issues, (2) student seems confused or unclear about the nature of his or her concerns, (3) student seems unable to analyze her or his own behavior accurately, and (4) there is a lack of congruence between the presenting problem and the intensity of emotion or actual behavior.

After establishing a helping relationship, the RA must determine where the resident's concerns fall on the developmental-remedial continuum. If diagnosed as developmental, RAs should be able to assist the resident in initiating appropriate actions or help the resident make connection with programs and services available to address the concerns. If diagnosed as remedial, the RA's principal response should be to ensure that the resident is put in direct contact with the appropriate helping professional or agency or the RA's supervisor. In cases of traumas, such as sexual attacks or other forms of assaults, accidents, serious illness, or threats of suicide, RAs should be trained in the use of the emergency referral and intervention processes worked out for the campus. When the concerns are unclear, the RA must first listen carefully, give the resident support in exploring the problem by acting as a sounding board, and encourage active problem solving. Eventually, the RA will need to determine whether the concern is basically developmental or remedial and take appropriate action based on that diagnosis. It is important that RAs be trained not to make snap judgments but to listen carefully to residents' concerns, because residents sometimes will present a "safe," relatively inconsequential matter as a concern to determine whether the RA is worthy and capable of helping.

As the above description suggests, if RAs are expected to function as peer helpers they require a substantial amount of inital training, close continuing supervision, and continued training through in-service education. Of all the functions RAs are called on to perform, peer counseling is one of the most complicated to execute effectively and often causes anxiety (especially for some men, who are unaccustomed to relating to their peers as peer helping models advocate). As noted earlier, if RAs are expected to function as disciplinarians as well, a built-in conflict will exist in the minds of some—though not all—residents that will preclude them from seeking help with personal concerns from the RA.

In addition to helping individual residents confront and deal with their problems, RAs are also generally expected to intervene in conflicts between residents, to mediate conflicts or differences between groups or cliques of residents, and to intervene in crisis situations. Consequently, in addition to interpersonal helping skills, RAs need training in analyzing conflict situations—that is, in determining whether they are capable of dealing with the situation effectively, whether someone else (such as a supervisor) needs to come into the situation, or whether the conflict can best be handled by the parties involved without outside involvement. Upcraft and Pilato (1982) offer eight guidelines RAs can use to help them be more effective mediators: (1) Listen to both parties. (2) Do not take sides. (3) Define the problem. (4) Keep the parties talking to one another. (5) Keep control of the situation. (6) Spell out alternatives. (7) Let the parties solve their own conflict. (8) Recognize limitations. Training programs should include simulations and role plays that permit RAs to practice the mediator role and receive feedback about intervention strategies.

Contributing or Assisting with Educational Programming

Some residential life programs expect RAs to possess programming skills and to have some degree of involvement in the conceptualization and/or execution of educational programs. The degree of involvement can vary widely; possibilities include being a (1) promoter of attendance at programs and workshops in the halls or elsewhere on campus; (2) sponsor of programs led by faculty or staff members that are imported into the living unit; (3) adviser to hall government groups or hall residents interested in developing programs; (4) planner and executer of programs for hall residents (these may be "packaged programs" developed by the professional staff that RAs are trained to present or original programs developed by individual RAs). The greater the degree of initiative in programming RAs are expected to take, the more extensive the knowledge and expertise required, and therefore the more intense the training and supervision required.

One should be careful in the assignment of primary responsibility to RAs for developing programs designed to directly affect personal development. As Barr (1985, p. 64) points out, "the astute student services professional should be knowledgeable about the political environment and use that knowledge to develop, maintain, and implement quality . . . programs." It is unrealistic to expect RAs to possess the background and sophistication needed to avoid serious public relations blunders. How programs are titled and advertised is an important political consideration on many campuses. It is equally unrealistic to expect RAs to conduct formal needs assessments and to use the results of that process in determining which programs are most appropriate for which categories of residents.

We hold that it is more realistic to assign responsibility to RAs for organizing social events and intramural sports teams that will encourage the acquaintance process among residents and can help build a sense of identity for the living unit and a feeling of esprit de corps. It also seems appropriate for RAs to be trained to present "tightly scripted" or "packaged" programs, perhaps utilizing media such as videotapes or films, which are then followed by group discussion/processing of the information presented. RAs are often essential ancillary personnel for programs. The success of almost any residence hall program depends on RAs' support, encouragement of residents to attend, and distribution of advertising. RAs can often be valuable sounding boards for potential program ideas because they have a good understanding of likely resident response. It may be desirable to expect RAs to help residents select outside resource persons (perhaps from a list of interested faculty members, community persons, clergy, government agency personnel, institutional administrators, and campus services and programs staff that has been compiled by the professional staff) to invite into the hall to present programs.

The Staffing Process

The staffing process involves the interrelated processes and activities of recruitment, selection, training, supervision, and evaluation. As in the familiar chain, the effectiveness of an RA program is determined by the weakest link in its recruitment-through-evaluation staffing practices. Without highly motivated, conscientious, talented undergraduates who are committed to the goals of the housing program, there can be no quality paraprofessional program. Likewise, if these talented individuals are not trained adequately, supervised properly, and evaluated accurately, the paraprofessional program will never reach its full potential to contribute to the housing department's student development goals.

Recruitment

A principle factor in determination of paraprofessional effectiveness is the identification established through shared characteristics (such as age, academic major, and background) of paraprofessionals and the students with whom they work. ("The RA is like me; therefore, she or he is someone who can understand what is happening to me.") For this reason, it is important that

the RA staff as a whole approximately reflect the demographic characteristics of the resident population. If there are categories of residents who
are not adequately represented on the RA staff, special efforts should be
made to solicit applications from them. Using the Myers-Briggs Type Indicator in a study of over 100 RAs at the University of Maine, Anchors and Hay
(1990) determined that RAs were somewhat dissimilar from the resident
population from which they were selected, which made role modeling quite
difficult. They argue for sensitivity to variables such as culture, gender, and
personality differences when selecting paraprofessionals.

Recruitment should include announcements, notices, personal invitations (especially from the current RA staff), and other forms of publicity.
These announcements should clearly spell out the characteristics, experiences, and backgrounds that will be considered in the application and
selection process, such as successful completion of a training course, group
and individual interviews, role plays, and simulations.

Selection

Criteria for selection should be based on an analysis of position responsibilities and should be correlated directly with the variables examined in the
selection process, such as previous experience, references, grades, performance on simulated tasks, and personal characteristics necessary to satisfy
job expectations. Careful analysis of position expectations and training and
supervision resources are required before beginning the recruitment and
selection process. Some criteria must be built into the selection process—for
example, personal characteristics (such as gender and race), personality
traits (such as approachability and tolerance of differences), and academic
achievement—because it is unrealistic to attempt to change them to a significant degree through training. Other attributes important to being a good
RA, such as knowledge of resources, ability to give facilitative responses, and
program development skills, can be influenced substantially through effective training, and therefore it is not essential that applicants possess them
prior to selection.

Winston and Ender (1988) report that the following played a role in
the selection process of the sixty-five housing programs surveyed: test of
academic ability—SAT or ACT (12 percent), personality instruments (19
percent), grades (86 percent), previous leadership experience (95 percent),
recommendations from faculty and/or staff (85 percent), peer ratings (68
percent), performance in training (28 percent), academic major (5 percent),
and successful apprenticeship (8 percent). When deciding on what data to
request from applicants, make sure that everything requested is relevant to
the selection process and will be *used*. (If a piece of information is not going
to play a part in the decision-making process, do not request it.)

If references are required, make sure that the persons who are asked to
provide the information know what information is sought. For example, if

unguided, faculty members frequently speak to academic performance alone, which is often of limited interest in the selection process. If information about leadership skills, contributions to group assignments, prevalent modes of interaction with peers, and fulfillment of responsibilities on time are what are of interest, those expectations must be clearly communicated. When generalizations about personality traits or behavioral patterns (for example, honesty, punctuality, and interaction style with peers and authority figures) are solicited, it is advisable to request the reference to explain in some detail or to provide an example to illustrate how he or she came to the conclusion. Ordinarily, it is good practice to request the applicant's RA to provide information about the applicant's life in the living unit and an assessment of his or her potential to become a "good" RA.

In their study of paraprofessional utilization, Winston and Ender (1988) report that 97 percent of all programs used individual interviews in the selection process, 75 percent used group interviews, 43 percent used simulations, and 32 percent used completion of training as a selection criterion. Several points need to be kept in mind during the selection process. First, interviews favor students with good verbal skills (and probably those students who have had the most experience in such situations) and are anxiety producing for some students. Interview skills, however, may not be crucial to success as an RA (German, 1979). Second, interviews can produce valid information useful in making good personnel decisions, but staff members responsible for selection should keep in mind the full set of responsibilities and expectations associated with the RA position — many of which are not easily assessed through interviews.

There have been frequent attempts to identify and measure personality variables associated with success as an RA. For example, scales from the Personal Orientation Inventory (Graff and Bradshaw, 1970; Mullozzi and Ortenzi, 1971; Atkinson, Williams, and Garb, 1973; Schroeder and Willis, 1973; Kipp, 1979), the Edwards Personal Preference Schedule (Holbrook, 1972), the Myers-Briggs Type Indicator (Wachowiak and Bauer, 1977), the California Personality Inventory (Morton, 1975–76; Hall and Creed, 1979), and the Gordon Personal Inventory (Hayes and Burke, 1981) have been used as predictor variables. None of them, however, have produced consistently reliable results, due in some measure to the vagueness of the criteria that define success in the RA position. It is probably much more important to understand how potential RAs relate to people and solve problems and whether these strategies are generally successful in situations likely to be encountered in the RA position than it is to seek any particular set of characteristics or traits.

If it is possible to have potential RAs complete a basic helping skills course (which includes a moderate level of self-disclosure and requires demonstration of the use of helping skills) prior to selection, observations made over the duration of the course usually provide more accurate information about how the candidate is likely to function as an RA than any other source.

Criteria for selecting RAs (based in part on suggestions from Delworth, Sherwood, and Cassaburri, 1974) include:

- Concern for and desire and ability to contribute to the academic, social, and personal development of peers
- Good communication skills
- Ability to create an emotional climate that communicates openness and facilitates self-exploration and personal growth
- Record of being able to manage one's own academic life successfully
- Adequate personal adjustment (RAs need to have at least as good mental health as those with whom they work)
- Good group facilitation skills
- Capacity to learn from training and to apply what is learned with peers
- Evidence of ego strength or sense of identity that allows the person to withstand peer pressure
- Ability to function well in ambiguous situations, emotionally charged circumstances, and crises
- Willingness to spend much of his or her free time in the residence halls (absent RAs are seldom helpful to residents)
- High energy level
- History of harmonious relationships with hallmates
- Evidence of *informal* leadership skills among fellow residents
- Basic agreement with the goals and philosophy of the housing program
- Specific skills (for example, program development, disciplinary skills, needs assessment, organizational leadership), as determined by the position responsibilities

Training

RA training can be divided into three categories: (1) preselection, (2) preservice, and (3) in-service.

Preselection training can be either a prerequisite for applying to be an RA or a requirement of successful completion prior to employment. This training should focus on generic peer helping or peer counseling skills and processes within the context of higher education. Upcraft and Pilato (1982) assert, and we wholeheartedly concur, that basic interpersonal facilitation or helping skills can best be learned prior to assuming the other responsibilities of the RA position, which almost always seem to have greater urgency or higher priority once on the job. Research by Winston and Buckner (1984) suggests that RAs who received training in helping skills prior to beginning work experience less stress after one term on the job than RAs who were simultaneously working as an RA and participating in training. The best situation is for the helping skills course (which carries regular academic credit like other courses) to be open to all students at the institution and to be taught in a way that has wide applicability, even for students who never apply for an RA position. Duration should be from thirty to forty-five class contact hours and should include completion of assignments outside of class. Successful completion of the course (grade of at least a B, for example) would be a prerequisite for being selected as an RA.

Content for the course should include the following (based in part on the suggestions of Ender, McCaffrey, and Miller, 1979; Upcraft and Pilato, 1982; and Blimling and Miltenberger, 1990).

1. Basic helping skills, based on a model such as Carkhuff (1969), Danish and Hauer (1973), Egan (1975), Ivey and Authier (1978), Gazda and others (1984), or Upcraft and Pilato (1982) — which includes extensive opportunities to practice using the skills (preferably with frequent use of videotape for receiving feedback)
2. Values clarification activities, especially as relating to topics such as ethnicity, sexual orientation, religious beliefs, drug and alcohol use, and sexual mores
3. Knowledge of cultural differences (including variables such as race, socioeconomic background, international students' cultural practices, and gender issues)
4. Basics of group dynamics and group leadership
5. Student development theories (focus on understanding principally through self-assessment and application of theories to self)
6. Crisis intervention (for example, threats of suicide and roommate conflicts)
7. Providing accurate information (include acquiring a working knowledge of services and programs available on the campus and selected institutional rules and policies)
8. Making effective referrals
9. Dealing with difficult circumstances or conflicts (for example, hostile, belligerent people, persons under the influence of alcohol or drugs, prejudice reactions, sexual issues, rape or other forms of physical assault)

It is very important to identify clearly the basic concepts to be mastered and the skills to be learned during each phase of training. There is a tendency to attempt to include too many topics and issues in preselection training, which may result in students becoming confused or feeling overloaded and, consequently, failing to master any. Above all else, preselection training should concentrate on teaching ways to create helpful interactions with peers and to intervene in potentially self-defeating situations. If this is to be successful, there must be extensive opportunity to practice in as realistic settings as possible and to receive honest feedback. These skills cannot be mastered during a weekend retreat or a few hours of classroom "instruction."

Training methodologies should include a diversity of instructional strategies, such as lectures, role plays, simulations, group discussions, structured group exercises, and videotape feedback. There should be a textbook, or at least a collection of duplicated materials, that students are expected to have read prior to class. The instructor(s) should provide students with syllabi and should have a clear and detailed plan of instruction. They may want to consider using an approach called *intentionally structured groups* as the principal means of instruction (Winston, Bonney, Miller, and Dagley, 1988).

Preservice training follows successful completion of preselection training. It concentrates on helping RAs acquire the specific information they need to open and run the halls, on providing RAs the opportunity to think about and practice dealing with difficult situations, and on developing relationships within the housing staff unit that will increase the likelihood of accomplishing student development goals. This training is generally held shortly before the opening of the halls in the fall. Duration may be from three days to two weeks.

RAs should be given a handbook or manual that details residence hall policies and procedures, includes copies of forms used and instruction for completing and processing them, and incorporates a well-organized guide to services and programs about which residents may need information. As much as possible, professional staff members should avoid spending training time on providing information that can be acquired through reading. (Training time should focus on discovering the less obvious implications of or uses for the information.) Opportunities should be available for RAs and the professional staff to deal with "what ifs"—if this happens, what should we do (or how can we handle the situation satisfactorily)? Details of who has responsibility for what need to be worked out and formalized.

Additional skills training may also be included in preservice training, including assertiveness training (Layne, Layne, and Schoch, 1977), review of human relations skills (Newton, 1974; Schroeder, Hill, Gormally, and Anthony, 1973; Zirkle and Hudson, 1975), stress management (Brunson and McKee, 1982), wellness (Snow, 1982), conflict resolution, or study skills (Ender, McCaffrey, and Miller, 1979; Blimling and Miltenberger, 1990), identifying and working with students who abuse alcohol and drugs, and educating residents about rape and sexually transmitted diseases (Blimling and Miltenberger, 1990).

Some attention should be directed at helping RAs who will be working together to get to know each other well and to develop working teams with the HDs and professional staff. Adventure training has proved to be one means of accelerating the acquaintance process and in developing cohesive work groups (Schroeder, 1976). Off-campus retreats, recreational activities, and social events can also serve this purpose, although they are seldom as intense an experience. These activities, however, cannot substitute for providing needed information and for helping RAs acquire specific skills that require a knowledge base and finesse in their use.

An unfortunate error of providing the same experiences for new RAs and returning RAs is sometimes made during preservice training. This can

prove to greatly undermine the effectiveness of the training, because returning RAs, who have "heard it all before," frequently act bored or create
distractions. There are several strategies for dealing with the need to present
certain materials to new RAs with which returning RAs are already familiar.
Returning RAs can be used to help present the material, serve on panels to
discuss the issues based on their experiences, give demonstrations, be role
players for the new RAs to practice with, or serve as facilitators of small-group
discussions of new RAs. Alternatively, separate programs can be presented to
new and returning RAs to ensure that fresh material is presented to everyone.

In-service training should go on throughout the academic year and is
generally most effective when it is problem or issue focused. The most
efficacious in-service training is designed to offer practical solutions to
problems that RAs experience during the course of the year and should be
identified through the supervision process (discussed in the following pages).
If RAs are involved in deciding on the topics and see that in-service training
is intended to help them do a better job, participation will be enthusiastic
and the learning immediate. On the other hand, if RAs see in-service training as contrived, ill-prepared, or not immediately applicable to their RA
duties, it will be resisted and viewed as a waste of valuable time.

Supervision

Supervision is sometimes a menacing word in residence halls because it
connotes being controlling, showing a lack of trust, and threatening punishment. The tendency has been for supervision to fluctuate between extremes:
from little or no control (or knowledge) of RAs' activities on the living unit to
stifling control that gives RAs no latitude in decision making and causes
them to spend much of their time concealing what they do from supervisors.
The situation is further complicated by two factors: (1) Many RAs are supervised by entry-level professionals who lack basic supervision skills and confidence in their abilities because of a lack of experience and who are unsure of
their authority within the housing system. (2) RAs are maturing young adults
who sometimes encounter developmental crises in their own lives that prevent them from hearing, much less dealing with, residents' concerns. As a
general rule, RAs cannot effectively assist residents in dealing with developmental issues that they themselves have not satisfactorily resolved.

Winston, Ullom, and Werring (1984) suggest that there are four different approaches to supervising RAs: maternalistic, authoritarian, laissez-faire,
and synergistic. Maternalistic supervisors want to be *liked* above all else; they
concentrate on being "buddies" with RAs but pay little attention to RAs' job
performance until problems reach crisis proportions. Unpleasant situations
or instances of poor judgment are ignored as long as possible in the hope
that they will correct themselves; this often results in supervision centering
around a series of crises.

Authoritarian supervisory styles are based on a belief that RAs require continuous attention because RAs are undependable or immature; they should be given very little authority to handle problems on their own. Major decisions are made by the supervisor; RAs' responsibilities are to do exactly as they are told. For entry-level professionals, this approach to supervision is sometimes rooted in insecurity and a desire to "look good" to their supervisors. This approach may also simply reflect the kind of supervision the entry-level professional is receiving or received as an RA himself or herself.

Laissez-faire supervision is based on a desire to allow RAs to run their own show without interference from the supervisor. RAs are instructed to come to the supervisor only when they have a problem they cannot handle but are seldom given instructions or advice on how to manage the living unit or deal with problems. To seek advice or direction from the supervisor requires the RA to first admit failure; therefore, supervisors are called in only when things have progressed to a serious state or have gotten completely out of hand. Supervision then becomes associated with crisis.

Synergistic supervision is a cooperative approach that makes the total efforts of the supervisor and RA have an effect greater than the sum of either's contributions. Emphasis is on both accomplishing organizational goals and on furthering the personal development of RAs. Problems brought to the supervisor's attention are seen as situations that require joint efforts to find solutions, not as failures. RAs are encouraged to talk openly about what is happening in the living unit; the emphasis is on preventing small disturbances or difficulties from escalating or on finding helpful interventions with individual residents who are experiencing difficulties. Synergistic supervision is difficult, if not impossible, unless the individuals selected to be RAs have a strong commitment to the housing program's goals and have completed rigorous preselection and preservice training programs.

We offer the following suggestions for supervisors who desire to employ synergistic supervision with RAs, which from our perspective is the most effective approach.

- Spend time in establishing rapport with RAs. Help them establish personal goals and goals for their living unit. Openness, respect, and genuineness are the characteristics that will create the kind of relationship that makes synergistic supervision possible.
- Schedule regular individual meetings for the sole purpose of providing supervision. We suggest that these sessions be scheduled at the beginning of each term for the same day and time throughout the term, no less frequently than alternate weeks. Be sure to focus attention on the status of the RAs' personal and living unit goals during these sessions.
- Spend time in the living units at night when residents are in their rooms. When RAs need to talk about an individual's problems, it is very helpful if the supervisor knows something about the resident and can contribute independent data and evaluations. The session can then truly be joint problem solving.

- Schedule group supervision sessions in which the RAs for whom the supervisor is responsible deal with issues and problems. These should be clearly differentiated from staff meetings, where the attention is generally on communicating information, making assignments, and hearing reports about past activities and plans for upcoming events.
- Give RAs systematic feedback about their performance since the last session, both positive and negative. Many supervisors may need to make a habit of keeping records of their observations of RAs' performance; otherwise, the tendency is to concentrate unfairly on only the most recent unlaudatory performance. Give RAs written feedback once a month within the context of the goals established at the beginning of the term.
- Solicit honest feedback from RAs about the supervisor's performance, both as a supervisor and as a housing professional in general.
- Reinforce RAs' use of skills and application of knowledge taught in training. The connections between training and practice need to be kept before RAs at all times; otherwise, RAs have the tendency to fall back on whatever had been their own personally preferred style of relating to others and solving problems.
- Spend informal time with RAs. Most RAs can relate better to supervisors who they also know as persons outside of their professional roles. Supervisors are cautioned, however, not to become *too* close; supervisors cannot be either intimate friends with or therapists for the RAs they supervise. "Such relationships compromise the supervisory relationship because of the inevitable conflict between the best interests of the RA and the best interests of students" (Upcraft and Pilato, 1982, p. 246).

Evaluation

The final component in creating effective RA programs is a system of fair, explicit, and valid evaluation of work performance. This is quite difficult to realize, however, because there is a great deal of ambiguity in job descriptions, resulting in a lack of clarity in performance criteria, and in any case, much of what RAs do cannot be directly observed by supervisors. This is further complicated by the unreliability of residents' evaluations, which are almost always greatly colored by the frequency of disciplinary problems in a unit and the nature of personal relationships with the RA. Residents tend to give uniformly positive evaluations to RAs they like and uniformly negative ones to RAs they dislike.

Upcraft and Pilato (1982) suggest four steps in an effective RA evaluation system: (1) providing a clear statement of job functions and expectations, (2) providing a clear statement of the sources of information that will be used in evaluations, (3) establishing clear goals for the job and the evaluation process, and (4) conducting evaluations only on the basis of stated criteria from previously identified sources.

Effective evaluation must be intimately connected to supervision. We suggest that evaluations be based on an operationalized version of the department's job description for RAs, specific goals for the living unit developed jointly by the RA and the supervisor, and specific personal growth goals developed by the RA and communicated to the supervisor (both of which have been discussed previously). By operationalizing the job description, we mean stating in specific terms what is meant by "provide personal help and assistance to residents," for instance. RAs could be asked to keep a record of instances when they became involved with a resident in dealing with a personal problem, the general nature of the problem, the technqiues used, and the outcome to the extent the RA can determine. There are confidentiality issues here, however, which would require use of strict guidelines to ensure the protection of residents' privacy. But supervisors must also exercise care to avoid onerous recordkeeping.

Sources of data used in evaluations include (1) supervisor's observations, (2) written resident evaluations that have been distributed and collected by neutral parties (for example, elected hall representatives), (3) observations of fellow RAs, and (4) RAs' own reports. We suggest that collection of data from residents be done well before the end of terms, when the press of examinations and assignments make completing evaluation forms a source of irritation. The results of all the evaluations need to be compiled and synthesized by the supervisor and shared in a private conference with the RA. The data should be frankly discussed, and RAs should have an opportunity to challenge evaluations with which they disagree. (Residents' rating should be kept in perspective, given the tendency of many residents to render evaluations based on the degree of personal affinity for the RA.) An important outcome of this conference should be the formulation of new living unit goals in light of the evaluation data and development of specific plans of action for accomplishing the agreed-on goals.

It is important to note that the quality of the relationship between a professional staff member and individual RAs gives RAs clear and direct cues as to how they are expected to interact with residents on the floor. A developmental approach to this relationship provides excellent modeling, as well as creating an environment that supports healthy, positive growth. In essence, just as residents observe and evaluate RAs, RAs in turn observe, evaluate, and often emulate professional staff members. In all cases, hypocrisy and duplicity can produce disastrous results for those committed to the goals of student development.

Advantages and Limitations of Using Paraprofessionals

The use of paraprofessionals in residence halls can greatly expand the impact of college attendance on residents' lives. Effective paraprofessional programs, however, require considerable time and expertise on the part of the professional staff. Without clear, realistic expectations of RAs and effective recruitment and selection processes that ensure a cadre of highly motivated and talented individuals—who are representative of the resident population and who are extensively trained, carefully supervised, and fairly evaluated—the resulting effect is likely to be marginal to negative. Effective RA programs require the commitment of substantial resources by the housing program.

References

Anchors, S., and Hay, S. "Resident Assistants: Are They Similar or Dissimilar to the Students from Whom They Are Selected?" *Journal of College and University Student Housing*, 1990, *20*, 18–21.

Atkinson, D. R., Williams, T. D., and Garb, E. "The Personal Orientation Inventory as a Predictor of Resident Assistant Effectiveness." *Journal of College Student Personnel*, 1973, *14*, 326–332.

Barr, M. J. "Internal and External Forces Influencing Programming." In M. J. Barr, L. A. Keating, and Associates, *Developing Effective Student Services Programs: Systematic Approaches for Practitioners*. San Francisco: Jossey-Bass, 1985.

Blimling, G. S., and Miltenberger, L. J. *The Resident Assistant: Working with College Students in Residence Halls*. (3rd ed.) Dubuque, Iowa: Kendall/Hunt, 1990.

Brunson, B. I., and McKee, K. D. "Crisis Intervention and Stress Management: Giving Resident Advisors What They Need." *Journal of College Student Personnel*, 1982, *23*, 547–548.

Carkhuff, R. R. *Helping and Human Relations: A Primer for Lay and Professional Helpers*. 2 vols. Troy, Mo.: Holt, Rinehart & Winston, 1969.

Danish, S. J., and Hauer, A. L. *Helping Skills: A Basic Training Program*. New York: Behavioral Publications, 1973.

Davis, L., Hamer, B., and Hanson, D. "Student Perceptions of Head Resident Effectiveness." *Journal of College and University Student Housing*, 1972, *2*, 20–23.

Deluga, R. J. "The Relationship Between Resident Assistants' Characteristics and Leadership Style and Students' Influencing Behavior." *Journal of College and University Student Housing*, 1989, *18*, 7–11.

Delworth, U., Sherwood, G., and Cassaburri, N. *Student Paraprofessionals: A Working Model for Higher Education*. Washington, D.C.: American College Personnel Association, 1974.

Egan, G. *The Skilled Helper*. Pacific Grove, Calif.: Brooks/Cole, 1975.

Ender, S. C. "Student Paraprofessionals Within Student Affairs: The State of the Art." In S. C. Ender and R. B. Winston, Jr. (eds.), *Students as Paraprofessional Staff*. New Directions for Student Services, no. 27. San Francisco: Jossey-Bass, 1984.

Ender, S. C., McCaffrey, S. S., and Miller, T. K. *Students Helping Students: A Training Manual for Peer Helpers on the College Campus*. Athens, Ga.: Student Development Associates, 1979.

Fenske, R. H. "Evolution of the Student Services Profession." In U. Delworth, G. R. Hanson, and Associates, *Student Services: A Handbook for the Profession.* (2nd ed.) San Francisco: Jossey-Bass, 1989.

Forsyth, C. J. "A Method for Determining the Organizational Perception of the Role of the Resident Assistant." *Journal of College and University Student Housing,* 1983, *13*, 20–23.

Gardner, J. W. "Building Community." *Kettering Review,* 1989, 7, 73–81.

Gazda, G. M., and others. *Human Relations Development: A Manual for Educators.* (3rd ed.) Needham Heights, Mass.: Allyn & Bacon, 1984.

German, S. C. "Selecting Undergraduate Paraprofessionals on College Campuses: A Review." *Journal of College Student Personnel,* 1979, *20*, 28–33.

Graff, R. W., and Bradshaw, H. E. "Relationship of a Measure of Self-Actualization to Dormitory Resident Assistant Effectiveness." *Journal of Counseling Psychology,* 1970, *17*, 502–505.

Greenleaf, E. A. "The Role of Student Staff Members." In D. A. DeCoster and P. Mable (eds.), *Student Development and Education in College Residence Halls.* Washington, D.C.: American College Personnel Association, 1974.

Hall, M., and Creed, W. "The Use of the CPI in the Evaluation and Selection of Resident Assistants." *Journal of College and University Student Housing,* 1979, *9*, 10–13.

Hayes, J. A., and Burke, T. "Predicting the Success of Undergraduate Resident Hall Assistants." *Southern College Personnel Association Journal,* 1981, *3*(3), 6–11.

Hersey, P., and Blanchard, K. H. *Management of Organizational Behavior: Utilizing Human Resources.* (4th ed.) Englewood Cliffs, N.J.: Prentice Hall, 1982.

Holbrook, R. L. "Student Volunteers as Helpers in Residence Halls." *Journal of College Student Personnel,* 1972, *13*, 559–561.

Hornak, J. "Resident Assistant Burnout: A Self-Defeating Behavior." *Journal of College and University Student Housing,* 1982, *12*, 14–16.

Ivey, A. E., and Authier, J. *Microcounseling: Innovations in Interviewing, Counseling, Psychotherapy, and Psychoeducation.* (2nd ed.) Springfield, Ill.: Thomas, 1978.

Kipp, D. J. "The Personal Orientation Inventory: A Predictive Device for Resident Advisors." *Journal of College Student Personnel,* 1979, *20*, 382–384.

Knouse, D. R., and Rodgers, D. T. "An Analysis of the Resident-Assistant Position Based on the Behaviorally Anchored Rating-Scales Technique." *Journal of College Student Personnel,* 1981, 22, 396–400.

Kuh, G. D., and Schuh, J. H. "Perceptions of the RA Role: Does a Year Make a Difference?" *Journal of College and University Student Housing,* 1983, *13*, 3–7.

Layne, R. G., Layne, B. H., and Schoch, E. W. "Group Assertiveness Training for Resident Assistants." *Journal of College Student Personnel,* 1977, *18*, 393–398.

Mable, P., and DeCoster, D. A. "The Role of Students as Staff Members and Leaders Within a Residence Community." In D. A. DeCoster and P. Mable (eds.), *Personal Education and Community Development in College Residence Halls.* Alexandria, Va.: American College Personnel Association, 1980.

Mable, P., Terry, M. J., and Duvall, W. H. "Student Development Through Community Development." In D. A. DeCoster and P. Mable (eds.), *Personal Education and Community Development in College Residence Halls.* Alexandria, Va.: American College Personnel Association, 1980.

Morton, L. J. "The CPI: Significance as a Resident Assistant Selection Aid." *Journal of College and University Student Housing,* 1975–76, *5,* 16–21.

Mullozzi, A., Jr., and Ortenzi, A. "Factors in Selecting Residence Hall Fellows." *Journal of the National Association of Women Deans and Counselors,* 1971, *34,* 185–190.

Newton, F. B. "The Effect of Systematic Communication Skills Training on Residence Hall Paraprofessionals." *Journal of College Student Personnel,* 1974, *15,* 366–369.

Powell, J. R., Plyler, S. A., Dickson, B. A., and McClellan, S. D. *The Personnel Assistant in College Residence Halls.* Boston: Houghton Mifflin, 1969.

Sanford, N. "Developmental Status of the Entering Freshman." In N. Sanford (ed.), *The American College: A Psychological and Social Interpretation of the Higher Learning.* New York: Wiley, 1962.

Schroeder, C. C. "Adventure Training for Resident Assistants." *Journal of College Student Personnel,* 1976, *17,* 11–15.

Schroeder, C. C., and Willis, B. S. "An Attempt to Use a Measure of Self-Actualization in the Selection of Resident Assistants." *Journal of College and University Student Housing,* 1973, *3,* 30–32.

Schroeder, K., Hill, C. E., Gormally, J., and Anthony, W. A. "Systematic Human Relations Training for Resident Assistants." *Journal of College Student Personnel,* 1973, *14,* 313–316.

Schuh, J. H., and Shipton, C. W. "Abuses Encountered by Resident Assistants During an Academic Year." *Journal of College Student Personnel,* 1983, *24,* 428–432.

Schuh, J. H., Shipton, W. C., and Edman, N. "Counseling Problems Encountered by Resident Assistants: A 15-Year Study." *Journal of College and University Student Housing,* 1988, *18,* 21–27.

Schuh, J. H., and others. "The RA Role Revisited: Differences in Perspectives of RA Responsibilities." *College Student Affairs Journal,* 1982, *4*(1), 13–22.

Snow, L. J. "Wellness Programming on a Small College Campus." *Journal of College Student Personnel,* 1982, *23,* 554–555.

Tannenbaum, R., and Schmidt, W. "How to Choose a Leadership Pattern." *Harvard Business Review,* 1960, *3,* 95–101.

Upcraft, M. L., with the collaboration of Pilato, G. T. *Residence Hall Assistants in College: A Guide to Selection, Training, and Supervision.* San Francisco: Jossey-Bass, 1982.

Wachowiak, D., and Bauer, G. "Use of the Myers-Briggs Type Indicator for the Selection and Evaluation of Residence Hall Advisors." *Journal of College and University Student Housing,* 1977, *6,* 34–37.

Winkelpleck, J. M., and Domke, J. A. "Perceived Problems and Assistance Desired by Residence Hall Staff." *Journal of College Student Personnel*, 1977, *18*, 195–199.

Winston, R. B., Jr. "Counseling and Advising." In U. Delworth, G. R. Hanson, and Associates, *Student Services: A Handbook for the Profession*. (2nd ed.) San Francisco: Jossey-Bass, 1989.

Winston, R. B., Jr., Bonney, W. C., Miller, T. K., and Dagley, J. C. *Promoting Student Development Through Intentionally Structured Groups: Principles, Techniques, and Applications*. San Francisco: Jossey-Bass, 1988.

Winston, R. B., Jr., and Buckner, J. D. "The Effects of Peer Helper Training and Timing of Training on Reported Stress of Resident Assistants." *Journal of College Student Personnel*, 1984, *25*, 430–436.

Winston, R. B., Jr., and Ender, S. C. "Use of Student Paraprofessionals in Divisions of College Student Affairs." *Journal of Counseling and Development*, 1988, *66*, 466–473.

Winston, R. B., Jr., Ullom, M., and Werring, C. J. "The Housing Graduate Assistantship: Factors That Affect Choice and Perceived Satisfaction." *Journal of College Student Personnel*, 1983, *24*, 225–235.

Winston, R. B., Jr., Ullom, M. S., and Werring, C. J. "Student Paraprofessionals in Residence Halls." In S. C. Ender and R. B. Winston, Jr. (eds.) *Students as Paraprofessional Staff*. New Directions for Student Services, no. 27. San Francisco: Jossey-Bass, 1984.

Zirkle, K. E., and Hudson, G. "The Effects of Residence Hall Staff Members on Maturity Development for Male Students." *Journal of College Student Personnel*, 1975, *16*, 30–33.

Chapter Fourteen

Legal and Regulatory
Concerns

Donald D. Gehring

There is probably a greater potential for legal liability in college and university housing than in any other area of student affairs. Student affairs professionals working in housing must deal with the physical aspects of buildings, student government, activities and programming, discipline, interpersonal conflicts, and a variety of personal problems. Each of these responsibilities is fraught with potential legal issues. However, these risks can be managed. To minimize potential liability, housing professionals must be familiar with the legal parameters involved in daily housing operations. The best way to manage risks is to identify potential dangers before they become problems. Administrators need not be attorneys, but knowing how to locate cases, statutes, rules, and constitutional provisions can be useful. A helpful guide is provided by Gehring (1991b).

This chapter furnishes an overview of the legal relationships that exist between residents and the institution as represented by the housing office. Housing professionals who understand these legal relationships should be able to better recognize the rights of those involved.

The information contained in this chapter is not designed to provide legal advice. There is no substitute for obtaining the advice of competent legal counsel, and where time permits, staff should seek such counsel. Often, however, college housing staff must respond immediately to situations. Thus, a basic knowledge of the legal parameters involved in a situation is imperative to minimize potential liability.

When time permits consultation with an attorney, administrators should understand the role of legal counsel. As Bickel (1974) points out, there are many roles that college or university counsel can take on; however, none include making educational decisions. Counsel should advise. Administrators must be prepared to inform counsel of the course they wish to take and educational outcomes they want to achieve and then ask counsel what legal parameters and risks are associated with that action. Once that information is known, administrators can weigh the potential risks against the educational benefit to be derived and make a decision. There are risks associated with every activity, and administrators who abdicate their right to make educational decisions are doomed to live with legal decisions based not on educational benefits but on minimizing the legal risks. If, for example, you asked an attorney to make a decision about allowing students to build lofts in their rooms, the decision would probably be not to allow such activity because of the potential risk of liability. However, if you tell counsel you want students to be able to build lofts because of the effect it has on a student's environment, counsel can tell you the risks associated with the activity and can help you develop a plan to minimize those risks.

The legal relationship between resident students and the institution may be found in the rights derived from federal and state constitutions, contracts, federal and state statutes, and the concept of torts. One or more of these relationships may be involved in almost every situation in college housing.

The Constitution

The U.S. Constitution is the highest law of the land and nothing may supersede it. Thus, the Constitution may be considered as creating the preeminent relationship between residents and the institution. While the Constitution itself defines the relationship between the three branches of government, the amendments set forth the rights of the people. Generally, however, the rights enumerated in the amendments only pertain to the relationship between individuals and the federal or state government. The rights guaranteed by the Constitutional amendments do not apply to an individual's relationship with a private college or university. In other words, there simply is no Constitutional guarantee that one will, for example, be free from unreasonable searches and seizures at a private college or university. The U.S. Supreme Court has said that the Constitution "erects no shield against merely private conduct, however disciplinary or wrongful" (*Shelley* v. *Kraemer*, 1947, at p. 13). However, if a private institution is closely allied with the state so that its actions are essentially those of the state, then the Constitution would apply. This concept of a private institution becoming entwined with the state is known as *state action*. The courts have examined a variety of entanglements between private institutions and the state and have generally been consistent in failing to find state action. Courts have rejected state action where private institutions have received state funding (*Torres* v. *Puerto Rico Junior College*, 1969), received federal funding (*Grossner* v. *Trustees of Columbia University*, 1968), had contracts with the state (*Power* v. *Miles*, 1968), were granted tax-exempt status (*Browns* v. *Mitchell*, 1969), served a public function (*Counts* v. *Voorhees College*, 1970), were chartered by the state (*Blackburn* v. *Fisk University*, 1971), used local police as campus police (*Robinson* v. *Davis*, 1971), had state approval of courses (*Rowe* v. *Chandler*, 1971), and were granted state accreditation (*Berrios* v. *Inter American University*, 1976). However, where a private university had disciplined a student for vandalism to a building financed by the State Dormitory Authority, the court found the requisite state action and required the university to provide the student with due process. The court noted that the Dormitory Authority had required the university to develop rules for maintenance of the building, in addition to pointing to other indications of state involvement (*Ryan* v. *Hofstra University*, 1971). Although private institutions are not generally required to provide residents the guarantees of the Constitution, they may choose to do so.

The federal Constitution sets forth minimal standards. However, state statutes or constitutions may provide an individual with more, but never fewer, rights than are guaranteed in the federal document. The case of *Washington* v. *Chrisman* (1982) illustrates this point. In this case, a campus police officer standing in the open doorway of a student's residence hall room observed marijuana seeds and a pipe in the room. The officer then entered the room and informed the students of their rights. The students waived their rights, and the officer conducted a search of the room that uncovered more illegal drugs. The students were convicted of felonies, and their appeals ended at the U.S. Supreme Court. The Court held the search to be permissible under the Fourth Amendment to the U.S. Constitution. However, on remand to the Washington State Supreme Court, that court held that the Washington State constitution guaranteed a heightened protection against warrantless searches and that the officer's entry into the room was impermissible under the state constitution (*State* v. *Chrisman*, 1984). This chapter does not permit a discussion of the constitution of each of the fifty states, but housing professionals should become familiar with the constitution of the state in which they work.

The three primary federal Constitutional amendments housing officers must be familiar with are the First, Fourth, and Fourteenth Amendments.

First Amendment

The First Amendment, probably the most jealously guarded by the courts, states that "Congress shall make no laws respecting the establishment of religion or prohibiting the free exercise thereof; or abridging the freedom of speech or of the press; or the right of the people peaceably to assemble; and to petition the Government for a redress of grievance."

The prohibition against establishing a religion (establishment clause) and the guarantee of religious freedom (free exercise clause) have come into conflict in college housing. Students have asked to take advantage of common use space in residence halls to conduct religious services. Institutional officials, recognizing that to allow the celebration of religious services in a state facility would give the appearance of state sponsorship, have denied these requests. Students, on the other hand, have argued that to deny them the opportunity would amount to prohibiting their free exercise of religion. The Supreme Court viewed the use of the facility as an "incidental" benefit that would not violate the establishment clause. Rather than seeing it as an issue of separation of church and state, the Court viewed the situation as one of freedom of speech in which the college had allowed others to use the facility but denied its use to those whose speech was religious in nature. Therefore, the denial constituted a violation of the free speech clause of the First Amendment (*Widmar* v. *Vincent*, 1981; also see *Keegan* v. *University of Delaware*, 1975).

Students have also unsuccessfully attempted to use the free exercise clause to justify going door to door in the residence halls to propagate the Christian faith. The Fourth Circuit Court of Appeals has upheld a university rule denying a religious group permission to do door-to-door soliciting in the halls. The regulation prohibiting such solicitation was upheld as a reasonable time, place, and manner restriction and found not to violate either the free exercise clause or the free speech clause of the First Amendment. The Court held that the university had a legitimate interest in protecting residential students from door-to-door solicitation (*Chapman* v. *Thomas*, 1984).

The Supreme Court has created a test that may be used to determine whether the concept of separation of church and state would be violated. The test is known as the *three-pronged test*, beause it asks three questions: (1) Does the rule have a sectarian purpose? (2) Is the primary effect of the rule the advancement of religion? (3) Will the rule cause an excessive entanglement between church and state? (*Lemon* v. *Kurtzman*, 1971). A rule or decision must answer no to each question in order not to violate the concept of separation of church and state. This test was used by the Delaware Supreme Court in overturning a University of Delaware prohibition against a student group celebrating Catholic mass in a residence hall common area (*Keegan* v. *University of Delaware*, 1975).

The guarantees of freedom of speech and press contained in the First Amendment are nowhere more sacred than on college and university campuses. The courts refer to institutions of higher education as "the free marketplace of ideas." The guarantees of free speech and press, however, are not absolute. One cannot yell fire in a crowded theater simply as an expression of free speech, nor can one incite people to imminent lawless action with the protection of the First Amendment (*Siegel* v. *Regents of the University of*

California, 1970). Furthermore, speech that creates a "clear and present danger" is not protected by the First Amendment (*Schenck* v. *United States*, 1919). This "clear and present danger" rule, however, is strictly construed, and officials attempting to regulate speech under this doctrine bear a heavy burden of showing that a real danger exists. The mere fear or speculation that danger will ensue is not enough (*Tinker* v. *Des Moines*, 1969, and *University of Utah Students Against Apartheid* v. *Peterson*, 1986). But the same "clear and present danger" exception also applies to symbolic speech. Not all forms of symbolic speech are protected. Indiana University prohibits firearms in the residence halls, and an ex-Marine employed as a resident assistant (RA) was told by his supervisor to remove a weapon from his room. The RA claimed that the rifle, along with other memorabilia, was a symbolic political statement about the Vietnam War, and he wrote a somewhat testy letter to the supervisor. He subsequently checked the rifle into the housing office, later removing it and taking it off campus. He was not rehired for the following year based on his behavior toward his supervisor, his belligerent attitude, and his poor understanding of the role of an RA. The court upheld the non-renewal, although it noted that if the university had terminated the RA based on his political views, it would have violated the First Amendment. The court pointed out that displaying an automatic rifle in the room of an RA who "is charged with offering advice and counsel to students, some of whom doubt-less are anxious, agitated, homesick, depressed or otherwise disturbed, does not strike us as conducive to the maintenance of a tranquil academic atmosphere" (*Shelton* v. *Trustees of Indiana University*, 1989, at p. 167).

Housing administrators will encounter the exercise of pure speech as well as symbolic speech. In recent years, administrators have been confronted with the question of what to do about what is referred to as "hate speech," or expressions that demean others. Obviously, students who place signs in their windows when housing regulations prohibit such displays of any type or who deface property may be disciplined for violating regulations. However, the Supreme Court has said very clearly that the speech itself may not be curtailed simply because it offends "conventions of decency" (*Papish* v. *Board of Curators of University of Missouri*, 1973). Several institutions have attempted to regulate hate speech, only to have the courts hold the regulations to be in violation of the First Amendment right of free expression (*Doe* v. *University of Michigan*, 1989; *UWM Post* v. *Board of Regents of University of Wisconsin*, 1991). The expression of racist attitudes has also been upheld as a protected right. In *Joyner* v. *Whiting* (1973), the Fourth Circuit Court of Appeals affirmed the right of the editor of a student newspaper at a publicly funded, predominantly black college to espouse segregationist views opposing the admission of white students to the college. Another federal court has upheld the right of a fraternity to depict in an "ugly woman" contest a black woman with large breasts and hips (*Iota Xi Chapter of Sigma Chi Fraternity* v. *George Mason University*, 1991). The courts simply will not permit the censorship of speech—either pure or symbolic—based on its content, no matter how offensive that content.

The Supreme Court has, however, stated that "fighting words" are not protected by the First Amendment (*Chaplinski* v. *New Hampshire*, 1942). While "fighting words" may constitute a basis for disciplining students, the standard is difficult to meet. The words must be directed at an individual and must incite a breach of the peace. A breach of the peace has been interpreted to mean inciting the hearer of the words to a violent response. Insensitive speech or posters on bulletin boards that express racist, misogynist, homophobic, or other demeaning opinions not directed at a specific individual simply do not qualify as "fighting words." The Supreme Court has recently struck down a city ordinance that prohibited individuals from placing symbols, graffiti, or other objects that would "arouse anger, alarm or resentment in others on the basis of race, color, creed, religion or gender" on public or private property (*Welfare of R.A.V.*, 1991). The city attempted to characterize the ordinance as regulating "fighting words," a regulation permissible under the First Amendment. The court did not hold the ordinance to be a prohibition against "fighting words" and found the law to be a violation of the First Amendment, because it prohibited speech solely on the basis of the subject of that speech. The court also rejected the argument that the city's ordinance was justified by a compelling interest in ensuring basic human rights to groups that historically have been discriminated against. Housing administrators would do well to be informed by the court's statement that while burning a cross in someone's yard is reprehensible, the city had many other options to punish the *behavior* without treading on the First Amendment.

The First Amendment affords less protection to commercial speech than it does to pure speech, and residence halls are generally not considered to be public forums. Thus, colleges and universities may prohibit commercial solicitation in the common areas of the residence halls (*International Society for Krishna Consciousness, Inc.* v. *New Jersey Sports and Exposition Authority*, 1982; *American Future Systems* v. *Pennsylvania State University*, 1985). In addition, regulations narrowly tailored at Pennsylvania State University that prohibited commercial group sales demonstrations in individual student rooms have been upheld by the Third Circuit Court of Appeals. The Supreme Court has denied a request for a review, thus allowing the Third Circuit decision to stand (*Johnson* v. *Pennsylvania State University*, 1985).

Residence halls, with their high density of students, draw not only commercial vendors, but also those seeking to spread their political and religious beliefs. The courts have long recognized that residence hall living spaces are not public forums and that universities have a strong interest in preserving an educational environment conducive to study in these areas. Institutional prohibitions narrowly drawn and content neutral that ban door-to-door solicitation, even the solicitation of votes or propagating religious beliefs, have been upheld by the courts as reasonable (*National Movement for Student Vote* v. *Regents of University of California*, 1975; *Harrell* v. *Southern Illinois University*, 1983; *Chapman* v. *Thomas*, 1984).

Reasonable time, place, and manner restrictions may also be imposed on protected speech and activity. As stated above, residence halls are not public forums, nor are the hallways akin to public streets, where one might go door to door soliciting (*Harrell* v. *Southern Illinois University*, 1983). Time, place, and manner restrictions should, however, offer a reasonable alternative. An example of a reasonable restriction on speech and activity might include prohibiting the use of amplifying equipment (bullhorns) in or near residence halls. It might also be considered reasonable, on esthetic ground, to prohibit the placing of signs in residence hall windows; however, signs should not be prohibited simply based on the content or message.

Some residence hall programs include the publication of student newsletters or newspapers. Housing staff should differentiate between "in-house" staff publications and student publications. Student publications enjoy the protections of the First Amendment and "the mere dissemination of ideas—no matter how offensive to good taste—on a state university campus may not be shut off in the name alone of 'conventions of decency'" (*Papish* v. *Board of Curators of University of Missouri*, 1973, at p. 1199).

Finally, the First Amendment protects the right of students to peaceably assemble. As stated above, reasonable time, place, and manner restrictions may be applied to the exercise of this right. For example, in order to maintain a quiet atmosphere, college officials may prohibit students from gathering in the hallways after midnight. The right to assemble also has been interpreted to include the right to associate freely. Thus, where residence hall programming encourages internal student organizations, recognition may not be denied to a group simply because the staff does not like or agree with the group's purpose or goals (*Healy* v. *James*, 1972). The right to associate freely also includes the corollary that one may not be compelled to associate. Residence hall governing units sometimes make the unlawful assumption that each resident is a member of the Residence Hall Association. The Supreme Court of Washington has stated that "the university may not compel membership in an association . . . which purports to represent all the students at the University" (*Good* v. *Associated Students*, 1975, at p. 768).

The best advice in dealing with First Amendment rights is to be content neutral. Most First Amendment violations occur because someone finds the content of a speech, written text, purpose of an organization, or advocacy of a group demonstration to be offensive. While the ideas expressed or advocated may be offensive or lacking in taste or sensitivity, they may not be denied their expression. Justice Hugo Black said: "I do not believe that it can be too often repeated that the freedoms of speech, press, petition and assembly guaranteed by the First Amendment must be accorded to the ideas we hate or sooner or later they will be denied to the ideas we cherish" (*Communist Party of U.S.* v. *Sub. Act. Cont. Bd.*, 1961, at p. 1431).

Fourth Amendment

The Fourth Amendment is particularly important to college housing staff. The amendment states: "The right of the people to be secure in their persons, houses, papers and effects, against unreasonable searches and seizures, shall not be violated and no warrant shall issue, but upon probable cause, supported by oath or affirmation and particularly describing the place to be searched and the person or thing to be seized."

The amendment only prohibits "unreasonable" searches and seizures. Thus, a reasonable search and seizure would not violate the amendment. The question is, what constitutes a reasonable search? Clearly, when one consents to a search it is reasonable (*State* v. *Wingerd*, 1974). When a legitimate emergency exists, an immediate search without a warrant also would be considered reasonable. For example, if a person were to see smoke emanating from beneath a door of a student's room, he or she would have a legitimate safety emergency and could enter the room to determine the source of the smoke. Once staff members are lawfully in the room (either with the resident's consent, because of an emergency, or during a legitimate health and safety inspection) and they see contraband in "plain view," they may seize it without violating the Fourth Amendment. The seizure of contraband in "plain view" is considered a reasonable seizure (*People* v. *Lanthier*, 1971; *State* v. *Kappes*, 1976).

Federal courts disagree over whether a warrantless search by institutional officials constitutes a reasonable search permitted by the Fourth Amendment. In *Moore* v. *Troy State University* (1968), a U.S. District Court held that the search by a dean, who had reasonable cause to believe students had drugs in their room, was reasonable and students could be discipined based on the evidence seized. A year later, two students at the same institution were arrested and convicted when police made a warrantless search of their room and seized illegal drugs. The Fifth Circuit Court of Appeals, however, overturned the conviction. The police argued that the dean, who had a right to conduct a warrantless search based on "reasonable cause to believe," had delegated to them the right to search using this lower standard and that they therefore were not required to obtain a warrant. The court, however, differentiated between a college official conducting a warrantless search to maintain good order and discipline and a police search to obtain criminal evidence. The latter requires a warrant. The court said:

> We must conclude that a student who occupies a college dormitory room enjoys the protection of the Fourth Amendment. True, the University retains broad supervisory powers which permit it to adopt the regulation heretofore quoted, provided that regulation is reasonably construed [the regulation permitting a warrantless search by institutional officials who had "reasonable cause to believe" there was contraband in a room] and is limited in its application to further the University's function as an educational institution. The regulation cannot be construed or applied so as to give consent to a search for evidence for the primary purpose of a criminal prosecution. Otherwise the regulation itself would constitute an unconstitutional attempt to require a student to waive his protection from unreasonable

searches and seizures as a condition to his occupancy of a college dormitory room. [*Pizzola* v. *Watkins*, 1971, at p. 289]

Several courts have upheld warrantless searches by institutional officials who had "reasonable cause to believe" contraband was in a student's room and conducted a search to maintain good order and discipline (*United States* v. *Coles*, 1969; *Keene* v. *Rodgers*, 1970; *Ekelund* v. *Secretary of Commerce*, 1976). One court, however, has rejected this standard, established in *Moore* v. *Troy State University* (1968), and has stated that college officials must obtain a warrant prior to searching a student's room (*Smythe and Smith* v. *Lubbers*, 1975).

The Supreme Court will ultimately need to decide the issue of warrantless searches by college officials. The greater weight of judicial precedent, however, comes down on the side of permitting institutional officials to conduct a warrantless search if they have "reasonable cause to believe" there is activity taking place in the room or there is contraband in the room that contravenes the educational mission of the institution. Housing staff should review their search-and-seizure policy with institutional counsel to determine if it meets the standards established by judicial precedent in their area and to determine if it conforms to state requirements, which may be higher than those imposed by the federal Constitution (*Washington* v. *Chrisman*, 1982).

If police enter a residence hall to obtain criminal evidence (this includes campus police officers who are deputized state officers), they should have a warrant. As stated earlier, the lower "reasonable cause" standard applied to entry by college officials may not be delegated to police, who must show "probable cause" to obtain a warrant. In some jurisdictions, police are required to knock and give notice of their identity and purpose before they enter occupied premises to execute a search warrant (*Commonwealth* v. *McCloskey*, 1970). The Fourth Amendment also states that the warrant must describe the particular place to be searched. Where two or more rooms are joined by a common bathroom or study space, police who have a warrant to search one room may not search an adjoining space unless it is specified in the warrant (*City of Athens* v. *Wolf*, 1974).

Fourteenth Amendment

The Fourteenth Amendment contains two clauses of particular interest to housing staff. The due process clause requirements for college discipline were first set forth in *Dixon* v. *Alabama State Board of Education* (1961). Since *Dixon*, many cases refining the requirements of campus due process have been decided. Although there are some basic requirements, the parameters of due process are flexible. The process that is due depends on the nature of the right that one seeks to take away. The greater the right to be taken away, the more process is due. This is why most states have an automatic appeal process for persons condemned to death. Thus, where an official residence hall reprimand or warning is the maximum penalty to be imposed for all infractions, due process does not need to be as formal or exacting as where a violation might result in suspension from the hall or from the institution.

The *Dixon* case and the *General Order on Judicial Standards of Procedure and Substance in Review of Student Discipline in Tax Supported Institutions of Higher Education* (1968) both set forth basic principles administrators should follow in their disciplinary processes. Basically, students should receive a written notice of the charges against them, they must be given an opportunity to defend themselves against the charges, and any decision must be supported by the evidence. Courts consistently have held that student disciplinary proceedings are not criminal in nature and therefore need not conform to the standards of criminal jurisprudence. The *General Order* (1968) also sets forth what the court considers to be the lawful missions of higher education.

While procedures may vary with the nature of the infraction and the potential sanction, students should generally be informed in writing of the charges against them (*Esteban* v. *Central Missouri State College*, 1967). Putting the charges in writing requires that the staff be specific and give some thought to the charges. It also eliminates any future questions about what the student was actually charged with. The charges should be stated specifically enough to allow the student to prepare a defense against them. A charge of "misconduct" or "unwholesome conduct" is simply too vague (*Soglin* v. *Kaufman*, 1969; *Shamloo* v. *Mississippi State Board of Trustees*, 1980). The notice should also state the time, date, and place of the hearing (*Dixon* v. *Alabama*, 1961). The student should receive the notice in enough time prior to the hearing to permit the preparation of an adequate defense. Thus, the length of time can vary depending on the seriousness of the charge and the possible consequences. Finally, the notice should also include the nature of the evidence against the student (*Dixon* v. *Alabama*, 1961).

The hearing should provide an opportunity for both sides to present oral, written, or physical evidence to an objective person or panel. There is no requirement that there be more than one person to conduct the hearing. A hall director may conduct hearings. The only requirement is that the individual conducting the hearing be impartial (*Dixon* v. *Alabama*, 1961). Students do not have a right to be represented by counsel. However, to ensure fundamental fairness, where the institution is represented by counsel, students must be permitted to be represented by counsel (*French* v. *Bashful*, 1969). Furthermore, if a student is facing criminal charges stemming from the same offense, the student should be permitted to have counsel present for advice (*Gabrilowitz* v. *Newman*, 1978). Being advised by counsel does not mean that counsel represents the student, nor does it mean that counsel may address the hearing board. Finally, there is no absolute right to confront and cross-examine witnesses. Even in potential suspension situations, only where the case turns on questions of a witness's credibility might cross-examination be required (*Blanton* v. *State University of New York*, 1973).

When students are also charged with criminal violations and must appear in local court, the institution need not delay its own hearing until the criminal charges are resolved (*Nzuve* v. *Castleton State College*, 1975). There is also no double jeopardy involved in charging the student with a housing violation and proceeding with a disciplinary hearing where the student is also charged with a criminal violation by local officials arising from the same incident (*Hart* v. *Ferris State College*, 1983).

Certain offenses in housing do not lend themselves to the time-consuming procedures of due process outlined above. When a student is, for example, setting fires in the residence hall, responsible housing professionals would want to remove that student from the halls as quickly as possible. Generally, where students constitute a threat to the health, safety, or welfare of themselves or others, they may be suspended from the halls or from the institution on an interim basis pending a subsequent hearing, at which time they may present a defense as to why the suspensions should not continue (*Gardenhire* v. *Chalmers*, 1971; *Wallace* v. *Florida A&M University*, 1983).

Housing administrators, especially RAs and hall directors, inevitably come into contact with disruptive students—those students who require a great deal of staff time and concern, but who do not necessarily violate specific hall regulations. Students who constantly threaten suicide as well as those who suffer from depression or other mental disorders fall into this category. The question of how to respond to such students is one that housing administrators constantly face. While the immediate reaction is to initiate some sort of "psychiatric withdrawal" or "medical withdrawal," Pavela (1985) points out that such an approach, with its general lack of due process, would violate not only the Fourteenth Amendment but also the requirements of Section 504 of the Rehabilitation Act of 1973. This does not mean there are no alternatives. Where the behavior of the student violates hall regulations or disrupts the educational environment, disciplinary action may be taken in accordance with established procedures conforming to the due process requirements outlined above. Also, where students threaten harm to themselves or identifiable others, administrators may require a psychiatric evaluation of the student (Gehring, 1983). The college then becomes the client, and the results of the evaluation are provided to the institution. A hearing may be held to determine if the student is fit to continue, but the hearing should provide the student an opportunity to refute the findings. It is important to remember, too, that we each have the right to be "different."

The equal protection clause of the Fourteenth Amendment is also of particular concern to housing staff. This clause requires that persons who are similarly situated be treated alike. Thus, it would not be a violation of the Fourteenth Amendment to charge a kitchen use fee to those who live in a residence hall but do not participate in a board plan while not charging the same fee to those who do participate in such a plan (*Schare* v. *State University of New York at Stony Brook*, 1977).

The courts use two tests to determine if there has been an equal protection violation. The first is known as the *strict scrutiny* test and is applied where a suspect class (one based on race, national origin, or alienage) is created by the rule or regulation or where the rule will deprive someone of a fundamental right (voting, interstate travel, marriage, procreation, and equal treatment in criminal prosecutions regardless of wealth or property ownership status). Courts have specifically held that the pursuit of an education (*Mauclet* v. *Nyquist*, 1976) and living in college housing (*Bynes* v. *Toll*, 1975) are not fundamental rights. The strict scrutiny test requires that a "compelling state interest" be served by a classification that creates a suspect class or deprives someone of a fundamental right.

The second touchstone, known as the *rational relationship* test, is a much lower standard and is applied when neither a suspect class nor a fundamental right is involved. This test simply asks if there is a "rational relationship" between the legitimate interests of the state and the classifications established. This test has served as the basis for determining whether a required on-campus residency regulation violated the Fourteenth Amendment. In *Mollere* v. *Southeastern Louisiana College* (1969), the institution required all women but only freshmen men to live on campus. The court found no legitimate state interest in such a classification. The following year, students unsuccessfully challenged Louisiana Polytechnic Institute's rule requiring all undergraduate students to live on campus (certain exceptions were made for veterans, medical or financial handicaps, and space limitations). The institute based its requirement on the educational benefits to be derived from group living. The court, in upholding the rule, said: "If sound educational policies, as are shown here, dictate that the educational mission of the State is best carried out by providing for the great majority of student citizens of each State adequate housing and eating facilities at a cost which can be afforded by all students seeking entrance into a particular university, then we do not think it our place to decree otherwise" (*Pratz* v. *Louisiana Polytechnic Institute*, 1970, at p. 885).

A series of cases following *Pratz* have upheld the university's right to require all students under a particular age (*Cooper* v. *Nix*, 1974; *Poynter* v. *Drevdahl*, 1972) and in a particular college class (*Prostrollo* v. *University of South Dakota*, 1974) to live on campus. However, the courts have not upheld such rules where the classification was based solely on gender (*Texas Woman's University* v. *Chayklintaste*, 1975).

Bynes v. *Toll* (1975) also provides a good illustration of the application of the equal protection clause in a housing situation. In this case, the university had a residence hall for single students that it converted to married housing. Although there were no kitchen facilities in the hall, the university did allow married couples who lived there to cook on hot plates. This resulted in approximately fifty-two fires in an eighteen-month period. There were also major construction projects near the hall and traffic problems in the immediate vicinity. The university decided to limit housing in the building to married couples without children, and several students brought suit. The court found no suspect category created nor any fundamental right denied (housing is not a fundamental right) and therefore applied the rational relationship test. In upholding the university's regulation, the court said: "With a campus which has parking problems, no traffic lights and heavy construction in progress (one student fell to his death through an uncovered manhole), it is rational for the University, which will be legally responsible for its negligence, to postpone the residence of children until such time, if ever, that it can provide the housing it (and not the parents) deem adequate" (*Bynes* v. *Toll*, 1975, at p. 258).

Contracts

Contracts create the second major relationship between students and their institutions. Courts generally accept the relationship between students and their institutions to be contractual in nature. The terms and conditions of the contract are set forth in the college catalog and other institutional documents (*Basch* v. *George Washington University*, 1977). Unlike the rights derived from the Constitution, which generally only apply to the relationship between students and public institutions, the rights derived from a contractual relationship apply equally to both public and private institutions. Contracts, both expressed and implied, are at the very heart of the housing operation. Each state may follow different interpretations of contractual law, and a detailed discussion of these interpretations exceeds the scope of this chapter. However, there are several general principles with which the housing staff should be familiar. Knowledge of these principles, while no substitute for legal counsel, can be of help in managing the risks associated with actions that may create a potential breach of contract, either by the staff or by students.

A contract is "a promise or set of promises for the breach of which the law gives a remedy or the performance of which the law in some way recognizes a duty" (American Law Institute, 1981, p. 5). This definition makes it clear that a contract involves a promise or a set of promises. But what is a promise, and how does one know when a promise is made and accepted?

There are generally two types of contracts recognized by the law—unilateral and bilateral. A unilateral contract is one in which one party makes a promise to the public rather than to a particular individual. More common, however, is a bilateral contract, in which two parties of equal stature each promise to do something. There are several elements that must be present in order to have a valid bilateral contract. Having two parties of equal stature generally would not include bargaining with a minor. Although many states recognize a minor's right to contract for necessities, including housing, not all states do so, and where students are less than eighteen years of age, housing staff would be well advised to require parents to sign the housing agreement (Miller, 1983). The first requirement for a valid bilateral contract is an offer. This is essentially a promise that sets forth what is offered and under what conditions. Once an offer is made, there must be acceptance in terms of the offer. Of course, there could also be a rejection or a counteroffer. There also must be a meeting of the minds in which both parties have the same understanding of the specifics of both promises. Finally, there must be consideration in which each party has a benefit and a detriment. The Supreme Court of Illinois has held that the acceptance of an application fee by a university constituted a contractual obligation on the part of the institution to fulfill its promises to evaluate an applicant on the criteria advertised. The court said: "Here the description in the brochure containing the terms under which an application will be appraised constituted an invitation for an offer. The tender of the application, as well as payment of the fee pursuant to the terms of the brochure, was an offer to apply. Acceptance of the application and fee constituted acceptance of an offer to apply under the criteria the defendant had established. . . . The application fee was sufficient consideration to support the agreement between the applicant and the school" (*Steinberg* v. *Chicago Medical School*, 1977, at p. 639).

Simmons v. *Sowela Technical Institute* (1985) illustrates a situation where the court held that the elements of a bilateral contract did not exist. A nursing student at Sowela Technical Institute was suspended for unethical conduct and sued for breach of contract. Students at Sowela pay for their uniforms, books, and supplies but pay no tuition. The court found no contract to exist, since the student paid no fees and was free to leave at any time — there simply was no reciprocity of obligation.

Housing contracts are generally contracts of adhesion because they are very one sided, with the student expected to "take it or leave it." These types of contracts are scrutinized very carefully by the courts. Thus, it would be beneficial to be sure that the terms and conditions of the contract are very specific. The rules and regulations governing conduct in the halls need not be a part of the contract itself but should be incorporated in the agreement by reference. Students who violate the rules have therefore breached the contract, which can serve as a basis for terminating housing (*Miller* v. *Long Island University*, 1976). The institution, however, would be well served by specifying in the contract that a breach of the contract, in terms of a violation of the rules, constitutes grounds for terminating the contract.

A minor breach of a contract either by the housing office or the student is usually not grounds to terminate the contract. However, where a major breach occurs, the contract may be terminated and the contract no longer exists. Damages may also be assessed against the party causing the breach. Minor breaches are those that deny some service for a short period of time, such as a loss of air-conditioning while the unit is being repaired. A major breach might involve a student failing to pay the rent on time or the university failing to provide promised air-conditioning service for a longer period, making the space uninhabitable.

Contracts may also be implied. Many states recognize, either through specific statute or common law, an implied warranty of habitability. Generally, this means that the landlord guarantees that the property is habitable or livable. If it is not, because of the infestation of pests or filthy showers (*Winans* v. *Stimpson*, 1981), the tenants may withhold their rent under conditions that vary from state to state (see *Pugh* v. *Holmes*, 1979, for a good discussion of implied warranty of habitability and a listing of states that have such laws) or seek damages.

Although it is preferable to specify the terms and conditions of a contract in writing, the elements of a contract do not include the necessity for a written document. Oral statements can also constitute a contract, and staff must be careful what they promise. Officers at the U.S. Merchant Marine Academy promised the students that they could speak freely during a drug investigation, since nothing they said would be used against them. However, when the students admitted using drugs, they were disciplined. The court held that a promise was made, the offer was accepted, and consideration was present to constitute a binding contract. Thus, the statements made by the students could not be used against them (*Krawez* v. *Stans*, 1969). The best advice for housing staff in terms of contracts would be to "deliver everything you promise and don't promise anything you can't deliver" (Miller, 1979).

Statutes

Federal and state statutes constitute the third relationship defining the rights and responsibilities of students and their institutions. There are a variety of state laws affecting college housing, and housing staff should become familiar with them as part of their staff development. Specifically, alcoholic beverage laws, including social host liability, hazing laws, and state statutes defining the conditions under which an implied warranty of habitability would be breached would seem imperative to understand. Staff members should also be familiar with the application of state landlord-tenant laws to college housing (*Houle* v. *Adams State College*, 1976; *Cook* v. *University Plaza*, 1981).

State statutes pertaining to alcohol are particularly important, since a violation of these laws can result not only in criminal liability but also in civil liability (Gehring and Geraci, 1989). The law is also moving rapidly in the area of third-party liability such as dramshop and social host liability. These two types of third-party liability differ only in who can be held accountable for the injury to an innocent third person. In dramshop liability, generally a person must be a licensed vendor who serves alcohol to a minor or possibly an intoxicated adult, who then injures an innocent third party. Most states now have statutes or common law holding the vendor liable for the third party's injuries. The same situation arises when a nonlicensed person—a social host—serves a minor (usually not an intoxicated adult, but state laws vary). The social host could be liable for the third party's injuries in such a situation. Although a minority of states have social host liability, there is a trend toward holding hosts liable for third-party injuries (Gehring, 1992).

Many states have also enacted antihazing laws, which, like alcoholic beverage laws, can be used as a basis for civil as well as criminal liability. A violation of the statute could constitute negligence per se. Most of the states that have enacted antihazing statutes include an affirmative obligation to take action to prevent hazing. Even where a statute does not exist, the courts may find a duty (*Furek* v. *University of Delaware*, 1991).

There are several federal antidiscrimination statutes that directly affect college housing operations. These statutes apply to any institution that receives federal financial assistance (FFA). Even where the financial assistance flows directly to students, the statutes are applicable to the institution (*Grove City College* v. *Bell*, 1984). Furthermore, Congress declared in the Civil Rights Restoration Act of 1987 (P.L. 100-259) that if an institution received any federal aid, all programs operated by the institution were covered by the statutes. Several of these statutes, what they prohibit, and the source of their regulations are listed in Table 14.1. The regulations issued pursuant to the law have the force and effect of law. These regulations should be read by housing staff members to fully understand their prohibitions and procedures, since they constitute the essence of the statute itself. The regulations issued to enforce the law often create higher standards than those established by the Constitution. In *Robinson* v. *Eastern Kentucky University* (1973), the court upheld a housing curfew for women under the rational relationship test of the Fourteenth Amendment. Today, while not violating the Constitution, such a regulation would be in violation of Title IX.

Title IX regulations have a specific section (86.32) related to college housing operations. These regulations state that generally a recipient of federal financial assistance "shall not, on the basis of sex, apply different rules or regulations, impose different fees or requirements, or offer different services or benefits related to housing, except as provided in this section

Table 14.1. Federal Antidiscrimination Statutes Affecting College Housing.

Statute	*Prohibition*	*Regulations may be found at*
Title VI of the Civil Rights Act of 1964 (42 U.S.C. 2000d)	Discrimination on the basis of race, color, national origin in any educational program or activity receiving FFA	34 C.F.R. 100
Title IX of the Education Amendments of 1972 (20 U.S.C. 1681)	Discrimination on the basis of sex in educational programs or activities receiving FFA	34 C.F.R. 106
Section 504 of the Rehabilitation Act of 1973 (29 U.S.C. 794)	Discrimination against "otherwise qualified" handicapped persons in educational programs or activities receiving FFA	34 C.F.R. 104
Americans with Disabilities Act of 1990 (42 U.S.C. 12101)	Discrimination against qualified individuals with a disability in employment, public accommodations, and services	

(including housing provided only to married students)" (86.32(a)). The regulations cover not only on-campus housing but also off-campus housing where the institution provides assistance to students in finding accommodations through solicitation, listings, or approval of off-campus housing (86.32(c)(2)).

Otherwise qualified handicapped persons under Section 504 are those who are qualified in spite of their disability (*Doe* v. *New York University*, 1981). Such individuals must have access to all programs and activities. The regulations define a handicap as "a physical or mental impairment that substantially limits one or more major life activities" (84.3(j)). Persons who have, have had, or are regarded as having a handicap are protected under the law. Persons with contagious diseases are also considered to be handicapped (*School Board of Nassau County, Florida* v. *Arline*, 1987). The Section 504 regulations contain housing-specific requirements much like those cited above for Title IX, including requirements for off-campus housing. New-building construction and renovations must be designed to be readily accessible and usable by handicapped persons (84.32).

Section 504 requires that housing "shall be available in sufficient quantity and variety so that the scope of handicapped students' choice of living accommodations is, as a whole, comparable to that of non-handicapped students" 84.45(a)). A wheelchair-bound graduate student at New York University brought suit under this section of the regulations when he was charged double rent to live in a double room by himself. The student had requested this arrangement in undergraduate housing rather than applying for graduate housing space. The court held that the university did not violate Section 504 because the student failed to show that there was inadequate graduate housing available (*Fleming* v. *New York University*, 1989).

The Americans with Disabilities Act of 1990 is also important for housing administrators, because it expands the rights granted under Section 504 in the area of "public accommodations." Both public and private colleges and universities are considered to be "public accommodations" (42 U.S.C. 12181(7)(j)). Generally, this law prohibits discrimination on the basis of disability "in the full and equal enjoyment of goods, services, facilities, privileges, advantages of accommodations of any place of public accommodation" (42 U.S.C. 12182(a)). The law also requires that the goods, services, and accommodations be provided in "the most integrative setting appropriate to the needs of the individual" (42 U.S.C. 12182(b)(B)). Discrimination in public accommodations includes a failure to remove architectural or communication barriers unless the removal is not "readily achievable." The law has four basic criteria to be evaluated to determine if removal of the barriers is "readily achievable." These criteria include (1) the cost, (2) the financial resources available to the facility, (3) the financial resources available to the covered entity, and (4) the type of operation.

The Family Educational Rights and Privacy Act (known as the Buckley Amendment, 20 U.S.C. 1232(g)) is not an antidiscrimination statute, but it is designed to provide students access to their educational records (with some exceptions) and to prohibit disclosure of those records to third parties without the students' consent (with some exceptions). The regulations implementing the statute can be found at 34 C.F.R. 99. Although the statute applies to educational records, and one would not think housing operations would be affected, nothing could be further from the truth. Educational records include those records that "(1) are directly related to the student; and (2) are maintained by an educational agency or institution or by a party acting for the agency or institution" (99.3). Thus, all housing records pertaining to students—including room assignment information, applications, roommate preference information, and disciplinary files—are covered by the law.

There are exceptions to both the access and disclosure requirements. Directory information, which may include hall assignment and phone number, may be disclosed without students' consent if students have been informed of what the institution considers "directory information" and have been given an opportunity to delete any or all of their information from the data banks of directory information (99.37). An exception to the access requirements of the law is provided for "private notes" such as an RA or hall director might keep on a student. To be exempt, these notes must not be shared with anyone else (not even a secretary) except a short-term substitute (99.33 Education Records(b)(1)). There are many other exceptions to both the disclosure prohibition and the access requirement, and staff members should become familiar with the regulations to understand the requirements for exercising these exceptions.

Two recent pieces of legislation also affect housing operations. The Drug Free Schools and Communities Act of 1989 (with regulations at 34 C.F.R. 86) requires institutions to distribute the following to each student and employee: (1) standards of conduct that prohibit unlawful possession, use, and distribution of illicit drugs and alcohol; (2) a description of applicable local, state, and federal laws for unlawful possession, use, or distribution of illicit drugs and alcohol; (3) a description of the health risks associated with the use of illicit drugs and alcohol; (4) a description of rehabilitation and treatment programs available; and (5) a statement that the institution *will* impose sanctions for violations of its standards. The law also requires a biennial review of the effectiveness of the program and to determine if sanctions for violations have been consistently enforced. Housing administrators will be directly involved in enforcing standards as required by this law. It thus becomes imperative that housing staff members understand their responsibilities under this law. Housing officials should be involved in the biennial review process, since housing is most often where violations occur.

The Student Right-to-Know and Campus Security Act (P.L. 101-542) requires, in general, that institutions maintain statistics on graduation rates and major crimes. Housing administrators need to stay abreast of this law since, at this time, the secretary of education has interpreted "campus security" to include hall directors, and the law requires hall directors to make timely reports to the campus community when major crimes are reported to them. Some aspects of this requirement and the law generally are troubling (Gehring, 1991a). Final regulations have not been published at this writing; therefore, administrators should stay alert for them.

The final federal statutes to be discussed are the Copyright Revision Act of 1976 and the copyright laws generally appearing in Title 17 of the United States Code. These laws are designed to provide federal protection to the authors of original literary, dramatic, artistic, musical, and other intellectual works. Even though there is a fair use exception to the law, it is very specific and should be closely examined before making copies under the exception (see Pavela, 1989). Of particular interest to housing staff are the parameters surrounding the showing of videotapes in the residence halls. The owner of a copyrighted work has the sole prerogative to grant permission to copy or to provide a public display, regardless of whether the work has been rented, purchased, or licensed. Most videos that are rented or sold are for "home use only," and public displays are not authorized. A public display is usually characterized as one that takes place in a space open to the public or any place where a substantial number of people gather who are other than the normal family circle and its acquaintances. Thus, showing a rented video in a residence hall lobby where other students may come and go without restriction is probably a copyright violation. However, the court has upheld a hotel policy of checking out videodiscs to guests to view in their rooms. The court noted that while the hotel is open to the public, guest rooms are not. Thus, it appears that a residence hall could purchase a library of videos that could be checked out or rented to students to be viewed in their individual rooms (*Columbia Pictures* v. *Professional Real Estate Investors, Inc.*, 1989).

Torts

Probably the most important legal relationship existing between students and their institutions is defined by the concept of torts. The importance of this relationship stems from the potential financial liability for breaching the relationship. The law expects one to act as a reasonably prudent person and not to interfere with another person's property or reputation. The word *tort* comes from a Latin word meaning "twisted." Specifically, a tort is a civil wrong (as opposed to a criminal wrong)—other than the breach of a contract—for which the courts will provide a remedy (usually in the form of money damages). Thus, a tort is failing to act as a reasonable person and interfering with another's person, property, or reputation. There are many kinds of torts, but this discussion will be limited to negligence, since negligence is more likely than other types of torts to occur in the operation of college and university residence halls. Negligence is generally defined as failing to act with due care. Negligence does not require an intent to do harm but only an awareness of a risk or danger. In order to be found negligent, there must first be a duty to conform to a certain standard of care. If there is a duty and one fails to meet that duty, either by doing or failing to do something, then there is negligence. Not all negligence, however, results in liability. To be actionable, there must be an injury that is proximately caused by the failure to meet one's duty. Thus, the four elements that must all be present for liability to occur are (1) duty, (2) breach of duty, (3) injury, and (4) a close causal relationship between the breach of the duty and the injury.

Several duties are recognized by the courts through our common law. Housing staff members would be expected to provide proper instruction and proper supervision, maintain equipment in a reasonable state of repair, provide a reasonably safe environment, and warn or protect students against the criminal acts of third persons. Generally, "the risk reasonably to be perceived defines the duty to be obeyed" (*Palsgraf* v. *Long Island Rail Road Co.*, 1928, at p. 100). The "risk reasonably to be perceived" is also known as *foreseeability* and is a key concept.

The breach of one's duty need not be intentional and may be caused either by doing or failing to do something. In *Miller* v. *State* (1984), the failure to lock the exterior doors of a residence hall was held to be the proximate cause of a rape. The court held the university negligent since the operation of housing is a proprietary function and, where criminal activity was reasonably foreseeable, the university, as landlord, had a duty to provide a safe environment by taking the minimal requirement of locking the exterior doors. One may also do something that creates a risk of harm to another. In a married housing unit, the middle (screen) panel of a door had been replaced several times by maintenance personnel because the children living in the unit pushed on the panel to open the door. When maintenance was called again to repair the panel, they switched it with the upper glass panel. Shortly thereafter, in pushing the door again, a child put his hand through the glass and suffered severe injuries. In holding the university negligent, the court said the university had a duty to maintain its equipment, it was reasonably foreseeable that the children would not alter their habits, and the act of switching the screen with the glass panel created a foreseeable risk of injury (*Bolkhir* v. *North Carolina State University*, 1988).

Not only must buildings be maintained in a reasonable state of repair, but they must be inspected periodically to uncover defects. Ohio University was found to be negligent when a student was cut severely in attempting to open her room window, which was stuck shut. An inspection of the building had not been carried out in ten years. The court said: "Under these circumstances, it was reasonable for the trier of facts to infer that defendant [university] was negligent with respect to inspection and that a reasonable inspection would have revealed a defective dangerous condition. . . . The . . . finding is not unreasonable merely because the university may be required to check every dormitory window by making periodic reasonable inspections" (*Sheltina* v. *Ohio University*, 1983, at p. 590). Documented, periodic inspections with follow-up maintenance requests are essential in avoiding negligence. In a case where a visitor to a residence hall fell in an unlighted stairwell, the

Supreme Court of Kansas in assessing negligence against the university noted that it not only had a duty to maintain its premises but also "to exercise reasonable care to carry out that duty" (*Burch* v. *University of Kansas*, 1988, at p. 437).

Proper instruction in the residence halls would include such things as explaining to residents how to leave the building in case of a fire, how to operate extinguishers, and what to do in case of various emergencies. Residence hall programs that involve outdoor activities might require additional instruction, such as how to adjust ski bindings, using the proper stroke in a canoe, and being aware of warning signs.

The duty to provide proper supervision depends on the age of the students and the nature of the activity. Generally, colleges are under no duty to control the conduct of a student, especially when the student is a legal adult (*Bradshaw* v. *Rawlings*, 1979). Even where an institution, by its regulations, controls the behavior of students to some extent, the institution will not be held liable for the criminal conduct of that student (*Smith* v. *Day*, 1987). However, where an RA is charged with a duty to maintain order on a hall and fails to respond when things get out of hand and someone is injured in the melee, the RA could be held negligent. When high school students are on campus for special programs and live in the residence halls, the duty to provide supervision is heightened. Since high school students are usually minors, the university assumes a custodial role. Montana State University operated a special program to bring talented high school students to campus for the summer. The students lived in the residence halls, had a curfew, and were prohibited from consuming alcohol. A sixteen-year-old participant was injured in a motorcycle accident after attending a party where she consumed alcoholic beverages allegedly in view of her RA. The court said if the RA "did in fact know of or see drinking by minor MAP participants at the party, that knowledge would render her duty immediate. Her failure to act would be a breach of that duty and could be negligence" (*Graham* v. *Montana State University*, 1988, at p. 304).

Administrators may be familiar with the *Tarasoff* v. *Regents of the University of California* (1976) decision, which held that there is a legal duty to protect if a special relationship exists such as that between a therapist or counselor and a client and there is a serious threat of harm to the client or another readily identifiable victim. This duty to protect or to warn has not been held to apply to paraprofessional staff (*Nally* v. *Grace Community Church of the Valley*, 1987). Residence life staff who "counsel" with students are not held to the same standards as professionally trained and licensed therapists. Housing staff should also be aware of the difference between confidentiality and privileged communication. Confidentiality is a duty that arises from professional codes of ethics; it has no real legal basis and is not enforced by the courts. Privileged communication, on the other hand, is created legally by statute or common law. Even the communication between licensed counselors and their clients is not privileged in every state. Privileged communication means that unless the client agrees (and the privilege belongs to the client), the communication may not be compelled in court. Keep in mind, however, that the courts compelled the disclosure of information alleged to be privileged for national security reasons by President Nixon!

The institution, as landlord, also has a duty to provide a reasonably safe environment (*Mullins* v. *Pine Manor College*, 1983; *Nieswand* v. *Cornell University*, 1988), and although the university need not guarantee students' safety, it is not an innocent bystander (*Klein* v. *1500 Massachusetts Avenue Apartment Corp.*, 1970). "Where . . . the landlord has notice of repeated criminal assaults and robberies, has notice that these crimes occurred in the portion of the premises exclusively within his control, has every reason to expect like crimes to happen again, and has the exclusive power to take preventative action, it does not seem unfair to place upon the landlord a duty to take those steps which are within his power to minimize the predictable risk to his tenants" (*Klein* v. *1500 Massachusetts Avenue Apartment Corp.*, 1970, at p. 481).

The *Klein* court also stated that the standard of care to be adhered to was the same standard that was employed when the resident moved into the complex. In other words, the same relative degree of security should be maintained. North Carolina Central University was found liable for the death of a student who was shot to death in the stairwell of his residence hall on a weekend when all of the security guards assigned to that building were on vacation. In finding the university negligent, it was noted that "there was neither an officer nor a guard on the premises of either the parking lot or the dormitory itself. This was directly contrary to the standards the university itself had established that there would be a minimum of four guards on duty" (*Bullock* v. *Board of Governors of the University of North Carolina*, 1989, at p. 23).

An audit of residence hall facilities and policies followed up with appropriate changes can assist in reducing the risks of liability (Tuttle, 1990). Audits and inspections of both the interior and exterior of buildings should be performed at night as well as in daylight. As part of an audit, one should review campuses' police reports and use the information to determine if there are "conditions which create a likelihood of criminal attacks" (*Lille* v. *Thompson*, 1947). Policies and services should also be reviewed to ensure that they are reasonable and do not invite crime.

Conclusion

This chapter has provided a broad outline of some of the legal parameters involved in the operation of college and university housing. The information provided is not intended as legal advice, but rather to assist housing staff in recognizing situations with potential legal liabilities. Where counsel can be contacted, an understanding of the parameters will assist staff in knowing the questions to ask and in being able to respond to counsel. The nature of housing operations and the four primary relationships defining the rights and responsibilities of students and their institutions — involving federal and state constitutions, contracts, federal and state statutes, and the concept of torts — precipitate many potential liabilities. However, housing staff need not be timid in pursuing the development of programs or policies. There is potential liability in many things we do, but we attempt to minimize that potential by acting reasonably in light of the circumstances and within the parameters established by constitutions, statutes, and contracts. Housing professionals have a responsibility to make educational decisions, and while the advice of counsel may be a necessary factor in many decisions, housing officials should not abdicate their responsibility by allowing counsel to make those choices.

References

American Law Institute. *Restatement of Contracts*. (2nd ed.) St. Paul, Minn.: American Law Institute, 1981.

Bickel, R. "The Role of College or University Legal Counsel." *Journal of Law and Education*, 1974, *3*(1), 73–80.

Gehring, D. "The Dismissal of Students with Serious Emotional Problems: An Administrative Decision Model." *NASPA Journal*, 1983, *20*(3), 9–14.

Gehring, D. "Abreast of the Law." *NASPA Forum*, Dec. 1991a, p. 10.

Gehring, D. "An Introduction to Legal Research." In T. K. Miller and R. B. Winston (eds.), *Administration and Leadership in Student Affairs: Actualizing Student Development in Higher Education*. Muncie, Ind.: Accelerated Development, 1991b.

Gehring, D. "Abreast of the Law." *NASPA Forum*, Feb. 1992, p. 6.

Gehring, D., and Geraci, C. *Alcohol on Campus: A Compendium of the Law and a Guide to Campus Policy*. Asheville, N.C.: College Administration Publications, 1989.

Miller, S. T. "Contract Law for College Housing Officers." ACUHO-I Legal Issues Institute. Training institute conducted at University of Vermont, Bennington, 1979.

Miller, S. T. "Contracts and Their Use in Housing." In D. Gehring (ed.), *Administering College and University Housing: A Legal Perspective*. Asheville, N.C.: College Administration Publications, 1983.

Pavela, G. *The Dismissal of Students with Mental Disorders: Legal Issues, Policy Considerations and Alternative Responses*. Asheville, N.C.: College Administration Publications, 1985.

Pavela, G. "Copyright and Fair Use." *Synthesis*, 1989, *1*(4).

Tuttle, D. "Campus Security: A Checklist for the Audit of Campus Security Programs [Summary]." *Proceedings of the 11th Annual Conference on Law and Higher Education*. Clearwater Beach, Fla.: Stetson University Law School, 1990.

Cases Cited

American Future Systems v. *Pennsylvania State University*, 752 F. 2d 854 (3rd Cir. 1985).

Basch v. *George Washington University*, 370 A. 2d 1364 (D.C. App. 1977).

Berrios v. *Inter American University*, 535 F. 2d 1220 (1st Cir. 1976).

Blackburn v. *Fisk University*, 443 F. 2d 121 (6th Cir. 1971).

Blanton v. *State University of New York*, 489 F. 2d 377 (2nd Cir. 1973).

Bolkhir v. *North Carolina State University*, 365 S.E. 2d 898 (N.C. 1988).

Bradshaw v. *Rawlings*, 612 F. 2d 135 (3rd Cir. 1979).

Browns v. *Mitchell*, 409 F. 2d 593 (10th Cir. 1969).

Bullock v. *Board of Governors of the University of North Carolina*, I.C. No. TA-10433 (N.C. Ind. Comm. 1989).

Burch v. *University of Kansas*, 756 P. 2d 431 (Kan. 1988).

Bynes v. *Toll*, 512 F. 2d 252 (2nd Cir. 1975).

Chaplinsky v. *New Hampshire*, 315 U.S. 568 (1942).

Chapman v. *Thomas*, 743 F. 2d 1056 (4th Cir. 1984).

City of Athens v. *Wolf*, 313 N.E. 2d 405 (Ohio 1974).

Columbia Pictures v. *Professional Real Estate Investors, Inc.*, 866 F. 2d 278 (9th Cir. 1989).

Commonwealth v. *McCloskey*, 272 A. 2d 271 (Pa. Super. 1970).

Communist Party of U.S. v. *Sub. Act. Cont. Bd.*, 81 S. Ct. 1357 (1961).

Cook v. *University Plaza*, 427 N.E. 2d 405 (Ill. App. 2nd Dist. 1981).

Cooper v. *Nix*, 496 F. 2d 1285 (5th Cir. 1974).

Counts v. *Voorhees College*, 312 F. Supp. 598 (D.S.C. Charleston Div. 1970).

Dixon v. *Alabama State Board of Education*, 294 F. 2d 150 (5th Cir. 1961); cert. den. 386 U.S. 930 (1961).

Doe v. *New York University*, 666 F. 2d 761 (2nd Cir. 1981).

Doe v. *University of Michigan*, 721 F. Supp. 852 (E.D. Mich. 1989).

Ekelund v. *Secretary of Commerce*, 418 F. Supp. 102 (E.D. N.Y. 1976).

Esteban v. *Central Missouri State College*, 277 F. Supp. 649 (W.D. Mo. 1967).

Fleming v. *New York University*, 865 F. 2d 478 (2nd Cir. 1989).

French v. *Bashful*, 303 F. Supp. 1333 (E.D. La. N. Div. 1969).

Furek v. *University of Delaware*, 594 A. 2d 506 (Del. 1991).

Gabrilowitz v. *Newman*, 582 F. 2d 100 (5th Cir. 1978).

Gardenhire v. *Chalmers*, 326 F. Supp. 1200 (D. Kan. 1971).

General Order on Judicial Standards of Procedure and Substance in Review of Student Discipline in Tax Supported Institutions of Higher Education, 45 F.R.D. 133 (W.D. Mo. 1968).

Good v. *Associated Students*, 542 P. 2d 762 (Wash. 1975).

Graham v. *Montana State University*, 767 P. 2nd 301 (Mont. 1988).

Grossner v. *Trustees of Columbia University*, 287 F. Suppl. 535 (S.D. N.Y. 1968).

Grove City College v. *Bell*, 104 S. Ct. 1211 (1984).

Harrell v. *Southern Illinois University*, 453 N.E. 2d 971 (Ill. App. 5th Dist. 1983).

Hart v. *Ferris State College*, 557 F. Supp. 1379 (W.D. Mich., S.D. 1983).

Healy v. *James*, 92 S. Ct. 2338 (1972).

Houle v. *Adams State College*, 547 P. 2d 916 (Col. 1976).

International Society for Krishna Consciousness, Inc. v. *New Jersey Sports and Exposition Authority*, 691 F. 2d 155 (3rd Cir. 1982).

Iota Xi Chapter of Sigma Chi Fraternity v. *George Mason University*, 773 F. Supp. 792 (E.D. Va. 1991).

Johnson v. *Pennsylvania State University*, 473 U.S. 911 (1985).

Joyner v. *Whiting*, 477 F. 2d 456 (4th Cir. 1973).

Keegan v. *University of Delaware*, 349 A. 2d 14 (Del. 1975).

Keene v. *Rodgers*, 316 F. Supp. 217 (D. Maine N.D. 1970).

Klein v. *1500 Massachusetts Avenue Apartment Corp.*, 439 F. 2d 477 (D.C. Cir. 1970).

Krawez v. *Stans*, 306 F. Supp. 1230 (E.D. N.Y. 1969).

Lemon v. *Kurtzman*, 403 U.S. 601 (1971).

Lille v. *Thompson*, 322 U.S. 459 (1947).

Mauclet v. *Nyquist*, 406 F. Supp. 1233 (W.D. N.Y. 1976); af'd 97 S. Ct. 2120 (1976).

Miller v. *Long Island University*, 380 N.Y.S. 2d 917 (S. Ct. Sp. Term 1976).

Miller v. *State*, 478 N.Y.S. 2d 829 (1984).

Mollere v. *Southeastern Louisiana College*, 304 F. Supp. 826 (W.D. Ark., Fayetteville Div. 1969).

Moore v. *Troy State University*, 284 F. Supp. 725 (M.D. Ala. N. Div. 1968).

Mullins v. *Pine Manor College*, 449 N.E. 2d 331 (Mass. 1983).

Nally v. *Grace Community Church of the Valley*, 240 Cal. Rptr. 215 (App. 2nd Dist. 1987).

National Movement for Student Vote v. *Regents of University of California*, 123 Cal. Rptr. 141 (App. 2nd Dist. 1975).

Nieswand v. *Cornell University*, 692 F. Supp. 1464 (N.D. N.Y. 1988).

Nzuve v. *Castleton State College*, 335 A. 2d (Vt. 1975).

Palsgraf v. *Long Island Rail Road Co.*, 162 N.E. 99 (N.Y. 1928).

Papish v. *Board of Curators of University of Missouri*, 93 S. Ct. 1197 (1973).

People v. *Lanthier*, 97 Cal. Rptr. 297 (1971).

Pizzola v. *Watkins*, 442 F. 2d 284 (5th Cir. 1971).

Power v. *Miles*, 407 F. 2d 73 (2nd Cir. 1968).

Poynter v. *Drevdahl*, 359 F. Suppl. 1137 (W.D. Mich. N.D. 1972).

Pratz v. *Louisiana Polytechnic Institute*, 316 F. Supp. 872 (W.D. La. 1970); cert. den. 401 U.S. 1004 (1971).

Prostrollo v. *University of South Dakota*, 507 F. 2d 775 (8th Cir. 1974).

Pugh v. *Holmes*, 405 A. 2d 897 (Pa. 1979).

Robinson v. *Davis*, 447 F. 2d 753 (4th Cir. 1971).

Robinson v. *Eastern Kentucky University*, 475 F. 2d 707 (6th Cir. 1973); cert. den. 416 U.S. 982 (1973).

Rowe v. *Chandler*, 332 F. Supp. 336 (D. Kan. 1971).

Ryan v. *Hofstra University*, 324 N.Y.S. 2d 964 (S. Ct. Nassau Cty. 1971).

Schare v. *State University of New York at Stony Brook*, 437 F. Supp. 969 (E.D. N.Y. 1977).

Schenck v. *United States*, 249 U.S. 47 (1919).

School Board of Nassau County, Florida v. *Arline*, 107 S. Ct. 1123 (1987).

Shamloo v. *Mississippi State Board of Trustees, etc.*, 620 F. 2d 516 (5th Cir. 1980).

Shelley v. *Kraemer*, 334 U.S. 1 (1947).

Sheltina v. *Ohio University*, 459 N.E. 2d 587 (Ohio App. 1983).

Shelton v. *Trustees of Indiana University*, 891 F. 2d 165 (7th Cir. 1989).

Siegel v. *Regents of the University of California*, 308 F. Suppl. 832 (ND. Cal. 1970).

Simmons v. *Sowela Technical Institute*, 470 So. 2d 913 (La. App. 3rd Cir. 1985).

Smith v. *Day*, 538 A. 2d 157 (Vt. 1987).

Smythe and Smith v. *Lubbers*, 398 F. Supp. 777 (W.D. Mich. 1975).

Soglin v. *Kaufman*, 418 F. 2d 163 (7th Cir. 1969).

State v. *Chrisman*, 676 P. 2d 419 (Wash. 1984).

State v. *Kappes*, 550 P. 2d 121 (Ariz. App. Div. 1 Dept. A 1976).

State v. *Wingerd*, 318 N.E. 2d 866 (Ohio App. 1974).

Steinberg v. *Chicago Medical School*, 371 N.E. 2d 634 (Ill. 1977).

Tarasoff v. *Regents of the University of California*, 551 P. 2d 334 (Cal. 1976).

Texas Woman's University v. *Chayklintaste*, 521 S.W. 2d 949 (Texas App. 1975).

Tinker v. *Des Moines*, 393 U.S. 503 (1969).

Torres v. *Puerto Rico Junior College*, 298 F. Supp. 458 (D.P.R. 1969).

United States v. *Coles*, 302 F. Supp. 99 (D. Maine N.D. 1969).

University of Utah Students Against Apartheid v. *Peterson*, 649 F. Supp. 1200 (D. Utah C.D. 1986).

UWM Post v. *Board of Regents of University of Wisconsin*, 774 F. Supp. 1163 (E.D. Wisc. 1991).

Wallace v. *Florida A&M University*, 433 So. 2d 600 (Fla. D.C. 1st Dist. 1983).

Washington v. *Chrisman*, 102 S. Ct. 812 (1982).

Welfare of R.A.V., In Matter of, 464 N.W. 2d 507 (Minn. 1991).

Widmar v. *Vincent*, 102 S. Ct. 269 (1981).

Winans v. *Stimpson*, Law 86,887, Circuit Court Prince George's County, Md. (1981).

Chapter Fifteen

Professional Standards for Housing Programs

Theodore K. Miller
Michael E. Eyster

College and university housing and residential life programs exist almost exclusively within the context of bureaucratic organizations. Consequently, those responsible for implementing the programs and services, maintaining the physical facilities, and otherwise managing the housing enterprise carry out their responsibilities as institutional employees and not as self-employed professionals. This fact gives housing and residence life practitioners a unique professional character, as it does others in the field of student affairs. It may also provide something of a dilemma when it comes to working with and educating students. For instance, which has higher priority, the welfare of students or the welfare of the employing institution? What is the professional responsibility of the housing practitioner when faced with conflicting expectations, requests, or demands for action from the employing agency on the one hand and the student constituent to be served on the other? Resolving issues of professional ethics and practice within a bureaucratic organizational structure calls for peculiar measures and considerations often beyond the ken of mere mortals. Yet they must be handled appropriately and efficiently.

Likewise, housing and residential life programs exist for dissimilar purposes when viewed from the perspectives of different individuals within the institution. For example, some view housing simply as a necessary evil to provide students with affordable lodging options when attending college, whereas others see it as a vehicle designed to enhance the educational and developmental opportunities for students to learn and mature. From a purely objective perspective, both viewpoints have merit and relevance, for who can deny that students often require a place to dwell while in college, or that any enterprise sponsored and supported by an institution of higher learning should be justifiable on educational grounds? At issue is not who is right or wrong, but how one can best determine what is essential to a truly effective housing enterprise. Making such important judgments requires more than intuition or "best guesses," even when based on years of experience and considered opinions. Judgments are made on the basis of sound criteria, and the best available criteria for professional practice are in the form of professional standards and guidelines.

This chapter examines the role and function of professional standards as they relate to those responsible for housing and residence life programs and services. It is organized into six parts, each designed to focus on a specific aspect of professional standards for housing practitioners. These include (1) standards of professional practice, (2) credentialing, (3) relevant housing standards, (4) using standards in housing programs, (5) ethical considerations, and (6) future directions.

Standards of Professional Practice

Professional standards and guidelines for housing and residential life programs are of relatively recent vintage. It was not until the 1980s that serious initiatives were undertaken. The establishment of the Council for the Advancement of Standards for Student Services/Development Programs (CAS) in the fall of 1979 was the first concerted effort to develop comprehensive standards for student affairs, including housing functions. The Association of College and University Housing Officers-International (ACUHO-I) and the American College Personnel Association's (ACPA) Commission III, Student Residence Programs, were jointly involved in the CAS initiative to develop standards. Members of these organizations worked individually and collaboratively to create standards of practice for housing and residential life programs. CAS accepted draft versions from both organizations and unified them through its systematic standards development procedures. After considerable review by housing professionals throughout the country, the CAS Standards and Guidelines for Housing and Residential Life Programs (see Resource A) were published in 1986 in what has become familiarly known as the *CAS bluebook* (Council for the Advancement of Standard for Student Services/Development Programs, 1986), standards and guidelines for sixteen functional student affairs areas. As of spring 1992, CAS had published three additional functional-area standards and guidelines.

The unifying process that resulted in the final *CAS Standards* eliminated a number of highly specific statements from the standards originally proposed by ACUHO-I and changed many of the proposed requirements (*must* statements) to suggestions (*should* statements). Because it felt strongly that more stringent housing standards were needed for detailed internal audits, ACUHO-I published its own housing standards in 1985 and revised them in July 1991 (see Resource C). Consequently, there are currently two sets of housing standards available. Since they have evolved from the same beginnings, they have much in common, though they also have some unique characteristics as well.

The fact that two separate published standards for student housing operations exist leads to the obvious question of which is most appropriate and for what purposes. The answer is indicated by the processes and constituent bodies that were involved in the creation of the standards. CAS is a multiorganizational consortium of twenty professional student services and student development associations, whereas ACUHO-I is one of those member associations whose constituents are limited largely to housing and residential life professionals within the international higher education community. The ACUHO-I standards, therefore, reflect the criteria its members are expected to use to judge their housing programs for quality assurance purposes. The *CAS Standards*, on the other hand, have a much larger constituency, since they are for the benefit of the profession at large. The fact that they are aimed at a broad audience means that they cannot be as prescriptive as standards established for a professional association, whose members seek professional direction and support for a more limited, specialized area of endeavor. Although ACUHO-I can prescribe a specified level of functioning for its members' adherence, CAS is limited to establishing a set of standards that reflect a professionwide consensus of *minimally appropriate* behaviors, programs, and facilities for institutions of any size, type, or purpose.

Realizing the dilemma created by the existence of two sets of standards, the ACUHO-I executive board has recommended that its standards be used for detailed *internal* self-studies and that the *CAS Standards* be used when student housing operations are to be evaluated *externally* (for example, as part of a student affairs division's evaluation). But there are relatively few substantive differences between the two documents. And the most important point is that housing professionals now have professional standards and guidelines to which they can refer when those external to the housing program question or otherwise challenge the purposes and responsibilities of housing and residential life programs.

Credentialing

Professional standards and guidelines are often associated with the establishment of professional credentials for individuals, programs, or institutions.

Such credentials are designed to provide a reasonable level of quality assurance to those who seek help or service from the individual, program, or institution involved. When an individual is involved, credentials usually take the form of certification or licensure, which proclaims that the individual is qualified at a preestablished level of knowledge and competence to provide the help or service being sought. Certification is often established by government agencies, such as those concerned with teacher or counselor certification for the public schools. In recent years, nongovernmental certification programs have been established in specialties such as vocational, rehabilitation, and mental health counseling. Standards associated with certification programs typically require specified levels of formal education and practical experience, as well as successful completion of knowledge- and skill-based examinations. Licensure, on the other hand, is granted through a government agency. Through licensure, state governments legally define and regulate practice in areas such as medicine, law, psychology, and counseling. Licensure is a government's attempt to assure the public that designated practitioners are qualified through education, experience, knowledge, and skill to provide specialized services to the public. Legislation in this arena is usually designed to protect the public from unqualified practitioners.

Where academic programs, student services, and institutions are concerned, professional standards are typically associated with accreditation, a term familiar throughout American higher education. Accreditation represents formal peer recognition that an institution or academic program is in voluntary compliance with preestablished criteria. To be accredited, educational institutions and their programs must document, usually through a systematic self-study process, that their offerings, services, personnel, facilities, and other resources provide users with a high level of education and service.

In the United States, an "umbrella" accrediting body structure has been established. This voluntary hierarchical organization is coordinated by the Council on Postsecondary Accreditation (COPA), which is sometimes referred to as the accreditor of accrediting agencies. Currently, COPA recognizes in its constituent membership six national institutional and six regional institutional accrediting bodies and thirty-eight specialized accrediting bodies that focus on educational units and programs within institutions (Council on Postsecondary Accreditation, 1988). According to the same organization (Council on Postsecondary Accreditation, 1989, p. 4), the functions of accreditation at the postsecondary level have been and are to:

- foster excellence in postsecondary education through the development of uniform national criteria and guidelines for assessing educational effectiveness;
- encourage improvement through continuous self-study and review;

- assure the educational community, the general public, and other agencies or organizations that an institution or program has clearly defined and appropriate objectives, maintains conditions under which their achievement can reasonably be expected, is in fact accomplishing them substantially, and can be expected to continue to do so;
- provide counsel and assistance to established and developing institutions and programs; and
- endeavor to protect institutions against encroachments which might jeopardize their educational effectiveness or academic freedom.

Although the housing standards of both ACUHO-I and CAS have great utility for accreditation self-study purposes, neither organization has sought to accredit programs. That process is left to COPA and its accrediting agencies. If, on the other hand, student affairs programs or institutions of higher learning wish to use the standards for accreditation self-study purposes, CAS and ACUHO-I see this as desirable, because these standards are intended for voluntary use by practitioners for program evaluation, development, and self-study purposes.

Relevant Housing Standards

The unique character of housing and residential life programs presents a certain level of difficulty to those wishing to apply professional standards. There are at least two characteristics that distinguish student housing from other student affairs agencies in colleges and universities. First, it is generally true that student housing programs entail a broader range of specialized functions than is common to most other student affairs programs. Second, most housing operations have functioned in largely nonstandardized ways over the years. These two features in combination have made it difficult to develop operational standards flexible enough on the one hand to encompass the variety of functions and responsibilities common to the enterprise yet specific enough on the other to ensure quality. The following discussion elaborates on these characteristics and on how the resulting dilemma faced by housing practitioners has been resolved within the context of the housing standards.

Broad Range of Specialized Functions

Because of the complexity of housing programs and services and the importance of addressing residents' needs comprehensively, on many campuses student affairs functions that are designated as separate administrative units—together with other campus support services—are contained within and are a responsibility of the housing and residential life program. These include such functional areas as physical plant management, repair, and renovation; educational programming for student residents; resident student activities, recreation, sports, and government programs; food service and catering; budget management; crisis intervention programs; conference and hotel services; apartment housing; off-campus housing; staff selection, supervision, in-service education, and professional development; judicial policy enforcement; and student safety and security programs and procedures. Student housing operations with responsibilities for many of these functions often employ specialists from a broad range of fields, such as student development education, counseling, interior design, engineering, architecture, research and evaluation, and dietetics. Specialists are also drawn from business management and accounting, real estate management and marketing, information systems management, safety sciences, human resource training and development, and human resource management.

To the extent that each of these specialty areas reflects a community of concerned professionals, standards of practice and ethical codes of behavior have been promulgated by relevant professional associations. For example, the National Association of Student Personnel Administrators (NASPA) has established *Standards of Professional Practice* (1991) for student affairs administrators. (See Resource F.) Obviously, the complexity of housing and residential life programs calls for a broad range of knowledge, skills, and competencies that few individuals could possess on their own. Because the area of college and university residence life is typically concerned with all aspects of students' education and development, the more comprehensive programs tend to be grounded in holistic human philosophies and developmental theories. They are, in short, important components of their institution's educational programs.

Nonstandardized Nature of Operations

A second notable difference between student housing and many other student affairs programs and services concerns the variety of responsibilities assigned to the student housing operation at different institutions. Standards of practice for housing programs should take this variation into account. The ACUHO-I *Standards* foreword emphasizes that "the membership of ACUHO-I is diverse, including large, small, public, and private colleges; universities; junior and community colleges; and technical schools throughout the world. This standards statement is written to reflect that diversity. The diversity of the membership of the Association limits the degree to which individual statements of standards can be specific" (1991, p. i).

The specific mission of the student housing operation varies considerably from campus to campus, depending on institutional factors such as size, type, and educational philosophy. An added complication for ACUHO-I is the fact that it has constituent members from institutions throughout the world, requiring that its functional standards must be designed to encompass student housing operations in various countries with different cultural heritages. Factors such as these result in even greater diversification of the roles and responsibilities in student housing that standards must accommodate. Some housing departments purposefully emphasize programmatic areas, while others focus on the contribution housing can make to students' classroom learning experiences or behavioral patterns and self-discipline. Still others emphasize educational support services, or revenue generation, or student retention, or a variety of other focal points. One thing is abundantly clear: *the role of student housing varies considerably among institutions, and to be relevant, professional standards must take such differences into account* .

Specificity of Standards

A major difficulty lies in writing standards that are specific enough to provide guidance to policy makers and practitioners but that also take into account the wide variety of functions performed by student housing professionals and the diversity of responsibilities assigned to student housing operations by different institutions.

Both ACUHO-I and CAS addressed the resulting dilemma through their attempts to develop standards of practice designed to identify *minimal* expectations. The intent to establish minimal standards of practice was clearly stated in the introductions to both sets of standards. CAS (1986, p. 2) indicated that "standards specify the minimum essential elements expected of any institution and its student services and student development programs [and] are the essential components of an acceptable practice, not necessarily the ideal, most desirable, or best practice." By identifying standards as minimal expectations, these organizations included only those aspects they considered essential to *all* operations. An obvious problem with this approach is that minimal standards may not make reference to areas of responsibility that a particular student housing operation has been assigned, because those particular functions are not common to "most" student housing operations.

To more effectively address the problem of inclusion, both the ACUHO-I and CAS standards provided guidelines to accompany the standards. "Guidelines describe recommended, but not essential, elements of programs and practice. They are used to explain, amplify, or interpret the meaning of standards through the use of examples and more detailed explanations" (Council for the Advancement of Standards for Student Services/Development Programs, 1986, p. 2). The use of guidelines permits flexibility that accommodates the wide variety of approaches used in different student housing operations. The main difference between standards and guidelines is that standards reflect requirements and use the auxiliary verbs *must* and *shall*, whereas guidelines are recommended but not required for compliance and use the auxiliary verbs *should* and *may*. For purposes of clarity and easier understanding, both ACUHO-I and CAS have used different typefaces to distinguish between standards and guidelines in their statements.

Using Standards in Housing Programs

CAS President Theodore K. Miller pointed out that the *CAS Standards* will only be effective to the extent practitioners view them as relevant and use them in their daily work. In writing about the *CAS Standards*, which were soon to be published, Miller (1984, p. 415) predicted that "institutional leaders and student affairs practitioners will be exposed to a new challenge that will strengthen their capacity to stimulate the development of students and to offer support services that will better meet the needs of those students. The opportunity for the field of student affairs to move to new levels of professionalism will be enhanced. A new challenge will have to be faced. But the most important implication is that individual practitioners, program directors, and institutions will have to decide whether or not to follow."

Two years after publication of the *CAS Standards*, Marron (1989) collected data for a doctoral dissertation in which he studied the extent to which the standards were being used by practitioners. His findings indicated that eighteen months after publication, relatively little practical use had been made of them. When describing how the *CAS Standards* were being utilized, Marron noted that they did not appear to be having the impact on the field of student affairs that the six years of development and the document's obvious high quality would dictate. He also indicated that initiating use of the *CAS Standards* at most institutions was largely dependent on the level of support and encouragement of the chief student affairs administrator. "Particularly disappointing is the lack of self-study and implementation of change that is taking place. . . . The primary need is to increase awareness of the document. Increased visibility must become the number one priority of CAS if the standards are ever to reach the utilization level that I believe they deserve and to which the organization professes to aspire" (Marron, 1989, pp. 80–81). Marron's research was instrumental in causing CAS to delay a planned standards revision initiative and instead mount an effort to make the standards more utilitarian for practitioners. In a more recent study, Marron (1991) reports that increasing numbers of institutions are using the *CAS Standards* for self-study purposes. A number of institutional contacts are identified in the appendix of a monograph on standards by Bryan, Winston, and Miller (1991).

Program Self-Study Evaluation Strategies

Marron's research (1989) verified that simply having standards in place would not ensure their use and that making the standards more "user friendly" would likely pay dividends. On the basis of this reasoning, CAS developed a series of self-assessment guides, one for each of the nineteen functional areas for which standards have been adopted. The *CAS Housing and Residential Life Programs Self Assessment Guide* (Miller, Thomas, Looney, and Yerian, 1988), for example, translates the *CAS Standards* into a relatively simple format designed specifically for self-study purposes. ACUHO-I (1991a) has also developed a self-assessment guide for its recently revised standards. These guides provide a series of criteria that practitioners can use to determine the extent to which their individual programs conform to the standards. The CAS guide also includes the full text of the *CAS Standards* as an appendix. In addition, a training manual (Yerian and Miller, 1988) was developed to assist those who wish to learn about or instruct others in the use of the CAS standards and self-assessment guides. This manual includes thirty-one transparency masters that can be copied for use as graphic displays for training purposes.

ACUHO-I has published a monograph on ACUHO-I standards (Daley, 1989) that covers pertinent topics. These include the following: (1) establishing the need for a program review, (2) determining goals and purposes, (3) establishing terminology and definitions, (4) implementing an internal program review, (5) implementing an external program review, and (6) conducting program review follow-up activities. Two major issues Daley raises deserve special attention: types of program review options and program review methodology.

Daley identifies three types of program reviews. The first is an *internal program review*, defined as a review conducted by members of the campus community of which the housing unit is a part. In this context, community is taken to include students' parents and alumni, in addition to the institution's faculty, staff, and students. The second type is the *external program review*, which involves data collection, data analysis, reporting, and recommendations compiled and completed by individuals *not* affiliated with the institution in which the housing organization is established—for example, a regional accrediting agency. The third is the *focused program review*, which attends to one particular functional component within the housing organization. This type of review may be useful when a detailed analysis of a single program such as educational programming, physical plant operations, food service, or business management is desired. Focused reviews may also be used to evaluate even more specific subsections such as family housing operations, housekeeping services, conference services, or computer applications. Obviously, each type of program review has both strengths and shortcomings. In large part, selection of the most appropriate approach for a given institution or situation depends on the purposes for which the review is being initiated.

The section on implementing an internal review is of particular value to practitioners because it describes several specific methods for collecting program data. Many of these methods are useful for external reviews as well. Each method describes a way in which a housing and residential life unit can be measured by a particular ACUHO-I standard. The methods of ACUHO-I standards data collection identified by Daley (1989) follow, as do the procedures from the *CAS Housing and Residential Life Programs Self Assessment Guide* (Miller, Thomas, Looney, and Yerian, 1988).

The Big Six Method. This method reflects the approach taken by six institutions using the *ACUHO-I Standards* as a basis for self-studies of housing programs. Participating institutions included the University of Florida, Indiana University, the University of Vermont, the University of California at Davis, the University of Texas at Austin, and Iowa State University. The approach used in these studies was based on the work of Grimm and Blansett (1985).

Outline of the Big Six Method (adapted from Daley, 1989, p. 4)

Example Standard. Each full-time employee and paraprofessional has a written job description.

a. Does the housing organization meet this standard?
    1. If yes—go to parts b through d below.
    2. If no—go to part e below.
b. Is this standard met intentionally by planned programs, policies, and procedures? Is it met naturally through physical, societal, or environmental factors? Is it met through a combination of intentional and natural occurrences?
c. In what ways does the organization meet this standard?
d. How well or to what degree is the housing program meeting the standard?

Excellent	Good	Average	Fair	Poor
5	4	3	2	1
100–85%	85–65%	65–35%	35–15%	15–0%

e. If this standard is not being met, is there a future plan to meet this standard? What are the goals and objectives of this future plan?

Syracuse University Method. In the *ACUHO-I Standards* self-study completed at Syracuse University, the following process developed by Baker, Decker, and Kohr (1986) was used to establish a data collection method.

Outline of the Syracuse University Method
(adapted from Daley, 1989, p. 5)

a. Develop
    1. Worst-possible case statement
    2. Worst-known case statement

3. Best-known case statement
4. Best-possible case statement

b. Develop criteria that describe minimum acceptable standards plus criteria that indicate above-average performance.

c. List the housing unit's operational components (policies, procedures, activities, publications, budgetary allocations, and so on) that demonstrate a commitment to meeting the standard.

d. Evaluate the level of the housing unit's commitment in relation to the standard.

Far below standard	Does not meet standard	Meets standard	Exceeds standard	Far exceeds standard

e. List suggested improvements.

The ACUHO-I and CAS Self Assessment Guide Method. In both the *CAS Self Assessment Guide* (Miller, Thomas, Looney, and Yerian, 1988) and the *ACUHO-I Assessment Guide* approaches, the following data collection procedures are used.

Outline of the CAS/ACUHO-I Self Assessment Format

a. Rate each assessment criterion measure using the scale below.

1	2	3	4	5	UK
Noncompliance			Compliance		Unknown

b. Cite any guidelines to be assessed as an institutional criterion (standard).

c. Identify documentation and rationales that support the evaluation.

d. If rated other than "compliance," describe the discrepancies in detail.

e. Actions required for compliance.

f. Actions recommended for program enhancement.

g. Follow-up action plan
   1. Identify the areas in which the program excels.
   2. List each assessment criterion identified as not being in compliance with the *Standards*.
   3. List each of the specific actions identified as being required to bring the program into compliance with the *Standards*.
   4. Prioritize the required actions needed to bring the program into compliance on the basis of their overall

importance to achieving the program's mission and
primary goals and objectives.

5. List each of the specific actions recommended to
strengthen and enhance the program.

6. Prioritize the recommended actions for enhancement
on the basis of their desirability and feasibility for
achievement.

7. Establish an action plan for initiating and implementing the changes required to bring the program into
compliance with the *Standards*.

8. Set dates by which specific actions are to be completed.

9. Identify the parties responsible for completing the action tasks.

A Self-Assessment Example

Assume that the task of initiating a comprehensive self-study of the student
housing program has been assigned. How might such a task be accomplished? First, the evaluator must answer the following questions: (1) What
are the primary goals and functions of the housing program? (2) What
criteria exist to judge the extent of program goal accomplishment? Prior to
the development of housing standards, these questions were nearly impossible to answer because there were no formal standards available against which
to make considered judgments. Establishment of the ACUHO-I and CAS
standards and guidelines has made program evaluation comparatively simple, for now the criteria on which judgments can be made are easily accessible to professionals at all operational levels.

The initial assessment criterion statement listed in the *CAS Housing and
Residential Life Programs Self Assessment Guide* (Miller, Thomas, Looney, and
Yerian, 1988, p. 1) is as follows:

Part 1: Mission

1.1 There exists a well developed, written set of housing and
residential life goals that are consistent with the stated
mission of the institution.

This assessment criterion statement is based on the housing and
residential life programs standards and guidelines reported in the *Guide*'s
appendix. Here is an excerpt from the standard on which the criterion is
based: "The institution and its residential life program must develop, review,
and disseminate regularly their own specific goals for student services/
development, which must be consistent with the nature and goals of the
institution and with the standards in this document" (Miller, Thomas,
Looney, and Ycrian, 1988, p. 21).

Note that the quoted standard does not specify the exact nature or direction of the mission but instead indicates that each institution's student housing program must have a statement of purpose based on specific program goals. Further, the standard requires that such a mission statement be consistent with that of the institution in which the program is established. Careful reading of the full statement, however, shows that the standard includes requirements that exceed criterion statement 1.1. Therefore, three additional criterion statements are used to cover all requirements called for in the standard. These are as follows:

1.2   Housing and residential life has a well-developed, written set of goals that are consistent with the stated student services/development goals of the institution.

1.3   Program goal statements are reviewed and disseminated on a regular basis.

1.4   The housing and residential life goals and objectives are consistent with the CAS Standards [Miller, Thomas, Looney, and Yerian, 1988, p. 1].

Because of the comprehensive nature of the standard, four separate criterion statements were required to incorporate all aspects of that single statement for evaluation purposes. The self-assessment guides present each criterion for the sole purpose of judging a single observable part of the standard. Through this highly detailed approach, the eighty-two criterion statements ensure that each part of each standard can be observed and judged on its own merits. Individual criterion measures are designed to be rated on five-point scales by evaluators who judge the extent to which the program meets that particular criterion. A rating of 1 indicates that the program is not in compliance with that part of the standard, while a rating of 5 indicates that the program is in or exceeds compliance. Ratings of 2, 3, and 4 reflect judgments that a program has been evaluated as being somewhere between noncompliance and compliance with respect to a particular standard.

Assessment criterion statements are not concerned directly with the guidelines included in the standards. This does not mean that the guidelines are unimportant, but it does indicate that from the standpoint of compliance evaluation, the nonsubstantive guidelines are included for explanation and amplification purposes only. A particular program, however, may decide to use selected guideline statements as criterion measures for self-study purposes. For example, Part 2, *Program*, of the housing and residential life standards and guidelines includes a guideline statement that reads as follows: "Maintenance/renovation programs should be implemented in all housing operations and may include: (a) a preventive maintenance program designed to extend the life of the equipment and facilities, (b) a program designed to repair in a timely manner equipment and building systems as they become inoperable, and (c) a renovation program that modifies physical facilities and building systems to make them more effective, attractive, efficient, and safe" (Miller, Thomas, Looney, and Yerian, 1988, p. 22).

Because this statement is printed in regular type and uses the auxiliary verb *should* rather than *must*, it can become a criterion measure only if those responsible for the self-study decide to use it in that fashion. If that decision is made, the guideline is treated as a standard, with the verb *should* being changed to *must* for rating purposes. The statement then would read as follows: "Maintenance/renovation programs must be implemented in all housing operations, including a preventive maintenance program designed to extend the life of the equipment and facilities." For self-study rating purposes, this new standard might be evaluated from two perspectives. Two additional criterion measures could be written as (1) the housing and residential life program has a systematic physical facilities renovation component in place, and (2) a preventive maintenance program designed to extend the life of the housing program's equipment and facilities has been established. These statements, which are substantively part of criterion 2.12 on page 3, would then be placed in the space provided with the instruction "Cite any CAS Guidelines to be assessed as an institutional criterion for the self-study" (Miller, Thomas, Looney, and Yerian, 1988, p. 4). They would be treated like any other standard assessment criterion for rating purposes.

Before a final rating is made on any of the assessment criterion statements, it is first necessary to identify and review all documentation that supports the rating and provides it with a rationale. It is important that the evaluative data and support documents be clearly identified and made available to the evaluators before the rating process is initiated.

A well-developed, written set of housing and residential life program goals are called for in assessment criterion measure 1.1, as previously noted. This requires that to be in compliance with the standards, a formal statement defining and describing the mission and goals of the housing program must exist. Such a statement may be published in the college's catalogue and/or student handbook, incorporated in the housing policies and procedures manual, or simply kept in a drawer of the program director's desk. On the other hand, a formal statement may not be readily found, or there may be a question about whether such a statement has ever existed. Program accountability and the ability to support whatever is called for in the standards with tangible evidence are at the heart of the documenting requirement, and so it must be viewed with deliberation by those responsible for judging the quality of a particular program.

If a mission statement cannot be found, either because it does not exist or because no one knows its location, there would clearly be no way to show that the program was in compliance with this particular standard. However, even when a purpose statement is available and printed in an institutional publication, that fact alone does not ensure automatic compliance with the standard. There are several possible limitations that may militate against compliance. For example, the statement may be out of date, inconsistent with the institution's stated purpose, limited in scope, or unknown to most practitioners. In other words, the quality of the evidence used to document a particular criterion measure is an important consideration when judging compliance. If it appears the standard is not met, whether in fact or in spirit, it is incumbent on the evaluators to rate the criterion measure accordingly and note the discrepancies found between the "good practice" as described in the standards and the actual practice observed. If discrepancies are found, they should be listed in the space provided and expanded on elsewhere as needed. At this point in the self-assessment process it is possible to determine whether the program fully meets, partially meets, or does not meet the minimum standards of practice. Further, it should also be possible to make the necessary judgments and rate the criterion measures reflecting that particular standard.

If no discrepancies between program practice and the written standards are found, no actions are required for achieving compliance. If, however, discrepancies are noted, the actions required to bring the program into compliance must be determined. For example, assume that a program goals statement exists but that it is outdated and has gone unreviewed in recent years. There may be several actions that could be initiated to deal with this discrepancy. The bases for such actions, however, depend on the raters' ability to identify and document relevant evidence and their competence in interpreting that evidence objectively and accurately. In this instance, a task force to study the current statement, revise it as necessary, and initiate a campuswide review process for the revised statement may be the best solution.

Even though a program is judged to be in compliance with the standards, additional actions for its enhancement can often be identified. In the current example, decisions to increase program mission reviews or expand the number of constituent groups involved in the goal review process might be deemed desirable. These and other enhancement action proposals may be written in the space provided in the *Guide*.

A comprehensive self-assessment process requires considerable time, campus resources, and personal commitment to implement. The extensive process outlined above was required to judge only one of four assessment criterion measures used to evaluate a single standard statement. Further, the standard and criterion measure used in the example is actually easier than many other housing standards to evaluate because, apart from information in existing documents, no data need to be collected. Many of the other housing standards focus on issues and concerns that will require implementation of additional data collection procedures. For instance, assessment criterion statement 11.3 of Part 11, *Multi-Cultural Programs and Services*, focuses on an area typically requiring the collection of data not readily available. This assessment criterion measure reads as follows:

11.3   Housing and residential life assists minority students to identify, prioritize, and meet their unique educational and developmental needs [Miller, Thomas, Looney, and Yerian, 1988, p. 13].

In most cases, it would not be possible to access an available data base or published document to evaluate this criterion. Objective evaluation will likely require special quantitative and qualitative data collection. What programs currently exist that can help minority students address their unique educational and developmental needs? Further, what are those needs, how were they determined, and what initiatives has the housing program designed for identified minority student populations? These and many other questions must be answered before an objective evaluation can be made. In many instances, it may be necessary to collect basic data to determine the current status of the minority students involved, let alone their special needs. Accurate information may exist in campus data bases on the number of African-American, Native American, and international students living in student housing. However, what about nontraditional-age students, returning students, and gay, lesbian, or bisexual students? Increased student diversity promotes increased complexity in identifying the various cultures and heritages associated with higher education today. Consequently, there is a growing need for housing personnel to carry out assessment initiatives to obtain data from self-study-initiated research and evaluation programs. These data may come from student surveys, ratings, and follow-ups as well as from theory-based research designed to use the *CAS Standards* as measurement criteria. No self-study is complete without relevant data and documentation to support rater judgments. The collection of additional data is a basic requirement of the typical self-study process.

Following a comprehensive program evaluation, a self-study follow-up action plan should be created. Such plans incorporate all aspects of the self-study and are based on three of its primary outcomes: (1) identified areas of program excellence, (2) the actions required to overcome the discrepancies judged to exist between the program as practiced and the standards' criterion measures, and (3) the voluntary actions proposed to enhance the program beyond actions required for compliance. Using these self-study outcomes as a foundation, follow-up plans are designed to initiate and implement the changes required to bring the program into compliance with the standards and to strengthen it beyond compliance. Such a plan prioritizes the desired actions so that adequate and appropriate resources can be utilized, establishes a schedule for bringing about the required changes, identifies the parties reponsible for completing the action tasks, and establishes the criteria to be used for evaluation purposes when the changes are complete. When the follow-up plan has been implemented, it may be time to begin the self-study process over again as the natural recycling process evolves.

Ethical Considerations

Other aspects of professional standards that have not been discussed so far concern the ethical principles and guidelines that underlie many of the judgments and choices housing personnel must make on an almost-daily basis. Failure to consider one's ethical responsibilities when working with staff and faculty colleagues as well as students can lead to unfortunate, even disastrous, consequences. As Kitchener (1985, p. 17) notes, "we must consider ethical principles and theories in order to make reasoned and ethically defensible judgments in student affairs." No matter what their position title, housing personnel have the education as well as the general welfare of resident students to consider. The interactions and relationships experienced in this arena may well influence those involved in meaningful ways, for human values are predominant in educational environments and the modeling effect of staff members on students is often more powerful than imagined. Fundamentally, students' residence life experiences are significant factors in their overall education, and the moral, ethical, and social learning that occurs in college can last a lifetime. If residence hall staff members are in the business of shaping students' lives, as Chickering (1981) contended that everyone associated with higher education must be, the ethical judgments and choices made and actions taken will impact the students' living and learning environments in significant ways. In other words, failure to incorporate professional ethics in daily activities will be fraught with difficulty and may well lead to malpractice. The quality of professional practice in the field of student affairs is greatly influenced by the degree of adherence to ethical principles and standards.

Significant concerns, however, revolve around issues relating to the nature of the ethics used to guide professional practice, the agreement or lack of it among practitioners as to what those ethics truly are, and sanctions established and implemented by the profession when unethical behavior is observed. Fortunately, ethical codes are available, and wide professional consensus exists that they should be adhered to.

The CAS Standards and Guidelines for Housing and Residential Life Programs, for example, emphasized the important role of ethical standards: "All persons involved in the provision of housing and residential life programs to students must maintain the highest standards of ethical behavior. Residential life program staff members must develop and adopt standards of ethical practice addressing the unique problems that face personnel in that area. The standards must be published and reviewed by all concerned. In the formulation of those standards, ethical standards statements previously adopted by the profession at large or relevant professional associations may be of assistance and must be considered" (Miller, Thomas, Looney, and Yerian, 1988, p. 27).

These published standards expand on the ethical considerations requisite to professional practice in this setting. They specify, for instance, the importance of maintaining confidentiality, of respecting institutions' policies on research with human participants, of guaranteeing fair and equitable access by students to institutional resources, of avoiding conflicts of interest, of preventing sexual harassment of all types, and of recognizing the limits of personal qualifications and of making referrals when appropriate. Although essential to the quality of professional practice, these stated ethical standards are, in and of themselves, insufficient as a comprehensive guide to ethical practice on the part of residence life staff members.

As noted in the standards quoted above, it is essential that each institution's residence life staff collectively establish and adopt an agreed-on set of ethical standards to guide their practice. This clearly implies that although every housing staff is expected to adopt ethical standards, *there is no single set of ethical standards that every program must follow*. There are, however, a number of ethical considerations that all programs should incorporate into their adopted standards in some fashion, if for no other reason than that the profession at large views them as essential to professional practice.

Everyone should seek to incorporate the fundamental ethical principles that underlie the agreed-on standards. The most recent *Statement of Ethical Principles and Standards* of the American College Personnel Association (ACPA) (1989) incorporates ethical principles articulated by Kitchener (1985). These principles, although offered as guides to everyday practice, are action oriented and represent assertiveness on the part of practitioners as opposed to simply reacting to situations after the fact. The five principles are as follows:

- Act to the benefit of others.
- Promote justice.
- Respect autonomy.
- Be faithful.
- Do no harm.

Promulgation of these basic ethical principles underscores the prevailing notion that ethical decisions should be generalizable and that they should be consistent with decisions made by others who face similar situations (Winston and Saunders, 1991). It is suggested that whatever codification is adopted to guide ethical practice in a given housing program, these principles should be carefully considered as a foundation on which to build.

Well-constructed ethical codes usually include several major categories that reflect the focus and breadth of concern common to professional practice in the areas under consideration. The ACPA (1989) ethical standards referred to previously are formatted around four primary constituencies with which student affairs professionals typically are concerned. These include the professional practitioner, the student, the educational institution, and the larger society. How one decides to respond to and interact with each of these constituent groups reflects both personal and professional values and ethical considerations. As Brown (1977) notes, there are at least three value conflicts that student affairs practitioners can expect to encounter in their work: (1) a dissonance between one's individual liberty and social responsibility, (2) a conflict between one's hedonistic needs and one's desire to behave altruistically, and (3) one's continuing search for the meaning of being human. How one responds to these ever-present value conflicts is relevant to one's ethical perspectives. But it is of paramount importance that all practitioners, individually and collectively, determine and follow to the best of their ability an agreed-on set of ethical guidelines. Establishing such an ethical code to guide behavior is a constructive endeavor that all housing practitioners should consider to be a professional trust.

Most professionals would agree that if appropriate mechanisms do not exist for monitoring and enforcing ethical behavior, ethical standards have limited value for practitioners and the profession at large (Cannon and Brown, 1985; Herlihy and Golden, 1990; Winston and Saunders, 1991). Unfortunately, to date, the field of student affairs and its primary professional associations have neither developed nor agreed on a comprehensive set of ethical guidelines for the profession at large. Granted, as noted earlier, ACPA, NASPA, ACUHO-I (1992), and other professional organizations have promulgated ethical standards for their members, but the profession as a whole has not reached that level of maturity. Obviously, if there are no agreed-on ethical codes across the profession, it is difficult to monitor, much less enforce, appropriate ethical behavior among its constituent groups. Therefore, professional housing staffs must establish, maintain, and manage their own expectations as to appropriate ethical behavior on the part of individual staff members.

Staff development programs in which ethical problems and dilemmas, such as those presented by Cannon and Brown (1985), Herlihy and Golden (1990), and Winston and Saunders (1991), are examined and discussed in detail can be most informative and have great utility for a housing staff. If staff members are expected to exhibit high degrees of ethical behavior in their daily work, it is incumbent on residence life leaders to provide them with the wherewithal to do so. What Winston and Saunders (1991, p. 340) note for the field of student affairs as a whole is also true for housing practitioners: "Whether the profession chooses to accept the challenge to deal with these important [ethical] issues will determine whether student affairs will move beyond its emerging professional status to become a true profession." If housing practitioners desire to achieve comparable status as professionals, it is essential that they take the responsibility for quality ethical practice into their own hands in their own programs and then *demand* that their professional associations do the same for the profession at large.

Brown (1985) challenges student affairs professionals, including those primarily responsible for programs of residence life and student housing, to consider their professional responsibilities for creating and establishing ethical communities. Brown's contention is that practitioners must begin by establishing an ethical agenda in order to fulfill their missions. From this perspective, the community norms established by all individuals associated with the residence life program have a great influence on the quality of residence life, as reflected by the common good achieved when students, faculty, and staff members alike encounter the campus residence environment. To accomplish this objective as Brown conceives it, however, there must be a concerted effort on the part of all concerned to intentionally create the kind of living and learning environment that is conducive to the development of ethical viewpoints and behavior.

Brown (1985, p. 72) notes that ethical concerns for professional practice can affect the ethical climate of an institution or parts of it and that endeavors to enhance ethical behavior can be increased by implementing a "checklist for creating an ethical community." This topical checklist approach identifies an educational framework that includes when, how, who, and the desired impact on members of the community. It is extremely useful for housing professionals who want to establish a living environment in which its members will be encouraged to become increasingly more humane, respectful and accepting of diversity, and socially concerned. Providing several examples, which can be readily tailored and expanded for a given residence life community, Brown argues that higher education in general badly needs new ways of thinking and acting on the ethical principles it promotes among its constituents. It behooves those associated with the college and university housing profession to review their roles, functions, and purposes in regard to both professional and community ethics. We may be doing both our student constituents and our professional colleagues a major disservice if we do not attend to the ethical quality of the residence environments and the ethical agendas that are being promulgated in them.

Future Directions

The development of professional standards and guidelines has been and will continue to be a boon to the emergence of student affairs as a recognized profession, because they help practitioners keep sight of high purposes and good practice. These standards and guidelines come from various sources thorughout the higher education community, and housing practitioners can benefit from their use as a complement to standards of practice that focus on housing programs and services alone. For example, the National Association of College and University Food Services (NACUFS) (1991) has developed professional standards concerned with the food service components so often associated with housing programs. Likewise, the National Association of College and University Business Officers (NACUBO) (1990) has published a financial accounting and reporting manual that represents criteria that can be used as standards to guide the business and accounting operations in housing. Housing professionals need to look to colleagues in the higher education arena for guidance and support when implementing specific management responsibilities. Reinventing the wheel is not a particularly efficient way to use increasingly limited resources.

Housing and residential life personnel, however, cannot afford to wait for others to set the priorities and make the plans if they wish to maintain leadership in their field of endeavor and command loyalty among their peers. As Larson (1977) notes, failure to establish either standards of practice or preparation in a profession will seriously limit the establishment of that profession as a recognized field of endeavor. By creating standards and guidelines for housing and residential life programs, ACUHO-I and CAS and their residence life colleagues have taken giant steps forward toward the professionalization of the field of housing in particular and student affairs in general.

Acting on and complying with those standards and using allied professional standards and guidelines when appropriate is the essence of professional practice. Until practitioners at all levels know about the standards, adhere to them thoughtfully, and apply them in their daily activities, the professionalization that many seek will not become a reality. This is not to suggest that professional standards are a panacea or an end all in themselves, for they are not. It is to suggest, however, that only when housing practitioners find ways to do better what they have been doing for years will student housing programs become recognized as possessing both the character and the quality of excellence that both institutional leaders and student constituents deserve. The ACUHO-I and CAS standards, among others—which include food service, business affairs, and facilities management standards and guidelines—can guide them and help them assess their practices on many levels.

Quality housing practice will develop only as high standards become the benchmark of professional practice. As institutions of higher learning seek to establish more effective educational and developmental environments designed to expose students to the essentials of a high quality of life, the professional housing standards can become increasingly relevant to promoting that end. Using professional standards to format annual reports, for instance, has great utility for program planning purposes as well as in encouraging analysis and evaluation from within. Institutional goals can be systematically enhanced through the use of professional standards to guide their achievement. The ability to show institutional leaders the connections between their goals and the educational and developmental goals of housing and residential life programs through published standards goes far toward enhancing the image and professional recognition so essential to continued success. The more institutional leaders understand the educational role and function of housing programs, which can be orchestrated to help achieve institutional ends, the more support will be forthcoming to achieve all the tasks assigned.

Careful attention must be paid to professionwide endeavors to create relevant standards as an important aspect of the housing profession's evolution. Housing standards should not become overly prescriptive to the point of specifying details that might better be left to the uniquely creative imaginations of the practitioners who know their programs, personnel, and facilities best. What the standards should do is provide professional staff members with criteria against which to judge the quality of their endeavors and the extent to which they are successful in capturing the essence of excellence in their daily routines.

It is essential that quality programming and leadership be based on carefully considered and continuing self-study over time. Answers to questions such as the following are especially important.

- What theory base is being used to guide practice, and to what end?
- What are the educational goals that guide the program's direction, and how are they determined?
- What type of environment is most conducive to the goals of the program, and how can that environment best be created to the benefit of the student constituents?
- What are the program and funding priorities that guide policy management and decisions about the housing approach used?
- How are qualified personnel selected, trained, and retained?

These are important questions that professional standards can help answer and whose answers will clearly guide the quality of the programs provided. It is no longer necessary for practitioners to be guided primarily by their best estimates of what should or could be. If the professional standards are used with care, housing staff members have the benefit of a thoughtfully developed foundation that is difficult for institutional leaders to resist or reject.

Standards that have wide acceptance throughout higher education provide excellent leverage for enhancing programs and obtaining funding for essential services and personnel that otherwise may go wanting for lack of support. Economic exigencies being what they are, of all the things in the higher education milieu that demand recognition by superiors and subordinates alike, appropriate and well-developed, tested, and established standards of practice are at the forefront. If carefully used, high standards of practice, quality, and integrity are powerful forces that can help practitioners move the mountains that confront them regularly.

References

American College Personnel Association. *A Statement of Ethical Principles and Standards of the American College Personnel Association.* Alexandria, Va.: American College Personnel Association, 1989.

Association of College and University Housing Officers-International. *Standards for College and University Student Housing.* Columbus, Ohio: Association of College and University Housing Officers-International, 1985.

Association of College and University Housing Officers-International. *Self-Assessment Guides for Standards for College and University Student Housing.* Columbus, Ohio: Association of College and University Housing Officers-International, 1991a.

Association of College and University Housing Officers-International. *Standards for College and University Student Housing* (Rev. ed.). Columbus, Ohio: Association of College and University Housing Officers-International, 1991b.

Association of College and University Housing Officers-International. *Ethical Principles and Standards for College and University Student Housing.* Columbus, Ohio: Association of College and University Housing Officers-International, 1992.

Baker, B., Decker, S., and Kohr, D. "ACUHO-I Professional Standards: A Model for Departmental Review." Paper presented at the 38th annual convention of the Association of College and University Housing Officers-International, Cullowhee, N.C., July 1986.

Brown, R. D. "Professional Development and Staff Development: The Search for a Metaphor." In R. P. Wanzek (ed.), *Staff Development.* DeKalb: Northern Illinois University, 1977.

Brown, R. D. "Creating an Ethical Community." In H. J. Cannon and R. D. Brown (eds.), *Applied Ethics in Student Services.* New Directions for Student Services, no. 30. San Francisco: Jossey-Bass, 1985.

Bryan, W. A., Winston, R. B., Jr., and Miller, T. K. (eds.). *Using Professional Standards in Student Affairs.* New Directions for Student Services, no. 53. San Francisco: Jossey-Bass, 1991.

Cannon, H. J., and Brown, R. D. (eds.). *Applied Ethics in Student Services.* New Directions for Student Services, no. 30. San Francisco: Jossey-Bass, 1985.

Chickering, A. W. "Introduction." In A. W. Chickering and Associates, *The Modern American College: Responding to the New Realities of Diverse Students and a Changing Society.* San Francisco: Jossey-Bass, 1981.

Council for the Advancement of Standards for Student Services/Development Programs. *CAS Standards and Guidelines for Student Services/Development Programs.* Iowa City, Iowa: Council for the Advancement of Standards for Student Services/Development Programs, 1986.

Council on Postsecondary Accreditation. *Directory of Recognized Accrediting Bodies.* Washington, D.C.: Council on Postsecondary Accreditation, 1988.

Council on Postsecondary Accreditation. *The Balance Wheel for Accreditation.* Washington, D.C.: Council on Postsecondary Accreditation, 1989.

Daley, M. K. *Prospectus: Using the ACUHO-I "Standards" as an Aid to Program Evaluation and Enhancement.* Columbus, Ohio: Association of College and University Housing Officers-International, 1989.

Grimm, J. C., and Blansett, S. C. (eds.). *Self Study Model for Housing Organizations*

Using ACUHO-I Standards. Columbus, Ohio: Association of College and University Housing Officers-International, 1985.

Herlihy, B., and Golden, L. B. *Ethical Standards Casebook.* (3rd ed.) Alexandria, Va.: American Association for Counseling and Development, 1990.

Kitchener, K. S. "Ethical Principles and Ethical Decisions in Student Affairs." In H. J. Cannon and R. D. Brown (eds.), *Applied Ethics in Student Services.* New Directions for Student Services, no. 30. San Francisco: Jossey-Bass, 1985.

Larson, N. S. *The Rise of Professionalism: A Sociological Analysis.* Berkeley: University of California Press, 1977.

Marron, J. M. "A Study of the Utilization of the Council for the Advancement of Standards for Student Services/Development Program Standards at Four Year Undergraduate Degree-Granting Colleges and Universities." Unpublished doctoral dissertation, George Peabody College for Teachers, Vanderbilt University, Nashville, Tenn., 1989.

Marron, J. M. "Example Applications of the CAS Standards." In W. A. Bryan, R. B. Winston, Jr., and T. K. Miller (eds.), *Using Professional Standards in Student Affairs.* New Directions for Student Services, no. 53. San Francisco: Jossey-Bass, 1991.

Miller, T. K. "Professional Standards: Whither Thou Goest?" *Journal of College Student Personnel*, 1984, *25*, 412–416.

Miller, T. K., Thomas, W. L., Looney, S. C., and Yerian, J. (eds.). *CAS Housing and Residential Life Programs Self Assessment Guide.* Iowa City: Council for the Advancement of Standards for Student Services/Development Programs, 1988.

National Association of College and University Business Officers. *Financial Accounting and Reporting Manual for Higher Education.* Washington, D.C.: National Association of College and University Business Officers, 1990.

National Association of College and University Food Services. *Professional Standards Manual.* (2nd ed.) East Lansing, Mich.: National Association of College and University Food Services, 1991.

National Association of Student Personnel Administrators. *Standards of Professional Practice.* Washington, D.C.: National Association of Student Personnel Administrators, 1991.

Winston, R. B., Jr., and Saunders, S. A. "Ethical Professional Practice in Student Affairs." In T. K. Miller, R. B. Winston, Jr., and Associates, *Administration and Leadership in Student Affairs: Actualizing Student Development in Higher Education.* (2nd ed.) Muncie, Ind.: Accelerated Development, 1991.

Yerian, J., and Miller, T. K. *Putting the CAS Standards to Work.* College Park, Md.: Council for the Advancement of Standards for Student Services/Development Programs, 1988.

Chapter Sixteen

Strengthening Programs
Through Evaluation
and Research

Robert D. Brown
Diane L. Podolske

Scenario 1. Sam Practicality, director of housing at Functional University, read all the chapters of this handbook and is particularly struck by the chapters that provide helpful clues for staffing, reducing conflicts, and responding to legal concerns. He puts together a staff training program that focuses on these topics. He wants to determine if other topics should be added, if his program works as he intends it to, and how the training program might be improved.

Scenario 2. Susan Ivorytower, director of housing at Theoretical University, has also read all the chapters in this handbook and is eager to conduct a research study. She would like to compare the relative effectiveness of developmental and person-environment theories by training half of the residence hall staff in understanding and implementing one developmental theory as it applies to residence life and the other half of the residence hall staff in understanding and implementing one of the person-environment theories. At the end of the school year, she will compare students who live in the respective residence halls on a student developmental measure, on a sense-of-community scale, on academic achievement outcomes, and on records of damage reports and retention rates. She would like the results to be useful for other campuses.

Susan and Sam have different goals. Sam wants to evaluate his program to see if it works and to determine how to make it work better. Susan wants to conduct research and make generalizations. She wants to publish her findings, whereas Sam is interested in documenting his managerial skills. They may use similar data collection strategies and instruments, and they may confront similar barriers and hurdles. It is important to remember, however, that their purposes are different. This chapter will help readers who, like Susan, want to conduct theoretically derived research, and it will also help readers who, like Sam, want to gather information to help make decisions about a program.

The chapter is divided into four sections. The first section presents important definitions and distinctions that will be helpful to those who are wondering whether they want to engage in research or evaluation. The next section outlines several approaches to inquiry and discusses how to decide which is most relevant for a given setting. The third section looks at how the different stages of residence hall program development lead to different research and evaluation questions. The final section presents a perspective on needed research and evaluation activities in housing for the next decade. Readers will benefit the most from this chapter if they keep in mind a specific research or evaluation question as they read the chapter.

Definitions and Distinctions

To allow for common points of reference, it is important to define and provide examples of key terms used in evaluation and research. These terms have sometimes been used inappropriately, leading to considerable confusion among practitioners.

Definition of "Program"

A definition of *program evaluation* in the context of residence hall life needs to be preceded by a definition of the term *program*. A program is any activity or arrangement that involves an intentional design and is aimed at a specific outcome. A program could be a formally planned educational workshop on study skills or AIDS prevention. It could be an orientation program for new resident assistants (RAs) or a leadership workshop for hall government leaders. A program can also be a procedure for handling telephone calls through the switchboard, a plan for arranging the furniture in the lounges, a policy of having student health aides available during weekends, or the format for training hall directors. Given this definition of *program*, what is evaluation?

Definition of "Evaluation"

Evaluation is making judgments about the worth of an entire residence hall program or elements of that program. The worth of a residence hall program is ultimately determined by its impact on the residents, the campus community, and those within the immediate environment. Examples of criteria for determining worth include the extent of the program's impact on the participants and others, the number of students or other persons affected, and the cost of the program in dollars, time, and energy. Worth can be determined by comparing the residence program's outcomes to its intended goals, by comparing the outcomes to those of other programs, or by comparing the outcomes to other standards. Once a determination of worth has been made, the evaluative judgment usually leads to decisions that have a direct impact on whether the residence program is continued, expanded, reduced, or otherwise changed. The evaluative judgment can be formal and explicit, based on an intentional and extensive data collection process, and can result in a publicly announced decision. Because evaluation is a natural human activity, it can also be informal, based on whatever information is available at the moment, can be private, and can be influenced by powers and pressures of the political process (Brown, 1978, p. 14).

Residence hall staff and administrators make evaluative judgments every day as they go about their professional life. When they decide there is a need to increase the living options available to students by designing special interest floors or when they make decisions about what educational programs to offer next year, they are making evaluative judgments. Noticing that students in one hall perform significantly less well academically than students in nearby halls, the residence hall staff may decide to offer programs in study skills for the struggling students. Hearing at a recent convention that another college campus had success with special interest floors for computer buffs may prompt the housing staff to see if there is interest among students on their campus for a a similar arrangement. Staff members may gather information informally, and the judgments and decisions may also be informal. Information is often collected in the form of casual observations and conversations. Opinions of others are collected and weighed. Assessments are made of the worth of past programs, and decisions are made about what needs to be done in the future. These informal evaluative judgments staff make influence program planning as well as decisions about retaining or dropping programs.

There are also times when evaluation needs to be more formal and systematic. When the college president wants to know how effective the residence hall staff has been in reducing racial tensions, informal opinions probably will not be enough. When a residence hall staff wants to know whether or not they should consider organizing an AIDS education program based on the experiences of staff from another campus, more than the whims or intellectual interests of the staff members need to be considered. When the regents or parents want a justification for the decision to have condom dispensers available in the residence halls, "hard data" have to be available that support the need for this service. When the residence hall staff want to know how to improve the learning environment on an honors program hall floor, the student health director wants to know if the residence hall health aide program is worth the expense, or the vice president for student affairs wants to decide if the program having parents living in the hall during the summer orientation program is worth keeping, casual opinions and impressions may not be sufficient. These are situations where more formal and systematic evaluation is required.

Formative Versus Summative Evaluation. Formative evaluation provides information for program planners during the development and early implementation of a program. Information is collected in an ongoing fashion so that changes and improvements can be made along the way. The information needs to be timely so that a program that is off course can be corrected before too much time has passed. Often, the collected information relates to the process rather than the outcomes. Process questions focus on the program itself: Were the speakers on time? How many students showed up? Was there enough time? A formative evaluation is usually conducted by the program staff members involved in the day-to-day decision making. Decisions are made about ways to improve the program or respond to nagging glitches. Reports are informal, often consisting of queries and discussions at weekly staff meetings.

Summative evaluation, in contrast, aims to provide evaluative information to persons external to the program. External persons could be the director of housing, the dean of students, the vice president for student affairs, the president, or even the governing board. The evaluator is often an unbiased third person, and the evaluation takes place at a critical point in the program. Decisions conceivably could result in the termination of the program. In summative evaluations, the evaluator usually makes a formal report to the key decision makers, and the data collected focus on program outcomes rather than processes: Did students learn something? Did the damage reports go down? Were reported racial incidents less frequent?

Residence hall staff will find a formative evaluation more useful and responsive to their information needs for decision making than a summative evaluation. This is especially true if they are involved in the evaluation's design and data gathering. The staff are familiar with the purposes of the program, the local idiosyncracies, and steps that can realistically be taken to improve the program. A summative evaluation, conducted by an outsider who will be less familiar with the program, seldom provides internal staff members with new or immediately useful information. But staff are not the intended audience for this evaluation; the information is meant to provide external decision makers with objective and unbiased information.

The decision makers, whether they are from within the specific residence hall, at the housing director's office, or at the vice president's office, need to distinguish carefully between formative and summative evaluation. Too often the questions asked and the amount of energy expended for a

summative evaluation could be better directed toward a formative evaluation. Because decisions about how to improve existing programs are more
frequent than decisions about whether a program should be kept or terminated, the focus of most evaluations should be on finding ways to improve the
program. If the staff members planning the evaluation keep in mind questions like, "Should the health aide training programs include sessions on
suicide crises or not?", or "What can be done to strengthen the hall floor
governments?", they can gather more useful information than if they ask
questions like, "Is our health aide training program effective?" If the decision
makers appear to be locked into determining whether or not the program is
"effective," it helps if the evaluator probes and determines the indicators of
effectiveness and the decisions the decision makers might make. By focusing
on what could possibly be changed or redirected, the evaluation information
can be more useful.

Research Versus Evaluation. In Scenario 2 at the beginning of the chapter
Susan was characterized as doing research. Sam (Scenario 1), on the other
hand, was portrayed as conducting an evaluation. It is important to distinguish clearly between these two purposes and activities. The researcher is
trying to establish or test a theory and hopes to generalize it to other settings.
Questions of utility and feasibility or even of values are not a primary
consideration. In contrast, evaluation focuses on questions of worth and the
everyday decisions that must be made about residence hall life. Evaluation
encompasses a broader spectrum of concerns or variables. The researcher
may want to know whether or not the health aide program that used a
consultative approach was more effective in reducing cold and flu symptoms
among residents than the program based on a prescriptive model. The
evaluator, on the other hand, recognizes that cost-effectiveness, staff and
student morale, and even campus politics must be considered in determining whether the consultative or prescriptive approach is retained. The researcher hopes to reach conclusions that suggest her findings are generalizable to similar residence halls and to other campuses. The evaluator is more
concerned with having the information be useful in making a decision at his
campus.

Selecting an Approach to Conducting Research and Evaluation

Investigators in all academic disciplines have access to a multitude of approaches. Historians use interviews, soil samples, economic indicators, and
even statistics to answer a particular research question. Anthropologists
gather data at exotic locales, even garbage dumps. Though there are no
reported studies of residence hall garbage, the researcher or evaluator investigating residence hall life has many approaches from which to choose. It is
important to match the appropriate approach with the investigator's questions. Most approaches fall into three categories: (1) descriptive, (2) issue-
resolving, and (3) cause-and-effect.

Descriptive Approaches

Case-study descriptive approaches to research and evaluation have gained increasing prominence and credibility in the past decade. Educational researchers have recently recognized that the tools and techniques of anthropologists have applicability and usefulness for them as well. Anthropologists make extensive use of interviews, observations, participant observation, and photography to obtain information for the purpose of describing a setting or a culture. Many who use what are referred to as *naturalistic inquiry* or *qualitative* approaches (Guba and Lincoln, 1981; Lincoln and Guba, 1985; Strauss and Corbin, 1990) have a different perspective on human behavior and reality that influences how a researcher or evaluator uses these strategies. As contrasted to the positivist paradigm or traditional experimental approaches to research, qualitative investigators see reality as more holistic, believe the researcher influences results in the act of collecting data, and develop working hypotheses rather than testing predetermined hypotheses. The qualitative researcher or evaluator also is more likely to aim for rich and full descriptions of events and recognizes that values cannot be separated completely from a presentation of findings. Description is the predominant goal, in contrast to testing cause-and-effect relationships.

Interviews help the qualitative investigator describe the setting with the voices of the participants. The subjective views of the program participants and others in the setting are important in this approach. Quotes from students about their reactions to a program on acquaintance rape can be as meaningful as reporting mean scores on an attitude survey. The investigative reporter and the anthropologist are helpful metaphors for thinking about the role of the inquirer who uses interviews. (For useful information about selecting people to interview and framing interview questions, see Bradburn, Sudman, and Associates, 1979; Spradley, 1979; Agar, 1980; Machovec, 1989; Johnson, 1990.)

Observation through direct or indirect participation helps the researcher or evaluator have a good sense of what residence hall life is like. Good research or evaluation reports provide the reader with a sense of place, and the most effective reports come close to providing a vicarious experience for the reader. Numbers or words are seldom as descriptive as being there in person. (See Hartmann, 1982; Miles and Huberman, 1984; Merriam, 1988.)

Good examples of research using such descriptions include *Involving Colleges: Successful Approaches to Fostering Student Learning and Development Outside the Classroom* (Kuh, Schuh, Whitt, and Associates, 1991) and *Coming of Age in New Jersey: College and American Culture* (Moffatt, 1989). Kuh, Schuh, Whitt, and their associates intensively analyzed eight colleges characterized as institutions that involve students in many facets of college life. An appendix provides a detailed listing of the questions and processes used by the authors when they visited the campuses. Moffatt (1989) presents an anthropologist's insider view of residential hall life as a participant observer.

Residence hall staff hardly need to live in (although, of course, many do) to discover what residence hall life is like. This strategy can be useful, however, for others. Having faculty members, administrators, or board members live in for a day will certainly provide a direct experience of what residence hall life is like in a way that numbers and charts cannot.

Photography is a data gathering device that, like interviews and observations, lends itself readily to unique ways of presenting results. Having participants take photographs of what they see as important and using photographs to evoke response from participants, for example, can provide data not collectible in any other form. (For additional information about the use of photography in evaluation, see Bogdan and Biklen, 1982; Brown, Petersen, and Sanstead, 1980; Fang and Ellwein, 1990.) Anthropologists have used the camera for many years; it is time educational researchers recognize its value.

All the data gathering approaches used for descriptive purposes have inherent problems relating to sampling, obtrusiveness, and objectivity. The same problems also arise for more traditional data gathering approaches, such as questionnaires, but educational researchers tend to forget or gloss over them. Do not be fooled by the apparent softness or ease of using these approaches; numerous techniques can enhance the reliability and validity of these methods and can make their credibility quite high (Miles and Huberman, 1984). Anyone who has conducted a thorough descriptive study that measures up to its highest standards can testify that it is not easy or quick.

Descriptive approaches to evaluation or research are particularly appropriate when knowing what the program participants think and feel is important, when presenting case-study data with photographs or quotations will serve a dramatic as well as a descriptive purpose, and when it is more appropriate to generate hypotheses than to test them.

Issue-Resolving Approaches

Programming for residence halls often either emanates from or results in controversy. As a result, a staff member, a student, or a parent often will not like what is being done. The governing board may fear that sponsoring programs against gay bashing is suggesting the college supports gay lifestyles. Parents may feel that if condoms are available, the residence halls are not an appropriate living environment for their son or daughter. If the purpose of the inquiry is to respond to these issues, an evaluation approach is most likely to be more appropriate than a research approach, and the evaluation needs to be focused directly on the issues. This is essential if the decisions will be based on how important stakeholders feel about the issues. Two closely related evaluation models focus on issue resolution: responsive evaluation and transactional evaluation.

A *responsive* approach to evaluation (Stake, 1975; Worthen and Sanders, 1987) emphasizes concentrating on program issues and program activities.

This is in contrast to the emphasis placed on outcomes by other evaluation approaches and by a research approach. The responsive evaluator attempts to identify the key issues, to determine what information is needed to respond to those issues, and to obtain the perspectives that different stakeholders (for example, parents, students, and staff) have on the issues. The evaluator using this approach spends considerable time visiting with staff, administrators, students, and others to share perspectives, to validate interpretations, and to determine if the issues remain the same over time. The responsive evaluator reacts to the needs of the moment. Stake (1975) characterizes the responsive approach as emergent in its design and focus and unlike the experimental design approaches that are preordinate.

An evaluator who is asked to assess whether or not condoms should continue to be available through the desk lobby or a vending machine in the canteen area is in a situation where the responsive approach would be highly applicable. The decision makers are going to want to know how people think and feel about this issue, as well as about possible outcome data such as frequency of sales or the number of unwanted pregnancies. This is an issue question that is value loaded. When controversy is a likely outcome, the evaluator will want to consider the responsive approach.

Transactional evaluation (Rippey, 1973; Worthen and Sanders, 1987) emphasizes working on conflict resolution as well as issue identification. There can be many reasons why a residence hall program fails, but prominent ones could be overt or covert hostility. Staff can resist role changes, student government can be upset about the power implications of who made the decisions, and administrators may look for any ammunition to kill a controversial program. The transactional evaluation approach is similar to the tactic many administrators use when they toss a controversial issue to a committee encompassing members representing diverse views. If the committee does the job, the heat of the arguments will have been worked through before they get out of the committee. Similarly, the transactional evaluator identifies the program proponents and antagonists and uses their viewpoints to gather the evidence that will be convincing to both. All sides determine the important criteria, how the data will be collected, and who will get what results.

Both the responsive and transactional approaches require evaluators to have good interpersonal skills, be good conflict resolvers, and be persons who can survive, if not enjoy, working in a politically charged environment. The issue-resolving approach is most appropriate in situations in which there is clearly a controversial issue. These can seldom be determined ahead of time, even with a thorough review of the literature. What is a straightforward and an obviously needed program on one campus may provoke an entire community to protest on another campus. So even if an issue-resolving approach is not adopted as a primary evaluation or research strategy, program designers, evaluators, and researchers need to be alert to and flexible enough to attend to these sources of resistance and potential controversies.

This may mean even abandoning a research design or a preordinate evaluation and switching to a more responsive approach.

Cause-and-Effect Approaches

The purpose of scientific research is to develop theory, reach conclusions about cause-and-effect relationships, and make generalizations that apply to other situations and settings (Borg and Gall, 1989). A person conducting scientific research on residence hall life examines theories about students; how students form friendships, how a sense of community is established, what developmental issues students confront, how interventions might facilitate development, or how behavioral norms are established and maintained. These theories stimulate new programs, procedures, or policies for residence halls — providing guidance on how students are assigned to halls, floors, or roommates, suggesting how floor governments might be structured, and providing program ideas for coed or single-sex halls. To make cause-and-effect connections between the innovations derived from the theories and the outcomes in student or staff behavior, it is often necessary to have strict control over many extraneous variables. This may be achieved only in a laboratory-like environment and may demand random assignment of students to the different halls. These conditions are seldom possible in college residence halls.

Three basic research designs — the randomized control group, the nonequivalent comparison group, and the self-comparison design — are described so that the readers, as well as Susan Ivorytower, will know what to consider as research projects are designed.

1. *Randomized control-group* designs require random assignment of students to experimental and control groups. If the researcher wants to compare the psychosocial development of college students in coed residence halls and single-sex residence halls, for example, he or she would randomly assign students applying to the residence halls to a coed residence hall (experimental group) or a single-sex residence hall (control group). This design provides the investigator with the most confidence that the outcome (psychosocial development) was due to living in either a coed or a single-sex residence hall. Randomness is a critical feature. It is the best guarantee the students assigned to the different halls were initially the same on psychosocial development and other variables that may be related, such as class standing, family background, and past experiences.

The confidence the investigator has in the two groups being initially the same is increased as the sample size gets larger. Obviously, if 10 male students were randomly assigned from a pool of 20 to a coed residence hall and compared to the remaining 10 randomly assigned to a single-sex residence hall, the investigator would be less confident they were initially similar on key characteristics than if the initial pool was 100 male students and 50 were randomly assigned to each hall. The researcher may pretest students on an outcome variable prior to their random assignment. If the student groups are significantly dissimilar, it is possible to employ statistical procedures, such as covariant procedures, to control for the initial differences.

Implementing this research design poses a significant problem for the investigator if it is not feasible or ethical to randomly assign students to different residence halls or different residence hall floors. Is it possible, for example, to randomly assign students to a coed residence hall or a single-sex residence hall? Is it politically feasible to randomly assign students to a residence hall close to the library or one a half mile from the library without interfering with a policy that specifies a first-come, first-served assignment procedure?

If the assignment of students to a control group means those students are not going to receive a customary or needed service, it may be unethical to withhold the service from the control group (American College Personnel Association, 1990). When resources are limited and such services can only be provided for a limited number of students, it might be ethical to make the service available to a random group of students. Another possibility is to delay the service for the control group, if this can be done without harm. Students in one residence hall or on one floor of a residence hall can be scheduled to have an experimental program on study skills during February, and the control-group floor can have the program scheduled for March. Students in both the experimental and control groups might be tested or queried on the criterion measure in January, at the end of February, and again at the end of March. (The researcher might want to replicate the study in reverse order the next year, because it may be possible that student motivation to learn and use study skills is greater in March than in February.)

The researcher or evaluator should never make decisions alone about what is ethical and what is not ethical. She or he should find out what campus policies and procedures exist to determine whether or not appropriate safeguards are present to protect students from harm and to respect their privacy. Many campuses have institutional review boards to conduct ethical reviews. Where official review groups do not exist, the investigator should consult available resources such as Buckner (1988) and Ebbers (1988), who review the legal issues related to residence hall life; they should also consult with respected colleagues and published professional ethical guidelines (American College Personnel Association, 1990).

2. *Nonrandomized comparison-group* studies involve comparing students who are already a part of an intact group. These approaches to research or evaluation are referred to as *quasi-experimental* designs (Borg and Gall, 1989). The major difference from the randomized control-group design is that it is not possible to assign students randomly to a program or treatment group and a control group. The program or treatment must be provided to an intact group of students—that is, to students who live in one hall or on one floor. Quasi-experimental research designs are more feasible than the fully randomized control-group approach. The investigator interested in studying

residence hall life usually has to work with intact groups of students who already live on a particular residence hall or floor. He or she can never really know whether there are systematic differences between students in the halls to be studied unless a premeasure is obtained. Even if the premeasure comparisons yield no significant differences, he or she may not be aware of other variables that may also be related. For example, the investigator may find that pretest measures of attitudes regarding use of condoms result in no statistical differences between students in a coed or a single-sex hall. It may be, however, that the students in the single-sex hall are older, or more sexually active, and that these factors make them more receptive to an AIDS education program.

Two statistical procedures can be used to patch up these designs, and both require a premeasure. One procedure is called *covariance* (Borg and Gall, 1989). This procedure is not a substitute for randomization, but it adjusts the postexperiment outcome measures on the basis of the initial status of the two groups. Covariance is roughly analogous to adding a bowling handicap to an amateur bowler's score and comparing the augmented total score of that bowler to a professional competitor's score. In residence hall research, this might mean, for example, using ACT scores of students as a covariant when comparing the academic achievement of students who live on career-focused floors to those with the same career goals who live on mixed floors. Because of a selection factor, the students who chose career-focused floors may have higher initial grade-point averages (GPAs) than the students who live on regular floors. The initial GPA could be used as a covariant for comparing their end-of-year GPAs. Similarly, ACT scores, which would be expected to be related to academic performance, could also be used as covariants. This statistical procedure is not perfect, but it does help make a more valid comparison possible.

Another statistical procedure is to calculate gain or difference scores between the students in the experimental condition and those in the control condition. If GPA was the important outcome measure, comparisons would be made between the differences in the initial and final GPA of the experimental group and the initial and final GPA of the control group. It is possible to collect premeasures on most outcome variables. If attitude change or hall damage is of interest, it is possible to collect initial attitude information or examine the record of hall damage prior to an intervention program and again after the program. A premeasure on the outcome variable is needed before a comparison can be made. If the residence hall program is aimed at racial attitudes and outcome measures include the number of racial incidents as well as attitude changes, it is essential to have residents of the hall in which the program is being piloted and the control-group hall be given a pretest of attitudes. Records of the number of racial incidents also need to be available prior to program implementation. A major difficulty with analysis of gain or difference scores is that the reliability of the difference score is weaker than the reliability of the initial measures themselves (Cook and Campbell, 1979).

3. *Self-comparison* designs are used when it is not possible to have a comparison group and the researcher or evaluator must compare the impact of a program within one residence hall. If self-comparison is the only comparison possible, a premeasure or baseline measure is needed so comparisons can be made between end-of-program measures and preprogram measures. If a new policy is established regarding false fire alarms, it is helpful to have a record of the number of false fire alarms for several months and ideally for the same period a year ago. If a change is made in visitation hours that is expected to have an impact on the sense of community within the hall, it is helpful to have an indicator of sense of community before the change is instituted. Though this research design does not provide as strong evidence as do those with a random sample control group, the evidence can still be convincing.

Cause-and-effect approaches to research and evaluation questions are most applicable when the investigator wants to generalize the findings to other residence halls or other campuses. Testing theory is usually a primary goal. None of the three research designs are perfect, if practicality is an important criteria, since often the purest research design is the least practical. With some creative thinking, however, it is possible to use these designs in a fashion that is both practical and scientifically sound. (For an instructive discussion of the philosophical and technical issues of quasi-experimental designs, see Cook and Campbell, 1979.)

Evaluation and Research at Different Stages of Program Development

Questions and decisions about residence hall programs differ depending on the developmental stage of the program. Four program stages interact with the questions and decisions: program establishment, program installation, program improvement, and program assessment. The audience for the results, the relevant questions that need answering, and the strategies for collecting data and conducting research and evaluation vary depending on the stage. Formative evaluation is most often the goal during the first three stages, and summative evaluation and research are often the primary focus in the final stage.

Stage 1: Establishing Programs

Planning an evaluation or a research project should begin before a decision has been made to start the program. The impetus for a new program for the residence halls may originate from a staff member who senses a need based on her or his experience with students last year or so far this year, an administrator who may bring the idea to campus from a previous work setting, a hall director who is stimulated by a journal article, or a student group that may express a need for a program or service. There are three questions that must be considered during this stage: Is there a need for the program? Is the program feasible? Is the campus climate receptive?

Is There a Need for the Program? There is no formula that provides a ready answer to questions of need. Though attempts can be made to weight differentially the opinions and assessments of students, staff, and experts, need is ultimately determined on the basis of a subjective judgment. Needs must first be distinguished from wants (Lenning and McAleenan, 1979; Stufflebeam, 1985). Students may indicate they "want" to have condoms accessible through vending machines in the residence halls, but this does not necessarily mean they "need" them. Whenever a mismatch exists between students' wants and their real needs, the staff must focus on the educational goal of helping students distinguish between the two. If the need exists for information on AIDS but students appear not to want it, the staff must first create a want. If the want exists for computer terminals on each residence hall floor but administrators do not see the value because terminals are available in a nearby library, the staff must work with one or both groups to reconcile the differences.

Needs assessment is a frequently used term that too often implies little more than sending out a survey that lists a variety of topics or programs and asks students to indicate their degree of interest in each. This democratic approach to conducting a needs assessment may provide useful information, but it is not sufficient information to launch major programmatic efforts. The results will provide a fair estimate of the "wants" of the students, but other information must be collected before a true needs assessment exists.

Needs assessment information should be sought from a variety of sources. Polling students in particular halls or on specific floors is one way of determining students' expressed needs. This can be done directly through listing program possibilities and asking students to rank their importance. It is also helpful to gather information about the format and timing of the program activity. Would they prefer a presentation, discussion, or debate? Would they like to have the program on weekends or on an evening during the week? These added bits of information can help program planners. But "needs" identified by students through such approaches often do not translate into attendance at programs related to the "needs."

Another useful source for determining needs is to compare the current residence hall environment with what staff and students consider to be the ideal residence hall. This is referred to as a *discrepancy* form of needs assessment. Is the sense of community as strong as it should be? Is the climate supportive of good study behavior? Are there racial tensions that need to be reduced? When conducting this form of needs assessment, it is helpful to be as behavioral as possible. It is not much help to ask students whether or not they want a program on "Community Life." Ask direct behavioral questions instead: How many students on the floor do they know? Who eats together? Where do they study? The program planners might ask staff members and student leaders for their views on the meaning of the information and whether or not the results warrant intervention.

An analytical approach to needs assessment requires a different process. Numerous information sources are involved. For example, the student health center may report a disturbing increase of sexually transmitted diseases (STD). Discussion among the student affairs staff suggests a good way to reach students about this concern is through the residence halls. Thus, program planning on STDs is clearly based on a need, but no information was obtained directly from students during the decision process. Similar needs assessment information could be obtained from finding out what is happening on other campuses, attending to what experts report, and noting local campus trends such as in grades, attrition rates, and drug and alcohol abuse behavior. Whether the new program is planned to meet a student need or for research purposes, the planners should always check the literature on the topic. What has been done on other campuses may seldom be directly applicable to a particular campus, but it can save time and energy and prevent program planners from taking a wrong path.

Needs assessment can also be used for making decisions about how students are assigned to residence halls, how the physical characteristics of the residence halls can be remodeled, and numerous other aspects of residence hall life.

Two major errors are frequently made when considering needs assessment for residence halls. The first involves the assumption that a needs assessment always necessitates a questionnaire surveying students' "wants." Judy Garland and Mickey Rooney in the "Andy Hardy" movies used to solve their money woes by saying almost in unison, "I know what we need to do, let's put on a show." So it is in student affairs; in unison, staff say, "Let's do a needs assessment by sending out a questionnaire." These questionnaires often become massive undertakings taxing the staff's time and energy to construct, mail, process, and tabulate the returns. Frequently, the questionnaires have dubious validity and meager returns, so generalization to the population is unwarranted. The approaches to needs assessment described in this chapter offer alternatives to questionnaires and surveys. Examination of records, a show of hands at floor meetings, and interviews with a few insightful students who have a sense of what other students think are useful, quick, and valid ways of gathering needs assessment information.

A second error in processing needs assessment data is the failure to recognize that politics play an important role in decisions made about what programs to implement in response to a needs assessment. If the college president suggests a need or a regent or board member finds a fault, these must be responded to regardless of others' perceptions of the needs. If a donor makes money available for athletic equipment for the residence hall intramural teams or a new lounge, that money probably cannot be spent on condom vending machines even though that may be a greater need in the eyes of some. It is important to recognize the political nature of decision making about needs, whether it involves different opinions among student groups, among staff, or between students and staff.

A negotiation process for making decisions about needs assessment information can be a useful educational opportunity within the residence halls. Making good use of needs assessment and following up on the information provided can help build a sense of involvement by students and other stakeholders who are queried. (For further discussion of needs assessment, see Stufflebeam, 1985.)

Is the Program Feasible? Feasibility plays an important role in determining whether an innovative residence hall program will be started and what form it will take. Are the resources available to offer the program? If it is an educational program, are staff members trained to offer the program or are other campus resources readily available? Is special funding necessary? A helpful way to approach feasibility is to construct lists of potential program topics, audience, and available resources. If one is planning an AIDS education program, she or he will want to have preliminary or ongoing discussions regarding the dimension of the topic the program will focus on. Will it emphasize behavior, attitudes, knowledge, or some combination? Program planners will also want to note the intended audience—females, males, freshmen, seniors? Eventually, the topic, audience, and resource lists must be matched up. Staff members will want to note the level of training and knowledge of the residence hall staff and the availability of resource persons from student health, the counseling center, and other campus or community experts. Perhaps the library has books or a media center has video materials on the topic.

Costs must also be considered. For a one-time program, start-up costs will be the primary expense. For a longer-term program, maintenance costs must be determined. Certainly, dollar costs must be noted. Are the presenters or resources available cost free, or is some honorarium expected? Are there equipment or rental costs? There is also the added expense of staff time. How much effort is going to be needed to organize, implement, and maintain this program? Is the staff motivated to put in the necessary time? Out of whose "hide" does this program come? Relative priorities must be considered as well. Even though there may be no apparent new dollar costs and staff time may be available, program planners need to consider what other activities or programs are not being offered because this one is.

Is the Campus Climate Receptive? A first consideration is whether the residence hall staff is receptive to the proposed program. The staff members on the firing line are usually the persons implementing the program or surviving the aftershocks. How receptive are they to new and possibly additional responsibilities? If the staff is supportive and eager, what about the rest of the campus and community? Residence halls do not exist in isolation from other dimensions of campus or community life. The director of housing may have sufficient power to launch a program, even if it means realigning her or his staff's responsibilities. But what about other political implications? Condoms in the residence halls and sexual orientation awareness workshops are potentially controversial program issues. There are many other topics that may prove to be controversial.

Stage 2: Program Installation

The focus of evaluation at this stage is to assist the residence hall staff in improving the established residence hall programs. This evaluation is formative and informal. The primary audience for the evaluation is internal to the organization — the housing director and staff. These are the people who will have daily contact with students and other staff who are affected by the program. Two questions need to be asked at this point: Who is served by the program? Are the intended programs being implemented?

Who Is Served by the Program? When program planners design a program, they usually specify the intended audience so that the program presenters know the characteristics of the audience. Too often, programmers get caught up in the number of students who attend rather than considering their characteristics. Staff may believe the more students who participate the better, since the success of the program rests on having good attendance. This criterion is difficult to ignore, and no doubt in many instances it is an important one. More critical, however, is the question of whether or not the right students participate. It is not unusual to offer a study techniques workshop and have the students who attend have higher GPAs than the students who did not attend. If the indicator of success is the number of students who attend, this would gloss over the fact that the targeted students did not participate.

Finding that the attending audience was different from the intended audience may indicate a need the residence hall staff were unaware of during the planning stage or problems in the marketing for the program. The planners may have to rethink whether the originally intended audience still needs the program, and if they do, how the program should be marketed or revised so the intended audience is reached.

Are the Intended Programs Being Provided? Many programs fail because they are not implemented in the intended fashion. The residence hall staff may decide to focus on having RAs visit with each floor resident during the first month of school. The staff believes this will encourage community development in the halls and increase the number of students who see the RA as a valuable resource person. The degree to which this program is implemented as intended could vary dramatically; it could include everything from the RA who perfunctorily stops by each room on her or his floor to the RA who spends twenty to thirty minutes with each set of roommates.

If the housing director is going to make decisions about how to improve the program or whether to even offer the program again, it is essential to know if the program was implemented and how well the implementation matches the expected events. This requires the housing director to stress to the staff the importance of follow-through and to consider ways of directly observing the program or indirectly monitoring implementation through staff logs or diaries. The monitoring process should be started early in the program implementation stage. Discovering the breakdowns or unexpected barriers early leaves time for problem-solving behavior to occur and the program to be salvaged.

Stage 3: Ongoing Program Improvement

After the program has been installed and has survived a shakedown period of initial changes and corrections, it is natural for interest and concern about evaluation to diminish. Periodic checks need to be made, however, to determine whether the program continues to run smoothly. The constant attention to program improvement yields payoffs for program effectiveness and efficiency. Two primary sources of information for ongoing, formative evaluation purposes are the students and the staff.

Gathering Student Opinion. Before designing a survey to administer to all residence hall students, other options should carefully be considered. Alternatives or supplements to the customary survey stuffed in student mailboxes or squeezed underneath doors include using student focus groups, such as a student advisory panel, to provide useful information and to involve students in the evaluation design process. Focus groups are small groups of program participants, in this case residence hall students, who have a stake in the outcome of the evaluation and who represent a broad spectrum of opinion. Small-group discussions can save the evaluator time, but more important, the interchange of ideas and opinions among the group members makes it possible for the interview to clarify statements and validate conclusions across several individuals. Student focus groups can provide information to help the evaluator decide what questions need answering, as well as furnishing student opinions. (For more on this topic, see Merton, Fiske, and Kendall, 1990; Morgan, 1988; Stewart and Shamdasani, 1990.)

Key questions to ask the students in the focus groups could include the following: What are students doing in the program? Are they attending with interest, as well as being in attendance physically? What do they see as the purpose of the program? How would they describe the program to another resident? Does the program seem to be addressing their needs? What suggestions do they have for program improvement? How do they see themselves being affected by the program?

Staff Input. The evaluator must set a tone so staff members see evaluation as a process, not as an event. Evaluation should not be something that is only done at certain times in the term or in early stages of a program; evaluation must be ongoing if it is to be useful. Staff members must have frequent opportunities to give input, and the program administrators must follow up on staff suggestions. An ideal administrative environment for effective on-going evaluation is one that is receptive to evaluative comments in an open, nonjudgmental, problem-solving manner. The program administrator should be able to say, "Let's talk about how things are going. What's working and not working?" and receive a response that is candid and constructive rather than defensive and hypercritical.

Stage 4: Assessing Impact

Programs in residence halls are seldom victims of an administrative ax so much as they often fade away as staff members depart and new ones take their place. Nevertheless, there are times when a budget crunch may force a cut or when a skeptical new director wants evidence that a program is having the intended impact. Occasionally, programs are tried on an "experimental" basis with the intention that they be evaluated after a trial period. Early efforts to establish coed residence halls often took this form (Brown, 1973). The possible decisions range from program termination to expansion or limitation. If the decision alternatives are termination or retention, this evaluation activity is clearly summative. As noted earlier, summative decisions are usually made by persons external to the immediate program being evaluated and are often conducted by external personnel.

Three questions need to be asked: Who are the decision makers? What are the criteria for assessing worth? What instrumentation is appropriate? The first question is of most interest to the person conducting an evaluation; the second and third questions are of interest to both the researcher and the evaluator. All the questions should be asked and answered before the program begins.

Who Are the Decision Makers? It is important in all stages of evaluation to know who is going to make decisions about the program. Are the decisions going to be made by the staff of the housing director's office, by the housing director alone, by the dean of students or vice president for student affairs, by a faculty group, or by a governing board? The evaluation may be proposed or requested by one person or group, and yet the ultimate decision making may rest in the hands of another person or group. The key decision makers should be identified before an evaluation plan is developed.

What Are the Criteria for Assessing Worth? It is essential to find out from the decision makers what criteria they will use to make judgments about the residence hall program. It does not help to collect information on how many students attend the program if the housing director wants information about the cost of the program compared to similar programs. It does not help to inform the vice president for student affairs that a recent survey indicates students in the experimental residence halls report great satisfaction with residence hall life when she or he wants to know how the halls compare on records of hall damage. It is essential to know the criteria for judging the worth or success of the program before the program is initiated. Though it is important to focus the evaluation on prespecified criteria, it should not be limited to these preselected variables. Consider collecting information about possible side effects of the program, both positive and negative. A training program for RAs aimed at increasing responsiveness to maintenance concerns (for example, where the light bulbs are or what to do when a toilet overflows) may reduce student complaints but may also mistakenly leave the impression with staff that educational programming on the floors is less important. Perhaps an intensive effort at reducing racial incidents in the halls appears to be successful, but as a result, there is extensive staff burnout and attrition. These negative side effects do not mean the program should be dropped, but rather provide indications of the need for refinements or adaptations so that the negative side effects are limited.

There may also be instances in which the side effects are positive. As a result of a hall having a mentoring program for new students, the new students may show no evidence of achieving higher grades or adjusting to college life any better, but roommate dissatisfaction might drop and more students might indicate they want to be in the same hall next year. The mentoring program may not appear to be having the impact it was expected to have, but it may be having other useful and positive effects.

What Instrumentation Is Appropriate? The primary concern for the investigator will usually be the impact a program has on students. Does the program affect student attitudes or behaviors? Are they more satisfied? Is the residence hall a better setting for studying? Is the students' psychosocial development different in a coed residence hall than in a single-sex residence hall? Do students who reside on special interest hall floors progress in their career development at a faster rate than those not on special interest hall floors?

It is helpful to think of student change as a sequence that runs through attention, knowledge, attitudes, and behaviors. The ultimate goal of a program is to change student behavior: students study more and have a higher GPA, or there is less acquaintance rape on campus. But for the program to have an impact, students must first participate in the program and be attentive in their participation, they must gain new knowledge, and their attitudes must change. Too often, researchers and evaluators jump to one end of the continuum—behavioral change—without assessing whether the program took place as intended, whether what was expected to occur did occur, whether the students gained knowledge, and whether their attitudes were affected.

Contrasted to the researcher's interest in assessing the impact on students, criteria for a summative evaluation of a residence hall program should include the impact the program has on residence hall environment, students, and staff and should provide cost-benefit information. The summative evaluator is going to be looking for a broader awareness of measures than just those that measure student outcomes.

When selecting instruments, a critical decision is whether to design an instrument that is applicable to the specific question and setting or to use a standardized instrument. Often this decision is determined by the balance between having an instrument directly applicable to the local setting and one that has greater credibility for an external audience. Check available references for tests and instruments to see what is available. The *Mental Measurements Yearbooks*, published by the University of Nebraska Press, provide objective, critical reviews of commercial tests. *Test Collection Bibliographies*, published by the Educational Testing Service, describe many unpublished as well as published instruments. If possible, read the test manual that provides validity and reliability data to see if what the instrument purports to measure is similar to the program's hoped-for outcomes. It is essential that the instrument measures what the researcher or evaluator wants it to measure and that what is measured relates directly to the intervention or program strategy. (Instrument names often are not accurate guides to what they actually measure.) The most valid instrument is not useful if it measures career maturity and the researcher wants to measure ego identity. If the researcher plans to publish the findings, editors will want to know the reliability and validity of the instrument, which are usually stronger in standardized measures than in homemade instruments. (For a discussion of instruments available for assessing student development and college environments, see Huebner and Lawson, 1990; King, 1990; Miller and Winston, 1990. Also see Chapters Three to Five of this volume.)

Sometimes, especially for evaluation purposes, it is necessary to construct a homemade instrument to meet the specific needs for a local study. Think first about what unobtrusive behavioral measures might answer the research or evaluation questions before considering a questionnaire or survey. If you are concerned about student satisfaction, ask what behaviors satisfied and dissatisfied students might exhibit and then devise a plan for gathering related data. Before surveying students, consider using roommate changes, retention rates, and vandalism and damage reports as indicators.

If you have to design a questionnaire, consider focusing as much as possible on behavioral indicators rather than on attitude surveys. The later often end up being little more than happiness indexes, which are helpful if the returns are all negative but not of much use otherwise. Rather than asking, "Are you satisfied with life in this residence hall?", ask questions about intentions to return to the hall, willingness to recommend the hall to a friend, and the amount of leisure time spent in the hall with other residents. These and similar behavior-focused questions (Who do they eat with? Who do they go to movies with? Are they on a hall intramural team? Do they use the lounge? How many residents do they know?) are often more accurate and descriptive information sources than the more typical Likert-type (Strongly Agree — Strongly Disagree) questions.

Reliability and validity remain important and should not be slighted because the evaluator is not thinking of publishing the results in a journal. Like the researcher, the evaluator must first see if an available standardized instrument suits his or her purpose. If the evaluator needs to construct an instrument, scales should include more than one item. As a minimum, this permits the evaluator to look at the reliability through calculation of Cronbach's alpha coefficient, an indicator of internal consistency (Borg and Gall, 1989). Someone should always read over the instrument to determine clarity and if possible to check it out for content validity; the person should decide whether it seems to be measuring the appropriate behaviors, attitudes, or opinions. (For excellent guidelines on questionnaire design, see Sudman and Bradburn, 1982.)

If Susan or Sam successfully collected useful data through these four program stages, their task would not be finished but would start all over again. This puts Susan back at looking at her theory and wondering if still another theory might have different effects and Sam back at deciding whether or not to continue his program, revise it, or change to another program. Both are back at stage 1: establishing programs. (For more discussion of evaluation approaches, see Madaus, Scriven, and Stufflebeam, 1983; Posavac and Carey, 1989; Rossi and Freeman, 1989.)

Research Agenda for Housing for the Next Decade

Housing research for the past three decades focused on two goals: (1) making residence hall life more humane, and (2) intentionally promoting student learning and development through the residence living experience. These goals interact, but they can be examined separately. Studies that investigate efforts to enhance roommate compatibility and those that look at the impact of person-environment matches and mismatches are driven by the goal of making the residence hall a more humane living environment. (See Burchill and Stiles, 1988; Carey, Stanley, and Biggers, 1988; Janosik, Creamer, and Cross, 1988.) Studies that examine the impact of having classes in the residence halls, the effect of having living units become centers for special student groups (for example, career hall floors, halls giving special attention to moral-ethical development), and many studies of coeducational residences are part of the living-learning tradition that evolved twenty-five years ago and continues today. (See Clarke, Miser, and Roberts, 1988.)

The need for studies that focus on these two goals still exists and will continue to be important through the next century. These goals and the need for research are analogous to those of psychologists who study marriage and family concerns and those of sociologists who study community living.

Because of changing times and circumstances, researchers will never determine what matchups make for the perfect marriage or what will promote the development of the ideal community. Each new generation, and decade, brings with it new problems and new opportunities. Given the constancy of these needs, the quality of life in the residence halls of the twenty-first century will be significantly enhanced if the research and evaluation activities of the next decade emphasize the following methodologies and research topics.

Needed Methodologies

There are a number of measures that, if taken, could improve the quality and quantity of evaluation and research studies in today's residence halls. Specifically, there need to be more formative evaluations, greater use of qualitative research methods, and studies that focus on both process and outcome.

More Formative Evaluations

Residence hall staff need support and encouragement to improve the everyday life in their residence halls through ongoing evaluations that monitor the day-by-day needs and moods of students. They need to assess what is going right and what is going wrong in the halls and with their program interventions in an ongoing manner, rather than waiting until the end of a program or the end of the academic term.

Greater Use of Qualitative Research Methods

Formative evaluation lends itself to using qualitative methods. An important first step is to try to describe what has happened. How many students attended a program? How did the leaders react? What happened after the meeting? What did the students do when they discovered the game room closed? What were students thinking and feeling when they heard about the suicide attempt? Case studies that illustrate critical incidents in successful or unsuccessful programs or interventions can be useful for research or evaluation purposes. (See Patton, 1990, for helpful guidelines.)

Studies That Focus on Both Process and Outcome

The predominant focus of past studies has been on retention and GPA as the primary and often sole outcome variables. These are important variables, but they are influenced by the complex interaction of many factors besides living circumstances, and they do not fully reflect the developmental goals of residence hall educators. There is also the danger that by focusing exclusively on outcome variables, which certainly have market value to other campus administrators, residence hall educators will neglect important process variables that must be in place to facilitate changes in the academic outcome measures. Attention to staff development and staff burnout prevention is needed if the residence hall staff hopes to have an impact on the academic achievement of the residents. Also, by overemphasizing the outcome variables—particularly academic achievement—to the exclusion of other outcomes, researchers and evaluators are not giving needed attention to the processes that enhance the quality of campus life. These include building a sense of community, promoting faculty-student interactions, and providing students with experiences in cultural diversity.

Needed Research and Evaluation Topics

Research on residence hall life during the past several decades has focused on questions of person-environment fit, roommate compatibility, retention, and governance structures. These will remain important questions for the future. The relatively heavy emphasis this chapter has on evaluation in contrast to research and on process in contrast to outcomes reflects the need for residence hall staff to be continually thinking about their specific local situation. Findings from research at a large, public institution may not apply to a small, private institution. Results from a women's residence hall may not apply to a men's or a coed hall. It is important to find out what works in the *local*, specific campus setting.

The research and evaluation needs for the next decade center on two critical topics: (1) making the residence hall an ethical learning community, and (2) increasing efforts to apply theory to practice. The specific questions within these topics are best determined by the context of each college campus. Here are several examples:

Making the Residence Hall an Ethical Learning Community

Finding ways to improve the sense of community within the residence hall promises to be an important research goal for as long as there are residence halls. Important concerns for the next decade include ways to reduce the racism that still manifests itself on college campuses. Violence—especially rape—is another campus concern warranting extensive research. Much more research is also needed on how to best ensure that students with disabilities are an important part of the residence hall community.

Residence hall staff can never become complacent about these concerns. These are campuswide concerns, not just residence life concerns. Staffs must work in concert with faculty and administrators. This may require extensive political work to convince the rest of the campus community that what happens in one residence hall is the concern of the entire community, not just the staff in that hall. Case studies of how residence hall staffs work toward these goals would be extremely useful as starting points, if not models, for other campuses.

It is incumbent on the residence hall staff to be responsible not only for designing intervention programs and hall environments that promote the development of an ethical community, but also for evaluating their efforts in a professional manner. The evaluation and research strategies described earlier in this chapter, coupled with the other suggested resources, are starting points for residence life professionals to garner and use the necessary expertise to make their residence halls humane learning environments and to provide their professional colleagues with useful hypotheses to initiate changes on their campuses.

Increasing Efforts to Apply Theory to Practice

Theory might be compared to the sand along a stretch of beach. The sand is mostly untouched, but a shovel, a pail, and a child's playful imagination (sometimes modeling an adult's childlike constructions) can make castles and moats come to life. Student development and person-environment theories are the sand. It is relatively untouched, and the tools to shape and mold the sand are themselves mostly untested. A few creative walkers along the sand (researchers and evaluators) have dug with their pails and shovels (their theories and measures) with some success (Stonewater, 1988) and provide guidelines for future castle builders (Winston, 1990).

Researchers in the future will continue to rely on relatively few theoretical models in trying to understand student life in residence halls and in determining how to design humane learning environments. Residence hall staff members conducting research and evaluations will find these models and guidelines helpful, but the beach is long and the sand plentiful. Every staff member must construct his or her own theory and search out its implications and applicability to a specific campus setting. Real progress into the twenty-first century will not be indicated fully by how the new theories are formulated or what research supports them. Real progress will be indicated by how successful the Sams and Susans are in using their imaginations to construct their own castles with the unique interpretations they have and using the best resources available to them.

References

Agar, M. H. *The Professional Stranger: An Informal Introduction to Ethnography.* New York: Academic Press, 1980.

American College Personnel Association. "Statement of Ethical Principles and Standards." *Journal of College Student Development*, 1990, *31*(3), 197–202.

Bogdan, R. C., and Biklen, S. K. *Qualitative Research for Education: An Introduction to Theory and Methods.* Needham Heights, Mass.: Allyn and Bacon, 1982.

Borg, W. R., and Gall, M. D. *Educational Research.* (5th ed.) White Plains, N.Y.: Longman, 1989.

Bradburn, N. M., Sudman, S., and Associates. *Improving Interview Method and*

Questionnaire Design: Response Effects to Threatening Questions in Survey Research. San Fransisco: Jossey-Bass, 1979.

Brown, R. D. "Student Development in a Co-Ed Residence Hall: Promiscuity, Prophylactic, or Panacea?" *Journal of College Student Personnel*, 1973, *14*, 98–104.

Brown, R. D. "How Evaluation Can Make a Difference." In G. R. Hanson (ed.), *Evaluating Program Effectiveness.* New Directions for Student Services, no. 1. San Francisco: Jossey-Bass, 1978.

Brown, R. D., Petersen, C., and Sanstead, M. "Photographic Evaluation: The Use of the Camera as an Evaluation Tool for Student Affairs." *Journal of College Student Personnel*, 1980, *21*, 558–563.

Buckner, D. R. "Residence Life Programs." In M. J. Barr and Associates, *Student Services and the Law: A Handbook for Practitioners.* San Francisco: Jossey-Bass, 1988.

Burchill, S.A.L., and Stiles, W. B. "Interactions of Depressed College Students with Their Roommates: Not Necessarily Negative." *Journal of Personality and Social Psychology*, 1988, *55*, 410–419.

Carey, J. C., Stanley, D. A., and Biggers, J. "Peak Alert Time and Rapport Between Residence Hall Roommates." *Journal of College Student Development*, 1988, *29*, 239–244.

Clarke, J. H., Miser, K. M., and Roberts, A. O. "Freshman Residential Programs: Effectiveness of Living-Learning Structure, Faculty Involvement, and Thematic Focus." *Journal of College and University Housing*, 1988, *18*, 7–13.

Cook, T., and Campbell, D. T. *Quasi-Experimentation.* Skokie, Ill.: Rand McNally, 1979.

Ebbers, L. H. "Management and Use of Student Records." In M. J. Barr and Associates, *Student Services and the Law: A Handbook for Practitioners.* San Francisco: Jossey-Bass, 1988.

Fang, W. L., and Ellwein, M. C. "Photography and Ethics in Evaluation." *Evaluation Review*, 1990, *14*(1), 100–105.

Guba, E. G., and Lincoln, Y. S. *Effective Evaluation: Improving the Usefulness of Evaluation Results Through Responsive and Naturalistic Approaches.* San Francisco: Jossey-Bass, 1981.

Hartmann, D. P. (ed.). *Using Observers to Study Behavior.* New Directions for Methodology of Social and Behavior Science, no. 14. San Francisco: Jossey-Bass, 1982.

Huebner, L. A., and Lawson, J. "Understanding and Assessing College Environments." In D. G. Creamer (ed.), *College Student Development: Theory and Practice for the 1990s.* Alexandria, Va.: American College Personnel Association, 1990.

Janosik, S. M., Creamer, D. G., and Cross, L. H. "The Relationship of Resident Halls' Student-Environment Fit and Sense of Competence." *Journal of College Student Development*, 1988, *19*, 320–326.

Johnson, J. C. "Selecting Ethnographic Informants." *Qualitative Research Methods*. Newbury Park, Calif.: Sage, 1990.

King, P. M. "Assessing Development from a Cognitive-Developmental Perspective." In D. G. Creamer (ed.)., *College Student Development: Theory and Practice for the 1990s*. Alexandria, Va.: American College Personnel Association, 1990.

Kuh, G. D., Schuh, J. H., Whitt, E. J., and Associates. *Involving Colleges: Successful Approaches to Fostering Student Learning and Development Outside the Classroom*. San Francisco: Jossey-Bass, 1991.

Lenning, O. T., and McAleenan, A. C. "Needs Assessment in Student Affairs." In G. D. Kuh (ed.), *Evaluation in Student Affairs*. Cincinnati, Ohio: American College Personnel Association, 1979.

Lincoln, Y. S., and Guba, E. G. *Naturalistic Inquiry*. Beverly Hills, Calif.: Sage, 1985.

Machovec, F. J. *Interview and Interrogation: A Scientific Approach*. Springfield, Ill.: Thomas, 1989.

Madaus, G. F., Scriven, M. S., and Stufflebeam, D. L. *Evaluation Models: Viewpoints on Educational and Human Services Evaluation*. Boston: Kluwer-Nijhoff, 1983.

Merriam, S. B. *Case Study Research in Education: A Qualitative Approach*. San Francisco: Jossey-Bass, 1988.

Merton, R. K., Fiske, M., and Kendall, P. L. *The Focused Interview: A Manual of Problems and Procedures*. (2nd ed.) New York: Free Press, 1990.

Miles, M. B., and Huberman, A. M. *Qualitative Data Analysis: A Sourcebook for New Methods*. Newbury Park, Calif.: Sage, 1984.

Miller, T. K., and Winston, R. B., Jr. "Assessing Development from a Psychosocial Perspective." In D. G. Creamer (ed.), *College Student Development: Theory and Practice for the 1990s*. Alexandria, Va.: American College Personnel Association, 1990.

Moffatt, M. *Coming of Age in New Jersey: College and American Culture*. New Brunswick, N.J.: Rutgers University Press, 1989.

Morgan, D. L. *Focus Groups as Qualitative Research*. Newbury Park, Calif.: Sage, 1988.

Patton, M. Q. *Qualitative Evaluation and Research Methods*. Newbury Park, Calif.: Sage, 1990.

Posavac, E. J., and Carey, R. G. *Program Evaluation: Methods and Case Studies*. (3rd ed.) Englewood Cliffs, N.J.: Prentice Hall, 1989.

Rippey, R. M. (ed.). *Studies in Transactional Evaluation*. Berkeley, Calif.: McCutchan, 1973.

Rossi, P. H., and Freeman, H. E. *Evaluation: A Systematic Approach*. (4th ed.) Newbury Park, Calif.: Sage, 1989.

Spradley, J. P. *The Ethnographic Interview*. Troy, Mo.: Holt, Rinehart & Winston, 1979.

Stake, R. E. *Evaluating the Arts in Education: A Responsive Approach.* Columbus, Ohio: Merrill, 1975.

Stewart, D. W., and Shamdasani, P. M. *Focus Groups: Theory and Practice.* Newbury Park, Calif.: Sage, 1990.

Stonewater, B. B. "Informal Developmental Assessment in the Residence Halls: A Theory to Practice Model." *NASPA Journal*, 1988, *25*, 267–273.

Strauss, A. L., and Corbin, J. M. *Basics of Qualitative Research: Grounded Theory Procedures and Techniques.* Newbury Park, Calif.: Sage, 1990.

Stufflebeam, D. L. *Conducting Educational Needs Assessments.* Boston: Kluwer-Nijhoff, 1985.

Sudman, S., and Bradburn, N. M. *Asking Questions: A Practical Guide to Questionnaire Design.* San Francisco: Jossey-Bass, 1982.

Winston, R. B., Jr. "Using Theory and Performing Research in Everyday Practice." In D. D. Coleman and J. E. Johnson (eds.), *The New Professional: A Resource Guide for New Student Affairs Professionals and Their Supervisors.* Monograph Series, no. 10. Washington, D.C.: National Association of Student Personnel Administrators, 1990.

Worthen, B. R., and Sanders, J. R. *Educational Evaluation: Alternative Approaches and Practical Guidelines.* White Plains, N.Y.: Longman, 1987.

PART THREE

Responsive Programming for Today's Students

Housing professionals' identity and the value they bring to individual campuses rests to a large degree on their ability to design and implement high-quality programs and services that meet students' needs and address institutional concerns. Because each campus is unique—made up of a particular mix of students, faculty, and staff, set in an institution with a history, and surrounded by a distinctive local community that has complex relationships with the college—there can be no "generic" programs or services that can be transported uncritically from campus to campus. The six chapters in this part offer practical suggestions and advice about creating programs and services that meet residents' needs and address some of today's societal problems within the specific context of the individual campus.

In Chapter Seventeen, Schuh and Triponey offer direction for creating personal enrichment, educational, social, and recreational programs designed to meet the specifications of the particular campus. Based on Astin's involvement theory, they provide guidance for developing programs that include awareness of the institution's mission, use of needs assessment data, involvement of students in planning and delivery, allocation of resources, and evaluation.

Wellness models have given many practitioners conceptual frameworks that have broadened their views of students and the possibilities for residential life programming. In Chapter Eighteen, Leafgren describes a multidimensional wellness model that includes psychosocial, health, recreational, nutrition, academic, and spiritual development. He describes how the various dimensions interact, offers guidance in implementing a wellness model and communicating its concepts to students, and identifies campuses that have used this approach to residential life programming successfully.

Much of the residence life staff's work directly or indirectly focuses on building and maintaining a sense of community within the residence halls. As Anchors, Douglas, and Kasper indicate in Chapter Nineteen, however, creating community is not a value-free activity. They identify many of the ethical issues associated with this activity, offer a process model for building community based on the research on the stages of group development and how norms are created and enforced, and discuss how the physical environment can inhibit or promote a sense of belonging among residents.

In Chapter Twenty, Werring, Robertson, and Coon explore some of the thorny issues associated with interpersonal conflicts, specifically clashes between parental expectations and institutional policies that address hate speech, racism, homophobia, and education about sexually transmitted diseases. The authors identify fundamental issues and describe programs designed to address them.

In Chapter Twenty-One, Janosik discusses criminal conduct in residence halls, including theft, vandalism, use of controlled substances, and the activities of religious cults. He also suggests policy strategies for confronting these problems and describes programmatic efforts on a variety of campuses.

In Chapter Twenty-Two, Schroeder takes a long-range perspective. He identifies future trends and challenges in higher education, offers responses that student affairs divisions might make, and proposes an integral role for residential life programs.

Chapter Seventeen

Fundamentals of
Program Design

John H. Schuh
Vicky L. Triponey

It would be difficult to find many people on the contemporary college campus who would not agree that developing a comprehensive program to meet the needs of residential students is essential to creating an environment in which students can learn and grow. A series of reports (Chickering, 1974; Astin, 1977, 1985) have underscored the value of the residential learning experience for students and have emphasized the value of student involvement on the college campus—both in and out of the classroom.

Given that there seems to be a consensus among housing administrators that the residential setting provides a potentially rich environment for student involvement, the next logical steps in developing that environment center on understanding the process of program development. This chapter is dedicated to providing information related to program development in the residential setting and is designed especially for entry- and mid-level residence life professionals. Specifically, the chapter has three purposes. First, it provides a brief overview of involvement theory as a framework within which to examine student program development. This book is quite concerned with the linkage between theory and practice in residence hall work, and this chapter will emphasize the need for programmers to have a solid theoretical foundation on which to build residential programs. Second, the chapter describes a variety of programming models. In the view of the authors, there is no *best* model to use as a guide for developing programs. Instead, each person who is responsible for developing programs ought to have a model in mind to frame her or his work. Third, this chapter describes a variety of factors or ingredients that will enhance programming efforts. Given all the responsibilities typically assumed by staff who work with residential students, numerous hints and tips for programmers are provided so that their work can be more efficient and effective.

Involvement Theory

Even though the benefits of student involvement in their college experiences were popularized by the report *Involvement in Learning: Realizing the Potential of American Higher Education* (Study Group on the Conditions of Excellence in American Higher Education, 1984), a variety of studies related to student involvement antedated that publication. For example, involvement was found to be related positively to community service after graduation and to postcollege income (Pace, 1979), to lower attrition rates (Astin, 1977; Pascarella and Terenzini, 1977, 1978), and to social and intellectual development (Astin, 1977; Pace, 1987; Astin and Scherrei, 1980). Kuh, Krehbiel, and MacKay (1988) conclude that personal development is associated with participation in one or more out-of-class activities (for example, social, cultural, or political activities).

Involvement as a concept was defined by the Study Group on the Conditions of Excellence in American Higher Education (1984) and then expanded on by Astin (1985). The Study Group's report concluded: "The fact that more learning occurs when students are actively engaged in the learning process has implications for every faculty member and administrator in every institution" (p. 19). Two important implications were that (1) the amount of learning and personal development associated with any educational program is directly proportional to the quality and quantity of student involvement in that program, and (2) the effectiveness of any educational policy or practice is directly related to the capacity of that program to increase student involvement in learning. The charge, then, to those who are responsible for residence hall programming is not only to determine ways to plan effective programs for students that best meet their needs, but perhaps more important, to plan programs that enable students to develop their own program planning skills (Kuh, Schuh, Whitt, and Associates, 1991).

Astin (1985, pp. 135–136), who was a member of the Study Group that produced the report mentioned above, offers five postulates that comprise student involvement theory:

1. Involvement refers to the investment of physical and psychological energy in various objects that might be quite general or very specific.

2. Involvement occurs along a continuum.
3. Involvement has both quantitative and qualitative dimensions. Time on task is not necessarily the only criterion used to measure student involvement. The effectiveness of the time spent on task also is crucial.
4. The amount of student learning and development from any educational program is related to the student involvement in that program.
5. The effectiveness of any educational policy or practice is directly related to the ability of that policy or program to increase student involvement.

Using the concept of involvement as a framework within which to develop programs, the challenge to residence life practitioners is to develop programs that increase student involvement. The residential setting provides a number of inherent advantages that improve the potential for success of various kinds of programs. Residential students tend to have more time to devote to their educational endeavors than commuters; they live in a structure that encourages involvement; they have the advantage of substantial peer support, which often is not available to the commuter; and they can take advantage of many services geared specifically to encourage student involvement (Schuh, 1989). As a result, the residential setting provides an excellent opportunity for student growth. The programmer needs to make use of these advantages and provide a truly stimulating, growth-producing environment for the residents. "Educational communities which are committed to their students and which reach out and involve them in the community's educational life also generate student involvement in learning and eventually student commitment to the goals of the education" (Tinto, 1987, p. 88). To provide that environment, the programmer should first choose a model for program development. To expedite that selection, we briefly discuss a variety of models.

Programming Models

Initially, we consider the conceptual model of intervention strategies (Morrill, Hurst, and Oetting, 1980). Then we present several other models that can be employed in the development of programs for residential students, including the campus ecology manager model (Banning, 1989), the health and wellness model (Mosier, 1989), and a five-stage program development model (Moore and Delworth, 1976).

Hurst and Jacobson (1985) offer several criticisms of the programming that occurs on college campuses that underscore the importance of adopting a program development model. They point out that the student affairs profession went through a long period when it did not have a theoretical underpinning or conceptual foundation. As a result, they argue that the programming that occurred may not have been related to the education and development of students. Program development without the framework of a theory occurred on the basis of the staff's personal interests, skill areas, or professional backgrounds; emerging crises; professional fads; political expediency; and special interest groups and traditions. Hurst and Jacobson (1985, p. 123) conclude that "the identification and commitment to this shared theoretical/conceptual approach to program development is essential to student services as a profession. The programs offered by student services are, after all, the clearest statement of the substance and vitality of the profession." The crucial factor for the residence hall programmer is not to adopt a specific theoretical approach that anyone else recommends for planning and delivering programs to students as a matter of orthodoxy. Rather, each person ought to have a theoretical framework that he or she is comfortable with and that produces the desired results consistently.

Model of Intervention Strategies

Morrill, Hurst, and Oetting (1980) describe a three-dimensional model of interventions for student development that can be particularly attractive to those responsible for developing residence hall programs. The model was introduced in 1974 and then was the focus of a book released in 1980. This model provides a comprehensive view of the three-dimensional approach to programming for student development. The dimensions of the model include the following: (1) the target of the intervention, (2) the purpose of the intervention, and (3) the method of intervention. A brief explanation of each dimension follows. (Those who seek detail beyond that provided here should consult Hurst and Jacobson, 1985.)

In the model, students are the target of intervention. The model, however, provides for various ways of aggregating students for programming purposes—for example, by primary groups, associational groups, and communities. Placed in the context of the residential hall, residence hall programs can be directed at individual residents, roommates (a primary group), members of the living unit such as the floor or wing (associational groups), or the entire residence hall or residence hall system (communities).

Three purposes or types of programs are identified: (1) *Remedial programs* are designed to correct problems that currently exist, such as providing tutoring in the floor lounge for residents who are having difficulty with college-level mathematics. (2) *Preventive programs* attempt to anticipate problems before they occur and suggest ways that students can avoid difficulties. A good example of a preventive program would be one designed to provide information for floor officers on how to plan a responsible social activity, including information about state and local laws concerning the possession and consumption of alcoholic beverages, alternative beverages, the availability of food items, and other risk management strategies. (3) *Developmental programs* are those designed to result in student growth and development. An example of developmental programming might be a program that results in the acquisition of a skill or a new way of approaching a problem. Programs focusing on improving one's understanding of nutrition could be defined as developmental, although one might also make the case that since a good diet frequently is related to the prevention of illness— obviously the objective of a preventive program—a program on nutrition could have preventive qualities.

The method of intervention is the third aspect of this model. Such methodological categories as direct interventions (delivering a program), training and consultation (teaching students how to deliver their own programs), and media (the use of print, audio, and video materials, for example) are identified. Leadership development programming for floor officers is a good example of the training/consultation method of intervention.

Most programs that are offered in residential settings fit well with the model suggested by Morrill, Hurst, and Oetting (1980). It is a clear, easily understood means of describing the objectives of offering programs in residence halls. One can look at this model and realize right away that there is a conceptual framework that makes intuitive sense as to what the programmer is attempting to accomplish by devoting time and effort to residential programming.

Campus Ecology Manager Model

Banning developed a model that can be applied to residence hall programming that is based on work completed by the Western Interstate Commission for Higher Education (1973), Banning and Kaiser (1974), Aulepp and Delworth (1976), and others. This model relies heavily on the concept of assessing student environments and then planning interventions to deal with aspects of the environment that are not consistent with student needs and expectations. Using this approach, students become participants in the process of designing environments that best meet their needs.

In his description of the campus ecology manager (for our purposes, read "programmer"), Banning (1989) makes the case that the environment of students should be developed using the ecosystem approach. The ecosystem approach involves the application of a seven-step theoretical model to assess and redesign student environments. The seven steps are (1) developing values intended for the inhabitants of the environment (the residence hall, in this case); (2) setting goals based on the values identified for the environment; (3) developing programs that implement the goals and values; (4) fitting the campus to the student; (5) mapping (that is, measuring students' perceptions of the environment); (6) observing student behavior in the environment; and (7) giving feedback, determining if the data support the values identified in the first step of this process.

This model has excellent potential for the residence hall setting. Values that undergird the residential living experience (for example, academic pursuits of the residents will take precedence over social activities) are developed, and programs to meet those goals are planned. The residential environment is tailored to meet the needs of the residents. Students' perceptions of the residence hall environment are measured, preferably using the ecosystem method of environmental assessment (see Schuh, 1990, for an application), and student behavior in the environment is observed. (For instance, are there many disciplinary reports? Are students being retained by the residential system from year to year? Is there a large proportion of roommate problems and requests for transfer?) Student feedback is sought using formal and informal methods to complete the application of this model to the residence hall setting.

Banning (1989, p. 316) concludes that "campus ecology management calls for a shift in the perspectives and attitudes of student services personnel." Many aspects of this approach to program design are attractive to the residence hall programmer. It provides a systematic way of planning programs for residence halls where the development of environments that meet students' needs is the focus.

Health and Wellness Model

Mosier (1989) presents a nine-stage model based on the health and wellness movement that can be applied to programming in the residential setting. His steps include the following:

1. Determine a theoretical frame of reference.
2. Ensure that staff (both professional and paraprofessional) understand the theoretical frame of reference.
3. Assess students' levels of wellness.
4. Develop a wellness curriculum.
5. Provide instruction to staff on how to use specific wellness programs.
6. Introduce the wellness model to students.
7. Provide adequate support to staff to allow them to function directly with students.
8. Provide a system of recognizing growth in students and staff along the six wellness dimensions (see below).
9. Implement an ongoing system of evaluation and goal review.

Wellness, according to Hettler (1980), has six dimensions. A well-balanced array of programs based on the wellness dimensions include programs that address the following aspects of development: emotional development, intellectual development, physical development, social development, occupational development, and spiritual development. To use the wellness model, one would need to follow the model sketched above and plan programs in each of the six areas of wellness, the proportions of which would depend on student needs. The University of Wisconsin at Stevens Point, for example, has done an excellent job of implementing the wellness model. (For greater detail on using wellness as a programming model, consult Chapter Eighteen.)

Student Service Program Development Model

Under the auspices of the Western Interstate Commission for Higher Education, a model for developing student services programs was introduced (Moore and Delworth, 1976). This model is particularly attractive to people who are responsible for developing residence hall programs but who have limited experience with planning for major programmatic initiatives that affect large numbers of students. This model fits best in a situation where a fairly large array of program activities are aggregated, such as a three-day residence hall orientation process or the development of a living-learning center, as opposed to a single presentation like having a speaker address a group of residents on career planning strategies. The model employs the theoretical base outlined by Morrill, Oetting, and Hurst (1974). Certainly, it is not the only model for program planning that one might wish to employ (see also Hughes, 1985; Miller and Prince, 1976), but it does provide an easily understood, practical approach to systematically developing programs for residence hall students as well as others.

Based on the material cited above and on our combined thirty years of practical experience in residence hall work, student activities, and student affairs administration, we recommend a number of elements that should be part of a program planning model. We maintain that regardless of whether residence hall programmers adopt one of the models identified in this chapter or develop their own, these elements should be a part of their thinking as they develop programs for and with residential students. Programmers should always:

- Be aware of the institution's mission.
- Plan programs with the model in mind.
- Conduct periodic assessments.
- Involve students in the planning and delivery of programs.
- Provide a balance of different types of programs.
- Provide adequate resource support.
- Include an evaluation component.

Those who plan programs should be aware of the institution's mission and the role that student housing plays in supporting the institution's efforts to achieve that mission. The programs that are offered should be consistent and supportive of the mission. For example, if the institution's mission places a heavy emphasis on the development of citizenship skills for its students, a strong residence hall governance structure ought to be planned.

Program planners should have a program development model in

mind as they go about their work. Staff with the strongest programming skills tend not to operate from an atheoretical base or to lack a vision of what they intend to accomplish. Rather, they understand that there is a theoretical or conceptual goal that can be attained by developing a specific program. For example, they know that developing programs that facilitate career planning can help students address vector five (freeing interpersonal relationships) of Chickering's (1969) theory of student development, and they plan programs accordingly. There is no *best* program development model, but we hold that those who do plan programs well normally use a program development model.

Those who program well undertake periodic assessments of residents' needs, attitudes, and environmental perceptions. How often these assessments are conducted and their exact nature vary widely. At times, assessments can be accomplished through the use of questionnaires, but alternatively, assessments can be conducted by talking with students in groups or individually and by analyzing data at hand (for example, incident reports from student staff) or observing students (in the dining hall or game room, for instance). The point is that programmers should understand the needs of students rather than planning programs arbitrarily.

In the best set of circumstances, students are involved in the planning and delivery of programs. At least as much effort ought to be expended in teaching students how to do programming for themselves as is expended in doing it for them. Over an academic year, if this is done well, the importance of the resident assistant as programmer, for example, may decline (Kuh and Schuh, 1983).

Residential programmers are advised to provide a balance of programs so that students can make progress on the various developmental tasks they face. A variety of taxonomies of programs exist, some of which could be applied to the general objectives for student housing identified by DeCoster and Mable (1980). Chickering's (1969) vector theory could also be applied in specific programming efforts (Komives and Schuh, 1988).

Adequate support is necessary for those who plan programs. In most situations, student paraprofessionals can play significant roles in planning and delivering programs. They can require technical help and adequate resources to do their work well. For example, to expect the student staff to generate a substantial resource base to support them in program development is unrealistic. Some mix of support from a programming fund that is controlled by professional staff along with student residence hall activity fees expended by student governing or programming boards and participation fees is an appropriate way to finance programs. Advice and support are also important in ensuring the success of residential programs. And the personal touch of the professional staff member attending a program, even if just for a few minutes, can be invaluable.

Finally, a programming model should include an evaluation component. Normally, the success of a program will be evaluated against the expressed objectives for developing it. Other techniques, such as determining the cost-effectiveness of a program or measuring the student learning that has resulted from participating in a program, can be employed. (Brown and Podolske offer excellent ideas about evaluation in Chapter Sixteen of this book.)

Program Enhancement Factors

Regardless of which programming model residence hall programmers adopt, several key ingredients essential in planning a variety of student programs have the potential to influence their success. Although no standard recipe exists that guarantees successful programs, the following ingredients, if blended appropriately, can increase the potential for success and help students and staff gain greater satisfaction and growth from their programming efforts.

Involvement of Appropriate People in Program Planning

Traditionally, the paraprofessional staff, the hall or community government, the hall's governmental organization (for example, the residence hall association), and/or the professional staff have assumed responsibility for planning the programs within the residence halls. Frequently, the programs sponsored by any one of these groups address a specific need or serve a specific purpose identified by the group planning the programs. For instance, the paraprofessional staff may identify adjustment problems confronting residents and may offer programs on understanding differences and interpersonal communication. The hall government officers may observe that visitation hours are being violated, which is resulting in security concerns, and might decide to hold a community meeting to review the hall's rules and regulations and to educate residents on security precautions. The residence hall association's interest survey could show that a majority of the students would like to attend a hall dance, take a trip to a nearby city for a concert, and participate in a mud volleyball tournament. The residence hall association could subsequently choose to sponsor these activities throughout the term. Finally, the professional staff, having knowledge of student development theory and programming models, may identify specific programs that can help their residents address Chickering's first three vectors: achieving competence, managing emotions, and developing autonomy.

Although this kind of segmented programming is common in the residence halls and in other campus activities, the programming needs of students may be served best through cooperative programming efforts. In presenting a rationale and model for coordination of campus activities, Mills (1989, p. 40) suggests that "by coordinating activities across departmental lines, staff can meet students' needs. Rather than leaving students on their own to select helpful activities, the coordinative approach designs activities to meet students' overall educational goals while assisting in the achievement of institutional objectives." Although this approach is suggested for campus-wide efforts to integrate programming and activities, the model is applicable in the residence halls as well. Whether it is the professional staff working cooperatively with the paraprofessionals or an academic department, or the residence hall association working with other student organizations, community service agencies, or the career planning office, coordinating activities outside of the traditional boundaries allows for the development of a more comprehensive educational community and allows students to view their activities "as a unified whole" (Mills, 1989, p. 41).

Ideally, *all* persons and offices on campus who are interested in enhancing a student's education through campus activities should be involved in coordinative programming endeavors to maximize the effect on student growth. Such comprehensive involvement, however, frequently is impractical and even impossible in specific programming efforts. Therefore, it is recommended that cooperative endeavors be undertaken with appropriate offices and groups whenever feasible, but it is advisable to always involve students in planning and implementing the programs in the residence halls. Student involvement in programming efforts will provide opportunities for the enhancement and development of the skills and leadership abilities of the student programmers, while also increasing student support for the programs. The more students are involved in planning their activities, the more ownership they assume and the more enthusiasm they generate among their fellow residents, which, in turn, can result in increased attendance and increased involvement in the programs. Additionally, students involved in planning their own programs can offer valuable insights regarding the needs and interests of fellow residents and can safeguard against programs that result solely from the interests, concerns, or expertise of the staff involved. A potential hazard of student involvement, however, is that some students can become so engrossed in these kinds of activities that they lose sight of their academic goals. Residence hall staff would be well advised to remind students to maintain a balance between their activities in and out of the classroom.

Mills (1989, p. 43) recommends that staff members engage student-determined groups (that is, special groups, hall communities, freshmen, specific academic majors, or wings/floors of a hall) in planning and implementing programs because this "allows considerably more specificity in marketing programs and services." It is not necessary that every program in the residence hall be sponsored by a formalized organization or by the elected "leaders" of the hall. In fact, the interests expressed by the officers of the hall government may not reflect the needs of less involved residents. Therefore, it may be more prudent to involve residents who do not hold officer or staff positions in specific programming efforts, so that they may share in the opportunity to develop valuable skills while providing programs for what may be the "silent majority" in the halls. Regardless of who initiates specific programming efforts within the residence halls, it is very important for programmers to explore the many opportunities for cooperative efforts to meet the varied needs and interests of residents.

Preparation and Training of Programmers

Along with the many skills and competencies that are required of residence hall professionals, it is crucial that programming skills be recognized and developed. The *CAS Standards* (Council for the Advancement of Standards for Student Services/Development Programs, 1986, p. 52) state that "the director and other professional staff members must have an appropriate combination of graduate course work, formal training, and supervised work experience," and these professionals should find the same balance as they prepare for programming responsibilities. It is important that residence hall professionals have a thorough understanding of student development theories and programming models, and it also is critical that they have practical experience translating those models into specific programs. Although a professional staff member undoubtedly can learn how to plan and implement programs "on the job," it is preferable to have previous experience (as an undergraduate or graduate student) with seeing a program through from identifying a need or interest, conceptualizing the program idea, and planning the event to implementing the details. Additionally, the responsibility of preparing student programmers usually rests with the professional staff. Consequently, if the personal programming skills of a professional staff member have been well developed, the task of preparing student programmers will be much easier and more effective.

Specific skills needed by professionals as well as student programmers are numerous and diverse. Perhaps first and foremost is a familiarity with the campus. Answers to such questions as "where to go" and "who to call" provide essential pieces of information as programmers undertake necessary arrangements for a program. Other skills to be developed include goal setting, communication (written and oral), effective promotion, time management, running meetings, organizing/planning and attending to detail, delegating, evaluating needs and interests, contracting/developing agreements, recognizing/utilizing resources, and exercising leadership. It is also extremely helpful for programmers to have at least a basic understanding of the concept of student development so that they can grasp the underlying purpose of programming in the residence halls and on campus. Ender and Winston (1984) provide a general model for the training of paraprofessionals that can be adapted to include the development of programming skills. (Also see Chapter Thirteen for a more detailed discussion of using paraprofessionals in hall programming.) Because programmers are expected to lead others to participate in their programs as planners and/or participants, leadership skills are essential. Roberts (1981) provides a model for leadership education, training, and development that is useful in formulating a training agenda for student programmers.

Whether student programmers are members of the paraprofessional staff, the hall government, or an informal group undertaking programming efforts, they need prior and ongoing training to refine their programming skills. If a formalized group such as the hall government or the paraprofessional staff plan to be engaged in ongoing programming efforts, they should be trained in many of these areas prior to beginning their jobs. If less involved students are engaged in planning a specific program, however, it may be more appropriate to train them on the job to develop the skills mentioned previously. A common concern among professional and paraprofessional staff members who oversee student programmers is how much direction and intervention they should provide as an advisor. The situational leadership model (Hersey, 1984) provides valuable guidance. By determining a programmer's level of readiness and willingness to complete a task, the advisor can then provide the appropriate amount of direction (task behavior) and support (relationship behavior) so that the student will succeed and eventually develop to a level where independent work is possible.

One final source of instruction for residence hall programmers is previous programming endeavors. Much can be learned from the success of other programmers. Repetition of previous mistakes can be avoided when programmers review the records (program evaluations, annual or quarterly reports, journal notes and files) of their predecessors. Although programmers should be mindful that the environment and needs of the residents are evolving constantly and should be open to new ideas as a result, they can also enhance their endeavors if they take time to review and evaluate the programs of the past. Additionally, by tapping the expertise of advisors and previous practitioners, programmers can develop some continuity and new programmers will gain greater insight into their roles.

Identification of the Needs and Interests of Residents

It is obvious that programs that meet the needs and interests of the target audience are destined for success. However, the personal preferences, current concerns, or personal interests of staff members and student leaders frequently dominate the decision-making process when selecting residence hall programs. Therefore, it is advisable for programmers to undertake a careful assessment of the needs and interests of their residents *before* selecting the programs to be offered.

Barr and Cuyjet (1983, p. 453) provide three methods to "assess student needs for program interventions: a study of the demographic characteristics of the student body, unobtrusive measures, and obtrusive measures." They recommend that a combination of all three methods be used to ensure that "an accurate measurement is made of the real needs of students" (p. 452). While staff members with an understanding of developmental theories should identify general programming needs based on the various stages of development common among students at different academic levels, this knowledge should be supplemented with data gathered from the students at that institution.

An understanding of the demographic characteristics of the residents, such as their ethnic background, academic major, and age, provides valuable insight into the needs of a particular hall or community and allows for adaptation of programs as the population changes. Whether this information is maintained through the residence life office or is obtained from admissions and/or enrollment reports, "an analysis of these sources can provide a composite picture of who students are and focus attention of the program staff on identifiable student subgroups that may need service" (Barr and Cuyjet, 1983, p. 453).

Through formal and informal interaction with students, staff members can gather valuable information concerning student needs. These unobtrusive measures (Barr and Cuyjet, 1991) enable programmers to observe the number of students attending specific programs, the characteristics of the attendees, and their levels of engagement in the program. Valuable observations are made regarding the times of day, week, and year when students are most likely to attend programs, and this information should be used in assessing residence hall programs. Moreover, "other student affairs staff members and faculty colleagues can provide a wealth of information through both their formal and informal contact with students" (p. 453). This information should be solicited and used by programmers to accurately assess, on an ongoing basis, the needs of the students on campus and in the residence halls.

Finally, "obtrusive measures such as questionnaires, entrance and exit interviews, and standardized environment assessment instruments can provide solid information for program planners" (Barr and Cuyjet, 1983, p. 453). Programmers should learn and practice research and evaluation techniques and call on the talents of other persons on campus who have expertise in this area. Whether assessment instruments are standardized (developed and used in many settings with comparisons to normative data) or customized (developed for a specific situation), they provide a mechanism for programmers to identify needs and assess the level of interest students have in a specific topic. An informal survey might be conducted by asking a group of students for their ideas for residence hall programs. However, this informal process presents two problems. First, it assumes that students are aware of all of their needs, and it does not allow for unrecognized needs for which an interest may have to be developed or nurtured. Second, an informal survey of student interests almost guarantees that the programmer will hear from the vocal members of the group—perhaps at the expense of the "silent majority." Therefore, it is recommended that obtrusive measures of students' needs and interests be conducted on a regular basis in a systematic manner.

By combining what is known about the students (demographic characteristics) with what has been observed in their behavior (unobtrusive measures) and by adding what students have expressed concerning their needs (obtrusive measures), the residence hall programmer will be well equipped to select, plan, and implement a variety of programs the residents need and want. Additionally, involving students extensively in the process of planning and implementing residence hall programs for themselves and their fellow students will provide an ongoing evaluation of whether the plans and ideas are "on target" or "off base."

Utilization of Available Resources

A wealth of resources are available to the programmer. Recognition and effective utilization of these resources can enhance the programs and the experience gained by the programmer. Human resources, facilities, time, and financial resources available on campus and in the community all should be explored and tapped to their potential.

An abundant but frequently underutilized resource at the disposal of the residence hall programmer is human resources. There are countless people on campus and in the local community who are willing and able to present or facilitate programs for college students on a wide variety of topics. However, residence hall staff frequently are unaware of such people or fail to ask for their assistance. Students majoring in the performing arts, for example, can provide top-quality but inexpensive entertainment while gaining valuable experience, and students who are unknown comedians are flattered to be asked to perform for their fellow residents. Faculty members who have a special hobby or recreational interest might welcome the opportunity to share their expertise with others and might appreciate the opportunity to interact with students outside of the classroom. Staff members (secretaries, hall directors, and deans, for instance) may be shy about their special talents and interests but might be flattered to perform or conduct a workshop in an area of special expertise. It is important, therefore, for residence hall programmers to become aware of the extensive human resources available on campus so that they can capitalize on the "home-grown" talent.

The programmer should also explore opportunities to share in the valuable human resources available in the surrounding area. Whether it is talent from the local entertainment community, civic organizations, high schools, or other insitutions of higher education, these resources may be abundant and can assist in meeting the needs and interests of college students. If regional or national figures are sought for an engagement on campus, these community resources might be prospective event cosponsors, they may have a relationship with the desired speaker, or they might be planning to bring the speaker to town for another event and would allow you to "block book" by paying a discounted fee to have the person perform on campus during the same visit. Local talent and local contacts can be priceless resources for the residence hall programmer.

Another resource that can have a significant effect on the success of a residence hall program is the facility. Even though it may seem easiest to hold most programs in the residence halls, some programs may be offered more appropriately in an alternative location on campus or in the surrounding community. Therefore, a programmer should become acquainted with potential sites for different kinds of programs and identify the procedures for reserving such facilities. Local church camps or state parks, lobbies in other residence halls, the student center, an art gallery or museum, an open-air patio, or other locations can provide a welcome change of scenery for a variety of programs. Programmers should consider the physical requirements, setup needs, costs, convenience to participants, and expected attendance for a program and deliberately choose a facility that provides the necessary arrangements.

Astin (1985, p. 143) observes that "the theory of student involvement suggests that the most precious institutional resource may be student time" and proposes that how students spend their time will have a direct impact on how well they actually develop their talents. As programs are developed to meet the needs and interests of students in the residence halls, programmers must be mindful of the demands on students' time and should be committed to making the most effective use of this time.

Programmers should identify the "impossible times" when students are preparing for mid-term or final examinations, but they also must consider the most appropriate times when topics such as stress management should be covered. They should avoid scheduling activities against other "big events" such as athletic competitions, holidays, campuswide celebrations, and community traditions. If a campuswide calendar of events is not coordinated on campus (for example, by the student activities office, student affairs office, or university relations office), it is recommended that the residence life office and/or the hall staff coordinate such a calendar for the benefit of their programmers and the residents. By coordinating a calendar of the many activities available to students, programmers will be able to ensure that their events do not compete with other valuable programs and can be better equipped to provide students with guidance on making the most effective use of their time.

Because few, if any, programmers have unlimited resources at their disposal, it is crucial for residence hall programmers to make the most of the available financial resources. Whether it is for a specific activity or an entire year's agenda, student and professional programmers must develop the skills of budgeting and managing funds. Hennessy and Lorenz (1987) provide helpful advice to student organization advisers on budgeting and financial management, and most campuses have financial officers available to advise their personnel on budgeting issues. Programmers should consult these resources and assist students involved in planning specific programs with the development of a realistic budget for the event. Additionally, as traditional sources of funding (student activity fees, room-and-board charges, and general institutional funds) become more limited, alternative sources of funding

for residence hall programs must be sought. Whether residence halls cospon-
sor more programs with the office of student activities or other campus
organizations, find corporate sponsors, or assess residents a special fee to
cover program costs, creativity will be necessary in developing the financial
resources available for residence hall programs.

Promotion of Programs and Activities

Involving the appropriate people in planning programs, preparing and
training the programmers, identifying the needs and interests of residents,
and utilizing the available resources can be exercises in futility if a residence
hall program is not promoted effectively. Through effective promotion,
programmers can turn their activity into an "event" and "can break the
multitude of day-to-day student distractions, short circuit apathy problems,
and earn the respect of the students for which they plan programs" (Caruso,
1985, p. 47). Effective promotion is accomplished by carefully planning *well
in advance* (usually at least four weeks) to reach the target audience with
messages that can convince them that the program offers something unique
and interesting and of special value to them. Programmers need to identify
their target audience and use "formal and informal advertising. . . 'eleventh
hour' resources such as teasers and the physical arrangements of the venue"
(Caruso, 1985, p. 47) to reach that audience.

Imaginativeness is essential in promoting campus events. A valuable
resource in this area is the *Campus Activities Programming* magazine, which is
published nine times each year by the National Association of Campus
Activities (NACA) for its members. This publication usually is available in the
student activities office or the campus union and frequently provides creative
ideas and tips about promotion. The national and regional conferences of
NACA can also provide professional and student programmers with virtually
unlimited programming ideas and opportunities to enhance a variety of
programming skills. If residence hall programmers are not able to participate in this organization or its activities, they may find that the student
activities personnel on their campus will be eager to share the valuable
information on a regular basis.

Other very useful resources to the professional staff are Commission
III (Student Residence Programs) of the American College Personnel Association (ACPA) and the Educational Programs Committee of the Association
of College and University Housing Officers-International (ACUHO-I). These
two groups can provide excellent assistance and materials to staff interested
in developing resources for programming. If the staff member is not involved
with either of these organizations, chances are that the dean of students is a
member of ACPA and that the chief housing officer is the institutional
representative to ACUHO-I.

One effective form of promotion that should not be overlooked is word of mouth. "While printed materials inform about a function, personal influence legitimizes it. . . . To be successful, word-of-mouth or informal advertising must involve those individuals who marketing professionals refer to as 'opinion leaders'" (Caruso, 1985, p. 48). By equipping student programmers and other campus personnel (including secretaries, custodial staff, and faculty) with appropriate information about an event and by convincing them of its merits, enthusiasm for the event will become contagious throughout the residence hall and even the campus.

Even though it may be helpful to have a publicity chairperson for residence hall programs, it is important that all persons involved in planning the event assume responsibility for the promotional resources at their disposal (that is, campus newspapers, campus calendars, bulletin boards, table tents, electronic bulletin boards, radio stations, newsletters, and cable television). They should find opportunities where a captive audience is available (for instance, hall meetings, sporting events, and dining hall during rush hour) and seize the moment to make creative announcements or presentations to promote the event. By scheduling and finalizing details of a program *well in advance*, the programmers can develop an effective promotional campaign that should guarantee that their efforts will be appreciated by a full and enthusiastic audience at a successful event.

This chapter has focused on the development of programming in campus residence halls. The chapter has stressed that involvement theory provides an excellent framework within which to develop residential programs. Several programming models have been presented that can be applied to residence halls. Our view is that the programmer ought to have a model in mind when developing programs and activities. There is no best model, but offering programs without a model is a mistake. Finally, the chapter has presented a number of ideas that address several practical dimensions associated with programming—training paraprofessionals, assessing needs, utilizing resources, and promoting activities. The information presented in this chapter should provide excellent resources for the residence hall programmer and an excellent point of departure as programs are planned in campus residence halls.

References

Astin, A. W. *Four Critical Years: Effects of College on Beliefs, Attitudes, and Knowledge.* San Francisco: Jossey-Bass, 1977.

Astin, A. W. *Achieving Educational Excellence: A Critical Assessment of Priorities and Practices in Higher Education.* San Francisco: Jossey-Bass, 1985.

Astin, A. W., and Scherrei, R. A. *Maximizing Leadership Effectiveness: Impact of Administrative Style on Faculty and Students.* San Francisco: Jossey-Bass, 1980.

Aulepp, L., and Delworth, U. *Training Manual for an Ecosystem Model: Assessing and Designing Campus Environments.* Boulder, Colo.: Western Interstate Commission for Higher Education, 1976.

Banning, J. H. "Creating a Climate for Successful Student Development: The Campus Ecology Manager Role." In U. Delworth, G. R. Hanson, and Associates, *Student Services: A Handbook for the Profession*. (2nd ed.) San Francisco: Jossey-Bass, 1989.

Banning, J. H., and Kaiser, L. "An Ecological Perspective for Campus Design." *Personnel and Guidance Journal*, 1974, *52*, 370–375.

Barr, M. J., and Cuyjet, M. J. "Program Development and Implementation." In T. K. Miller, R. B. Winston, Jr., and W. R. Mendenhall (eds.), *Administration and Leadership in Student Affairs: Actualizing Student Development in Higher Education*. Muncie, Ind.: Accelerated Development, 1983.

Barr, M. J., and Cuyjet, M. J. "Program Development and Implementation." In T. K. Miller and R. B. Winston, Jr. (eds.), *Administration and Leadership in Student Affairs: Actualizing Student Development in Higher Education*. (2nd ed.) Muncie, Ind.: Accelerated Development, 1991.

Caruso, M. A. "The Event No One Will Miss." *Campus Activities Programming*, 1985, *18*(6), 47–49.

Chickering, A. W. *Education and Identity*. San Francisco: Jossey-Bass, 1969.

Chickering, A. W. *Commuting Versus Resident Students: Overcoming Educational Inequities of Living Off Campus*. San Francisco: Jossey-Bass, 1974.

Council for the Advancement of Standards for Student Services/Development Programs. *Standards and Guidelines for Housing and Residential Life Programs*. Iowa City, Iowa: Council for the Advancement of Standards for Student Services/Development Programs, 1986.

DeCoster, D. A., and Mable, P. "Residence Education: Purpose and Process." In D. A. DeCoster and P. Mable (eds.), *Personal Education and Community Development in College Residence Halls*. Cincinnati, Ohio: American College Personnel Association, 1980.

Ender, S. C., and Winston, R. B., Jr. (eds.). *Students as Paraprofessional Staff*. New Directions for Student Services, no. 27. San Francisco: Jossey-Bass, 1984.

Hennessy, T. J., and Lorenz, N. "Budget and Fiscal Management." In J. H. Schuh (ed.), *A Handbook for Student Group Advisors*. Alexandria, Va.: American College Personnel Association, 1987.

Hersey, P. *The Situational Leader*. New York: Warner Books, 1984.

Hettler, W. "Wellness Promotion on a University Campus." *Family and Community Health Promotion and Maintenance*, 1980, *3*(1), 77–95.

Hughes, M. H. "Effective Examples of Systematic Program Planning." In M. J. Barr, L. A. Keating, and Associates, *Developing Effective Student Services Programs: Systematic Approaches for Practitioners*. San Francisco: Jossey-Bass, 1985.

Hurst, J. C., and Jacobson, J. K. "Theories Underlying Students' Needs for Programs." In M. J. Barr, L. A. Keating, and Associates, *Developing Effective Student Services Programs: Systematic Approaches for Practitioners*. San Francisco: Jossey-Bass, 1985.

Komives, S. R., and Schuh, J. H. *Student Development Applications to Greek Letter*

Organizations. Bloomington, Ind.: Center for the Study of the College Fraternity, 1988.

Kuh, G. D., Krehbiel, L. E., and MacKay, K. *Personal Development and the College Student Experience: A Review of the Literature.* Bloomington: Department of Educational Leadership and Policy Studies, School of Education, Indiana University, 1988.

Kuh, G. A., and Schuh, J. H. "Perception of the RA Role: Does a Year Make a Difference?" *Journal of College and University Student Housing,* 1983, *13*(2), 3–7.

Kuh, G. D., Schuh, J. H., Whitt, E. J., and Associates. *Involving Colleges: Successful Approaches to Fostering Student Learning and Development Outside the Classroom.* San Francisco: Jossey-Bass, 1991.

Miller, T. K., and Prince, J. S. *The Future of Student Affairs: A Guide to Student Development for Tomorrow's Higher Education.* San Francisco: Jossey-Bass, 1976.

Mills, D. B. "Campus Activities Coordination." In D. C. Roberts (ed.), *Designing Campus Activities to Foster a Sense of Community.* New Directions for Student Services, no. 48. San Francisco: Jossey-Bass, 1989.

Moore, M., and Delworth, U. *Training Manual for Student Services Program Development.* Boulder, Colo.: Western Insterstate Commission for Higher Education, 1976.

Morrill, W. H., and Hurst, J. C., with Oetting, E. R. *Dimensions of Intervention for Student Development.* New York: Wiley, 1980.

Morrill, W. H., Oetting, E. R., and Hurst, J. C. "Dimensions of Counselor Functioning." *Personnel and Guidance Journal,* 1974, *52,* 354–359.

Mosier, R. "Health and Wellness Programs." In J. H. Schuh (ed.), *Educational Programming in College and University Residence Halls.* Columbus, Ohio: Association of College and University Housing Officers-International, 1989.

Pace, C. R. *Measuring Outcomes of College: Fifty Years of Findings and Recommendations for the Future.* San Francisco: Jossey-Bass, 1979.

Pace, C. R. *Good Things Go Together.* Los Angeles: Higher Education Research Institute, UCLA, 1987.

Pascarella, E. T., and Terenzini, P. T. "Patterns of Student-Faculty Informal Interaction Beyond the Classroom and Voluntary Freshman Attrition." *Journal of Higher Education,* 1977, *48,* 540–552.

Pascarella, E. T., and Terenzini, P. T. "Student-Faculty Informal Relationships and Freshman-Year Educational Outcomes." *Journal of Educational Research,* 1978, *71,* 183–189.

Roberts, D. C. *Student Leadership Programs in Higher Education.* Carbondale, Ill.: American College Personnel Association, 1981.

Schuh, J. H. "A Framework for Student Involvement." In J. H. Schuh (ed.), *Educational Programming in College and University Residence Halls.* Columbus,

Ohio: Association of College and University Housing Officers-International, 1989.

Schuh, J. H. "Streamlining the Ecosystems Approach to Residence Hall Environmental Assessment." *NASPA Journal*, 1990, *27*, 185–191.

Study Group on the Conditions of Excellence in American Higher Education. *Involvement in Learning: Realizing the Potential of American Higher Education*. Washington, D.C.: National Institute of Education, 1984.

Tinto, V. *Leaving College: Rethinking the Causes and Cures of Student Attrition*. Chicago: University of Chicago Press, 1987.

Western Interstate Commission for Higher Education. *The Ecosystem Model: Designing Campus Environments*. Boulder, Colo.: Western Interstate Commission for Higher Education, 1973.

Chapter Eighteen

Wellness as a Comprehensive
Student Development
Approach

Fred Leafgren

Since its inception, American higher education has been committed to the total individual and her or his development. Presidents of the first colleges not only emphasized intellectual growth, but attended to students' moral and personal development as well. Rules and regulations, living arrangements, and mentoring relationships created an environment considered essential for students' well-being.

The advent of the positions of dean of men and dean of women resulted in the development of the student affairs profession, with higher education designating specific personnel in clearly identified roles and positions to direct and provide environments for the optimal growth and development of students. In recent decades, theorists such as Havighurst (1953), Chickering (1969), and Sanford (1964, 1967) have made important contributions to the philosophical and psychological understandings of human development in the academic setting. Contributions from the disciplines of psychology, sociology, and communications have also increased knowledge and provided resources and directions for student affairs professionals committed to establishing developmental models for students' growth.

The recent introduction into higher education of the concept of wellness provides another model that can serve student affairs professionals. Even though many colleges and universities have a clearly stated commitment to influencing students' development, a program that helps them accomplish this goal is often elusive. Furthermore, communicating student development goals to students in a way that shows them how they can participate in and influence their own development is essential. The wellness model seems well suited to accomplishing both of these objectives. Since it is holistic, student affairs practitioners can use this model to conceptualize their tasks. Also, through a wellness model students can readily perceive how they can be actively involved in their own development.

Wellness models seem particularly appropriate for use in residential life programming. Because they are comprehensive and relatively easy to explain to undergraduates, they have proven effective in residence halls across the country.

In this chapter, wellness is defined and a model of wellness programs is presented with example applications from colleges and universities around the country. Finally, wellness as a comprehensive approach to addressing student development goals in residence halls is discussed.

Defining Wellness

Halbert A. Dunn (1961) is credited by many with giving impetus to the current, rapidly growing wellness movement. He defined wellness as an integrated method of functioning that is oriented toward maximizing the potential of the individual within his or her particular environment. Hettler (1980) expands this definition and describes wellness as a process of becoming aware and making choices that contribute to a more balanced and healthy life-style. This definition contains four important components: awareness, choices, personal responsibility, and balance. The awareness of choices is important for the decision process. Individuals must take personal responsibility for the choices they make. Ideally, the choices result in optimal health and living.

Motivating students to adopt a healthy life-style requires communication of information and knowledge. Students need to understand the effects of their present behaviors and the benefits to be gained from a wellness life-style. Adopting this life-style does not limit but instead expands participation and involvement in the total academic and out-of-class offerings of colleges and contributes significantly to students' development.

There are many models that can be used to introduce the wellness concept. I have selected the model developed by Hettler (1980). It is comprehensive and provides in-depth coverage of each dimension as well as a means of assessing each of these dimensions. Hettler identifies six dimensions of wellness: (1) emotional, (2) intellectual, (3) physical, (4) social, (5) occupational, and (6) spiritual. These six dimensions are defined as follows.

Emotional Wellness

Emotional wellness emphasizes an awareness and acceptance of one's feelings. This type of wellness includes the degree to which one feels positive and enthusiastic about oneself and life in general. It encompasses the capacity to manage one's feelings and related behaviors, including the realistic assessment of one's limitations, development of autonomy, and ability to cope effectively with stress. The emotionally well person maintains satisfying relationships with others.

Intellectual Wellness

This dimension of wellness encourages creative, stimulating mental activities. An intellectually well person uses the resources available to expand his or her knowledge and improve skills, along with expanding the potential for sharing with others. Such a person takes advantage of the intellectual and cultural activities in the classroom and cocurriculum, combined with the human resources and learning resources available within the university community and the larger community.

Physical Wellness

The encouragement of cardiovascular flexibility and strength through regular physical activity is a goal of physical development. It also encourages knowledge about food and nutrition and discourages the use of tobacco and drugs and excessive alcohol consumption. It encourages activities that contribute to high-level wellness, including medical self-care and appropriate use of the medical system.

Social Wellness

Social wellness involves contributing to the human and physical environment for the common welfare of the community. It emphasizes interdependence with others and nature and includes the pursuit of harmony in one's family.

Occupational Wellness

The preparation for work in which one will gain personal satisfaction and find enrichment is part of occupational development. It is related to one's attitude about work.

Spiritual Wellness

Spiritual wellness involves seeking meaning and purpose in human existence. It includes the development of an appreciation for the depth and expanse of life and natural forces that exist in the universe.

The importance of *all six dimensions* cannot be overemphasized. A lack of wellness in any one of these dimensions affects other dimensions, diminishing the person's well-being in all areas.

Challenges for Residence Hall Staffs

A challenge faced by residence hall professionals is to develop systems by which the wellness model can be introduced to all students as they enter the institution. Students need to be made aware of the importance a wellness lifestyle has for their present and future welfare. If wellness is the programming model adopted by a residential life program, the staff have a responsibility to provide information, resources, programs, facilities, and community and individual support that enable students to be actively involved in pursuing a wellness-oriented life-style. The challenge is more than providing information. It involves teaching skills, as well as creating and maintaining programs and services.

Ties Between National and Campus Goals

The Office of Disease Prevention and Health Promotion, a branch of the U.S. Public Health Service, has sponsored a report on the health objectives of the nation. *Healthy People 2000: National Health Promotion and Disease Prevention Objectives* (1991) has significant implications for institutions of higher education. Some of the objectives that directly address students include the following:

- Increase years of healthy life to at least sixty-five years
- Increase life expectancy to at least seventy-eight years
- Reduce drug abuse–related emergency room visits by at least 50 percent
- Reduce occasions of heavy drinking of alcoholic beverages by college students to no more than 32 percent of current use
- Reduce by at least 50 percent the use of alcohol, marijuana, and/or cocaine among young people
- Increase to at least 50 percent the proportion of higher education institutions with institutionwide programs that provide health education and health promotion activities for students, faculty, and staff

Healthy People 2000: National Health Promotion and Disease Prevention Objectives (1991), also encourages institutions of higher education to establish wellness programs as an integral part of student services.

Colleges and universities are the training ground for the nation's future leaders, health professionals, and public health personnel. It is imperative that future leaders and professionals embrace health promotion and disease prevention concepts. Institutions of higher education are one of the few settings outside the military where large numbers of eighteen- to twenty-four-year-olds can easily be reached. Currently, 5 percent of the U.S. population is enrolled in colleges and universities. Health beliefs and health practices are still developing during the college years. It is important to model, encourage, and support life-styles conducive to good health. The campus environment—especially residence halls—provides unique opportunities for classes, interventions, and student service programs. Colleges and universities often have ready access to health professionals who can provide the necessary knowledge and expertise. Furthermore, colleges offer students opportunities to be involved in health promotion through volunteer programs, as employees, and through internship experiences.

The Six Dimensions of Wellness on Campus

The six dimensions of wellness can be viewed in terms of student development goals. Following are descriptions of wellness programs that can and have been implemented in colleges of all types throughout the country.

Emotional Wellness

An excellent way to contribute to students' emotional development is to increase their understanding of themselves and of how their personality influences their relationships with people, processing of ideas, and attitudes about things. The Myers-Briggs Type Indicator is a superb instrument for this purpose (see Briggs and McCaulley, 1985). It can be easily administered and scored. Interpretations of the results can enhance students' awareness of their preferred style of behavior and a recognition of other personality types. This awareness can contribute to increased acceptance of their own strengths and create a better understanding of others' strengths. It can contribute to improved relationships with roommates, professors, parents, "significant others," and the residence hall staff.

Another method of assessing personality type has been introduced by Lowery (1991) in a program called "True Colors." This approach uses cards and an assessment/interpretation booklet to determine personality type. Manuals have been developed to assist professional staff in programs that can facilitate student involvement. Students have been receptive to this approach, which can be used with large or small groups.

The increase in self-awareness is useful for students' development emotionally, socially, and intellectually, as well as in career planning. Provost and Anchors (1987) identify many other applications of personality type in higher education. Auburn University, St. Louis University, and the University of Wisconsin at Stevens Point use the Myers-Briggs Type Indicator and/or True Colors in programming and also for research on student outcomes.

Programs on feelings, autonomy, stress, and relationships contribute to students' emotional wellness and development. They can be offered by residence hall staff who are trained to present this type of program or by other professionals within the college or university. These programs stimulate students' discussion and encourage further self-exploration. Residence hall staff can encourage and support students' exploration in these areas.

Emotional well-being can be enhanced by clarification of gender-role issues, a significant developmental issue for students at this point in their development. Most campuses have women's resource centers, which can provide materials and programs for residence hall students. Men's programs are only beginning to develop. A male support group has been formed among freshmen living in residence halls at San Jose State University. The group was designed to provide support systems for men and help them answer questions concerning maleness. A related course is being taught at the University of Wisconsin at Milwaukee. The course discusses the contribution of schools in forming male identity and the changing expectations of men in work, the family, and society. Many publications on this topic are available. Robert Bly's *Iron John* (1990) is one of the best-known books on men and can serve as an impetus to discussions and workshops. *Problem Solving Strategies and Interventions for Men in Conflict* (Moore and Leafgren, 1990) covers a wide variety of topics on male issues and provides an extensive bibliography of resources.

Intellectual Wellness

Colleges and universities provide a vast array of opportunities for intellectual development, both inside and outside the classroom. Outside the classroom, cultural programs, speakers, workshops, and seminars all promote intellectual development. Academic experiences that stimulate additional learning contribute to intellectual growth.

The role of the residence hall staff is to keep students informed about the opportunities available. Staff can encourage students' participation and attendance. They can also serve as models by their active participation in academic programs and cultural events.

Currently, most residence halls offer speakers, and other educational programs can be presented in the residence hall. When the students from a given living unit attend these programs together, it provides a common experience for dialogue. Faculty liaisons or faculty mentors for the residence hall also can increase faculty-student interaction and encourage intellectual dialogue and activities.

California Polytechnic State University at San Luis Obispo keeps students informed about activities that are scheduled for each of the six dimensions of wellness. If a student is interested in knowing about the intellectual programs available on a given day, this information is available. This is an excellent method of encouraging student participation, and students know they have a reliable source of information available to them.

Physical Wellness

The physical dimension of wellness includes physical activity, nutrition, substance abuse, sexual activity, and skin care. Major risk factors identified for the health of the eighteen- to twenty-five-year-old population are smoking, lack of seat belt use, excess body weight, too little exercise, and high blood cholesterol. A study (Hettler, Elsenrath, and Leafgren, 1990) of 3,630 college-age students indicated that 17 percent were smoking, 28 percent did not use seat belts 80 percent of the time or more, 61 percent exceed ideal body weight by 10 percent or more, 27 percent exercise less than once a week, and 19 percent have blood cholesterol levels above 200 milligrams.

Students need to know that smoking, obesity, inactivity, high blood cholesterol, and high blood pressure are harmful to the heart. In contrast, exercise, proper nutrition, stress management, social and mental activities, not smoking, moderate alcohol intake, avoiding drugs, personal safety, adequate sleep, and avoiding excessive sun exposure prevent or reduce chronic ailments (Center for Corporate Health Promotion, 1989). These life-style behaviors help prevent chronic ailments such as arthritis, cancer, cataracts, depression, diabetes, heart disease, high blood pressure, kidney disease, obstructive lung disease, osteoporosis, periodontal disease, and stroke.

Students generally are interested in their physical well-being. A health inventory to identify health-related issues with which students would like assistance was administered to 1,700 incoming freshmen students at the University of Wisconsin at Stevens Point. The four topics mentioned most frequently out of a list of forty-three health-related issues were (1) exercise programs, (2) stress reduction, (3) weight reduction, and (4) nutrition. Twenty percent of the students were seeking personal assistance in these areas.

Opportunities for physical activity are extensive, permitting students the option of selecting something they enjoy. The physical activities menu includes walking, hiking, climbing, jogging, running, swimming, surfing, bicycling, weight lifting, yoga, jumping rope, roller skating, and skiing. It includes sports such as tennis, racquetball, handball, basketball, baseball, golf, sailing, volleyball, soccer, and hockey. Rigorous physical work should not be overlooked as a healthy form of physical activity. This can include chopping wood, vigorous housework, yard work, and other forms of strenuous physical labor. Exercise programs designed to increase cardiovascular capacity, flexibility, strength, and endurance are increasing in popularity.

Dancing is an excellent source of physical activity. Organized physical activities often keep students actively involved because they can serve a social need as well.

There are many benefits to physical activity. These include keeping the heart and lungs healthy, increasing strength and flexibility, controlling weight, improving one's personal appearance, controlling blood pressure, reducing stress, reducing depression, preventing diabetes, contributing to smoking cessation, providing social benefits, and helping a person feel good. Muscle tone is improved, lung capacity is enhanced, and heart muscles are strengthened. The circulatory system is improved. There are recognizable increases of energy, and sleep is more restful. The individual feels better about himself or herself and has higher self-esteem and a more positive self-image and outlook on life. People who are physically active consume fewer substances that are harmful to the body such as drugs, coffee, tea, alcohol, and tobacco. They find these things inconsistent with a physically active life-style.

Physical fitness programs are often the first wellness programs established on campuses. Organized programs in residence halls or other campus facilities attract the attention of students and can encourage them to join. The traditional physical fitness programs are often expanded with aerobic exercise and other high-participation activity programs.

At the University of Maine at Orono, the Hilltop Health Club, housed in the basement of a coeducational residence hall, provides weight-lifting equipment for a comprehensive program that encourages physical development for college students by implementing a framework of goal-setting assessment and instruction.

Students at the University of Wisconsin at Stevens Point enroll in a class titled "The Healthy American." This class gives a comprehensive overview of the wellness life-style as well as requiring participation in a variety of activities to enhance physical well-being.

Portland State University has developed a health-and-fitness-for-life laboratory manual focused largely on physical well-being. It is in a workbook format that contains educational information and data as well as an opportunity for individuals to assess their own wellness levels.

Central Florida University has established a comprehensive wellness program with the goals of Healthy Campus 2000. It includes physical fitness programs, assessment programs, and informational programs with student involvement and support.

Hettler and Weston of the University of Wisconsin at Stevens Point developed a fitness testing unit called FIT Stop. It is a portable unit that can be easily moved about the campus. It provides testing for blood pressure, resting pulse, muscular strength, muscular endurance, flexibility, stress, percentage of body fat, and vital lung capacity. This form of assessment also serves as a motivating force, encouraging people to become involved in physical fitness activities.

Eastern Washington University established an on-campus fitness center called the Body Shop. For a fee of $80 a year, students have access to individualized workout programs. The center is open eighty-four hours per week. Computerized videos provide students with information on growth and change. It serves as a wellness resource center as well. More people at Eastern Washington University are involved in the center than in all other physical activities combined. Over 400,000 individual visits to the Body Shop have been recorded.

Nutrition. Nutrition is a very important area of physical wellness. The federal government's dietary goals for the nation are as follows:

1. Increase complex carbohydrate consumption to account for 55 to 60 percent of the energy (caloric) intake.
2. Reduce overall fat consumption from approximately 40 to 30 percent of energy intake.
3. Reduce saturated fat consumption to account for about 10 percent of total energy intake and balance that with polyunsaturated and monounsaturated fats, which should account for about 10 percent of energy intake each day.
4. Reduce cholesterol consumption to about 300 milligrams a day.
5. Reduce sugar consumption by about 40 percent to account for about 15 percent of total energy intake.
6. Reduce salt consumption by about 50 percent to 85 percent to approximately three grams a day.

Programs that educate students about basic nutrition need to be presented. To be effective, programs should relate nutritional goals to actual food choices and food consumption. Most students are not knowledgeable about the amount of fat, carbohydrate, and protein in the foods they consume. Information should be provided in a manner and at a time that can facilitate making "good" food choices. The dining service, for instance, can use labels to indicate the amount of carbohydrate, protein, and fat content in the food items, as well as reporting the number of calories per serving. Poster displays of frequently consumed food items illustrating the amount of sugar, salt, and fat are an effective educational tool as well. Food fairs are another way of informing people about good nutrition. Articles in the campus newspaper that focus on food and nutrition also are means of communicating nutrition information.

A government-endorsed report recommends an ambitious effort by food companies, physicians, and individuals to improve health by reducing fat and cholesterol in the national diet. The result, says the expert panel that produced the report, would be a 20 percent reduction in coronary heart disease. "The American Public should have a greater range of low-saturated fatty acid, low-fat and low-cholesterol food options available, and they should have the information to establish healthy eating patterns," states James Cleeman, coordinator of the National Cholesterol Education Program ("'Low-Fat' Diet Endorsed by Health Groups," 1990, p. 14).

Programs to help students maintain appropriate weight are a necessity for a comprehensive program of physical wellness. To maintain or reduce body weight, calories consumed from food and beverages must not exceed calories used for normal body functions and physical activity. Weight loss requires eating less, exercising more, or both. There are no quick and easy solutions to weight loss.

Charles Kuntzleman has long advocated the importance of combining both nutrition and physical activity as the primary means of weight control. A year-long study showed that diet, exercise, and stress reduction can open arteries and save lives (Hagar, Joseph, and Shapiro, 1990). Students who are interested in controlling weight need to combine both a diet program and a physical activity program. It is the combination of these two that ultimately can control weight. Exercise burns calories in more ways than one. Muscles burn more calories than fat. The more exercise one engages in, the more muscle is built and the more fat one loses. The body will burn more calories to maintain itself.

Appropriate eating habits include avoiding eating disorders. Although eating disorders are more common among women, some studies suggest that 5 to 10 percent of those who seek help for eating disorders are men (Van Pelt, 1987, p. 56). A male support group for eating disorders has been established at St. Francis Medical Center in Pittsburgh. Female support groups are more common across the country.

Substance Abuse. Research has shown that the use of alcohol, marijuana, and cocaine poses significant health risks for youth and young adults (*Tufts University Diet and Nutrition Letter*, 1989). These mind-altering and addictive substances have been shown to jeopardize physical, mental, and social development during a person's formative years and to endanger the successful transition from school to the workplace. Moreover, the use of most substances is illegal for young people and thus may have long-term implications for employment and education. Research also indicates that the use of alcohol and marijuana increases the risk of use of other illicit drugs. The use of these drugs is correlated with other health problems, including adolescent suicide, homicide, school dropouts, motor vehicle crashes, delinquency, early sexual activity, sexually transmitted diseases, and problem pregnancy.

Baldwin-Wallace College has a club called the Student Activities Center or the SAC, which is designed to serve as an alternative to the bar scene (Collison, 1990). Alcohol-free clubs like this are gaining popularity as colleges struggle to combat alcohol abuse and find alternatives to bars for students who are under twenty-one. "We're trying to compete with the bar scene. We are trying to have a youthful, creative atmosphere where the focus is not on booze" (Collison, 1990, p. A31). Alcohol and drug abuse prevention

materials are available through state and federal agencies as well as community agencies. Films and speakers on the topics can increase awareness of
these issues associated with drug abuse. Wellness-oriented physical activities
provide attractive alternatives to social events involving substance abuse. A
combination of many programs is probably necessary to have the greatest
impact on substance abuse. The most successful programs are those that
include students as the primary leaders of the activity.

No amount of smoking is ever healthy. The American Heart Association, the American Lung Association, and the American Cancer Society have
resources and materials that institutional stop-smoking programs can utilize.
Educational information, stop-smoking programs, institutional policies on
smoking, and support systems are means of impacting students' lives. Establishing policies regarding smoking in the residence halls is important because of the negative effects of secondary smoke.

Eight of the thirty-four residence halls at Ball State University in
Indiana encourage an alcohol-free, tobacco-free, and drug-free environment
that focuses on the physical and mental well-being of its residents. These
residence halls provide students with a unique living environment that
supports healthy habits. All of the residence halls have fitness centers. The
dining halls provide a "healthier alternative" menu. Daily testing of blood
pressure, cholesterol, and body fat are provided for the students.

Sexual Behavior. Students need accurate information regarding sexually
transmitted diseases. These include gonorrhea, syphilis, genital herpes,
chlamydia, genital warts, pubic lice, and acquired immune deficiency syndrome (AIDS). Residence hall staff can solicit help in providing information
and presenting programs from the health center, counseling center, and
academic departments involved in health education, as well as from community agencies. Student response to these programs is usually excellent. There
is high interest. Resource materials are readily available.

Physical concerns around women's health issues deal with breast cancer and the need for breast self-exam, for mammograms, and for pap smears.
Women students should be informed about the availability of the services on
the campus and encouraged to utilize these services.

Men need knowledge on proper testes self-exam techniques. Research
on a group of 1,723 men in a self-report study revealed 61 percent did not
know the proper techniques or were unsure of the proper techniques for
testes self-exam. Of the same group, 57 percent indicated that they rarely or
never undertook such an examination (Hettler, Elsenrath, and Leafgren,
1990).

Skin Cancer. The incidence of skin cancer is soaring. Skin cancer is now the
most common form of cancer in the United States. The chances of getting
skin cancer in one's lifetime are about one in seven. Cases of malignant
melanoma—the deadliest form of skin cancer—have been doubling each

decade. More than 90 percent of all skin cancer is caused by excessive exposure to the sun's radiation (Bachman and Preston, 1990). Tips for minimizing the risk of skin cancer should be communicated, especially before vacation breaks.

Social Wellness

Social wellness involves participation in one's community. "Community" includes the residence hall, the campus, and the town or city in which the college or university is located. Students have opportunities for involvement in residence hall governing and program groups as well as campus organizations, and they are usually welcomed as participants in community organizations and endeavors.

Student involvement creates a sense of belonging. This involvement contributes to retention and ultimately graduation. It also enhances students' social development. Residence hall staff can encourage student involvement by making the opportunities for involvement known to them. Faculty can encourage student involvement by making it course related when appropriate: they can often make involvement in relevant activities part of a specific course requirement, a project, or independent study.

Social wellness also includes the environment. Teaching students about environmental needs is important for everyone's welfare. Educational programs can be presented in the residence hall or through specially designed outdoor experiences. The College of Natural Resources at the University of Wisconsin at Stevens Point has developed excellent training programs in environmental awareness.

Residence hall programs promoting recycling should be implemented. Students can become aware of how they can contribute to environmental wellness on a daily basis.

Social wellness involves living in such a way that one contributes positively to the welfare of others. The residence hall is an ideal place to learn the importance of sharing, being supportive toward others, and being willing to ask for help when necessary. Residence halls provide opportunities to teach tolerance, cooperation, and mutual respect in a community where individuals with different life-styles and from diverse backgrounds must interact on a daily basis. A heterogeneous population can enhance the learning opportunities. Residence hall staff have many opportunities for that teachable moment as students confront one another. The opportunities for positive interventions are continuous.

Occupational Wellness

Many students find selecting a career to be a difficult task. On-campus and off-campus job opportunities can facilitate the career selection process, since they enable students to gain a sense of themselves in a work environment.

Students can identify more clearly those tasks that bring satisfaction and fulfillment and often begin to know themselves better as they must interact with others, both as supervisors and subordinates.

Career exploration and planning can be facilitated through the use of a multitude of assessment instruments and other programs. An assessment instrument often used for self-exploration is the Strong Vocational Interest Inventory, which helps students identify their interests and compare their preferences to samples of persons who actually work in different occupations. Holland's *The Self-Directed Search* (1985) can also be useful in residence hall programming, because it is self-scoring and can be easily understood by residents with minimal assistance from professionals.

Residence hall staff are encouraged to request programming assistance from offices assigned the task of helping students with career planning. Professionals working primarily in career planning welcome opportunities to present programs to students that facilitate students' exploration and decision-making process. These programs are often well received when they are presented in residence halls. Again, they promote ongoing discussion among the residents.

Spiritual Wellness

Spiritual development is a lifelong process. Campus and community religious organizations provide opportunities for affiliation and involvement in religious life. Courses on religion and philosophy are offered on most campuses. Students will find many resources for spiritual exploration and growth.

Members of the faculty, clergy, and religious educators are usually willing to make presentations and hold discussions in the residence halls on a wide variety of topics. These topics may be more specifically focused on religious faith or may emphasize current social problems. These presentations can stimulate further dialogue and exploration by students. It is important that students accept spiritual well-being as an important aspect of their total developmental process.

There is currently a resurgence of interest in mythology. Programs on mythology can be an interesting way to explore values, purposes, meanings, and ethics. Joseph Campbell prepared a series of audiocassettes entitled *The Wisdom of Joseph Campbell* (1991). These tapes are a collection of dialogues on creative living and the world of myth. The program can encourage students to explore and better understand the myths that direct their lives.

Roles for Residence Hall Staff

The dimensions of wellness have been identified. Becoming knowledgeable about these dimensions and engaging in behaviors and activities that support optimal wellness are goals for many residence hall programs.

If the wellness programming model is adopted, residence hall staff should be trained to provide leadership for all six dimensions of wellness. The techniques utilized to promote other kinds of programs for students in the residence hall are also applicable to wellness programs. The programs should be communicated with enthusiasm. Students need to be challenged to become involved. Physical wellness is the easiest wellness dimension to introduce and often gets a good response in terms of participation. Most students are seeking opportunities to be involved in physical activities. These activities contribute positively to their physical well-being and also give them a sense of belonging, identification, and good feeling about themselves. Recognizing the importance of physical wellness for their total well-being can help them understand the significance of the other dimensions of wellness for their total development.

Residence hall staff provide the clearest leadership when they are engaged in wellness activities themselves. It is important for staff to model wellness to other students. There are four major challenges for residence hall staff to be aware of to maximize students' participation in wellness programs and activities.

1. *Encourage the participation of students who have not been involved in these programs before.* One approach in motivating students to participate in wellness programming is to send a consistent message, according to Hettler (1986). The message Hettler conveys to entering students at the University of Wisconsin at Stevens Point is that "we are interested in your growth and development; we are interested in your success; we believe that wellness is a desirable role for everyone." Students are encouraged to experiment with a variety of activities and programs.

Numerous assessments of wellness are available in the marketplace. By administering such instruments, student affairs professionals can generate interest in development. Awareness is a first step in bringing students into the wellness program. These instruments can inform students about their present level of wellness and can provide a clear picture of their present wellness levels compared with peers. Students can set priorities regarding the dimension or dimensions they would like to emphasize for their own growth. Wellness requires self-responsibility, and students must determine the direction and amount of commitment they are willing to undertake.

The greatest demand on the residence hall staff is education. The staff must inform students about opportunities available for their growth in all wellness dimensions. They must provide information and develop programs for students' involvement and participation. This becomes the essence of the work of the residence hall staff and requires knowledge, skills, and competencies in wellness and development. It also requires commitment to promotion, communication, and support. Organized programs in residence halls and other campus facilities increase the visibility of these programs and serve as a promotion device.

2. *Provide support systems to avoid potential dropouts.* Wellness programs

are defined at three levels: awareness, behavioral change, and supportive environments. Each of these is distinct, and all are exceedingly important. The first step is to heighten awareness of the value of a behavior. "College's aim, of course, [is] to transmit culture, to bring about changes in the values and beliefs with which students arrive" (Sanford, 1964, p. 23). The principle Sanford advocates also applies to wellness development.

Behavioral change itself involves additional educational opportunities, motivational assistance, and skill-building programs. Educational programs give students the information that will influence their decision to make a behavioral change. Wellness fairs and workshops are excellent ways to showcase health and wellness issues and programs. These fairs offer a chance for students to be introduced to new information, new programs, new skills, and new approaches to fitness and well-being.

Environments should teach, encourage, and support the wellness practice. These environments include not only people who will provide support but the facilities, food, and other prerequisites necessary to bring about change. The goal is to have students involved in new behaviors for a long enough time so that the new behaviors become habitual and are incorporated into their life-style.

3. *Set up a reward system for those who are going to stay with the program.* Students need and like recognition. Most college students have received recognition in the past. This reward system can be continued. Residence hall staff can recognize participants by displaying their names and accomplishments prominently. This is especially true for the physical dimension. Pictures are excellent means of recognition as well. Videotaping activities for the participants is often well received. Accomplishments can be recorded with names on plaques, recognition T-shirts, hall banquets, a Hall Book of Records (like the Guinness Book of Records), and special privileges. Public recognition reduces dropouts.

Self-recognition can also have an important impact on student persistence. People who are engaged in activities to further their development generally have a better sense of well-being, a livelier enjoyment of the world around them, and a greater number of options in their life-style.

4. *Provide opportunities for participants to assess their growth and change.* The participants' growth process can be motivated by reassessment and a recording of the change that has taken place. Wellness assessments can involve pencil-and-paper methods, self-report forms, physical activity, body measurement, and records of participation. Recording this information keeps the student aware of changes. These assessments can be made as often as seems appropriate. Recording accomplishments can provide self-reward and can be used for public recognition as well.

Ingredients of Wellness Programs

We are rapidly moving into the Information Age. In the past, many people relied on the health care professional to take care of them. But in the 1970s, a significant change got underway with the advent of self-care books: *The Aerobics Way* by Ken Cooper (1977) and *High Level Wellness; An Alternative to Doctors, Drugs, and Disease* by Don Ardell (1977) sounded wake-up calls for many Americans. These books empower the individual to assume responsibility for proactive behavior.

Many opportunities exist for residence hall professionals to serve as authority models and as partners in wellness and developmental endeavors. Staff must focus on cultural norms, which include traditional behavior, expected behavior, supported behavior, accepted behavior, and written or unwritten rules of the institution and community. They need to identify any negative norms and begin to change these norms by promoting a desired culture characterized by positive norms. Residence hall professionals can describe specific behaviors that will accomplish the desired goals.

Ideally, members of the residence hall community should participate in establishing and owning these goals and objectives. It is important that a sense of community, a shared vision, exist. It is usually necessary to change group or organizational cultures to support wellness-oriented life-styles. "Asking people to change their health practices without changing their culture is like asking them to reach over the Twinkies for the celery and the carrots" (Allen, 1989). Allen suggests the following six-step intervention process that can bring about change for the individual (p. 4):

1. Get the facts about the life-style area.
2. Develop a plan for change.
3. Find or build a supportive subculture.
4. Put your plan into action.
5. Reward yourself and have fun.
6. Reach out to help others.

Allen has also identified eight cultural factors that may determine which norms take hold in a culture (p. 4):

1. How will formal and informal leadership model desired behavior?
2. How will desired behavior be rewarded and recognized in the culture?
3. How will desired behavior be better integrated? What is being communicated by members of the culture?
4. How will positive interpersonal relationships develop around desired behavior?
5. How will human and material resources be allocated differently to support desired norms?
6. How will new people be oriented to desired behavior?
7. How will people get the skills they need to practice desired behavior?
8. How will people who support the desired culture be recruited from an external culture?

Allen points out that in Western countries, the culture is usually overlooked when attempting to plant the seeds of life-style change. This is why many attempts at life-style change bear sparse fruit. To reduce the cycle of frustration and broken promises, residence hall staff must focus simultaneously on the individual and the culture.

Travis and Ryan (1981, p. 1) write,

> Wellness is a choice—a decision you make to move toward optimal health. Wellness is a way of life, a lifestyle designed to achieve your highest potential for well-being. Wellness is a process—a developing awareness that there is no end point, but that health and happiness are possible in each moment, here and now. Wellness is an efficient channeling of energy—energy received from the environment, transformed within you, is sent on to affect the world outside. Wellness is the integration of body, mind, and spirit—the appreciation of everything you do, and think, and feel, and believe has an impact on your state of health. Wellness is a loving acceptance of yourself.

There are few today who are not aware of the focus on wellness and health. College and university residence halls possess the three essentials for wellness promotion: a captive audience, reasonably motivated participants, and the opportunity to incorporate wellness activities into the total residence hall program to further student development.

References

Allen, J. *Wellness Management.* National Wellness Association conference newsletter, Stevens Point, Wis., 1989, (4), 4.

Ardell, D. *High Level Wellness: An Alternative to Doctors, Drugs, and Disease.* Emmaus, Pa.: Rodale Press, 1977.

Bachman, D., and Preston, M. "Preventing Skin Cancer—Exercise Your Right with Good Sense." *Stevens Point Journal,* May 26, 1990, p. 17.

Bly, R. *Iron John.* Reading, Mass.: Addison-Wesley, 1990.

Briggs, I. B., and McCaulley, M. H. *A Guide to the Development and Use of the Myers-Briggs Type Indicator.* Palo Alto, Calif.: Consulting Psychologists Press, 1985.

Campbell, J. *The Wisdom of Joseph Campbell.* San Francisco: New Dimensions Foundation, 1991. Audiotapes.

Center for Corporate Health Promotion. *Taking Care,* 1989, 2(4), 11.

Chickering, A. W. *Education and Identity.* San Francisco: Jossey-Bass, 1969.

Collison, M. "Alcohol-Free Clubs Gaining Popularity on Some Campuses." *Chronicle of Higher Education,* May 23, 1990, p. A31.

Cooper, K. *The Aerobics Way.* New York: Bantam Books, 1977.

Dunn, H. A. *High Level Wellness.* Arlington, Va.: Betty, 1961.

Hagar, M., Joseph, N., and Shapiro, L. "A New Menu to Heal the Heart." *Newsweek,* July 30, 1990, p. 58.

Havighurst, R. J. *Human Development and Education.* White Plains, N.Y.: Longman, 1953.

Hettler, W. "Wellness Promotion on a University Campus." *Family and Community Health Promotion and Maintenance,* 1980, *3*(1), 77–95.

Hettler, W. "Strategies for Wellness and Recreation Program Development." In F. Leafgren (ed.), *Developing Campus Recreation and Wellness Programs.* New Directions for Student Services, no. 34. San Francisco: Jossey-Bass, 1986.

Hettler, W., Elsenrath, D., and Leafgren, F. *Lifestyle Assessment Questionnaire.* Stevens Point, Wis.: National Wellness Institute, 1990.

Holland, J. L. *The Self-Directed Search.* Odessa, Fla.: Psychological Assessment Resources, 1985.

Lowery, D. *True Colors: Positive Attitudes in America.* Corona, Calif.: Communication Companies International, 1991.

"'Low-Fat' Diet Endorsed by Health Groups." *Stevens Point Journal,* Feb. 28, 1990, p. 14.

Moore, D., and Leafgren, F. *Problem Solving Strategies and Interventions for Men in Conflict.* Alexandria, Va.: American Association for Counseling and Development, 1990.

Office of Disease Prevention and Health Promotion, U.S. Public Health Service. *Healthy People 2000: National Health Promotion and Disease Prevention Objectives.* Washington, D.C.: U.S. Government Printing Office, 1991.

Provost, J. A., and Anchors, S. *Applications of the Myers-Briggs Type Indicator in Higher Education.* Palo Alto, Calif.: Consulting Psychologists Press, 1987.

Sanford, N. *College and Character.* New York: Wiley, 1964.

Sanford, N. *Where Colleges Fail: A Study of the Student as a Person.* San Francisco: Jossey-Bass, 1967.

Travis, J., and Ryan, R. *Wellness Workbook.* Berkeley, Calif.: Ten Speed Press, 1981.

Tufts University Diet and Nutrition Letter, 1989, *3*(10), 7.

Van Pelt, D. "Keeping Tabs on the Risk of Everyday Radiation." *Insight,* Aug. 3, 1987, p. 56.

Chapter Nineteen

Developing and Enhancing
Student Communities

Scott Anchors
Katie Branch Douglas
Mary Kay Kasper

The challenge of developing and enhancing community is not unique to higher education. According to Hamilton (1985, p. 7), "the concept of community has been one of the most compelling and attractive themes in modern science, and at the same time one of the most difficult to define." In residence halls, "community" is evidenced in a variety of ways. In its most limiting (and often destructive) form, a residential community is a kind of clique, or even gang, that thrives on exclusiveness. In a healthier sense, community can be an *inclusive*, vital, essential context for promoting tolerance and acceptance of diversity, self-exploration, and other student development goals. This latter sense of community aims at promoting the common good, imparts a sense of belonging, and supports the ultimate goal of encouraging students' personal development. Gardner (1989, p. 73) writes: "We know that where community exists it confers upon its members identity, a sense of belonging, and a measure of security. . . . Communities are the ground-level generators and preservers of values and ethical systems. The ideals of justice and compassion are nurtured in communities." In his prescription for improving the quality of higher education, Boyer (1987, p. 69) asserts that "throughout an effective college education, students should become personally empowered and also committed to the common good." This is most likely to occur when student affairs professionals devote thought and energy to creating healthy communities and is a *major challenge* for contemporary residence hall programs that espouse student development goals.

Historically, on-campus community was rooted in the philosophy of in loco parentis. Houseparents, faculty members, and other adults were expected to direct, monitor, and support students. Community was an extension of the leadership provided by those in charge, who were expected to create a family atmosphere. It was an idea based on an authoritarian family structure. In recent decades, the focus has turned more sharply toward "community development," which emphasizes the "adult" status of students. They can be members of a community of their own making. The perspectives of these recent decades are serving as the foundation for emerging paradigms in both the physical and social sciences. These paradigms seek to integrate multiple perspectives into constructs that accommodate greater complexity, inclusiveness, and pluralism with respect to community.

Effective residence halls are not educationally neutral; they create environments and purposive interventions that are designed to enhance the academic experience and personal lives of students. (See Chapter Two.) This chapter surveys different strategies that have been employed to build and maintain community in residence halls. Theoretical foundations for community development (such as the establishment of norms in groups, behavioral management, and student leadership development) are outlined, a process model for developing community is offered, the physical environment's impact on students and their community is examined, and ethical implications are explored. Interwoven with each topic is a discussion of our conviction that every intrusion into the lives of students, no matter how subtle, is value laden and that we should be forthright about the values we hold and promote. Readers should consult other chapters in this volume for additional perspectives on some of these and related topics, such as programming (Chapter Seventeen), housing alternatives (Chapter Ten), and addressing interpersonal relationships and conflicts (Chapter Twenty).

Foundations for Community Development

The Student Personnel Point of View (American Council on Education, 1949) highlights the significance of the individual as a complex, whole person developing in context. The residence hall community is one of the out-of-the-classroom environments, or contexts, where students are often challenged to explore the benefits and risks of sharing their emerging selves. The struggles between individual and group identities fuel this development, frequently caused by a confrontation with diversity and the working out of ways to respond. One might conclude, then, that student affairs divisions, especially housing programs, have a responsibility to aid in the creation of new communities or to strengthen existing communities that enrich the educational experience and personal development of students.

If we accept the premise that community development is a *responsibility* for housing programs, there are multiple theoretical and philosophical perspectives that can inform practitioners as they conceptualize their tasks.

The "New Paradigm"

The emergence of qualitative approaches to research as "valid" alternatives to quantitative, "positivist" approaches (Lincoln and Guba, 1985) and the growing influence of ideas about humanistic organizational leadership have had significant impacts on how community development is conceptualized. When studying these concepts in the framework of a "paradigm shift" or alternative worldview that recognizes the significance of context, multiple ways of meaning making, diversity, and change, many new possibilities arise in interpretation and implementation. Ogilvy and Schwartz (1979) describe this paradigm as "the foundation for future values and belief systems." Kuh, Whitt, and Shedd (1987, p. xi) note that "in the emergent paradigm, some aspects of human development are interpreted as unfolding in a spontaneous, uncontrollable, unpredictable manner."

Gilligan (1982) encourages the recognition of ways of looking at the world that are less hierarchical and more connected, based on relational values. In a similar vain, Noddings (1990) calls for an ethics of care. She argues that people, as well as the situational effects of decision making about people, should come before specific predefined principles. These congruent themes point toward the emerging paradigm shift of the intentional, inclusive community.

Understanding How Groups Form and Develop

When residence hall communities are explored through such a dynamic lens, the holistic process of developing a synergistic community becomes the focal point. Tuckman (1965) presents the traditional view of the group development process in four stages: forming, storming, norming, and performing. As a group forms, members begin to make initial contacts to establish working relationships and learn the purposes of their entry into that group. Tension may begin to form as members clarify the tasks and goals of both individuals and the group and as differences in personality and approaches emerge. Commonality and norms for acceptable behavior are established, and the group proceeds toward the performing stage.

Additionally, Peck (1987) offers four stages of development in groups where community making is intentional: pseudocommunity, chaos, emptiness, and community. A pseudocommunity, a kind of insta-community, is created when participants act with a veneer of friendliness in order to avoid addressing any underlying conflict. In many residence halls, especially at the beginning of an academic year, examples of pseudocommunity are abundant. These include residents' initial politeness, sharing personal possessions, eating all meals together, and making the same new friends. Eventually, groups move on to the chaos stage. While intensity varies, this part of the process is characterized by conflict and the expression of many issues that are perceived as inhibiting movement toward community. After chaos is emptiness. In emptiness, people begin to realize that converting others to their viewpoints and blocking communication are ineffective and promote sameness and boredom. Within emptiness, acceptance begins to grow and communication becomes more fluid. This exploration of differences enhances the development of an inclusive community. In the last of Peck's stages, that of community, participants recognize that differences among individuals cannot only be appreciated but must also be nurtured to enhance movement toward a pluralistic, holistic community.

Peck's stages of community making philosophically parallel Crookston's (1980) ideas about intentional democratic community for residence halls. Crookston's innovative project at the University of Connecticut found the following elements to be of particular significance in the development of residence hall community: social contracts, primary groups, shared goals and values, boundaries, power, work, commitment, transcendence, communion, and meaningful processes. Crookston (1980, p. 58) argues that "as the individual contributes to the enrichment of community, so the community is able to enrich the individual."

Marginality and Mattering

Some additional perspectives enrich or broaden the multidimensional foundation for understanding person-environment interaction theories (see Chapter Five). Schlossberg's (1989) concepts of marginality and mattering and Peck's (1987) stages of intentional community making further expand the framing and implementation of person-environment interaction theories as they relate to student and community development in a group setting. Schlossberg, Lynch, and Chickering (1989, p. 21) define *mattering* as "the belief people have, whether right or wrong, that they matter to someone else, that they are the object of someone else's attention, and that others care about them and appreciate them." Students have feelings of marginality when they do not think that they *matter*; they feel out of place, alienated, not central, lack connections, or feel as if they do not belong. It is principally through rituals in community settings that a sense of mattering is reinforced. Individuals frequently feel marginal, or as if they do not matter, during transitions in their lives. This is often true, for example, of the freshman as he or she moves into a residence hall. Rituals, such as Welcome Weeks and graduation ceremonies, can help people through the transition process and increase perceptions of mattering. As Schlossberg (1989, p. 13) states, "The problem is that we have no rituals. We ritualize the entry to and final departure from the college environment, but for many transitions—completing a project or program for a student organization, selecting a major, separating from a relationship—we have no rituals."

Psychosocial Development Constructs

Two of the intrapersonal struggles captured in Chickering's (1969) developmental vector model—autonomy and interdependence—often are experienced in the residence hall environment. Supportive communities offer a safe environment to explore the balance between retaining personal identity and seeking interdependence with others. Such a community atmosphere allows participants to work on these developmental tasks simultaneously, rather than in distinct linear stages. The dynamic interchange among responsibility to self as well as to others is experienced as an important part of the whole.

A Community Development Process Model

A community's effectiveness and success are based, in part, on its ability to listen to and respond to the voices of those who are unable to speak, or whose voices are drowned out by the more aggressive, self-assured members of the community. In order to do that, the community must acknowledge that the voiceless individuals exist, must make a commitment to seek these individuals out, and must be skilled in its ability to draw these individuals into a dialogue that addresses their needs. Such individuals may be members of typical student leadership groups, or they may be students who are not part of such traditional groups. In listening to the silent voices, the staff can design strategies that realistically encompass the broader concepts of the inclusive community. The utilization of this perspective offers a unifying mission that requires staff to remain accountable to their residential life department's goals.

The model outlined in this section is intended to facilitate the goal of listening to a community. This model consists of four phases, which can be utilized either as an integrated process or as independent activities: assessment, design, implementation, and evaluation. These phases imply a continuous process of developing and enhancing residence hall communities. The model integrates the concepts of student development and residential life standards of practice through clarifying community needs, setting goals, designing and implementing services, and evaluating the process.

The transient and diverse nature of the student population requires a model that is inclusive and process oriented. Yanikoski (1980) conceptualized a progressive model of assessment that is process oriented rather than outcome directed. Change is the most enduring feature in developing communities for a transitory student population. It is, therefore, vital to develop a model that is flexible, comprehensive, and ongoing.

Assessment

Assessment is the process of gathering information. Its goal is to identify and clarify the needs of students and other constituencies. Assessment is a continuous process that provides facts, details, and opinions about specific issues and concerns that arise in the residence community on a daily basis. Despite the perceived complexity of the assessment task, its undertaking is accomplished by simply recognizing the broader techniques that can be used. Later in this section, we will provide a discussion of those techniques.

In designing an assessment plan, it is important to build a foundation that is inclusive of all students and all aspects of residential living and that is flexible. Aulepp and Delworth's (1976) ecosystem approach to environmental assessment offers five steps in which to plan and implement a thorough assessment process:

1. Determine what to assess.
2. Organize a planning team.
3. Develop techniques to accomplish the assessment.
4. Conduct the assessment and analyze the data.
5. Redesign the environment based on the data.

When deciding what is to be assessed, a comprehensive format should be utilized. Moos's (1979) work on environmental assessment provides a formal set of domains numerous residence hall researchers have used successfully. Three of the four domains are integrated into this assessment model: (1) human aggregate, (2) physical, and (3) social/organizational.

The first domain, *human aggregate*, concentrates on the characteristics of the student population who live in an identifiable area—for example, a wing of a building or a whole residence hall. Specific student characteristics to be considered include gender, race, ethnicity, religion, class standing, kind of disability, sexual orientation, academic major, socioeconomic background, and personality types, traits, or preferences.

The second domain, *physical environment*, includes the physical layout of the building or buildings, grounds around the buildings, structure of the building (which includes fire alarm locations, locks on doors, and accessibility to phones), recreational facilities, locations of bathrooms, and study areas.

The last domain is the *social/organizational* makeup. This includes hall traditions, values, social structure, rules and policies, and staff commitments. The organizational structure of the residential life department impacts community development. The variety of concerns and differences in each domain complement and influence the perceived commonality of the community experience. Because of this, it is important to remember that human and physical domains will interact and influence each other. An obvious example could include the interrelationship between a student using a wheelchair and the accessibility of a hall.

Students, resident assistants, hall directors, area coordinators, peer helpers, involved faculty, and administrators can conduct assessments. The tools and techniques for assessment are available through a variety of campus and community resources. Although not a substitute for formal assessment methods, intuitive approaches and the use of everyday data from routine management materials — such as occupancy reports and floor layouts — can be useful. Staff often use standardized surveys or design a specific tool, which can then be adapted to obtain a variety of data. Formal techniques utilizing those tools include observing social atmosphere, studying layouts and maintenance reports, analyzing campuswide services, or conducting surveys of activities. Walking through a residence hall, talking with students on Friday night, or holding one-on-one meetings to gather information on pertinent perceptions can add "words and meanings" to hard data.

Timing is essential to the data gathering process. Clearly, assessing for social needs at the end of the second semester provides valid data; however, program planning and implementation are irrelevant, because most students leave for the summer. Students tend to "create" a totally new world for themselves at the start of each academic year.

The collected data can be used to develop community-building projects, justify programming decisions, meet students' needs, design plans for the next semester or year, and offer clarification of staff roles and responsibilities.

Design

The process of design emphasizes the planning of flexible structures by which to create community within residence halls. When planning, keep in mind the following factors:

1. The need to define goals and objectives while remaining sensitive to process and product issues
2. The importance of ongoing identification of student and community needs
3. Available resources (physical, budget, staff, materials)
4. Staff ability to meet planning/training needs
5. Staff commitment to implementation

Implementation

Implementation of the third, most visibly active phase in the model is carried out by conducting a program, which may include altering the physical environment, establishing hall governments, supervising staff, using bulletin boards, or addressing incidents of harassment. Buying floor T-shirts, arranging for floor dinners, creating study breaks, and forming intramural teams are further examples of community-building activities. Leaders should use these events and experiences to establish commonalities in experience as the foundation for community. These are the acts of building community. However, these things in themselves do not necessarily build community. A sense of community develops from a variety of interwoven acts with individuals who share common meaning and connection. Goals need to be set, and these activities should be ways of reaching those goals. Many residence halls have these activities and never build a sense of community. Some specific items to remember are the following:

1.   Timing and scheduling
2.   Coordination with other programs and organizations
3.   Marketing to students (advertising, participation)
4.   Contingency plans

Evaluation

The final phase in the community development process model is evaluation. The evaluation phase systematically determines the effectiveness of the process. Were the goals achieved? Was a sense of community fostered? While formal instruments such as evaluation forms and open forums are most often used to assess goal attainment, other nonintrusive means should also be included. Formal instruments of evaluation identify excesses and limitations and provide insights into the development and enhancement of residence hall communities. The data collected from an evaluation provide staff with relevant feedback (both positive and critical) from many voices. The data can be used to guide decisions concerning the continuation of projects and programs, to develop alternative interventions, to determine the need for additional resources, and to design new strategies that will reinforce the emergence of the informed community. Evaluation identifies current and future concerns of the staff and students.

      Utilizing the following criteria maximizes the effectiveness of an evaluation:

1.   Appropriately defined goals for the evaluation
2.   Knowledgeable and committed evaluators
3.   Previously designed criteria specific for each situation
4.   Appropriate instruments
5.   A system that will disseminate results of the evaluation

      Residence life staff need to remain objective regarding the meaning of the evaluation for the intended community. When developing an evaluation process, incorporating student needs, staff needs, and the role of community in the residence hall can be essential. Evaluation, like assessment, is also an ongoing process and a significant component of the process model (see Chapter Sixteen).

Typically, the model is presented as a step-by-step method, but all facets can occur simultaneously. The community development process model is open by design. This process is utilized to assess, design, implement, and evaluate the creation and enhancement of the intended residence hall community.

Establishing and Monitoring Norms

Commonality is often the perceived basis of community. A challenge for residence hall staff is to create, identify, or develop perceived commonalities that nurture a sense of belonging. Also, while searching for common understandings, people often discover their differences and the uniqueness of each individual. Staff have a significant role in this exploration process by helping to foster basic commonalities while teaching skills needed to develop meaningful relationships in a pluralistic world. Three ways this can be addressed are through the processes of roommate matching, roommate contracting, and group norming.

Roommate Matching

Roommate relationships are core building blocks of community that can be supported intentionally through staff involvement. Matching individuals who appear to be compatible in life-styles, academic and personal interests, or individual characteristics can serve as a starting point to help roommates discover their commonalities. Possible questions to ask in assisting with matching individuals by life-style preferences can include the following:

- Do you prefer to live in a coed or single-sex environment?
- What size community would you like to be a part of?
- Would you prefer a smoking or nonsmoking environment?
- What are your preferences about the legal possession of alcohol in your room? Its consumption?
- During what time of day do you prefer to have visitors?
- How does sound affect your personal habits? Sleep habits?
- What hours do you prefer to study?

Some questions to ask when considering matching by academic and personal interests include:

- What is your intended major? What majors are you interested in exploring?
- What career choices are you interested in?

- Are you pursuing honors studies?
- Are you interested in learning more about a specific culture?
- Are you interested in living with an English-as-a-second-language student?
- What are your hobbies?
- What do you like to do in your free time?

Roommate matching by individual characteristics can include housing students according to similar class levels (for example, assigning first-year students together), assigning roommates together by their birth order within their family, and using preference scores on the Myers-Briggs Type Indicator. Schroeder and Jackson (1987, p. 67) note that "the *Myers-Briggs Type Indicator* has proven to be an extremely useful tool for structuring conditions that enhance the 'fit' between students and their resident hall environments. The *Indicator* has been successfully utilized in matching roommates, suitemates, and floormates."

Roommate Contracting

The intentional matching process tries to ensure connections prior to the arrival of students to campus. Once roommates meet, a process of developing agreements or understandings for the current living situation begins. This process takes place not only within individual rooms but also expands out toward the suite, section, floor, house, or hall. Residence hall staff members play key roles in helping to find perceived commonalities, and the reasons for promoting such efforts need to be communicated to residents through both words and actions. Forced methods and lack of flexibility in adjusting the process to fit differing situations, as well as viewing the staff role as purely an administrative function rather than an educational endeavor, can negatively impact the process.

Roommate contracting can be a useful way to help students identify commonalities as well as explore the rich diversity of other people, especially for first-year residents. Through this process, roommates can share and negotiate expectations, developing a set of mutual understandings that they will choose to monitor and to renegotiate. To begin roommate contracting, a staff person, at an initial meeting, introduces topics of forming positive interpersonal relationships; understanding different communication styles; negotiating differences, disagreements, and preferences; and taking responsibility for the living environment.

Once this has been completed, a list of questions designed to get individuals thinking about what they value in themselves and what they expect from others is distributed to community participants. Anticipatory and thought-provoking ideas can include queries about the following:

1. Use and borrowing of personal items such as clothes, television sets, and computers

2. Noise, particularly in regard to study habits and sleeping
3. Visitors, especially regarding length of visit and gender of guests
4. Smoking, including whether and where visitors can smoke
5. Personal hygiene, such as cleaning the room, showering, placement of dirty laundry, and the taking out of trash
6. Communication patterns, such as where phone messages are kept, what outgoing message to leave on an answering machine, and how conflict will be handled

Once individuals have had time to review and think about these questions, the staff person usually sets up a meeting with each pair or group of roommates to develop a roommate contract. If residents previously have taken part in roommate contracting, staff involvement may be limited to reviewing the contract after students have completed meetings on their own. The roommates share their thoughts and feelings about each category and negotiate terms that are written into the roommate contract. A form can be used that has general categories as subheadings that match the sections developed for the personal questionnaire described previously. When complete, all roommates sign the contract. The staff involved in this process help the roommates if the roommates seem reluctant to confront differences (a common occurrence at the beginning of roommate relationships) or are overly constrictive. If sensitive areas, such as personal hygiene, seem to be overlooked or if an individual seems to be under- or overinvolved in the contracting session, staff can be an intrusive resource (or process observer that points out what appear to be inequities). Roommates should be encouraged to record their own expectations and to discuss any other issues they might have. They should also be reminded that the contract holds only until renegotiation takes place, which may be initiated by either party. Renegotiation can take place at any time (or only at specified times), and this also can be highlighted in the contract to avoid perpetuating dualistic thoughts and behavior. If a conflict develops, the roommate contract serves as a foundation for mediation strategies and renegotiation.

Group Norming

Group norming, which is sometimes called unit, section, or floor norming, is similar to the roommate contracting process. The concepts of seeking commonalities, exploring differences, and developing understandings for parameters of behavior are now extended to a broader group of residents. To begin this process, residence hall staff can review both formal and informal policies and procedures to develop a survey for helping a group set its own standards for community living. The purpose of a group norming assessment survey is to gather input and to encourage resident involvement in setting and monitoring norms, while communicating organizational boundaries. For example, if a residence life department has a policy stating that quiet hours begin no later than 11:00 P.M. and are in effect until 7:00 A.M., questions can be developed for a norming survey that suggest an earlier time to start quiet hours and that suggest that they remain in effect until a later time in the morning and be modified on the weekends. Residents can be asked what kind of information they would like to see posted on bulletin boards or walls and in what locations. Use of common physical space can be established, and time parameters could be added by residents. Community members can decide what noise means to them. Do conversations in a hallway at 2:00 A.M. constitute noise? Is exercising in the hallway acceptable?

The surveys can point out and help narrow options to be discussed at the meeting, but they should be thought of primarily as an assessment tool that can be used to start discussion. Voting, or simply taking the response with the highest rating, should be avoided. The process of consensus decision making, which is a focus in group norming, emphasizes the values of modification and compromise. Additionally, the importance of including the non-dominant viewpoints is stressed.

Once a group establishes its set of norms, community members participate in monitoring the observance of the norms. The community helps shape appropriate responses to violations of community standards. General community standards should be clearly and concisely posted to reinforce values and permit visitors to learn what behaviors and values are operating within that environment. Periodically, throughout the life of a floor unit and particularly as other voices join and emerge from the group, these norms can be discussed and renegotiated by using the same process. The significance is not necessarily the specific "products" of processes such as roommate contracting and group norming, but that a communication process has been established, discussed, and modeled. If the methods of resolving conflict established by roommates, or a group of residents such as a floor, are not being effective, other behavioral management techniques need to be considered. These alternatives should emulate and be congruent with the ideals of a process-oriented educational community. Some examples are mediation models, peer review boards, educational assignments, and community service.

Using a mediation model and setting up peer review boards for dealing with roommate and other group disputes are two ways community participants remain responsible for and to community standards. An example of an effective use of mediation is when a conflict between floors about noise coming through pipes is dealt with by the staff of a specific building through individual and group meetings that focus on conflict resolution strategies. Peer review boards allow for participation of several students in deciding if another student has infringed on community standards and, if so, how that individual should be held accountable for his or her behavior.

Educational assignments, either as part of in-hall follow-up or as part of a more formal judicial process, are a way of addressing or redressing negative behaviors that infringe on community standards and of giving "offending residents" a chance to provide service to the community. When used as part of a judicial process, these assignments can be coupled with traditional discipline sanctions to help provide education and build investment. An example of an educational assignment is having a person who activated a smoke detector do research and write a brief paper about who was affected in the community, how those people responded, and why they needed to implement those responses when the device was activated by that individual. Such an assignment is not only congruent with the academic mission of the institution, but also with the philosophies of community and student development.

A crucial component of educational assignments is the exchange that takes place between the person who has violated a policy or procedure that is part of the community standards and the person in the staff role. A firm, caring attitude and the willingness of staff members to try to work for the student's interests can help promote educational engagement in sanctioning. (Chapters Twenty and Twenty-One, on fostering mature interpersonal relations and responding to criminal conduct, respectively, further explore ways in which to deal with a wide range of behaviors.)

Student Leadership Development

Leadership programs provide structures in which students are encouraged to participate in their evolving communities. Student leaders play a dynamic role in the development and enhancement of residence hall communities. Through participation, many students experience situations parallel with future roles. Without student involvement, community development is not possible. Staff members cannot replace students' involvement.

According to Striffolino and Saunders (1989), the benefits of developing and promoting a strong leadership program are immense. Leadership programming provides a framework that encourages students to visibly participate in the design and implementation of community-enhancing projects. Students who participate in decision-making processes are more likely to take ownership in the outcome and are inclined to encourage other students to participate in the activity.

Leadership programs also help students individually and collectively realize their visions. Students are able to take responsibility for integrating community values and norms through their own projects. This empowers them to continue exercising their intellectual, social, and leadership skills.

Within a leadership program, a variety of traditional and alternative approaches can exist. Types of traditional leadership programs that impact residence hall communities are hall governments, floor councils, programming committees, student office workers, resident-operated academic resource centers, recreational rooms, and store facilities. More specifically, hall governments create that link between staff and students that can be utilized to initiate cooperative communication and to develop and implement community-enhancing projects. Hall governments can be used to market innovative ideas, initiate change in policies, deal with conflicts, and make hall decisions. They may operate as a hierarchy with officers or use consensus-based decision-making processes. Both have proven successful; however, changing culture encourages and requires a consensual decision-making process.

Consensus Model

This type of leadership design is based on equal status. All participants hold positions equal to each other. Decisions must be unanimous and not strongly opposed. For example, members can give approval to implement a decision they do not agree with. Members take an active role in supporting and encouraging everyone's participation. Members may be appointed by the entire body to various roles (Bartoo, 1978). An example of this approach to leadership is an appointed committee consisting of one respresentative from each floor. Members share job responsibilities equally, and all decisions are made by consensus. Each floor would have an open forum meeting facilitated by a committee member. All floor residents can attend, and decisions also are made by consensus.

Hierarchical Model

This system is run by elected officers. The officers hold positions of authority in a graded series. Decisions are made by majority rule, and *Robert's Rules of Order* (Robert, 1983) is used, or some formalized procedure is followed, to conduct meetings. An example of this is a traditional hall government structure run by a president, vice president, secretary, and treasurer.

A more inclusive view of leadership provides additional experiences not easily categorized or measured as tangibly as traditional types. Informal leadership behaviors often are not recognized because the student is not in a formalized leadership position. These leaders are equally supportive of the hall community. Alternative examples include specific types of student behaviors that influence a section, floor, or hall. They can be initiating a social gathering, calling a meeting, voicing a concern, helping staff gather students together for a program, or getting a movie for others to watch. The whole concept of leadership recognizes this variety of student presence and its influence on the community in a residence hall. Leadership programs in all forms must be acknowledged, nurtured, and celebrated, so as to challenge communities to develop fully.

In developing and implementing a leadership program, the areas of design, marketing, and maintenance must be considered. Within these areas, two primary goals established through Duvall and Ender's (1980) work in student leadership can be incorporated. These goals are assisting students in developing personal awareness of their leadership skills and in sharpening their organizational skills. The following offers a list of factors to consider when developing each area.

Design begins with the definition of goals and objectives. The use of background research on leadership theories can be very instrumental in goal development and must not be overlooked. The planner should also be cognizant of all organizational structures and resources available to assist in the design. In addition, staff commitment to implementation of the leadership program must be assessed.

Marketing a program is a process of gathering all pertinent and marketable information as well as creatively designing a marketing strategy that targets a broad range of students. All available resources that will assist in effectively marketing to a diversity of students should be explored.

The maintenance of the program protects its integrity and contributes to its longevity. Maintenance also affirms staff commitment to leadership and therefore motivates students to continue their involvement. Several things must happen to maintain the program. Motivating students is essential. Providing students with training, adequate advising, intrinsic and extrinsic awards, semester-long involvement in community-building activities, and awareness of changing student leadership roles is vital to creating and maintaining that motivation. Assessment and evaluations of the program should be conducted on a regular basis. Information obtained as the result of an evaluation (feedback) can be recycled back into the original design after appropriate alterations have been made. Implementation of changes will both enhance the program and motivate students to continue their involvement.

Committing staff to participate in leadership development is essential to bridging gaps between staff and students. Bridging these gaps allows for unique opportunities to enhance collaborative work with staff and students. If students feel supported by staff, they are more likely to invest efforts in community development through leadership positions and participate in sponsored activities. Recognizing this important connection highlights the need to encourage staff commitment to student leadership programming.

The Physical Environment

Students have a natural connection to the physical environment—that is, the "bricks and mortar" of physical layout of the student residence. The physical environment has consistently been shown to impact student behavior and community. For example, Mehrabian (1976) demonstrated that students residing on the ground floor of a residence hall had a broader familiarity with other hall residents than those living on the top floor. Student residential communities with high retention rates often have low damage, high satisfaction, and positive student development outcomes. Student personalization of rooms and hallways has been linked to increased retention, overall satisfaction, and higher grade-point averages (Schroeder, 1976). Supporting these connections is one way to respond to Grant's (1980) perceived individual needs for freedom, order, control, and stimulation. These needs have differing intensities across the student population, with the environment allowing these needs to be met differentially. For example, those with a need to listen to loud music (stimulation) may elect to cover their walls with egg crates.

Facilitating student empowerment through the use of space is a tangible expression of involvement, ownership, mattering, and establishing identity through intentional actions. During the 1970s and 1980s, residence educators implemented Grant's notions through "territoriality" projects. Students were encouraged to "personalize their space" through painting their rooms and hallways, as well as to regulate their privacy by creating lofts, partitions, and other natural barriers to discourage encroachment by outsiders. This concept has been articulated as a primal concern of some students to "stake out their turf." This perspective has been supported by numerous anthropologists, who feel that many social animals—particularly aggressive ones—stake out mating or feeding territories that they defend against all other members of their species, except their mate and offspring. Males most frequently evidence these tendencies. It is also not uncommon for male residents to make strong statements about potential or actual use of their rooms through constructing drinking bars, partitions, or other room dividers.

The emergence of such behavior has been well documented among students. It has been shown that among individuals and in groups, space is "staked out" in libraries, residence halls, and dining areas, as well as within individual rooms (Schroeder, 1976). But rather than necessarily considering this behavior as territorial, it can be viewed as representing a physical extension of personal identity that is gender and culture dependent. Female students may decorate a room collaboratively with the intention of sharing about themselves and encouraging human connections to other residents. An international student may use a wall hanging to decorate a space, as well as for a personal religious ceremony.

Traditional residence hall architecture often needs humanization. The cell-like rooms, built-in furniture, and double-loaded corridors are often decorated in such a manner that they all look identical. The consequence is that students may exist in an environment saturated with a boring, programmed atmosphere. The message of these environments is that all students and communities are alike, so that a state of continual marginality is experienced.

The act of personalizing space (rooms, hallways, and other common space) is a significant expression of identity for students in transition who may feel marginal. According to Astin (1984, p. 298), "the effectiveness of any educational practice or policy is directly related to the capacity of that policy or practice to increase student involvement." Decorating a room or hallway with important symbols such as posters from home, quilts on the wall, and pictures of loved ones is important behavior because it contributes to a successful transition from home to residence hall living. Lofts or bunk beds also give students a chance to shape personal environments in ways that maximize freedom.

This transition is often referred to as a ritual, custom, or rite of passage of an individual from one phase to another. Students use significant symbols and activities to make the transition successful. Anchors, Schroeder, and Jackson (1978) suggest numerous strategies and activities that students can be encouraged to use in making this transition. Some are as elaborate as painting a wall mural or constructing a loft, while others are as simple as bringing a favorite chair or pictures from home.

In cooperation with architects, the residential life staff can design buildings that have personal space, create humane interactions, and support the development of community in natural ways. For example, at the University of Maine, the Doris Twitchell Allen Village was designed to accommodate 200 students in spaces that met the criteria outlined in this chapter as well as in other recent writings (Anchors and Moore, 1992). A goal was to create physical residence space that required minimal intrusion by staff while maximizing the development of community.

Understanding the role and importance of the physical environment is an important thread for weaving community. Through consideration of the physical environment, we can understand student development and nurture community. These objectives should be kept in mind:

1. Establishing residence hall policies that encourage students to express themselves within the physical environment
2. Creating student culture that supports positive rituals and rites of passage from home to the residence hall by encouraging transition from marginality to mattering
3. Using common physical space to support overall community development goals
4. Familiarizing staff with the layout, plan, and nuances of facilities of the physical environment
5. Understanding how gender and other characteristics impact the concept of territoriality
6. Welcoming residents and guests of varying physical abilities and diversity

Ethical and Values Implications

As previously noted in this chapter, the process of weaving community is not value free. Ethical issues abound and challenge everyone involved in residential life and housing. Communities developed on campus are influenced by the values of the institution, departmental mission, the staff that manage the halls, and most centrally, the residents. When students arrive on campus, they bring certain expectations about freedom from constraint and supervision different from what they found at home. These include the freedom to choose whether to eat, sleep, go to classes, wear certain type of clothes, drink alcohol, experiment with drugs and sex, attend religious services, or participate in community activities.

Along with these freedoms and other choices come responsibilities for actions involving others. Student development is facilitated through interaction within a community. Students develop personal identities while learning about interdependence, independence, and dependence within a group. Community does not have to be a threat to the expression of individuality. Personal growth occurs most richly within the context of a caring community.

In recent years, challenges for the development of communities in the future have been highlighted in conferences and publications. These challenges suggest that the health and richness of campus communities depend on whether a community has the following characteristics:

1. A wholeness that includes pluralism and diversity within a developmental and purposeful framework
2. A commonality of shared experiences, culture, and goals
3. Effective internal communication between residents, the staff, and the outside community
4. A sense of caring, trust, and teamwork among residents and staff
5. The involvement and shared leadership by students in the governance process
6. An overall recognition of the centrality and importance of the academic mission to the residence and housing program

Several ethical and professional dilemmas await housing practitioners charged with developing and enhancing community. Addressing them is essential to moving ahead as a housing profession. Throughout this book, responses to these dilemmas emerge:

1. Do we impose community or let it develop? If it does not develop, have we failed as professionals?
2. What values are communities based on? Are they compatible with the institution's mission?
3. How do we balance community welfare with individual rights?
4. Is the community inclusive of diversity?

Clearly there are a multitude of answers to these questions. This chapter, along with the rest of the book, poses some responses, challenges, and responsibilities for residence educators. Staff, faculty, and students need to address these questions within the context of their respective environments.

References

American Council on Education. *The Student Personnel Point of View.* Washington, D.C.: American Council on Education, 1937.

American Council on Education. *The Student Personnel Point of View.* (Rev. ed.) Washington, D.C.: American Council on Education, 1949.

Anchors, S., and Moore, S. "Doris Twitchell Allen Village: The University of Maine's Response to Student Needs of the Future." Paper presented at the convention of the Association of College and University Housing Officers-International, Boston, 1992.

Anchors, S., Schroeder, C. C., and Jackson, S. *Making Yourself at Home: A Practical Guide to Restructuring and Personalizing Your Residence Hall Environment.* Washington, D.C.: American College Personnel Association, 1978.

Astin, A. W. *Four Critical Years: Effects of College on Beliefs, Attitudes, and Knowledge.* San Francisco: Jossey-Bass, 1977.

Astin, A. W. "Student Involvement: A Developmental Theory for Higher Education." *Journal of College Student Personnel,* 1984, *25,* 297–308.

Aulepp, L., and Delworth, U. *Training Manual for an Ecosystem Model: Assessing and Designing Campus Environments.* Boulder, Colo.: Western Interstate Commission for Higher Education, 1976.

Bartoo, G. *Decisions by Consensus: A Study of the Quaker Methods.* Chicago: Progressive, 1978.

Boyer, E. L. *College: The Undergraduate Experience in America.* New York: Harper-Collins, 1987.

Chickering, A. W. *Education and Identity.* San Francisco: Jossey-Bass, 1969.

Crookston, B. "A Design for an Intentional Democratic Community." In D. A. DeCoster and P. Mable (eds.), *Student Development and Education in College Residence Halls.* Washington, D.C.: American College Personnel Association, 1980.

Duvall, W., and Ender, K. L. "A Training Model for Developing Leadership Awareness." In F. B. Newton and K. L. Ender (eds.), *Student Development Practices: Strategies for Making a Difference.* Springfield, Ill.: Thomas, 1980.

Gardner, J. W. "Building Community." *Kettering Review,* 1989, *7,* 73–81.

Gilligan, C. *In a Different Voice: Psychological Theory and Women's Development.* Cambridge, Mass.: Harvard University Press, 1982.

Grant, W. H. "Humanizing the Residence Hall Environment." In D. A. DeCoster and P. Mable (eds.), *Personal Education and Community Development in College Residence Halls.* Cincinnati, Ohio: American College Personnel Association, 1980.

Hamilton, P. "Introduction." In A. P. Cohen (ed.), *The Symbolic Construction of Community.* Chichester, England: Horword, 1985.

Kuh, G. D., Whitt, E. J., and Shedd, J. *Student Affairs Work, 2001: A Paradigmatic Odyssey.* Alexandria, Va.: American College Personnel Association, 1987.

Lincoln, Y. S., and Guba, E. G. *Naturalistic Inquiry.* Newbury Park, Calif.: Sage, 1985.

Mehrabian, A. *Public Places and Private Spaces*. New York: Basic Books, 1976.

Moos, R. H. *Evaluating Educational Environments: Procedures, Measures, Findings, and Policy Implications*. San Francisco: Jossey-Bass, 1979.

Noddings, N. Paper presented at the convention of the American College Personnel Association, St. Louis, Mo., Apr. 1990.

Ogilvy, J., and Schwartz, P. *The Emergent Paradigm: Changing Patterns of Thought and Belief*. Analytical Report No. 7, Values and Lifestyles Program. Menlo Park, Calif.: SRI International, 1979.

Peck, M. S. *The Different Drum: Community Making and Peace*. New York: Simon & Schuster, 1987.

Robert, H. M. *Robert's Rules of Order*. New York: Jove Books, 1983.

Schlossberg, N. K. "Marginality and Mattering: Key Issues in Building Community." In D. C. Roberts (ed.), *Designing Campus Activities to Foster a Sense of Community*. New Directions for Student Services, no. 48. San Francisco: Jossey-Bass, 1989.

Schlossberg, N. K., Lynch, A. Q., and Chickering, A. W. *Improving Higher Education Environments for Adults: Responsive Programs and Services from Entry to Departure*. San Francisco: Jossey-Bass, 1989.

Schroeder, C. C. "New Strategies for Structuring Residential Environments." *Journal of College Student Personnel*, 1976, *17*, 51–57.

Schroeder, C. C., and Freesh, P. N. "Applying Environmental Management Strategies in Residence Halls." *National Association of Student Personnel Administrators Journal*, 1975, *15*, 19–22.

Schroeder, C. C., and Jackson, S. "Designing Residential Environments." In J. A. Provost and S. Anchors (eds.), *Applications of the Myers-Briggs Type Indicator in Higher Education*. Palo Alto, Calif.: Consulting Psychologists Press, 1987.

Striffolino, P., and Saunders, S. "Emerging Leaders: Students in Need of Development." *National Association of Student Personnel Administrators Journal*, 1989, *27*, 51–58.

Tuckman, B. "Developmental Sequence in Small Groups." *Psychological Bulletin*, 1965, *6*, 384–399.

Yanikoski, R. A. "Value of College." Presentation made at the Illinois Association for Institutional Research, Champaign, 1980.

Chapter Twenty

=====

Fostering Interpersonal
Relationships and
Reducing Conflicts

Charles J. Werring
Diana L. Robertson
Carolyn V. Coon

The residence hall environment is dynamic. Students have the ability to interact with each other in many ways. Pascarella and Terenzini (1991) assert that on-campus living might be the most consistent influence on students during their college experience. They further note that "residential living is positively, if modestly, linked to increases in aesthetic, cultural, and intellectual values; a liberalizing of social, political, and religious values and attitudes; increases in self-concept, intellectual orientation, autonomy, and independence; gains in tolerance, empathy, and ability to relate to others; persistence in college; and bachelor's degree attainment" (p. 611).

Carey, Hamilton, and Shanklin (1986) note that the residence hall experience is the most profound for students as they move away from the family unit. Many students encounter interpersonal relationship issues as they test their ability to adapt to new ways of viewing society. Pruett and Brown (1990, p. 3) indicate that "the freshman entering a college or university environment must cope with many changes. For many of college age, separation is necessary from parents and other family members, high school peers, and home town familiarity." How students in general view themselves and others affects how they make social adjustments and view their external social environment and the world (Pascarella and Terenzini, 1991).

Most students in residence halls will be living with a roommate for the first time in their lives, while at home they probably did not even share a room with a sibling. Shipton and Schuh (1982) report that resolving roommate conflicts in residence halls consumes a great deal of time for residence hall staff. Rapport between roommates, therefore, is essential in creating the potential for a positive growth experience for student relationship building in residence halls (Stanley, Werring, and Carey, 1988).

In this chapter, we address some of the principal interpersonal relationship issues that students face in contemporary residence halls and offer suggestions or examples of successful strategies for dealing with conflicts and problem areas. Specifically, we focus on problems or issues related to parent concerns and security; relationship violence; sexual behavior; and race relations.

Parent Concerns and Security

Parents play an important role in the interpersonal relationships that are established among residence hall students. As Newman and Newman (1992, p. 61) note, "Life in the residence halls brings students face-to-face with hundreds of decisions they may never have made before. Students have to ask each other to hold down the noise, to take shorter showers, or to make shorter phone calls. Students depend on one another to take phone messages, to find another room for a night or two if a guest is visiting, and to share toothpaste or shaving cream in an emergency."

Colleges and universities are reevaluating their residence hall policies and procedures to address the concerns of parents. Parents are not necessarily seeking the in loco parentis approaches of the 1950s and 1960s; however, there is more interest in monitoring the social, educational, and value development of their children in the higher educational environment today than there used to be (Couburn and Treeger, 1988). Students and their parents are seeking more structure, support, and a sense of community in the college environment, knowing that the student will be separated from the perceived securities of the home environment (Wood, 1991).

Campus safety today is critical in the process by which both parents and students choose a college or university. The current Student Right to Know and Campus Security Act is an example of a conscientious effort to help parents and students make constructive choices (Sautter, 1991). Residence hall administrators and paraprofessionals have aggressively promoted strategies that can assist students in understanding the shared responsibility of creating a safe and secure residential environment. Simpson (1991) outlines a number of issues related to facilities, policy and procedures, and programmatic and staff training methodologies to help housing professionals develop a plan for a safe and secure residence hall living experience.

Residence hall administrators have responded with a variety of facility interventions, including magnetic door lock systems, computerized card entrance programs, additional external lighting, security screens for room windows, and surveillance cameras. Also, institutions are adding more student security patrols, twenty-four-hour paraprofessional staff coverage, student escort programs, and safety and security specialists to conduct educational seminars to prevent crime on campus. Many residence hall programs have reevaluated policies and procedures to include more stringent regulations on visiting guests, hours of entrance and exit from a building, and required "neighborhood watch" strategies. (See Chapter Twenty-One.)

Relationship Violence

Violence on campuses has become an important topic for residence hall educators, parents, students, faculty, and staff. Cowley (1934) outlines a history of violence in residential settings specially directed toward residence hall staff dating from the colonial period. Another type of violence—relationship violence—is also a major concern for students and staff today. Rickgarn (1989, p. 30) describes relationship violence as "campus domestic violence," which incorporates two concepts: "Violence is a violation of the individual's personal space and/or property. This violence includes physical [injury] (injury of person or destruction of property), psychological [injury] (threats and intimidation), or both. The second concept is that residence halls are domiciles where relationships of varying levels of intimacy are formed."

A cooperative effort among college and university administrators, faculty, and staff should be implemented to address the issues of violent acts in residence halls. Torrey and Lee (1987) describe a number of programs that attempt to prevent and intervene in relationship violence situations. Rickgarn (1989) also suggests a number of prevention strategies to help residence hall educators plan programs and train staff in preventing violent acts.

Institutions have varied educational mission statements that influence how policies and procedures will be designed and implemented. Today, numerous colleges and universities have written policies on violence, racism, substance abuse, sexual conduct, personal safety, and security. These policies and procedures translate to the residence hall setting. Residence hall staff must be trained to educate students to the realities of a residence hall environment that represents a microcosm of the larger society. Residence hall and institutional disciplinary procedures should reflect the culture of the campus setting (Smith, 1989).

Violence in Dating Relationships

Dating relationships in the college and university setting have come under close scrutiny by student affairs administrators, student health center personnel, and campus security staff (Bogal-Allbritten and Allbritten, 1991). Roark

(1989) discusses the impact of sexual violence on students and how colleges and universities can respond with prevention techniques and interventions. He summarizes institutional responses to campus violence according to certain levels of prevention: "(1) tertiary prevention to limit the damage of a situation that has already taken place; (2) secondary prevention to identify existing problems and to bring about effective correction at the earliest possible time; and (3) primary prevention to prevent new cases of victimization by addressing causes and changing actions and attitudes that contribute to the prevalence of sexual violence" (p. 44).

Hate Speech

Also, the emerging issue of hate speech in residence halls has affected the relationships between students. Gender, ethnic, racial, and sexual-preference harassment is on the rise. Verbal slurs and offensive posted messages and materials are becoming commonplace in a number of residential settings. Terrell and Ehrlich (1989) suggest that conflict among residence hall students is on the increase due to the intolerance on the part of students of diverse backgrounds who are housed in close proximity and may not have had the developmental training to deal with their differences.

Residential life professionals are continually debating the issues of hate speech that oppose concerns with legal issue perspectives. Janosik (1991) argues that students should be able to express their First Amendment rights of free speech, press, and peaceful assembly, while Palmer (1991) contends that college and university administrators should be developing policies and procedures that, within legal boundaries, discourage such speech from being part of the institutional environment.

Residence hall administrators need to examine their policies and procedures related to hate speech practices. Mission statements must include a residential philosophy that reflects the institutional and departmental approaches to hate speech behaviors on the part of students. Both Janosik (1991) and Palmer (1991) provide residence hall administrators with resources that can assist them with the development of standards regarding harassment issues.

Interpersonal Conflicts

Confrontation and conflict among residence hall students is a common occurrence. Blimling and Miltenberger (1990) outline a number of strategies dealing with confrontation and disciplinary counseling models for students and staff. Upcraft and Pilato (1982) report a wealth of information on how residence hall educators, including administrators and professional and paraprofessional residence hall staff, can assist in the development of strategies to help students with conflict resolution and problem solving. Engram

(1989) provides a workable definition for residence hall student confrontation procedures that delineates the differences between negotiation, mediation, and arbitration. All of these processes are critical in the planning of a judicial system that is effective not only for residential life staff but for college and university judicial officers as well. As noted earlier, the sense of community being sought by students in residence halls depends strongly on the students' ability to communicate with each other.

Sexual Behavior

A relationship issue of importance to residence hall students is sexual activity. College is a time of social relationship building and, as Chickering (1969, p. 15) describes it, a time when students learn to "free interpersonal relationships." Students learn to be more open and accepting of one another, hence they are able to establish close friendships and intimate relationships. At the same time, students also are learning to "manage emotions" and are seeking to express aggression and sexual feelings in appropriate ways. Understanding oneself as a sexual being is likely to be one of the more challenging undertakings that a college student experiences.

Many students begin to experiment sexually during their college years. Estimates of the number of college students who are sexually active vary, but fairly distinct trends have developed over the past two decades. Studies indicate that during the 1970s, between 50 and 75 percent of all college students were sexually active. Men were more sexually active than women, although the double standard (of men's premarital sexual experimentation being acceptable, while women were to remain virgins until marriage) began to weaken and decline (Hildebrand and Abramowitz, 1984; Murstein, Chalpin, Heard, and Vyse, 1989). The 1970s were a decade of increasing liberal attitudes and behaviors. Approximately 20 percent of college students were willing to have sex with strangers or to "pick up" someone for a one-night stand (Hildebrand and Abramowitz, 1984).

Sexually Transmitted Diseases

The onset of genital herpes and the emergence of the acquired immune deficiency syndrome (AIDS) epidemic during the early 1980s are thought to have curbed the frequency of casual sexual liaisons somewhat (Abler and Sedlacek, 1989; Murstein, Chalpin, Heard, and Vyse, 1989; Renshaw, 1989). During the 1980s, the number of students who were sexually active stopped growing so rapidly, although the number did not decline (Hildebrand and Abramowitz, 1984; Murstein, Chalpin, Heard, and Vyse, 1989).

Health practitioners and student affairs professionals began to educate college students with the facts regarding human immunodeficiency virus (HIV) and AIDS. While students' knowledge of AIDS (its symptoms and the risky sexual behaviors that increase the likelihood of its transmission) was generally good, college students did not seem to think that herpes or AIDS would affect them personally (Abler and Sedlacek, 1989; Hildebrand and Abramowitz, 1984; Murstein, Chalpin, Heard, and Vyse, 1989; Renshaw, 1989). Nonetheless, studies suggest that one-night stands have become less common than in recent decades, and students are more likely than before to establish monogamous relationships and practice safer sex (Abler and Sedlacek, 1989; Murstein, Chalpin, Heard, and Vyse, 1989; Renshaw, 1989).

Although between 50 and 75 percent of today's students are likely to be sexually active, they often overestimate how frequently their peers engage in sexual activity (Abler and Sedlacek, 1989; Hildebrand and Abramowitz, 1984). Developing their identity as sexual beings, then, becomes complicated by misperceptions.

College women's sexual identity development has been thought to be influenced by their family of origin and the religiosity of their upbringing. Women who have close relationships with their parents are more likely to delay sexual activity until marraige. The religiosity of one's upbringing, however, seems to have less impact on the level of women's sexual activity than it did in the past (Hildebrand and Abramowitz, 1984; Murstein, Chalpin, Heard, and Vyse, 1989).

The implication of this overview of college students' sexual activity is that professional staff members can assist students by developing programs that focus on the reality of college students' sexual activity levels, thereby easing the perceived need or peer pressure to be sexually active. Professional staff members need to talk comfortably and openly with students about intimacy and sexuality. Such program development and dialogue require that professional staff members become comfortable with their knowledge level and their ability to discuss such issues.

Students today have a high knowledge of HIV/AIDS, which may be attributed to any of the following: (1) the growing awareness of the general public, (2) AIDS education programs, (3) professional and lay literature on the topic, and (4) media coverage and television advertisements for safer sex (Roscoe and Skomski, 1989). The concern is that although increasing students' knowledge base is a start, it may not lead sexually active students to change or stop risky sexual behaviors. College students see a relatively low incidence of AIDS among their peers and therefore see AIDS as a problem that is not going to affect them personally (Crawford, 1990).

The challenge for professional staff members is to move HIV/AIDS education beyond the level of "theory" to address the real consequences of risky sexual behavior (Roscoe and Skomski, 1989). Elevating and personalizing students' awareness of AIDS may help lead students to change their sexual behaviors. Educational programs need to be geared toward emphasizing the increasing rate of AIDS among teens and young adults (Crawford, 1990). Keeling (1992) recommends discussing difficult and personal situations, such as the impact felt by learning that a friend, lover, or relative has AIDS. Giffore and Kallen (1990) suggest that providing a visual image of

AIDS deterioration evokes strong emotions and may help bring about change in sexual behavior.

The sixteen-campus University of North Carolina system provides an example of a comprehensive approach to educating campus constituents about AIDS (Bryan and Robinson, 1988). The president of the system convened a task force that developed guidelines for addressing the AIDS epidemic educationally and in regard to policy concerns. An AIDS information team was established by the president to visit each of the sixteen campuses, preparing key administrators to implement the guidelines and plan strategies for addressing any anticipated concerns. These efforts serve as a model for other universities and state systems.

Keeling (1992) thoroughly addresses strategies for educating college students during this second decade of the AIDS epidemic. He presents principles for effective educational programming, along with factors to be considered in assessing the environment and context of the problematic target behaviors. Building students' skill levels (particularly in regard to assertiveness, communication, active listening, decision making, negotiation, and values clarification) can assist them in making wise sexual behavior choices.

Brown (1990) emphasizes the need to focus on at-risk behaviors, not at-risk groups. On many campuses, peer educators have proven an effective means of educating college students, and professional staff members are encouraged to involve students in creating both written and audiovisual programming materials. The goals of the higher education community, according to Brown, must be to increase awareness and provide education to prevent the further spread of AIDS, as well as providing appropriate crisis intervention in a sensitive manner.

Keeling (1992) addresses the new and challenging array of issues involved in working with students who test HIV positive, including the counseling process for HIV intervention. He offers tips for speaking and preparing written material about the topic of AIDS and includes steps for cultural sensitivity. The needs of the specific subpopulations of women, people of color, and men who have sex with other men are also outlined. Keeling emphasizes the importance of creating a spirit of community among all campus groups in order to provide education about and prevent AIDS.

Sexual Orientation Issues

Much effort goes into training residence life professional and paraprofessional staff members, seeking to raise their awareness levels and to increase their sensitivity to students whose values, beliefs, backgrounds, or life-styles may differ from their own. Gay, lesbian, and bisexual issues should receive concentrated attention in training sessions on many campuses today, because at least 50 percent of the male population and 28 percent of the female population engages in some homosexual behavior at some time in their lives (Gramick, 1983).

Many studies over the years have indicated that homonegativism, defined as "the entire domain of anti-gay responses" (Hudson and Ricketts, 1980, p. 358), is certainly evident on American campuses (Herek, 1988; Iyriboz and Carter, 1986; Kite and Deaux, 1986; Kurdek, 1988; Young and Whertvine, 1982). Findings indicate that one's gender and conception of the proper gender roles have an effect on attitudes about homosexuals. Conservative gender-role attitudes among heterosexuals lead to less tolerance and acceptance of homosexuality (Whitley, 1987; Yarber and Yee, 1983; Young and Whertvine, 1982). Male students have typically been more homophobic than females (D'Augelli, 1989, 1990; Herek, 1984, 1988; Kurdek, 1988; Nyberg and Alston, 1977; Young and Whertvine, 1982). It is also common that students hold more negative attitudes toward homosexuals of their own gender (Nyberg and Alston, 1977; Herek, 1984, 1988; Kurdek, 1988).

Studies show that gay and lesbian students are sometimes more alienated from their peers than bisexual and heterosexual students (Greenberg, 1973; Reynolds, 1989). Additionally, societal pressures and stigmatization that gay and lesbian students experience lead to special concerns for these students (Thompson, Candless, and Strickland, 1971; Nuehring, Fein, and Tyler, 1974). Some of these concerns may include finding compatible roommates, encountering derogatory comments by peers, and verbal and/or physical harassment (Nelson and Baha, 1990). With the development of community as a common goal for residence halls, it is important that professional and paraprofessional staff members seek to create a campus climate that is comfortable for and accepting of all students, including the gay, lesbian, and bisexual populations.

Effectively training the paraprofessional staff members in residence halls is the first step toward developing comfortable and accepting living environments for gay, lesbian, and bisexual students. Robertson (1990) surveyed resident assistants (RAs), RA candidates, and non-RA students to assess their attitudes toward homosexuality. Findings revealed that females were less homophobic than males, and RAs were less homophobic than RA candidates, who in turn were less homophobic than residents in general. Although all three groups scored within a "homophobic" range, Robertson (1990) suggests that the lower homophobic levels of the RAs may be attributable to the training of paraprofessionals.

Limited studies have been conducted to assess the training needs of RAs. Bowles (1981) devised and administered a questionnaire to 151 RAs, the result of which was an overwhelming request for additional training to enable them to assist gay and lesbian students better. D'Augelli (1989) surveyed RA candidates, again determining that male candidates were more homophobic than female candidates. Less than half of the students surveyed knew a homosexual, and most displayed an inconsistent knowledge of gay and lesbian issues. D'Augelli suggests that RAs might benefit from greater exposure to, and knowledge of, gay men and lesbians.

Homosexuality can be a difficult topic for administrators to tackle. The nature of the institution (public or private), the degree of religiosity or conservatism, and in some cases, state sodomy laws are factors that need careful attention and consideration. Various publics view homosexuality in different ways. Some parents, alumni, religious groups, legislators, and ad- ministrators may see it as "immoral," "illegal," and "distasteful," whereas some students, faculty, and staff are supporting efforts to increase the sensitivity to this issue through planned forums, rallies, campus committees, and policy revisions. The formulation of action or response plans for situations that may surface will vary among different institutions based on their particular circumstances.

Miltenberger (1984) suggests informative movies or gay and lesbian guest speakers as means of raising awareness and acceptance levels of homo- sexual peers among college students. Miltenberger and Miltenberger (1989) reemphasize the importance of the paraprofessional staff member's comfort level with discussing the topic of homosexuality through interactive discus- sion programs, case studies, and examples of training programs.

Numerous studies have indicated that attitudinal change can and does result from educational programming efforts on the topic of homosexuality, both in and out of the classroom (Kirby, 1980; Goldberg, 1982; Taylor, 1982; Cerney and Polyson, 1984; Serdahely and Ziemba, 1984; Iyriboz and Carter, 1986; Wells and Franken, 1987). Evans and Wall (1991) provide educators with many suggestions for developing program ideas designed to educate students about gay, lesbian, and bisexual issues. The development of gay- positive professional and paraprofessional staff recruitment, selection, and training procedures is also addressed.

Race Relations

Race relations among students in general and within residence hall popula- tions in particular continue to be a matter of concern. Campus racial uprisings were believed to have been an issue of earlier decades. During the past thirty years it was not unusual to read about or to witness incidents involving physical fights, verbal abuse, or campus demonstrations that were sparked by racist remarks or acts. A review of the current campus press makes the reader well aware that campus racial activism has returned, and violent episodes are once again a reality for many campuses (Henley and Arnold, 1990; Dalton, 1991). Finding ways of preventing and resolving race-based conflict is again on the agenda of student affairs professionals.

As students of the 1990s are different from students of the 1960s, so are their reasons for feeling and expressing racism. Students now place more emphasis on their personal success, rather than being motivated by altruistic and social concerns (Levine, 1989; Dalton, 1991). The traditional-age white college student today has only read about the struggle for civil rights and can only imagine the extreme forms of discrimination imposed on persons of color prior to the 1964 Civil Rights Act. European-American students generally lack awareness about the racist conditions of the past, but they still possess some of the negative feelings and stereotypes toward other ethnic or racial groups (Cheatham, 1991b).

Since current college students may not have witnessed the extreme inequalities of the past, they struggle to accept the efforts of reparation. Students and paraprofessionals may view affirmative action and minority preference programs as being racist because they are designed to help specific groups. Students who are not eligible for the benefits of these services label them acts of reverse discrimination and believe they give an unfair advantage to people of color and women (Steele, 1990). Difficult economic times and scarce resources may have contributed to the escalation of the problem, as did the conservatism of the Reagan and Bush administrations (Bourassa, 1991; Cheatham, 1991a; Dalton, 1991; Harris and Nettles, 1991).

The perspective of students of color is often much different from that of white students. Even though they did not take part in the civil rights movement of the 1960s, students of color are able to identify with the struggle. They themselves have usually experienced many forms of racism, and they have heard stories, seen pictures, and read enough about the past to feel a part of those events. Many parents are able to describe the situation firsthand to their children. These parents can help them understand the need for programs like affirmative action, special admissions, and special scholarships. Parents and students of color believe they are getting what has been long overdue (Steele, 1990).

Many racial conflicts currently happening on campuses are different from those of earlier decades, and they are being acted out in various ways. The forms of racism are typically no longer as blatant as cross burnings and beatings, although of course such cases still exist. The "new racism" is likely to be much more subtle and occurs in many environments, including residence halls. This form of racism is often expressed by taking advantage of the established system to create a racist environment (Bennett, 1989; Cheatham, 1991a). College and university systems help create racist environments by not insisting that multiculturalism be incorporated into the curriculum, by refusing to respect differences, and by not being clear about their affirmative action goals and purposes (Cheatham, 1991a).

The National Institute Against Prejudice and Violence views new racism as *ethnoviolence*, which includes any act done because of prejudice with the intent of causing mental or physical harm to another person (Clay and Sherrill, 1991). Ethnoviolent acts can be as subtle as passing comments or as blatant as physical assault. Since racism is now usually more subtle, it is sometimes more difficult for college officials to identify the source of the problem (Bennett, 1989; Cheatham, 1991a). Often there are a series of covert racist acts that cause tension to slowly mount until a violent act occurs. The omission of persons of color on institutional committees and task forces, policies and procedures that are designed to be broad statements circumventing the needs of multicultural students, questionable levels of commitment to recruit and retain faculty, staff, and students of color, and a lack of communication training within the institutional setting are some examples of these covert acts. By the time staff become aware of the problem, it may have grown into a more serious situation.

Residence halls are prime areas for racial conflicts to arise. The nature of residential living creates an atmosphere where persons from different backgrounds are brought together to share a common living environment. Students are assigned to rooms and floors with other students who they often do not know. A diversity of students are asked to share bedrooms, dining rooms, showers, and restrooms. In some cases, students may be asked to live with a person against whom they are prejudiced. Residence halls can also be prime areas for the development of understanding racial differences. The challenge is for residence life staff to design creative educational programs that teach students how to understand and appreciate differences and diversity.

Position Statement About Racism

One way to demonstrate an institutional position on racism is through a clearly articulated position statement. Residence hall student leaders can express their stance in written form and communicate it to all new and returning residents. A position statement that emphasizes respect for others and that discourages ethnoviolence could also be incorporated into a residence hall orientation program.

Orientation is the time when many of the attitudes and values about college are formed (Boyer, 1987; Perigo and Upcraft, 1989). The orientation to residential living also sets the tone for attitudes and values that are important to the residential community. It is critical that the residence life staff make it clear that acts of ethnoviolence will not be tolerated. Orientation is also the time to let students and parents know that being equal members of the campus and residential community carries with it certain responsibilities. Residents should be made aware of their obligation to show sensitivity and respect for the needs of all others. Programs that promote the feeling of community and group responsibility should be incorporated into hall-opening and orientation activities. Programming could include viewing videotapes like the Anti-Defamation League's *Facing Differences: Living Together on Campus*. This videotape is designed to be used during orientation to make students aware of some of the kinds of prejudices that they may experience or observe on college campuses. The videotape and follow-up discussions give them the opportunity to express their concerns in a less threatening environment.

An early message can also be sent by distributing literature similar to the University of Wisconsin at Madison's brochure *Racism—Let Us Know.* A publication like this lets the students know that the issue of racism is taken seriously and that the institution will act on reports of racial conflict. Students need to know that if they or others are victimized, they should report it to the appropriate authorities. Students may hesitate to risk reporting incidents if they perceive that follow-up actions will not be taken (Rickgarn, 1989). A key element is to get students involved and invested in the residence hall community as early as possible. They need to take ownership of the positive and negative situations they encounter.

Training RAs

Paraprofessional staff can be catalysts in promoting and maintaining positive race relations in the residence halls. Their attitudes are observed and mimicked by other residents. Paraprofessional staff will likely be the primary source of intervention in situations of personal conflict. They can also serve as educators for the residents on their floor. Since paraprofessional staff play such a critical role in responding to and teaching about ethnoviolence, it is important that they have an understanding of the causes and appropriate responses to the problem (Jakobsen, 1991). They should be trained in the appropriate ways of dealing with ethnoviolent episodes.

Before residence hall staff begin working with students, it is important that they have an understanding of their own racial attitudes. Residence hall staff training should include values clarification, conflict resolution, psychosocial exploration, and other methods that help paraprofessionals understand their own views of tolerance (VanBebber, 1991). (See also Chapter Thirteen.)

Sherrill (1989) offers guidelines for how to deal with numerous situations involving campus violence effectively, including the importance of examining campus judicial codes, the use of the court system, and counseling techniques to help the victims and perpetrators deal with ethnoviolent occurrences.

One example of how diversity and racism training can be incorporated into paraprofessional staff training can be drawn from Bowling Green State University (Vickio, Dings, and Leopold, 1989). During a one-day training session, the paraprofessional staff were required to wear a blue or an orange armband, which represented their social class status. The participants went through their daily events being treated as persons of that status in society. At the end of the day, the staff reported a heightened awareness of prejudice. Iasenza and Troutt (1990) describe an exercise that involves word association and problem solving to be used as a part of staff training.

There are a number of reasons for including the topic of ethnoviolence as a primary component of ongoing staff training. First, paraprofessional staff should be reminded of the seriousness and importance of racial issues.

Racism will continue to be on their minds, and their awareness and sensitivity can be heightened as a result. Second, the paraprofessional staff need to be made aware that students' racial awareness occurs in stages much like those proposed by student development theorists (Mann and Moser, 1991). Paraprofessionals can be taught racial awareness models that can be integrated with student development models to better assess student needs. This will help them be better programmers and paraprofessional counselors because they will have a sense of students' racial awareness.

Programming Models

Hughes (1987) presents a six-level model for creating an ethnically diverse and racially aware community. Each stage has certain types of behavior and actions that reflect the person's developmental level. The stages include the following: (1) having a negative view of diversity, (2) looking for creative ways to understand and learn about diversity, (3) increasing acceptance and tolerance of diversity, (4) testing the principles of diversity, (5) valuing diversity in a positive way, and (6) building community. These stages can be incorporated into a residence hall programming model in order to encourage diversity from a developmental perspective. Staff should plan programs that meet the needs of residents at various stages of racial awareness development.

Jakobsen (1991) recommends using Cross's model for racial identity development. This model could be incorporated into a series designed to study how attitudes are developed toward different racial and ethnic groups. Bourassa (1991) has described programs at Indiana University and Pennsylvania State University that have implemented Katz's six-stage model focusing specifically on helping white persons understand their racial awareness.

Proactive Interventions

The key to any racism reduction program is the involvement of the whole community. All members should be given the opportunity to help develop the program. Success depends on the commitment from students, faculty, and staff and on support from the institution. Racism cannot be categorized as only a residence hall problem.

One method of increasing involvement and commitment is by creating intentional peer groups. These groups are comprised of members of all parts of the community. Their job is to educate others on issues related to racism, ethnoviolence, and prejudices of all kinds. Peer groups are effective ways of helping the community, especially residence hall communities, realize that students can individually and collectively make a difference. The power and ownership to influence racial awareness education for the campus and the residence hall environment is given to the students themselves.

Brown and Mazza (1991) make recommendations for effective peer groups. The peer groups should be made up of students, faculty, and staff from a variety of racial and ethnic backgrounds. It is important for the peer groups to represent the diversity of the campus. The purpose of the groups is to take a proactive, educational approach to dealing with problems of campus racism. They are not to function as a crisis intervention team but can be used as a resource if problems arise. The programs presented by the peer groups can vary depending on the needs of the campus or residence hall community. The groups should keep in mind that their goal is to increase awareness and appreciation of differences—not point fingers or raise the tension level. The core peer group should assess the needs of the community and work with the general population on developing programs and services; its purpose, however, is not to solve the problems or assume the responsibility for campus racism.

Responding to Acts of Racism

The programs and suggestions presented so far are geared toward prevention of the problem of racial or ethnic conflict. Unfortunately, ethnoviolent situations sometimes occur in spite of our best preventive efforts. When a situation does arise, it is important that the institution and the residence life staff be familiar with and be able to communicate the institutional response procedure. It is critical that policies and procedures be in place and that they be articulated to all members of the residence hall community. Immediate follow-up is a top priority and should be done fairly and judiciously. It is important for the residence hall community to be aware that a conflict has arisen and that it is being acted on. One cannot allow involved parties to perceive that the judicial system for residence halls is not responding in a timely manner. Everyone who is a member of the residential community is affected by the situation in some way. Hall community meetings where students are allowed to share their feelings in a productive and appropriate way can be beneficial. Unaddressed tension can grow and develop into more serious situations that undermine efforts to build trust and awareness.

Colleges and universities across the country are developing creative ways of responding to the increase in ethnoviolence. As these programs are being designed, it is important for educators to remember that student involvement in setting community standards is essential. It is critical for the entire college and university environment to share the ownership of the problem and the solution. If we can help residence hall students accept and understand the differences between each other, we can help educate our entire institutional community.

Interpersonal Relations in the Future

This chapter has identified a number of areas affecting students' relationships with each other. As Jacoby (1991) illustrates, student demographics are rapidly changing. The increasingly diverse needs of students demand varying programmatic, policy, and procedural responses by the entire institution and the specific subcommunities that comprise the institution (Kuh, Schuh, Whitt, and Associates, 1991). The residence hall community faces numerous challenges not only in dealing with changing student relationship issues and conflict resolution, but also in planning effective student development programs, facility management strategies, and training responses to positively affect student growth through the 1990s and beyond.

References

Abler, R. M., and Sedlacek, W. E. "Freshman Sexual Attitudes and Behaviors Over a 15-Year Period." *Journal of College Student Development*, 1989, *30*, 201–209.

Bennett, C. "Issues of Race and Culture on the College Campus." In G. S. Blimling (ed.), *The Experienced Resident Assistant: Readings, Case Studies, and Structured Group Exercises for Advanced Training*. Dubuque, Iowa: Kendall/Hunt, 1989.

Blimling, G. S., and Miltenberger, L. J. *The Resident Assistant: Working with College Students in Residence Halls*. (3rd ed.) Dubuque, Iowa: Kendall/Hunt, 1990.

Bogal-Allbritten, R. B., and Allbritten, W. L. "Courtship Violence on Campus: A Nationwide Survey of Student Affairs Professionals." *NASPA Journal*, 1991, *28*, 312–318.

Bourassa, D. M. "How White Students and Students of Color Organize and Interact on Campus." In J. C. Dalton (ed.), *Racism on Campus: Confronting Racial Bias Through Peer Interventions*. New Directions for Student Services, no 56. San Francisco: Jossey-Bass, 1991.

Bowles, J. K. "Dealing with Homosexuality: A Survey of Staff Training Needs." *Journal of College Student Personnel*, 1981, *22*, 276–277.

Boyer, E. L. *College: The Undergraduate Experience in America*. New York: Harper-Collins, 1987.

Brown, C., and Mazza, G. "Peer Training Strategies for Welcoming Diversity." In J. C. Dalton (ed.), *Racism on Campus: Confronting Racial Bias Through Peer Interventions*. New Directions for Student Services, no. 56. San Francisco: Jossey-Bass, 1991.

Brown, V. B. "The AIDS Crisis: Intervention and Prevention." In H. L. Pruett and V. B. Brown (eds.), *Crisis Intervention and Prevention*. New Directions for Student Services, no. 49. San Francisco: Jossey-Bass, 1990.

Bryan, W. A., and Robinson, R. H. "A University System Response to AIDS: Development of Community Policy and Educational Programs." *Student Services: Responding to Issues and Challenges*. Chapel Hill: General Administration, University of North Carolina, 1988.

Carey, J. C., Hamilton, D. L., and Shanklin, G. "Development of an Instrument to Measure Rapport Between College Roommates." *Journal of College Student Personnel*, 1986, *27*, 269–273.

Cerney, J. A., and Polyson, J. "Changing Homonegative Attitudes." *Journal of Social and Clinical Psychology*, 1984, *2*, 366–371.

Cheatham, H. E. "Affirming Affirmative Action." In H. E. Cheatham (ed.), *Cultural Pluralism on Campus*. Alexandria, Va.: American College Personnel Association, 1991a.

Cheatham, H. E. (ed.). *Cultural Pluralism on Campus*. Alexandria, Va.: American College Personnel Association, 1991b.

Chickering, A. W. *Education and Identity*. San Francisco: Jossey-Bass, 1969.

Clay, C. A., and Sherrill, J. M. "Racial Violence on Campus." In H. E. Cheatham (ed.), *Cultural Pluralism on Campus*. Alexandria, Va.: American College Personnel Association, 1991.

Couburn, K. L., and Treeger, M. L. *Letting Go: A Parents Guide to Today's College Experience*. Bethesda, Md.: Adler and Adler, 1988.

Cowley, W. H. "The History of Residential Student Housing." *School and Society*, 1934, *40*, 705–712, 758–764.

Crawford, I. "Attitudes of Undergraduate College Students Toward AIDS." *Psychological Reports*, 1990, *66*, 11–16.

Dalton, J. C. "Racial and Ethnic Backlash in College Peer Culture." In J. C. Dalton (ed.), *Racism on Campus: Confronting Racial Bias Through Peer Interventions*. New Directions for Student Services, no. 56. San Francisco: Jossey-Bass, 1991.

D'Augelli, A. R. "Homophobia in a University Community: Views of Prospective Resident Assistants." *Journal of College Student Development*, 1989, *30*, 546–552.

D'Augelli, A. R. "Homophobia in a University Community: Attitudes and Experiences of Heterosexual Freshmen." *Journal of College Student Development*, 1990, *31*, 484–491.

Engram, B. E. "Mediation and Conflict Resolution." In G. S. Blimling (ed.), *The Experienced Resident Assistant: Readings, Case Studies, and Structured Group Exercises for Advanced Training*. Dubuque, Iowa: Kendall/Hunt, 1989.

Evans, N. J., and Wall, V. A. *Beyond Tolerance: Gays, Lesbians, and Bisexuals on Campus*. Alexandria, Va.: American College Personnel Association, 1991.

Giffore, R. J., and Kallen, D. J. "AIDS and College Students: Toward Effective Prophylactic Use of Condoms." *College Student Journal*, 1990, *24*, 341–344.

Goldberg, R. "Attitude Change Among College Students Toward Homosexuality." *Journal of American College Health*, 1982, *30*, 260–268.

Gramick, J. "Homophobia: A New Challenge." *Social Health*, 1983, *19*, 137–141.

Greenberg, J. "A Study of Self-Esteem and Alienation of Male Homosexuals." *Journal of Psychology*, 1973, *83*, 137–143.

Harris, S. M., and Nettles, M. T. "Racial Differences in Student Experiences and Attitudes." In J. C. Dalton (ed.), *Racism on Campus: Confronting Racial*

Bias Through Peer Interventions. New Directions for Student Services, no. 56. San Francisco: Jossey-Bass, 1991.

Henley, B., and Arnold, M. S. "Unlearning Racism: A Student Affairs Agenda for Professional Development." *Journal of College Student Development*, 1990, *31*, 176–177.

Herek, G. M. "Attitudes Toward Lesbians and Gay Men: A Factor Analytic Study." *Journal of Homosexuality*, 1984, *10*, 39–52.

Herek, G. M. "Heterosexuals' Attitudes Toward Lesbians and Gay Men: Correlates and Gender Differences." *Journal of Sex Research*, 1988, *25*, 451–477.

Hildebrand, M., and Abramowitz, S. "Sexuality on Campus: Changes in Attitudes and Behaviors During the 1970's." *Journal of College Student Personnel*, 1984, *25*, 534–538.

Hudson, W. W., and Ricketts, W. A. "A Strategy for the Measurement of Homophobia." *Journal of Homosexuality*, 1980, *5*, 357–372.

Hughes, M. S. "Black Students' Participation in Higher Education." *Journal of College Student Personnel*, 1987, *28*, 532–545.

Iasenza, S., and Troutt, B. V. "A Training Program to Diminish Prejudicial Attitudes in Student Leaders." *Journal of College Student Development*, 1990, *31*, 83–84.

Iyriboz, Y., and Carter, J. A. "Attitudes of a Southern University Human Sexuality Class Toward Sexual Variance, Abortion, and Homosexuality." *College Student Journal*, 1986, *20*, 89–93.

Jacoby, B. "Today's Students: Diverse Needs Require Comprehensive Responses." In T. K. Miller and R. B. Winston, Jr. (eds.), *Administration and Leadership in Student Affairs: Actualizing Student Development in Higher Education.* (2nd ed.) Muncie, Ind.: Accelerated Development, 1991.

Jakobsen, L. "Promoting Diversity Among New Students in Predominantly White Residence Halls." In W. Zeller, D. Zeller, and B. Barefoot (eds.), *Residence Life Programs and the Freshman Year Experience.* Monograph No. 5. Columbia: University of South Carolina, 1991.

Janosik, S. M. "Additional Regulations for Hate Speech in Residence Halls." *Journal of College and University Student Housing*, 1991, *21*, 25–26.

Keeling, R. P. (ed.). *Effective AIDS Education on Campus.* New Directions for Student Services, no. 57. San Francisco: Jossey-Bass, 1992.

Kirby, D. "The Effects of School Sex Education Programs: A Review of the Literature." *Journal of School Health*, 1980, *50*, 559–563.

Kite, M. E., and Deaux, K. "Attitudes Toward Homosexuality: Assessment and Behavioral Consequences." *Basic and Applied Social Psychology*, 1986, 7, 137–162.

Kuh, G. D., Schuh, J. H., Whitt, E. J., and Associates. *Involving Colleges: Successful Approaches to Fostering Student Learning and Development Outside the Classroom.* San Francisco: Jossey-Bass, 1991.

Kurdek, L. A. "Correlates of Negative Attitudes Toward Homosexuals in Heterosexual College Students." *Sex Roles*, 1988, *18*, 727–738.

Levine, A. "Who Are Today's Freshmen?" In M. L. Upcraft, J. N. Gardner, and Associates, *The Freshman Year Experience: Helping Students Survive and Succeed in College*. San Francisco: Jossey-Bass, 1989.

Mann, B. A., and Moser, R. M. "A Model for Designing Peer-Initiated Activities to Promote Racial Awareness and an Appreciation of Differences." In J. C. Dalton (ed.), *Racism on Campus: Confronting Racial Bias Through Peer Interventions*. New Directions for Student Services, no. 56. San Francisco: Jossey-Bass, 1991.

Miltenberger, J. "Sexuality." In G. S. Blimling and L. J. Miltenberger (eds.), *The Resident Assistant: Working with College Students in Residence Halls*. (2nd ed.) Dubuque, Iowa: Kendall/Hunt, 1984.

Miltenberger, J., and Miltenberger, L. J. "Sexuality." In G. S. Blimling (ed.), *The Experienced Resident Assistant: Readings, Case Studies, and Structured Group Exercises for Advanced Training*. Dubuque, Iowa: Kendall/Hunt, 1989.

Murstein, B. I., Chalpin, M. J., Heard, K. V., and Vyse, S. A. "Sexual Behavior, Drugs, and Relationship Patterns on a College Campus Over Thirteen Years." *Adolescence*, 1989, *93*, 125–139.

Nelson, R., and Baha, H. E. "The Educational Climate for Gay, Lesbian, and Bisexual Students." Paper presented at meeting of the Association for Institutional Research, Louisville, Ky., May 1990.

Newman, B. M., and Newman, P. R. *When Kids Go to College: A Parent's Guide to Changing Relationships*. Columbus: Ohio State University Press, 1992.

Nuehring, E., Fein, S. B., and Tyler, M. "The Gay College Student: Perspectives for Mental Health Professionals." *Counseling Psychologist*, 1974, *5*, 64–72.

Nyberg, K. L., and Alston, J. P. "Homosexual Labeling by University Youths." *Adolescence*, 1977, *12*, 541–546.

Palmer, C. J. "Additional Regulations for Hate Speech in Residence Halls." *Journal of College and University Student Housing*, 1991, *21*, 27–30.

Pascarella, E. T., and Terenzini, P. T. *How College Affects Students: Findings and Insights from Twenty Years of Research*. San Francisco: Jossey-Bass, 1991.

Perigo, D. J., and Upcraft, M. L. "Orientation Programs." In M. L. Upcraft, J. N. Gardner, and Associates, *The Freshman Year Experience: Helping Students Survive and Succeed in College*. San Francisco: Jossey-Bass, 1989.

Pruett, H. L., and Brown, V. B. "Crisis Intervention and Prevention as a Campus-as-Community Mental Health Model." In H. L. Pruett and V. B. Brown (eds.), *Crisis Intervention and Prevention*. New Directions for Student Services, no. 49. San Francisco: Jossey-Bass, 1990.

Renshaw, D. C. "Sex and the 1980's College Student." *Journal of American College Health*, 1989, *37*, 154–157.

Reynolds, A. J. "Social Environmental Conceptions of Male Homosexual Behavior: A University Climate Analysis." *Journal of College Student Development*, 1989, *30*, 62–69.

Rickgarn, R.L.V. "Violence in Residence Halls: Campus Domestic Violence." In J. M. Sherrill and D. G. Siegel (eds.), *Responding to Violence on Campus*.

New Directions for Student Services, no. 47. San Francisco: Jossey-Bass, 1989.

Roark, M. L. "Sexual Violence." In J. M. Sherrill and D. G. Siegel (eds.), *Responding to Violence on Campus.* New Directions for Student Services, no. 47. San Francisco: Jossey-Bass, 1989.

Robertson, D. L. "Resident Students' Homophobia: Implications for Staff Selection and Training." Unpublished master's thesis, Western Illinois University, Macomb, 1990.

Roscoe, B., and Skomski, G. "Residence Hall Students' Knowledge and Attitudes Related to AIDS and AIDS Education Programs." *College Student Journal,* 1989, *23,* 59–66.

Sautter, J. A. "Residence Life Programs and the First-Year Experience: Personal Safety and Security." In W. Zeller, D. Fidler, and B. Barefoot (eds.), *Residence Life Programs and the First Year Experience.* Columbus, Ohio: Association of College and University Officers-International, 1991.

Serdahely, W. J., and Ziemba, G. J. "Changing Homophobic Attitudes Through College Sexuality Education." *Journal of Homosexuality,* 1984, *10,* 109–116.

Sherrill, J. M. "Models of Response to Campus Violence." In J. M. Sherrill and D. G. Siegel (eds.), *Responding to Violence on Campus.* New Directions for Student Services, no. 47. San Francisco: Jossey-Bass, 1989.

Shipton, W. C., and Schuh, J. H. "Counseling Problems Encountered by Resident Assistants: A Longitudinal Study." *Journal of College Student Personnel,* 1982, *23,* 246–251.

Simpson, J. A. "Developing a Safety/Security Program for Residence Halls." In J. Grimm (ed.), *Residence Hall and Apartment Housing Safety and Security.* Columbus, Ohio: Association of College and University Housing Officers-International, 1991.

Smith A. F. "The Resident Assistant and Discipline." In G. Blimling (ed.), *The Experienced Resident Assistant: Readings, Case Studies, and Structured Group Exercises for Advanced Training.* Dubuque, Iowa: Kendall/Hunt, 1989.

Stanley, D., Werring, C. J., and Carey, J. C. "Level of Rapport and Frequency of Change in Self-Selected and Randomly Assigned Roommate Pairs." *Journal of College and University Student Housing,* 1988, *18,* 21–24.

Steele, S. *The Content of Our Character: A New Vision of Race in America.* New York: St. Martin's Press, 1990.

Taylor, M. E. "A Discriminant Analysis Approach to Exploring Changes in Human Sexuality Attitudes Among University Students." *Journal of American College Health,* 1982, *31,* 124–129.

Terrell, A., and Ehrlich, H. "Climate of Ethnoviolence on Campus: Strategies for Improving Diversity." Paper presented at Virginia Polytechnic Institute and State University, Blacksburg, Nov. 1989.

Thompson, N., Candless, B., and Strickland, B. "Personal Adjustment of Male and Female Homosexuals and Heterosexuals." *Journal of Abnormal Psychology*, 1971, *78*, 237.

Torrey, S. S., and Lee, R. M. "Curbing Date Violence: Campus-Wide Strategies." *Journal of the National Association of Women Deans, Administrators, and Counselors*, 1987, *51*, 3–8.

Upcraft, M. L., with G. T. Pilato. *Residence Hall Assistants in College: A Guide to Selection, Training, and Supervision.* San Francisco: Jossey-Bass, 1982.

VanBebber, R. "Integrating Diversity into Traditional Resident Assistant Courses." In H. E. Cheatham (ed.), *Cultural Pluralism on Campus.* Alexandria, Va.: American College Personnel Association, 1991.

Vickio, C., Dings, J., and Leopold, T. "Diversity and Discrimination: An Intensive Staff Development Workshop." *Journal of College Student Development*, 1989, *30*, 85–86.

Wells, J. W., and Franken, M. L. "University Students' Knowledge About and Attitudes Toward Homosexuality." *Journal of Humanistic Education and Development*, 1987, *26*, 81–95.

Whitley, B. E. "The Relationship of Sex Role Orientation to Heterosexuals' Attitudes Toward Homosexuals." *Sex Roles*, 1987, *1*, 103–113.

Wood, S. A. "Toward a Renewed Collegiality: The Challenge of the 1990's." *NASPA Journal*, 1991, *29*, 2–9.

Yarber, W. L., and Yee, B. "Heterosexuals' Attitudes Toward Lesbianism and Male Homosexuality: Their Affective Orientation Toward Sexuality and Sex Guilt." *Journal of American College Health*, 1983, *31*, 203–208.

Young, M., and Whertvine, J. "Attitudes of Heterosexual Students Toward Homosexual Behaviors." *Psychological Reports*, 1982, *51*, 673–674.

Chapter Twenty-One

Dealing with Criminal Conduct and Other Deleterious Behaviors

Steven M. Janosik

Residence halls have been long thought to be a positive influence on the development of the students who live in them (Spencer, 1972; Astin, 1977). In particular, researchers suggest that coeducational housing patterns have a beneficial impact on campus climate, since they may enhance the maturity level and social development of students (Greenleaf, 1962; Borger, 1971; Gerst and Moos, 1971; Lynch, 1971; Locher, 1972; Brown, Winkworth, and Braskamp, 1973; Schroeder and LeMay, 1973; MacInnis, Byrne, and Fraser, 1980). But even though many student affairs practitioners can be justifiably proud of the difference a well-conceived residence hall program can make in the development of students, there is a darker side that must be addressed.

Astin's work (1977) underscored the contribution residence hall living makes to students' development, but he also found that living in a residence hall is associated with "greater-than-expected increases in hedonism" (p. 79). For purposes of his study, hedonism included such behaviors as drinking beer or wine, smoking, oversleeping, missing classes, and gambling. That hedonism pales in comparison to the self-destructive and dangerous behaviors that exist on today's campuses. For example, incidents of gender and racial harassment are being reported with greater and greater frequency.

Over 250 colleges and universities have reported such incidents on their campuses within the last three years ("Virginia's Colleges Battle Rising Ride of Campus Racism," 1989).

Instances of intergroup conflict include the letters KKK being painted on the room walls of five Asian women and the words "Death Nigger" carved on the office door of a hall counselor (Ehrlich, Pincus, and Morton, 1987). Terrell and Ehrlich (1989) suggest that residence halls are becoming fertile ground for increasing incidents of ethnoviolence on college campuses. They argue that conflict is bound to increase when students of dissimilar backgrounds are brought together in close proximity, especially when these students have not been prepared to deal with these differences.

Other crimes on campuses are reported with increasing regularity. During the mid 1980s, colleges reported over 2,000 crimes of personal violence, which includes aggravated assault, forcible rape, forcible robbery, manslaughter, and murder. Over 100,000 serious property crimes (including arson, burglary, larceny, and auto theft) also were reported (Federal Bureau of Investigation, 1985). Smith (1988) reports that crimes of violence and thefts of property and of information are soaring. Many of these incidents occur in residence halls.

Many practitioners argue that the college community, including residence halls, is a reflection of the larger society and that higher education is not immune to these negative events. Regardless of the cause, the problem is real, the problem is here, and the problem is escalating.

The purpose of this chapter is to report on the current status of campus crime and other troublesome activity that jeopardizes the safety and well-being of students, comment on the increasing public sensitivity to campus safety issues, and highlight the strengths and weaknesses of the administrative response to these concerns. For the practitioner, the chapter also includes recommendations for practice, resources, and successful program ideas.

Criminal Activity in Residence Halls

Murder

Fortunately, homicide does not occur frequently in residence halls. It is, however, an area of growing concern. In a *USA Today* survey, one-fourth of the nation's colleges and universities reported thirty-one homicides ("Campus Crime," 1988). A fatal shooting at an on-campus fraternity house at a large state university in the South, a murder-rape at a small college in the Northeast, and a fatal stabbing of a student by four or five youths in an apparent robbery attempt in the West are all reminders that homicides can occur in collegiate residence halls.

These horrible crimes and others like them may be linked to alcohol and other drugs, domestic arguments, or robbery. Regardless of the cause, such incidents generally receive national attention and can change the ethos of the campus for years to come.

Rape

Although the legal definition of rape may vary from state to state, it is usually defined as sexual intercourse that is perpetrated against the will of the victim. Rape is by far the most prevalent, serious violent crime reported on college campuses (Adams and Abarbanel, 1988). Even though the number of reported homosexual rapes is increasing, the vast majority of rapes involve men raping women (Blimling and Miltenberger, 1990).

In a recent survey, one out of every six females report having been a victim of rape or attempted rape. One of every fifteen male students reports committing rape or attempting rape during the same period (Koss, Gidycz, and Wisniewski, 1987). The State Council for Higher Education in Virginia reports that 15 percent of college women responding to a 1991 survey had given in to unwanted sexual activity, 7 percent had been sexually assaulted, 5 percent had been victims of attempted rape, and 2 percent had experienced rape during their college years (Virginia State Council for Higher Education and the Task Force on Campus Rape, 1992).

Rape can occur at any time, but most incidents take place on weekends between the hours of 9:00 P.M. and 2:00 A.M.. The vast majority occur indoors, and over half the victims know their assailants (Blimling and Miltenberger, 1990). Leo (1987) reports that the number of women who have been involved in acquaintance rape may run as high as one in five. Regrettably, residence halls are a prime location for this crime of violence. One of the most tragic outcomes of sexual assaults on campus is that most victims do not seek the medical and psychological help they need, and only about 10 percent report their assaults to the police.

Resident assistants (RAs) can help prevent rape by sponsoring or conducting antiviolence programs for males and programs that teach women about personal safety. Programs that teach men and women about defining limits in their relationships may help address the problem of acquaintance rape as well.

If rape does occur, RAs should encourage the victim to see the police or campus authorities immediately. The appropriate campus administrators should also be contacted. The person who has been attacked should be encouraged not to wash, change clothes, or disturb the scene where the incident took place. Medical attention should be obtained quickly. Hospital personnel should be informed of the rape or assault so that they can take the appropriate steps to preserve any evidence found. There will be cases where victims will decide not to make a formal complaint. In these cases, RAs and other university staff should make sure the victim is fully aware of all the alternatives and probable consequences of different lines of action. Many college campuses provide for the informal reporting of assaults and make available a wide range of support services for victims.

Concerned college administrators have responded to this type of criminal activity by developing programs that specifically address rape on campus. The staff at the University of Maryland at Baltimore County has produced a video to address campus crime. *Not a Sanctuary* teaches students how to be more security conscious. Programs designed to support the victim and programs designed to educate men are common. "Man to Man," a Syracuse University–based organization of male volunteers, speaks to college students nationwide about ending men's violence against women. The Sexual Assault Victims Emotional Support (SAVES) Group, an organization of faculty, staff, and students at Virginia Tech University, responds to victims of sexual assault and delivers a wide variety of educational programs on rape to students. A program at Texas A&M University titled "Creating Attitudes for a Rape-Free Environment" attempts to minimize misunderstandings that may foster a rape culture and to provide men and women with an understanding of how they can assertively communicate their sexual limits in a dating relationship. These educational programs address the legal definitions of rape and sexual assault, victims' responses, and relationship issues, among other things. They can go a long way in helping college students understand rape and its consequences.

Theft

Theft is cited as a moderate to major problem by 47 percent of college presidents in one survey (Carnegie Foundation, 1989). Contrary to the conventional wisdom, most thefts are committed by students and not by those outside the collegiate community (Center for the Study of Campus Violence, 1988).

Fennelly (1985) reports that theft of personal articles from students is a common campus occurrence. Items left unattended such as purses, wallets, and knapsacks are reported stolen most frequently. More expensive items such as cameras and jewelry taken from unlocked student rooms were reported next most often. While many of these losses are covered by parents' homeowner insurance policies, campus morale is affected when this type of petty larceny is not addressed and guilty parties identified.

Students and parents should be reminded of the possibilities of property loss. They should be encouraged to secure additional riders on their homeowner's insurance policies to cover personal possessions brought to the campus. Once on campus, students should receive information on how to protect their personal property.

Many campus police departments offer a free engraving service to students so that personal property can be marked with a social security number and inventoried. This program, referred to as "Operation ID" on many campuses, discourages theft and aids in the recovery of stolen property.

The use of "electronic keys" for entry into residence halls and/or individual rooms may also increase security. These plastic key cards offer several advantages over the mechanical locking system. In the case of the plastic key card, a single card can be invalidated. Other individuals using the same "key" are not inconvenienced. Changing mechanical hardware and issuing new keys are not necessary. The result can be tighter key control and greater security. The use of "computerized key control programs" can be used to track important key control information such as location of cores and keys, department key lists, individual key lists, core marks, and key cuts. Software programs, specially designed for housing and residence life applications, are available commercially and can be used to increase key control and security.

Vandalism

The destruction or the defacing of institutional property is a serious concern on a number of campuses. Statistics on its frequency are difficult to come by, since vandalism does not usually result in a police report (Smith, 1988). Students, however, indicate wide disapproval of destruction of campus property and graffiti. They believe that such behavior is most often group behavior that may be influenced by the use or misuse of alcohol (Roberta, 1983).

Vandalism is not a victimless crime. When vandalism goes unreported or unrepaired, it may contribute to an increase in the level of disrespect for property and persons. A number of institutions have developed neighborhood watch programs and instituted peer patrols to help curb this type of crime. In cooperation with the campus housing office, the Florida State University police have instituted a program that tries to involve the student population in crime prevention by reestablishing a traditional neighborhood police beat in each of the school's twelve residence halls. The program at Florida State University is referred to as the "Adopt a Cop" program. The "Student Nighttime Auxiliary Patrol (SNAP)" uses students to patrol the grounds immediately surrounding university residence halls at Virginia Tech University. They report suspicious behavior to a dispatcher by radio. Campus police officers respond and make the investigation or arrest. At Florida International University, residents participate in a program similar to the Neighborhood Watch program developed by police departments in any number of communities.

Vandalism to fire safety equipment in residence halls is common. A product called the "Stopper II" can be used to reduce this type of vandalism. The device consists of a clear Lexan tamperproof shield that covers the fire alarm pull station. A horn sounds if the cover is lifted. This signal is not connected to the building alarm system.

Illegal Use and Misuse of Alcohol and Other Drugs

The illegal use and misuse of alcohol and other substances by college students continues to receive national attention. Because the federal government is focusing its attention on drugs other than alcohol, most administrators agree that the illegal use and misuse of beverage alcohol is by far the drug problem of greatest concern for college communities. Substance abuse (primarily alcohol) is listed as one of the greatest concerns by two-thirds of college presidents (Carnegie Foundation, 1989).

The connection between alcohol and campus crime is well established. Student affairs professionals, campus police personnel, and residence hall staff representing 1,100 institutions report in a national study on campus crime that 41 percent of sexual assaults, 40 percent of physical assaults, 43 percent of hazing violence, and 43 percent of all vandalism involves the use or misuse of beverage alcohol (Center for the Study of Campus Violence, 1988). In another study, Bogal-Allbritten and Allbritten (1985) report that about 50 percent of the assailants in dating violence had consumed beverage alcohol before or during the incident. In their interviews, campus police reported that alcohol is a very large part of campus violence.

In response to the growing concern about alcohol and other drugs, many institutions have created offices of alcohol and drug education, hired full-time staff to help educate students, developed intervention programs, written new policy statements, and developed a wide variety of other strategies. Despite these efforts, in general, data suggest that only slight gains have been made (Gonzalez, 1988). College student drinking behavior has not changed in any substantial way over the last ten years. From an administrative perspective, it is disturbing to note that 25 percent of chief student affairs officers still indicate that their institutions never use checklists to review event standards with party sponsors who plan events where alcoholic beverages will be present, never require party sponsors to acknowledge their responsibility in writing, never meet with presidents of student organizations to discuss state law or recent court decisions regarding alcohol, and never meet with party sponsors to discuss social host liability or how to deal with drunks and party crashers (Janosik and Anderson, 1989). Although college administrators report progress on this issue, many remain unconvinced.

Other Troublesome Activity

Other areas of illegal or problematic behavior that are widespread on campuses nationally include gender and racial harassment and the presence of cults that attempt to recruit students.

Harassment

The Carnegie Foundation (1990) suggests that civility on college campuses is breaking down. One indicator of this is the more frequent reporting of abusive behavior within the college community. Gender, ethnic, and general verbal harassment among college students seems to be increasing. Over 60 percent of presidents at research and doctorate-granting institutions, for example, report that racial tensions and hostilities are a moderate to major problem on their campuses. Sixty percent of the same group reports that gender harassment is a problem as well (Carnegie Foundation, 1989).

In response to this increased tension, a variety of programs have been developed. A videotape developed by the University of Maryland at Baltimore County entitled *Still Burning* suggests methods or approaches for dealing with ethnoviolence. Freshmen entering the University of Vermont attend a two-day orientation and workshop on race relations and cultural diversity. The program addresses racial harassment issues. After a number of racist and misogynist incidents, the University of Wisconsin at Madison developed a comprehensive plan to deal with racism and sexism and at the same time celebrate diversity. The plan gives administrators better disciplinary tools, provides a means of dealing with faculty and staff who may perpetrate such incidents, and establishes guidelines for disciplining student organizations.

Student staffs also are not immune to such harassment. Durant, Marston, and Eisenhandler (1986) report that over 83 percent of RAs who responded to a national survey had experienced harassment in the form of abusive language at least once or twice. Over 24 percent reported threats to their person or property. Roughly 10 percent of this group indicated that they had experienced harassment based on gender, sexual preference, or religion. Among nonwhite RAs, almost 60 percent reported some type of racial-ethnic harassment.

Such behavior has a chilling effect on the developmental climate in residence halls. It creates fear, inhibits the ability of residents to move freely within that environment, and prevents them from learning more about one another. (See Chapter Twenty for descriptions of programs that have successfully dealt with many of these issues.)

Cults

In the past five years, cult activities on college campuses have increased at an alarming rate ("Special Report: Satanic Groups and Cults on Campus," 1989). It is estimated that almost three million young people between the ages of eighteen and twenty-one are active in religious cults in the United States today (Blimling and Miltenberger, 1990). Cults pose special problems for residence hall staff. Even though all cults may not engage in illegal activities, they present a serious mental health risk to students, their families, and the institution and often interfere with students' educational progress.

A destructive cult is defined by the Cult Awareness Network (CAN) (1987) as a closed group whose followers have been recruited deceptively and retained through the use of manipulative techniques of thought reform or mind control (undue influence).

Generally, cult groups may be placed in one of four categories: (1) new religious groups, (2) therapeutic or pseudotherapeutic self-help groups, (3) neopolitical groups, or (4) commercial enterprises offering "training seminars." Destructive cults also may pose as legitimate student organizations. In many instances, it is extremely difficult to obtain information about groups that recruit residence hall students or meet in residence hall space. Even when a destructive cult is identified, it may be difficult to respond to this menace. This is especially true at public institutions, where the rights of assembly and association are protected under the Constitution. (See Chapter Fourteen.)

Individuals are particularly vulnerable to the influence of cults during normal transitions in their lives, such as the first year away from home, when they are lonely or away from friends, or when making new friends and trying new things is encouraged (Rokos, 1989). Many residents fall into all three of these categories during their freshmen year! Residence hall staff should be aware of the existence of cults and the warning signs connected with such activity. Students falling under the influence of destructive cults may exhibit or experience some or all of the following:

- Loss of free will and control over one's life
- Return to dependency
- Loss of spontaneity
- Inability to form intimate or flexible relationships with others
- Decreased intellectual ability
- Physical and psychological deterioration
- De facto slavery
- Neurotic, psychotic, or suicidal tendencies

Dealing with this contemporary issue in residence life requires good communication. There can be no substitute for good staff training activities and consultation with local experts. Mental health staff and religious leaders in the community are most likely to have the best information about cult activity in and around the college campus. These professionals are in the best position to provide training and develop intervention strategies.

Public Concern and the Legislative Agenda

Public concern over crime on campus has been steadily increasing (Atwell, 1988). The media are focusing more and more attention on campus violence. As a result of serious incidents that have occurred and the increased publicity about them, parents and other concerned citizens are demanding more accountability from colleges. Despite good responses from many vice presidents, deans of students, and directors of housing and the initiation of additional security programs on many campuses, many parents and students are convinced that such action has been inadequate and too slow in coming. Out of frustration, a number of individuals have forced the issue. The efforts of the parents of one of the victims of a particularly horrible crime, for example, led to a state law in Pennsylvania that requires all colleges and universities to prepare and distribute detailed campus crime statistics to all student and employee applicants. More recently, Congress passed the Crime Awareness and Campus Security Act of 1990 under section 438(b) of the General Education Provisions Act. Provisions of this act require institutions to report selected crime statistics and summarize the institutional response to crime on campus annually (Title II, Section 204 Crime Awareness and Campus Security Act of 1990).

Drafting laws to deal with problems on college campuses is not new. Many states have passed laws against hazing that were a direct result of abuse in Greek-letter social organizations. The Drug Free Schools and Communities Act of 1989 and the Higher Education Amendments Act of 1991 contain language that require institutions to respond to criminal activity in a specific manner.

Although some may argue with the potential impact of these laws on institutional policy and student behavior, the intent seems clear. The public and some elected officials at the state and federal levels seem to be saying with a louder voice than ever, "If you do not deal with criminal behavior on your campuses, we will do it for you."

Why College Administrators Fail to Respond to Campus Crime

Despite all the staff training and discussion devoted to crisis management and campus crime, college administrators are brought under criticism frequently for their inability to deal with these issues. The following example illustrates this point.

After a series of incidents involving the harassment of gay students in a residence hall at a large state university in Ohio, one student was quoted as saying, "there have been incidents all year long and [officials] had names early on but didn't do anything about it" (Leib, 1990, p. 1). Now, after taking action to remove a number of residents from the affected floor, the university may face a class-action suit initiated by those who feel they were moved unfairly (Doulin, 1990).

Unfortunately, scenarios such as these are all too common on college campuses. It would appear that in this instance, those responsible for these residence halls could not satisfy anyone. They were criticized for not acting in one instance and then overreacting in the next. Why is it that administrators fail to deal with campus security and campus crime issues effectively?

Communicating Poorly

In many ways, the student affairs profession is stronger than it has ever been. There are more qualified professionals practicing than ever before. Still, many of the organizational structures we use lack effectiveness. It may be that the elaborate departmental hierarchies that include RAs, assistant hall directors, hall directors, assistant area coordinators, and area coordinators are too cumbersome to respond to campus crime and other crises. Boyer (1987, p. 199) suggests that in residence halls, in particular, "responsibility has been delegated so far down the administrative ladder that leaders on the campus have little idea about what goes on in these facilities." When criminal activity does occur in residence halls, it may go unreported for some time. Once reported, it may move through a multilayered organizational structure slowly, as each administrative layer attempts to deal with the problem.

Although many undergraduates do exemplary work as RAs across the country, some student affairs professionals are beginning to question if they can any longer do the job (Dodge, 1990). RAs are not necessarily at fault. The job is simply becoming more and more demanding as difficult problems such as alcoholism, suicide, homophobia, racism, acquaintance rape, and stress become more common. Young adults who are employed on a part-time basis may not be in a position to observe incidents or to receive reports from residents when incidents take place. In either case, the ability to respond to a crisis situation is delayed and ineffective.

Listening to the Wrong People

Many student affairs professionals are committed to a participatory management style. It is not an uncommon practice for a task force composed of students, faculty, and staff members to be asked to review residence hall policies and procedures. Students, in particular, are often in favor of extended visitation hours or supporting procedures that allow for maximum flexibility, freedom of choice, and freedom of movement. In some instances, administrators rely on "majority vote" or opinion polls to increase their sensitivity to students' wants and desires. Even though such procedures and practices may support important developmental constructs like fostering autonomy and independence, they may not address important safety and security needs. Establishing an open campus creates free access for crime ("Open Access," 1990). In some instances, residence hall administrators find themselves doing what is convenient or popular, not what is prudent.

Conflicting Needs with Other Campus Agencies

Campus crime is an extremely sensitive subject. In the past, there has been little agreement on how to share information about criminal activity. There are those who, for good reason, want to minimize public discussion about incidents on their campuses. Admissions officers, law enforcement personnel, institutional development officials, and public relations officers have a legitimate concern about how such information is shared with the public. It could affect the number of admissions applications received, the ability to solve a crime, the amount of money contributed, or the public's perception of the institution. As students and parents become more consumer oriented, institutions are reponding by paying more and more attention to marketing themselves so as to attract the greatest number of students, dollars, and other resources. Finding the balance of what and how much to share for everyone's well-being is not an easy task. In some cases, we may not share enough information with residents and others for fear that it may be used against the institution.

Denying the Problem Exists

When crimes occur in residence halls, many college administrators are tempted to dismiss the situation as "an isolated incident." This phrase frequently appears in all types of media when administrators are first made aware of a problem. It may be an accurate statement. More often than not, however, such a statement is made as a substitute for not having better information or not having a plan to respond to the crisis. In some instances, such a statement may be made in the hope that given a little time, the problem will go away or be solved by someone else.

A theft in an individual room, a single voyeur reported in a women's bathroom, or a report of a harassing phone call may be isolated incidents, but over time these incidents become trends that must be identified as early as possible. When campus crime is viewed in its proper context, no incident is isolated. The connection cannot be ignored.

Defining Crime as a Low Priority

Reducing campus crime is an expensive proposition. Refitting locks, installing security devices, establishing key control systems, and hiring additional security personnel do not fit easily into today's budgets. The truth may also be that given a choice, residence life professionals would rather spend money on items or programs that attend to the positive aspects of college life than protecting against the negative. Regrettably, in many instances, this type of expenditure moves up the priority list only after a tragedy occurs.

Institutional Strategies to Reduce Crime

To successfully address campus crime, residence hall professionals must be prepared to view the issue in both macro and micro perspectives. The macro perspective attends to institutional/departmental philosophy and policy. A comprehensive crime prevention plan should be developed for residence halls. This plan should be integrated into the institution's reponse to the issues. Such a plan must include a review of the campus environment and the education of those who participate in it.

Developing a Comprehensive Plan

In 1985, the American Council on Education (ACE) and the American College Personnel Association (ACPA) endorsed a document titled *Achieving*

Reasonable Campus Security. This document suggests a number of sound administrative steps that colleges and universities can take to minimize the likelihood of violent crime. Professionals in residence life should adopt these guidelines as minimum standards for reducing crime in residence halls. They include the following:

1. Providing residents with information about security risks and precautions applicable to areas of campus they may frequent. This information should be provided at all orientation programs, in brochures and fliers, and as part of the regular residence hall programming activities. The topics of assault, harassment, rape, substance abuse, theft, and vandalism should be addressed in candid detail.

2. Informing residents about the procedures for summoning aid in the event of a security emergency.

3. Informing residents of the importance of reporting all criminal activity immediately.

4. Examining residence hall entrances, parking areas, outdoor communication facilities, and major campus pathways for plant growth, debris, and other obstacles that may detract from security.

5. Reviewing the adequacy of all outdoor lighting from a security point of view. Residence halls should be sufficiently illuminated after dusk to permit observation of persons loitering in the vicinity. Additional lighting should be provided for those areas in immediate proximity to residence halls, including parking areas, bus stops, and recreational areas.

6. Developing a strict and comprehensive key control system. Access to master keys should be restricted. A procedure for replacing lost or stolen keys should be implemented, and a key coding system that prevents the easy identification of residence hall keys should be instituted.

7. Screening all residence hall personnel for maturity and judgment. Conduct background checks before employment.

8. Including seminars on campus crime and campus security in staff training programs for all residence life personnel. This training should be commensurate with the staff members' responsibility for security.

9. Examining regulations that affect access to residence halls. Assess the feasibility and desirability of having and enforcing rules restricting the access of nonresidents to student housing (adapted from the American Council on Education, 1985).

In addition to following these guidelines, residence life staff should seek to develop close and supportive relationships with the campus and local law enforcement agencies. Determining appropriate jurisdictions for criminal activities is a critical step in developing a comprehensive crime reduction and prevention plan.

The development of a standing committee on security in residence halls that includes students, staff, and faculty should also be used to evaluate needs and progress in each of these areas on a continuous basis. Such a strategy can serve to focus attention on security issues throughout the academic year. Involving student security staff, police, judicial staff, and the campus escort staff in these activities can result in higher levels of security.

Examples of these comprehensive approaches to security planning are numerous. The office of housing and residential life at San Diego State University completes a security review every five years. The model includes a review of current procedures, a comprehensive staff survey, and a housing operation telephone survey, among other measures. Northeastern University, in Massachusetts, uses a comprehensive approach to residence hall security that addresses access control, key control, and door propping. Criminal activity and institutional liability may be reduced through good planning.

Philosophy and policy, however, are only half of the solution. The broader view must be incorporated into the day-to-day operation of the residence halls. The latter is the micro perspective. Together, they compose a complete strategy to limit campus crime.

Responding to Crime on a Daily Basis

The development of sound administrative policy and programs does not ensure that incidents occurring in residence halls will be handled promptly and correctly. From a micro perspective, any plan must be operationalized through the development of clear and concise lines of authority, decision making, and communication. Such procedures will allow professional staff to respond to a security crisis in a confident and prompt manner.

Hammond (1987) suggests that emergencies be responded to on two levels. The institutional level emphasizes notification of personnel, fact finding, risk/loss evaluation, and report generation. The human level focuses on the needs of the victims. This level emphasizes caring for and supporting all of the individuals affected by the incident. Depending on the crime, this may include the victim, the roommate, hall residents, parents and other significant others, and residence hall staff. Both levels should be attended to when responding to crime in residence halls.

As a staff considers its procedures, the following guidelines are offered:

1. Separate forms should be developed to report crime in residence halls from those used to report violations of the conduct code, which are not significant criminal violations. Copies of these forms should be sent to designated personnel in the residence life office and other appropriate agencies simultaneously. Routing should be avoided, since it delays communication.

2. These forms should not only include space to record who, what, when, and where but should also allow the person completing the form to list all of the contacts made, actions taken, and follow-ups conducted relative to the incident.

3. All security-related incidents should be monitored and tracked.

Residence life staff should be made aware of the criminal activity in their building and area on a regular basis. Residents should be made aware of this activity as soon as prudently possible.

4. Security response teams should be established. These teams should include the on-site RA and hall director, the investigating police officer, and a representative from the central housing office. In cases where the crime is particularly traumatic, a member of the counseling center staff should also be included. A member from the public affairs office might be included if the event is likely to receive extensive media attention. The highest administrative-level person from the residence life staff (or other agreed-on representative) should assume responsibility for keeping other college officials informed, contacting parents, and responding to the media if appropriate.

5. This team should meet immediately on notification of the incident to develop a response strategy. In minor cases involving theft, a meeting to make staff aware might be scheduled, a notice of the criminal activity might be posted for residents, and a hall program on protecting personal property might be scheduled. In serious cases involving rape, other forms of assault, or murder, more complex strategies must be developed. In all cases, the actions taken should be well documented.

6. The number of people contacting the victim, parents, and significant others should be minimized to avoid confusion.

7. Contact with others made by institutional staff should be done with the victim's permission in accordance with institutional policy or the appropriate state law. (See Chapter Fourteen.)

8. If parents plan to visit the campus as a result of the incident, senior staff in the resident life office should meet with them immediately on their arrival on campus to review the incident and the actions taken.

9. If room changes or withdrawals from college are requested, every possible step should be taken to expedite the process for the victim. Refunds, if appropriate, should be made without delay.

The outlook for future criminal activity in residence halls is not positive. Indications point to further increases in crimes of all sorts. Residence life professionals must move campus security issues to a higher priority within their organizations and attack the problem aggressively. Because successful efforts will vary with the special needs of respective institutions, large investments in technology, personnel, and training must be made if residence halls are to be a safe environment in which students can live, learn, and grow.

References

Adams, A., and Abarbanel, G. *Sexual Assault on Campus*. Santa Monica, Calif.: Rape Treatment Center, 1988.

American Council on Education. *Achieving Reasonable Campus Security*. Washington, D.C.: American Council on Education, 1985.

Astin, A. W. *Four Critical Years: Effects of College on Beliefs, Attitudes, and Knowledge*. San Francisco: Jossey-Bass, 1977.

Atwell, R. H. *A Letter to College and University Presidents*. Washington, D.C.: American Council on Education, Aug. 16, 1988.

Blimling, G. S., and Miltenberger, L. J. *The Resident Assistant: Working with College Students in Residence Halls*. (3rd ed.) Dubuque, Iowa: Kendall/Hunt, 1990.

Bogal-Allbritten, R. B., and Allbritten, W. L. "The Hidden Victims: Courtship Violence Among College Students." *Journal of College Student Personnel*, 1985, *26*, 201.

Borger, J. "Coed Housing." *Today's Education*, 1971, *60*, 35–36.

Boyer, E. L. *College: The Undergraduate Experience in America*. New York: Harper-Collins, 1987.

Brown, R. D., Winkworth, J., and Braskamp, L. "Student Development in a Coed Residence Hall: Promiscuity, Prophylactic, or Panacea?" *Journal of College Student Personnel*, 1973, *14*, 98–104.

"Campus Crime." *USA Today*, Oct. 4, 1988, pp. A1, A2.

Carnegie Foundation. *National Survey of College and University Presidents*. Lawrenceville, N.J.: Princeton University Press, 1989.

Carnegie Foundation. *Campus Life: In Search of Community*. Lawrenceville, N.J.: Princeton University Press, 1990.

Center for the Study of Campus Violence. *National Campus Violence Survey General Report*. Towson, Md.: Towson State University, 1988.

Cult Awareness Network. *Cult Awareness Network*. Chicago: National Office of the Cult Awareness Network, 1987.

Dodge, S. "The Demanding Job of Resident Assistant: Has It Grown Too Big for Students?" *Chronicle of Higher Education*, Feb. 21, 1990, pp. A1, A38–A41.

Doulin, T. "Parents of Displaced Sons May Sue OSU." *Dispatch* (Columbus, Ohio), May 29, 1990, p. 3.

Durant, C. E., Marston, L. L., and Eisenhandler, S. *Findings from the 1985 National RA Harassment Survey*. Amherst: University of Massachusetts, 1986.

Ehrlich, H. J., Pincus, F. L., and Morton, C. *Ethnoviolence on Campus: The UMBC Study*. Institute Report No. 2. Baltimore, Md.: National Institute Against Prejudice and Violence, 1987.

Federal Bureau of Investigation. *Uniform Crime Reports*. Washington, D.C.: U.S. Department of Justice, 1985.

Fennelly, L. J. "Crime Problems on College Campuses." *Security Management*, Sept. 1985, p. 122.

Gerst, M., and Moos, R. "A University Residence Environment Scale." *Western Interstate Commission for Higher Education Newsletter*, Apr. 1971, pp. 1–2.

Gonzalez, G. M. "Should Alcohol and Other Drug Education Be a Part of Comprehensive Prevention Policy? The Evidence from the College Campus." *Journal of Drug Issues*, 1988, *18*, 355–365.

Greenleaf, E. A. "Co-Educational Residence Halls: An Evaluation." *National Association of Women Deans and Counselors Journal*, 1962, *25*, 51–57.

Hammond, E. "Risk Management Workshop." Paper presented at the joint annual meeting of the American College Personnel Association and the National Association of Student Personnel Administrators, Mar. 1987.

Janosik, S. M., and Anderson, D. S. "An Assessment of Alcoholic Risk Management Practices on the College Campus." *NASPA Journal*, 1989, *26*, 193–201.

Koss, M. P., Gidycz, C. A., and Wisniewski, N. "The Scope of Rape: Incidence and Prevalence of Sexual Aggression and Victimization in a National Sample of Higher Education Students." *Journal of Consulting and Clinical Psychology*, 1987, *55*, 2.

Leib, K. L. "Residents Ousted for Threats to Gays." *Lantern* (Columbus, Ohio), May 24, 1990, p. 1.

Leo, J. "When the Date Turns into Rape." *Time*, Mar. 23, 1987, p. ••.

Locher, N. C. "Administrative Attitudes Toward Coeducational Housing at Sixteen Small Colleges." *Journal of College Student Personnel*, 1972, *13*, 395–401.

Lynch, R. C. "A Comparison of Activities and Behaviors in Coeducational and Non-Coeducational Residence Halls." Unpublished manuscript, Department of Residence Life, University of Maryland, College Park, 1971.

MacInnis, M. C., Byrne, T. D., and Fraser, J. A. "Opinions of Students, Parents, Faculty, and Community Concerning Coeducational Residence Halls." *Journal of College and University Student Housing*, 1980, *10*, 30–34.

"Open Access." *College Security Report*, 1990, *2*, 4.

Roberta, L. "Campus Destructiveness in the 1980s: A Survey of American College Students." Paper presented at the annual meeting of the Association for the Study of Higher Education, Mar. 1983.

Rokos, M. G. *Do You Know When Your Teenager Is in Danger?* Joppa, Md.: Copley Parish, 1989.

Schroeder, C. C., and LeMay, L. W. "The Impact of Coed Residence Halls on Self Actualization." *Journal of College Student Personnel*, 1973, *14*, 105–110.

Smith, M. C. *Coping with Crime on Campus*. New York: Macmillan, 1988.

"Special Report: Satanic Groups and Cults on Campus." *College Security Report*, Nov. 1989, pp. 5–9.

Spencer, E. F. "A Study of Coeducation Residence Halls at the University of Delaware." Unpublished manuscript, Department of Residence Life, University of Delaware, 1972.

Terrell, A., and Ehrlich, H. "Climate of Ethnoviolence on Campus: Strategies for Improving Diversity." Paper presented at Virginia Polytechnic Institute and State University, Nov. 1989.

"Virginia's Colleges Battle Rising Tide of Campus Racism." *News and Observer* (Raleigh, N.C.), Dec. 27, 1989, p. 3B.

Virginia State Council of Higher Education and the Task Force on Campus Rape. *Sexual Assault on Virginia's Campuses*. Senate Document No. 17. Richmond: Virginia State Council for Higher Education and the Task Force on Campus Rape, 1992.

Chapter Twenty-Two

=============

Conclusion: Creating Residence Life Programs with Student Development Goals

Charles C. Schroeder

Although the history of higher education is marked by change, growth, and adaptation, colleges and universities now face unprecedented challenges. Student affairs and housing professionals must understand and respond to these challenges if they are to effectively educate students and serve their institutions. To address these issues successfully, residence life staff must examine traditional assumptions, create new organizational roles, and broaden their sphere of influence within their campus community. This chapter delineates these challenges and opportunities and offers responses appropriate for residence life programs with student development goals.

Challenges Facing Higher Education and Student Affairs

Parents of today's college students had a collegiate experience radically different from that of their children. In the late 1950s and early 1960s, the opportunity to attend college was a privilege and was available primarily to white middle-class youngsters seeking to be liberally educated. As a group, these students were academically well prepared, serious about the educational enterprise, and convinced that college attendance would ensure a successful career. Their relationship with their institutions was governed by the doctrine in loco parentis, with the college or university assuming responsibility for all aspects of their welfare. This doctrine was manifest in numerous rules and regulations that included dress codes, no public displays of affection, curfews for female students, rigid adherence to state and federal laws concerning alcohol consumption by minors, and the prohibition of intervisitation by members of the opposite sex. Astin's (1977) research suggests that college students in the 1960s and early 1970s valued liberal learning, were concerned about developing a philosophy of life, and struggled with such major social and political causes as civil rights, the Vietnam conflict, and the women's movement. Few students worked to pay their college expenses, and most had considerable discretionary time to invest in various campus life opportunities. Although many campuses did not provide formal placement services, employment was virtually guaranteed for the vast majority of graduates.

In less than thirty years, higher education has been transformed. The elitist perspective of earlier decades has been replaced with an egalitarian movement that opened institutional doors to large segments of the population previously neglected. The access revolution, fueled in part by a 6,000 percent increase in financial aid (Merante, 1987), has resulted in creating the most diverse student populations in history. Many students enter college today without the knowledge, skills, and attitudes necessary for success. As a result, gaps between ideal academic standards and actual student learning are widening.

In response to burgeoning enrollments and an extremely diverse clientele, institutions have become increasingly complex and specialized. As differences between constituencies, programs, and services have been accentuated, organizational structures have become more fragmented, compartmentalized, and encapsulated. Within the student affairs profession, roles and functions are becoming more segmented, to the point that it is difficult to focus on commonalities and transcendent values. As Boyer (1987) points out, colleges and universities today are characterized by an absence of a sense of community.

Higher education institutions are faced with other pressing challenges as well. Changes in the economic agendas at both the federal and state levels are placing greater financial burdens on many schools, and severe budget cuts, retrenchment, layoffs, and furloughs are becoming commonplace. The dramatic decline in the number of traditional-age college students has resulted in fierce and intense competition, an alarming trend particularly for private colleges and universities that are tuition driven and extremely vulnerable to subtle enrollment shifts. A related concern is the recruitment and retention of minority students. Although the number of minorities in America is increasing dramatically, their participation and completion rates in higher education continue to decline. Those members of minority groups who enroll experience chilly campus environments characterized by increased incidents of intolerance and racism.

Although the 1970s and 1980s were characterized by a perspective that affirmed equity of access, current public demand for quality and accountability has rekindled a focus on excellence (Mayhew, Ford, and Hubbard, 1990). In response, many states are requiring public institutions to develop systematic methods for demonstrating their impact on students. These expectations have spawned a nationwide assessment movement that has gained tremendous momentum. Unfortunately, the movement has focused almost exclusively on academic outcomes, summarily neglecting many powerful impacts associated with residential living arrangements and other out-of-class experiences.

Public concern for quality and accountability has also focused increased attention on the nature of undergraduate education. Major reports commissioned by the Carnegie Foundation, the Education Commission of the States, and the National Institute of Education argue for the renewal of the undergraduate experience. These reports express concern about the fragmented and specialized curriculum, the lack of clarity about goals and purposes, and the need to integrate out-of-class experiences with the educational mission of the college. The reports stress the need to make connections, to integrate undergraduate experiences in the service of student learning and development.

Finally, a great deal of confusion exists regarding the student-institution relationship. Although students and faculty alike celebrated the demise of in loco parentis and the paternalistic control it symbolized, there is great uncertainty about what should replace it. The benevolent authoritarian approach to rule enforcement that prevailed in earlier decades has been replaced on many campuses by a sense of indifference, as students and faculty go their separate ways. This point is cogently illustrated in Boyer (1987, p. 204). While Boyer was conducting student interviews at DePaul University, a student said, "We'd like you to understand one thing. We don't want the university to interfere in our lives, but we want someone in the university to be concerned with our lives."

These challenges offer unique opportunities for student affairs and housing professionals to foster not only the development of their students, but the development of their institutions as well (Garland, 1985). Effective responses require new roles, perspectives, and commitments because current organizational approaches to residence life programs are often inadequate. The fragmentation and compartmentalization typical of formal academic programs are also reflected in contemporary approaches to residence hall education. As a result, there are few connections and points of integration between the educational priorities of the institution and the programs and services offered in residence halls. To address these issues, residence life programs must do the following:

- Contribute to the quality of students' academic experiences
- Foster the creation of authentic residential communities
- Contribute to institutional enrollment management initiatives
- Prudently utilize limited resources
- Demonstrate the value of programs and services

Even though the preceding opportunities will be discussed separately, they are highly interdependent and synergistic.

Contribute to the Quality of Students' Academic Experiences

Although colleges and universities exist for a variety of purposes, most people would agree that the academic mission of the institution is preeminent (Blake, 1979; National Association of Student Personnel Administrators, 1987). Indeed, a fundamental assumption of this book is that "effective residence halls are not educationally neutral but intentionally create environments and proactive interventions designed to enhance the academic experience and to enrich the personal lives of residents" (Chapter Two). Traditionally, staff have attempted to accomplish this objective through providing a variety of "educational programs" that often reflect the particular interests and skills of staff rather than the academic goals and priorities of the institution. Such programs rarely focus on academic skill enhancement, clarification of academic values, or improvement of performance in specific academic curricula. Outcomes such as these are more readily influenced by certain environmental conditions than by traditional, top-down staff programming initiatives.

Structure Environments to Respond to Academic Needs.

Responding to the academic needs of students must be a priority of residence life programs with student development goals, particularly since this generation is uniquely different from previous ones. Compared to their more traditional predecessors of the 1950s and 1960s, students today are less independent in thought and judgment, are more passive, have less tolerance for diversity, are more dependent on immediate gratification, and exhibit more difficulty with basic academic skills (Davis and Schroeder, 1982; Schroeder, DiTiberio, and Kalsbeek, 1988). They also experience more difficulty understanding relationships between various academic disciplines and integrating different knowledge bases. When characteristics such as these interact with demanding expectations of faculty, many students become overwhelmed and disillusioned and choose not to persist.

Residence halls can be academically rich environments, providing students with broad-based learning opportunities that reflect specific academic objectives of the institution. A critical component of such environments is appropriate degrees of support that enable students to meet rigorous academic challenges effectively. For freshmen in particular, intrusive support is often essential. Although many institutions have attempted to provide such support through the creation of freshman-year-experience courses (Upcraft, Gardner, and Associates, 1989), with few exceptions, the "freshman experience" is highly fragmented and lacks substantive integration and coherence. Residence hall environments can be structured to provide such integration and coherence. For example, students that participate in freshman seminar groups are often assigned to such groups on a random and unsystematic basis. Since students in these groups are rarely assigned common courses, they have few, if any, opportunities to develop ongoing relationships characterized by high degrees of peer support. Instead of randomly assigning students to freshman seminar groups, homogeneous assignments could be developed from floor rosters in the residence halls. For instance, students living on the same floor would be assigned to the same freshman seminar group. Furthermore, these students could be assigned at least two other courses in common, selected from the general education or "core" requirements of the institution.

In large colleges and universities, students might also be offered homogeneous housing options designed around common educational aspirations or academic themes (for example, engineering or allied health). Residence life staff working in conjunction with academic administrators could identify the traditionally most challenging and demanding "high-risk" courses within these academic areas. Outstanding upperclass residence students or resident advisers with particular skills in these courses could be selected to serve as peer tutors to assist freshmen. If space for these "study partner" or peer tutoring programs is provided in each residential unit, students with common academic interests and concerns would have easy access to support systems designed to facilitate their academic achievement. These support systems would be enhanced through the creation of faculty affiliate programs that encourage frequent faculty-student interaction (Jackson and Stevens, 1990). Such arrangements would provide freshmen with a truly "common" experience, one characterized by high degrees of peer support, integration, and coherence.

Encourage Community Service and Civic Responsibility. As stated in Chapter Two, residence life programs committed to student development goals must help students become responsible, contributing members of a society of multiple communities and must foster ideals of altruism and social justice. Many faculty members, particularly those in liberal arts institutions, would agree that these are admirable objectives of undergraduate education. Opportunities for community service, however, are generally provided through centrally coordinated volunteer program offices administratively linked to either academic or student affairs. Due to the often fragmented and isolated nature of such programs, their academic and social impact on students in residence halls is limited. One way of addressing this issue is to encourage students in a particular residence hall to sponsor an ongoing service project that reflects their collective commitment to altruism, social justice, and community service. An example of just such an approach is the Adams School project at Saint Louis University. Students living on nine floors of a high-rise building chose to "adopt" Adams School, an inner-city, predominantly African-American elementary school located within ten minutes of the campus. The school, which is over a hundred years old, is suffering from years of deferred maintenance and inadequate academic achievement of students.

Every day, residents from each floor go to Adams to provide tutorial services for approximately fifty youngsters identified by their teachers as needing special, individualized attention. On Saturday mornings, residence hall students devote their time and energy to plastering and painting the interior of the school. Housing maintenance personnel have joined with other staff and students to help their Adams School neighbors improve the school's physical and educational environments.

The impact of this community service project, both on Saint Louis University students and the children, is profound. Teachers at Adams report dramatic academic and social gains on the part of the children being tutored. Residence life staff report a range of impacts on the college students who give freely of their time and energy, including the following: clarifying and, at times, changing one's academic major; greater understanding and appreciation of cultural differences; and enhanced understanding of one's obligations as a citizen of a larger community. Such impacts are the direct result of students in a specific residence hall working together on a specific ongoing community service project. By having opportunities to discuss their experiences through daily interactions on their floors, a "carryover" effect is created, and this appears to be the primary basis for the transformational nature of the project.

The success of the Adams School project has spawned other initiatives that can integrate residence life programming with other academic priorities. For example, faculty in the social sciences are being encouraged to offer students a fourth-credit option if they participate in a volunteer activity such as the Adams School project. Students in a three-credit psychology or sociology class, for example could obtain a fourth credit in exchange for participation in community service activities. The real opportunity here is to use experiential, volunteer service activities to integrate theory and practice—in other words, to connect informal, value-oriented residence hall learning opportunities with the formal academic emphasis of the disciplines in meaningful ways.

The preceding examples are only a few illustrations of ways residence life programs can contribute to enhancing the academic experience of students. To achieve such results, residential life staff must develop collaborative relationships with academic administrators and faculty. Such approaches enable residence life programs to be integrating agents within the campus environment—that is, they can help students understand and appreciate the interrelatedness of different aspects of their educational experience.

Foster the Creation of Authentic Residential Communities

The need to establish a sense of community is one of the most critical issues facing higher education during this decade. The absence of community has been related to such factors as changing enrollment configurations; highly specialized, fragmented, and compartmentalized organizational structures; and the lack of a shared purpose and of transcendent institutional values. Residence life programs with student development goals are in a unique position to foster the creation of authentic communities. To achieve this objective, however, staff must abandon, or at least adapt, many traditional approaches to community development.

Create New Approaches to Community Development. The traditional approach to developing community residence halls is usually some variant of a programmed-implementation strategy (Berman, 1979) grounded in a reductionist, essentially bureaucratic model. Those in authority (staff) define goals and objectives, which are transmitted downward through the residence hall organization to those in the trenches (resident assistants). An attempt is made to create a sense of community through tightly coupled programs addressing clearly stated and shared goals (determined by staff) and state-of-the-art technologies (such as programs based on developmental theory). Such an approach to community development is unlikely to result in conditions that encourage broad-based student involvement, participation, and influence. What is encouraged, however, is a sense of ownership on the part of staff for "their" housing program. Under such conditions, it is not surprising that student attrition rates are so high or that vandalism, hostile interaction, and other inappropriate behavior tend to characterize many residence halls throughout the country.

Numerous elements are involved in fostering a sense of authentic community. The most fundamental components include similar interests, common purpose, peer influence, social interaction, stability, and self-determination. Also, community is nurtured when members collaborate to create their own standards and commit themselves to maintaining satisfactory interactions among members through personal contact, not through rules and regulations. Hence, within broad institutional value parameters, floor residents must be challenged to develop mutually shared standards. In contrast to institutional rules, mutually shared standards make explicit the behavioral limits that already exist so as to define the parameters within which groups can function effectively. To develop such standards, floor residents must consider common values, goals, and aspirations.

Although the literature is replete with references to the relationship between peer influences and certain learning and personal development outcomes (DeCoster and Mable, 1980; Blimling and Schuh, 1981; Kuh, Schuh, Whitt, and Associates, 1991; Pascarella and Terenzini, 1991), residence life staff often fail to understand the powerful influences of peer culture, because so much of their time and energy is devoted to implementing formal programs for students at a macro level (system or hall level). They need instead to encourage the emergence of facilitative conditions within each floor in every residence hall in the system. Clearly, such an approach encourages the emergence of community from a "bottom-up" rather than the traditional bureaucratic "top-down" approach.

A Model for Creating Authentic Communities. There are a number of ways of conceptualizing community development in residence halls (Mable, Terry, and Duvall, 1977; Newton, 1980; Schroeder and Jackson, 1987). A rather simplistic, yet effective, approach utilizes the four I's—involvement, influence, investment, and identity. These elements can be considered guidelines for encouraging the emergence of floor communities as well as criteria for evaluating the degree of community within floors. Briefly, the elements are defined as follows:

1. *Involvement.* A true community encourages, expects, and rewards broad-based member involvement. The environment is characterized by a high degree of interaction, with students, *not staff,* assuming a multitude of roles. As a consequence, everyone is important and everyone is needed. Returning residents assume responsibility for orienting and integrating "new" members through formal and informal rites of passage. High-involving floors are characterized by supportive interactions, with students naturally helping one another with personal and academic problems.

2. *Influence.* In floor units that exhibit a high degree of influence, control is vested in members, and students exert maximum control over their physical and social environments. For example, residents are encouraged and expected to personalize their rooms and hallways, through painting and decorating them, and to recruit and assign members. They are also expected to develop a social contract whereby group standards are affirmed, both individually and collectively. In such units, students feel important, their perspective is valued, and their contributions are essential to the welfare of the group.

3. *Investment.* Investment is a reflection of psychological ownership and flows naturally from involvement and influence. Students care about one another and their group. Boundaries with respect to other groups are clear, and group or institutional property is guarded rather than being damaged. Interactions are often characterized by gentle confrontation rather than polite or passive-aggressive behaviors. Students are simply unwilling to have staff assume responsibility for them—they understand and appreciate the need for open, honest, and assertive communication with one another. Finally, there are clear variations in status and roles, as well as longevity of association. Rewards are provided for being a "good" member.

4. *Identity.* Floor units characterized by a high degree of identity are ones that focus on commonalities and transcendent values. Students in such units have shared symbols, similar to those fraternities and sororities use to signify their identities. In such living units, members describe themselves in collective terms such as *we* and *us*, not *I* or *they*, thereby reflecting their emphasis on common purposes and unity.

As illustrated in previous chapters, residence life staff can encourage the creation of conditions that promote community development through such processes as determining room and floor assignments, making the physical environment responsive to students' basic needs, and encouraging students to self-select living groups with explicit themes related to academic aspirations and priorities. These conditions can help facilitate authentic communities; however, staff must encourage and expect students to assume primary responsibility for the quality of their residence hall experience. When a model based on the four I's is implemented, students become the architects of authentic communities, while staff assume such supporting roles as consultant, advisor, and teacher.

Contribute to Institutional Enrollment Management Initiatives

Dramatic declines in the number of high school graduates, substantial demographic changes, and growing competition for increasingly limited resources have caused colleges and universities to realize the importance of strategically managing their enrollments. Although many other definitions exist, enrollment management is generally considered an integrated, systems approach to influencing college enrollments. Hossler (1986, p. 10) defines it as "a process or activity that influences the size, shape, and characteristics of a student body by directing institutional efforts in marketing, recruitment, and admissions as well as pricing and financial aid." This definition contains no mention of housing or residence life programs. Indeed, many student affairs and housing professionals consider enrollment management to be the sole responsibility of admissions and financial aid offices. Herein lies the problem and the opportunity.

Historically, housing and residence life departments have functioned as independent units expending considerable energy on a variety of internal issues, thereby neglecting important external challenges central to the vitality of their institutions. Clearly, stabilizing enrollment is an imperative for most institutions, and housing programs should play a key role in addressing this challenge. To do so, housing and residence life staff must assume new organizational roles, including a "boundaries spanning perspective" (Garland, 1985). Such a perspective focuses on forming alliances with important constituencies to integrate student and institutional development. Enrollment management is an institutional system that by design impels student affairs and residence life staff to serve an integrator role in influencing enrollment development.

Institutions committed to stabilizing and hopefully expanding their enrollments generally focus their efforts on two fundamental processes: recruitment and retention. As a process, enrollment management is similar to environmental management—that is, institutions must understand factors that influence students' choices to enroll and persist. The focus must be on the entirety of the student experience and not simply on organizational structures that fragment the experience in the service of administrative efficiencies. A key to effective enrollment management is creating a tightly coupled system that systematically links all policies and functional areas that have an impact on student enrollments (Hossler, Bean, and Associates, 1990).

Develop Programs for Recruiting Students. With regard to recruitment efforts, housing and residence life staff can make major contributions. For example, the process of college choice is often an exercise in determining the probability of a "good fit" between the prospective students' needs and aspirations and opportunities provided by the institutions to meet them. It is a process that, at its best, should lead to an informed choice. Campus visits, with overnight stays in residence halls, are ideal mechanisms for helping students make "informed choices." Residence life staff, working through resident assistants and student leaders, can develop campus host/hostess programs that help prospective students learn about the nature of undergraduate campus life and the value of residential living. In addition, residence hall students can be actively involved in telemarketing efforts to provide prospective students with information about residential living, the undergraduate experience, and academic expectations. On campuses that use student-to-student telemarketing programs, telephone calls are followed by personal letters with invitations to visit the campus and stay overnight in a residence hall.

Because financial accessibility is a crucial enrollment issue, housing staff, working in conjunction with admissions and financial aid personnel, can develop targeted "housing grants" that can be awarded to prospective students on the basis of merit and/or need. As part of an overall financial aid package, housing grants can be the difference between making a college education accessible or inaccessible to students with specific characteristics and needs. Targeted housing grants also contribute to increasing retention and persistence rates by providing financial incentives to remain in campus housing.

As previously stated, the recruitment and retention of minority students is an increasing concern for most colleges and universities. From an enrollment management perspective, it is critically important for special populations such as African Americans, Hispanic Americans, and Asian Americans to establish an early identification with their preferred institution. Residence life staff, in conjunction with admissions officers and academic administrators, should jointly sponsor summer institutes for such specially targeted populations. By offering these initiatives between the ninth and eleventh grades, staff can give these students opportunities for academic skill enhancement, precollege orientation, and personal development. Certain national organizations committed to minority talent development, such as INROADS, Inc., have been quite successful in cosponsoring such programs with various colleges and universities.

Focus More Attention on Retaining Students. Although the recruitment of new students is a critical dimension of the enrollment management program, college administrators are quick to admit that it is much more cost effective to retain students than to recruit new ones. Retention is a function of a number of critical variables; however, Tinto (1975) has suggested that the greater the degree of academic and social integration students experience, the greater the likelihood of their continued enrollment. An appropriate focus of retention efforts is the nature of the interaction of the individual student with specific aspects of the campus environment. Simply put, if students' needs and aspirations are fulfilled through their participation in residence hall communities, there is a significant probability that they will choose to stay, not only in those communities, but in the institution as well.

As highlighted in previous chapters, residence life programs that offer diverse living arrangements, often built around academic themes or homogeneous groupings, tend to achieve higher student retention and persistence rates than usual. Such units are typically characterized by high degrees of student involvement, peer support, influence, and social stability—factors essential for students' academic and social integration.

If residence life staff are to play an even more dramatic role in the retention of students, they must understand persistence and attrition patterns within their housing systems. This requires well-developed assessment and information management technologies. For example, housing staff, working in conjunction with academic administrators, should identify segments of the student population most "at risk." Students within these segments could be offered housing options specially designed to help them develop the requisite skills and attitudes necessary to ensure their success. Important services provided by departments such as counseling, career planning and placement, and learning skills centers could be integrated into these units on an outreach basis. As a result, students at risk could be provided with more extensive support to increase the probability of their success, thereby increasing retention.

Improved retention rates strengthen the financial viability of colleges and universities. During this decade, both public and private institutions will struggle to meet rising costs while resources diminish. Housing and residence life programs are not immune to these challenges. Indeed, to address them, residence life programs with student development goals must prudently utilize limited resources in the service of specific and well-developed goals.

Prudently Utilize Limited Resources

Housing programs on many campuses are struggling to provide high-quality services and effective programs without adequate resources. As stated in Chapter Eight, the deferred maintenance of the past decade alone is estimated to be a $300 billion problem for higher education. Facilities that were rapidly constructed during the 1950s and 1960s when enrollments were expanding are now in need of major refurbishing. To cut the cost of construction, many of these facilities were designed with built-in furniture, small cell-like rooms, and limited space for social interaction, particularly on individual floors. Many of these facilities are not meeting the new, though sometimes unrealistic, expectations of today's students, who are much more materialistic and expect a host of amenities not provided to students of previous generations. Furthermore, as technology continues to expand, many students and faculty expect residence halls to provide easy access to new technological tools, such as computer workstations, electronic mail, and other items that require major outlays of capital.

Engage in Systematic Strategic Planning. To address the preceding issues, housing and residence life staff must commit themselves to an ongoing process of strategic planning. Such a process requires residence life programs to have a well-developed mission statement, a thorough understanding of internal and external environmental factors that impact their ability to accomplish their mission, clearly stated goals and priorities, and mechanisms for strategically allocating resources in the service of objectives. Perhaps the most significant challenge of strategic planning is clarifying the basic purposes of the housing and residence life programs. During this decade, staff simply cannot be all things to all people. Difficult choices must be made on the basis of rational criteria. Furthermore, housing and residence life strategic plans must be congruent with strategic initiatives of the division of student affairs and the institution at large.

   In some colleges and universities, the strategic planning process is being driven by a commitment to total-quality management (TQM). The TQM perspective includes a number of themes, the most relevant being a focus on quality, an absolute commitment to customer satisfaction, an emphasis on continuous improvement, utilization of information to determine results, and empowerment of staff to act responsibly by giving them appropriate authority. Although TQM is relatively new on the higher education scene, Marchese (1991) believes that it is more than a passing fancy and will be adopted by many institutions during this decade. A principal benefit of TQM is that it impels staff to focus on fundamental issues of purpose and quality improvement, using strategic planning and information technology as means of accomplishing these ends. In reviewing TQM applications to date, Seymour (1991) found that quality improvement was most frequently initiated in nonacademic areas and that student housing procedures and physical maintenance of residence halls were often included in the TQM program. Housing and residence life professionals could find TQM a helpful tool in prudently utilizing diminishing resources.

On the surface, TQM appears to focus exclusively on a service orientation with students. Some professionals argue that TQM conjures up an image of residence halls as "supermarkets," where staff "serve up" various programs and services with the greatest customer appeal. Perhaps it is more fruitful to view TQM from the perspective of Maslow's hierarchy of needs. Residence life programs have an obligation to provide students with effectively managed basic services that meet their physiological, safety, and security needs (housekeeping, maintenance, dining, and so on). Higher-order needs, such as belonging, affiliation, self-esteem, and self-actualization, can also be addressed through a TQM program, particularly one that focuses on creating powerful transactions between individuals and groups.

For residence life programs with student development goals, the TQM model does not focus exclusively on a service orientation, but rather accepts high-quality services as an essential component of the learning environment. Such variables as academic achievement, persistence, and personal development are clearly outcomes of a total-quality residence life program. The key to implementing TQM is to simply accept the necessary and appropriate balance between a service orientation and a commitment to student development, often reconciling, in the process, the dialectic between what students want and what they need. Clearly, personal development can be challenging and, at times, painful. From an educational perspective, total quality assumes that personal development and learning are the most important outcomes of a collegiate residence hall experience.

Develop Entrepreneurial Initiatives. In prior decades, housing programs benefited from a phenomenon associated with the popular movie *Field of Dreams*: "build it and they will come." In the future, when enrollments are projected to decline along with state and federal support for higher education, housing and residence life programs must become much more entrepreneurial if they are to raise the capital to fund renovations necessitated by past deferred maintenance and meet the customer-driven needs and wants of contemporary college students. After determining crucial needs through the strategic planning process, housing administrators should work with staff in their development or institutional advancement offices to ensure that their needs are included as goals in capital campaigns. In some universities, such as Colorado State and Arizona State, chief student affairs officers have been very successful in hiring their own development officers, who solicit contributions to fund important student life projects. Former student leaders, resident assistants, and alumni from various halls are often eager and willing to donate funds to help the housing program.

The strategic planning process should help housing professionals develop strategies for reducing costs as well as generating new sources of income. Because most institutions incur costs over a twelve-month period but generate income in only nine of those months, housing staff should consider developing comprehensive summer conference programs and aggressively marketing them to youth groups, senior citizens, and academic administrators. By maintaining certain occupancy levels throughout the fiscal year, adequate resources can be generated to finance needed improvements.

Utilize New Technology. Residence life programs committed to student development goals are recognizing the profound implications of technology in accomplishing educational objectives. Many institutions, such as Dartmouth, Drake, the University of Maine, Bradley, and Georgia Tech, among others, have sophisticated computer and information technology networks integrated within their residence halls. At Georgia Tech, for example, students can make room change requests and complete the formal contracting process through on-line access from their rooms. Such a process has many advantages, including eliminating lines and input errors as well as providing this option around the clock. Georgia Tech students also have the opportunity to register for classes using computer clusters with on-line access in their living units.

In 1991, Washington State University unveiled plans to install one of the country's most ambitious fiber optic networks under a $25 million program to integrate voice, video, and data telecommunications services. The system connects more than 125 buildings on the Pullman campus, handling the communication needs of 15,000 students as well as 5,000 faculty and administrative staff. The system connects several hundred departmental terminals, personal computers, workstations, minicomputers, and the mainframe complex. The residence halls are a primary beneficiary of the new network, with on-line capability for residents.

Finally, Georgia Tech is implementing interactive computer programs in various residence halls to assist students in conducting self-assessments of their personal skills and competencies. Following the assessment, students use their personal computers to scan a menu of various campus involvement opportunities that focus on the acquisition of specific skills and competencies. After participating in the desired campus activities, students obtain certificates acknowledging that they have acquired the desired attributes. As a result, residents can present prospective employers with a personal development portfolio that complements their academic transcript.

Both internal and external support for housing and residence life programs in the years ahead will be determined, to a large extent, by the degree to which these programs can demonstrate value to their students and their institutions. Demonstrating such value requires well-developed assessment and information management programs.

Demonstrate the Value of Programs and Services

In a decade of tight budgets and rapidly diminishing resources, institutions are forced to make difficult decisions concerning the value of various programs and services. Questioning the value of student affairs divisions is becoming more commonplace as tight budgets demand tough decisions. Although staff in housing and residence life programs occasionally evaluate the quality of their efforts, in general, most programs do a relatively poor job of examining and documenting their impact on students and their institutions. Indeed, arguments based on theoretical models or professional literature are often unconvincing in the face of limited resources and competitive pressures. What is needed is an ongoing and systematic approach to assessing program effectiveness and evaluation.

Develop Ongoing Assessment and Evaluation Efforts. Perhaps the most significant first step in implementing an ongoing assessment and evaluation initiative is helping housing professionals understand the kinds of questions worth asking, the information worth having, and the available means for generating the information to address the critical questions. For residence life programs with student development goals, some of the most crucial questions are as follows:

1. What are the desired outcomes of a residential living experience?
2. What should students learn as a result of living in residence halls?
3. How does a residential experience contribute to the broader educational goals of the institution?
4. How do different types of students (for example, African Americans and women) experience residential living?
5. How satisfied are students with certain services, programs, and activities?
6. What patterns characterize students' movement through the residence hall system?
7. What are students' contributions to their residence hall experience?
8. What specific contributions do residence halls make to students' learning and personal development?
9. Are there real differences between resident and commuter students regarding retention, academic achievement, and personal development?
10. Are certain student subpopulations overrepresented or underrepresented in residence halls?

To answer many of these questions, housing and residence life staff must become experts on their students. They must understand students' expectations, needs, and interests and how they interact with different aspects of the residential experience. As suggested in Chapter Sixteen, staff can utilize a variety of evaluation and assessment techniques to generate information for answering these questions. Such techniques might include unobtrusive measures as well as qualitative and quantitative approaches.

Take a Broad View of Assessment. Although the recent assessment movement has focused a great deal of attention on "outcomes," assessment should provide fundamental information that helps staff and students improve the quality of the learning environment within residence halls. Hutchings (1989) argues for an expanded view of assessment, one that emphasizes understanding variations in the way different students learn and develop and how these variations are affected by different environmental conditions. Such a perspective not only focuses on what happens to students, but more important, on how it happens and under what conditions.

Housing and residence life professionals who demonstrate the value of their programs and services to major institutional stakeholders (that is, senior administrators, faculty, academic deans, and governing boards) will be less vulnerable to shifting economic agendas and diminishing resources. Furthermore, although assessment and evaluation have generally been considered optional for many programs, as argued in Chapter Sixteen, most accrediting agencies are now requiring institutions to demonstrate their overall impact on students. By including assessment as part of professional standards and accreditation expectations, student affairs divisions and housing units will be compelled to address this issue. Although compliance with external demands is increasingly required, one should not lose sight of the real reason for evaluating the quality of residence life programs—to improve student learning and personal development. Indeed, housing and residence life staff have a professional obligation to ensure that their efforts are achieving these desired results. (See also Winston and Moore, 1991, for further discussion of outcomes assessment in student affairs.)

New Challenges and Opportunities

This chapter has delineated a number of challenges and opportunities for residence life programs with student development goals. Implicit throughout the chapter is the notion that staff must examine traditional assumptions about their professional practice and the nature of the students they are called on to serve and educate. In response to growing enrollments and greater institutional complexity, housing programs have become increasingly specialized, compartmentalized, and distant from the educational mission of the institution. Too much staff energy is devoted to supporting such traditional structures as resident assistants, judicial boards, programming councils, developmental programs, and hall councils. The proliferation of these efforts and the amount of staff time devoted to them are reminiscent of Woodrow Wilson's comment on the expansion of the extracurriculum during his tenure as president of Princeton in 1909. He stated that "'the sideshows are so numerous, so diverting—so important, if you will—that they have swallowed up the circus'" (in Brubacher and Rudy, 1968, p. 120). Though residence halls have attempted to become more educationally and developmentally viable settings, their programs and services are still often viewed as removed from the core of undergraduate education, being regarded as marginal or peripheral to the educational priorities of the institution.

A number of responses for residence life programs concerned about challenges facing higher education, student affairs, and their institutions have been suggested that expand traditional roles for housing. To successfully address these challenges, residence life staff must venture beyond the predictable and secure organizational boundaries within which they routinely operate. They must develop authentic partnerships with academic colleagues and staff from other institutional divisions. They must engage in ongoing planning efforts and strategically utilize limited resources in the service of well-developed goals and priorities. Finally, they must celebrate the fundamental purpose of a college or university—to promote learning—and shape educationally powerful environments that ensure student learning and personal development.

References

Astin, A. W. *Four Critical Years: Effects of College on Beliefs, Attitudes, and Knowledge.* San Franciso: Jossey-Bass, 1977.

Berman, P. "A New Perspective on Implementation Design: Adaptive Implementation." In P. D. Hood (ed.), *New Perspectives on Planning, Management, and Evaluation in School Improvement.* San Francisco: Far West Laboratory for Educational Research and Development, 1979.

Blake, E. "Classroom and Context: An Educational Dialectic." *Academe,* 1979, *65,* 280–292.

Blimling, G. S., and Schuh, J. H. (eds.). *Increasing the Educational Role of Residence Halls.* New Directions for Student Services, no. 13. San Francisco: Jossey-Bass, 1981.

Boyer, E. L. *College: The Undergraduate Experience in America.* New York: HarperCollins, 1987.

Brubacher, J. S., and Rudy, W. *Higher Education in Transition.* New York: HarperCollins, 1968.

Davis, M., and Schroeder, C. "New Students in Liberal Arts Colleges: Threat or Challenge?" In J. Watson and R. Stevens (eds.), *Pioneers and Pallbearers: Perspectives on Liberal Education.* Macon, Ga.: Mercer University Press, 1982.

DeCoster, D. A., and Mable, P. (eds.). *Personal Education and Community Development in College Residence Halls.* Cincinnati, Ohio: American College Personnel Association, 1980.

Garland, P. H. *Serving More Than Students.* Washington, D.C.: Association for the Study of Higher Education, 1985.

Hossler, D. *Creating Effective Enrollment Management Systems.* New York: College Entrance Examination Board, 1986.

Hossler, D., Bean, J. P., and Associates. *The Strategic Management of College Enrollments.* San Francisco: Jossey-Bass, 1990.

Hutchings, P. *Behind Outcomes: Context and Questions for Assessment.* AAHE Assessment Forum Resource Paper. Washington, D.C.: American Association for Higher Education, 1989.

Jackson, S. G., and Stevens, S. "Incorporating Faculty and Staff into Residence Halls." *Journal of College and University Student Housing,* 1990, *20*(1), 7–10.

Kuh, G. D., Schuh, J. H., Whitt, E. J., and Associates. *Involving Colleges: Successful Approaches to Fostering Student Learning and Development Outside the Classroom.* San Francisco: Jossey-Bass, 1991.

Mable, P., Terry, M., and Duvall, W. J. "A Model of Student Development Through Community Responsibility." *Journal of College Student Personnel,* 1977, *18*, 50–56.

Marchese, T. "TQM Reaches Academe." *AAHE Bulletin,* 1991, *44*(3), 3–9.

Mayhew, L. B., Ford, P. J., and Hubbard, D. L. *The Quest for Quality: The Challenge for Undergraduate Education in the 1990s.* San Francisco: Jossey-Bass, 1990.

Merante, J. A. "Organizing to Manage Enrollment." *College Board Review,* 1987, *145*, 14–17, 31–33.

National Association of Student Personnel Administrators. *A Perspective on Student Affairs.* Washington, D.C.: National Association of Student Personnel Administrators, 1987.

Newton, F. B. "Community Building Strategies with Student Groups." In F. Newton and K. Ender (eds.), *Student Development Practices.* Springfield, Ill.: Thomas, 1980.

Pascarella, E. T., and Terenzini, P. T. *How College Affects Students: Findings and Insights from Twenty Years of Research.* San Francisco: Jossey-Bass, 1991.

Schroeder, C. C., DiTiberio, J. K., and Kalsbeek, D. H. "Bridging the Gap Between Faculty and Students: Opportunities and Obligations for Student Affairs." *NASPA Journal,* 1988, *26*, 14–20.

Schroeder, C. C., and Jackson, S. G. "Creating Conditions for Student Development in Campus Living Environments." *NASPA Journal,* 1987, *25*, 45–53.

Seymour, D. T. "TQM on Campus: What the Pioneers Are Finding." *AAHE Bulletin,* 1991, *44*(3), 10–13.

Tinto, V. "Drop Out from Higher Education: A Theoretical Synthesis of Recent Research." *Review of Educational Research,* 1975, *43*, 89–125.

Upcraft, M. L., Gardner, J. N., and Associates. *The Freshman Year Experience: Helping Students Survive and Succeed in College.* San Francisco: Jossey-Bass, 1989.

Winston, R. B., Jr., and Moore, W. S. "Standards and Outcomes Assessment: Strategies and Tools." In W. A. Bryan, R. B. Winston, Jr., and T. K. Miller (eds.), *Using Professional Standards in Student Affairs.* New Directions for Student Services, no. 53. San Francisco: Jossey-Bass, 1991.

Resource A

========

Council for the Advancement of Standards for Student Services/Development Programs: Standards and Guidelines for Housing and Residential Life Programs

Part 1: Mission

The institution and the residential life program must develop, review, and disseminate regularly their own specific goals for student services/development, which must be consistent with the nature and goals of the institution and with the standards in this document.

The residential life program is an integral part of the educational program and academic support services of the institution. The mission must include provision for educational programs and services, residential facilities, management services, and, where appropriate, food services.

To accomplish the mission, the goals of the program must provide:

- **a living-learning environment that enhances individual growth and development;**

- facilities that ensure well-maintained, safe, and sanitary housing conditions for students, and otherwise accommodate residential life programs;
- management services that ensure the orderly and effective administration of all aspects of the program; and
- food, dining facilities, and related services that effectively meet institutional and residential life program goals in programs that include food services.

Part 2: Program

Residential life programs must be (a) purposeful, (b) coherent, (c) based on or related to theories and knowledge of human development and learning characteristics, and (d) reflective of the demographic and developmental profiles of the student body.

The residential life program must promote student development by encouraging such things as positive and realistic self-appraisal, intellectual development, appropriate personal and occupational choices, clarification of values, physical fitness, the ability to relate meaningfully with others, the capacity to engage in a personally satisfying and effective style of living, the capacity to appreciate cultural and esthetic differences, and the capacity to work independently and interdependently.

The residential life program must assist students in overcoming specific personal, physical, or educational problems or skill deficiencies.

The residential life program must identify environmental conditions that may negatively influence welfare and propose interventions that may neutralize such conditions or improve the environment.

The educational experience of students consists of both academic efforts in the classroom and developmental opportunities through residential life. Institutions must define the relative importance of these processes.

To effectively fulfill its mission and goals, the program must provide the following:

1. Individual and group educational and developmental opportunities

Opportunities should include activities and/or experiences in:

- living cooperatively with others;
- developing and clarifying values;
- developing independence and self-sufficiency;
- developing appreciation for new ideas, cultural differences, and life style differences;
- enhancing respect for self, others, and property;
- exploring and improving interpersonal relationships;

- making educational and career decisions;
- acquiring and using knowledge;
- understanding and managing personal health requirements, personal finances, and time:
- developing and exercising leadership skills;
- exploring and managing the use of leisure time;
- promoting and demonstrating responsible social behavior such as non-exploitive and nondiscriminatory racial and sexual relationships; and
- promoting and demonstrating a proper understanding of the results of drug and alcohol use.

Educational programming, advising, and supervisory activities of the residential life staff should address developmental objectives and will vary in accordance with locally assessed needs. Examples include:

- introduction and orientation of students to services, facilities, staff members, and staff functions;
- education on safety, security, and emergency precautions and procedures;
- encouragement of student participation in institutional and residence hall programs;
- encouragement of an atmosphere conducive to academic pursuits;
- explanation of institutional and residential living policies, procedures, and expectations;
- provision of information about relevant civil and criminal laws;
- provision of written institutional disciplinary policies and procedures;
- encouragement of students to develop a sense of responsibility for their community through:
  - participation in policy decisions,
  - confrontation of and education about inappropriate and disruptive behavior,
  - participation in mediating conflict within the community,
  - assessing fair charges to individual(s) responsible for damages, and
  - participation in evaluating the housing program;
- provision of academic information;
- provision of a planned array of social, recreational, educational, and cultural programs;
- assessment of needs for special interest populations;
- making appropriate referrals;
- provision of individual advising or counseling support; and
- provision of student consumer information.

2. *Residential facilities that are clean, safe, well maintained, reasonably priced, attractive, comfortable, properly designed, and conducive to study.*

Functions associated with this goal include: maintenance and renovation, equipment replacement, custodial care, energy conservation, and grounds care.

- Maintenance/renovation programs should be implemented in all housing operations and may include: (a) a preventive maintenance program designed to extend the life of the equipment and facilities, (b) a program designed to repair in a timely manner equipment and building systems as they become inoperable, and (c) a renovation program that modifies physical facilities and building systems to make them more effective, attractive, efficient, and safe.
- Systematically planned equipment replacement programs should exist for furnishings, mechanical systems, maintenance equipment, carpeting, draperies, and kitchen equipment, where applicable.
- Regularly scheduled cleaning of public areas should be provided.
- Energy conservation efforts should be implemented through educational programs, as well as through timely renovation and replacement of inefficient equipment and obsolete facilities.
- Grounds, which may include streets, walks, and parking lots, should be safe, clean, and attractively maintained.

3. Management functions including planning, personnel, property management, purchasing, contract administration, financial control, and, where applicable, conference administration.

Financial reports should be available to all responsible offices and should be utilized to provide an accurate financial picture of the organization, and to provide clear, understandable, and timely data on which housing officers and others can base decisions and make plans.

Representatives of the residence hall and family housing communities should be given the opportunity to comment on proposed rate increases and operating budgets. Rate increases should be announced and discussed well in advance of their effective date.

Purchasing and property management procedures should be designed to ensure value for money spent, security for supplies and furnishings, and maintenance of proper inventories.

Clear and comprehensive communications and written individual housing agreements should be utilized to establish terms applicable to students and to the institution. There should be clear communication to students, other interested members of the campus community, and potential residents of the procedures and priorities for securing a room and/or board contract. Procedures for canceling, subleasing, or being released from a contract should be written and distributed, if there are provisions for such release.

All service functions should be efficiently and effectively managed. Any off-campus housing referral or information service and any conference operation should be administered in a manner consistent with the mission and goals of the institution.

4. Food services, where applicable, which provide high quality, nutritious, and reasonably priced meals

Food services should include provision of a variety of nutritional meals, secure and sanitary food storage, recipes which ensure appetizing food, good customer relations, pleasant dining environments, and safe and sanitary conditions.

Part 3: Leadership and Management

[Institution level only, See General Standards]

Part 4: Organization and Administration

The residential life program must develop its own set of policies and procedures that include a detailed description of the administrative process and an organizational chart showing the job functions and reporting relationships within and beyond the program.

An effectively unified organizational structure, including both management and program functions, should be employed. In this way, the entire organization can function to meet all the housing needs of students, rather than through multiple and separate organizational lines of communication and authority. Where the campus organization dictates a split structure, it is the joint responsibility of the program and the management staffs to establish and maintain effective communication.

Part 5: Human Resources

The residential life program must have adequate and qualified professional staff to fulfill its mission and to implement all aspects of the program. To be qualified, professional staff members must have a graduate degree in a field of study relevant to the particular job in question or must have an appropriate combination of education and experience. In any residential life program in which there is a full-time director, that director must possess levels of education and/or professional experience beyond that of the staff to be supervised.

Preprofessional or support staff members employed in the residential life program must be qualified by relevant education and experience. Degree requirements, including both degree levels and subject matter, must be germane to the particular job responsibilities. Such staff members must be trained appropriately and supervised adequately by professional staff.

Paraprofessionals must be carefully selected, trained with respect to helping skills and institutional services and procedures, closely supervised, and evaluated regularly. Their compensation must be fair and any

voluntary services must be recognized adequately. Paraprofessionals must recognize the limitations of their knowledge and skills and must refer students to appropriate professionals when the problems encountered warrant.

To ensure that professional staff members devote adequate time to professional duties, the residential life program must have sufficient clerical and technical support staff. Such support must be of sufficient quantity and quality to accomplish the following kinds of activities: typing, filing, telephone and other receptionist duties, bookkeeping, maintaining student records, organizing resource materials, receiving students and making appointments, and handling routine correspondence.

Salary level and fringe benefits for staff must be commensurate with those for similar professional, preprofessional, and clerical positions at the institution and in the geographic area.

To ensure the existence of suitable and readily identifiable role models within the campus teaching and administrative ranks, staff employment profiles must reflect representation of categories of persons who comprise the student population. However, where student bodies are predominantly nondisabled, of one race, sex, or religion, a diverse staffing pattern will enrich the teaching/administrative ranks and will demonstrate institutional commitment to fair employment practices.

The residential life program must have a regular system of staff selection and evaluation, and must provide continuing professional development opportunities for staff including inservice training programs, participation in professional conferences, workshops, and other continuing education activities.

The staff must consist of one or more professionals who is aware of the goals, objectives, and philosophy of the residential life program.

All housing professional staff members should strive to develop and maintain staff relations in a climate of mutual respect, support, trust, and interdependence, recognizing the strengths and limitations of each professional colleague.

The director and other professional staff members must have an appropriate combination of graduate coursework, formal training, and supervised work experience.

Professionally-Trained Staff Members

An effective housing staff consists not only of professionally trained staff members but also paraprofessional, technical, clerical, and other support staff members. Qualifications for housing officer positions can be gained through formal academic preparations, workshops, self-study, work experience, participation in professional organizations, and in-service training.

Chief housing officers (i.e., director) should have attained a graduate degree in higher education, business administration, or a behavioral science, or possess an appropriate combination of education and experience.

The director should have knowledge of and experience with human behavior and business management. Recommended concentration areas for preparation are (a) human behavior (e.g., learning theory, philosophical foundations, social psychology, American college student, contemporary issues, minority concerns) and (b) business management (e.g., accounting, statistics, marketing, budgeting and report analysis, computers, and business management functions such as planning, organization, staffing, directing, and controlling).

The housing officer in charge of physical plant administration should possess at least a bachelor's degree and related experience in engineering and maintenance. This officer should coordinate residential staff and students' interactions with the functions of construction, maintenance, and custodial work. This includes all areas of construction and maintenance of residential facilities. These functions should be carried out with full cognizance and in support of educational goals, under the direction of the chief housing officer. Recommended academic areas related to preparation for this position include (a) architecture and design principles; (b) construction and engineering principles, and (c) prevention maintenance theory and practice.

The administrator in charge of food service should have earned at least a bachelor's degree in dietetics or hotel and restaurant administration and have substantial experience in the food services.

It is the responsibility of the food services officer to manage those functions that are necessary to provide wholesome, appetizing, and nutritious meals for students, conferees, and guests. The functions should be carried out with food services staff and in support of residential education, under the direction of the chief housing officer. Preparation for this position may include courses in (a) dietetics and menu planning, (b) principles of public health and sanitation, and (c) institutional food services management.

The administrator in charge of educational programming should possess at least a master's degree in college student personnel, counseling or related field, or an appropriate combination of education and experience.

Demonstrated skills of leadership and communication, maturity, a well developed sense of responsibility, sensitivity to individual differences, a positive self-concept, academic success, and an obvious interest and enthusiasm for working with students are desirable characteristics for both professional and paraprofessional staff members.

Educational programming should provide for interaction with academic faculty so that students' living experiences complement and reinforce classroom learning. Recommended courses for preparation for programming positions may include: (a) developmental psychology, (b) group theory, (c) American college student, (d) contemporary issues, (e) minority concerns, and (f) principles of management.

The housing officer in charge of central office administration should possess a graduate degree in any of the areas previously cited as well as significant administrative experience. Recommended courses for preparation for office administration may include: (a) introduction to college housing principles, (b) college law and landlord/tenant law, (c) labor relations, (d) organizational theory, (e) communications, (f) personnel administration, (g) public relations, (h) higher education administration, (i) research and evaluation, (j) management principle, (k) organizational development, and (l) principles of college student development.

Resident Assistants (Paraprofessionals)

Residential life operations are highly dependent upon the use of part-time student employees (the most common example being resident assistants) for the implementation of all programs that impact student residents. The resident assistants are expected to contribute to the accomplishment of the following functions: (a) educational programming, (b) administration, (c) group and activity advising, (d) leadership development, (e) discipline, (f) role modeling, and (g) paraprofessional counseling.

Part 6: Funding

The residential life program must have funding sufficient to carry out its mission and to support the following, where applicable: staff salaries; purchase and maintenance of office furnishing, supplies, materials, and equipment, including current technology; phone and postage costs; printing and media costs; institutional memberships in appropriate professional organizations; relevant subscriptions and necessary library resources; attendance at professional association meetings, conferences, and workshops; and other professional development activities. In addition to institutional funding commitment through general funds, other funding sources may be considered, including: state appropriations, student fees, user fees, donations and contributions, fines, concession and store sales, rentals, and dues.

Funding should be adequate to provide for continuous upkeep of facilities, major maintenance and renovation of facilities, educational programming, and services to residents. Adequate reserves for essential repairs, replacement, and capital improvements should be provided.

Student governance units (e.g., hall or campus-wide residential councils) should have access to accounting offices and services to effectively carry out their functions. Dues collected from students for programs and services should be managed within the institution. Fees collected through the use of housing facilities should be dedicated to the support and improvement of housing programs and facilities.

Part 7: Facilities

The residential life program must be provided adequate facilities to fulfill its mission. As applicable, the facilities for residential life programs must include, or the program must have access to, the following: private offices or private spaces for counseling, interviewing, or other meetings of a confidential nature; office, reception, and storage space sufficient to accommodate assigned staff, supplies, equipment, library resources, and machinery; and conference room or meeting space. All facilities must be accessible to disabled persons and must be in compliance with relevant federal, state, and local health and safety requirements.

Facilities must provide sufficient and appropriate space to accommodate program goals and objectives and meet students' needs for safety and security. Facilities must be maintained at optimal levels of cleanliness, repair, and decor. Spaces provided must include adequate areas for study, office functions, lounging, recreation, and group meetings.

Individual rooms should be adequately furnished to accommodate all occupants assigned to the room. All community bathrooms and other public areas should be cleaned at least daily on week days. Ramps, bathrooms, elevators, room fixtures, and other appropriate special provisions to accommodate mobility-impaired students should be well maintained, clearly marked, and their availability thoroughly communicated to current and potential students. Public common areas such as study rooms, exercise rooms, TV rooms, and kitchens, should be adequately furnished to accommodate a planned number of residents. Sufficient space for maintenance work and storage should be available in close proximity to the assigned area of the maintenance and custodial staff. Residence halls should be furnished and maintained in a manner designed to provide security, comfort, and an atmosphere conducive to study, as well as providing facilities that promote individual growth and development. Adequate office space and equipment for staff should be provided. Laundry facilities should be provided within or in close proximity to living areas.

Part 8: Legal Responsibilities

Staff members must be knowledgeable about and responsive to relevant civil and criminal laws and must be responsible for ensuring that the institution fulfills its legal obligations. Staff members in residential life must be well versed in those obligations and limitations imposed on the operation of residential life programs by local, state, and federal constitutional, statutory, regulatory, and common law, and by institutional policy. They must utilize appropriate policies and practices to limit the liability exposure of the institution, its officers, employees, and agents. The institution must provide access to legal advice to professional staff as needed to carry out assigned responsibilities.

Part 9: Equal Opportunity, Access, and Affirmative Action

The residential life program must adhere to the spirit and intent of equal opportunity laws in all activities. The program must ensure that its services and facilities are accessible to and provide hours of operation that respond to the needs of special student populations, including traditionally under-represented, evening, part-time, and commuter students.

Personnel policies shall not discriminate on the basis of race, sex, color, religion, age, national origin and/or handicap. In hiring and promotion policies, student services professionals must take affirmative action that strives to remedy significant staffing imbalance, particularly when resulting from past discriminatory practices. The residential life program must seek to identify, prevent and/or remedy other discriminatory practices.

Part 10: Campus and Community Relations

The residential life program must maintain good relations with relevant campus offices and external agencies, which necessarily requires regular identification of the offices with whom such relationships are critical.

Particular efforts should be made by the staff to develop positive relationships with campus and off-campus agencies responsible for student counseling services, student health services, student activities, security and safety, academic advising, campus mail and telephone services, physical plant services, institutional budgeting and planning, vendors and suppliers of products used in residence halls, and private and commercial housing operators.

Representatives of the residence hall and family housing communities should be given the opportunity for comment on proposed rate increases and the operating budget.

Housing staff members should be particularly aware of and supportive of the role of faculty. Faculty members should be encouraged to become involved in the residential program by presenting workshops, lectures, symposia, or by other means. Possibilities for faculty members to reside for a scheduled time in the residence halls as a community building activity or to accomplish a specific program objective should exist.

Part 11: Multi-Cultural Programs and Services

The institution's residential life program must provide to members of its majority and minority cultures' educational efforts that focus on awareness of cultural differences, self-assessment of possible prejudices, and desirable behavioral changes.

The residential life program must provide educational programs that help minority students identify their unique needs, prioritize those needs, and meet them to the degree that numbers of students, facilities, and resources permit. The program must orient minority students to the culture of the institution and promote and deepen their understanding of their own culture and heritage.

Part 12: Ethics

All persons involved in the provision of housing and residential life programs to students must maintain the highest standards of ethical behavior. Residential life program staff members must develop and adopt standards of ethical practice addressing the unique problems that face personnel in that area. The standards must be published and reviewed by all concerned. In the formulation of those standards, ethical standards statements previously adopted by the profession at large or relevant professional associations may be of assistance and must be considered.

Certain ethical obligations apply to all individuals employed in student services/development programs, for example: All staff members must ensure that confidentiality is maintained with respect to all communications and records considered confidential. Unless written permission is given by the student, information disclosed in individual counseling sessions must remain confidential. In addition, all requirements of the Family Educational Rights and Privacy Act (Buckley Amendment) must be complied with and information contained in students' educational records must not be disclosed to third parties without appropriate consent, unless one of the relevant statutory exceptions applies. A similar dedication to privacy and confidentiality must be applied to research data concerning individuals.

All staff members must be aware of and comply with the provisions contained in the institution's human subjects policy and in any other institutional policy addressing ethical practice.

All staff members must ensure that students are provided access to services on a fair and equitable basis. All staff members must avoid any personal conflict of interest so they can deal objectively and impartially with persons within and outside the institution. In many instances, the appearance of a conflict of interest can be as damaging as an actual conflict. Whenever handling funds, all staff must ensure that such funds are handled in accordance with established and responsible accounting procedures.

Staff members must not participate in any form of sexual harassment. Sexual harassment is defined to include sexual advances, requests for sexual favors, as well as other verbal or physical conduct of a sexual nature if

(1) submission to such conduct is made either explicitly or implicitly a term or condition of an individual's employment,

academic progress, or any other outcome of an official nature,
(2)...is used as the basis for such decisions or outcomes...,
(3)...has the purpose or effect of unreasonably interfering
with an individual's work performance or creating an intim-
idating, hostile, or offensive working environment [29 Code of
Federal Regulations, C.F.R., Section 1604.11 (a)].

**All staff members must recognize the limits of their training, exper-
tise, and competence and must refer students in need of further expertise
to persons possessing appropriate qualifications.**
The housing professional should acknowledge a special responsibility
for the welfare of resident students. Because of the enormity of time spent in
the residential setting and the breadth of impact that it can have on the life of
the student, an extraordinary sense of concern for successful study and
development is appropriate.
All housing professionals have an obligation to understand the educational goals of the institution and to aid in the support and realization of
these goals.
Each housing professional should accept students as individuals, each
with rights and responsibilities, each with goals, and needs, and with this in
mind seek to create and maintain a group living environment that enhances
learning and personal development.

Part 13: Evaluation

**There must be systematic and regular research on and evaluation of the
overall institutional student services/development program and the residential life program to determine whether the educational goals and the
needs of students are being met. Although methods of evaluation may vary,
they must utilize both quantitative and qualitative measures. Data collected must include responses from students and other significant constituencies. Results of these regular evaluations must be used in revising and
improving the program goals and implementation.**

Resource B

CAS Standards and Guidelines
for Student Services/Development Programs:
Housing and Residential Life Programs
Self Assessment Guide

CAS developed the Self Assessment Guide to be used in conjunction with the 1986 and 1987 *CAS Standards and Guidelines*. A separate Self Assessment Guide has been prepared for each of the seventeen CAS Functional Area Standards and Guidelines. Each Guide reprints, in an integrated format in the appendix, the CAS General Standards and the CAS functional area standards and guidelines with which it is to be used. The guide is designed to aid interpretation and evaluation of the CAS Standards during a self-study process.

This document is a product of the Council for the Advancement of Standards. Those primarily responsible for its development and editing are: Theodore K. Miller, CAS President, University of Georgia; William L. Thomas, CAS Secretary, University of Maryland; Sara C. Looney, CAS Treasurer, George Mason University; Jean Yerian, CAS Board of Directors, Virginia Commonwealth University.

CAS Member Associations

American Association for Counseling and Development (AACD)

American College Personnel Association (ACPA)

Association of College and University Housing Officers-International (ACUHO-I)

Association of College Unions-International (ACU-I)

Association for Counselor Education and Supervision (ACES)

Association of Fraternity Advisors (AFA)

Association on Handicapped Student Services Programs in Post-secondary Education (AHSSPPE)

Association for School, College and University Staffing (ASCUS)

Association of University and College Counseling Center Directors (AUCCCD)

College Placement Council (CPC)

National Academic Advising Association (NACADA)

National Association of Campus Activities (NACA)

National Association of College Admission Counselors (NACAC)

National Association of Student Personnel Administrators (NASPA)

National Association for Women Deans, Administrators and Counselors (NAWDAC)

National Clearinghouse for Commuter Programs (NCCP)

National Council on Student Development (NCSD) [A Council of AACJC]

National Intramural-Recreational Sports Association (NIRSA)

National Orientation Directors Association (NODA)

Southern Association of College Student Affairs (SACSA)

This document [is] produced and disseminated for CAS under the auspices of ACT, American College Testing Program, 2201 North Dodge Street, Iowa City, Iowa 52243. Copies of the CAS Self Assessment Guides can [also] be obtained from: CAS, Office of Student Affairs, 2108 North Administration Building, University of Maryland, College Park, MD 20742.

I. Purpose and Organization of the Guide

This Self Assessment Guide translates the *CAS Standards and Guidelines* (1986) into a format for self-study purposes. By following this Guide, an institution can gain an informed perspective on its strengths and deficiencies and then plan for program improvement.

The first section of the Guide introduces the CAS Standards and Guidelines and details the roles of documentation and assessment in the self-study process. It also outlines the steps for developing a follow-up action plan to assure maximum benefit from time spent on the self-study.

The second section is in worksheet format. Each of its thirteen parts includes the following:

- Assessment criteria for determining the extent to which the program is in compliance with the Standards
- Space for including selected CAS Guidelines as additional assessment criteria for the self-study
- A scale for rating compliance judgments
- Space for identifying and summarizing evaluation evidence [documentation]
- Space for describing discrepancies between assessment criteria and actual program practice
- Space for delineating required corrective actions that need to be taken
- Space for recommending special actions for program enhancement

A note at the close of the Guide's rating and narrative worksheets reinforces the need for a follow-up plan and refers once more to the step-by-step action plan development process outlined in the first section.

The final section of the Guide is a reprint of the CAS Standards and Guidelines for this functional area in integrated format.

It is important to note that rating the assessment criteria in the Guide is not the end point of the self-study process. Ratings, whether done on an individual or a collective basis, constitute a necessary, but not sufficient, part of any self-study. The process also requires documentation and action planning.

II. Standards and Guidelines

The CAS Standards are requirements for minimal practice; CAS Guidelines, however, are suggestions for practice and are provided as an elaboration of the Standards. In the 1986 and 1987 *CAS Standards and Guidelines* and in this Self Assessment Guide, statements that reflect the CAS Standards [requirements] are printed in **BOLD** type. CAS Guidelines, which accompany the Standards, are printed in regular type and are intended to explain, amplify, or interpret the meaning of those Standards through the use of examples and more detailed descriptions. The Guidelines describe elements of programs and practice that are recommended, but which are not essential for a program to exhibit to be evaluated as being in compliance with the standards.

The CAS Standards assessment criteria in this Guide are organized into thirteen component parts and are presented in the following order:

1. Mission
2. Program
3. Leadership and Management
4. Organization and Administration
5. Human Resources

6. Funding
7. Facilities
8. Legal Issues
9. Equal Opportunity, Access, and Affirmative Action
10. Campus and Community Relations
11. Multi-Cultural
12. Ethics
13. Evaluation

Special Note: For further explanation about incorporating CAS Guidelines into the self-study process, consult Section V of this document.

III. Documentation

The collection, documentation, and inclusion of supporting evidence is an essential first step in the assessment process. No self-study is complete without relevant data and related documentation to support staff judgments. It is important to remember that completion of the Self Assessment Guide rating scales does NOT represent a full self-study.

Examples of the types of data that can and should be used to support evaluative judgments include the following:

1. *Relevant publications* (e.g., mission statements, catalogs, handbooks, staff manuals, policy manuals, annual reports)
2. *Descriptions of existing progams and interventions* (e.g., Career Development Center, alcohol awareness workshop, test anxiety reduction groups, new student orientation, Advising Center)
3. *Relevant institutional and other data* (e.g., student profiles, quantitative data, student needs assessment, theory-based assessments, and state, regional, and national data for comparisons)
4. *Program evaluation data* (e.g., surveys, ratings, interviews, reports, summaries)
5. *Self-study initiated research and evaluation data* (e.g., student surveys, ratings, follow-ups, and theory-based research studies designed to evaluate various aspects of the program/department/division using CAS Standards as measurement criteria)
6. *Resumes, job descriptions, performance evaluations, budgets, organization charts, and similar documents.*

Evaluations might include both quantitative data such as responses on a questionnaire and qualitative data such as a written summary of student evaluations obtained in group interviews to support a judgment on the effectiveness of a given program. The primary point is that some type of documentation and rationale to support the rater's judgments needs to be summarized in the Guide's narrative section, with the actual documented evidence appended as part of the self-study.

In many instances the self-study rating process will identify the need to collect additional data in order to evaluate a given criterion or to document the importance for providing new program offerings where none currently exist. When a criterion statement is obviously not met, evaluators should note *discrepancies* between the standards and the self-study findings and recommend corrective actions to be taken.

Because the primary purpose of the self-study is for program evaluation and development, virtually all student services/development programs self-studies will identify some needed changes, whether they be to address compliance of the standards or program enhancement. Few institutions will find that none of their services and programs require additional attention.

IV. Standards Assessment

Assessment Criteria are used to make judgments about the extent to which the program under study has met the various standards. Each statement reflects an essential element of the standard and can be rated using the following scale:

1	2	3	4	5	UK
Noncompliance				Compliance	Unknown

This rating scale provides a vehicle to obtain subjective estimates of the degree to which a given criterion has been met. The primary intention of any self-study process is to evaluate an institution's programs and services to determine how effective they are and to identify areas or component parts that can be improved. Only when a program or service is completely and fully in compliance with a particular standard should a "5" rating be made. To mark "5" when additional documentation is required, or when additional criteria need to be met for even minimal practice to be achieved, does a disservice to the institution and tends to invalidate the self-study.

Individual staff members can initially complete the Guide independently, and later the individual ratings can be combined to determine the extent to which the total staff believes the unit is in compliance with the various standards. Alternatively, independent judgments can be used to identify differences in perception and a group consensus can be sought.

While a numerical, quantitative rating scale provides rater(s) with a simple, yet standardized way to report and compare judgments, consistency among raters is not automatic. Raters should use relatively similar criteria when making judgments and so some type of rater "training" is helpful. Probably the simplest way to do this is to bring the raters together in a group to discuss the rating scale in an attempt to reach consensus on the process to be used *before initiating the rating process*.

Some institutions will wish to include certain CAS Guidelines in the self-study and may desire to write criterion statements for evaluators to document and rate in a fashion similar to that used for evaluating the CAS Standards. Space is made available to append such criteria following the assessment criterion statements in each part of the Guide.

V. Guidelines Assessment

Determination of compliance or noncompliance with program standards is minimally effective in the self-study process. CAS Guidelines provide additional examples of good practice. In many instances, program leaders will wish to use the CAS Guidelines as well as the CAS Standards in the self-study. Because the Self Assessment Guides do not include the CAS Guidelines, using the Guidelines will require special effort. The following example, from the Organization and Administration section of the CAS Research and Evaluation Standards, demonstrates one way to use both the CAS Standards (requirements) and CAS Guidelines (recommendations).

Standard: Since research and evaluation efforts are conducted on most campuses in cooperation with other institutional research and evaluation efforts, the chief student affairs officer must be central to the establishment of specific objectives for student services research and evaluation.

Guideline: Research and evaluation objectives should result from a collaborative effort between the chief student affairs officer, those responsible for the various student services programs, and others responsible for institutional research evaluation efforts.

Rating: The criterion statement reflecting this Standard is presented on page 4 of the *CAS Research and Evaluation Standards Self Assessment Guide* and reads as follows:

1	2	3	4	5	UK
Noncompliance				Compliance	Unknown

4.4   *The chief student affairs officer is central to the establishment*
      of objectives for student services' research and evaluation
      efforts.   4.4 _____

When rating the level of compliance with this Standard, the rater(s) can make their rating anywhere along the five-point continuum from noncompliance to compliance. If the Chief Student Affairs Officer (CSAO) has had nothing to do with any research and evaluation efforts, the rating would be "1." If the CSAO has sought to be kept minimally informed but has turned the task over to others, the rating might be "2," "3," or "4," depending upon the extent of the CSAO's involvement. If the CSAO has made special efforts to guide, inform, coordinate, and otherwise take leadership in the research and evaluation effort, the rating would probably be "5." It must be noted, however, that the criterion statement is designed to rate the observed behavior of the CSAO as required in the CAS Standards rather than to assess the *nature or quality* of his or her involvement such as the CAS Guidelines may suggest.

Interpretation: The Standard, in this example, is met when there is evidence that the CSAO has taken a primary role in specifying goals and objectives for the student services/development prorams research and evaluation effort. How the CSAO accomplishes this task, however, is not specified in the Standard. It is conceivable that one CSAO might do this without involving others in the institution while another CSAO might establish a task force of faculty members, student affairs staff members, and members of the institutional research office. Both might be judged as being in compliance with the Standard, but the latter also follows the collaborative pattern recommended in the Guideline. In effect, a program may be in compliance with the Standard, yet not meet the *quality* of practice suggested by the Guidelines.

VI. Follow-up Action Plan

After explaining the nature of a given program, reviewing all documentation, and recommending specific actions, the self-study committee needs to prepare a statement of overall action, a *Self-Study Follow-Up Action Plan.* This plan identifies future directions on the basis of comparing past performance with desired outcomes. The self-study should develop priorities for implementing those recommended actions. The following outlines a recommended CAS Standards Self-Study Follow-Up Action Plan.

A. *Areas of Excellence*

1. Review the self-study and identify the areas in which the program excels.

B. *Required Actions*

2. Review the completed self-study and *list each assessment criterion identified* as not being in compliance with the Standards [note discrepancies as well].
3. Review the completed self-study and *list each of the specific actions identified* as being required to bring the program into compliance with the Standards.
4. *Establish priority of required actions* needed to bring the program into compliance with the Standards *on the basis of their overall importance* to achieving the program's mission and primary goals and objectives.

C. *Program Enhancement Actions*

5. Review the completed self-study and *list each of the specific actions* recommended to strengthen and enhance the program beyond the essential

requirements needed to bring the program into compliance with the standards.

6. *Establish priority of the recommended actions* for program enhancement on the basis of their desirability for program enhancement and feasibility for achievement.

D. *Program Action Plans*

7. Establish an *Action Plan* for initiating and implementing the *changes required to bring the program into compliance with the standards* that also incorporates actions to introduce the recommended program enhancement changes.
8. Set dates by which specific actions are to be completed.
9. Identify responsible parties to complete the action tasks.

Special Note: Users will note that there are several functional areas common to student affairs practice that are not addressed directly in the CAS Standards and Guidelines. The fact that a particular functional area such as student health services, international student services, or financial aid programs is not included should not be construed to mean it is unimportant. Rather, it means that standards have been developed elsewhere and CAS did not develop duplicate standards.

When a college does not incorporate a particular functional area in its student services and development programs, use of the *CAS Self Assessment Guide* for that area would be inappropriate. However, institutions which do not provide student services and development programs for which CAS standards and guidelines exist should review their programs carefully and the nonexisting functional area(s) should be considered for future development.

CAS *Housing and Residential Life Programs*
Standards Self Assessment Guide

Rater: _____

Institution: _____

Instructions: Use this scale to rate assessment criteria listed below. Place rating score in the space to the right of each criterion statement. Use Unknown (UK) response only if documentation or other information is unavailable.

1	2	3	4	5	UK
Noncompliance				Compliance	Unknown

Part 1: Mission

Assessment Criteria:	*Scale*	*Score*
1.1 There exists a well developed, written set of housing and residential life goals that are consistent with the stated mission of the institution.	1.1	_____
1.2 Housing and residential life has a well developed, written set of goals that are consistent with the stated student services/development goals of the institution.	1.2	_____
1.3 Program goal statements are reviewed and disseminated on a regular basis.	1.3	_____
1.4 The housing and residential life goals and objectives are consistent with the CAS Standards.	1.4	_____
1.5 Housing and residential life is an integral part of the institution's educational and academic support services program.	1.5	_____
1.6 A mission of housing and residential life is to provide for educational programs and services.	1.6	_____
1.7 A mission of housing and residential life is to provide management and facilities for student housing and, where applicable, food services.	1.7	_____
1.8 The goals of housing and residential life include providing a living-learning environment that enhances individual growth and development.	1.8	_____

1	2	3	4	5	UK
Noncompliance				Compliance	Unknown

1.9   The goals of housing and residential life include
providing facilities which ensure well-maintained,
safe, and sanitary housing conditions for students
and programs.   1.9   _____

1.10   The goals of housing and residential life include
providing management services that ensure orderly
and effective administration.   1.10 _____

1.11   Where appropriate, the housing and residential life
goals include providing food, dining facilities, and
related services to meet institutional and residential
life program needs.   1.11 _____

Cite any CAS Guidelines to be assessed as an institutional criterion for the
self-study:

_____

_____

_____

Identify documentation and rationale that support evaluations:

_____

_____

_____

If other than compliance, describe the discrepancies in detail:

_____

_____

_____

Actions needed [required] for compliance:

_____

_____

_____

Actions recommended for Housing and Residential Life enhancement
including suggestions from CAS Guidelines:

_____

_____

_____

1	2	3	4	5	UK
Noncompliance				Compliance	Unknown

Part 2: Program

Assessment Criteria: *Scale*   *Score*

2.1   Housing and residential life services and programs
      are purposeful.   2.1   _____

2.2   Housing and residential life services and programs
      are organized in a coherent, logical fashion.   2.2   _____

2.3   The programs are based on a relevant theoretical
      foundation that incorporates knowledge of human
      development and learning characteristics.   2.3   _____

2.4   The program is responsive to the developmental
      and demographic profiles of the students served.   2.4   _____

2.5   The program promotes student development by
      encouraging:

    2.5A   positive and realistic self appraisal   2.5A   _____

    2.5B   intellectual development   2.5B   _____

    2.5C   appropriate personal and occupational
       choices   2.5C   _____

    2.5D   clarification of values   2.5D   _____

    2.5E   physical fitness   2.5E   _____

    2.5F   the ability to relate meaningfully to others   2.5F   _____

    2.5G   an enhanced capacity to engage in a person-
       ally satisfying and effective style of living   2.5G   _____

    2.5H   appreciation of cultural and esthetic
       differences   2.5H   _____

    2.5I   an enhanced capacity to work independently
       and interdependently   2.5I   _____

2.6   Housing programs assist students to resolve per-
      sonal, physical, and educational problems.   2.6   _____

2.7   Housing and residential life assists students to
      overcome skill deficiencies.   2.7   _____

2.8   Housing and residential life provides intentional
      interventions designed to improve the environment
      and neutralize negative environmental conditions.   2.8   _____

1	2	3	4	5	UK
Noncompliance				Compliance	Unknown

2.9   The institution recognizes that the educational
      experience of students consists of both academic
      efforts in the classroom and developmental oppor-
      tunities through housing and residential life pro-
      grams and services.   2.9   _____

2.10 Housing and residential life helps the campus
      community understand the importance and rela-
      tionship of both formal academic activity and
      student services/development program activity to
      students' development.   2.10 _____

2.11 Housing and residential life provides opportunities
      for both individual and group education and
      development.   2.11 _____

2.12 Residential facilities are clean, safe, well maintained,
      reasonably priced, attractive, comfortable, properly
      designed, and conducive to study.   2.12 _____

2.13 Program management functions include planning,
      personnel, property management, purchasing, con-
      tracts, financial control, and, where appropriate,
      conference administration.   2.13 _____

2.14 Any food services managed provide high quality,
      nutritious, and reasonably priced meals.   2.14 _____

Cite any CAS Guidelines to be assessed as an institutional criterion for the
self-study:

_____

_____

_____

Identify documentation and rationale that supports evaluations:

_____

_____

_____

If other than compliance, describe the discrepancies in detail:

_____

_____

_____

1	2	3	4	5	UK
Noncompliance				Compliance	Unknown

Actions needed [required] for compliance:

_____

_____

_____

Actions recommended for Housing and Residential Life enhancement including suggestions from CAS Guidelines:

_____

_____

_____

Part 3: Leadership and Management [Institutional Level]

[No Criterion Measures for Housing and Residential Life]

Part 4: Organization and Administration

Assessment Criteria:	*Scale*	*Score*

4.1   There exists a clearly written set of housing and
       residential life policies and procedures.   4.1   _____
4.2   There exists a detailed description of the adminis-
       trative processes for housing and residential life.   4.2   _____
4.3   There exists an organization chart showing job
       functions and reporting relationships within and
       beyond housing and residential life.   4.3   _____

Cite any CAS Guidelines to be assessed as an institutional criterion for the self-study:

_____

_____

Identify documentation and rationale that support evaluations:

_____

_____

_____

If other than compliance, describe the discrepancies in detail:

_____

_____

_____

1	2	3	4	5	UK
Noncompliance				Compliance	Unknown

Actions needed [required] for compliance:

_____

_____

_____

Actions recommended for Housing and Residential Life enhancement including suggestions from CAS Guidelines:

_____

_____

_____

Part 5: Human Resources

Assessment Criteria: *Scale*   *Score*

5.1   There exist sufficient numbers of professional staff members to carry out all aspects of housing and residential life.   5.1   _____

5.2   All professional housing staff members are qualified for their positions on the basis of relevant graduate education or an appropriate combination of education and experience.   5.2   _____

5.3   The director of housing and residential life is qualified for the position beyond the level of staff members to be supervised.   5.3   _____

5.4   Members of the support staff are qualified by education and experience.   5.4   _____

5.5   Preprofessional staff members have an academic preparation germane to job responsibilities.   5.5   _____

5.6   Adequate training and supervision is provided for support and preprofessional staff.   5.6   _____

5.7   Paraprofessional members of the housing staff are carefully selected.   5.7   _____

5.8   Paraprofessional members of the staff are appropriately trained to carry out their duties.   5.8   _____

5.9   Paraprofessional members of the staff possess a clear understanding of their limitations.   5.9   _____

5.10   Paraprofessional staff members are adequately compensated and/or recognized for their work.   5.10   _____

1	2	3	4	5	UK
Noncompliance				Compliance	Unknown

5.11   Paraprofessional staff members are adequately su-
        pervised and evaluated regularly.   5.11 _____

5.12   There are adequate numbers and kinds of clerical
        and technical support staff members to assure that
        professional staff members can carry out their
        assigned responsibilities.   5.12 _____

5.13   Salary and fringe benefits for all program staff
        members are adequate and commensurate with
        similar positions in the institution and the region.   5.13 _____

5.14   There is evidence of a diverse staffing pattern
        reflective of cultural and heritage factors within the
        student population.   5.14 _____

5.15   A diverse staffing pattern exists that provides
        identifiable role models and demonstrates a com-
        mitment to fair employment practices.   5.15 _____

5.16   Systematic procedures for staff selection and evalua-
        tion are used.   5.16 _____

5.17   Housing and residential life provides adequate and
        appropriate professional development oppor-
        tunities for staff members including:
        5.17A   inservice education.   5.17A _____
        5.17B   support to attend professional development
                 activities.   5.17B _____

5.18   The institution has at least one professionally
        qualified staff member who is knowledgeable about
        the goals, objectives, and philosophy of housing and
        residential life.   5.18 _____

Cite any CAS Guidelines to be assessed as an institutional criterion for the
self-study:

_____

_____

_____

Identify documentation and rationale that support evaluations:

_____

_____

_____

1	2	3	4	5	UK
Noncompliance				Compliance	Unknown

If other than compliance, describe the discrepancies in detail:

_____

_____

_____

Actions needed [required] for compliance:

_____

_____

_____

Actions recommended for Housing and Residential Life enhancement including suggestions from CAS Guidelines:

_____

_____

_____

Part 6: Funding

Assessment Criteria: *Scale*   *Score*

6.1   Funding is adequate to carry out the designated
        mission of housing and residential life.   6.1   _____
6.2   The program attempts to identify and utilize all
        appropriate sources of funds.   6.2   _____

Cite any CAS Guidelines to be assessed as an institutional criterion for the self-study:

_____

_____

_____

Identify documentation and rationale that support evaluations:

_____

_____

_____

If other than compliance, describe the discrepancies in detail:

_____

_____

_____

1	2	3	4	5	UK
Noncompliance				Compliance	Unknown

Actions needed [required] for compliance:

_____

_____

_____

Actions recommended for Housing and Residential Life enhancement including suggestions from CAS Guidelines:

_____

_____

_____

Part 7: Facilities

Assessment Criteria: *Scale*   *Score*

7.1 The program has adequate facilities to carry out its mission.   7.1 _____

7.2 All housing facilities are accessible to physically disabled persons and are in compliance with all legal requirements.   7.2 _____

7.3 Housing facilities provide sufficient and appropriate space to achieve goals and objectives of housing and residential life.   7.3 _____

7.4 Housing facilities meet students' needs for safety and security.   7.4 _____

7.5 Housing facilities are well maintained at optimal levels of cleanliness, repair, and decor.   7.5 _____

7.6 Adequate space is provided resident students for study, lounging, recreation, and group meetings.   7.6 _____

7.7 Adequate space is provided for office functions.   7.7 _____

Cite any CAS Guidelines to be assessed as an institutional criterion for the self-study:

_____

_____

_____

Identify documentation and rationale that support evaluations:

_____

_____

_____

1	2	3	4	5	UK

Noncompliance   Compliance   Unknown

If other than compliance, describe the discrepancies in detail:

_____

_____

_____

Actions needed [required] for compliance:

_____

_____

_____

Actions recommended for Housing and Residential Life enhancement
including suggestions from CAS Guidelines:

_____

_____

_____

Part 8: Legal Responsibilities

Assessment Criteria: *Scale*   *Score*

8.1   Housing and residential life staff members are
      knowledgeable about and responsive to relevant
      civil and criminal laws related to their role and
      function in the institution.   8.1   _____

8.2   Staff members are well informed and regularly
      updated about the obligations and limitations
      placed upon the institution by constitutional, stat-
      utory, and common law, external governmental
      agencies, and institutional policy.   8.2   _____

8.3   Professional housing and residential life staff mem-
      bers are provided access to legal advice as needed to
      implement assigned responsibilities.   8.3   _____

8.4   Staff members utilize policies and practices that
      limit liability exposure for the institution and its
      agents.   8.4   _____

Cite any CAS Guidelines to be assessed as an institutional criterion for the
self-study:

_____

_____

_____

1	2	3	4	5	UK
Noncompliance				Compliance	Unknown

Identify documentation and rationale that support evaluations:

_____
_____
_____

If other than compliance, describe the discrepancies in detail:

_____
_____
_____

Actions needed [required] for compliance:

_____
_____
_____

Actions recommended for Housing and Residential Life enhancement
including suggestions from CAS Guidelines:

_____
_____
_____

Part 9: Equal Opportunity, Access, and Affirmative Action

Assessment Criteria: *Scale*   *Score*

9.1 Both the spirit and intent of equal opportunity laws
     are evident throughout housing programs.   9.1   _____

9.2 Housing and residential life services and facilities
     are readily accessible to all residence hall and
     dining students, including traditionally under-
     represented, evening, part-time, and commuter
     students.   9.2   _____

9.3 Nondiscriminatory housing and residential life per-
     sonnel policies regarding race, gender, religion, age,
     national origin, color, and handicap have been
     developed and are practiced regularly.   9.3   _____

9.4 Hiring and promotion policies exist to assure that
     affirmative action will be taken to overcome staff
     imbalances where they exist.   9.4   _____

9.5 The program seeks to identify, prevent, and/or
     remedy other discriminatory practices.   9.5   _____

1	2	3	4	5	UK
Noncompliance				Compliance	Unknown

Cite any CAS Guidelines to be assessed as an institutional criterion for the self-study:

_____

_____

_____

Identify documentation and rationale that support evaluations:

_____

_____

_____

If other than compliance, describe the discrepancies in detail:

_____

_____

_____

Actions needed [required] for compliance:

_____

_____

_____

Actions recommended for Housing and Residential Life enhancement including suggestions from CAS Guidelines:

_____

_____

_____

Part 10: Campus and Community Relations

Assessment Criteria: *Scale*   *Score*

10.1   There is evidence of systematic efforts to maintain
        effective working relationships with campus and
        community agencies whose operations are relevant
        to the designated mission of housing and residential
        life.   10.1   _____

Cite any CAS Guidelines to be assessed as an institutional criterion for the self-study:

_____

_____

_____

1	2	3	4	5	UK
Noncompliance				Compliance	Unknown

Identify documentation and rationale that support evaluations:

_____

_____

_____

If other than compliance, describe the discrepancies in detail:

_____

_____

_____

Actions needed [required] for compliance:

_____

_____

_____

Actions recommended for Housing and Residential Life enhancement including suggestions from CAS Guidelines:

_____

_____

_____

Part 11: Multi-Cultural Programs and Services

Assessment Criteria: *Scale*   *Score*

11.1 The program helps the institution in providing an
      environment that enhances awareness of cultural
      differences.   11.1 _____

11.2 The program helps the institution in providing
      opportunities for individuals to assess their per-
      sonal views and biases regarding cultural differ-
      ences and need for behavioral change.   11.2 _____

11.3 Housing and residential life assists minority stu-
      dents to identify, prioritize, and meet their unique
      educational and developmental needs.   11.3 _____

11.4 Housing and residential life assists minority stu-
      dents in understanding the institution's culture.   11.4 _____

11.5 Housing and residential life assists minority stu-
      dents to understand their unique cultures and
      heritages.   11.5 _____

1	2	3	4	5	UK
Noncompliance				Compliance	Unknown

Cite any CAS Guidelines to be assessed as an institutional criterion for the self-study:

_____

_____

_____

Identify documentation and rationale that support evaluations:

_____

_____

_____

If other than compliance, describe the discrepancies in detail:

_____

_____

_____

Actions needed [required] for compliance:

_____

_____

_____

Actions recommended for Housing and Residential Life enhancement including suggestions from CAS Guidelines:

_____

_____

_____

Part 12: Ethics

Assessment Criteria: *Scale*   *Score*

12.1   Professional housing and residential life staff members have identified and implemented an appropriate set of ethical standards to guide professional practice.   12.1   _____

12.2   The adopted ethical standards are available in written form and reviewed on a regular basis.   12.2   _____

12.3   Housing and residential life policies and procedures are consistent with the ethical standards.   12.3   _____

12.4   Appropriate measures to assure privacy of individuals and confidentiality of information, including research data, have been implemented.   12.4   _____

1	2	3	4	5	UK
Noncompliance				Compliance	Unknown

12.5   Staff members are informed about the institution's
       human subjects research policy and other policies
       addressing ethical practice.   12.5 _____

12.6   Staff members comply with the provisions of these
       policies when doing research.   12.6 _____

12.7   All students are provided access to services on a fair
       and equitable basis.   12.7 _____

12.8   Staff members avoid personal conflicts of interest,
       or the appearance of such.   12.8 _____

12.9   All funds handled by housing and residential life
       staff members are handled in accordance with
       established and responsible accounting procedures.   12.9 _____

12.10 Housing and residential life staff members avoid all
       forms of sexual harassment.   12.10 _____

12.11 Housing and residential life staff members recog-
       nize their limitations and make appropriate refer-
       rals when necessary.   12.11 _____

Cite any CAS Guidelines to be assessed as an institutional criterion for the
self-study:

_____

_____

_____

Identify documentation and rationale that support evaluations:

_____

_____

_____

If other than compliance, describe the discrepancies in detail:

_____

_____

_____

Actions needed [required] for compliance:

_____

_____

_____

1	2	3	4	5	UK
Noncompliance				Compliance	Unknown

Actions recommended for Housing and Residential Life enhancement
including suggestions from CAS Guidelines:

_____

_____

_____

Part 13: Evaluation

Assessment Criteria: *Scale*   *Score*

13.1 A program of regular and systematic research and
      evaluation exists within the program to determine
      whether the educational goals and the needs of
      students are being met.   13.1   _____

13.2 Relevant quantitative and qualitative data obtained
      as a result of the research and evaluation are used to
      revise and improve program goals and implementa-
      tion processes.   13.2   _____

13.3 Evaluation data includes responses from students
      and other significant constituencies.   13.3   _____

Cite any CAS Guidelines to be assessed as an institutional criterion for the
self-study:

_____

_____

_____

Identify documentation and rationale that support evaluations:

_____

_____

_____

If other than compliance, describe the discrepancies in detail:

_____

_____

_____

Actions needed [required] for compliance:

_____

_____

_____

1	2	3	4	5	UK
Noncompliance				Compliance	Unknown

Actions recommended for Housing and Residential Life enhancement including suggestions from CAS Guidelines:

_____

_____

_____

_____

Special Self-Study Follow-Up Action Note

Using the "Actions needed [required] for compliance" and "Actions recommended for program enhancement" entries in this Self Assessment Guide, proceed to develop a *Follow-Up Action Plan*.

_____

_____

_____

_____

_____

_____

Resource C

═══════════════

Association of College and University Housing Officers-International: Standards for College and University Student Housing

The following statement of standards reflects a commitment by ACUHO-I to further the professional development of the field of college and university student housing. Several points of information are presented to the reader as an orientation to the document.

Diversity of Membership. The membership of ACUHO-I is diverse, including large, small, public, and private colleges; universities; junior and community colleges; and technical schools throughout the world. This standards statement is written to reflect that diversity. The diversity of the membership of the Association limits the degree to which individual statements of standards can be specific.

Standards and Guidelines. The ACUHO-I *Standards for College and University Student Housing* contains both standards and guidelines. *Standards* are in bold print, indicating that all colleges/universities operating student housing should comply with these statements in order to meet a minimum level of acceptable performance. *Guidelines* are in italics, indicating practices and/or policies that are recommended, but not necessarily required, to meet a minimum level of performance.

Format. There are four major components of the ACUHO-I *Standards for College and University Student Housing.* They are: (a) Mission, (b) Functional Areas, (c) Ethics, and (d) Qualifications. Standards and guidelines appropriate to each of these topics are presented under each heading.

Intended Use. There are a number of possible uses for the standards statement. A few of them are: staff training, graduate preparation programs, program evaluation, assisting in the explanation of the mission of Housing and Residence Life to others in the university community, assisting outside agencies such as the courts, labor arbitrators, and government agencies (that might be called upon to make rulings that would affect college/university housing operations), and self-study.

Applications. As more housing and residence life staff members become familiar with the *Standards*, they will no doubt think of applications not anticipated by the Professional Standards Committee. It is also likely that in some instances the *Standards* may generate questions. Questions, comments, and suggestions are welcomed and should be directed to the Chair of the Professional Standards Committee or the ACUHO-I Central Office. The Committee will attempt to keep the membership informed of the unique applications being made of the standards statement, while updating the *Standards* on a timely basis.

Revisions. The ACUHO-I standards statement was originally adopted by the ACUHO-I Executive Board July 19, 1984. The Executive Board recognized that revision would be necessary. The following document represents the first revision of the ACUHO-I *Standards.* There is little question that this document also will require revision. Proposals for revision should be submitted to the Chair of the ACUHO-I Professional Standards Committee, ACUHO-I Central Office, 101 Curl Drive, Suite 140, Columbus, Ohio 43210-1195.

Sources of Information. Some of the standards statements in this document have been adopted from the Council for the Advancement of Standards for Student Services/Development Programs (CAS) Housing and Residence Life Programs Self-Assessment Guide, 1988. Other standards statements in this document have been adopted from the American Council on Education (ACE) Statement entitled, "Achieving Reasonable Campus Security," 1985.

Mike Eyster, Co-chair
ACUHO-I Professional Standards Committee

Mission

The Housing and Residence Life program exists as an integral part of the educational program and academic support services of the institution. The mission of Housing and Residence Life includes:

1. providing reasonably priced living environments which are clean, attractive, well maintained, comfortable, and which include safety features.
2. ensuring the orderly and effective administration of the program through effective management.
3. providing a learning environment and related cocurricular programs which promote maturity and academic success. Programs and staff interventions designed to promote maturity are grounded in human development and student development theory.
4. providing, in programs that include food services, a variety of nutritious and pleasing meals, in pleasant surroundings, at a reasonable cost.

Functional Areas

The mission of the college/university housing program is accomplished through the coordination of three interdependent specialized function areas of college/university housing: (a) Business/Management, (b) Physical Plant, and (c) Education/Programming. Many college/university housing operations are also responsible for one or more of the following additional specialized functional areas: food service, apartment/family housing, conference housing, special interest housing, off-campus housing, and faculty/staff housing. Standards in this document apply to those specialized functional areas, as well as to the areas of traditional responsibility of Housing and Residential Life.

Where campus administrative structures require that any of these functional areas report to agencies other than the student housing organization, it is the responsibility of management staff to ensure effective communication and working relationships.

The most effective housing operations are composed of staff who have expertise in at least one of the specialized knowledge areas and a general knowledge of all the other areas.

Business/Management

The management functions performed by housing officers fall into the following categories: planning, personnel, accounting/finance, property management, contract administration, and, in some cases, conference administration, information systems management, and/or off-campus housing services.

A. *Planning*
    1. A mission statement and a set of goals and objectives supportive of that mission statement are an integral part of the program.

They are reflected in job descriptions, policy statements, and guidelines for effective administration of the system.

2.   The mission statement and goals are consistent with the mission of the institution. They are reviewed and disseminated regularly.

3.   The mission statement and goals are consistent with the ACUHO-I *Standards for College and University Student Housing*.

4.   Evaluation of the organization is based on progress toward the achievement of short-range and long-range organizational and individual goals. Planning should be adequate to project and accommodate future needs.

5.   Each management employee has a written plan which reflects and supports the goals and objectives of the organization and areas for personal improvement.

6.   Managers' jobs are defined to provide adequate time for planning as well as implementation.

B.   *Personnel*

1.   There must be at least one professional staff member responsible for the administration/coordination of the Housing and Residence Life Program. This person must be knowledgeable about the goals and mission of the program.

2.   An organizational chart defines both the responsibilities and relationships of staff members.

3.   A written job description is provided to each full-time employee.

4.   Training, supervision, and resources to accomplish assigned tasks are provided each staff member.

5.   A written performance appraisal is provided each full-time and paraprofessional employee at least annually.

6.   Policies and procedures are contained in a manual which is accessible to staff, reviewed annually, and updated when appropriate.

7.   The rationale for policies and procedures is readily available and is related to the organization's mission statement, goals, and objectives.

8.   Staff have a working knowledge of all policies and procedures.

9.   Appropriate measures are taken to ensure that when preprofessional and/or paraprofessional staff members are employed, they are adequately trained and supervised.

10. Procedures for filing, hearing, and processing employee grievances are written and available to all employees.

11. Sufficient numbers of professional staff members are present to carry out the mission of Housing and Residence Life.

12. Adequate numbers and kinds of clerical and technical support staff are present to assure that professional staff can carry out their assigned responsibilities. Support staff must be of sufficient quantity and quality to accomplish the following activities:

operation of electronic data processing machines, filing, telephone and reception duties, bookkeeping, maintaining files and confidential records, making appointments, and handling routine correspondence.

13. Salary and benefits for all Housing and Residence Life staff members are adequate and commensurate with similar positions in the institution and region.

14. Paraprofessional staff members are adequately compensated and recognized for their work.

15. Adequate and appropriate professional development opportunities exist for staff including in-service education. Support is provided for staff to attend professional development and continuing education programs.

16. Staff members are knowledgeable about and remain current with respect to the obligations and limitations placed upon the institution by constitutional, statutory, and common law, and by external governmental agencies and institutional policies.

17. Professional staff members are provided access to legal advice as needed to implement their responsibilities.

18. Staff members utilize policies and practices that limit liability exposure for the institution and its agents.

19. Both the spirit and intent of equal opportunity laws are evident throughout the housing and residence life program.

20. Non-discriminatory personnel policies regarding race, gender, religion, age, national origin, color, sexual orientation, and handicap have been developed and are followed routinely.

21. Hiring and promotion policies exist to assure that affirmative action will overcome staff imbalances where they exist.

22. Policies are in place to encourage the hiring of a multicultural staff.

23. All staff members ensure that students are provided access to services on a fair and equitable basis.

24. The Housing and Residence Life program seeks to identify, prevent, and/or remedy other discriminatory practices.

25. There is evidence of systematic efforts to maintain effective working relationships with campus and community agencies whose operations are relevant to the mission of Housing and Residence Life.

26. Staff members abstain from all forms of sexual harassment.

27. Staff members abstain from personal conflicts of interest, or the appearance of such.

28. Staff members recognize their limitations and make appropriate referrals when necessary.

29. Staff members are informed about the institution's human subjects research policy and other policies addressing ethical practice.

30. Staff members comply with the provisions of the above policies when conducting research.

31. All policies/procedures related to safety/security are periodically reviewed and modified as appropriate.

32. Staff members employed by housing and residence life with safety and security responsibilities are carefully selected and provided with training and supervision.

C. *Accounting/Finance*

1. All funds administered by housing and residence life are handled in accordance with established, responsible accounting procedures.

2. Financial reports provide an accurate financial picture of the organization, and provide clear, understandable, timely data on which housing officers and others can base decisions and make plans.

3. The budget is used as a planning and goal setting document, which reflects commitment to the mission and goals of the housing organization and the institution. Budgets are flexible and capable of being adjusted during the year.

4. Representatives of the college/university housing community are given the opportunity for comment on proposed rate increases and the operating budget.

5. Information regarding the use of Housing and Residence Life funds is available to the college/university community.

6. When the student housing and/or dining operation is an auxiliary enterprise, funds from those operations are not used to support parts of the university not related to the auxiliary enterprise that generated the funds.

7. Adequate funding is available to carry out the mission of Housing and Residence Life including reserves for repairs, replacement, and capital improvements.

8. *Rate increases are announced at least 90 days in advance of their implementation.*

9. *ACUHO-I recommends the use of the procedures developed and published by the National Association of College and University Business Officers (NACUBO), with regard to financial reporting and accounting.*

D. *Purchasing/Property Management*

1. Purchasing procedures are designed to be consistent with institutional policies and ensure that the institution receives the best value for dollars spent.

2. Appropriate steps are taken to secure college/university housing property and furnishings.

3. Procedures are present to ensure reconciliation between goods paid for and goods ordered and received.

4. *An up-to-date inventory of college/university housing property and furnishings is maintained.*

E. *Contract Administration*
1. A clear and thorough written agreement between the resident and the university conveys mutual commitments.
2. The procedures and priorities for obtaining housing and/or meal options are clearly communicated to students, other interested members of the campus community, and potential residents.
3. Procedures for cancelling, subleasing, or being released from the housing and/or dining agreement are written and distributed, if there is a provision for such release.

F. *Service*
1. Services (such as telephone, reception desk, vending, laundry, housing information, etc.) are managed efficiently and in a professional manner.
2. If an off-campus housing referral/information service is provided, it is operated efficiently and in a professional manner. Equal opportunity principles and fairness are used in administering an off-campus housing service.
3. Housing and residence life facilities and services are readily accessible to all residence and dining students, including traditionally underrepresented, evening, part-time and commuter students, as required by institutional policy.

G. *Conference Administration*
1. Conference housing is administered to support the mission of the Housing Department and the university/college.
2. Live-in supervision is provided when housing conferees are of high school age or younger.
3. Conference housing is administered in an efficient and professional manner.
4. The conference operation is ancillary to the student housing operation when student residence hall facilities are used for conferences.

H. *Evaluation*
1. A program of regular and systematic evaluation exists within the Housing and Residence Life program to determine the extent to which the mission is being met.
2. Evaluation data are gathered from students and other significant constituencies.
3. Evaluation data are used to revise and improve the housing and residence life program.

Physical Plant

Administration of the college/university housing and/or dining physical plant is designed to make the physical environment attractive, conducive to academic success, functional, in compliance with codes, and provide safety features. Physical plant administration can be divided into five general areas: maintenance/renovation, equipment replacement, custodial care, energy conservation, and grounds care. The following must be in evidence in all college/university housing and dining operations:

1. Facilities are adequate to carry out the mission. Facilities must include: private offices for counseling, interviewing, or other meetings of a confidential nature; office, reception, and storage space sufficient to accommodate assigned staff, supplies, equipment, library resources, and machinery; and conference room or meeting space. Facilities must be accessible to disabled persons and must be in compliance with federal, state, and local health and safety requirements.

2. A maintenance/renovation program is implemented in all housing operations, in three major areas:
   a. a preventive maintenance program designed to realize or exceed the projected life expectancy of the equipment and facilities,
   b. a program designed to repair or upgrade equipment/building systems as they become inoperable or obsolete, and
   c. a renovation program which modifies physical facilities and building systems to make them more effective, attractive, efficient, and/or safe.

3. A systematically planned equipment replacement program exists for furnishings, mechanical systems, maintenance equipment, carpeting and draperies, and dining equipment (in systems that operate food service or provide kitchens).

4. A housekeeping program to provide a clean and orderly environment in all housing facilities operated by the college/university exists. This refers to the cleaning of public areas of the housing system, although systematic cleaning of all areas should be performed on a regularly scheduled basis.

5. A program exists to provide that housing grounds, including streets, walks, recreational areas, and parking lots, are attractively maintained and include safety features.

6. Periodic inspections are made to: (a) ensure compliance with fire/safety codes; (b) identify and address potential safety/security hazards (i.e., fire extinguisher charged; exit doors working properly; lighting outside of buildings; identifying potentially dangerous spaces, such as isolated laundry rooms; identifying areas where shrubbery might conceal an assailant, etc.).

7. A system of key control is in place which provides for frequent monitoring of keys and identification of potential security hazards related to keys.

8. Waste disposal and handling and storage of chemicals and hazardous

materials shall be in compliance with federal, state, and local health, safety, and environmental protection requirements.

9. *A systematic energy conservation program should be implemented through programming, education, renovation, and replacement.*

The following general minimal standards should be a part of every housing operation:

1. **Measures are taken to promote a safe and secure environment in and around the residence and dining halls.**
2. **Ramps, bathrooms, elevators, room fixtures, and other appropriate special provisions made for mobility impaired residents are well maintained, clearly marked, and their availability is thoroughly communicated to residents and potential residents.**
3. **Public, common, study, and recreational areas, as well as individual living quarters are adequate to accommodate the projected number of mobility impaired residents requesting space, and are available and fully accessible.**
4. **Public, common, study, and recreational areas are adequately furnished to accommodate the number of residents who use them.**
5. **All community bathrooms, as well as other public areas, are cleaned at least daily on week days.**
6. **Adequate space is provided for student study, lounging, recreation, and group meetings.**
7. **Sufficient space for custodial work and storage is available in close proximity to the area of custodial responsibility.**
8. *Individual rooms/apartments are furnished/equipped to accommodate the designated number of occupants.*
9. *Residence halls/apartments are furnished and maintained in a manner designed to provide security, comfort, and an atmosphere conducive to study, growth, and development.*
10. *Laundry facilities are provided within or in close proximity to the residence halls/ apartments.*
11. *Suggestions from residents are regularly and consistently sought and considered regarding physical plant improvements and renovations to college/university housing and dining facilities.*
12. *Whenever possible, physical plant renovations shall be scheduled to minimize disruption to residents and diners.*

Education/Programming

The residential learning environment provides educational opportunities for students and other members of the campus community. Staff involvement in educational opportunities ensures that learning experiences are oriented toward promoting maturity and are grounded in human/student development theory and research. Educational opportunities should include activities and/or experiences in:

A. *Educational Opportunities*
    Educational opportunities shall include activities and/or experiences in a wide variety of areas.
    1. Students will have opportunities to develop a mature style of relating to others.
    2. Students shall have opportunities to live cooperatively with others.
    3. Students will be provided opportunities for analyzing, forming, and/or confirming values (including spiritual development).
    4. Activities to develop independence and self-sufficiency will be provided.
    5. Activities and experiences to develop a sense of respect for self, others, property, and a sense of fairness will be provided to students.
    6. Opportunities for the development of appreciation for new ideas, cultural differences, and life-style will be presented.
    7. Students will have access to programs designed to help them acquire and use knowledge.
    8. Students will have opportunities to make educational and career choices through planned opportunities.
    9. Students will have opportunities to explore and manage the use of leisure time.
    10. Students will have opportunities to engage in self-management (health, personal finances, time).
    11. Students will have opportunities to identify, develop, and/or confirm a sense of identity.

B. *Staff Activities*
    Educational programming, advising, and supervisory activities of the staff will vary with locally assessed needs, but will include multiple functions.
    1. Staff members will introduce and orient residents to services, facilities, staff members, and staff functions.
    2. Staff members will provide information on safety, security, and emergency procedures.
    3. Staff members shall encourage an atmosphere conducive to academic pursuits.
    4. Staff members shall provide written institutional policies and rationale for policies, procedures, and expectations which affect residents including the potential consequences for violation.
    5. Staff members shall promote and demonstrate responsible social behavior.
    6. Staff members shall provide academic information.

7. Staff members shall make appropriate referrals.

8. Staff members shall provide individual advising or counseling support.

9. Staff members shall treat confidential information appropriately.

10. Staff members shall assist African American, Asian American, Hispanic American, Native American, and other students of color to personally identify, prioritize, and achieve educational goals and developmental needs.

11. Staff members shall provide educational programs that focus on awareness of cultural differences, self-assessment of possible prejudices, and desirable behavior changes.

12. Staff members shall assist minority students in understanding their culture and its impact on diversity issues.

13. Staff members shall promote majority students' understanding of unique cultures and heritages.

14. Staff members shall involve residents in programming and policy development.

15. Staff members shall provide information about appropriate civil law as well as policies consistent with civil law.

16. Staff members shall encourage residents to exercise responsibility for their community through confrontation of inappropriate/ disruptive behavior, participation in mediating conflict within the community, and participation in evaluating the Housing and Residence Life program.

17. Staff members shall assess the feasibility and desirability of having and enforcing policies restricting access of non-residents in residence halls.

18. Staff members shall ensure that the safety and security of residence hall students/apartment occupants and their property is taken into consideration as policies are developed.

19. Staff members shall ensure that data regarding security incidents are reviewed to determine the need for corrective action.

20. *Staff members shall promote and demonstrate an educationally sound perspective of the results of drug and alcohol use.*

21. *Staff members shall assess needs of the housing population annually, specifically addressing the needs for special interest programming and for upgrading or modifying facilities.*

22. *Staff members shall encourage residents to learn and exercise their rights as tenants and consumers.*

23. *Staff members shall provide educational experiences in leadership development and decision making.*

Food Service

In campus operations where food is a part of or related to the housing program, the purposes of food service are to provide high quality, nutritious meals at a reasonable cost and to support the programmatic and educational mission of the campus.

ACUHO-I recommends the use of the standards and procedures developed and published by the National Association of College and University Food Services (NACUFS) as guidelines for operating campus food service operations. Whether developed by NACUFS, a specific campus, or otherwise, general standards should include:

1. Management shall ensure menu planning to provide optimum nutrition and variety.
2. Management shall purchase high quality food products.
3. Management shall ensure orderly, secure, and sanitary food storage.
4. Management shall provide recipes and preparation processes which ensure appetizing food.
5. Management shall ensure the existence of safety provisions and sanitary conditions.
6. Management shall ensure that fiscal policies and procedures are consistent with those stated in the Business/Management section of this document.
7. Management will provide policies and practices which ensure timely delivery of services and products.
8. Management will provide hours of dining service operation sufficient to reasonably accommodate student needs.
9. *Staff members should practice positive attitudes and good customer relations.*
10. *Management should ensure the provision of a pleasant environment in dining areas.*
11. *Management should ensure food service involvement in educational programming that contributes to human development and resident satisfaction.*
12. *Management should seek suggestions and input from diners regarding menu selection and satisfaction with the dining program.*

Ethics

1. A set of ethical standards is identified and implemented which guides professional practice.
2. The adopted ethical standards are available in written form and reviewed regularly.
3. Policies and procedures are consistent with the ethical standards.

ACUHO-I has adopted professional and ethical standards which guide the behavior of housing professionals, stimulate concern for the ways they function, and serve as guides to the conduct of housing staff members.

These standards recognize: the need to make referrals when specialized skills are needed; the importance of providing materials which fully represent the services and programs offered; expectations held; regulations and policies of the housing program; the need to respond appropriately to issues of confidentiality; and the importance of demonstrating respect, integrity, and caring for others. A copy of "Ethical Standards for the Housing Professional" is available from the ACUHO-I Central Office.

Qualifications

1. All professional staff members are qualified for their positions on the basis of relevant graduate education or an appropriate combination of education and experience.
2. Members of the support staff are qualified by education and experience.
3. Preprofessional staff members are qualified for their positions on the basis of written criteria established by the institution.
4. Paraprofessional staff members are qualified for their positions on the basis of written criteria established by the institution.

Qualifications for housing officer positions can be gained through formal academic preparation, workshops, self-study, work experience, participation in professional organizations, and in-service training. Well-rounded and effective housing officers gain knowledge through each of these methods.

The following qualifications for the respective housing officer positions are recommended:

1. *Chief housing officer — a terminal degree in higher education, business administration, or human behavior related fields, such as counseling, in addition to related experience; OR, a master's OR bachelor's degree in a similar field AND significant experience in housing.*
2. *Housing officer in charge of physical plant administration — a bachelor's degree AND related experience in engineering and maintenance.*
3. *Housing officer in charge of food service — a bachelor's degree in hotel and restaurant administration or dietetics AND significant experience.*
4. *Housing officer in charge of programming — a master's degree in college student personnel, counseling, or related field; OR, a bachelor's degree AND significant experience.*
5. *Housing officer in charge of central office administration, conference housing, or apartment/family housing — a degree in any of the above areas, assuming the person has significant experience in the general area of responsibility.*

Demonstrated skills of leadership and communication, maturity, a well-developed sense of responsibility, sensitivity to individual differences, a positive self-concept, academic success, and an obvious interest and enthusiasm for working with students are desirable characteristics for professional, preprofessional and paraprofessional staff members.

Bibliography

*1. "The Ideal Housing Organization: Its Structure and a Rationale for Its Choice," by Dr. Dorian Sprandel. Position paper presented at 1984 ACUHO-I Annual Conference.

*2. "Recommended Guidelines for the Development of Professional Housing Officers," ACUHO News/April 1980.

*3. "Prospectus: Using the ACUHO-I Standards as an Aid to Program Evaluation and Enhancement."

 4. "CAS Standards and Guidelines for Student Services/Development Programs—Self-Assessment Guides."

* Available at ACUHO-I Central Office, 101 Curl Drive, Suite 140, Columbus, Ohio 43210-1195; (614) 292-0099.

Resource D

================

Housing and Residential Life Resources

Professional Standards

The reader is referred to Resources A and C in this book for the most recent professional standards statements related to college and university housing and residence life practice. Those resources also include examples of other professional standards.

Although many institutions use or have used both the ACUHO-I *Standards for College and University Student Housing* and the CAS *Standards and Guidelines for Housing and Residential Life Programs* for program review, self-study, and development purposes, relatively little published information on housing standards is available. Contacts that may be of assistance include the following:

The Central Support Services Office (CSSO) of ACUHO-I, 101 Curl Drive, Suite 140, Columbus, OH 43210-1195. Phone: (614) 292-0099, Fax: (614) 292-3205. Publishes *Ethical Principles and Standards for College and University Student Housing* in a three-ring-binder format, which includes four ACUHO-I standards documents and the ACPA *Statement of Ethical Principles and Standards.*

The Council for the Advancement of Standards for Higher Education (CAS), Office of Student Affairs, 2108 Mitchell Building, University of Maryland, College Park, MD 20742-5221. Phone: (301) 454-2925. Publishes *CAS Standards and Guidelines* for nineteen student affairs/service functions, including the CAS *Housing and Residential Life Programs Self Assessment Guide.*

American College Personnel Association (ACPA) Commission III, Student Residence Programs, One Dupont Circle, Suite 360A, Washington, DC 20036. Phone: (202) 835-2272.

Ethics Committee, American College Personnel Association (ACPA), 5999 Stevenson Avenue, Alexandria, VA 22304. Phone: (703) 823-9800. Developed *A Statement of Ethical Principles and Standards of the American College Personnel Association* and responds to professional ethical issues and concerns of ACPA members.

Publications Office, National Association of College and University Business Officers (NACUBO), P.O. Box 96164, Washington, DC 20090-6164. Publishes the NACUBO *Financial Accounting and Reporting Manual for Higher Education.*

Executive Director, National Association of College and University Food Services (NACUFS), 1405 South Harrison Rd., Suite 303–304, Manly Miles Building, Michigan State University, East Lansing, MI 48824. Phone: (517) 332-2494. Publishes NACUFS' *Professional Standards Manual.*

Division of Career Development and Professional Standards, National Association of Student Personnel Administrators (NASPA), 1875 Connecticut Avenue, N.W., Suite 418, Washington, DC 20009-5728. Phone: (202) 265-7500. Publishes the NASPA *Standards of Professional Practice.*

The Council on Postsecondary Accreditation (COPA), One Dupont Circle, Suite 305, Washington, DC 20036. Phone: (202) 452-1433. Represents national and regional accrediting agencies for both institutions and academic programs. COPA is the national-level accreditor of accrediting bodies.

Renovation and Construction Planning Resources

ACUHO-I Research and Information Reports. ACUHO-I Central Office, Jones Tower, Suite 140, Columbus, OH 43210-1195. The central office of ACUHO-I is a source of reports on issues relating to construction and renovation plan trends and costs. Over twenty reports are available through this office.

Anchors, S., Schroeder, C., and Jackson, S. *Making Yourself at Home.* American College Personnel Association, 5999 Stevenson Avenue, Alexandria, VA

22304. 1977. This guidebook establishes a theoretical and practical base for supporting students in their use and design of personal space. Practical solutions are offered for design problems, and creative ways to think of physical space differently are proposed.

Bates, K. *Computerized Maintenance Management Systems*. ACUHO·I Central Office, Jones Tower, Suite 140, Columbus, OH 43210-1195. 1977. Strategies for using technology in creating an efficient and effective maintenance program are the theme of this brief article.

Braver, R. *Facilities Planning*. American Management Association, 135 W. 50th St., New York, NY 10020-1201. 1986. Pragmatic nuts-and-bolts details for facilities planning issues are the heart of this publication.

Coons, M., and Milner, M. *Creating an Accessible Campus*. Association of Physical Plant Administrators of Colleges and Universities, 1446 Duke St., Alexandria, VA 22314-3492. 1979. Strategies for making the entire campus accessible are the central theme.

Dillow, R. (ed.). *Facilities Management: A Manual for Plant Administration*. Association of Physical Plant Administrators of Colleges and Universities, 1446 Duke St., Alexandria, VA 22314-3492. 1989. This comprehensive manual reflects the collected knowledge and efforts of the members of the organization that publishes it. It is a major resource on general administration, human resources management, facilities planning, design, construction, work management and control, and other topics related to colleges and universities. It also offers basic principles and suggestions to help individuals meet the requirements unique to their residence and dining program.

Gates, W. *Planning is the Key to Successful Construction or Renovation Projects*. ACUHO·I Talking Stick. ACUHO·I Central Office, Jones Tower, Suite 140, Columbus, OH 43210-1195. 1991. A practicing housing officer offers tips in a friendly, easily understandable manner on how to carry out a successful project.

Grimm, J., and Mosier, R. (eds.). *Successful Management of Facilities in College and University Residence Halls and Apartment Housing*. ACUHO·I Central Office, Jones Tower, Suite 140, Columbus, OH 43210-1195, 1992. This monograph has nine chapters that deal with different but related aspects of a housing management system. Topics include upkeep and maintenance, refinancing, design and management of renovations, new construction, mileu management programs, and future directions.

Lewis, B. *Developing Maintenance Time Standards*. Boston: Farnsworth, 1967. This publication provides standards for developing and performing maintenance of all aspects of various types of buildings. An excellent guide for the technically oriented.

Murphy, M. *Complying with the ADA*. ACUHO·I Talking Stick. ACUHO·I Central Office, Jones Tower, Suite 140, Columbus, OH 43210-1195. 1992. This article informs readers on what they have to do to comply with the Americans with Disabilities Act.

Robinette, G. *Barrier Free Exterior Design*. New York: McGraw-Hill, 1985. Excellent resource for staff who are responsible for helping meet the requirements of the Americans with Disabilities Act. Contains information and design concepts.

Sleeper, H. R. *Building Planning and Design Standards*. New York: Wiley, 1955. General as well as specific guidelines are offered for creating design standards for all types of buildings.

Staten, G. *Renovation and Construction: Tips for a Successful Project*. ACUHO-I Talking Stick. ACUHO-I Central Office, Jones Tower, Suite 140, Columbus, OH 43210-1195. 1991. A practical article helpful in the renovation and construction area.

Resource E

American College Personnel Association: Statement of Ethical Principles and Standards*

Preamble

The American College Personnel Association (ACPA) is an association whose members are dedicated to enhancing the worth, dignity, potential, and uniqueness of each individual within post-secondary educational institutions and thus to the service of society. ACPA members are committed to contributing to the comprehensive education of the student, protecting human rights, advancing knowledge of student growth and development, and promoting the effectiveness of institutional programs, services, and organizational units. As a means of supporting these commitments, members of ACPA subscribe to the following principles and standards of ethical conduct. Acceptance of membership in ACPA signifies that the member agrees to adhere to the provisions of this statement. This statement is designed to address issues particularly relevant to college student affairs practice. Persons charged with duties in various functional areas of higher education are also encouraged to consult ethical standards specific to their professional responsibilities.

* As revised and approved by the ACPA Executive Council, July 1989. Used with permission.

Use of This Statement

The principal purpose of this statement is to assist student affairs professionals in regulating their own behavior by sensitizing them to potential ethical problems and by providing standards useful in daily practice. Observance of ethical behavior also benefits fellow professionals and students due to the effects of modeling. Self-regulation is the most effective and preferred means of assuring ethical behavior. If, however, a professional observes conduct by a fellow professional that seems contrary to the provisions of this document, several courses of action are available.

Initiate a private conference. Because unethical conduct often is due to a lack of awareness or understanding of ethical standards, a private conference with the professional(s) about the conduct in question is an important initial line of action. This conference, if pursued in a spirit of collegiality and sincerity, often may resolve the ethical concern and promote future ethical conduct.

Pursue institutional remedies. If private consultation does not produce the desired results, institutional channels for resolving alleged ethical improprieties may be pursued. All student affairs divisions should have a widely publicized process for addressing allegations of ethical misconduct.

Contact ACPA Ethics Committee. If the ACPA member is unsure about whether a particular activity or practice falls under the provisions of this statement, the Ethics Committee may be contacted in writing. The member should describe in reasonable detail (omitting data that would identify the person(s) as much as possible) the potentially unethical conduct or practices and the circumstances surrounding the situation. Members of the Committee or others in the Association will provide the member with a summary of opinions regarding the ethical appropriateness of the conduct or practice in question. Because these opinions are based on limited information, no specific situation or action will be judged "unethical." The responses rendered by the Committee are advisory only and are not an official statement on behalf of ACPA.

Request consultation from ACPA Ethics Committee. If the institution wants further assistance in resolving the controversy, an institutional representative may request on-campus consultation. Provided all parties to the controversy agree, a team of consultants selected by the Ethics Committee will visit the campus at the institution's expense to hear the allegations and to review the facts and circumstances. The team will advise institutional leadership on possible actions consistent with both the content and spirit of the *ACPA Statement of Ethical Principles and Standards*. Compliance with recommendations is voluntary. No sanctions will be imposed by ACPA. Institutional leaders remain responsible for assuring ethical conduct and practice. The consultation team will maintain confidentiality surrounding the process to the extent possible.

During the transitional period associated with the disaffiliation of

ACPA from AACD, policies and procedures regarding the adjudication of ethical complaints will be developed. These policies and procedures will be reflected in the next revision of the *Statement of Ethical Principles and Standards*.

Ethical Principles

No statement of ethical standards can anticipate all situations that have ethical implications. When student affairs professionals are presented with dilemmas that are not explicitly addressed herein, five ethical principles may be used in conjunction with the four enumerated standards (Professional Responsibility and Competence, Student Learning and Development, Responsibility to the Institution, and Responsibility to Society) to assist in making decisions and determining appropriate courses of action.

Ethical principles should guide the behaviors of professionals in everyday practice. Principles, however, are not just guidelines for reaction when something goes wrong or when a complaint is raised. Adhering to ethical principles also calls for action. These principles include the following.

Act to benefit others. Service to humanity is the basic tenet underlying student affairs practice. Hence, student affairs professionals exist to (a) promote healthy social, physical, academic, moral, cognitive, career, and personality development of students; (b) bring a developmental perspective to the institution's total educational process and learning environment; (c) contribute to the effective functioning of the institution; and (d) provide programs and services consistent with this principle.

Promote justice. Student affairs professionals are committed to assuring fundamental fairness for all individuals within the academic community. In pursuit of this goal, the principles of impartiality, equity, and reciprocity (treating others as one would desire to be treated) are basic. When there are greater needs than resources available or when the interests of constituencies conflict, justice requires honest consideration of all claims and requests and equitable (not necessarily equal) distribution of goods and services. A crucial aspect of promoting justice is demonstrating an appreciation for human differences and opposing intolerance and bigotry concerning these differences. Important human differences include, but are not limited to, characteristics such as age, culture, ethnicity, gender, disabling condition, race, religion, or sexual/affectional orientation.

Respect autonomy. Student affairs professionals respect and promote individual autonomy and privacy. Students' freedom of choice and action are not restricted unless their actions significantly interfere with the welfare of others or the accomplishment of the institution's mission.

Be faithful. Student affairs professionals are truthful, honor agreements, and are trustworthy in the performance of their duties.

Do no harm. Student affairs professionals do not engage in activities that cause either physical or psychological damage to others. In addition to their personal actions, student affairs professionals are especially vigilant to assure that the institutional policies do not: (a) hinder students' opportunities to benefit from the learning experiences available in the environment; (b) threaten individuals' self-worth, dignity, or safety; or (c) discriminate unjustly or illegally.

Ethical Standards

Four ethical standards related to primary constituencies with whom student affairs professionals work—fellow professionals, students, educational institutions, and society—are specified.

1. *Professional Responsibility and Competence.* Student affairs professionals are responsible for promoting students' learning and development, enhancing the understanding of student life, and advancing the profession and its ideals. They possess the knowledge, skills, emotional stability, and maturity to discharge responsibilities as administrators, advisors, consultants, counselors, programmers, researchers, and teachers. High levels of professional competence are expected in the performance of their duties and responsibilities. They ultimately are responsible for the consequences of their actions or inaction.

As ACPA members, student affairs professionals will:

1.1 Adopt a professional lifestyle characterized by use of sound theoretical principles and a personal value system congruent with the basic tenets of the profession.

1.2 Contribute to the development of the profession (e.g., recruiting students to the profession, serving professional organizations, educating new professionals, improving professional practices, and conducting and reporting research).

1.3 Maintain and enhance professional effectiveness by improving skills and acquiring new knowledge.

1.4 Monitor their personal and professional functioning and effectiveness and seek assistance from appropriate professionals as needed.

1.5 Represent their professional credentials, competencies, and limitations accurately and correct any misrepresentations of these qualifications by others.

1.6 Establish fees for professional services after consideration of the ability of the recipient to pay. They will provide some services, including professional development activities for colleagues, for little or no remuneration.

1.7 Refrain from attitudes or actions that impinge on colleagues' dignity, moral code, privacy, worth, professional functioning, and/or personal growth.

1.8 Abstain from sexual harassment.

1.9   Abstain from sexual intimacies with colleagues or with staff for whom they have supervisory, evaluative, or instructional responsibility.

1.10   Refrain from using their positions to seek unjustified personal gains, sexual favors, unfair advantages, or unearned goods and services not normally accorded those in such positions.

1.11   Inform students of the nature and/or limits of confidentiality. They will share information about the students only in accordance with institutional policies and applicable laws, when given their permission, or when required to prevent personal harm to themselves or others.

1.12   Use records and electronically stored information only to accomplish legitimate, institutional purposes and to benefit students.

1.13   Define job responsibilities, decision-making procedures, mutual expectations, accountability procedures, and evaluation criteria with subordinates and supervisors.

1.14   Acknowledge contributions by others to program development, program implementation, evaluations, and reports.

1.15   Assure that participation by staff in planned activities that emphasize self-disclosure or other relatively intimate or personal involvement is voluntary and that the leader(s) of such activities do not have administrative, supervisory, or evaluative authority over participants.

1.16   Adhere to professional practices in securing positions: (a) represent education and experiences accurately; (b) respond to offers promptly; (c) accept only those positions they intend to assume; (d) advise current employer and all institutions at which applications are pending immediately when they sign a contract; and (e) inform their employers at least thirty days before leaving a position.

1.17   Gain approval of research plans involving human subjects from the institutional committee with oversight responsibility prior to initiation of the study. In the absence of such a committee, they will seek to create procedures to protect the rights and assure the safety of research participants.

1.18   Conduct and report research studies accurately. They will neither engage in fraudulent research nor will they distort or misrepresent their data or deliberately bias their results.

1.19   Cite previous works on a topic when writing or when speaking to professional audiences.

1.20   Acknowledge major contributions to research projects and professional writings through joint authorships with the principal contributor listed first. They will acknowledge minor technical or professional contributions in notes or introductory statements.

1.21   Not demand co-authorship of publications when their involvement was ancillary or unduly pressure others for joint authorship.

1.22   Share original research data with qualified others upon request.

1.23   Communicate the results of any research judged to be of value to other professionals and not withhold results reflecting unfavorably on specific institutions, programs, services, or prevailing opinion.

1.24   Submit manuscripts for consideration to only one journal at a time. They will not seek to publish previously published or accepted-for-publication materials in other media or publications without first informing all editors and/or publishers concerned. They will make appropriate references in the text and receive permission to use if copyrights are involved.

1.25   Support professional preparation program efforts by providing assistantships, practica, field placements, and consultation to students and faculty.

As ACPA members, preparation program faculty will:

1.26   Inform prospective graduate students of program expectations, predominant theoretical orientations, skills needed for successful completion, and employment of recent graduates.

1.27   Assure that required experiences involving self-disclosure are communicated to prospective graduate students. When the program offers experiences that emphasize self-disclosure or other relatively intimate or personal involvement (e.g., group or individual counseling or growth groups), professionals must not have current or anticipated administrative, supervisory, or evaluative authority over participants.

1.28   Provide graduate students with a broad knowledge base consisting of theory, research, and practice.

1.29   Inform graduate students of the ethical responsibilities and standards of the profession.

1.30   Assess all relevant competencies and interpersonal functioning of students throughout the program, communicate these assessments to students, and take appropriate corrective actions including dismissal when warranted.

1.31   Assure that field supervisors are qualified to provide supervision to graduate students and are informed of their ethical responsibilities in this role.

2. *Student Learning and Development.* Student development is an essential purpose of higher education, and the pursuit of this aim is a major responsibility of student affairs. Development is complex and includes cognitive, physical, moral, social, career, spiritual, personality, and educational dimensions. Professionals must be sensitive to the variety of backgrounds, cultures, and personal characteristics evident in the student population and use appropriate theoretical perspectives to identify learning opportunities and to reduce barriers that inhibit development.

As ACPA members, student affairs professionals will:

2.1   Treat students as individuals who possess dignity, worth, and the ability to be self-directed.

2.2   Avoid dual relationships with students (e.g., counselor/employer, supervisor/best friend, or faculty/sexual partner) that may involve incompatible roles and conflicting responsibilities.

2.3   Abstain from sexual harassment.

2.4   Abstain from sexual intimacies with clients or with students for whom they have supervisory, evaluative, or instructional responsibility.

2.5   Inform students of the conditions under which they may receive assistance and the limits of confidentiality when the counseling relationship is initiated.

2.6   Avoid entering or continuing helping relationships if benefits to students are unlikely. They will refer students to appropriate specialists and recognize that if the referral is declined, they are not obligated to continue the relationship.

2.7   Inform students about the purpose of assessment and make explicit the planned use of results prior to assessment.

2.8   Provide appropriate information to students prior to and following the use of any assessment procedure to place results in proper perspective with other relevant factors (e.g., socioeconomic, ethnic, cultural, and gender related experiences).

2.9   Confront students regarding issues, attitudes, and behaviors that have ethical implications.

3. *Responsibility to the Institution.* Institutions of higher education provide the context for student affairs practice. Institutional mission, policies, organizational structure, and culture, combined with individual judgment and professional standards, define and delimit the nature and extent of practice. Student affairs professionals share responsibility with other members of the academic community for fulfilling the institutional mission. Responsibility to promote the development of individual students and to support the institution's policies and interests requires that professionals balance competing demands.

As ACPA members, student affairs professionals will:

3.1   Contribute to their institution by supporting its mission, goals, and policies.

3.2   Seek resolution when they and their institution encounter substantial disagreements concerning professional or personal values. Resolution may require sustained efforts to modify institutional policies and practices or result in voluntary termination of employment.

3.3   Recognize that conflicts among students, colleagues, or the institution should be resolved without diminishing appropriate obligations to any party involved.

3.4 Assure that information provided about the institution is factual and accurate.

3.5 Inform appropriate officials of conditions that may be disruptive or damaging to their institution.

3.6 Inform supervisors of conditions or practices that may restrict institutional or professional effectiveness.

3.7 Recognize their fiduciary responsibility to the institution. They will assure that funds for which they have oversight are expended following established procedures and in ways that optimize value, are accounted for properly, and contribute to the accomplishment of the institution's mission. They also will assure equipment, facilities, personnel, and other resources are used to promote the welfare of the institution and students.

3.8 Restrict their private interests, obligations, and transactions in ways to minimize conflicts of interest or the appearance of conflicts of interest. They will identify their personal views and actions as private citizens from those expressed or undertaken as institutional representatives.

3.9 Collaborate and share professional expertise with members of the academic community.

3.10 Evaluate programs, services, and organizational structures regularly and systematically to assure conformity to published standards and guidelines. Evaluations should be conducted using rigorous evaluation methods and principles, and the results should be made available to appropriate institutional personnel.

3.11 Evaluate job performance of subordinates regularly and recommend appropriate actions to enhance professional development and improve performance.

3.12 Provide fair and honest assessments of colleagues' job performance.

3.13 Seek evaluations of their job performance and/or services they provide.

3.14 Provide training to student affairs search and screening committee members who are unfamiliar with the profession.

3.15 Disseminate information that accurately describes the responsibilities of position vacancies, required qualifications, and the institution.

3.16 Follow a published interview and selection process that periodically notifies applicants of their status.

4. *Responsibility to Society.* Student affairs professionals, both as citizens and practitioners, have a responsibility to contribute to the improvement of the communities in which they live and work. They respect individuality and recognize that worth is not diminished by characteristics such as age, culture, ethnicity, gender, disabling condition, race, religion, or sexual/affectional orientation. Student affairs professionals work to protect human rights and promote an appreciation of human diversity in higher education.

As ACPA members, student affairs professionals will:

4.1   Assist students in becoming productive and responsible citizens.

4.2   Demonstrate concern for the welfare of all students and work for constructive change on behalf of students.

4.3   Not discriminate on the basis of age, culture, ethnicity, gender, disabling condition, race, religion, or sexual/affectional orientation. They will work to modify discriminatory practices.

4.4   Demonstrate regard for social codes and moral expectations of the communities in which they live and work. They will recognize that violations of accepted moral and legal standards may involve their clients, students, or colleagues in damaging personal conflicts and may impugn the integrity of the profession, their own reputations, and that of the employing institution.

4.5   Report to the appropriate authority any condition that is likely to harm their clients and/or others.

Reference

American Association for Counseling and Development. (1988). *Ethical Standards*. Alexandria, VA: Author.

Resource F

=======

National Association of Student
Personnel Administrators:
Standards of Professional Practice

The National Association of Student Personnel Administrators (NASPA) is an organization of colleges, universities, agencies, and professional educators whose members are committed to providing services and education that enhance student growth and development. The association seeks to promote student personnel work as a profession which requires personal integrity, belief in the dignity and worth of individuals, respect for individual differences and diversity, a commitment to service, and dedication to the development of individuals and the college community through education. NASPA supports student personnel work by providing opportunities for its members to expand knowledge and skills through professional education and experience. The following standards were endorsed by NASPA at the December 1990 board of directors meeting in Washington, D.C.

1. *Professional Services.* Members of NASPA fulfill the responsibilities of their position by supporting the educational interests, rights, and welfare of students in accordance with the mission of the employing institution.

Used with permission of the National Association of Student Personnel Administrators (NASPA).

2. *Agreement with Institutional Mission and Goals.* Members who accept employment with an educational institution subscribe to the general mission and goals of the institution.

3. *Management of Institutional Resources.* Members seek to advance the welfare of the employing institution through accountability for the proper use of institutional funds, personnel, equipment, and other resources. Members inform appropriate officials of conditions which may be potentially disruptive or damaging to the institution's mission, personnel, and property.

4. *Employment Relationships.* Members honor employment relationships. Members do not commence new duties or obligations at another institution under a new contractual agreement until termination of an existing contract, unless otherwise agreed to by the member and the member's current and new supervisors. Members adhere to professional practices in securing positions and employment relationships.

5. *Conflict of Interest.* Members recognize their obligation to the employing institution and seek to avoid private interests, obligations, and transactions which are in conflict of interest or give the appearance of impropriety. Members clearly distinguish between statements and actions which represent their own personal views and those which represent their employing institution when important to do so.

6. *Legal Authority.* Members respect and acknowledge all lawful authority. Members refrain from conduct involving dishonesty, fraud, deceit, and misrepresentation or unlawful discrimination. NASPA recognizes that legal issues are often ambiguous, and members should seek the advice of counsel as appropriate. Members demonstrate concern for the legal, social codes and moral expectations of the communities in which they live and work even when the dictates of one's conscience may require behavior as a private citizen which is not in keeping with these codes/expectations.

7. *Equal Consideration and Treatment of Others.* Members execute professional responsibilities with fairness and impartiality and show equal consideration to individuals regardless of status or position. Members respect individuality and promote an appreciation of human diversity in higher education. In keeping with the mission of their respective institution and remaining cognizant of federal, state, and local laws, they do not discriminate on the basis of race, religion, creed, gender, age, national origin, sexual orientation, or physical disability. Members do not engage in or tolerate harassment in any form and should exercise professional judgment in entering into intimate relationships with those for whom they have any supervisory, evaluative, or instructional responsibility.

8. *Student Behavior.* Members demonstrate and promote responsible behavior and support actions that enhance personal growth and development of students. Members foster conditions designed to ensure a student's acceptance of responsibility for his/her own behavior. Members inform and educate students as to sanctions or constraints on student behavior which may result from violations of law or institutional policies.

9. *Integrity of Information and Research.* Members ensure that all information conveyed to others is accurate and in appropriate context. In their research and publications, members conduct and report research studies to assure accurate interpretation of findings, and they adhere to accepted professional standards of academic integrity.

10. *Confidentiality.* Members ensure that confidentiality is maintained with respect to all privileged communications and to educational and professional records considered confidential. They inform all parties of the nature and/or limits of confidentiality. Members share information only in accordance with institutional policies and relevant statutes when given the informed consent or when required to prevent personal harm to themselves or others.

11. *Research Involving Human Subjects.* Members are aware of and take responsibility for all pertinent ethical principles and institutional requirements when planning any research activity dealing with human subjects. (See *Ethical Principles in the Conduct of Research with Human Participants*, Washington, D.C.: American Psychological Association, 1982.)

12. *Representation of Professional Competence.* Members at all times represent accurately their professional credentials, competencies, and limitations and act to correct any misrepresentations of these qualifications by others. Members make proper referrals to appropriate professionals when the member's professional competence does not meet the task or issue in question.

13. *Selection and Promotion Practices.* Members support nondiscriminatory, fair employment practices by appropriately publicizing staff vacancies, selection criteria, deadlines, and promotion criteria in accordance with the spirit and intent of equal opportunity policies and established legal guidelines and institutional policies.

14. *References.* Members, when serving as a reference, provide accurate and complete information about candidates, including both relevant strengths and limitations of a professional and personal nature.

15. *Job Definitions and Performance Evaluation.* Members clearly define with subordinates and supervisors job responsibilities and decision-making

procedures, mutual expectations, accountability procedures, and evaluation criteria.

16. *Campus Community*. Members promote a sense of community among all areas of the campus by working cooperatively with students, faculty, staff, and others outside the institution to address the common goals of student learning and development. Members foster a climate of collegiality and mutual respect in their work relationships.

17. *Professional Development*. Members have an obligation to continue personal professional growth and to contribute to the development of the profession by enhancing personal knowledge and skills, sharing ideas and information, improving professional practices, conducting and reporting research, and participating in association activities. Members promote and facilitate the professional growth of staff and they emphasize ethical standards in professional preparation and development programs.

18. *Assessment*. Members regularly and systematically assess organizational structures, programs, and services to determine whether the developmental goals and needs of students are being met and to assure conformity to published standards and guidelines such as those of the Council for the Advancement of Standards for Student Services/Development Programs (CAS). Members collect data which include responses from students and other significant constituencies and make assessment results available to appropriate institutional officials for the purpose of revising and improving program goals and implementation.

Name Index

Subject Index

M

Maine, University of: collaborative advising at, 30; food services at, 242; technology use at, 530

Maine at Orono, University of: community development at, 477; paraprofessionals at, 331; values at, 42; wellness program at, 450

Maintenance: deferred, 221–223; managing, 11–12, 45–46, 225–228; preventive, 226

Managing Emotions Inventory, 80

Manning theory, and residential environments, 148–149

Marginality. *See* Mattering and marginality

Marketing: of programs, 438–439; strategies for, 219–221

Maryland at Baltimore County, University of, crime prevention at, 504, 507

Mattering and marginality: in community development, 464–465; and psychosocial development, 86–87, 88

Maturity, model of psychosocial, 70–71

Mauclet v. Nyquist, 355, 368

Meal plans: debit card for, 239; declining balance plan for, 239; meal equivalency for, 238; point plan for, 238

Measure of Epistemological Reflection, 120

Mediation: of conflicts, 329; in group norming, 472

Men: and crowding, 139, 140; and residence orientations, 153; wellness programs for, 448, 452

Miami, University of, faculty-in-residence at, 257

Miami University, collaborative advising at, 30

Michigan, University of: in court case, 348, 367; history of housing at, 169; Martha Cook Hall at, 155

Michigan State College, housing construction at, 171

Michigan State University: Brody Hall at, 234; living-learning center at, 255

Middle East, moral development in, 110

Midwest Association of Residence Halls, 182

Midwest Dormitory Conference, 181

Miller v. Long Island University, 357, 368

Miller v. State, 363, 368

Mines-Jensen Interpersonal Relationships Inventory, 81

Minnesota: hate groups in, 3; and housing construction, 171

Minnesota, University of, history of housing at, 171

Mission: and food service, 246; of housing, 26; and program design, 429; of residence halls, 190; in self-study, 381–382, 383–384

Mississippi, court case in, 353, 368

Mississippi A&M College, housing construction at, 171

Missouri, University of, in court case, 348, 350, 368

Mollere v. Southeastern Louisiana College, 355, 368

Montana State University, in court case, 364, 367

Monthly operating statements, and budgets, 208–210

Moore v. Troy State University, 351, 352, 368

Moral development. *See* Intellectual and moral development

Moral Judgment Interview, 109

Morehouse College, Graves Hall at, 155

Morrill Act, 169

Mullins v. Pine Manor College, 365, 368

Multiculturalism: and residential environments, 2–5, 144–145; in self-study, 384–385

Murder, in residences, 502–503

Myers-Briggs Type Indicator (MBTI): and environment, 143, 145, 156; and intellectual and moral development, 118, 124; for paraprofessionals, 331, 332; for roommate matching, 470; and student development, 47; for support staff, 302; for wellness, 447–448

N

Nally v. Grace Community Church of the Valley, 364, 368

National Association of Campus Activities, 438

National Association of College and University Business Officers, 180, 221, 389, 393, 587

National Association of College and University Food Services, 180, 246, 247, 389, 393, 587

National Association of College and University Housing Officers, 177

National Association of College and University Residence Halls, 181–182, 252

National Association of College Auxiliary Services, 180

National Association of Educational Buyers, 180

National Association of Student Affairs Administrators, 38, 61